USING

Management Accounting Information 2e

A DECISION CASE APPROACH

Steven J. Adams
Professor, California State University, Chico

LeRoy J. Pryor
Professor, California State University, Chico

Donald E. Keller
Professor Emeritus, California State University, Chico

Mary E. Harston
Associate Professor, St. Mary's University

Australia · Canada · Mexico · Singapore · Spain · United Kingdom · United States

Using Management Accounting Information: A Decision Case Approach, 2e

Steven J. Adams, LeRoy J. Pryor, Donald E. Keller, Mary E. Harston

Editor-in-Chief:
Jack W. Calhoun

Team Leader:
Melissa S. Acuña

Acquisitions Editor:
Sharon Oblinger

Developmental Editor:
Sara E. Wilson

Marketing Manager:
Mignon Tucker

Production Editor:
Heather A. Mann

Manufacturing Coordinator:
Doug Wilke

Printer:
Patterson Printing
Benton Harbor, MI

Design Project Manager:
Rik Moore

Cover Design:
Rik Moore

Cover Photo Source:
PhotoDisc, Inc.

Printed in the United States of America
1 2 3 4 5 05 04 03 02

For more information contact South-Western, 5191 Natorp Boulevard, Mason, Ohio 45040.
Or you can visit our Internet site at: http://www.swcollege.com

ISBN 0-324-11462-1

USING MANAGEMENT ACCOUNTING INFORMATION: A DECISION CASE APPROACH

Table of Contents

		Page
Preface		v
Authors' Message		ix
About the Authors		xvii
MODULE 1 - TRANSITION FROM FINANCIAL ACCOUNTING		1
Module 1	Introduction	3
Reading 1-1	Using the Income Statement and Balance Sheet for Decisions	5
Case 1-1	J & J Corporation: Evaluation of Financial Performance	25
Group 1-1	How is J & J Corporation Doing?	29
Reading 1-2	Using the Statement of Cash Flows for Decisions	31
Case 1-2	J & J Corporation: Statement of Cash Flows	53
Reading 1-3	Cost, Volume, and Profitability Decisions	57
Case 1-3	J & J Corporation: Opening a New Store	71
Case 1-4	J & J: Cash Flows for the New Store	75
Group 1-4	Is it a "Grand" Opening?	79
Module 1	Peer Evaluation of Group Members	81
MODULE 2 - TRADITIONAL PRODUCT COSTING AND PRICING		83
Module 2	Introduction	85
Reading 2-1	California Car Company and Its Environment	89
Case 2-1	California Car Company Background	107
Case 2-2	California Car Company Production Line Simulation	113
Group 2-2	Assembling Cars at California Car Company	127
Case 2-3	Production Problems at California Car Company	129
Reading 2-4	Estimating Manufacturing Costs	131
Case 2-4	Development of Product Cost Estimates for 2002	143
Reading 2-5	Pricing and Profitability Decisions	149
Case 2-5	Profitability Issues at California Car Company	169
Group 2-5	Saudi Golf Cart Order	173
Reading 2-6	Job-Order Costing	175
Case 2-6	Job-Order Costing at California Car Company	189
Reading 2-7	Performance Budgets	195
Case 2-7	Variance Controversy at California Car Company	205
Group 2-7	Overdone Overhead?	209
Module 2	Peer Evaluation of Group Members	213
Module 2	Review	215
MODULE 3 - COST MANAGEMENT SYSTEMS		219
Module 3	Introduction	221
Reading 3-1	Activity-Based Costing	223
Case 3-1	Activity-Based Costing at California Car Company	241
Group 3-1	A Cost by Any Other Name	247
Reading 3-2	Process Management and Accounting	249
Case 3-2	Implementing a Quality Program at California Car Company	269

Case 3-3 Cost of Quality at California Car Company 271
Reading 3-4 JIT and Process Improvement 277
Case 3-4 Implementing Just-in-Time at California Car Company 293
Group 3-4 Just-in-Time Simulation at California Car Company 301
Case 3-5 Just-in-Time Costing at California Car Company 303
Group 3-5 A Cost is a Cost is a Cost? 309
Module 3 Peer Evaluation of Group Members 311
Reading 3-6 Careers in Accounting 313
Module 3 Review 321

MODULE 4 - PLANNING AND PERFORMANCE EVALUATION 323

Module 4 Introduction 325
Reading 4-1 Budgeting and Control 329
Case 4-1 California Car Company: Plans for 2003 347
Case 4-2 California Car Company Plans: for 2003 (Continued) 355
Group 4-2 The Best Laid Plans 359
Reading 4-3 Ethical Considerations in Decision Making 361
Case 4-3 Ethical Decision at California Car Company 369
Reading 4-4 Capital Budgeting 371
Case 4-4 Capital Budgeting at California Car Company 387
Reading 4-5 Standard Setting, Performance Evaluation, and the Balanced Scorecard 391
Case 4-5 The Balanced Scorecard at California Car Company 407
Group 4-5 Setting Standards for 2004 411
Module 4 Peer Evaluation of Group Members 413
Module 4 Review Problem 415

MODULE 5 - ANALYSIS OF FINANCIAL STATEMENTS IN A GLOBAL ECONOMY 419

Module 5 Introduction 421
Reading 5-1 Global Business and Foreign Exchange Rates 423
Case 5-1 RF Circuit's Contract With Osaka Components 439
Group 5-1 "Exchanging" Thoughts 441
Reading 5-2 Translation and Consolidation of Foreign Subsidiaries 443
Case 5-2 Opening a Foreign Subsidiary at California Car Company 453
Case 5-3 The Mexico Subsidiary After One Year 459
Reading 5-4 Reading and Interpreting Annual Reports 463
Case 5-4 Analysis of Ford Motor Company's Annual Report 481
Case 5-5 Comparison of Ford and California Car Company Financial Statements 485
Group 5-5 Financial Horsepower 487
Module 5 Peer Evaluation of Group Members 489
Module 5 Review 491

APPENDIX, GLOSSARY AND INDEX

Appendix Instructions for Microsoft® Excel 495
Glossary 503
Index 519

PREFACE

Many authoritative groups have called for different and expanded learning objectives in the first accounting courses. This preface presents the overall objectives for this book, which include decision making, accounting literacy, and business knowledge objectives, as well as problem-solving, interpersonal, and computer skill objectives. The objectives are followed by an explanation of why and how we designed the introductory texts. The preface concludes with a review of how to participate effectively in groups and the steps involved in decision making.

GLOBAL LEARNING OBJECTIVES

Individuals in today's society inevitably become members of many different organizations, including businesses, governmental units, social clubs, charities, etc. All such organizations share a common problem: *limited resources are available for pursuing organizational goals.* Consequently, individuals are continually confronted with the need to make important economic decisions. Accounting information generally will be a vital input to those decisions. Hence, individuals need to know how to use accounting information effectively in making economic decisions. In short, individuals in today's society need to become "accounting literate."

This text will provide students with exposure to a broad range of economic decision problems that arise in a variety of organizational contexts and with various types of accounting and other information that is relevant in addressing those problems. Specific objectives to be met regarding decision making, accounting, and business are as follows:

Economic Decision Making—Introduce students to a broad range of decision-making problems that arise in various organizational settings and to approaches for dealing with such problems, including their ethical considerations.

Accounting Literacy—Introduce students to the role of accounting in a global market economy and to fundamental accounting concepts that underlie the development and communication of information that supports economic decision making.

Business/Organization Literacy—Assist students in gaining a basic understanding of the business/organizational contexts in which economic decision making takes place.

To become effective economic decision makers in today's society, individuals not only need to meet the three "knowledge acquisition" objectives presented above, but also must develop skills in the following three key areas related to decision making:

Problem Solving—Assist students in enhancing their analytical/problem-solving skills by engaging them in a variety of real world, relatively unstructured cases that require problem definition and clarification, data collection, interpretation, analysis, and defense of proposed solutions.

Interpersonal—Assist students in improving their abilities to communicate and to work together with others by engaging them in frequent writing exercises, oral presentations, and group activities.

Computer—Assist students in becoming more adept in the use of computers by engaging them in frequent computer applications in business, accounting, and economic decision-making activities.

The relevance of these skills to decision making is clear and immediate. First, the possession of creative problem-solving skills is obviously desirable. In business, economic decision problems neither present themselves in nicely structured, clearly defined terms; nor do they typically lead to well-defined solutions with a single, correct answer. Instead, real problems are ill-structured and "messy," and solutions often involve several defensible positions. Students need to recognize these complexities and gain practice in dealing with them.

Second, most (if not all) significant economic decision-making activities involve interpersonal relationships. In real settings, problems are mostly addressed by teams rather than individuals. Problem analyses generally have to be communicated to others, both orally and in writing. Proposed courses of action may need to be vigorously defended in open debate or in position papers. Thus, it is clear that such interpersonal skills play a critical role in economic decision making. *Using Management Accounting Information* includes several extensions of case assignments which require a group solution.

Finally, it should also be clear that computers, particularly personal computers, play an increasing role in economic decision-making activities. *Using Management Accounting Information* is designed to enhance skills in using a computer for analysis and decision making.

Course Modules

Using Management Accounting Information is divided into the following five modules:

1. Transition from *Using Financial Accounting Information*
2. Traditional Product Costing and Pricing
3. Cost Management Systems
4. Planning and Performance Evaluation
5. Analysis of Financial Statements in a Global Economy

Each module focuses on decision scenarios that students must address as the module progresses. These decision problems provide the context and rationale for studying related accounting and business subjects. The authors extend a warm welcome to you with the hope that you have a successful academic experience.

SUPPLEMENTS

Faculty Supplements

Instructor's manual. This manual is a combination of an instructor's resource manual and a solutions manual. It is an excellent resource to help the instructor plan and teach the course. The manual includes a suggested syllabus and course schedule, an overview of each case, teaching notes for each reading and case, and PowerPoint transparency thumbnails. Suggested solutions to all cases and case reading exercises and problems are also a part of this package.

Test bank. This resource book contains a wide variety of questions and question formats. There are multiple choice questions, structured problems, unstructured problems, and written response problems. Many of the test bank questions are formatted similar to the materials in the text. There are quizzes for the end of each reading and sample test questions for each module. An electronic version of the test bank is available.

Web site. The web site for this book is an excellent resource for both faculty and students. The web site contains considerable information that is useful in teaching this course. Faculty will be able to visit the site to secure solutions to exercises and problems (in addition to the solutions in the instructor's manual).

PowerPoint Slides. PowerPoint presentations for each Reading are available for instructors at the web site.

WebCT Course. The authors have independently created a WebCT site as a supplement for their students. The authors will supply any instructors with a CD containing the content of this site. For more information, please contact Steve Adams at sjadams@csuchico.edu.

Student Supplements

Web site. Students find the web site (http://adams.swcollege.com) to be a very important resource for this book. The wide variety of items contained in the site include:

1. Helpful hints for completing the case assignments,
2. Solutions for selected problems and cases,
3. Accounting career information,
4. Links to corporation data,
5. Self-testing quizzes over the material in the book,
6. Audio and PowerPoint presentations covering topics in the book, and
7. A video showing student roles in the simulation.

Students should visit this site at least once a week to see what new materials may have been added.

Self-Grading Templates. Excel templates for the quantitative portions of most cases are provided. Numerous check figures in each case are compared to the solution and students receive instant feedback on whether their answer is correct. The instant feedback reinforces learning and encourages students to invest time in mastering the material.

Revisions for the Second Edition

The second edition maintains the same case-based pedagogy that provides a relevant decision context for students. The topical sequencing also remains the same as in the first edition. Major changes in the second edition follow.

- Significant expansion of text material. Discussions of topics including cost-volume-profit, performance evaluation, the balanced scorecard, and capital budgeting have been expanded. New topics, such as enterprise resource planning (ERP) systems, activity-based budgeting, and Six Sigma, have been added.

- The number of end-of-reading exercises and problems has been doubled. Existing exercises and problems have been revised.
- The California Car Company serial case has been completely revised with all new numbers, improved clarity, and more of a focus on solving mistakes made by the company.
- Sophisticated, color-coded, self-grading templates have been prepared for the quantitative portions of most cases. The instant feedback provided by these templates reinforces student learning and has been found to significantly increase student time on task.

Acknowledgments

The original development of this material was derived from a Fund for the Improvement of Post Secondary Education (FIPSE) grant from the U.S. Department of Education to the accounting faculty at California State University, Chico. We thank the U.S. Department of Education for their confidence in us and our research concept and the following CSU, Chico faculty who were originally involved in developing much of this material: Sally L. Adams, Curtis L. DeBerg, Paul Krause, Richard B. Lea, and Brock Murdoch. We also wish to thank James M. Emig, Villanova University, for reviewing the test bank, solutions manual, and text.

We also gratefully acknowledge the contributions of the following persons who have shared ideas and comments on various parts of the materials:

Sherri Anderson	Sonoma State University
Angele Brill	Castleton State College
Janet Cassagio	Nassau Community College
Dianna Coker	St. Mary's University
Joe Colgan	Fort Lewis College
Jack Flanagan	Australian Catholic University
Glenn W. Goodale	Castleton State College
Bob Harrington	Fort Lewis College
Norma C. Holter	Towson State University
Thomas Madison	St. Mary's University
Lynn Mazzola	Nassau Community College
Patrick Reihing	Nassau Community College
Alan Taylor	Australian Catholic University

The following person has developed or otherwise contributed to the development of the materials indicated. We thank her for the extensive comments and contributions.

Readings 1-1, 1-2, and 1-3 Sally L. Adams

We also thank the Accounting and Tax Team of South-Western Thomson Learning for their hard work and dedication. And finally, we thank our families for their encouragement, patience, and support in this labor of love.

Steve Adams
Lee Pryor
Don Keller
Mary Harston

AUTHORS' MESSAGE TO INTRODUCTORY ACCOUNTING STUDENTS

THE FIRST ACCOUNTING COURSE

For many of you (particularly those who have not worked with *Using Financial Accounting Information*), studying how accounting is used to support management decisions will be a new and different college learning experience. As a result, it may take you a couple of weeks to feel comfortable with the learning environment your instructor has developed. The authors believe strongly that you will find the experience more rewarding if you understand why this text is designed to parallel real-life business situations.

Change in Accounting Education

As a student, you are attending college at a time of revolutionary change in higher education. Nowhere is that change more pervasive than in business education in general and accounting education in particular. Most of the elite business schools are radically changing the curriculum and the way business courses are taught. Hundreds of other schools also are involved in reengineering their business programs. *Reengineering* is a common business term that means redesigning a process from scratch. This redesign is normally facilitated through the installation of computer hardware and software.

The Accounting Education Change Commission

The major impetus for accounting education change came from the formation of the Accounting Education Change Commission (AECC). The AECC was funded in the amount of $4 million by several large certified public accounting (CPA) firms. The AECC's charge is to stimulate radical change in accounting education. The reason the CPA firms were willing to put up so much of their own money was that they were unhappy with the educational background of the students they were hiring. The AECC has issued a statement describing what the first-year accounting course should be like. *Using Management Accounting Information* closely follows the AECC's recommendations.

Employers of Business School Graduates

CPA firms are not the only employers concerned about the educational background of business graduates. Throughout the nation employers are demanding that business schools change the curriculum and the way courses are taught.

Employer demands typically include the following knowledge, skills, and personal attributes:

- Demonstrate a strong work ethic and the ability to take the initiative,
- Become financially literate so they can understand the business implications of what they do and changes they suggest,

- Learn group interaction skills, including the ability to work with employees in other functions and with diverse backgrounds, and
- Develop computer and analytical skills to use newly available information on their jobs.

Alumni Surveys

Alumni surveys of business school graduates who have worked from two to five years in professional jobs also indicate a need to change business education. When asked what should have been covered more extensively in college, alumni frequently cite:

- More writing integrated into the curriculum,
- More practical applications and examples,
- More exposure to information technology found in practice, and
- More unstructured, "real world" problems.

U.S. Department of Education

Because major changes in the introductory accounting courses are felt to be a critical step in improving business education, the U.S. Department of Education (DOE) awarded a $200,000 grant that helped support development of the text you are now using. The grant was made through DOE's Fund for the Improvement of Post-Secondary Education (FIPSE) program.

Text Design

Real-life cases form the core learning experience in this course. The cases provide the business decision context in which accounting information is used. The cases have been carefully designed to promote active learning, emphasize decision uses of accounting information, stimulate collaborative learning, improve problem solving-skills, and integrate the use of computer software.

Active Learning

The philosophy behind active learning stems from the old, but true, adage:

Tell me .... and I will forget,
Show me .... and I will remember,
Involve me ..... and I will understand.

Research shows (and common sense validates) that students retain information much better if they learn it for themselves, rather than passively receiving the information from the instructor. Although active learning places more of the responsibility on the students, we are convinced that you will retain the information much better. Better retention will help you in your future courses and in the business world. Please remember that the substantial work required to create an active learning environment was not done to create anxiety or frustration, but to improve your education. In addition, recall that the first employer demand of college graduates focuses on employee initiative and independence. Development of these critical "learning how to learn" skills is another key benefit of active learning.

Decision Uses of Accounting Information

The readings and cases in this text are built around important "real world" business decisions. Accounting concepts are presented as you need them to address a specific decision. By learning accounting in a relevant decision context normally found in businesses, accounting will make more sense and should be more interesting and meaningful.

The authors have experimented with many different approaches to introductory accounting. The design of the readings, cases, web page, and other supplementary materials is based upon successful results from several years of in-class testing. We found that typical college students gain a better mastery of introductory accounting concepts if they understand the relevant business context.

To illustrate the importance of context, consider the 2-point conversion strategy in football. Most coaches would agree that the 1-point conversion (kicking the ball through the goal posts) has a higher probability of success than the 2-point conversion (running or passing the ball into the end zone). Yet there are times when the coach will call for the 2-point conversion. To the observer who does not know the game of football, the 2-point strategy may not make sense due to a lack of context.

Suppose you were to describe to your friend, a football neophyte, a situation where Team A has just scored a touchdown and is one point ahead of Team B. There are two minutes left to play in the game and Team B has an excellent field goal kicker. Team A's coach must decide whether to go for the 1-point or 2-point conversion. You explain to your friend that if Team A makes the 1-point conversion followed by Team B making a field goal (three points) in the closing seconds of the game, Team A will lose by one point. Instead, if Team A makes the 2-point conversion followed by Team B's field goal, the score would be tied, giving Team A a chance to win in overtime. By providing the context, your friend is in a position to understand the rationale of the coach's decision to take the riskier 2-point strategy. Your friend would have a better understanding of the game of football than if you had just taught the rules.

Collaborative Learning

Research shows that students who participate extensively in study groups enjoy their college experience more and earn better grades. In addition, employers and alumni both believe that students should develop effective group interaction skills during college. *Using Management Accounting Information* is, therefore, structured to include group activities. Remember that groups are most effective when every member comes to every meeting prepared. Group members who don't pull their weight soon create undesirable tension within the group.

Problem-Solving Skills

Solving unstructured, "real world" problems is one of the most sought-after skills in business. It is also a skill that both employers and recent alumni believe is insufficiently developed in college. As a result, many of the cases in this course are somewhat unstructured and have no single "correct" answer. The football illustration is an example of an unstructured problem. With different assumptions, the 1-point strategy could be deemed the "correct" or "incorrect" decision.

Use of Computer Software

The cases in *Using Management Accounting Information* require you to use word processing and spreadsheet software. If you are not yet minimally proficient with these two types of software, you may have to spend some additional time this semester learning them. Remember, however, that you will need these skills in future courses and on the job once you graduate.

How to Succeed in This Course

Understanding the uses of accounting for decision making will require that you:

- Carefully read case readings,
- Complete all course assignments on time,
- Work diligently with members of you group,
- Take extensive notes of in-class discussion of lectures and case discussions,
- Ask questions when you do not understand a concept, and
- Make frequent visits to this book's web site.

How Will You Benefit From the Changes?

If we have been successful in developing this text and you are diligent in completing the assignments, you should:

- Retain the material better,
- Have a more realistic and positive view of what accountants do,
- Develop important job-market skills, and
- Find the course more interesting and relevant.

ECONOMIC DECISION MAKING

An economic decision-making process may be divided into the seven steps shown in Exhibit I-1 and described briefly below.

Exhibit I-1
Economic Decision Making

1. Define the problem.
2. Specify the goal(s).
3. Identify feasible alternatives (mutually exclusive and exhaustive set).
4. Predict possible outcomes (mutually exclusive and exhaustive set for each alternative).
5. Collect additional relevant quantitative data.
6. Identify relevant qualitative considerations.
7. Make the decision.

Define the Problem

The economic decision-making process begins with a careful statement of the problem being addressed. What is the problem? That is, sales have declined, but why? Because prices are too high? Because quality has deteriorated? Due to ineffective advertising? Asking the right questions at this step clarifies the problem and removes some of the surrounding ambiguities.

Specify the Goal(s)

Goals (objectives) are statements of what an organization wants to achieve. Is the goal to maximize profit, minimize cost, or attain a particular quality level? If two or more goals are specified, the decision maker must determine which goals act as constraints—for example, maximize profit subject to a specified impact on the environment.

Identify Feasible Alternatives

A decision involves the choice among two or more mutually exclusive, feasible alternative courses of action. An alternative that might be infeasible would be a level of advertising that exceeds the company's current level of available resources.

Predict Possible Outcomes

For each particular alternative course of action, the decision maker must identify or predict a set of mutually exclusive and exhaustive outcomes that may occur and the nature of the costs and benefits associated with those outcomes. Because the future is uncertain, a particular alternative course of action may lead to two or more different outcomes. For example, the alternative of increasing advertising for a particular product may lead to competitors' retaliation, which in turn may lead to a reduction in sales volume.

Collect Additional Relevant Quantitative Data

Quantitative estimates (predictions) are needed for costs and benefits. In general, more effort should be devoted to obtaining accurate estimates of those costs or benefits that are most critical to the decision.

Identify Relevant Qualitative Considerations

Important economic decisions rarely depend solely on quantitative analysis. Significant qualitative considerations, which are factors that cannot be measured effectively in numerical terms, generally are important. For example, the effect of a decision on the morale of company employees is a qualitative consideration.

Make the Decision

The alternative is selected that appears to "best" satisfy the decision maker's specified goal(s), taking into account both quantitative and qualitative considerations. In this course we spend much of our time on steps five, six, and seven in the decision process. You should keep in mind, however, that decision makers must progress through the first four steps if they are to make sound decisions. Note that the ability to address the first four steps well often requires experience in the industry for which the business decision is being made.

Auto Loan Example

These concepts may be illustrated by considering a decision problem involving a personal car loan. Exhibit I-2 presents an analysis of this problem from the perspectives of two different decision makers—the auto loan officer in a bank and the individual car buyer.

Exhibit I-2
Steps in Decision Making

Decision Elements/Steps	Loan Officer	Borrower
The Problem	• Must decide whether to approve the auto loan	• Needs a car and related bank financing
The Goals	• Profit • Growth • Responsiveness to community funding needs	• Minimize cost of the auto purchase
The Alternatives	• Do not lend • Lend money, but determine: --Interest rate --Repayment period --Default provisions	• Bank A vs. Bank B • Don't purchase car
Possible Outcomes	• If money is not lent: --no profit, etc. • If money is lent: --Timely repayment --Default/repossession	• Repay loan • Default: --Future credit --Lose car
Relevant Data	• Borrower's financial condition • Competitors' offerings • Bank funds available for lending	• Financial condition • Bank A vs. Bank B deal
Qualitative Considerations	• Is the borrower a special case (e.g., granddaughter of the bank president)?	• How "good" a car is needed?
Decision	• Lend?	• Borrow?

GROUP ACTIVITIES

The ability to work effectively in groups has become one of the key skills employers are looking for when they recruit college graduates. In order to understand why, you should refer back to the "The First Accounting Courses" section of this introduction where recommendations of the AECC, business school alumni, and employers about the value of groups are discussed.

The "delayering" or flattening of the management structure that has swept the private sector in the United States has pushed much of the decision making traditionally done by individual managers down to groups of employees actually doing the work. A survey reported in *The Wall Street Journal* found that two-thirds of 1,811 employers nationwide are using formal teams to conduct work.[1] Also, the increased complexity of the business world has resulted in a situation where no single employee has the breadth of knowledge necessary to make many

[1] *The Wall Street Journal*, November 28, 1995, p. 1.

decisions. Therefore, a team with a diverse set of skills relevant to the problem at hand usually will arrive at better decisions than do individual managers.

You may have noticed the use of the terms "groups" and "teams" in the above discussion, and wondered how they differ. A commonly used distinction is that a group is a number of people assigned to a particular task. A team is a group that has learned to work together effectively on various projects. It is not easy for a group to become an effective team, and many groups never develop into a team.

Your instructor may ask you to complete the Student Information Sheet located at the end of this section. The information collected on this form will help your instructor create diverse groups. The diversity of background should allow you to learn from your group members, as well as from your instructor and the assigned materials. The amount you learn from your group depends on how well your group functions, and whether it becomes a true team.

An important outcome of this course is for you to learn how to build an effective team. The key to creating an effective team is to follow the guidelines for group participation presented in Exhibit I-3. As soon as possible after your group has been created, it should meet and discuss each of the points in Exhibit I-3 in detail. If your group is having difficulty working together, the group should ask your instructor for assistance immediately. Conflicts can escalate quickly and destroy your group.

SUMMARY

Major changes are occurring in the way introductory accounting is taught. The changes include the accounting topics covered, as well as the economic decision making and business knowledge a student is expected to acquire. The changes involve the better development of problem-solving, interpersonal, and computer skills. The basic problem-solving and group skills reviewed in this introduction will be used throughout the course.

Exhibit I-3
Group Assignments
Guidelines for Participation

1. Everyone must contribute to the group's consensus solutions of assigned problems. No sandbaggers (free riders) or dominators allowed.
   - To participate effectively in a group, each group member is individually responsible for doing the assigned advance preparation.
   - Each group member is responsible for making sure that everyone contributes.
   - Peer evaluation sheets will be completed by each group member to monitor individual contributions.
2. Each group member is responsible for all other team members' learning. Help each other to understand your group's solution.
   - Each group member is responsible for making sure that everyone understands the group's consensus solution.
   - The instructor will frequently call on group members at random to explain the group's solution.
   - The objective of each group assignment is not to finish first, but to have all group members master the materials.
3. You can criticize ideas, but not the person presenting the ideas. Keep disagreements at a professional level. Work hard to resolve conflicts in a "team spirit."
4. Each member brings unique knowledge and skills to group tasks, e.g., computer skills. Look for ways to create sharing opportunities through monitoring relationships, both before and during in-class group activities.
   - The group's computer consultant is "officially" responsible for assisting other group members on computer assignments.
5. You can't participate unless you attend class.
   - Bonus points will be given for good attendance in group activities, both in class and outside of class.
   - The group's "recorder" is responsible for recording attendance on each group assignment form before it is turned in to the instructor.

ABOUT THE AUTHORS

Steven J. Adams

Steven J. Adams is professor of accounting at California State University, Chico. He teaches undergraduate and graduate courses in managerial accounting. He has been the Associate Dean of the College of Business, as well as Graduate Coordinator. He was Co-Director of a project funded by U.S. Department of Education's Fund for the Improvement of Post-Secondary Education (FIPSE) to disseminate changes in the first year introductory courses.

Professor Adams is a Certified Management Accountant (CMA), Certified Public Accountant (CPA), and holds a Ph.D. from the University of Cincinnati. Prior to becoming an academic he was a cost analyst for a Fortune 500 company and has consulted for firms in the electronics, retail, and equipment manufacturing industries. Dr. Adams has published in numerous journals in the areas of management control systems and accounting education. Dr. Adams received the joint American Accounting Association/Institute of Management Accountants 1997 James Bulloch Award for Innovations in Management Accounting Education. The Bulloch Award was for the California Car Company case contained in this book. He has also won the College of Business Outstanding Faculty Award, the College of Business Outstanding Research Award, and the MBA Outstanding Teacher Award.

Professor Adams lives with his wife, Sally, and their two children, Jennifer and Kristen. He is a life master duplicate bridge player and enjoys basketball, backpacking, and travel with his family.

LeRoy J. Pryor

LeRoy J. Pryor is professor of accounting and management information systems at California State University, Chico. He teaches courses in accounting information systems, financial accounting, and managerial accounting. He has served as chair of the Department of Accounting and Management Information Systems and is a member of the Accounting Education Advisory Committee and the Corporate Accounting Policy Committee of the American Accounting Association. In 1998, he served as Director of Continuing Professional Education for the American Accounting Association.

Lee is a Certified Public Accountant and holds a Doctorate in Business Administration from the University of Southern California and an MBA with distinction from DePaul University. His undergraduate degree was awarded by the University of Illinois. Prior to entering academe, he worked in public accounting as an auditor for an international firm. He has consulted in many types of businesses, principally in the design of their accounting systems. Dr. Pryor has published articles in *the Journal of Accountancy, Management Accounting, Issues in Accounting Education*, and in several other journals. Dr. Pryor received the joint American Accounting Association/Institute of Management Accountants 1997 James Bulloch Award for Innovations in Management Accounting Education. The Bulloch Award was for a unique pedagogical approach called the California Car Company case. He has received his college's Outstanding Faculty Member Award.

Lee is married to Cathy Sweet. He has a son, Steven, daughter, Ashlee, and three grandchildren, Cooper, Berlyn, and Perris. His hobby is competitive sailing.

Donald E. Keller

Donald E. Keller is Professor Emeritus and past chair of the Department of Accounting and Management Information Systems at California State University, Chico. Before joining CSU, Chico, he was professor and chairman, Department of Accounting and Finance at Seton Hall University, South Orange, New Jersey. From 1974 to 1982, he was Director of Technical Services for the National Association of Accountants (now the Institute of Management Accounts) in New York City. His prior experience includes positions with the American Institute of CPAs, California State University, Northridge, University of Arizona, University of Southern California, San Diego State University, and an international public accounting firm.

Dr. Keller teaches managerial and financial accounting courses at both the graduate and undergraduate levels. He has published in *Management Accounting* and has been author or editor of nine accounting books.

His education includes a B.S. degree from the University of Arizona, an M.S. degree from San Diego State University, and a D.B.A. from the University of Southern California. Dr. Keller is a CPA and a CMA and past president of the Chico Area Chapter of the Institute of Management Accountants, National Director of the Institute of Management Accountants, and is an active member of the American Institute of CPAs, American Accounting Association and the California Society of CPAs.

Professor Keller lives with his wife, Merlene, in San Marcos, California. The Kellers have three children and three grandchildren. His favorite pastime is playing golf.

Mary E. Harston

Mary E. Harston has been teaching at St. Mary's University for eleven years, where she is currently Chair of the Accounting Department. Dr. Harston also has been the project coordinator for the re-engineering of introductory accounting courses at St. Mary's University. She is a Certified Public Accountant in Texas and has worked in both public and corporate accounting. A graduate of the doctoral program at the University of North Texas, her research interests include teaching methodologies, the history of the accounting profession, and ethics in the accounting profession. She is published in all three of these areas. Professor Harston is the 1997 recipient of the Texas Society of Certified Public Accountants Outstanding Educator Award for small universities.

MODULE ONE

TRANSITION FROM USING FINANCIAL ACCOUNTING

Information

Module 1 Introduction

TRANSITION FROM *USING FINANCIAL ACCOUNTING INFORMATION*

MODULE OVERVIEW

Most students using this text have completed a course in financial accounting. Before presenting the body of concepts in management accounting, the authors believe that a brief review in Readings 1-1 and 1-2 of the basic principles underlying financial statements will benefit students. Reading 1-3 introduces students to basic managerial concepts used throughout the book. Module 1 also serves to introduce students who did not use *Using Financial Accounting Information: A Decision Case Approach* in their previous accounting course to a decision case approach.

Learning Objectives

After completing Module 1, you should be able to:

1. Be an informed user of the income statement, the balance sheet, and financial ratios to evaluate the performance of companies.

- Reading 1-1	Using the Income Statement and Balance Sheet for Decisions
- Case 1-1	J & J Corporation: Evaluation of Financial Performance
- Group Assignment 1-1	How is J & J Corporation Doing?
- Exercises and Problems	Exercises and Problems at the end of Reading 1-1

2. Be an informed user of the statement of cash flows by making decisions relating to operating, investing, and financing activities.

- Reading 1-2	Using the Statement Cash Flows for Decisions
- Case 1-2	J & J Corporation: Statement of Cash Flows
- Exercises and Problems	Exercises and Problems at the end of Reading 1-2

3. Determine the relative profitability and breakeven points of segments of a business, as well as costs that are relevant to decisions.

- Reading 1-3	Cost, Volume, and Profitability Decisions
- Case 1-3	J & J Corporation: Opening a New Store
- Exercises and Problems	Exercises and Problems at the end of Reading 1-3

4. Prepare an electronic spreadsheet showing the projected cash flows for a number of years in the future and to determine the payback period.

- Case 1-4	J & J Corporation: Cash Flows for the New Store
- Group Assignment 1-4	Is It a "Grand" Opening?
- Exercises and Problems	Exercises and Problems at the end of Reading 1-4

TERMINOLOGY LIST FOR MODULE 1

Accrual basis of accounting
Amortization
Assets
Book value
Breakeven point
Cash adequacy ratio
Cash flows
Contributed capital
Contribution income statement
Contribution margin
Contribution margin ratio
Current ratio
Debt-to-equity ratio
Entity concept
Financing assets ratio
Fixed costs
Going concern concept
Goodwill
Historical cost concept
Inventory turnover ratio
Liabilities
Liquidity
Market value
Matching principle
Mixed costs
Net income
Relevant cost
Relevant range
Retained earnings
Return on sales ratio
Return on equity ratio
Revenue recognition principle
Sales revenue
Shareholders' or stockholders' equity
Sunk costs
Variable costs

Reading 1-1

USING THE INCOME STATEMENT AND BALANCE SHEET FOR DECISIONS

INTRODUCTION

The publication of financial statements by corporations has become an accepted practice in market economies. People who need to make decisions about their investments require accurate economic information about the companies in which they have a financial stake. The investing public's trust in the system that conveys financial information from inside the corporation to external interested parties is the key to an efficiently running economy such as that of the United States. Reading 1-1 is a review of the information contained in the income statement and the balance sheet. This reading covers the basic analysis that can be made using the data contained in these two financial statements.

The income statement reports the revenues and expenses for a period of time. In doing so it measures the results of business operations for an interval of time such as a year, a quarter or a month. The balance sheet reports the assets, liabilities, and shareholders' equity at a point in time. It is a snapshot that can be used to assess the financial health of the business. Imagine bookends holding upright twelve volumes on a shelf. The bookends represent the beginning and ending balance sheets for the year just ended. Each volume contains a monthly reporting period for which planned and actual revenues and expenses are measured and analyzed. Because financial statements are generally published 60–90 days after the fiscal year end, footnotes may be needed to explain the effect of significant subsequent events and other disclosures. The analysis of data in balance sheets and income statements help managers and owners formulate plans to improve financial results. This financial information also helps managers make the necessary decisions to ensure sustainability and growth of the business.

INCOME STATEMENT

The income statement reports the revenues earned and the expenses incurred during a specific time period. Its purpose is to measure the profitability of the enterprise for that period of time. In equation form the income statement is simply:

Revenues – Expenses = Net income

The two determinants of net income are defined as follows:

Revenue of the enterprise is the total money or value received in exchange for providing customers with the goods and services they purchased in a specific time period.

Expenses are the cost of economic resources consumed in the process of earning revenues during a specific time period.

The measurement of revenues and expenses in published income statements is done in accordance with generally accepted accounting principles, referred to as GAAP. At the core of GAAP is the **accrual basis of accounting**, a method of recording assets, liabilities, revenues, expenses, and owners' equity based upon an objective view of legal and economic events rather than the payment or receipt of cash.

The Financial Accounting Standards Board (FASB) is charged with the responsibility to set the rules for financial reporting in the United Sates. In its nearly thirty-year history, the FASB has amended GAAP numerous times to ensure that financial reporting continues to win the trust and confidence of the investing public. At the time of this writing, the FASB has issued over 140 statements on accounting standards to be followed by corporations that have either issued securities in the United States or must meet the requirements of an independent audit by a certified public accountant.

Of particular importance to the income statement are the revenue recognition principle and the matching principle. The **revenue recognition principle** requires that revenue be reported in the accounting period in which the revenues were earned, not earlier or later. The cash flow associated with the revenue event is *not* the controlling factor. Typically, revenues are reported upon delivery of the goods or services that the customer purchased. Payment by the customer usually arrives after the revenue has been "earned." In a legal sense revenue is earned when title has transferred from the seller to the buyer. However, there are instances when the terms of the sale give the buyer the right to reverse the transaction. For example, some states have a "lemon law." A purchaser of a new car can return it to the dealer if defects are found and cannot be corrected in a timely manner. If the car manufacturer cannot reasonably estimate the cost of complying with the lemon law, it may defer the recognition of revenue until the legislated warranty period permitting return of the car has expired.

The **matching principle** requires that all expenses incurred in generating revenue be reported in the same accounting period as the revenues. The timing of expenses is similar to revenue. Expenses are reported on the income statement when they are incurred. *Incurred* means that the benefit of the expense has already produced an income-generating effect and that no future benefit from the expense is expected. For example, suppose a company pays $1,000 for insurance on its delivery trucks for the month of December 2002. Starting at midnight on December 31, 2002, the insurance expense has no future benefit. Therefore, the expense was incurred in December and must be reported accordingly.

Sample Income Statements

Exhibit 1-1.1 is a sample comparative income statement for Super Stereos. As is common in published financial statements, three years of comparative data are presented with the most recent year shown in the left-most column. Readers of these comparative income statements can easily identify positive and negative trends. For example, consider the trend in net sales (*net* refers to sales less returns). From 2000 to 2002 net sales increased from $486 million to $545 million. If this increase in sales is greater than the average of companies in the same industry, this is considered a positive trend. In contrast, note the gross margin on sales. Although the dollar amount of margin increased from 2000 to 2002, the margin rate as a percentage of net sales declined. This is generally considered a negative development, as investors are wary of competitive pressures that mean lower profits and dividends. An even worse trend is the declining net income in both dollar amounts and as a percentage of net sales. From 2000 to 2002 net income dropped from over $71 million to just under $51 million.

Exhibit 1-1.1

Super Stereos Comparative Income Statements Years Ended December 31 (000s omitted)						
	2002		2001		2000	
	$	%	$	%	$	%
Net sales	$ 545,000	100.00%	$ 505,000	100.00%	$ 486,000	100.00%
Cost of goods sold	330,000	60.55%	304,000	60.20%	286,000	58.85%
Gross margin on sales	$ 215,000	39.45%	$ 201,000	39.80%	$ 200,000	41.15%
Operating expenses	133,000	24.40%	93,000	18.42%	89,000	18.31%
Interest expense	9,450	1.73%	8,320	1.65%	8,380	1.72%
Earnings before income tax	$ 72,550	13.31%	$ 99,680	19.74%	$ 102,620	21.12%
Income tax at 30%	21,765	3.99%	29,904	5.92%	30,786	6.33%
Net income	$ 50,785	9.32%	$ 69,776	13.82%	$ 71,834	14.78%
Average shares outstanding	80,000		50,000		50,000	
Earnings per share	$ 0.63		$ 1.40		$ 1.44	

The Heading

The heading of the income statements indicates the period of time for which revenues and expenses are being reported. The reverse chronological order illustrated in Exhibit 1-1.1 is typical of published financial statements. Because the most recent fiscal year is of the greatest interest to investors, it is shown in the first column.

Net Sales

Sales revenue is the cash or other value received from customers in payment for the goods or services delivered. The word "net" in the income statement in Exhibit 1-1 refers to the fact that occasionally customers return the item they purchased. The detailed accounting records contain the total sales made and a separate record kept for returned sales, the relationship of which may be of interest to management.

Cost of Goods Sold

Cost of goods sold is the expense incurred in selling products to customers. For a retail business, cost of goods sold is the expense of the inventory sold to customers in a certain accounting period. For a manufacturing company, cost of goods sold is comprised of direct material, labor, and factory overhead expenses. Other phrases that caption this major expense are "Cost of Sales" and "Cost of Revenue."

Gross Margin on Sales

Gross margin on sales is a subtotal to measure the profit before selling, administrative, interest, and tax expenses. In the semiconductor industry, Intel's gross profit has reached 70 percent. Similarly, pharmaceutical companies have very high gross profit margins. In both cases their products are protected by patents and advanced technology that competitors do not yet have. In industries where there are many competitors and where product differentiation is slight, the gross margins are much lower. The steel and food distribution industries are examples where low margins on sales are typical.

Operating Expenses

Operating expenses is a category of expenses that contains such items as administrative salaries, insurance, rent, commissions to sales staff, and other nonfactory costs of doing business.

Interest Expense

Interest expense is the cost of borrowing. Super Stereos reports long-term notes payable of approximately $176 million on its 2002 balance sheet (see Exhibit 1-1.2). The interest rate on the borrowed funds caused this expense.

Income Tax

Income taxes are assessed by the federal government and by some of the states. The amount shown as income tax expense is based on a set of rules developed by the FASB and is a complex process. In the case of Super Stereos the effective tax rate is 30 percent, which is used to report this expense. Some companies are able to defer payment of a portion of the tax expense.

Net Income

Net income (or loss) is the residual of revenues less all expenses for a given accounting period, such as a year, a three-month quarter, or a month. Net income increases shareholders' equity and a net loss decreases shareholders' equity. Such changes in shareholders' equity are shown in the retained earnings account on the balance sheet. Net income is transferred to retained earnings once each year soon after the fiscal year has ended.

When companies publish their annual reports to shareholders they may use words that are synonymous with net income. "Earnings" and "profits" are two examples of terminology used to convey the concept of net income, namely revenues minus expenses.

Basic Earnings per Share

Earnings per share (EPS) is closely watched by financial statement users. Basic earnings per share is the net income less any dividends on preferred shares divided by the average number of common shares outstanding during the year. Super Stereos has not issued any preferred shares; only common stock has been issued. Therefore all of the reported net income is divided by the common shares outstanding each year (technical issues in arriving at the weighted average number of shares outstanding during a fiscal year are beyond the scope of this text).

Diluted Earnings per Share

Diluted earnings per share is net income divided by the number of common stock shares outstanding plus all potential new shares that could be issued to fulfill contractual arrangements. Of increasing importance is the modifying word "diluted" when reporting earnings per share. Contractual arrangements, which many corporations have with other parties, have the potential to increase the number of shares outstanding. The potential increase in shares is termed dilution. Stock options are an example of such an agreement. Employees of the company are given options to purchase shares at a fixed price for a number of years in the future. If the market price of the stock rises in the open market, the stock options held by employees become valuable because they enable the employees to purchase shares at the lower price. If an employee has a stock option for 1,000 shares at a price of $10 and exercises the option two years later when the market price is $25, the employee has enjoyed a gain of $15,000. Many companies are granting stock options to all employees, not just top management, in the hope that more employees will be motivated to make greater contributions to the corporate goals and become long-term employees.

Other examples of potential dilution are convertible bonds and preferred stock. Diluted EPS takes into account the prospect of the holders of these securities choosing to convert their bonds or preferred shares into common stock. For example, if conversion of one or both of the above securities could increase the number of shares outstanding by a material amount, the existing shareholders need to be informed about the potential dilution.

THE BALANCE SHEET

The balance sheet is so named because it is based upon the following equality:

Assets = Liabilities + Shareholders' equity

The definitions of the terms in the balance sheet equation follow.

Assets are probable future economic benefits owned or controlled by the company that result from past transactions or events. An example is a building used in conducting business. A building's useful life is twenty years or more. It appears on the balance sheet because the amount of its undepreciated cost is the accounting measurement of its future economic benefit.

Liabilities are obligations to transfer cash or other assets to other entities. When a company raises money from a bank or other creditor to purchase assets, the balance sheet reports the debt owed to the lender. Purchases of inventory and services on short-term credit are also shown as a liability until paid. The total liability amount appearing on a balance sheet can be viewed as the portion of the total assets that all creditors are financing.

Shareholders' (or **stockholders'**) **Equity** is the portion of a corporation's assets financed by the owners of the entity. This section of the balance sheet consists of two basic parts: the contributed capital and the retained earnings. **Contributed capital** is the amount invested in the corporation by shareholders. This contribution is a one-way street. The corporation is not legally required to pay back the amounts paid into the corporation. If shareholders want to recover their investment, they have the option of selling their shares in the open market such as that of the New York Stock Exchange. The number of shares traded daily exceeds 3 billion on these two exchanges, but this activity has no impact on the balance sheets of the corporations whose shares are traded. Rather, these transactions are between investors who are selling and buying these stocks. When a stock rises or falls for whatever reason, there is no recording of this event on the financial statements of the issuing corporation. The gains or losses sustained are instead reflected in the accounts of the investors who buy, sell, or own shares in the corporation's stock.

Retained Earnings in the stockholders' equity section is the cumulative net income (net of losses) less the total of dividends declared to shareholders since inception of the corporation. Although the phrase "retained earnings" may cause students to infer it is cash, it is not! Remember, retained earnings simply represents a portion of the assets financed by the owners of the corporations. Typically, the cash generated by the earning process, less dividends paid out, is used to purchase assets such as new equipment and inventory.

Investments in these assets are aimed at sustaining and expanding the business. Cash assets and retained earnings are on opposite sides of the balance sheet. Cash is one of the economic resources of a business; retained earnings is an ownership claim on the economic resources. Net income added to retained earnings does not normally result in similar additions to the cash assets of a company. In Reading 1-2, you will see how net income and changes in the balance sheet affect the cash flow of a company.

Key Concepts

There are three important concepts that guide the preparation of the balance sheet: the entity concept, the historical cost concept, and the going concern concept. The **entity concept** states that there must be a separation of the personal financial affairs of owners from those of the business entity. To allow a commingling of the personal and business transactions would destroy the information contained in financial statements. For example, prospective investors would not be able to judge whether a business is a financial success or whether it is the result of a subsidization by one who might be promoting the sale of shares.

The **historical cost concept** states that the assets should be reported at the actual price to acquire them. In addition, costs incurred to place an asset into service are part of historical cost. For example, a machine may cost $10,000 and the installation costs to get the machine working are $5,000. The historical cost of the machine will be shown on the balance sheet as $15,000. The proper measurement of historical cost of assets is important because the depreciation expense will be based on it.

The external market value for assets can rise above the asset's historical cost. Suppose that an asset such as land has appreciated in value because of the general growth in population surrounding the property. While this information is important to the business owners, balance sheets do not report market values because to do so would bring subjective opinion into the balance sheet. Without the historical cost concept, balance sheets would be based on guesswork and appraisals instead of on completed economic transactions and their associated facts.

There are instances when the market value of an inventory asset falls below the historical cost. For example, if a manufacturer with a large inventory of analog cell phones finds that the demand has shifted to digital cell phones, the disposal value of the analog phones may be lower than the cost to make them. Special accounting rules called lower of cost or market are designed to prevent inventory assets from being reported at historical cost when the reality is that they will be sold for less than that cost. In this case a loss must be reported when there is evidence that cost is higher than market, thus bringing the inventory down to its realizable value.

The **going concern concept** is an assumption that the business entity will continue for an indefinite future period. In other words, the valuation of assets and liabilities is not based upon the prospect of immediate liquidation, the selling of all assets and winding up the affairs of the business. Instead, the going concern concept is the assumption that the business will continue indefinitely and utilize its assets for the extent of their useful life. In the case of long-lived assets, the going concern concept justifies the allocation of historical cost of the asset to expense over its predicted useful life. This allocation is called depreciation expense.

Sample Balance Sheets

Exhibit 1-1.2 illustrates a sample comparative balance sheet. This exhibit is also labeled "comparative" because three snapshots of the financial position of Super Stereos are shown at the end of three years. Readers can identify trends or important changes in the assets or the way assets are being financed. The following is a discussion of the major sections of the balance sheet.

The Heading

The heading of the balance sheet always gives the date at which the reported values are effective. Because the most recent fiscal year is of the greatest interest to users, it is shown in the first column of comparative balance sheets.

Current Assets

Current assets are cash or equivalent items, such as certificates of deposit, and assets that are expected to be used or converted into cash within the next year. Of the total 2002 current assets of $328,950,000 in Exhibit 1-1.2, merchandise inventory comprises about half. Normally inventory turns over several times per year. Therefore, it is anticipated that most of the inventory on hand at December 31, 2002, will be sold within the next twelve months. When inventory items become obsolete, accounting rules require that such inventory be written down to its disposable value, which can be well below original cost. Similarly, accounts receivable must be adjusted for any uncollectable customer accounts. The "net" next to accounts receivable indicates that the adjustment had been made to allow for uncollectable accounts expense.

Property and Equipment

Property and equipment are the long-lived, physical assets of the company. They are reported at their historical cost. When an asset is sold, it is removed from the balance sheet so that only the original cost of the assets remaining is reported.

Accumulated Depreciation

Accumulated depreciation is the cumulative sum of all depreciation recorded for an asset since its purchase and placement into service. Land assets are not depreciated because land normally does not wear out or become obsolete. Therefore, the $122 million shown in Exhibit 1-1.2 for 2002 accumulated depreciation is the depreciation expense taken over the entire lives to date for all building and equipment assets owned by Super Stereos at December 31, 2002. To determine the amount of accumulated depreciation on each category of asset, refer to the footnotes to the financial statements, where more detailed information is often provided.

The subtotal below the accumulated depreciation, $392 million for 2002, is called net property and equipment. There is no suggestion that the market value is the same. The going concern concept and historical cost concept justify the use of original cost minus the systematic depreciation expense taken on the assets since they were acquired.

Exhibit 1-1.2

Super Stereos
Comparative Balance Sheets
December 31 (000s omitted)

	2002	2001	2000
Assets			
Current assets			
Cash	$ 48,500	$ 58,000	$ 52,000
Accounts receivable, net	89,000	76,000	68,000
Merchandise inventory	165,000	154,000	150,000
Prepaid expenses	26,450	28,650	28,650
Total current assets	$ 328,950	$ 316,650	$ 298,650
Property and equipment			
Land	$ 93,000	$ 68,000	$ 68,000
Building	325,000	154,000	154,000
Equipment	96,000	62,030	61,040
	$ 514,000	$ 284,030	$ 283,040
Accumulated depreciation	(122,000)	(86,120)	(86,000)
Property and equipment, net	$ 392,000	$ 197,910	$ 197,040
Other assets	13,320	13,320	13,320
Total assets	$ 734,270	$ 527,880	$ 509,010
Liabilities and Stockholders' Equity			
Current liabilities			
Notes payable	$ 40,050	$ 30,050	$ 10,000
Accounts payable	44,000	59,000	61,000
Accrued expenses	48,060	27,650	28,450
Income taxes payable	36,000	34,210	35,550
Total current liabilities	$ 168,110	$ 150,910	$ 135,000
Long-term liabilities			
Long-term notes payable	176,000	130,000	130,000
Total liabilities	$ 344,110	$ 280,910	$ 265,000
Stockholders' equity			
Common stock, $1 par	$ 80,000	$ 50,000	$ 50,000
Additional paid-in capital	150,000	70,000	70,000
Retained earnings	160,160	126,970	124,010
Total stockholders' equity	$ 390,160	$ 246,970	$ 244,010
Total liabilities and stockholders' equity	$ 734,270	$ 527,880	$ 509,010

Other Assets

Other assets are long-term assets not classified as property and equipment that are not expected to be converted into cash quickly. Examples include goodwill, patents, and other intangible assets.

Total Assets

As the caption suggests, this is the total of all assets as of the dates of the three balance sheets in Exhibit 1-1.2. Note the increase from 2001 to 2002. How this increase in assets was financed is answered in the information contained in the Liabilities and Stockholders' Equity section of the balance sheet.

Current Liabilities

Current liabilities are the debts and obligations that will be paid in cash or satisfied with other assets within the next year. The total of the four current liabilities for 2002 is slightly over $168 million; this is an increase from the previous year. Readers of balance sheets compare the level of current assets with the level of current liabilities because it is the former that normally is used to pay off the latter.

Long-Term Liabilities

Long-term liabilities are debts of a corporation that are not due within the next year. Companies issue bonds and notes with a maturity of ten years or more to finance the purchase of long-lived assets. Super Stereos has increased its long-term borrowing by $46 million in 2002. This partly explains how a portion of the increase in total assets in 2002 was financed. The interest expense on the income statement is the result of this and other debts on the balance sheet.

Stockholders' Equity

Stockholders' equity (also called shareholders' equity or owners' equity) reports the collective economic interest of the owners of the corporation. The values reported are the result of the various key concepts discussed above. The values also are the result of many accounting rules comprising GAAP. The values reported *are not* the total market value of all shares held by stockholders. Instead, the stockholders' equity is the sum of the actual amount invested in the corporation and the net earnings of the business after dividends have been paid out to shareholders. These amounts are the cumulative totals since inception of the corporation.

Financial analysts often refer to market capitalization (price per share × the number of shares outstanding) to compare differences between book value and market value of a company's shares. **Book value** for an entire firm is the accounting value of the firm's assets less the value of its liabilities. In other words, it is equal to the amount of a company's shareholders' equity. Price or market value per share is the quoted price of the share on the stock exchange. **Market value** is the product of investors' expectations about the company's economic future. In times of economic growth, low inflation, and low interest rates, many stocks' market prices exceed their book values. In times of recession, high interest rates, and deteriorating income prospects, market values often fall below book values.

Super Stereos has what might be called a simple capital structure because the corporation has issued only one class of stock, namely common stock. A number of companies issue another class of stock called preferred stock. Ways in which preferred stock differs from common stock include having a stated dividend rate and a first claim on payment of dividends. Many analysts treat preferred stock as debt because the features are very similar to that of a bond. Moreover, preferred shares do not possess voting rights as do common shares.

Common stock for Super Stereos has a par value of $1, which is an arbitrary amount set at the time the corporation was chartered. The comparison of the common stock account from 2001 to 2002 shows the increase of $30 million. This means that 30 million more shares were issued in 2002. Were they issued for $1 each? No. Note the additional paid-in capital account. It increased by $80 million from 2001 to 2002. Combining the two increases tells us that the shares were issued for a total of $110 million, or an average of $3.67 per share. This infusion of new capital into the corporation is a further explanation of how the increase in assets was financed.

The increase in retained earnings from 2001 to 2002 is less than the income for 2002. This suggests that a dividend was declared and paid to the shareholders. Recall that income was almost $51 million. The increase in retained earnings is approximately $33 million. This indicates that Super Stereos declared an $18 million dividend in 2002 (assuming no unusual events occurred in 2002 that caused an adjustment to retained earnings). Thus, $33 million of income for 2002 was reinvested in the business and is yet another explanation of how the increase in assets was accomplished.

INTANGIBLE ASSETS

An intangible asset is an asset that does not have a physical form. The value of intangible assets derives from its expected future benefits. Examples of intangible assets include trademarks, copyrights, and patents. Normally the appearance of intangible assets on a balance sheet is the result of a purchase transaction. If the seller has a bona fide legal and/or economic right to intangible assets, the buyer will benefit by purchasing the assets. An example is a patent that has 7 years remaining of the original 17 years protection granted by the federal government.

An intangible asset that expires soon will be of little value to the buyer. Like fixed assets, intangible assets are initially recorded in the accounting records at cost and that cost is allocated over all periods benefited. This allocation is called **amortization**. The amount shown at any given point in time for the intangible asset is its cost less its total amortization to date. Once again, this does not correspond in any way to market value. Determining the market value of intangible assets is a difficult and subjective task, often performed by consultants.

Goodwill

Another example of an intangible asset that may appear on the balance sheet of an existing business is called **goodwill**. Proper accounting practice restricts the creation of goodwill to that which arises from purchase transactions. It cannot be added to the balance sheet unless it is the result of a purchase of a going business. If the amount paid for an existing business exceeds the fair market value of the net assets acquired, then the excess is classified as an intangible asset called goodwill. Fair market value is an objective estimate of the price of assets that two parties seeking their own best financial well-being will agree to in a buy-sell transaction. Presumably the buyers, seeking their own best interests, would be willing to pay a premium over fair market value only when indications are that the business will earn above-average profits in the future. Above-average profits can result from the company having a unique competitive advantage such as proprietary technology, extraordinary employees, a strong, loyal customer base, or a very desirable location.

The buyer must be wary of any goodwill appearing on the balance sheet of an existing business because it may no longer be valuable. Goodwill was established when the company was purchased by its current owners, or when the company purchased other businesses. Also note that goodwill is not separable from the other assets on the balance sheet; its value, if any, is based upon the above-average future profitability.

A Case History of Goodwill

A local landmark bar and hamburger grill, the Madison Bear Garden, was purchased by North Valley Saloon (NVS) Inc. NVS's president, Jack Sterling, had done a great deal of research before making his offer to buy "The Bear." After several rounds of negotiation, a deal was finally struck.

Although Mr. Sterling did not disclose the details of his offer, let's assume the following:

- Sterling paid $50,000 cash and signed a 10-year, 8 percent note payable for $1,300,000. The note is a "simple interest" note with interest payable annually. The principal is due at the end of 10 years.

- He assumed an existing mortgage on the land and building with an outstanding balance of $250,000. The mortgage's interest rate is 7.8 percent, which reflects an interest rate similar to mortgage rates available in the current marketplace.

- The fair market value of all tangible assets (which included land, buildings, supplies, bar equipment, hamburger grills, furniture and fixtures, a computerized cash register, and wall artifacts) was $1,400,000. The fair market value was obtained by taking the average of two independent appraisals. There were no accounts receivable.

- The only outstanding debt to be assumed by Sterling was the mortgage.

Let's step back and take a look at what's happened here.

1. How much has Sterling "paid" for The Bear? **Answer**: $50,000 cash + $1,300,000 note payable + $250,000 mortgage payable, for a total of $1,600,000.

2. How much was the fair market value of the tangible assets acquired by Sterling? **Answer**: $1,400,000.

3. Why would Sterling be willing to pay $200,000 more for The Bear than the total fair value of the net assets acquired? **Answer**: Sterling believes that The Bear has some value that exceeds the sum of the individual assets acquired. This "value" to Sterling is recorded as goodwill on the opening balance sheet for the new business. The changes to the balance sheet of the acquirer are as follows:

Cash	Tangible Assets*	Goodwill	Notes Payable	Mortgage Payable
–$50,000	+$1,400,000	+$200,000	+$1,300,000	+$250,000

*Although $1,400,000 is shown as one entry here, each asset acquired would be recorded at its fair market value.

4. What are some of the reasons that goodwill exists? In other words, what would cause goodwill to be created? **Answer**: In The Bear's case, there are a few primary reasons why a prospective new owner would be willing to pay more for the business than its underlying net assets would suggest: location, standing in the community, and reputation for making one of the best burgers in town.

5. Assume that the previous owner of The Bear was the first and only owner since The Bear began operations. Could the previous owner show goodwill on its balance sheet? **Answer**: No, a business can reflect goodwill in the accounting records only when it acquires another entity at an amount greater than the fair market value of the net assets of that entity. Unlike other specifically identifiable assets, the components of goodwill cannot be sold separately. That is, all net assets are treated as a unit rather than being sold individually. Only when a business changes hands can the excess of the purchase price over the fair value of net identifiable assets be measured and recorded.

   Therefore, the goodwill shown on the balance sheet is *not* a measure of the economic value of goodwill for the entire company. It is only the unimpaired net amount paid in excess of fair market value of assets acquired. According to new financial accounting rules, goodwill no longer can be amortized and must be shown at its unimpaired value.

6. In The Bear's case, Sterling was willing to pay $200,000 more for The Bear than the underlying fair value of the net assets he acquired. How do you think he may have arrived at this figure? **Answer**: Clearly, the $200,000 was a result of the negotiations that ultimately led to a $1,600,000 sales price. In order to make that offer, Sterling must have felt that the future earning power of The Bear was sufficient to justify the $1,600,000 price.

   The assumption is that Sterling had a rational approach to arriving at the $1,600,000 purchase price. He could have sat down with his financial advisor and studied the previous owner's income statements. If the average net income over the past several years was greater than a typical bar/restaurant business in the area, and if Sterling expects these excess earnings to continue under his management, he could have computed the present value of these excess earnings by discounting them at the required rate of return for investments with similar risk. Or, more simply, if the excess earnings were $100,000 per year, Sterling may have agreed to pay for the next two years of excess earnings by paying a premium over the $1,400,000 appraisal value of the tangible assets

After Goodwill Is Recorded on the Balance Sheet

In the past GAAP has required the amortization of goodwill not to exceed 40 years. In the case of the Madison Bear Garden purchase by Jack Sterling, the $200,000 of recorded goodwill would have been expensed (amortized) over 40 years or less. If Sterling and his accountant thought it appropriate to amortize the goodwill over 20 years, $10,000 per year would have been expensed.

In 2001, the Financial Accounting Standards Board (FASB) adopted a change in the accounting for goodwill. Instead of the systematic amortization of goodwill over a period not to exceed 40 years, the FASB stipulated that goodwill be expensed only when there is evidence that the goodwill, acquired as part of an acquisition, has suffered impairment of (decrease in) value. The new rule also prohibits the continued amortization of goodwill purchased prior to the effective date of the 2001 FASB pronouncement. Now, management must make an annual review to justify reporting goodwill at its purchased amount and record a loss for the amount of any decline in value of purchased goodwill.

INCOME STATEMENT AND BALANCE SHEET LINKAGE

Exhibit 1-1.3 illustrates how the income statement and balance sheet tie together. You will notice that the income statement computes the profit of the company, called net income, and that this amount increases retained earnings, a balance sheet account. Retained earnings are decreased by dividends. These increases and decreases can be seen on the statement of retained earnings, often presented in a footnote to the financial statements or as part of the income statement. The ending retained earnings balance from the retained earnings statement is also shown in the owner's equity section of the balance sheet. The cash flow statement is not shown here.

Exhibit 1-1.3
The Links Connecting the Income Statement and Balance Sheet

Bouncing Bungies Company
Income Statement
Month Ended December 31, 2002

Revenues		
Ticket revenue		$8,525
Expenses		
Wage expense	$2,400	
Supplies expense	1,500	
Advertising expense	1,500	
Insurance expense	400	
Utilities expense	300	
Depreciation expense	100	
Interest expense	41	
Service charge	15	
Total expenses		6,256
Net income		$2,269

Bouncing Bungies Company
Statement of Retained Earnings
Month Ended December 31, 2002

Retained earnings, December 1, 2002	$ 0
Add Net income	2,269
Subtotal	2,269
Dividends	(43)
Retained earnings, December 31, 2002	$ 2,226

Bouncing Bungies Company
Balance Sheet
December 31, 2002

Assets			Liabilities and Owner's Equity		
Current assets			Current liabilities		
Cash	$ 8,141		Accounts payable	$ 2,000	
Accounts receivable	1,000		Gift certificates	25	
Supplies	500		Wages payable	2,400	
Prepaid insurance	4,400		Total current liabilities		$ 4,425
Total current assets		$ 14,041			
			Long term liabilities		
Fixed assets			Note payable		5,290
Bungies, net		7,900			
			Owner's equity		
			Contributed capital	10,000	
			Retained earnings	2,226	
			Total owner's equity		12,226
Total Assets		$ 21,941	Total Liabilities and Owner's Equity		$ 21,941

The heading of the statement of financial position (the balance sheet) tells us that the company name is Bouncing Bungies Company and that the statement date is December 31, 2002. To emphasize that retained earnings is not the same as cash or any other asset, note how income less dividends is transferred to the owner's equity section of the balance sheet, on the opposite side of the balance sheet from that of the assets. The income less dividends simply adds to the claim that the owners have on the assets. Small businesses often discover that to grow the business requires the reinvestment of income into various assets.

RATIO ANALYSIS OF FINANCIAL STATEMENTS

Users of financial statements, including shareholders, bankers, and management, often rely on ratio analysis to gain insight into the operations of a company. Ratios can be used to evaluate a company's performance over time, as well as to compare one company with other companies. In Module 1 we will use the following five key ratios to help us review financial statement relationships.

Current Ratio

The **current ratio** (CR) is a measure of a company's ability to meet its short-term debt obligations. A value of one would result if current assets were equal to current liabilities. A CR equal to 1 is considered marginal; the company possibly is having difficulty meeting scheduled payments to creditors. A CR of 4 means that there are four dollars of current assets for every dollar of current liabilities reported on the balance sheet. This favorable ratio gives the company much flexibility to manage its current assets and still have sufficient cash resources to pay short-term debts when due. In equation form,

$$CR = \frac{\text{Total current assets}}{\text{Total current liabilities}}$$

For many companies, a long-standing rule of thumb is that the current ratio should be no less that 2. For every dollar of current liabilities, there should be at least two dollars of current assets. However, there needs to be a careful assessment of the liquidity needs of the business. For example, in a highly seasonal business such as a holiday ornaments or fireworks manufacturer, it may be more prudent to have a significantly greater ratio because of the time it will take to manufacture the product, sell the product on credit, and collect the resulting accounts receivable. Conversely, an airline, which collects much of its revenue in advance of service, may not require a robust CR since it does not manufacture a product, thus precluding the need for inventory investments. Many electric and water utilities have a CR of less than 2.

The best approach to determining the range of CR that is appropriate is to compare the CR of the company being researched with its counterparts in the same industry. Because the financial characteristics of an industry will impact all companies in essentially the same way, a study of the CR exhibited by competitors will provide a good guide to the appropriate CR level.

Return on Equity Ratio

The **return on equity ratio** (ROE) is computed by dividing net income by average shareholders' (or stockholders') equity. Average equity is the sum of the beginning equity balance and ending equity balance divided by 2. In equation form,

$$ROE = \frac{\text{Net income}}{(\text{Beginning equity} + \text{Ending equity}) \div 2}$$

Return on equity is usually considered to be the primary measure of overall company performance. A high ratio compared to previous years and to companies that face similar risks is an indication of good performance.

Return on Sales Ratio

The **return on sales** (ROS), often referred to as profit margin percentage, is computed by dividing net income by sales revenue. In equation form,

$$ROS = \frac{\text{Net income}}{\text{Sales revenue}}$$

The operating performance ratio is a measure of the profit earned on each sales dollar. An increasing or high ratio relative to other companies in the same industry is usually an indication of efficient operations and good cost control. It is important to compare this ratio only with companies in the same industry, because it will vary greatly from industry to industry. For example, a reasonable ROS ratio might be .02 for a supermarket and .10 for a jewelry store. One reason for the difference is that supermarkets may generate several times the level of sales per dollar of investment than do jewelry stores. As a result, supermarkets need earn only a fraction of net income per dollar of sales relative to other industries in order to earn the same return on equity.

Inventory Turnover Ratio

The **inventory turnover ratio** (ITR) is computed by dividing cost of goods sold by average inventory. In equation form,

$$ITR = \frac{\text{Cost of goods sold}}{(\text{Beginning inventory} + \text{Ending inventory}) \div 2}$$

The inventory turnover ratio is a measure of how efficiently inventory is managed. An increasing or high ratio relative to other companies in the same industry is usually an indication of efficient inventory management. All other factors held constant, the higher a company's inventory turnover ratio, the lower its selling price and operating performance margin must be to earn the same return on equity. Later in this course we will learn that inventory turnover is also an important measure of flexibility and ability to meet customer needs.

Debt-to-Equity Ratio

The **debt-to-equity ratio** (DER) is computed by dividing the total debt by total equity at the balance sheet date. In equation form,

$$DER = \frac{\text{Ending total liabilities}}{\text{Ending stockholders' equity}}$$

The debt-to-equity ratio is a measure of a company's financial risk (likelihood of going bankrupt) and the extent to which a company is taking advantage of cheaper debt financing. Both a relatively high and a relatively low ratio are undesirable. Therefore, companies strive to achieve an optimum ratio.

An increasing or high debt-to-equity ratio relative to the industry indicates higher financial risk and greater use of debt financing. A decreasing or low ratio relative to the industry may mean that the company isn't utilizing lower-cost debt financing to the optimum extent. Companies with too low of a ratio may risk being taken over by other investors willing to finance with more debt. The debt-to-equity ratio is particularly important to bankers, bondholders, and other creditors.

SUMMARY

The income statement and balance sheet present two facets of financial health. The income statement enables the reader to evaluate operating performance. The balance sheet enables the reader to assess the overall health and financial risk of the entity. Five ratios were presented that facilitate the comparison of different companies. With these tools businesses of varying sizes can be analyzed to gain insights into their performance relative to one another and to the industry norms. In the case that follows, you are asked to evaluate the performance of J & J Corporation.

EXERCISES AND PROBLEMS

Exercises

Exercise 1 Revenue. Which accounting principle governs how revenues are reported? Apply the principle to airline tickets that are booked six weeks in advance of the scheduled flight.

Exercise 2 Expenses. Which accounting principle governs the timing of expenses in the income statement? Apply the principle to the cost of catered food service on a specific flight from San Francisco to Hong Kong.

Exercise 3 Income Statement. Explain the difference between cost of goods sold and operating expenses in the income statement. Give two examples of each expense category that you might find in a supermarket grocery.

Exercise 4 Gross Margin on Sales. Define gross margin in the income statement. What industries do you think are characterized by a high gross margin? What industries do you think are characterized by a low gross margin?

Exercise 5 Net Income. Define net income. Why is the heading of the income statement so important? What other terms might you expect to see in annual reports to convey the concept of income?

Exercise 6 Earnings per Share. Write the formula for earnings per share. What part of the formula is affected when dilution is possible?

Exercise 7 Balance Sheet. Define the three components of the balance sheet equation. What is contained in the heading of the balance sheet?

Exercise 8 Retained Earnings. Where is retained earnings found on the balance sheet? For a corporation that is profitable year after year and which pays dividends to its shareholders, why does the retained earnings amount continue to increase?

Exercise 9 Asset Recognition Concepts. What are the three concepts that guide the preparation of the balance sheet? Which concept prohibits the inclusion of the owners' personal assets from being included in the balance sheet?

Exercise 10 Asset Valuation. A balance sheet reports the asset land at $100,000. Is this what it could be sold for at the balance sheet date?

Problems

Problem 1 Income Statement. From the following list of transactions, prepare an income statement in good form for Dine Easy Restaurant, Inc., for the year 2002. (*Hint*: Not all transactions belong in the income statement.)

1. Total billings for all meals served in 2002: $65,000 during the twelve months ended December 31, 2002.
2. Owners were paid a dividend by Dine Easy of $10,000.
3. Fraudulent credit cards used to pay for meals, $2,000.
4. A new shareholder contributed $10,000 to the shareholder equity.
5. Rent on the building for 2002, $12,000.
6. A fire in the kitchen in 2001 was repaired in January 2002 for $3,000; there was no insurance coverage. Payment was made to the repair contractor in February 2002.
7. Depreciation of furniture, fixtures, and equipment for 2002, $7,000.
8. Wages for 2002 considered to be operating expenses, $30,000.
9. Food supplies purchased and used in 2002, $15,000.
10. Inventory of food supplies at January 1, 2002 was $1,000; inventory of food supplies at December 31, 2002 was zero.

Problem 2 Balance Sheet. Prepare a balance sheet in good form for Internet Service Co. as of December 31, 2002. All amounts are as of December 31, 2002, unless otherwise noted.

1. Accounts payable, $4,500.
2. Computer equipment original cost, $25,000; accumulated depreciation, $7,500.
3. Common stock, $20,000.
4. Computer supplies: January 1, 2002, $15,000; December 31, 2002, $4,000.
5. Shareholder's personal residence, $320,000.
6. Cash in the company checking account, $6,000.
7. New network server purchased on December 31, 2002 by credit card and not included in 1 and 2 above, $5,000.
8. Accounts receivable, $7,000.
9. Liability for alimony to shareholder's former spouse, $5,000.
10. Retained earnings at January 1, 2002, $3,500. No dividends were declared or paid in the 2002.
11. Net income for 2002, $6,500

Problem 3 Financial Statement Ratios. Use the financial statements in Exhibit 1-1.3 to calculate the return on equity, return on sales, and debt-to-equity ratios. If companies in the same industry have ratios of .10, .20 and .25, respectively, how would you evaluate profitability (ROE and ROS) and financial risk (DER)?

Problem 4 Balance Sheet and Income Statement Linkages. Perris Construction Company began business in January 2000. Complete the following table.

Totals as of	*December 31: 2000*	*2001*	*2002*
Assets	$ 46,000	$ 100,000	?
Liabilities	8,000	32,000	20,000
Shareholders' equity	?	?	?
Changes During Year:			
Net income (loss)	$ 20,000	?	$ 32,000
Dividends	?	16,000	12,000
Shareholder investment	$ 24,000	$ 10,000	$ 20,000

Problem 5 EPS, ROS, and Average Shares. Using the income statement for Texas Instruments (TI) in Exhibit 1-1.4:

a. Calculate the average shares used to compute basis earnings per share for each of the three years.

b. Comment on the change, if any, in the numbers of average shares used to compute EPS.

c. Comment on the difference between the average numbers of shares of basic versus diluted for EPS.

d. Compute ROS for each of the three years.

Problem 6 Analysis of the TI Balance Sheet. Using the data in Exhibit 1-1.5:

a. Compute the current ratio for each year. Comment on the change, if any, in the ratio.

b. Compute the inventory turnover ratio (ITR) for each year. *Hint:* Assume the beginning inventory for year 1999 was $700 million. Comment on any change in the ITR.

c. Compute the DER for each year. Comment on any change.

d. What was the main reason for the increase in retained earnings in 2000?

e. Calculate ROE for each year. *Hint:* You will need to use the net income for 1999 and 2000 in Exhibit 1-1.4. Assume that total stockholders' equity at the beginning of 1999 (end of 1998) was $9,000 million (9 billion). Comment on the change if any.

Exhibit 1-1.4

TEXAS INSTRUMENTS INCORPORATED AND SUBSIDIARIES Income Statement *(Millions of dollars, except per-share amounts.)*			
	For the years ended December 31		
Income	**2000**	**1999**	**1998**
Net revenues	**$ 11,875**	$ 9,759	$ 8,875
Operating costs and expenses:			
Cost of revenues	**6,120**	5,069	5,605
Research and development	**1,747**	1,379	1,265
Selling, general and administrative	**1,669**	1,556	1,549
Total	**9,536**	8,004	8,419
Profit from operations	**2,339**	1,755	456
Other income (expense) net	**2,314**	403	301
Interest on loans	**75**	76	76
Income before provision for income taxes and cumulative effect of an accounting change	**4,578**	2,082	681
Provision for income taxes	**1,491**	631	229
Income before cumulative effect of an accounting change	**3,087**	1,451	452
Cumulative effect of an accounting change	**(29)**	--	--
Net income	**$ 3,058**	$ 1,451	$ 452
Diluted earnings per common share:			
Income before cumulative effect of an accounting change	**$ 1.73**	$ 0.83	$ 0.26
Cumulative effect of an accounting change	**(.02)**	--	--
Net income	**$ 1.71**	$ 0.83	$ 0.26
Basic earnings per common share:			
Income before cumulative effect of an accounting change	**$ 1.80**	$ 0.86	$ 0.27
Cumulative effect of an accounting change	**(.02)**	--	--
Net income	**$ 1.78**	$ 0.86	$ 0.27

Problem 7 What If Analysis of Texas Instruments Financial Information. Using Exhibits 1-1.4 and 1-1.5 (assume the three items below retained earnings do not change in 2001):

a. If the board of directors of Texas Instruments set a goal of increasing the book value per share to $10 by the end of 2001, how much would net income have to be to achieve that goal?

b. If the management of Texas Instruments forecast net income to drop to $2 billion in 2001 and the board still wishes to increase total stockholders' equity to $16 billion, how much additional contributed capital would be needed to achieve that goal?

c. Assume your answer to (b) is $3 billion and the management in concurrence with the board does not wish to issue more than 75 million new shares, at what price would the shares need to be issued? Assess the feasibility of reaching this goal by researching Texas Instruments' stock price for 2001.

Exhibit 1-1.5

TEXAS INSTRUMENTS INCORPORATED AND SUBSIDIARIES
Consolidated Financial Statements
(Millions of dollars, except per-share amounts.)

	December 31	
BALANCE SHEET	**2000**	**1999**
Assets		
Current assets		
Cash and cash equivalents	$ 745	$ 781
Short-term investments	3,258	2,045
Accounts receivable, net of allowance for losses	2,204	1,909
Inventories	1,233	894
Prepaid expenses	80	109
Deferred income taxes	595	615
Total current assets	8,115	6,353
Property, plant, and equipment at cost	9,099	7,338
Less accumulated depreciation	(3,652)	(3,405)
Property, plant, and equipment (net)	5,447	3,933
Investments	2,400	4,205
Goodwill and other acquisition-related intangibles	961	502
Deferred income taxes	106	41
Other assets	691	393
Total assets	$ 17,720	$ 15,427
Liabilities and Stockholders' Equity		
Current liabilities		
Loans payable and current portion long-term debt	$ 148	$ 331
Accounts payable and accrued expenses	1,921	1,722
Income taxes payable	323	270
Accrued retirement and profit sharing contributions	421	374
Total current liabilities	2,813	2,697
Long-term debt	1,216	1,099
Accrued retirement costs	378	797
Deferred income taxes	469	998
Deferred credits and other liabilities	256	258
Stockholders' equity:		
Common stock, $25 par value	1,733	851
Paid-in capital	1,185	877
Retained earnings	9,323	6,406
Less treasury common stock at cost	(93)	(109)
Accumulated other comprehensive income	574	1,553
Deferred compensation	(134)	-
Total stockholders' equity	12,588	9,578
Total liabilities and stockholders' equity	$ 17,720	$ 15,427

Case 1-1

J & J CORPORATION: EVALUATION OF FINANCIAL PERFORMANCE

Case Objectives

1. Review the elements of an income statement and balance sheet
2. Review financial performance and ratio analysis

Decision: Does J & J need to take action to improve financial performance?

INTRODUCTION

J & J Corporation began with the merger of two businesses: a house painting service started by John Miller and an interior design firm run by Joanna Barnes. The stockholders consisted of John and Joanna. Their business strategy was based upon the marketing of quality service with the final test of success being that the customer perceived excellent value of the exterior house painting or interior remodeling for the money paid. If they could attain this customer satisfaction, they felt assured of repeat business and referrals and, of course, profits.

As J & J Corporation grew, the company expanded its scope of operations by the purchase of a retail paint and wallpaper store. This acquisition afforded J & J Corporation access to paint and other materials at wholesale prices, considerably below those experienced before the acquisition. It also provided for better inventory management since the retail store was generally stocking the items needed in the exterior and interior service businesses, causing a better inventory turnover.

It has been three years since J & J Corporation acquired the retail store. In this time the company has attained growth in both sales revenue and income. The company's most recent balance sheet and income statement are shown in Exhibits C1-1.1 and C1-1.2, respectively. The income statement shows performance for the company and each of its three divisions: exterior painting, interior remodeling, and retail. John and Joanna are concerned that the business is not doing as well as they had hoped. They ask you to give them your evaluation of the corporation's financial performance as shown on the accompanying financial statements.

J & J Corporation is a member of the Maintenance, Improvement, and Remodeling Association, a trade association. It supplies its members with selected financial ratios determined from a survey of its members. These ratios are presented on the next page.

Current ratio	3.15
Return on sales	.07
Inventory turnover ratio	2.40
Debt-to-equity ratio	1.30
Return on equity	.14

Requirements

1. Consider the following five relationships.

Current ratio	=	Current assets ÷ Current liabilities
Return on sales	=	Net income (earnings) ÷ Sales revenue
Inventory turnover	=	Cost of goods sold ÷ average inventory (see note below)
Debt-to-equity	=	Total liabilities ÷ Total stockholders' equity
Return on equity	=	Net income ÷ average stockholders' equity

Note: Average inventory means the sum of beginning-of-the-year inventory and end-of the-year inventory divided by 2. A similar computation is made to compute average liabilities and stockholders' equity.

   a. Compute the above ratios for J & J Corporation for 2002.

   b. On the basis of the computed ratios and the industry average ratios, how is J & J doing? Explain.

2. a. Which division of J & J is doing the best? Explain.

   b. Which division of J & J is doing the worst? Explain.

   c. What steps might the worst-performing division take in order to improve results next year? Explain.

3. J & J has $133,000 in goodwill recorded as an asset on its December 31, 2002 balance sheet. Economic goodwill occurs when the value of a company exceeds the value of its tangible assets less its liabilities.

   a. Explain how a company can be worth more than the assets shown on its balance sheet less the liabilities shown on its balance sheet.

   b. What event occurred to create the accounting goodwill on J & J's balance sheet?

4. Using information from J&J's financial statements, explain what caused retained earnings to increase during 2002.

Exhibit C1-1.1

J & J Corporation
Comparative Balance Sheets
December 31

	2002	2001
Assets		
Current assets		
Cash	$ 59,570	$ 52,000
Accounts receivable, net	72,000	60,000
Inventory	249,000	184,000
Prepaid expenses	2,500	3,000
Total current assets	$ 383,070	$ 299,000
Plant and equipment		
Service equipment	$ 190,000	$ 190,000
Retail building	400,000	400,000
Display and fixtures	232,000	198,000
	$ 822,000	$ 788,000
Less accumulated depreciation	(318,500)	(245,000)
Plant and equipment, net	$ 503,500	$ 543,000
Goodwill	133,000	133,000
Total assets	$ 1,019,570	$ 975,000
Liabilities		
Current Liabilities		
Accounts payable	$ 91,900	$ 161,000
Taxes payable	32,000	20,000
Wages payable	5,200	6,000
Total current liabilities	$ 129,100	$ 187,000
Notes payable	-	-
Mortgage payable	272,000	272,000
Total liabilities	$ 401,100	$ 459,000
Stockholders' equity		
Contributed capital	$ 200,000	$ 150,000
Retained earnings	418,470	366,000
Total stockholders' equity	$ 618,470	$ 516,000
Total liabilities and stockholders' equity	$ 1,019,570	$ 975,000

Exhibit C1-1.2

J & J Corporation
Contribution Income Statement
Year Ended December 31, 2002

	Divisions: Exterior Painting	Interior Remodeling	Retail	Total Company
Sales revenue	$ 160,000	$ 325,000	$ 558,000	$ 1,043,000
Cost of goods sold	65,000	162,500	332,000	559,500
Gross margin on sales	$ 95,000	$ 162,500	$ 226,000	$ 483,500
Operating expenses				
Salaries	$ 40,000	$ 70,000	$ 63,500	$ 173,500
Interest	-	-	10,000	10,000
Utilities	2,000	4,000	13,000	19,000
Property taxes	1,000	1,000	5,000	7,000
Insurance	6,000	3,000	5,000	14,000
Depreciation	8,000	15,000	50,500	73,500
Advertising	5,000	14,000	16,000	35,000
Total	$ 62,000	$ 107,000	$ 163,000	$ 332,000
Division profit	$ 33,000	$ 55,500	$ 63,000	$ 151,500
Corporate operating expenses				72,000
Income before taxes				$ 79,500
Income tax				27,030
Net income				$ 52,470
Division Assets	$ 168,000	$ 330,000	$ 385,500	

Group Assignment 1-1

HOW IS J & J CORPORATION DOING?

Group number ___________ **Signatures of group members participating:**

____

____

Objectives

1. Use financial ratios to compare a company's performance with the industry average.
2. Use financial ratios to evaluate the performance of divisions of a company.
3. Compute book value per share and interpret it in relation to market value per share.

Requirements

1. Your individual assignment was to compute five financial analysis ratios. Discuss the results of your analysis of the ratios. Record below the group's consensus of how well J & J is performing. Briefly state your reasons.

   Using the ratios presented in this case, in which areas is J & J's performance adequate? Explain your answer.

   Using the ratios presented in this case, in which areas is J & J's performance inadequate? Explain your answer.

2. Compute the book value per share of J & J Corporation as of the end of year 2002 (Stockholders' equity ÷ Number of shares). J & J has 8,000 shares outstanding at December 31, 2002.

J & J book value per share at Dec. 31, 2002: ____________________

3. The recent common stock price of Handy Supply, a large national chain and a J & J competitor, was $60 per share. Assume that J & J Corporation has 8,000 shares outstanding and your group can buy one share for $100. Handy Supply has a book value per share of $30. Based on book values, is Handy Supply a better value at $60 per share, or is J & J a better value at $100 per share? That is, are you getting more or less book value per dollar of share price with J & J? Show calculations.

4. Give two possible reasons why Handy Supply and J & J have different ratios of market price per share to book value per share. In other words, why would investors pay more for a share of Handy relative to its book value than they would for J & J?

Reading 1-2

USING THE STATEMENT OF CASH FLOWS FOR DECISIONS

INTRODUCTION

Your own checking account bank statement is like a statement of cash flows. It has the balance as of the beginning of the month, the cash deposits (inflows), the checks that were paid (outflows), and the ending balance. If you are surprised and disappointed that your cash balance has declined, the bank statement provides data to explain why that happened. If you are delighted by the increase in your cash balance you can gain insight into the transactions that helped produce this result. Similarly, the statement of cash flows gives the manager, owner, or investor a summary explanation of why the cash resources increased or decreased during the year.

An adequate level of cash is essential to the orderly operation of any business. Cash is often referred to as the lifeblood of business. The statement of cash flows is one of the three primary financial reports issued by companies (the income statement and the balance sheet are the others). **Cash flows** are increases or decreases in cash and equivalents to cash, such as interest-paying accounts and marketable securities. Many bank officers and financial analysts consider the statement of cash flows to be the most important financial statement. It augments the balance sheet and income statement by informing the reader how the resources of the company are being used. Three major uses of the statement of cash flows are to:

- Explain why cash increased or decreased during the year. The statement of cash flows highlights how a company earned and spent its cash. This information helps users assess whether the company has sufficient cash resources to carry out its business plan.

- Estimate future cash flows from operations, investments, and financing. Bankers and other creditors interested in a company's solvency use the statement to estimate future cash flows, and hence the risk of insolvency. There have been many instances where the statement of cash flows has signaled the financial decline of companies that were forced into bankruptcy several years later. Shareholders also are interested in future cash flows because they are the main source of future dividends.

- Determine the quality of earnings. All reported net income is not of equal quality. For example, if a company selects a long useful life for its assets and uses straight-line depreciation, it will report a higher net income (due to a lower depreciation expense) than if it selects a shorter useful life and uses accelerated depreciation. The higher reported income resulting from lower depreciation expense is said to be of lower quality. Analysts compare the level of cash flow from operations with income from operations to evaluate the quality of earnings. High net income coupled with low cash flow from operations is a warning sign of overstated income, poor asset management, or a combination of both.

STRUCTURE OF THE STATEMENT OF CASH FLOWS

The statement of cash flows tells the reader the causes of the change in the amount of cash from one balance sheet date to the next. It is not the bottom line of the statement that is of interest because one already knows the change in cash by looking at the comparative balance sheets. Of much greater interest to the reader are the specific transactions that had a material impact on cash. The statement of cash flows covers the same accounting period as does the income statement. For example, if the income statement reports the revenues and expenses for the calendar year 2002, the statement of cash flows must cover the same period. Similarly, if the income statement covers one quarter, the statement of cash flows would report the causes of the change in cash assets for the same three months.

The statement of cash flows is divided into three sections: cash flow from operations (CFO), cash flow from investing (CFI), and cash flow from financing (CFF). We will use Kmart Corporation's financial statement excerpts to illustrate the meaning and content of each of these three sections of the statement of cash flows.

- CFO (not to be confused with chief financial officer) is cash flow from operations. "Operations" refer to the day-to-day transactions such as selling goods or services and paying for inventory purchases and other expenses incurred in generating revenue. CFO is a summary of net income, depreciation, and the cash effects of changes in current assets and current liabilities. Exhibit 1-2.1 is an excerpt of Kmart's statement of cash flows. The exhibit shows the items that are adjustments to accrual basis net income to arrive at CFO. Kmart's statement of cash flows utilizes the indirect method as shown by the changes in the current assets and current liabilities.

  Note that Kmart incurred a net loss for its 2000 fiscal year. Despite this, there were several adjustments that were reported as expenses in the income statement that did not require cash to be disbursed (strategic actions and depreciation and amortization). There was also a reduction in the level of inventories that yielded $324 million in cash. These items were positive adjustments to accrual basis net income.

  Conversely, the bottom four adjustments reflect the fact that cash was not received at the same rate as revenue recognized (accounts receivable increase) and that cash was paid out at a greater rate than the expense reflected in the income statement (accounts payable, deferred taxes and other adjustments). These adjustments result from cash outflows greater than their related income statement expense item. Of greatest importance is this section's subtotal, which reports that Kmart was able to generate $1,154 million positive cash flow from operations during the fiscal year.

- CFI – Cash flow from investing activities. CFI summarizes the sources and uses of cash from the selling and buying of long-lived assets, investments, and other noncurrent assets.

  Exhibit 1-2.2 is the CFI section of Kmart's statement of cash flows. Kmart made investments in its stores and distribution system that cost over $1 billion during its fiscal year 2000. This is shown as a negative number ($1,087 billion) indicating that Kmart used cash in that amount to expand its facilities. It also made an investment of $55 million in its Internet sales operation called "BlueLight.com". As is typical of most companies, this section showed how cash was used to acquire new plant and equipment assets.

Exhibit 1-2.1
Kmart Corporation
Cash Flows from Operating Activities

Years Ended January 31, 2001, January 26, 2000 and January 27, 1999	**2000**	**1999**	**1998**
Cash Flows From Operating Activities			
Net income (loss) from continuing operations	**$ (244)**	$ 633	$ 518
Adjustments:			
One-time charge for strategic actions	**728**	--	--
Depreciation and amortization	**777**	770	671
Equity loss in BlueLight.com	**64**	--	--
Decrease (increase) in inventories	**324**	(565)	(169)
Increase in trade accounts payable	**84**	157	124
Increase in accounts receivable	**(103)**	(62)	(76)
Deferred income taxes and taxes payable	**(204)**	258	308
Cash used for store closings and other charges	**(102)**	(80)	(94)
Other adjustments	**(170)**	(24)	15
Net cash provided by continuing operations	$ **1,154**	$ 1,087	$ 1,297
Net cash used for discontinued operations	$ **(115)**	$ (83)	$ (60)
Net cash provided by operating activities	**$ 1,039**	**$ 1,004**	**$ 1,237**

The CFI section typically reports a negative cash flow because most business purchase new fixed assets on a fairly regular basis. However, it is certainly possible to report a positive amount in the CFI section. This is the result of a business selling fixed assets. The proceeds of the sale of fixed assets such as land, buildings, or long-term investments will be reported as a positive amount in the CFI section regardless of the gain or loss experienced on the sale.

- CFF - Cash flow from financing activities. CFF summarizes the sources of cash from the issuance of notes, bonds, or stock to investors or long-term creditors. CFF reports how cash was used to repay debt and to pay dividends to shareholders.

Exhibit 1-2.2
Kmart Corporation
Cash Flows from Investing Activities

Years Ended January 31, 2001, January 26, 2000 and January 27, 1999	**2000**	**1999**	**1998**
Cash Flows From Investing Activities			
Capital expenditures	$ **(1,087)**	$ (1,277)	$ (981)
Investment in BlueLight.com	(55)	--	--
Acquisition of Caldor leases	--	(86)	--
Proceeds from divestitures	--	--	87
Decrease in property held and other	--	--	99
Net cash used for investing activities	$ **(1,142)**	$ (1,363)	$ (795)

Exhibit 1-2.3 is Kmart's CFF section of its statement of cash flows. The largest item in Kmart's CFF section is the $397 million issuance of debt. Kmart borrowed that amount during the year by selling long-term bonds to the public. It also paid back some of its long-term debt and bought back a small amount of its common stock and preferred stock. The net additional cash from these transactions was $160 million. Kmart has not been paying a dividend to its shareholders in recent years but if it had, the cash out flow to pay dividends would be reported in CFF.

The following is a model of the cash flow statement:

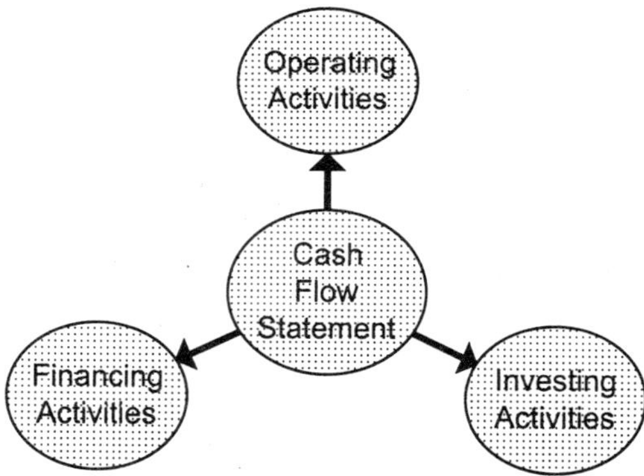

The basic structure of the statement of cash flows is the sum of these three categories as the following equation shows:

$$\text{Cash (beginning of period)} \pm \text{CFO} \pm \text{CFI} \pm \text{CFF} = \text{Cash (end of period)}$$

The cash amount at the beginning and end of an accounting period corresponds to that amount reported on the comparative balance sheets.

Exhibit 1-2.3
Kmart Corporation
Cash Flows from Financing Activities

Years Ended January 31, 2001, January 26, 2000 and January 27, 1999	**2000**	**1999**	**1998**
Cash Flows From Financing Activities			
Proceeds from issuance of debt	**$ 397**	$ 297	--
Issuance of common shares	**53**	63	$ 76
Purchase of convertible preferred securities	**(84)**	--	--
Purchase of common shares	**(55)**	(200)	(30)
Payments on debt	**(73)**	(90)	(188)
Payments on capital lease obligations	**(78)**	(77)	(88)
Net cash provided by (used for) financing activities	**$ 160**	$ (7)	$ (230)

Exhibit 1-2.4 contains Kmart's net change in cash and cash equivalents, which shows that the sum of CFO, CFI, and CFF is $57 million ($1,039,000 – $1,142,000 + $160,000) for year 2000. Adding that to the cash balance at the beginning of the year gives the cash balance at the end of the year. Does Kmart hold $401 million in a checking account? Certainly not. The excess funds not needed on a day-to-day basis are invested in short-term very liquid securities such as U.S. Treasury bills and notes, and are referred to as "cash equivalents."

Exhibit 1-2.4
Kmart Corporation
Changes in Cash

Years Ended January 31, 2001, January 26, 2000 and January 27, 1999	**2000**	**1999**	**1998**
Net change in cash and cash equivalents	**$ 57**	$ (366)	$ 212
Cash and cash equivalents, beginning of year	**344**	710	498
Cash and cash equivalents, end of year	**$ 401**	$ 344	$ 710

TWO TYPES OF STATEMENTS OF CASH FLOWS

There are two types of statements of cash flows: direct and indirect. Both are structured with the three CFO, CFI, and CFF sections. The difference lies in the formulation of CFO, cash flow from operations. Total CFO for a specific accounting period is the same in both types, but the steps shown to arrive at that total on the statement are different. CFI and CFF are identical in format for both the indirect and the direct statement of cash flows.

The direct method of arriving at CFO is an analysis of the operational cash disbursements and cash receipts generally categorized as follows:

Cash flow from operations:		
	Cash received from customers	xxxxx
	Cash paid to vendors	(xxxx)
	Cash paid to employees	(xxxx)
	Cash paid for interest on debt	(xxxx)
	Cash paid for other operating expenses	(xxxx)
	Cash Flow from Operations (CFO)	xxxx

The CFO subtotal can be positive or negative. A company that reports a negative CFO may be facing serious financial difficulties. To offset the drain on the cash resources, such a company will need to approach lenders or investors for additional funds. Many lenders will be wary of the risk of a company that has a chronic cash outflow from operations because the prospect of repayment is questionable.

While the direct method has the advantage of being relatively easy to understand, most companies have adopted the indirect method of presenting the CFO section of the statement of cash flows. Accordingly, this discussion is aimed at your mastery of the indirect statement of cash flows. This has the additional benefit of refreshing your thinking on the difference between the cash and accrual bases of recognizing revenues and expenses.

Indirect Method for Computing CFO

The key to the indirect approach is to understand the difference between accrual and cash accounting for items that impact depreciation, current liabilities, and most current assets. A description of the four adjustments that normally are most important for a retail company (the logic for a manufacturing company is more complicated) are:

1. Those arising from the difference between the amount of revenues recorded and cash collections from customers (these differences are reflected by the change in the accounts receivable balance);

2. Those arising from the difference between the cost of goods sold shown on the income statement and the amount of goods actually purchased (reflected by the change in the inventory balance);

3. Those arising from the difference between the amount of goods and services purchased and those actually paid for (reflected by the change in the accounts payable balance); and

4. Depreciation and amortization. Depreciation and amortization are adjustments because they are expenses on the income statement, but do not involve any cash outflows.

Other adjustments we will cover are required to account for the difference in (1) prepaid expenses included on the income statement and the cash paid for these prepaid items (reflected by the change in the prepaid account, which is a current asset), and (2) the expense shown on the income statement for taxes and wages and the actual cash outflow for these items (reflected by the change in the taxes payable and wages payable accounts).

In order to understand the direction of the adjustment, you must determine whether the adjustment item causes accrual income to be greater than or less than cash flow. If accrual income is less than cash flow, a positive adjustment must be made to bring net income up to the higher cash flow number. To illustrate, assume that T Corporation made cash sales of $500,000 in May 2001. It also collected $50,000 from a customer who purchased goods on credit in April, adding to CFO. The May income statement will report revenues of $500,000, the proper amount from which to deduct the expenses for the month. However, the statement of cash flows will show the collection of $50,000 of accounts receivable that existed at the end of April. The total collected from customers in May is $550,000.

Another example is wage expense and wages payable. If wage expense on the income statement is greater than wages actually paid employees (that is, the wages payable account increased), then a positive adjustment to CFO in the amount of the change in the wages payable account must be made to net income to reflect the actual, lower amount of cash paid to employees. Note that reducing wages from the higher accrual amount to the lower cash paid amount reduces expenses, which in turn increases cash-based net income; hence, the positive adjustment to net income to arrive at CFO.

Summary of Indirect Cash Flow Statement Adjustments

For our purposes, the indirect method requires the following adjustments to net income:

1. Amount of depreciation and amortization expense for the period:
   - Always a positive adjustment.
2. Change in accounts receivable beginning and ending balances:
   - Increase in the balance is a negative adjustment.
3. Change in inventory beginning and ending balances:
   - Increase in the balance is a negative adjustment.
4. Change in the prepaid expenses beginning and ending balances:
   - Increase in the balance is a negative adjustment.
5. Change in the accounts payable beginning and ending balances:
   - Increase in the balance is a positive adjustment.
6. Change in the taxes payable beginning and ending balances:
   - Increase in the balance is a positive adjustment.
7. Change in the wages payable beginning and ending balances:
   - Increase in the balance is a positive adjustment.

Note that all increases in current asset accounts result in negative adjustments to net income and all increases in current liabilities result in positive adjustments. Of course, just the reverse is true for decreases. Decreases in current asset accounts result in positive adjustments, while decreases in current liabilities result in negative adjustments. The investing and financing sections of the statement of cash flows are the same for the direct and indirect approaches.

Type of Account	Change in Account	Direction of Adjustment To Net Income
Current Asset	Increase	Subtracted
Current Asset	Decrease	Added
Current Liability	Increase	Added
Current Liability	Decrease	Subtracted
Depreciation	NA	Added

Cash Flow from Operations: An Illustration

Before continuing with the Super Stereos illustration, let's focus on just the CFO section of the statement of cash flows. Exhibit 1-2.5 presents the current asset and current liability portions of Lightner Corporation's balance sheets.

Exhibit 1-2.5

Lightner Corporation
Partial Balance Sheets
Years Ended December 31

	2002	2001	Change
Current assets			
Cash	$ 31,900	$ 6,000	$ 25,900
Accounts receivable	14,500	12,000	2,500
Inventory	18,700	23,000	(4,300)
Current liabilities			
Accounts payable	$ 31,100	$ 34,000	$ (2,900)

In addition, assume that depreciation expense for 2002 totaled $17,000, 2002 net income was $10,000, and Lightner had no cash flows from investing or financing activities during 2002. Exhibit 1-2.6 shows Lightner's statement of cash flows.

Exhibit 1-2.6

Lightner Corporation
Statement of Cash Flows—Indirect Method
Year Ended December 31, 2002

Operating Activities		
Net income		$10,000
Add (deduct) adjustments to cash basis:		
Depreciation expense	$ 17,000	
Increase in accounts receivable	(2,500)	
Decrease in inventory	4,300	
Decrease in accounts payable	(2,900)	15,900
Net Cash Flow From Operations		$25,900
Net Cash Flow from Investing Activities		0
Net Cash Flow from Financing Activities		0
Net increase in cash during 2001		$25,900
Add cash balance, January 1, 2001		6,000
Cash balance, December 31, 2001		$31,900

Lightner Corporation experienced CFO of $25,900 compared to net income of $10,000 for 2002. This is due primarily to the adjustment to add the depreciation expense. It is necessary to match this cost against the revenues each year to properly measure the income performance of the business. However, no cash is disbursed to recognize depreciation expense. Rather, the carrying value of the plant and equipment is reduced by the amount of the depreciation expense.

STATEMENT OF CASH FLOWS: AN EXAMPLE

Consider the financial statements of Super Stereos shown in Exhibits 1-2.7 and 1-2.8. The information needed to construct a statement of cash flows includes the income statement for the year in which cash flow is being analyzed, balance sheets at the beginning and end of the fiscal year, and certain additional information. For example, the balance sheets report an increase in equipment of $33,970 (we will also omit the 000's in the narrative discussion). There are two possible causes of this: (1) equipment with a cost of $33,970 was purchased in 2002, or (2) there were both purchases and sales of equipment with the cost of equipment purchased greater than the historical cost of equipment sold by the amount $33,970. Offsetting transactions are complex and require information directly from the company's records. The objective of this reading is for the student to be perceptive about cash flow data in published reports of companies. Therefore, we will assume that the balance sheets for Super Stereos do not include any offsetting transactions in the noncurrent assets, long-term liabilities, and stockholders' equity accounts.

Exhibit 1-2.7

Super Stereos

Income Statement

Year Ended December 31, 2002

(000's omitted)

Net sales	$ 545,000
Cost of goods sold	330,000
Gross margin on sales	215,000
Operating expenses	133,000
Interest expense	9,450
Earnings before income tax	72,550
Income tax at 30%	21,765
Net income	$ 50,785

Super Stereos' Statement of Cash Flows

Exhibit 1-2.9 is the statement of cash flows for Super Stereos. Exhibit 1-2.8 was used to categorize the various changes in balance sheet amounts. Take the time to trace the change column numbers to the statement of cash flows.

Exhibit 1-2.8

Super Stereos
Comparative Balance Sheets
December 31

	2002	2001	Change	Cash Effect	Type
Assets					
Current Assets					
Cash	$ 48,500	$ 58,000	$ (9,500)	$ (9,500)	CFO
Accounts Receivable, net	89,000	76,000	13,000	negative	CFO
Merchandise Inventory	165,000	154,000	11,000	negative	CFO
Prepaid Expenses	26,450	28,650	(2,200)	positive	CFO
Total Current Assets	328,950	316,650	12,300		
Property and Equipment					
Land	93,000	68,000	25,000	negative	CFI
Building	325,000	154,000	171,000	negative	CFI
Equipment	96,000	62,030	33,970	negative	CFI
Total property and Equipment	514,000	284,030	229,970		
Accumulated Depreciation	(122,000)	(86,120)	(35,880)	positive	CFO
Property and Equipment, net	392,000	197,910	194,090		
Other Assets	13,320	13,320	0	no change	CFI
Total Assets	$ 734,270	$ 527,880	$ 206,390		
Liabilities and Stockholders' Equity					
Current Liabilities					
Notes Payable	$ 40,050	$ 30,050	$ 10,000	positive	CFO
Accounts Payable	44,000	59,000	(15,000)	negative	CFO
Accrued Expenses	48,060	27,650	20,410	positive	CFO
Income Taxes Payable	36,000	34,210	1,790	positive	CFO
Total Current Liabilities	168,110	150,910	17,200		
Long-Term Liabilities					
Long-Term Notes Payable	176,000	130,000	46,000	positive	CFF
Total Liabilities	344,110	280,910	63,200		
Stockholders' Equity					
Common Stock, $1 par	80,000	50,000	30,000	positive	CFF
Additional Paid-In Capital	150,000	70,000	80,000	positive	CFF
Retained Earnings	160,160	126,970	33,190	none	
Total Stockholders' Equity	390,160	246,970	143,190		
Total Liabilities and Stockholders' Equity	$ 734,270	$ 527,880	$ 206,390		

Exhibit 1-2.9

Super Stereos **Statement of Cash Flows-Indirect Method** **Year Ended December 31, 2002**		
Operating Activities		
Net Income		$ 50,785
Add (deduct) adjustments to cash basis:		
Depreciation expense	$ 35,880	
Increase in accounts receivable	(13,000)	
Increase in merchandise inventory	(11,000)	
Decrease in prepaid expenses	2,200	
Increase in current notes payable	10,000	
Decrease in accounts payable	(15,000)	
Increase in accrued expenses	20,410	
Increase in income tax payable	1,790	31,280
Net Cash Flow from Operations		$ 82,065
Investing Activities		
Cash paid for land	$ (25,000)	
Cash paid for building	(171,000)	
Cash paid for equipment	(33,970)	
Net Cash Flow from Investing Activities		(229,970)
Financing Activities		
Cash received from long-term notes	$ 46,000	
Cash received from issuance of common stock	110,000	
Cash paid for dividends	(17,595)	
Net Cash Flow from Financing Activities		138,405
Net decrease in cash during 2002		(9,500)
Add cash balance, January 1, 2002		58,000
Cash balance, December 31, 2002		$ 48,500

How Was Cash Paid for Dividends Determined?

To answer this question requires a review of how the retained earnings account changes from the beginning of the year to the end. The basic formula for the retained earnings account is:

> Beginning retained earnings ± Net income (loss) – Dividends = Ending retained earnings

Applying this to Super Stereos:

> $126,970 + $50,785 – Dividends = $160,160
> Dividends = $17,595

Interpretation of Super Stereos' Statement of Cash Flows

The CFO is greater than net income, which is true of many companies. However, of some concern is that if one removes the effect of the depreciation add back, the remaining current asset and liability items are net users of cash. This is especially worrisome given the fact that there was an increase in notes payable of $10,000 adding to the CFO. By definition, current liabilities are those that must be repaid within one year. Super Stereos is facing major cash outflows to pay off $40,050 of short-term notes.

At the end of 2002, the company has only $48,500 in cash. This part of the statement is like the yellow light at the traffic intersection that warns of the need to be more vigilant about possible risks. Therefore, the **liquidity**, which means sufficient cash to meet current obligations, needs improvement. One item contributing to this illiquid condition is a large increase in accounts receivable, which is the amount of sales revenue not collected during the year. An increase in accounts receivable reduces positive cash flows. This can signify poor management of receivables. The overall objective is for management to generate a strongly positive CFO. Large increases in current assets such as receivables and inventory thwart that goal.

The CFI section explains the nature of the dramatic increase in assets during 2002. The investment in plant and equipment nearly doubled in the year. Time will tell whether this expansion strategy will be profitable. One thing is clear; it is a drain on the resources of the company.

The CFF section explains how cash was raised to pay for the aforementioned increase in assets. Note that the combined amount of new long-term notes payable and common stock ($46,000 + $110,000 = $156,000) were not sufficient to cover the cost of new plant and equipment (CFI = $229,970). Resources existing before the issuance of new securities must have been used to make up the difference.

Overall, the statement of cash flows for Super Stereos is giving warning signals of a thinly financed corporation. Management will need to implement a financial plan to ensure that the company has sufficient liquidity to meet these obligations to repay the debt. Another equally important step that management must take is to improve profitability, thereby improving CFO. To accomplish this, management must scrutinize the operations to determine areas of cost control, pricing opportunities, and product strategy that singularly or collectively can improve profit margins.

Two ratios can assist the user of the statement cash flows in determining the financial strength of the company study.

Cash Adequacy Ratio

The **cash adequacy ratio** (CAR) is cash flow from operations (CFO) divided by current liabilities (CL). It is a measure of the cash-generating muscle of the business compared to the short-term liabilities that must be paid within the coming year. The CAR augments the current ratio discussed in Reading 1-1 because it compares the cash actually realized in the previous year to the current liabilities that must be paid off in the subsequent year. The higher the ratio of CFO to CL is above one, the healthier is the company. A ratio of less than one indicates that insufficient cash is generated to pay current debts. In cases of chronic insufficiency of cash, the typical responses are long-term loans, infusions of contributed capital by shareholders, sale of assets, or sale of the company.

For Super Stereos:

$$CAR = CFO/CL = \$82,065 \div 168,110 = .488$$

Even though Super Stereos has a reasonable current ratio, the CAR gives us insight on how little liquidity is evident in its financial structure. This information should motivate management to develop aggressive plans to improve the weak financial state of the company. Among the steps to be taken are improve operations to increase income, minimize the investment in accounts receivable and inventory, schedule payments to creditors to avoid cash outages, and seek additional capital. The last alternative will be difficult due to the recent issuance of shares as noted in the CFF section of Super Stereos, statement of cash flows.

Financing Assets Ratio

The **financing assets ratio** (FAR) is CFO divided by the absolute value of CFI. A company with good cash flow from operations is able to pay for the purchase of new buildings and equipment with its internally generated cash, CFO. Strong CFO performance means borrowing that weakens the balance sheet or issuance of stock that dilutes current shareholder's interest is avoided. Also, its profitability is strengthened by reduced interest expense and increased capacity to generate revenues from the new long-term assets.

For Super Stereos:

$$CFO/CFI = \$82,065 \div |-\$229,970| = .357$$

The vast majority of companies report a positive CFO (if negative, the company is in real trouble). CFI is usually negative because it reports the cash used to purchase long-term assets, sometimes referred to as capital investments. However, if a company sold assets in amounts greater than those purchased, CFI is positive and the FAR is not relevant in those rare cases. The FAR is calculated using absolute values, ignoring the normal negative sign of CFI.

Obviously, Super Stereos falls short of paying for new long-term assets with its cash from operations. The CFF section of Super Stereos' statement of cash flows shows how the company raised the necessary cash to complete the purchase of land, buildings and equipment. Two consequences of this less than optimal financing strategy are apparent: (1) dilution of the ownership percentage of existing shareholders has occurred, assuming the issuance of new shares was to new shareholders, and (2) the added long-term notes will mean higher interest expense in future years, negatively impacting income and CFO.

Why Is the Indirect Method So Popular?

The indirect method is popular because it directly ties the net income amount per the income statement to the cash provided by operations. Users of the financial statements can easily see how much of the net income results in changes in operating cash flow. This helps the users predict future cash flow requirements. In addition, companies with thousands of cash transactions in a given period would find it tedious to classify and summarize all of them for the direct statement.

Why Is Cash Flow So Important to Financial Statement Users?

Most users of financial statements are particularly interested in the statement of cash flows. Although the statement of cash flows deals with current cash flow information, this data is especially helpful in predicting future cash flows of the company. Managers are involved in cash budgeting daily and must be constantly aware of the cash requirements of the business and how to meet those commitments. Creditors and owners or stockholders read the statement of cash flows very carefully. The primary concern for creditors is getting paid in a timely manner and the main concern for owners is profitability and the ability of the company to generate cash that they can then withdraw.

The price or value of the company's stock is basically determined by the "market's" estimation of the future cash that will be distributed by the company to the stockholders, reduced by an interest or discount factor (which is compensation for waiting to receive the cash flow). The operating section of the statement of cash flows emphasizes the fact that revenues are not the same as cash received and expenses are not the same as cash paid due to timing differences caused by accrual basis accounting. Having a net income for the period does not necessarily mean that there will be an increase in cash.

Besides cash flow generated by operations, cash changes can also be the result of the purchase or sale of fixed assets, the borrowing or repayment of debt, or the contributions or withdrawals of cash by the owner.

SUMMARY

The statement of cash flows is vital to assess the financial health of a business. It has the added benefit of allowing the reader to understand how the changes in the balance sheet were brought about. Many financial analysts view the statement of cash flows as a major determinant of how companies are valued in the stock market.

The three sections of the statement of cash flows are referred to as CFO, CFI, and CFF. Each section of the statement gives the reader a different facet of why the cash assets went up or down during the year. The CFO gives a picture of how the operations of the company would look if accounted for on a cash basis. The CFI shows the cash uses and sources to purchase and sell long-lived assets such as plant and equipment. CFF shows the cash effects of transactions with long-term creditors and shareholders.

Two ratios can provide insight into the financial strength of the company. The cash adequacy ratio (CAR) measures the coverage of current liabilities by the CFO. The financing assets ratio (FAR) measures the degree to which CFO is sufficient to finance the purchase of new long-term assets.

In the case that follows, you are asked to determine whether John and Joanna, as the only two shareholders, can pay themselves a dividend of $50,000. The statement of cash flows will be a key to the correct decision.

EXERCISES AND PROBLEMS

Exercises

Exercise 1 Statement of Cash Flows Basics. Answer the following cash flow questions.

1. Identify the three main sections of a statement of cash flows and give two examples of transactions that impact each section.
2. List and briefly explain three decision uses of the statement of cash flows.
3. List seven adjustments to net income that often must be made in order to compute cash flow from operations using the indirect method.

Exercise 2 Cash Flow Versus Net Income. Which of the two financial variables, cash flow or net income, is used to judge the "quality" of accounting methods used to measure earnings?

Exercise 3 Direct Method for CFO. List the major cash inflows and outflows that are found in the direct method of arriving at CFO.

Exercise 4 Data for the Direct Method of CFO. How would a company gather the data necessary to report the CFO using the direct method properly?

Exercise 5 Data for the Indirect Method of Statement of Cash Flows. What statements are needed to construct a statement of cash flows using the indirect method?

Exercise 6 Liquidity and CFO. Discuss how CFO relates to the liquidity of a company.

Exercise 7 CFI Transactions. Give an example of a transaction that increases cash and a transaction that decreases cash from investing activities.

Exercise 8 CFF Transactions. Give an example of a transaction that increases cash and an example that decreases cash from financing activities.

Exercise 9 Dividends and CFF. If retained earnings are $10,000 at the beginning of the year and $20,000 at the end of the year when income for that year is $18,000, what is the amount of the dividend that is declared? If the declared dividend was also paid in cash during the year, where is it found in the statement of cash flows?

Exercise 10 CFO and Net Income. Berlyn Industries Incorporated reported net income for 2002 of $50 million and CFO of $40 million. It reported depreciation expense of $35 million. During 2002, Berlyn's current assets increased by over $100 million. From this limited information, provide your interpretation of the change in Berlyn's balance sheet from the beginning of 2002 to the end of the year.

Problems

Problem 1 Types of Cash Flow Transactions. For each of the following transactions indicate in which section (CFO, CFI, or CFF) of the indirect statement of cash flows it is classified and indicate whether it has a positive or negative effect on the cash and equivalents. If the transaction does not appear on the statement of cash flows so indicate.

a. Sale of equipment at book value.
b. Cash collections of accounts receivable were greater than sales on account.
c. Payment of a dividend to shareholders.
d. Repayment of bonds issued ten years ago.
e. Goodwill of $100,000 was written off to expense.
f. Shares of common stock were issued to employees for 85 percent of the current market value.
g. Payments to accounts payable vendors were less than purchases on account.
h. Purchased 25 percent of the stock of a privately held corporation not listed on a public exchange.
i. Accrued wages payable at the end of the year were $500,000, to be paid on January 2 of the following year.
j. Received $10,000 on December 30 in advance for shipment of goods to occur on January 10 of the following year.

Problem 2 Simple Statement of Cash Flows. You have been elected treasurer of your school's Accounting Society and assume your duties in September 2002. At the time of your election, the Accounting Society is broke (it has no cash). It also has no assets or liabilities. In order to raise funds, you organize a sale of T-shirts with the Accounting Society logo. You oversee the following events:

- You order 250 T-shirts for $3,000 from a manufacturer. Terms of the purchase are payment in full on January 15, 2003.

- You sell 200 of the T-shirts at the December 10, 2002 banquet at $20 per shirt. Terms of the sales are full payment by January 15, 2003. You don't receive your first payment until January 5, 2003.

a. Prepare an Accounting Society income statement for the year ending December 31, 2002. The Accounting Society had no other transactions during the year and owns no fixed assets.

b. Can the Accounting Society make cash purchases of Christmas presents for the faculty on December 20, 2002?

c. Prepare an Accounting Society statement of cash flows for the year ending December 31, 2002. Use the indirect method.

Problem 3 Cash Flow from Operations. From the data given in Exhibit 1-2.10, determine the cash flow from operations of Buffet Tire Company for 2002. Net income for the year 2002 was $69,776. The company did not sell or dispose of any noncurrent assets during the year.

Problem 4 Statement of Cash Flows. Using the data in Problem 3 and in Exhibit 1-2.10, complete the statement of cash flows for 2002. In 2002, Buffet's board of directors chose to declare and pay a dividend of $66,816. Critique this decision in view of the fact that sales revenue declined 20 percent to $1 million and the gross profit margin declined from 40 percent in 2001 to 35 percent in 2002.

Exhibit 1-2.10

Buffet Tire Company
Comparative Balance Sheets
December 31

	2002	2001	Change
Assets			
Current assets			
Cash	$ 58,000	$ 52,000	$ 6,000
Accounts receivable, net	76,000	68,000	8,000
Merchandise inventory	204,000	150,000	54,000
Prepaid expenses	18,650	28,650	(10,000)
Total current assets	$356,650	$ 298,650	$ 58,000
Property and equipment			
Land	68,000	68,000	-
Building	154,000	154,000	-
Equipment	62,030	61,040	990
	$284,030	$ 283,040	$ 990
Accumulated depreciation	(126,120)	(86,000)	(40,120)
Property and equipment, net	$157,910	$ 197,040	$ (39,130)
Long-Term investments	13,320	13,320	-
Total assets	$527,880	$ 509,010	$ 18,870
Liabilities and stockholders' equity			
Current liabilities			
Notes payable	$ 30,050	$ 10,000	$ 20,050
Accounts payable	59,000	61,000	(2,000)
Accrued expenses	27,650	28,450	(800)
Income taxes payable	34,210	35,550	(1,340)
Total current liabilities	$150,910	$ 135,000	$ 15,910
Long-term liabilities			
Long-term notes payable	130,000	130,000	-
Total liabilities	$280,910	$ 265,000	$ 15,910
Stockholders' equity			
Common stock, $100 par	50,000	50,000	-
Additional paid-in capital	70,000	70,000	-
Retained earnings	126,970	124,010	2,960
Total stockholders' equity	$246,970	$ 244,010	$ 2,960
Total liabilities and stockholders' equity	$527,880	$ 509,010	$ 18,870

Problem 5 Completing the Balance Sheet. Complete the following 2003 and 2002 balance sheets for Gaylord Company.

Gaylord Company
Statement of Cash Flows
For Year Ended December 31, 2003

Cash Flows from Operating Activities		
Net income	$ 23,000	
Add (deduct) items not affecting cash:		
Depreciation expense	6,000	
Decrease in accounts receivable	8,000	
Decrease in accounts payable	(6,000)	
Net Cash Flow from Operating Activities		$ 31,000
Cash Flows from Investing Activities		
Purchase of store fixtures		(4,000)
Cash Flows from Financing Activities		
Repayment of long-term debt	(2,000)	
Payment of cash dividends	(5,000)	
Net Cash Flow from Financing Activities		(7,000)
Increase in cash for the year		$ 20,000

Gaylord Company
Balance Sheets
December 31

	2003	**2002**
Current Assets		
Cash	$ 37,000	$
Accounts Receivable		39,000
Total Current Assets		
Store Fixtures		$24,000
Less: Accum. Depreciation	(13,000)	
Net Store Fixtures		
Total Assets		
Accounts Payable		$ 18,000
Long-Term Debt	18,000	
Total Liabilities		
Owners' Equity		
Capital Stock		$20,000
Retained Earnings		
Total Owners' Equity		
Total Liabilities and Owners' Equity		

Problem 6 Statement of Cash Flows, Kmart Corporation. Reading 1-2 included the statement of cash flows for Kmart Corporation for 1999 and 2000. Use this data and Kmart's balance sheet shown in Exhibit 1-2.11 to answer the following questions:

a. Comparing the net income of each year with the CFO of the same year, is Kmart generating cash that exceeds accrual income? If yes, what are the two largest adjustments to net income to arrive at CFO? If no, what does the text suggest might be the reason for the gap?

b. Calculate CAR for 2000 and 1999. Comment on the result in terms of a measure of debt-paying ability.

c. Calculate FAR for 2000 and 1999. What is Kmart's ability to finance the purchase of new assets?

Exhibit 1-2.11

Kmart Corporation

Balance Sheets (000,000 omitted)

As of January 31, 2001 and January 26, 2000		2000		1999
Current Assets				
Cash and cash equivalents	$	401	$	344
Merchandise inventories		6,412		7,101
Other current assets		811		715
Total current assets	$	7,624	$	8,160
Property and equipment, net		6,557		6,410
Other assets and deferred charges		449		534
Total Assets	$	14,630	$	15,104
Current Liabilities				
Long-term debt due within one year	$	68	$	66
Trade accounts payable		2,288		2,204
Accrued payroll and other liabilities		1,256		1,574
Taxes other than income taxes		187		232
Total current liabilities	$	3,799	$	4,076
Long-term debt and notes payable		2,084		1,759
Capital lease obligations		943		1,014
Other long-term liabilities		834		965
Preferred stock		887		986
Common stock, $1 par value		487		481
Capital in excess of par value		1,578		1,555
Retained earnings		4,018		4,268
Total Liabilities and Shareholders' Equity	$	14,630	$	15,104

Problem 7 Statement of Cash Flows, EMC Corporation. Exhibit 1-2.12 presents the statement of cash flows for EMC Corporation for the quarter ending March 31, 2000 and 2001. Use this data to answer the following questions:

a. Comparing the net income of each year with the CFO of the same year, is EMC generating cash that exceeds accrual income? If yes, what are the two largest adjustments to net income to arrive at CFO? If no, what does the text suggest might be the reason for the gap?

b. Calculate CAR for 2001 and 2000. Comment on the result in terms of the measure of debt-paying ability of EMC in 2001. Current liabilities for EMC at the end of two years are shown on the balance sheet and were $2,113,647 and $1,397,915 for 2001 and 2000 respectively. The current liabilities are expressed in thousands of dollars, as are cash flow amounts.

c. Calculate FAR for each of the two years. What is EMC's ability to finance the purchase of new assets?

Exhibit 1-2.12

EMC CORP
CONSOLIDATED STATEMENTS OF CASH FLOWS
(IN THOUSANDS)
FOR THE THREE MONTHS ENDED

	MARCH 31, 2001	MARCH 31 2000
CASH FLOWS FROM OPERATING ACTIVITIES:		
Net income	$ 398,795	$ 331,987
Adjustments to reconcile net income to net cash provided/(used) by operating activities:		
Depreciation and amortization	144,931	116,166
Amortization of deferred compensation	5,256	3,589
Provision for doubtful accounts	8,989	4,943
Deferred income taxes	(7,743)	19,829
Net loss on disposal of property and equipment	1,324	7,514
Tax benefit from stock options exercised	90,315	64,939
Minority interest	29	951
Changes in assets and liabilities, net of acquired assets and liabilities:		
Accounts and notes receivable	188,603	16,748
Inventories	(75,507)	(59,813)
Other assets	(85,361)	(42,310)
Accounts payable	(43,002)	90,995
Accrued expenses	(37,429)	(25,517)
Income taxes payable	(113,949)	(6,838)
Deferred revenue	32,920	13,472
Other liabilities	3,130	(5)
Net cash provided by operating activities	$ 511,301	$ 536,650

Exhibit 1-2.12 (Continued)

CASH FLOWS FROM INVESTING ACTIVITIES:		
Additions to property, plant and equipment	$ (281,121)	$ (183,047)
Proceeds from sales of property, plant and equipment	17,128	--
Capitalized software development costs	(29,737)	(28,084)
Purchase of short-term and long-term available for sale Securities	(1,133,922)	(286,454)
Sale of short-term and long-term available for sale Securities	927,925	189,967
Maturity of short-term and long-term available for sale Securities	74,175	238,831
Business acquisitions, net of cash acquired	--	(198,251)
Net cash used for investing activities	$ (425,552)	$ (267,038)
CASH FLOWS FROM FINANCING ACTIVITIES:		
Issuance of common stock	54,835	64,256
Payment of long-term and short-term obligations	(8,484)	(7,225)
Issuance of long-term and short-term obligations	--	6,935
Cash portion of McDATA Corporation dividend	(141,981)	--
Net cash provided/(used) by financing activities	$ (95,630)	$ 63,966
Effect of exchange rate changes on cash	$ (3,735)	$ (3,486)
Net increase/(decrease) in cash and cash equivalents	(9,881)	333,578
Cash and cash equivalents at beginning of period	1,983,221	1,109,409
Cash and cash equivalents at end of period	$ 1,969,605	$ 1,439,501

Problem 8 Comparison of EMC and Kmart. Utilizing the statements described in Problems 6 and 7, prepare a spreadsheet showing the CAR and FAR for each of the two years for Kmart and EMC. Kmart's statements are for 2000 and 1999 while EMC's are for 2001 and 2000. Comment on which company shows better results. Kmart's balance sheet is shown in Exhibit 1-2.11. To calculate CAR for EMC Corporation, assume its current liabilities are $2 billion.

Case 1-2

J & J CORPORATION: STATEMENT OF CASH FLOWS

Case Objectives

1. Review the basic elements of a statement of cash flows
2. Review how financial statements interrelate
3. Review the decision usefulness of the statement of cash flows

Decision: Can J & J Corporation pay a dividend to John and Joanna?

NOTE: As you learned in your previous accounting course, the purpose of the statement of cash flows is to show a company's actual cash inflows and cash outflows during the past year for all operations. The statement of cash flows is both conceptually different and serves a different purpose than projected cash flows for one project, which will be covered in Case 1-4. The statement is a history covering the previous accounting period whereas the projection of cash flows looks several years into the future based upon a set of assumptions.

John and Joanna worked extremely hard to build J & J into a successful company. They feel good about the level of income achieved in the year 2002, and believe that they deserve a bonus in the form of a cash dividend of $30,000 each. They received some salary in 2002, which is included in the salaries item on the income statement. The problem, however, is that the cash balance for J & J on December 31, 2002 amounts to only $59,570, and John and Joanna believe that a minimum cash balance of $30,000 must be maintained. John and Joanna are puzzled. How could J & J start 2002 with a $52,000 cash balance, report a net income of $52,470, issue $50,000 worth of stock, and end the year with too little cash to pay a dividend of $60,000?

J & J Corporation's income statement for 2002 is presented in Exhibit C1-2.1. The company's comparative balance sheets for 2002 and 2001 are presented in Exhibit C1-2.2.

Requirements

1. Prepare a statement of cash flows using the indirect method in the format of Exhibit C1-2.3. Show all calculations to the right of the outlined area. Seven adjustments to income are necessary to compute net cash flow from operations. Enter the adjustment item (for example, accounts receivable) and whether you must add or deduct the adjustment. You also must determine net cash flow from investing activities and net cash flow from financing activities. All purchases of long-term assets were made for cash. No noncurrent assets were sold or disposed of during 2002.

2. Six of the seven operating activity adjustments to net income come from the balance sheet. What is the exception? Explain why it is an adjustment.

3. John and Joanna have gone to a bank to apply for a $60,000 loan so they have the cash to declare a $60,000 dividend. John and Joanna took J & J's income statement and balance sheet for 2002, but the bank also required that they have a statement of cash flows

   a. Why does the bank require a statement of cash flows?

   b. What do you think the bank's reaction to J & J's statement of cash flows will be?

4. John and Joanna did not receive the bank loan. They want to know how the financial statements would have been impacted if they had paid themselves a $30,000 dividend at the end of year 2002 instead of the original $60,000 amount they hoped to receive.

   a. Compute J & J's ending 2002 cash balance if a dividend of $30,000 had been paid to shareholders in 2002.

   b. If a $30,000 dividend had been paid by the J & J Corporation in 2002, identify which amounts in the income statement and the balance sheet would have changed, and to what amount they would change.

5. What operating problems are highlighted in J & J's statement of cash flows?

6. Joanna was brainstorming on the ways to improve cash flows so that she and John could get a dividend. She pointed out that J & J could depreciate the $34,000 in new equipment over three years (at $11,333 per year) instead of ten years (at $3,400 per year) as reflected in J & J's 2002 financial statements. Joanna noted that this would increase the amount added back to net income on the statement of cash flows using the indirect method. Evaluate Joanna's brainstorm.

Exhibit C1-2.1

J & J Corporation
Income Statement
Year Ended December 31, 2002

Sales revenue		$ 1,043,000
Cost of goods sold		559,500
Gross margin on sales		$ 483,500
Other expenses		
Salaries	$ 173,500	
Interest	10,000	
Utilities	19,000	
Property taxes	7,000	
Insurance	14,000	
Depreciation	73,500	
Advertising	35,000	
Other	72,000	
Total other expenses		404,000
Income before taxes		$ 79,500
Income tax		27,030
Net income		$ 52,470

Exhibit C1-2.2

J & J Corporation
Comparative Balance Sheets
December 31

	2002	2001
Assets		
Current assets		
Cash	$ 59,570	$ 52,000
Accounts receivable, net	72,000	60,000
Inventory	249,000	184,000
Prepaid expenses	2,500	3,000
Total current assets	$ 383,070	$ 299,000
Plant and equipment		
Service equipment	$ 190,000	$ 190,000
Retail building	400,000	400,000
Display and fixtures	232,000	198,000
	$ 822,000	$ 788,000
Less accumulated depreciation	(318,500)	(245,000)
Plant and equipment, net	$ 503,500	$ 543,000
Goodwill	133,000	133,000
Total assets	$ 1,019,570	$ 975,000
Liabilities		
Current liabilities:		
Accounts payable	$ 91,900	$ 161,000
Taxes payable	32,000	20,000
Wages payable	5,200	6,000
Total current liabilities	$ 129,100	$ 187,000
Notes payable	-	-
Mortgage payable	272,000	272,000
Total liabilities	$ 401,100	$ 459,000
Stockholders' equity		
Contributed capital	$ 200,000	$ 150,000
Retained earnings	418,470	366,000
Total stockholders' equity	$ 618,470	$ 516,000
Total liabilities and stockholders' equity	$ 1,019,570	$ 975,000

Exhibit C1-2.3

J & J Corporation
Statement of Cash Flows–Indirect Method
Year Ended December 31, 2002

Operating Activities		
Net Income		
Add (deduct) adjustments to cash basis:		
1. ______		
2. ______		
3. ______		
4. ______		
5. ______		
6. ______		
7. ______		
Net Cash Flow from Operations		
Investing Activities		
8. ______		
Financing Activities		
9. ______		
Change in cash during 2002		
Add cash balance, January 1, 2002		52,000
Cash balance, December 31, 2002		

Reading 1-3

COST, VOLUME, AND PROFITABILITY DECISIONS

INTRODUCTION

Financial planning is the formulation of future scenarios of a business organization. In order to make effective plans it is necessary for management to know how revenues and expenses respond to changes in activity levels. The foundation of profitability analysis is the separation of total costs into variable and fixed expenses and relating these cost behaviors with revenue assumptions in the planning process. The cost-volume-profit (CVP) analysis model used in financial planning is introduced. The importance of contribution margin and the contribution margin ratio is emphasized, as well as how these calculations are used in the computation of breakeven volume. The reading concludes by showing how breakeven analysis and the CVP model are used in making short-term business decisions.

REVENUE PLANNING

The revenue that a company earns is determined by the unit price times the number of units sold. The price that a company charges for its products must be competitive unless that product is unique and the buyer is willing to pay a premium to acquire it. In a department store, the price will depend on what the retailer (1) paid to acquire the inventory; (2) needs to cover other costs such as advertising, salaries, supplies, insurance, rent, etc.; and (3) adds to earn a reasonable profit. If the product is widely distributed, the individual pricing of the product on any given day may depend on the price that a competitor charges for that same item, any advertising specials, etc. For example, if a gas station operates in an area where there are many other gas stations, then customers tend to be more price sensitive. That gas station may need to lower its price to attract more customers. Unless the retailer is offering some additional services for the higher price, many customers will tend to shop at the retailer that offers the lower price. Additional services may include window washing, tire checks, or an easy access location.

Lowering the price on a product will usually increase the quantity sold. However, a thorough understanding of the effect that a change in volume will have on profit is only possible if the planner understands the behavior of its various costs.

COST PLANNING

The planned level of costs will depend on the nature of each cost and its behavior in relation to sales volume. Costs can be broken down into two categories: variable and fixed. Some costs are mixed, which means they have both a variable and a fixed component. An example is the cost of telephone service. A monthly fixed amount plus a variable charge for the minutes devoted to long-distance calls comprises the total charges. Mixed costs such as the total charge for telephone service must be broken down into their variable and fixed components.

Variable Costs and Contribution Margin

Variable costs are those that, in total, vary in proportion to changes in sales volume. The calculation of total variable cost is as follows:

Total variable cost = Variable cost per unit × number of units

Note that the variable cost per unit remains the same regardless of the number of units involved. For example, let's assume that we are selling a book for $40. The only variable cost is $25 to print the book. The variable cost would be $25 per unit and $75 for three units:

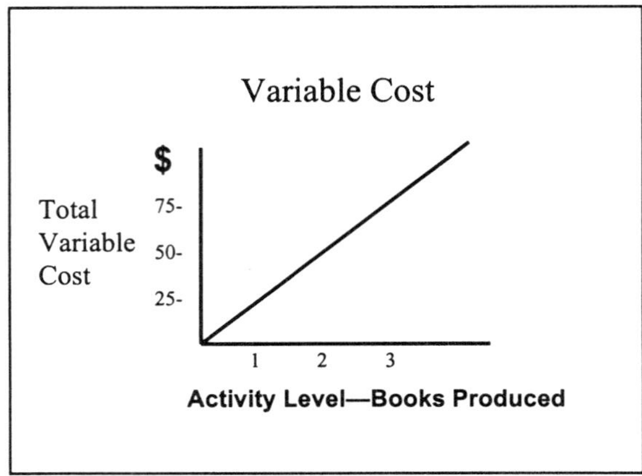

After identifying the variable costs, the company can determine the **contribution margin**.

	Sales =	Unit selling price (SP) × Number of units sold
–	Variable cost =	Unit variable cost (VC) × Number of units sold
	Contribution margin =	Unit contribution margin × Number of units sold

Apply this relationship to the book product. Assume a book sells for $40, and it costs $25 to print a book (printing is the only variable cost.). What is the CM per book?

CM = $40 SP - $25 VC = $15 per book
CM for 20 books is 20 × $15 = $300

The **contribution margin ratio** (CMR) is the contribution margin divided by sales revenue. For our book example, the contribution margin ratio is $15 ÷ $40 = 37.5 percent.

Contribution Margin Ratio (CMR)

	Per Book	20 books	%
Revenues	$ 40	$ 800	100.0%
Variable costs	25	500	62.5%
Contribution margin	$ 15	$ 300	37.5%

The example shows that the contribution margin is $15 per book. To complete the table for sales revenue for 20 books, 20 is multiplied by each line item: sales price per unit to arrive at sales, variable cost per unit to arrive at variable costs, and contribution margin per unit to arrive at the contribution margin for twenty books. Note that the contribution margin ratio can be calculated using either $15 ÷ $40 or $300 ÷ $800. Either calculation will result in a ratio of 37.5 percent, because the ratio always remains the same (within the relevant range) regardless of the number of units involved.

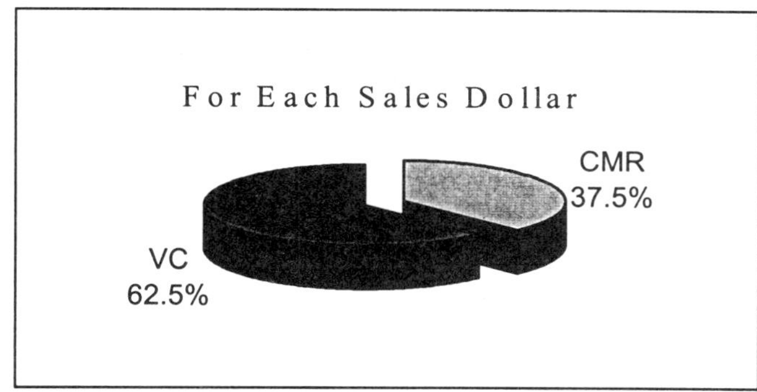

The contribution margin ratio indicates that for each sales dollar, 37.5 percent of that dollar is available to cover fixed costs and to provide a profit. The variable cost percentage of 62.5 percent means that 62.5 cents of each sales dollar covers variable costs.

Fixed Costs

Fixed costs are those that remain constant in total over a certain relevant range of activity, regardless of the activity level. The range of volumes over which fixed costs remain the same is known as the **relevant range**. As an example, rent for a building is usually a fixed cost for most companies. The amount of rent expense for the building stays the same (until the company expands its facilities), regardless of the number of units a company sells. Expanding to a new building would represent a new relevant range. The relevant range may differ for each type of fixed cost. Rent may not change but the addition of a night shift may introduce additional fixed costs for supervision.

Note that the fixed cost *per unit* changes as the volume involved changes. This sometimes confusing aspect of fixed costs is important in management accounting and will reappear throughout the course. The reason this concept is so important is that for many decisions the cost per unit is the critical focus, not total costs. Therefore, in order to provide relevant information to decision makers, fixed costs must be presented on a per-unit basis. To compute fixed cost per unit, however, a volume must be specified because a change in volume will change the fixed cost per unit.

Going back to our book example, the graphic designer's fee would be the same regardless of how many books were sold (within the relevant range). Let's assume that the graphic designer's fee and other fixed costs total $5,400.

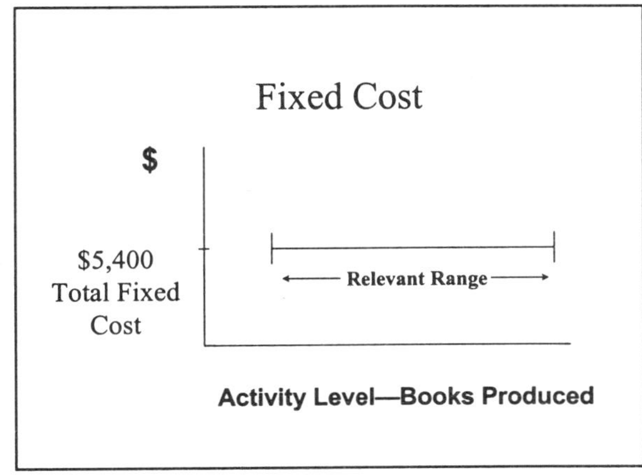

Mixed Costs

Mixed costs are those that are partially variable and partially fixed. The variable portion of the mixed cost varies with the activity level, and the remainder is fixed regardless of the activity level (within the relevant range). Good examples of mixed costs are telephone or electric bills. Your bill is based on a flat fee per month regardless of use, plus a fee based on how much of the utility you used.

A graph of mixed cost would look like this:

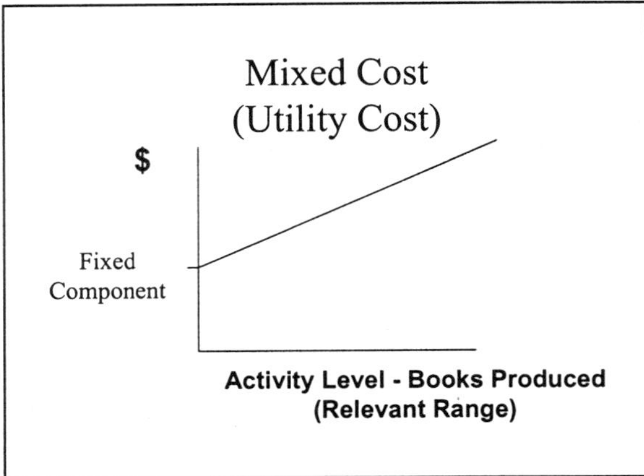

Notice that the line does not go through the origin. The line will intersect the *y* (or vertical) axis at the amount of fixed cost.

BREAKEVEN ANALYSIS

Breakeven analysis is a simple yet powerful tool for analyzing a company's performance. The concept underlying this tool is that, within a relevant range of volume (number of units produced or sold), some costs will in total remain unchanged (fixed costs) and some costs and revenues in total will vary in proportion to volume (sales revenue and variable costs). The basic question addressed is: At what level of sales is the company expected to earn exactly zero net income? This level of sales is called the **breakeven point**.

The breakeven point can be calculated in two ways: (1) breakeven in unit sales and (2) breakeven in dollar sales. The formula (labeled formula 1) for breakeven in unit sales is:

$$\text{Unit breakeven}^{1} = \frac{\text{Total fixed costs}}{\text{Contribution margin per unit}} \qquad (1)$$

[1]The unit breakeven formula is derived as follows:

Net income (NI) = (Unit sales – Unit variable costs)(Units) – Total fixed costs (TFC) = 0
Total fixed costs = (Unit sales – Unit variable costs)(Units)
Total fixed costs = (Contribution margin per unit)(Units)
Total fixed costs ÷ (Contribution margin per unit) = Units required to earn 0 net income

The formula (labeled formula 2) for breakeven in dollar sales is:

$$\text{Dollar breakeven} = \frac{\text{Total fixed costs}}{\text{Contribution margin ratio}} \quad (2)$$

For a company producing more than one product, only a dollar sales breakeven can be computed for the entire company. Computing a unit breakeven for the entire company by adding unlike units together isn't meaningful.

Industry Characteristics

Some types of businesses, such as passenger air carriers, typically have low variable costs. Processing tickets and in-flight food and drink are examples of common variable costs. The contribution margin for airlines is very large, but it needs to be because airlines have high fixed costs per flight such as salaries, depreciation on the airplanes, fuel, etc. Once a breakeven number of passengers are ticketed, every new passenger contributes his or her contribution margin directly to net income. In 1998, airline profits set new records largely because the planes were near full capacity on most flights. Conversely, in Fall 2001 airlines lost billions of dollars because of a steep decline in the number of passengers.

Kmart is an example of a company with high variable costs, mostly due to the cost of the inventory sold. Because of the high variable costs, Kmart has a low contribution margin. For this reason, the company needs to sell a large volume of merchandise to cover fixed costs. Advertised specials may be "loss leaders," which are designed to increase store traffic and thereby increase sales of regularly-priced merchandise.

Breakeven Example

To illustrate, assume that you are evaluating two multi-product companies, Alpha and Beta, in the same industry. Projected year 2003 contribution income statements for the two companies are presented in Exhibit 1-3.1. Contribution income statements are discussed later.

Exhibit 1-3.1

Alpha and Beta Corporations
Contribution Income Statements

	Alpha Corporation	%	Beta Corporation	%
Sales	$ 5,000,000	100%	$ 5,000,000	100%
Variable expenses	2,000,000	40%	3,500,000	70%
Contribution margin	$ 3,000,000	60%	$ 1,500,000	30%
Fixed expenses	2,400,000		900,000	
Net income	$ 600,000		$ 600,000	
Contribution margin ratio		0.60		0.30

Both companies have projected sales of $5,000,000 and net income of $600,000. Do they have the same breakeven sales revenue? Recall that the contribution margin ratio is the contribution margin divided by sales. Therefore, using equation (2), the sales revenue breakeven point for Alpha is $4,000,000 ($2,400,000 ÷ .60) and for Beta is $3,000,000 ($900,000 ÷ .30). Exhibit 1-3.2 presents contribution income statements for both companies at these breakeven sales levels. Note how the formulas create a sales level that results in zero net income.

Exhibit 1-3.2

Alpha and Beta Corporations Contribution Income Statements at Breakeven Levels				
	Alpha Corporation	**%**	**Beta Corporation**	**%**
Sales	$ 4,000,000	100%	$ 3,000,000	100%
Variable expenses	1,600,000	40%	2,100,000	70%
Contribution margin	$ 2,400,000	60%	$ 900,000	30%
Fixed expenses	2,400,000		900,000	
Net income	$ 0		$ 0	
Contribution margin ratio		0.60		0.30

Breakeven analysis gives decision makers a "feel" for the riskiness of an entire company, division of a company, or individual project or product. Savvy decision makers are interested in more financial information than just the projected profitability of the decision under consideration. They also want to know what will happen to profitability if estimates of future revenues and costs are different than projected. If the net income of a company, division, etc., is relatively unaffected by changes in cost and revenue estimates, it is said to be less risky than companies that are more impacted by changes.

Which company is at more risk of having a negative net income due to sales being less than expected, Alpha or Beta? Alpha is more at risk, because sales need to fall only 20 percent ($1,000,000) below expectations before income falls below the breakeven point. Sales for Beta, on the other hand, would have to fall 40 percent below expectations before it loses money. Conversely, Alpha is more likely to double net income to a level of $1,200,000 because to do this, sales need to increase by only $1,000,000 to $6,000,000. Beta would have to increase sales by $2,000,000 to $7,000,000 to double net income. Use formula (4) in the next section to verify the sales necessary for Alpha and Beta to earn an income of $1,200,000.

Many managers place the lowering of their company's breakeven point as a major goal of the organization. Why? Because by lowering the breakeven sales level, there is less risk of a company losing money (or at least losing large amounts of money) in an economic downturn. The airline industry is one example where managers work to lower breakeven sales levels. Due to intense competition in part due to deregulation of the airline industry, many airlines have seen actual revenues be much lower than projected. This, in turn, resulted in huge losses for some carriers during the economic recession of 1991–1992.

Including a Desired Profit Ignoring Income Taxes

Most decision makers are interested in the level of sales required to earn some desired profit, not merely to breakeven. Breakeven analysis is easily extended by simply adding a desired level of profit to total fixed costs in the numerator. The breakeven formula then computes the number of units or total dollar sales required to earn a desired profit. For example, the formula (labeled formula 3) to compute the number of units that must be sold to earn a net income of $144,000 is:

$$\text{Units for desired profit} = \frac{\text{Total fixed costs} + \$144{,}000}{\text{Contribution margin per unit}} \qquad (3)$$

The formula (labeled formula 4) to compute the dollar sales required to earn a net income of \$144,000 is:

$$\text{Dollar sales for desired profit} = \frac{\text{Total fixed costs} + \$144{,}000}{\text{Contribution margin ratio}} \qquad (4)$$

Impact of Taxes

Since corporations must pay tax on pre-tax income, the impact of taxes should be considered when the units or dollar sales required to earn an after-tax profit are computed. The complicating factor is that taxes are not a purely variable cost. Income taxes owed the government increase as sales increase and decrease as sales decrease, but taxes do not change in proportion to changes in sales.

As a result, income taxes need to be considered as a separate item in the breakeven formula.. Therefore, the desired income of \$144,000 in the previous formula must be replaced by the amount of pre-tax income that must be earned in order to produce an after-tax income of \$144,000. If a tax rate of 28 percent is assumed, the amount of pre-tax income (PTI) needed can be determined as follows:

$$\begin{aligned} \$144{,}000 &= \text{PTI} - .28\text{PTI} \\ \$144{,}000 &= \text{PTI} \times (1 - .28) \\ \text{or PTI} &= \$144{,}000 \div (1 - .28) \end{aligned}$$

In order to compute either the unit or dollar sales necessary to earn an after-tax income of \$144,000 with a tax rate of 28 percent, simply replace the \$144,000 in formulas (3) or (4) with \$144,000 ÷ (1 – .28), or \$200,000. Inserting this number captures the effect of income taxes and the sales necessary to earn \$144,000 after taxes.

THE CONTRIBUTION INCOME STATEMENT

Many organizations prepare income statements in two different formats. For external reporting purposes a traditional (also called an *absorption*) income statement is prepared. Generally accepted accounting principles require preparation of a traditional income statement. Therefore, all audited statements must be in the traditional format. For companies that have no special accounting events during the period (for example, extraordinary items, changes in accounting principles, or discontinued operations), the traditional format income statement contains nine major headings: Sales revenue; cost of goods sold; gross margin; selling, general, and administrative expenses; interest expense; extraordinary gains and losses; income before tax; income tax; and net income. An example of a condensed traditional income statement for J & J Corporation is presented in Exhibit 1-3.3 (J & J reported no extraordinary gains or losses in 2002). Most companies add more detail within some of these categories, but the format is similar.

The major division of expenses in a traditional income statement is between cost of goods sold above gross margin and selling, general, and administrative (SG&A) and other expenses below gross margin. Expenses in cost of goods sold are referred to as product costs because these costs are assigned to products (unlike SG&A expenses) and do not show up on the income statement until the product is sold. For example, managers at a retail paint store know their cost to purchase the can of paint you buy, but usually they have no idea of how much SG&A costs that can of paint created. Notice in Exhibit 1-3.3 that the cost of goods sold is the same in each format. This is because for a retail company, cost of goods sold consists entirely of variable expenses. In a manufacturing company, however, cost of goods sold also includes fixed manufacturing expenses. Therefore, in the traditional approach, fixed and variable costs are often mixed together in both the cost of goods sold and SG&A categories.

Exhibit 1-3.3
Comparison of Traditional and Contribution Income Statements

J & J Corporation Income Statements
Year Ended December 31, 2002

Traditional Income Statement		Contribution Income Statement	
Sales revenue	$ 1,040,000	Sales Revenue	$ 1,040,000
Cost of goods sold	559,500	Less variable expenses:	
Gross margin	$ 480,500	Variable cost of sales	491,500
Selling and administrative		Variable S&A	68,000
expense (S&A)	394,000	Contribution margin	$ 480,500
Interest expense	10,000	Fixed expenses[1]	404,000
Income before tax	$ 76,500	Income before tax	$ 76,500
Income tax	30,600	Income tax	30,600
Net income	$ 45,900	Net income	$ 45,900

[1] Fixed selling and administrative expenses plus interest.

In the **contribution income statement** illustrated in Exhibit 1-3.3, costs are arranged by variable and fixed categories rather than by cost of goods sold and SG&A categories. Note that the user can more easily determine the effects of changes in sales on net income than with the traditional statement. Net income will increase at a faster rate (percentage) than sales volume as units sold increase, and fall at a faster rate than sales volume as unit sales decline. Can you explain why this is so? Income tax is handled as a separate item. Income taxes aren't a variable cost because although they increase as sales increase, they do not increase in proportion to sales increases. Since income taxes are a major cost and are affected by changes in sales volume, decision makers usually want to include the impact of changes in income tax expense as "what if" and other scenarios are explored.

Why Use Contribution Income Statements?

Most management accountants argue that the contribution income approach better supports management decisions than does the absorption approach. The primary advantage of the contribution approach is that with fixed and variable costs readily determinable, breakeven and other "what if" questions managers use to assess risk are easily answered. These types of analyses cannot be done if only absorption income statement information is available. From the contribution income statement J & J's contribution margin ratio of about .462 can be computed ($480,500 ÷ $1,040,000). Dividing fixed expenses of $404,000 by the contribution margin ratio of .462 yields J & J's breakeven sales level of $874,459. A breakeven sales level cannot be computed using information from only the traditional income statement.

Why is absorption costing required for external financial statements? The best answer is probably tradition. Many financial analysts and bankers argue that they also need cost information in a contribution income statement format so they can perform breakeven and "what if" analysis. To date, however, most users of external financial statements have had to "guesstimate" companies' fixed and variable costs.

RELEVANT COSTS

Future costs are often the result of past decisions. The financial consequences of a past decision cannot be changed because the decision cannot be changed. For example, a past decision to construct a new plant sets up an accounting process that allocates depreciation expense over future periods. If later circumstances prove the new plant to have been a bad idea, the decision of whether or not to close the plant should not be based upon depreciation expense. The reason is that even if the plant is not profitable, depreciation expense will continue will continue to appear an expense on the income statement. The decision to close, or not to close, should be based upon the future costs relevant to the decisions, not on past depreciation or other costs.

To illustrate, if continuing to run the plant means next year's annual cash cost (labor, materials, occupancy costs, etc.) will be $10 million, depreciation expense will be $3 million and revenues from its production will be $12 million, what decision should be made? The total cost of the plant from an accounting perspective is $13 million. But that number includes $3 million, which is called a **sunk cost**; a cost stemming from a past decision. In this example, the plant should remain operating. The incremental future revenues will be $12 million, the incremental costs will be $10 million, and the contribution margin from continuing to operate the plant will be $2 million. In other words, the company is better off continuing to operate the plant than closing the plant by an amount of $2 million.

You may ask: "What about the $3 million depreciation?" A good question! The income statement for this plant will report a loss of $1 million. Total costs will be $13 million and the revenues will be $12 million. But because $3 million of the total cost is a sunk cost, it is not a relevant cost in considering whether or not to close the plant. A **relevant cost** is one that is incremental to a decision under study. In our example, $10 million represents the total relevant cost because it is the cost that can change as a result of the decision to keep operating the plant. This example illustrates how traditional financial statements can be misleading to management when making operating decisions. The loss reported in the income statement suggests closing the plant, which is the wrong decision financially. A management accounting analysis using relevant cost shows that *in the short term* the company is $ 2 million better off keeping the plant open.

Another example is a high-fashion retailer who purchases a large stock of seasonable merchandise at $40 per garment that is expected to sell quickly for $100 per garment. At the end of the season the unsold stock represents a sunk cost. Lets assume a liquidator, who will take the entire unsold inventory, offers the retailer $20 per garment for the stock of 200 unsold garments. An alternative is for the retailer to run a special clearance sale within the store. The retailer estimates that a "50% off clearance sale" will dispose of the unsold stock. Assume the costs per garment to run this clearance sale are:

Clearance tags on each garment	$3
New bar codes for clearance merchandise	1
Commissions to sales staff	5

In addition, the following expenses will be incurred to run this clearance sale:

Advertising on radio and TV	$4,000
New window display	1,000
Rearrange store layout of merchandise	1,000

Should the retailer sell to the liquidator? Or should the retailer run the clearance sale? Is the original cost of the garments relevant to the decision? What is relevant now is the net amount the retailer can recover from the unsold merchandise. Exhibit 1-3.4 presents the comparison of the two alternatives.

Exhibit 1-3.4

Fashion Retailer Alternatives

Alternative	Liquidator	Clearance Sale
Revenue from sale of inventory	$ 4,000	$ 10,000
Relevant costs (200 garments)	none	
Advertising		(4,000)
Window display		(1,000)
Store rearraging		(1,000)
Clearance tags @ $3 each		(600)
Bar codes@ $1 each		(200)
Commissions @ $5 each		(1,000)
Incremental income	$ 4,000	$ 2,200

Note that all the items listed in the analysis are future costs and revenues. The original cost of $40 per garment is not relevant because it is a sunk cost stemming from a past decision. Even though the clearance sale sounded like a good idea compared to the liquidator, the incremental costs of promoting and implementing a clearance sale make it a less desirable economic alternative.

SUMMARY

The separation of variable and fixed costs is a powerful planning tool. It enables the planner to gain insights into the way in which income will change in relation to sales. Breakeven can be computed in both units and sales dollars. For companies that produce more than one product, only breakeven in sales dollars can be computed for the entire firm. Cost-volume-profit (CVP) analysis extends simple breakeven calculations to include identification of sales levels required to earn desired income both before and after taxes. A contribution income statement is another CVP tool used in financial planning. You will have the opportunity to use all of these techniques throughout the rest of this book.

EXERCISES AND PROBLEMS

Exercises

Exercise 1 Cost Behavior. A hospital is studying four of its large costs: air conditioning, laundry, meals for patients, and X-ray supplies. The hospital's controller is trying to correlate the change in these costs with the number of admissions to the hospital. Explain which are likely variable costs and which are fixed costs.

Exercise 2 Breakeven Point. Define the term breakeven point.

Exercise 3 Breakeven: Units Versus Dollars. Explain the difference between breakeven units and breakeven sales revenue.

Exercise 4 Breakeven and Income Taxes. If desired net income is $100,000 and the income tax rate is 40 percent, how is the breakeven formula modified to give sales necessary to reach the goal?

Exercise 5 Simple Breakeven. Wildcat Company manufactures and sells two products: Psi and Rho. March 2003 cost and sales revenue information is as follows:

	Psi	Rho
Sales price	$9.00	$6.75
March sales	10,000 units	20,000 units
Variable costs	$6.75	$4.50
Fixed costs	$18,500	$28,000

a. Compute the unit contribution margin for each product.

b. Compute the contribution margin ratio for each product.

c. Compute the March breakeven point in units for each product.

d. Compute the March breakeven point in sales dollars for each product.

e. Compute the March breakeven point in sales dollars for the entire Wildcat Company (assume sales of Psi and Rho remain in the same proportion).

f. If Wildcat sells an additional 1,000 units of Psi in March at $9 per unit (total March sales of 11,000 units), by how much will its total net income increase?

Exercise 6 Desired Income and Taxes. Using the information in Exercise 5 for Wildcat Company, answer the following questions.

a. If taxes are ignored, what level of sales must Wildcat achieve in order to earn a net income of $30,000, assuming that sales of Psi and Rho remain in the same proportion?

b. If Wildcat faces a combined state and federal income tax rate of 35 percent, what level of sales must Wildcat achieve in order to earn an after-tax net income of $25,000, assuming that sales of Psi and Rho remain in the same proportion?

c. If all costs remain the same, at what price must Wildcat sell 10,000 Psi products in order to earn an after-tax March net income of $5,000 on the Psi products alone?

Exercise 7 Relative Product Risk. Using the information in Exercise 5 for Wildcat Company, answer the following questions.

a. Which product, Psi or Rho, has a higher risk of losing money due to a shortfall in sales revenue? Explain.

b. Which product, Psi or Rho, has a higher risk of losing money due to an increase in fixed costs? Explain.

c. Explain how Wildcat's managers can reduce Psi's breakeven sales level.

Exercise 8 Relationship of Income Tax and Sales. Buckeye Co. projects the following financial information:

Sales revenue	$2,500,000
Variable costs	1,000,000
Contribution margin	$1,500,000
Fixed costs	900,000
Income before tax	$ 600,000
Income tax (25%)	150,000
Net income	$ 450,000

a. If sales increase by 10 percent, will income tax increase by 10 percent? Explain your answer without performing any computations.

b. Create another income statement for Buckeye that reflects a 10 percent increase in sales revenue, but with the same variable costs per unit, same total fixed costs, and same income tax rate. By what percentage does income tax increase?

c. If Buckeye has the same variable costs per unit, same total fixed costs, and same income tax rate, by how much must sales revenue increase to increase net income to $600,000?

Problems

Problem 1 Contribution Income Statement and Pricing. Bravura Yachts Incorporated (BYI) began business in January 2002. In its first year, it plans to produce and sell 20 units of the Sportster 29, a luxury sailboat. Management has not yet set a price for the Sportster 29 and asks you to determine the price that is consistent with the following cost data and that will yield an after-tax net income of $120,000.

Direct materials per unit	$10,000
Direct labor per unit	1,000 hours at $15
Rent, interest, and annual fixed costs	$300,000
Tax rate on income	40%

Problem 2 Cost-Volume-Profitability Analysis. This is a continuation of Problem 1. Use the data from Problem 1 where appropriate.

Because of competitive pressures, Bravura wants to pursue a strategy of low price compared to other products on the market. Accordingly, management has reduced the target net income after taxes to $60,000. Management also realizes that it will need to give salespersons a commission of $4,000 for each unit they sell and commit to a year of magazine advertising, which will cost $50,000. Based upon these additional considerations, what is the resulting price based upon a plan to produce and sell 20 Sportster 29s?

Problem 3 Breakeven Cost-Volume-Profitability Analysis. This is a continuation of Problems 1 and 2. Use the data from these problems where appropriate.

In order to meet the competition, management has set the price of the Sportster 29 at $49,000. A plant for manufacturing the boats has been leased at a much lower rent and overhead than previously thought. This will lower fixed costs by $100,000. With this favorable development, management wants to know how many boats it must sell to earn an after tax net income of $90,000.

Problem 4 Cost and Profitability. VideoMax has introduced a new product that will record a library of 50 DVDs. The user can record 50 2-hour broadcasts. Once recorded, the user can easily edit out unwanted portions of the broadcast, such as commercials. VideoMax has made the following estimates for 2003:

Variable cost of manufacturing	$50
Variable selling expense per unit	5
Fixed expenses:	
Selling	$300,000
Administrative	200,000
Manufacturing	500,000
Expected sales volume for 2003	10,000 units
Selling price	$150
Tax rate	30%

a. What is the breakeven point for 2003?

b. What is the net income (loss) at the expected sales volume?

c. If VideoMax wants to earn $250,000 net income, how many units must it sell?

Problem 5 Multiple Product Profitability. Rock Climb Corp. makes two products: a titanium carbiner called T-Hook and a hardened aluminum carbiner called A-hook. Both are very light yet have a 1,000 pound breaking strength. The two products are manufactured in two separate but similar factories. Rock Climb Corp. has made the following projections for 2003:

	T-Hook	A-Hook
Price	$10	$7
Unit volume	40,000	30,000
Sales revenue	$ 400,000	$ 210,000
Costs:		
Variable	$6	$3
Fixed	$ 100,000	$ 100,000

Note: Corporate fixed expenses not traceable to either product are $60,000.

a. What is the contribution margin and profitability for each product?

b. What is the breakeven for each product?

c. What is the CMR if the actual sales for 2003 are as projected?

d. What is the breakeven for the Rock Climb Corp?

e. If sales of A-Hook reach 50,000 units in 2003, what is the new breakeven and income before tax for 2003?

f. Compare your answers for d and e. Comment on the causes of the difference.

Problem 6 Cost and Volume Profit Analysis. Motorsport Inc. makes an electronic engine control module that increases horsepower of auto engines by 20 to 30 percent. This after market product replaces the factory-installed control unit. Motorsport's income statement for 2002 is as follows:

Motorsport Incorporated Income Statement for 2002	
Sales (40,000 units)	$ 700,000
Variable costs	400,000
Contribution margin	$ 300,000
Fixed costs	150,000
Income before tax	$ 150,000
Income tax (20%)	30,000
Net Income	$ 120,000

For 2003 Motorsport will introduce an improved computer chip in its modules that will increase horsepower and get better fuel economy. The old chip cost $3 in each unit but the new chip will cost $4. In addition, new equipment is needed to robotically install the new chip in the module. The machine can be leased for $25,000 per year.

a. What was Motorsport's breakeven in units in year 2002?

b. What is Motorsport's projected breakeven for 2003?

c. How many units must be sold for Motorsport to earn net income of $165,000?

d. Motorsport can avoid leasing the new machine by adding a labor step that will add $0.50 to the variable cost of manufacturing. Should Motorsport use labor instead of leasing the machine?

e. Motorsport believes it can increase selling price to $20. If 40,000 units are sold, by how much must fixed expenses be reduced to earn an income of $180,000?

Case 1-3

J & J CORPORATION: OPENING A NEW STORE

Case Objectives

1. Review managerial uses of financial data
2. Review breakeven and contribution analyses

Decision: Should J & J Corporation open a new store?

An opportunity to further expand J & J Corporation has been identified by one of its shareholders, Joanna Barnes. A new retailing area is planned for development on the edge of town. Some of the stores planned are Wal-Mart, Kroger, Walgreen Drug, specialty and discount clothing stores, a tire/auto store, and various fast-food franchises. When the area is fully developed, an excellent customer traffic pattern is likely, which is an important consideration in retailing.

Joanna's proposal is to open a home improvement store. She proposes adding the following four departments:

- Gardening and landscaping
- Draperies, rugs, and pictures
- Furniture and appliances
- Paint and wallpaper

The scale of financial commitment and risk is considerably greater than J & J's existing business. For example, total assets of J & J Corporation are about $1 million (see Case 1-1). The funds needed to open the home improvement store are more than six times that level. Expansion will significantly alter its balance sheet. Consequently, John and Joanna are approaching the new venture with extreme caution. They are acutely aware that failure of the home improvement store would bankrupt their corporation. Yet the profit potential of this expansion is enormous—if sales reach sufficiently high levels.

Forecasts

J & J Corporation engaged the services of a retail marketing research company. Based upon an analysis of similar retail complexes in similar size cities, the consulting company's report, shown as Exhibit C1-3.1, provided forecast ranges for sales, contribution margin ratios, and fixed expenses for each of the four departments. The market research company believes that economic uncertainties in the region of the proposed store limit its ability to provide single point forecasts. Therefore, Exhibit C1-3.1 contains the best estimates of equally probable outcomes should J & J Corp. proceed with the project to open a home improvement store.

Exhibit C1-3.1
Home Improvement Store
Range of First Year Forecasts

Dice Roll	Paint & Wallpaper	Gardening	Draperies	Furniture	Total
		Projected Sales Volume			
5 or 6	$ 2,700,000	$ 2,400,000	$ 3,500,000	$ 6,100,000	$ 14,700,000
3 or 4	2,400,000	1,400,000	1,500,000	5,200,000	10,500,000
1 or 2	1,300,000	800,000	1,000,000	3,400,000	6,500,000
		Projected Contribution Margin Ratios			
5 or 6	0.68	0.72	0.54	0.38	
3 or 4	0.58	0.57	0.44	0.35	
1 or 2	0.48	0.46	0.38	0.32	
		Projected Fixed Expenses			
5 or 6	$ 600,000	$ 720,000	$ 480,000	$ 850,000	$ 2,650,000
3 or 4	500,000	620,000	420,000	820,000	2,360,000
1 or 2	420,000	510,000	380,000	730,000	2,040,000

How to Select Sales, Contribution Margin, and Fixed Expenses

By rolling a die (one of a pair of dice) twelve times, and selecting the corresponding values from Exhibit C1-3.1, you will create a personalized set of numbers. Your task is to use these values to prepare a projected income statement and breakeven point for the first year of operation for each of the four departments.

Example

To illustrate, determine the expected sales in the paint and wallpaper department by rolling the die. Suppose a 4 comes up; this means that the estimated sales revenue in that department is $2,400,000. Roll the die again; assume a 6 comes up. That means the contribution margin ratio for that department is .68. Next, determine the level of fixed expenses for the paint department by rolling the die. If a 2 is rolled, fixed expenses are $420,000. Combining these dice-roll selections yields the departmental income statement shown in Exhibit C1-3.2.

Exhibit C1-3.2

Paint And Wallpaper Department
Projected Contribution Income Statement
Year Ended December 31, 2003

Sales	$ 2,400,000
Variable cost of goods sold (.32)	768,000
Contribution margin (CMR = .68)	1,632,000
Fixed expenses	420,000
Pre-tax departmental income	$ 1,212,000

Breakeven Point for Paint and Wallpaper Department, New Store Proposal

$$\text{Breakeven sales} = \frac{\text{Fixed costs}}{\text{CMR}} = \frac{\$420{,}000}{.68} = \$617{,}647$$

Requirements

1. Roll the die three times for each department (twelve rolls total) to determine your values for sales, contribution margin ratio, and fixed expenses for the first year. Show the results of rolling the die by circling the selected estimates in Exhibit C1-3.1. *Note*: Since there are many combinations of data generated by the rolling of the die, each student should have a different answer.

2. Compile the relevant data into a contribution income statement for the first year on a computer spreadsheet. Exhibit C1-3.3 provides a template you can use as a guideline to prepare your Excel spreadsheet. For this requirement, you need only complete rows 6 through 10 and row 16. Print the template after completing this requirement and save your spreadsheet.

3. Using a "Save As" command, save your spreadsheet again but under a different name than you used in requirement 2. Assume for this requirement that all the dice rolls were a 3 or 4 and complete the spreadsheet again using these dice rolls for projected sales, contribution margin ratio, and fixed expenses for each department and for J & J in total.

Complete the remaining requirements on the template prepared in requirement 3, which assumed the midpoint rolls of 3 or 4.

4. A probable effect of the new home improvement store would be a reduction of sales at J & J's existing paint and wallpaper store across town. The report contained an estimate that the loss of sales at the old store would be $100,000 annually. The fixed expenses of $450,000 and a contribution ratio of .56 at the old store are not expected to change if the new store is opened. Compute the lost contribution margin at the existing store caused by the opening of the new store. Treat this lost contribution margin as a fixed expense

5. What is the total (income from new store less loss of contribution from existing store) after-tax first-year impact of the proposed home improvement store on J & J? Assume a tax rate of 26 percent.

6. What is the breakeven point in sales dollars for the new store, assuming each department's proportion of total sales remains the same as computed in requirement 3?

7. Assuming each department's proportion of total sales remain the same as computed in requirement 3, at what level of sales will the new store earn a net income after tax of $1,000,000? (Use the formula for desired after-tax income in Reading 1-3 to solve this requirement.)

Exhibit C1-3.3
J & J Corporation
Projected Contribution Income Statement
Year Ended December 31, 2003

	B	C	D	E	F	G	H
5		**Paint**	**Gardening**	**Draperies**	**Furniture**	**Total**	
6	Sales						
7	Variable costs						
8	Contribution margin						
9	Fixed costs						
10	Pretax income (loss)						
11	Lost CM at existing store						Requirement 4
12	Net pretax effect						
13	Income tax expense						
14	Net income (loss)						Requirement 5
15							
16	CMR (given)						Don't add across for total
17							
18	Breakeven						Requirement 6
19							
20	Target sales required to earn after tax profit of $1,000,000						Requirement 7

Case 1-4

J & J CORPORATION: CASH FLOWS FOR THE NEW STORE

Case Objectives

1. Understand the difference between net income and cash flows.
2. Translate business plans into multi-year cash flow projections.
3. Improve basic spreadsheet skills.

Decision: Based on the desire to recover the investment in the new store in 3–5 years, should J & J Corporation open a new store?

J & J Corporation's board of directors is charged with making the final decision on whether the company should embark on the home improvement store venture, scheduled to open January 1, 2003, as discussed in Case 1-3. Joanne Barnes, who is chairperson of the board, has convinced other board members of the need to review a five-year cash flow projection before deciding on the project. "From this type of analysis, the board can determine the nature of the cash inflows and outflows to better evaluate the quality of forecasts. Moreover, the board can assess the payback period of the project. When this financial indicator is matched against alternative investments that J & J Corporation could make, the board is in a better position to make strategic decisions that maximize the value of the corporation."

Board member Dr. James Smolen, an oil industry consultant, explained to the J & J board that payback period is the time it takes for cumulative cash flows from a project to equal the original cost of the investment. He shares his experience of the purchase of a producing oil well in Texas for which he paid $1 million.

Cash flow each year averaged $250,000 while net income averaged $100,000. The difference, he explained, was due to the depreciation expense on the oil well equipment and improvements. Dr. Smolen reported that the payback period was four years (original investment ÷ annual cash flow = $1,000,000 ÷ $250,000 = 4 years), even though the oil well continued to be in production an additional five years. He summarized by saying, "My $1 million investment returned a total of $2,250,000. I am aware that this doesn't take into account the time value of money. However, I can assure you that the internal rate of return (IRR function in Excel) was better than any other investment in my portfolio!"

Joanne stated to the board that the home improvement store is likely to have a similar pattern of cash flows because of the store's location in a growing population area. Nevertheless, she would like to see a payback in three years but feels that the project is still viable if payback is more than three but less than five years.

Financing the Home Improvement Store

The minimum asset investment required to begin operations is:

Building	0
Display fixtures	$1,250,000
Inventory	2,500,000

Ignore the results of Case 1-3. See below to determine the amount of cash needed at the opening of the new store on January 1, 2003.

Building

J & J Corporation has secured an agreement with a real estate investment group that is willing to finance the construction of the building and rent it to J & J for $360,000 per year plus 2 percent of sales revenue in excess of $8,000,000 per year. The rental period will be for five years. The base rent payment is due monthly in advance and the 2 percent override, if any, is to be paid in the following year. As part of the building rental agreement, J & J is required to have an annual audit performed by a certified public accounting firm. J & J has hired Isom and Kittredge, CPAs, to perform the annual audit at a cost of $51,000 per year. The fee is to be paid in the year following the one being audited, i.e., the audit of 2003 will be paid in 2004. The audit for each year will verify the amount of 2 percent override to be paid in the following year.

Inventory

J & J estimates that it will have to purchase and maintain a store inventory that will cost $2,500,000. This inventory level will remain constant throughout the life of the store. Since you are asked to conduct an analysis for a five-year time period, assume that the inventory is constantly replenished. This means that the $2,500,000 cash outflow to acquire the starting inventory is paid out as of the opening of the new store on January 1, 2003.

Equipment

J & J Corporation has been successful in locating an equipment manufacturer willing to sell the necessary display fixtures to J & J. The equipment supplier will need to be paid for the cost of the equipment on January 1, 2003. The terms of the sale are:

Purchase price	$1,250,000
Useful life of equipment	10 years
Salvage value at end of useful life	0

Operating the New Home Improvement Store

In order to facilitate the development of a five-year cash flow projection, the following estimates related to the five-year period have been made (the groups refer to the classroom groups to which you have been assigned by your instructor):

Estimated sales: Year 1 (ignore results of Case 1-3):

Group 1 team members	$10,500,000
Group 2 team members	10,600,000
Group 3 team members	10,700,000
Group 4 team members	10,800,000
Group 5 team members	10,900,000
Group 6 team members	11,000,000
Group 7 team members	11,100,000
Group 8 team members	11,200,000
Group 9 team members	11,300,000
Group 10 team members	11,400,000

Estimated sales: Years 2–5 — 3% annual growth

Contribution margin ratio for store (all years) — .35
(variable cost of sales is .65)

Fixed store operating expenses (salaries, wages, insurance, utilities, etc.):

Year 1	$2,300,000
Years 2–5	8% annual increase

Annual audit fees (each year)	$51,000
Reduced contribution margin at existing store (each year)	$50,000

Requirements (Ignore the effect of income taxes.)

1. Use a spreadsheet to develop a five-year cash flow projection for the net cash flow impact of the home improvement store (including the negative impact on the existing store, $50,000). A format for your spreadsheet is presented as Exhibit C1-4.1. The cells that are shaded should be left empty. You are required to hand in:
   a. A printout of your solution in the format presented.
   b. A printout of the formulas used in your solution.
2. From a payback period perspective only, should J & J invest in the new store? Explain.
3. At what level of first-year sales for the new store (with the second year and each year thereafter still increasing at 3 percent) will J & J attain a payback period of three years? *Hint*: If your spreadsheet is constructed properly with sales for years 2–5 represented by the appropriate formulas, you just need to change the first year's sales amount by the trial and error method until the cumulative net cash flows equal the original investment.

Exhibit C1-4.1
Five-Year Cash Flow Projection

	Now	December 31				
	Jan. 1, 2003	Year 1 2003	Year 2 2004	Year 3 2005	Year 4 2006	Year 5 2007
Cash inflows						
Sales						
Total cash inflows						
Cash outflows						
Opening inventory	(2,500,000)					
Store equipment	(1,250,000)					
Variable cost of sales (.65)						
Audit fee			51,000	51,000	51,000	51,000
Base rent expense		360,000	360,000	360,000	360,000	360,000
Rental override						
Lost margin – old store		50,000	50,000	50,000	50,000	50,000
Fixed expenses		2,300,000				
Total cash outflows	(3,750,000)					
Net cash flows	(3,750,000)					
Cumulative cash flow	(3,750,000)					

Note: Data in all blank cells are based upon your starting sales amount.

Group Assignment 1-4

IS IT A "GRAND" OPENING?

Group number ___________ **Signatures of group members participating:**

____

____

Objectives

1. Discuss the J & J Corporation home improvement store project to arrive at a consensus of whether the project meets the payback goal.
2. Determine the feasibility of launching the project by completing a pro forma balance sheet (as if the project was approved and the associated cash flows occurred).

Requirements

1. Based only on your group's individual solutions to Case 1-4, should J & J open the new store? Explain on a separate sheet of paper how you used the payback period to make the decision.

2. Complete the boxes for changes caused by the proposed home improvement store in the pro forma (projected) balance sheet provided in this assignment, assuming that the home improvement project is approved. You are to enter changes caused by the new store in the middle column, and prepare a new balance sheet in the third column. J & J Corporation's current (December 31, 2002) financial position from Case 1-1 is completed. Note that the ending balance sheet for 2002 also is the beginning position for the first year that includes operation of the new home improvement store, January 1, 2003. The following entries to reflect the home improvement store must be made:

    a. Assume that J & J acquires the store inventory of $2,500,000 and must pay $500,000 on January 1, 2003 and sign a note payable for $2,000,000 due on March 1, 2003.

    b. The display equipment was acquired by signing a two-year note payable of $1,250,000.

3. Ignore your answer to requirement 1. Using the pro forma balance sheet, should the board of directors approve this project? On a separate sheet of paper, explain all aspects of your decision, including profitability and risk. What information does the balance sheet provide that payback period doesn't?

J & J Corporation
Projected Balance Sheet
January 1, 2003

	Existing Business Dec. 31, 2002	Home Improv. Store Jan. 1, 2003	Combined Jan. 1, 2003
Assets			
Current assets:			
Cash	$ 59,570		$
Accounts receivable, net	72,000		72,000
Inventory	249,000		
Prepaid expenses	2,500		2,500
Total current assets	383,070		
Plant and equipment:			
Service equipment	190,000		190,000
Retail building	400,000		400,000
Display and fixtures	232,000		
	822,000		
Less accumulated deprec.	(318,500)		(318,500)
Plant and equipment, net	503,500		
Goodwill (net of amortization)	133,000		133,000
Total assets	$ 1,019,570		$
Liabilities			
Current liabilities:			
Accounts and notes payable	$ 91,900		$
Taxes payable	32,000		32,000
Wages payable	5,200		5,200
Total current liabilities	129,100		
Notes payable	-		
Mortgage payable	272,000		272,000
Total liabilities	401,100		
Stockholders' equity			
Contributed capital	200,000		200,000
Retained earnings	418,470		418,470
Total stockholders' equity	618,470		618,470
Total Liabilities and Equity	$ 1,019,570		$

Module 1

Peer Evaluation of Group Members	Class Section	Group No.

Evaluator's Name ____________________

Module 1

In the table below, please indicate your estimate, in percentage terms, of the contributions that individual group members made to each of the group assignments listed. Each column should add to 100 percent. For example, if there are five members in your group and all were present for Group Assignment 1-1, you would divide the 100 percent among the five members, including yourself. If you felt that all group members were prepared to discuss the assignment and contributed equally to the solution, you would give each person 20 percent. If only four members were present and you felt that one particular member contributed twice as much as the other three, you would give the heavy contributor 40 percent and the other three members 20 percent. <u>Any group member who was absent should be listed and given zero percent.</u>

	Group Assignment Number	
Group Members (List)	**1-1**	**1-4**
Myself		
Totals	**100**	**100**

Fill in this sheet after each group assignment is completed and turn in at the completion of Group Assignment 1-4.

MODULE TWO

TRADITIONAL PRODUCT

Costing and Pricing

Module 2 Introduction

TRADITIONAL PRODUCT COSTING AND PRICING

MODULE OVERVIEW

For about the next 10 weeks you will be applying management, or managerial, accounting concepts to a fictitious firm, California Car Company (CCC), that will be used in Modules 2, 3, and 4 to illustrate problems found in a manufacturing firm. **Management accounting** provides and analyzes the information necessary for management decisions that are made within the firm rather than for those decisions made by stakeholders external to the company. CCC is a serial case, which means that each assignment builds on what you have learned in previous assignments. A serial case is designed so that you have sufficient background to perform accounting analyses in the context of a real-world decision situation of one company. Someday you will encounter accounting information in the workplace. Hopefully, as you work the case assignments, you will grow to understand that a business consists of interrelated systems and processes that must function together if the company is to succeed. In addition, the CCC serial case will enable you to see that accounting information is used by management to plan and measure success. By presenting accounting in a relevant decision context, we hope that accounting will be (1) more interesting and relevant, (2) easier to learn, and (3) more likely to be retained and used by you in your more advanced courses.

By the end of the serial case you should have the background to analyze sophisticated problems faced by CCC and make reasonable decisions based on your analyses. A primary determinant of how much you will learn from the case is how well you keep up with the assignments. Because later tasks build on what you learned in earlier work, falling behind, not completing earlier assignments, or completing assignments but not understanding what you did will create more difficulty for you with later case execution. As you work each case you should think about what decision(s) it is addressing. You also should concentrate on how accounting information supports CCC's decisions.

In this module, you will become familiar with CCC's production process by participating in a simulation of the company's daily production activities. You also will be introduced to the major inputs used in production processes and shown how the costs of those inputs are associated with particular products and used in decision-making activities involving specific products.

This module emphasizes five major decisions faced by CCC:

1. *Operating Decisions*—How to improve the efficiency and effectiveness of operations.
2. *Planning Decisions*—How to prepare and plan for the coming year. What are CCC's estimated costs?

3. *Pricing Decisions*—How to set a price for each car model, how to determine what mix of products to sell, and how to determine product profitability. Are markups competitive for its two products? Should CCC reduce the price of its compact vehicle when responding to a special order and, if so, what is the lowest price the company can entertain to maintain an overall profitable position?
4. *Financial Reporting Decisions*—How to report financial information to shareholders and creditors.
5. *Performance Evaluation Decisions*—How to evaluate performance of individuals, groups, and departments. Is CCC's performance adequate? Where is the performance deficient? Which department performed best?

Module 2 stresses four categories of learning objectives. Details of those learning objectives and their relationship to specific case readings and cases follow.

Learning Objectives

After completing Module 2, you should be able to:

1. Understand the basic elements of manufacturing costs (direct materials, direct labor, and manufacturing overhead); understand the flow of manufacturing costs from raw materials to work-in-process, to finished goods, to cost of goods sold; understand the concept of a predetermined overhead rate and how it is used to assign overhead to units of production; understand why overhead costs are erratic and why applied overhead is added to the cost of products instead of the actual amount; and understand how the production process fits into the overall value chain of a manufacturing company.

   - Reading 2-1 California Car Company and Its Environment
   - Reading 2-4 Estimating Manufacturing Costs
   - Reading 2-6 Job-Order Costing
   - Case 2-1 California Car Company Background
   - Case 2-4 Development of Product Cost Estimates for 2002
   - Case 2-6 Job-Order Costing at California Car Company
   - Exercises and Problems Exercises and Problems at the end of Readings 2-4 and 2-6

2. Understand the roles of direct laborers, indirect laborers (setup and maintenance personnel, inspectors, and material handlers), and management personnel in production processes; understand how the costs of various personnel are assigned to units of production; analyze particular production processes; and identify major strengths and weaknesses in the design of those processes.

   - Case 2-1 California Car Company Background
   - Case 2-2 California Car Company Production Line Simulation
   - Case 2-3 Production Problems at California Car Company
   - Group Assignment 2-2 Assembling Cars at California Car Company

3. Understand how manufacturing costs are planned for a period (month, year); understand how actual results may be compared to planned manufacturing costs for the purpose of determining variances; and understand how problems involved in the physical production process translate into cost variances.

- Reading 2-4	Estimating Manufacturing Costs
- Reading 2-7	Performance Budgets
- Case 2-4	Development of Product Cost Estimates for 2002
- Case 2-7	Variance Controversy at California Car Company
- Group Assignment 2-7	Overdone Overhead?
- Exercises and Problems	Exercises and Problems at the end of Readings 2-4 and 2-7

4. Understand how cost information may be used to set prices for special orders.

- Reading 2-5	Pricing and Profitability Decisions
- Case 2-5	Pricing Problems at California Car Company
- Group Assignment 2-5	Saudi Golf Cart Order
- Exercises and Problems	Exercises and Problems at the end of Reading 2-5

TERMINOLOGY LIST FOR MODULE 2

Applied overhead
Bill of materials
Cost driver
Cost object
Cost of goods manufactured and sold
Cost-plus pricing
Cost pool
Direct labor
Direct material
Finished goods inventory
Indirect labor
Indirect material
Job
Job-order costing
Job-order cost sheet
Make-or-buy
Management, or managerial, accounting
Manufacturing overhead
Markup
Material requisition form
Normal cost system
Overapplied overhead
Overhead (or service) department
Performance (flexible) budget
Period cost
Planning (static) budget
Plantwide overhead rate
Predetermined overhead rate
Process costing
Product cost
Production department
Production process
Responsibility center
Special order
Standard cost system
Target cost
Target price
Time ticket
Traditional overhead allocation
Transfer pricing
Underapplied overhead
Value-added activity
Value chain
Variance
Work-in-process inventory

Reading 2-1

CALIFORNIA CAR COMPANY AND ITS ENVIRONMENT

INTRODUCTION

The purpose of Reading 2-1 is to introduce the hybrid gasoline-electric vehicle industry, provide you with an overview of a hybrid vehicle production company, discuss manufacturing processes that add value for customers (value chain), and to define the type of accounting terminology used in the manufacturing environment. This first reading describes California Car Company's (CCC) production structure and cost accounting system. CCC is a car manufacturing company that builds low-emission vehicles (LEVs). The management of this company, entrepreneurs at heart, has experience in auto manufacturing and envisions a great future for hybrid vehicles. Text material introduces the value chain concept and explains how the production function fits into the value chain. The content of this reading should help you understand the importance and purpose of appropriate accounting information, define basic accounting terms that you will use in preparing cost data reports for CCC decision making, and supply the necessary background on CCC to help you answer the Requirements of Case 2-1. The reading also provides necessary background information to prepare you for the production simulation in Case 2-2.

THE HYBRID VEHICLE INDUSTRY

The internal combustion engine, using gasoline or diesel fuel, has not been the only means to supply power to vehicles. Many of the early cars that traveled the roads in the first decades of the last century were electric or steam powered. In 1897, the biggest selling model in motor vehicles was electric. Electric streetcars and buses were also common sights at one time in many U.S. cities, and San Francisco still has numerous electric buses in service. The higher production and operating costs, however, limited traveling range, inconvenience, and poor acceleration that characterized electric vehicles quickly triggered a loss in their popularity. Steam engines proved to be inferior to gasoline-powered cars as they used more petroleum plus large amounts of water. Disadvantages of both the electric and steam vehicles led to the almost universal domination of gasoline and diesel cars that were faster, cheaper, more convenient, and, from an engineering perspective, more adaptable to technological improvements.

Gasoline engines were not without disadvantages. Studies showed that motor vehicles were a major source of air pollution, which surfaced as a major ecological and societal concern during the final quarter of the twentieth century. Clearly, a need had arisen for an alternative to the internal combustion engine. Lack of success in developing convenient storage batteries and inconsistent operating capability of steam vehicles indicated that the alternative to the gasoline car needed to be something other than the electric or steam-powered motor. Despite the post World War II interest in auto technological innovation, inventors had not seriously thought of combining electricity and gasoline to fuel cars with reduced pollution emissions. Now, however, the need to squeeze more miles out of a gallon of gasoline has produced the hybrid vehicles.

Current Market Situation

Today's drivers want vehicles that maintain speed in traffic with a range of at least 300 miles between refuelings. The gasoline-powered car meets this criteria but produces pollution and gets low mileage per gallon. Most users, however, only need an engine large enough to accelerate and perform at peak capability less than one percent of road time. A smaller engine would run more efficiently, weigh less, and require less fuel. The hybrid gasoline-electric engine provides advantages over both the solely electric and solely gasoline-fueled vehicle. The hybrid has both an electric motor and battery and a gasoline engine, but utilizes only one energy system, electric or gasoline, for routine travel and the second to provide the "burst" of power necessary for acceleration and special situations.

Currently, only two car manufacturers, Toyota and Honda, produce hybrid gasoline-electric vehicles for sale in the United States. The Honda Insight was first introduced in the United States in 2000. The Insight has the better mileage of the two and drives like a conventional car because of the highly efficient gasoline engine, but it is a small two-seater. The Toyota Prius was introduced in 1997, is a four-door sedan that seats five people, and is about the size of a Toyota Corolla. Because the car can use its electric motor to maintain a speed of 15 mph without the gasoline engine kicking in, it is more environmentally conscious than the Honda Insight. An additional advantage to the Prius is that its batteries never need recharging since a built-in generator accomplishes that task.

As mentioned in the previous section, purely electric alternative vehicles to the gasoline car are uncompetitive for cost and performance reasons. The small number that are sold or leased are primarily tiny electric commuter cars with very limited range and power, or retrofitted traditional cars and vans that are much more expensive than their gasoline-powered relatives. The two market sectors in which electric vehicles compete successfully are the golf cart and U.S. postal service mail delivery vehicle segments. In a way, these successes have hindered the industry because they have led to a public perception of electric vehicles as novelty or specialty items, more like toys than means of serious highway transportation.

Future Demand

The future of alternative vehicles, powered by non-gasoline sources, was changed radically in 1990 by the California Air Resources Board. This state agency set a 1998 target that 2 percent of all new cars sold in California (about 40,000 cars) be zero-emission vehicles (ZEVs). It also mandated that in the year 2000 5 percent (about 100,000) of all new cars be ZEVs. The original year 2003 requirements for ZEVs were 10 percent (about 200,000) of all cars sold. In addition, after California's action several other states, such as New York and Massachusetts, representing almost 40 percent of the market for new cars, indicated that they would take similar action. Large automotive manufacturers began designing concept electric cars during the 1990s. General Motor's eye-catching EV1 celebrated its first birthday in December 1997, and has been redesigned and improved during the last five years.

Standards have been relaxed somewhat in recent years, indicating the need for LEVs rather than vehicles that are totally free of pollution emissions. For instance, California regulators have recommended lowering the 2003 goal of 10 percent ZEVs to 2 percent and substituting a requirement for 8 percent hybrid vehicles. This could mean that within the next ten years the demand for LEVs in the United States could approach one million cars per year. Although there are other experimental nonhybrid LEVs, such as the experimental hydrogen-powered cars, from a practical perspective, environmental requirements for LEVs will mean hybrid gasoline-electric vehicles for the foreseeable future. As a result, global auto makers such as DaimlerChrysler, Ford, and General Motors, in addition to Toyota and Honda, all have projects underway to develop attractive hybrid vehicles. Ford Motor Company plans to release its hybrid electric SUV, the Escape, in 2003. DaimlerChrysler also is working on a hybrid version of its Dodge Durango SUV plus a concept hybrid electric vehicle, the Citadel. Additionally, the large car manufacturers, DaimlerChrysler, Ford, and General Motors, established an association in 1992 called the United States Council for Automotive Research (USCAR) to jointly develop improved LEV technology. In an effort to accelerate the development of environmentally clean vehicles, the U.S. government joined this group in 1993 to form the Partners for a New Generation of Vehicles (PNGV) that continues as the cooperative global organization for LEV research.

Despite the interest of the world's major auto companies, many believe that because the technology is still immature and because the hybrid vehicle is significantly different, there is room in the industry for smaller, entrepreneurial companies.

STRATEGY OF CALIFORNIA CAR COMPANY

CCC's overall strategy is to use the flexibility and diligence of a small company to establish and maintain a technology and quality advantage in the marketplace. CCC plans to appeal to consumers who are interested in quality and special features. They do not plan to compete head on with the major auto manufacturers in the mass market for hybrid vehicles. CCC views themselves as more like a Volvo than a Ford or Toyota. The development of a compact hybrid car is a natural result of this strategy. Although more expensive than a traditional hybrid compact, this car will appeal to consumers who want a sporty-looking model, but who are still environmentally sensitive.

Marketing strategy is a critical part of CCC's plans. CCC hopes to develop an environmentally aware, high-quality image. As a result, CCC plans to price their products at or a little above average, but hopes customers will perceive that the extra features of its cars are worth much more than the increased price. If all goes well, CCC will build a loyal following of customers who will make repeat purchases. Ideally, a kind of "cult following" will develop similar to Volkswagon's bug. A second aspect of CCC's marketing plan is to reach an agreement with a major auto company such as Toyota or Honda, whereby another auto company would sell CCC cars under its nameplate. Such an agreement would give CCC access to a huge dealer network.

HISTORY OF CCC AND ITS MANAGEMENT STRUCTURE

The purpose of this section is to give you an idea of how CCC came into being and the background that might be representative of the top managers in an entrepreneurial manufacturing firm like CCC. The company initially was established as a research and development organization and gradually was transformed into the operating company that exists today. CCC is divided into the following four administrative areas, each of which is headed by a vice president (see Exhibit 2-1.1):

- Production
- Marketing
- Finance
- Engineering

Exhibit 2-1.1
California Car Company Organization Chart

- **President**
  - Vice President - Engineering
    - Design
    - Develop-ment
  - Vice President - Marketing
    - Marketing Research
    - Sales
    - Customer Service
  - Vice President - Production
    - Plant Manager
      - Chassis Assembly
      - Final Assembly
      - Inspection
      - Maintenance
      - Setup
      - Material Handling
      - General Factory
  - Vice President - Finance
    - Treasury (Treasurer)
    - Accounting (Controller)
    - Management Information
    - Human Resources
    - General Office

David Gomez—President of California Car Company

David graduated with a bachelor's degree in engineering from St. Mary's University in San Antonio, Texas, and went to work for General Dynamics, a large aerospace firm. David worked in the quality control area and after six years was named plant manager of quality control. After two years in this position, David decided that he wanted to move into a higher management position. Therefore, he left General Dynamics and enrolled in the manufacturing management master of business administration program at the Massachusetts Institute of Technology. After graduation, David accepted a position as assistant plant manager at General Motors (GM) in Lordstown, Ohio. Four years later he was promoted to plant manager at GM's Fremont, California, plant.

Shortly after his arrival at Fremont, GM entered into negotiations with Toyota to establish a joint venture called New United Motor Manufacturing, Inc. (NUMMI). Meshing the Toyota and GM way of manufacturing cars was a tremendous challenge, but also an incredible learning experience. David spent a considerable amount of time in Japan being trained in Toyota's production philosophy. He likens this experience to earning a Ph.D. in production management. Five years later David was named vice president of production for NUMMI.

The production management system at NUMMI was a smashing success. NUMMI took what was GM's least productive and least automated factory and kept what was universally considered to be GM's worst factory labor force. Within a couple of years, with very little new equipment investment, NUMMI became GM's most productive plant with the best labor relations.

Despite NUMMI's success, David was becoming restless. For one thing, he had become intrigued with the prospects of the electric or hybrid electric/gas vehicle industry. It appeared to him that by 1998 environmental and legal forces, particularly in California, would catapult vehicles that did not rely solely on the gasoline engine to the status of a major industry. David had tried to interest GM in transferring him to its electric vehicle development group, but without success. Secondly, David had always dreamed of starting his own business and being his own boss. David began discussing his interest in forming a hybrid vehicle company with Sally Swanson, production manager at NUMMI, over a few after-work beers. Sally also was enthusiastic about hybrid vehicles and was very excited at the prospect of starting a company.

David and Sally, with their personal funds, hired a consulting firm to prepare a business plan. The manager in charge of their business plan, Jena Butler, took a special interest in their project and put them in contact with a large venture capital partnership she had done work for in the past. Much to David and Sally's surprise, the venture capital firm liked their idea and initially put up $3,500,000 and eventually invested a total of $14,000,000. The agreement left David and Sally with a combined 30 percent ownership in CCC.

As president, David has final responsibility for the performance of the entire company; this includes hiring and evaluating the top managers and solving major problems that arise. Second, he reports CCC's performance, prospects and problems to the board of directors, venture capitalists, and bankers. Third, he is involved in negotiations with major customers, vendors, and the union. David must use accounting reports extensively in performing his duties. For example, he must assess the performance of CCC and its managers based partially on financial reports. He must present CCC's financial position to the board and to others, and he must negotiate prices with major customers and vendors based on cost accounting information.

Sally Swanson—Vice President of Production

Sally graduated from Baylor University in Waco, Texas, with a bachelor of science in business with a concentration in production and operations management. After graduation, she took a position with GM as a production management trainee. After three years as an assistant manager, she was named manager of the Transmission Assembly Department. In this capacity she oversaw 150 employees who produced about $125,000,000 worth of transmissions per year.

During her fourth year as manager, Sally became interested in moving up to a higher management position, and realized that an MBA from a top school would enhance her prospects significantly. Therefore, Sally left GM after four years and enrolled in the Stanford MBA program. After receiving her MBA, Sally accepted a position as assistant plant manager at New United Motors Manufacturing, Inc. (NUMMI), the General Motors-Toyota joint venture in Fremont, California. This position required that Sally support the plant manager in a wide array of tasks, including investigating and recommending solutions for problems in production scheduling, quality, bottlenecks, and cost areas. Her most important assignment, however, was to oversee the continuous improvement efforts of work groups in NUMMI's just-in-time environment.

During Sally's third year at NUMMI, the position of production manager opened up and her previous hard work was rewarded with a promotion to that job. In her second year as production manager, Sally left NUMMI for the opportunity to help form an exciting new company that planned to produce hybrid vehicles: California Car Company.

Sally is responsible for hiring and evaluating the performance of all department managers in the manufacturing area. She has final responsibility for the plant design and purchase of equipment for the plant. She also oversees a staff responsible for scheduling production, assuring quality, reporting manufacturing accounting information, and purchasing parts and materials from vendors.

George Olson—Vice President of Marketing

George received his bachelor of science degree in engineering from Colorado State University in Fort Collins, Colorado, and went to work at Ford Motor Co. in the product design area. After two years at Ford, George decided that he really enjoyed marketing and sales more than product development. Therefore, he left Ford and enrolled in the MBA program at the University of Michigan.

Upon receipt of his MBA, George took a sales position with Eaton Corp., a large auto parts supplier. After eight years at Eaton, George moved up to marketing manager for a major division. George saw great potential in the hybrid vehicle industry. Consequently, he devoted considerable time in trying to establish a partnership between Eaton and CCC because he thought that CCC might grow to be a major Eaton customer. The more George talked to David Gomez and Sally Swanson, the more excited he became about CCC's prospects. As a result, when George was offered the vice president of marketing position, he accepted without hesitation.

George's major responsibilities at CCC are to develop a marketing strategy, to hire and train a sales force, and to oversee the development of a dealer network. George also is heavily involved in pricing decisions, in presenting customer needs in design decisions, and in advertising decisions.

Jena Butler—Vice President of Finance

Jena Butler received a bachelor of science in accounting and a bachelor of arts in history from Castleton State College in Castleton, Vermont. She started college as a history major, but decided it was prudent to take a few business courses to enhance her job prospects. She enjoyed using computers, and to her surprise liked the introductory accounting courses. Jena then took the intermediate and cost accounting courses and declared a second major in that field. After graduation, she accepted a position as a staff auditor in a Big Six (now the Big Five) international accounting firm. After four years and a promotion to senior auditor, Jena decided she preferred a career in consulting.

She took a two-year leave of absence and enrolled in the master of science in accountancy program at California State University in Chico. This program emphasized the accounting applications of information technology and production management. Upon graduation she returned to the same accounting firm, although in the management consulting area of the San Francisco office.

For the next several years Jena worked extensively with venture capital firms in helping fast-growth, high-tech companies solve their accounting and production systems problems. This work with entrepreneurs and new ventures created an interest in participating in a start-up company as a manager and part owner rather than as a consultant. Jena received several employment offers from clients, but none of them felt right until, after supervising the development of a business plan for CCC, she was offered the position of vice president of finance and an ownership stake. Although partnership in the accounting firm and a $250,000 annual salary seemed imminent, she quickly accepted CCC's offer.

Jena is responsible for all the external report preparation, including CCC's financial statements, tax reports, and other regulatory filings. She hires and evaluates the performance of the treasurer, controller, management information systems director, manager of human resources, and the office manager. Jena, and the cost analysts that work for her, work closely with all other CCC managers and provide information needed to make decisions. The other top managers view her as an internal consultant to be called in when major decisions are made. She spends much of her time planning and overseeing the implementation of CCC's management information systems. Note that the controller of a firm is the person with the responsibility for ensuring that all events affecting CCC are properly recorded and reflected in the financial statements. The treasurer is the person responsible for the control of the firm's assets, including cash, inventory, and machinery.

PHYSICAL STRUCTURE OF CCC

Because CCC began as a research and development company then evolved into a manufacturing concern, the physical structure of the facilities was not planned with an eye for the future of automotive manufacturing or the storage of inventory. This layout evolved through time, with new activities being assigned to vacant space as they were created. The physical layout of the production and operations facility for CCC is shown in Exhibit 2-1.2.

Plant Layout

Building 1, the original facility, now contains all administrative, marketing and finance functions, as well as certain engineering and production functions such as the final assembly, inspection, maintenance and setup, finished goods (outgoing) inventory storage and shipping activities, and engineering. Building 2 houses all other production activities, including receiving, parts inventory storage, chassis assembly, and various other production support functions. The plant layout diagram is drawn to scale. Notice that assembly and inventory storage together occupy more than 50 percent of the total manufacturing space.

Production Process

The plant layout described represents a traditional, departmentalized **production process** that manufactures both CCC sedan and compact models. A production process is a sequence of events involved in the manufacturing activities necessary to complete a product, including the delivery of materials and the cutting, assembly, finishing, and inspection of units. The administration of CCC production is divided into seven manufacturing responsibility centers—two assembly departments and five overhead departments. A **responsibility center** is a unit of an organization that holds its manager accountable for specific activities and outcomes that may include costs, revenues, or profits. The production departments are Chassis Assembly and Final Assembly. Inspection, Maintenance, Setup, Material Handling, and General Factory are classified as overhead departments. As Exhibit 2-1.2 indicates, production begins in the Chassis Assembly Department.

Inventories

From chassis assembly, unfinished vehicles move to work-in-process inventory storage where they are then drawn into final assembly as needed. **Work-in-process inventory** consists of all partially completed units. After final assembly, completed units pass through inspection and then to outgoing storage called finished goods inventory where they stay until shipped to customers. **Finished goods inventory** contains all the completed units waiting to be sold or shipped to customers.

Work-in-process and finished goods are not the only inventories in manufacturing. All incoming parts are received and inspected in the Receiving Department. After inspection, parts are moved by material handlers to inventory storage, called the **materials inventory**, to await their use in chassis or final assembly. The Materials Inventory Storage Department maintains an adequate stock of all parts needed for the production of sedans and compacts. Parts quantities are monitored through the use of computerized economic order quantity (EOQ) models. EOQ models signal to purchasing managers when to order parts and how many parts to order at one time. Management is quite proud that parts inventory and ordering have been automated. A list of parts used in the manufacture of sedans and compacts appears in Case 2-1.

THE MANUFACTURING VALUE CHAIN

CCC's strategy to achieve flexibility and an advantage in the marketplace requires management to concentrate on improving quality at all levels of the company's operations. Ensuring quality necessitates the establishment of a **value chain** that optimizes the use of resources and promotes the efficient exchange of information. An organization's value chain consists of the set of interdependent processes that adds value to a product or service provided to customers. **Value-added activities** are those processes that increase customer satisfaction and enhance quality. These activities also may reduce delivery times and/or reduce prices charged for products and services. In contrast, *nonvalue-added* activities may exist that accomplish none of these things and most likely increase sales prices. Therefore, once identified, they should be eliminated. Note that value is essentially a *customer-oriented* concept. In this context, value should be measured in terms of nonfinancial goals, such as reduced defects, as well as more traditional financial measures, such as price.

Exhibit 2-1.2
California Car Company
Traditional Plant Layout

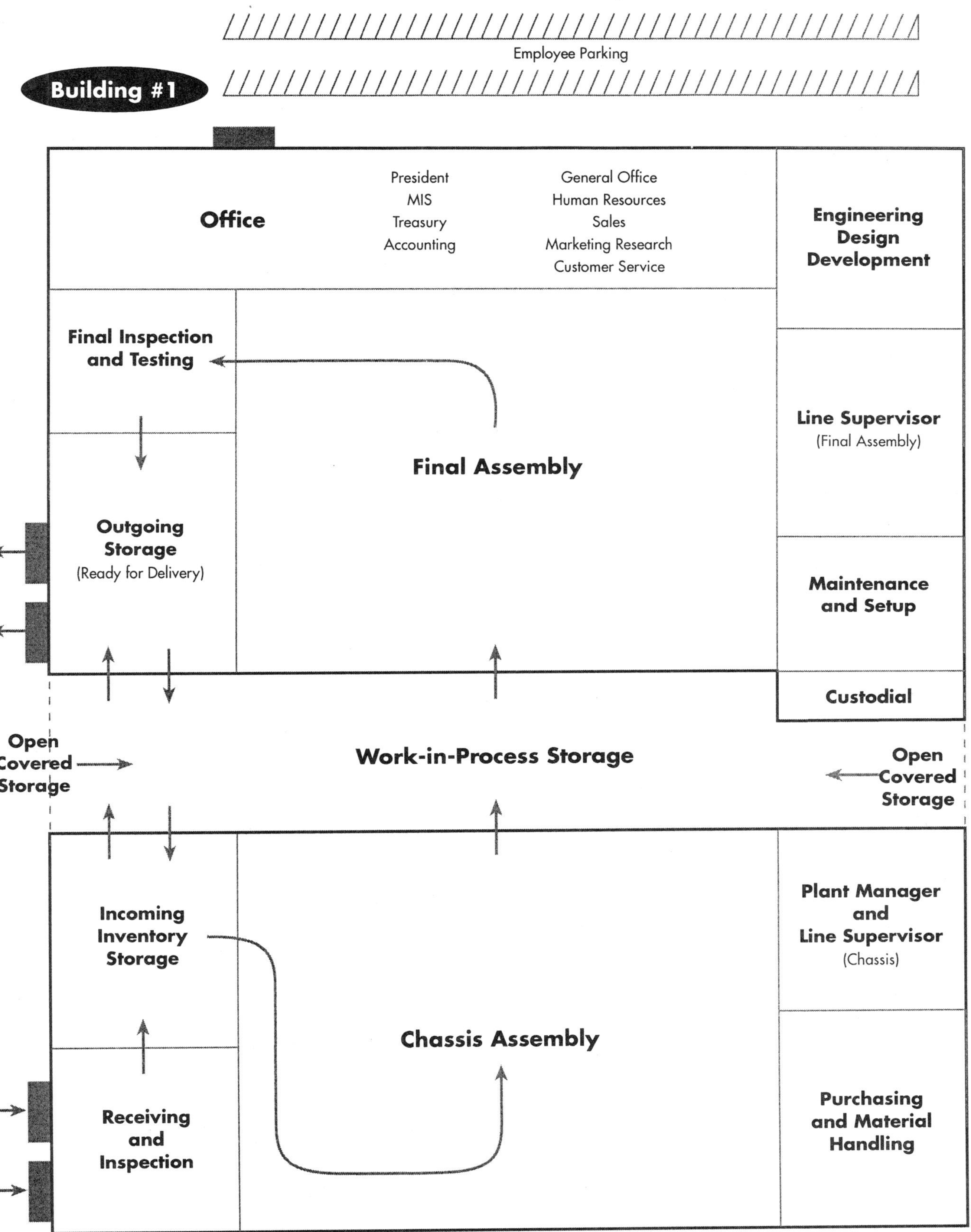

A value-added focus is of great importance to all organizations striving to be competitive in today's global economy. As a newcomer to this competitive market, CCC is well aware of today's emphasis on quality and is in the process of identifying the value-added activities within its own organization structure. The company has identified the following major activities as comprising its value chain illustrated in Exhibit 2-1.3:

- Research and development,
- Product design,
- Production,
- Marketing,
- Distribution, and
- Customer service.

Exhibit 2-1.3
Manufacturing Value Chain

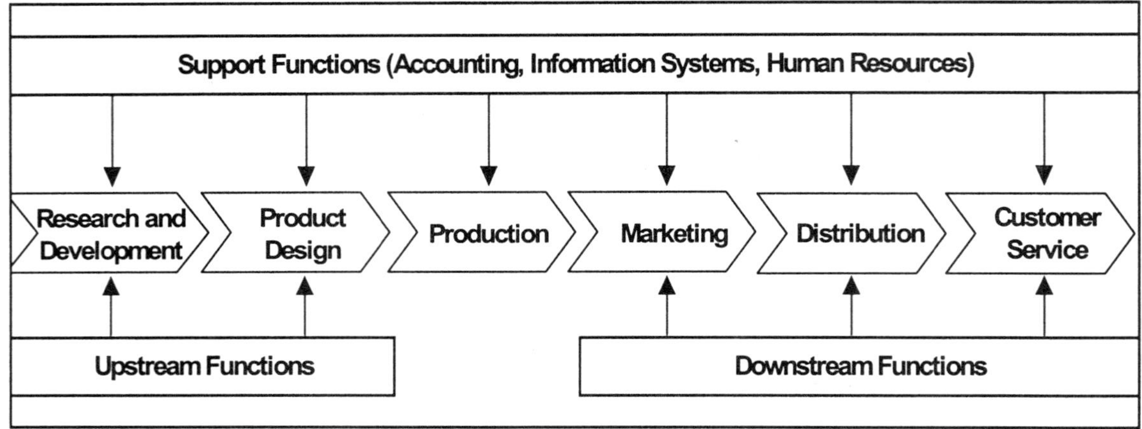

Extending the Value Chain Concept Beyond Company Boundaries: An Example from the Business World

The concept of a value chain may be extended beyond the boundaries of a particular company. For example, in the case of CCC, lying "upstream" are suppliers of raw materials and parts and delivery companies bringing those items to the company. Likewise, lying "downstream" are auto dealers and finally, at the end of the line, the customers of the dealers. Value can be added to CCC's vehicles at any step in this comprehensive value chain, which includes both internal and external activities. An example from the Hewlett-Packard (HP), Roseville, California, operation illustrates how a value chain can be extended to units outside the company.

HP defines its internal value-added operation as the assembly of component parts and the delivery of a finished product. The company made major efforts to farm out the manufacture of component parts. Consequently, nonrelated companies at distant locations now manufacture many parts. HP works very closely with only a few parts suppliers to ensure quality and timely delivery of parts.

HP even has gone so far as to work out changes in delivery packaging with its unrelated trucking firm to eliminate nonvalue-added costs. HP receives molded plastic cases from a firm in Oregon. In the past, cases were packaged in cardboard cartons to prevent marring during shipment. Upon arrival at HP, the cartons were removed, folded, and sent back to the supplying firm. Notice that handling of the cardboard cartons is a good example of a nonvalue-added activity. Once a nonvalue-added activity is identified, management can work towards elimination of that activity and its related cost, which is exactly what HP did. Working with both the manufacturer of the plastic cases and the trucking firm, HP developed a method of shipping the plastic cases without any additional packaging, eliminating the need for and handling of the nonvalue-added shipping carton.

A second example of external value chain analysis involves the following problem recently addressed by HP. Trucks were arriving full at the HP plant, but had no designated loads for the return trip to Oregon. The trucks often made the return trip empty. This deadheading of returns was a cost that was indirectly being passed on to HP through the shipping charge for plastic cases. Realizing this was a nonvalue-added activity being performed externally, HP worked with the trucker and found return loads from another HP supplier. The net result of this value chain analysis was that HP was happy because of the lower cost of their one-way shipments, the supplier was happy because it found a reliable and low cost shipper, and the trucking company was happy because it now had two-way loads and increased revenue.

These examples illustrate that managers, who expand their views of value-added activities beyond the traditional production-oriented emphasis, may realize substantial gains. The examples also suggest that the types of information useful to managers who are involved in value chain analyses must be considerably broader than the financial information contained in a traditional income statement.

ACCOUNTING FOR MANUFACTURING

Before managers can make beneficial decisions that determine value-added activities, they must have a basic understanding of production flow and the cost terminology associated with manufacturing. The cost accounting system at CCC was originally designed to provide information to management about product costs for the purpose of valuing the year-end inventories of parts, work-in-process, and finished goods. As production volume increased, managers found it increasingly difficult to keep track of activities by direct observation. Consequently, the cost accounting system gradually has been modified to produce monthly "responsibility center" reports that allow management to evaluate performance at various operating levels. The cost accounting system at CCC measures the following three inputs to the manufacturing process and combines them to determine product costs for the sedan and compact:

- Direct materials
- Direct labor
- Manufacturing overhead

Direct Costs

Direct material and direct labor costs occur only in the Chassis Assembly and Final Assembly departments. **Direct material** represents the cost of parts that are included in the cars. **Direct labor** cost represents the pay of production workers who work assembling vehicles or vehicle components. Each assembly department has a supervisor who is responsible for the operation of that department and the control of direct material and direct labor costs. Departments in which direct material and direct labor occur are termed **production departments**.

Manufacturing Overhead Costs

Manufacturing overhead consists of all remaining manufacturing costs that are incurred in producing the LEVs. These are indirect in that they represent the costs for manufacturing activities that, while necessary, do not physically or directly affect the produced unit. As shown in Exhibit 2-1.4, CCC has created the following overhead departments into which all manufacturing costs, other than direct material and direct labor, are collected:

- *Inspection*—All costs of inspecting cars and fixing defective ones. Repairing defects discovered before products leave the factory is known as rework.
- *Maintenance*—All costs of fixing and maintaining equipment, including salaries and parts, plus all equipment depreciation charges.
- *Setup*—All costs of changing the factory equipment to switch production from one model to another.
- *Material Handling*—All costs of ordering and receiving parts and materials, of loading cars on trucks, and moving work-in-process inventory in the plant.
- *General Factory*—All other manufacturing costs including building occupancy costs, plant support costs such as cost accounting and manufacturing engineering, and plant management.

Exhibit 2-1.4
California Car Company
Flow of Costs to the Income Statement

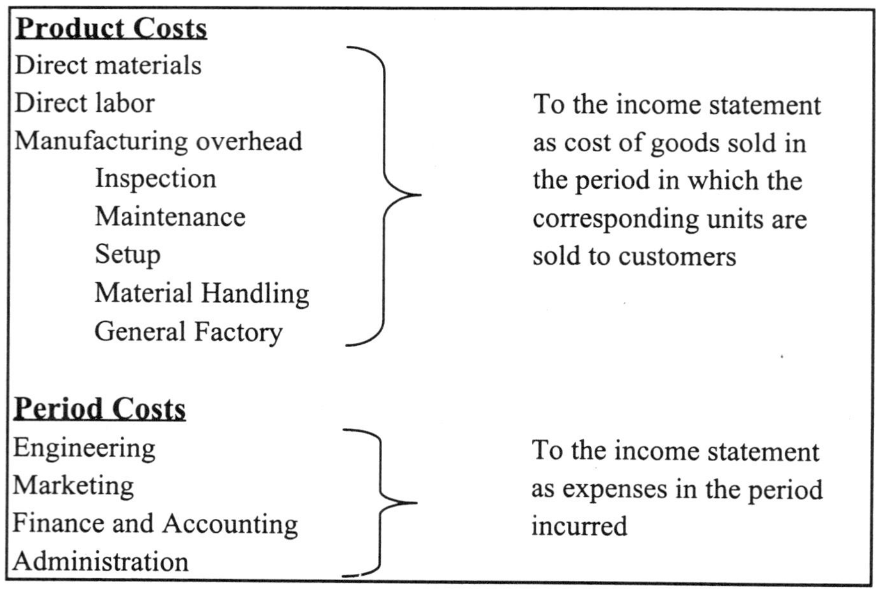

Manufacturing overhead costs initially are collected in the overhead departments and the overhead department managers have primary responsibility for controlling these costs. Overhead costs eventually are allocated to each car manufactured. The Chassis and Final Assembly department managers are responsible for controlling the total manufacturing cost.

Note that all costs incurred in the various production departments are considered to be **product costs** and therefore can be included in inventory. When units of production are sold, these costs appear as cost of goods sold on the income statement. Conversely, all marketing and administration costs, including engineering, are considered to be **period costs** and are therefore recognized as expenses in the period incurred. Exhibit 2-1.4 summarizes the company's cost flows and shows how they enter into the yearly measurement of net income. Product costs for all partially completed goods not yet sold are collected in the work-in-process inventory account. The cost of completed, but unsold, goods remains in the finished goods inventory account. Costs at the end of an accounting period for all three inventories—materials, work-in-process, and finished goods—appear on the balance sheet.

SUMMARY

The reading first furnishes a brief description of the hybrid vehicle industry and introduces CCC and its top management in order to provide you with a background for the case assignments of Module 2. CCC's elements of a manufacturing value chain are identified, their importance explained, and an example of a value chain concept from the real business world is presented. Where Module 1 emphasizes published financial reports used by investors and creditors, Reading 2-1 stresses the importance of accounting for management decision-making and introduces accounting terminology used in manufacturing.

EXERCISES AND PROBLEMS

Exercises

Exercise 1 Demand for Cars. Discuss why the gasoline or internal combustion engine has become the favorite of motorists over alternative forms of power. Also discuss why future demand for a hybrid vehicle may be increasing.

Exercise 2 CCC's Strategy. List CCC's four primary goals to meet the current market situation in the vehicle industry.

Exercise 3 Advantages of Motor Vehicles. Indicate whether each of the following items is an advantage of a gasoline-powered vehicle (g) or an advantage of an electric-powered vehicle (e) or is not relevant (n) to the comparison of gasoline with electric-powered vehicles.

a. Longer traveling range
b. Adequate maintenance of speed in traffic
c. High mileage per unit of power
d. Convenience of operation
e. Less expensive to manufacture
f. Accelerates easily
g. More environmentally friendly
h. Adaptable to technological improvements
i. Consistency of operation
j. Uses large amounts of water

Exercise 4 Disadvantages of Motor Vehicles. Indicate whether each of the following items is a disadvantage of a gasoline-powered vehicle (g) or a disadvantage of an electric-powered vehicle (e) or is not relevant (n) to the comparison of gasoline with electric-powered vehicles.

a. Limited traveling range
b. Slow acceleration

c. Costly to manufacture
d. Source of air pollution
e. Inconsistent operating ability
f. Bulky storage of power supply
g. Low mileage per unit of power
h. Frequent refueling
i. Uses large amounts of water
j. Difficulty in adapting to technological improvements

Exercise 5 Responsibilities of CCC Management Positions. Indicate whether each of the following officer job responsibilities belongs to the position of the president (p), the vice president of finance (vf), or does not apply to either officer (n). If the responsibility applies to both positions, write (p) and (vf) as your answer.

a. Oversees the preparation of all external reports including the financial statements
b. Hires and evaluates top officers
c. Hires and evaluates the treasurer, controller, and management information systems director
d. Oversees the development of a dealer network
e. Reports the company performance and financial position to the board of directors
f. Negotiates prices with major customers and vendors
g. Schedules production
h. Uses accounting information
i. Controls the firm's assets
j. Controls the recording and reflection of events in the financial statements
k. Works closely with cost accountants and other CCC managers to provide relevant information for decision making.

Exercise 6 Responsibilities of CCC Management Positions. Indicate whether each of the following officer job responsibilities belongs to the position of the vice president of marketing (vm), vice president of production (vp), or does not apply to either officer (n). If the responsibility applies to both positions, write (vm) and (vp) as your answer.

a. Oversees the preparation of all external reports including the financial statements
b. Hires and evaluates managers of manufacturing
c. Hires and trains the sales force
d. Oversees the development of a dealer network
e. Makes final decision for plant design
f. Negotiates prices with major customers and vendors
g. Schedules production
h. Uses accounting information
i. Involved in pricing, customer needs, and advertising decisions
j. Controls the recording and reflection of events in the financial statements
k. Oversees the purchasing of parts and materials

Exercise 7 CCC's Responsibility Centers. List CCC's manufacturing responsibility centers. State which are production departments and which are overhead centers.

Exercise 8 Activities Classification in a Value Chain. Component costs of a value chain may represent activities that extend beyond the boundaries of a particular company or production department. For each of the following items, indicate (u) for those costs or activities that would occur upstream of the production function, (d) for those that would occur downstream of the production function, and (n) for neither upstream or downstream costs of activities.

a. Drawing blueprints for a new model car
b. Repairing a dishwasher sold to a customer the previous year
c. Choosing the product to manufacture that will maintain a lucrative competitive advantage
d. Testing a prototype (model) of a product
e. Putting the final coat of paint on a car product
f. Hiring market representatives
g. Running initial laboratory tests on an antibiotic produced by a pharmaceutical company
h. Paying commissions to the sales force of a manufacturing company
i. Adding steel doors to a car on an assembly line
j. Delivering a dishwasher to a customer's home

Exercise 9 Activities Classification in a Value Chain. Component costs of a value chain may represent activities that extend beyond the boundaries of a particular company or organization. Universities also should be conscious of value chains within the educational process. For each of the following items involved in education, indicate (u) for those costs or activities that would occur upstream of the classroom experience, (d) for those that would occur downstream of the classroom experience, and (n) for neither upstream or downstream costs of activities.

a. Attending classes in a state university
b. Searching for a job after graduation
c. Producing and dispersing glossy brochures to recruit students to the university
d. Administering final exams
e. Faculty implementing a new curriculum
f. Sending of transcripts after graduation
g. State government investigating the need for a new university
h. Students deciding which school to attend
i. Paying faculty salaries
j. Faculty writing letters of recommendation for a graduate's job search two years after graduation

Exercise 10 Product Value. Assume that you just purchased a new car. List three items involved with the car purchase that did not add value. State why each of your stated three items did not add value.

Exercise 11 Product Value. For each of the following items state two elements of value that the product supplies.

a. Recently released movie
b. Car
c. Television set
d. College night course
e. Fast-food meal
f. Off-campus apartment
g. Dormitory room
h. Campus cafeteria
i. Business suit
j. CD player

Exercise 12 Activity Value. Indicate whether each of the following activities from the customer's perspective adds value (a) or does not add value (n).

a. Work-in-process inventory
b. Product design
c. Inspection
d. Defect-free manufacturing
e. Quick delivery
f. Accounting
g. Product marketing
h. Human Resources employee support
i. Warranty service
j. Machine repair

Exercise 13 Activity Value. Indicate whether each of the following activities from the student's perspective adds value (a) or does not add value (n).

a. Faculty research
b. Computer center
c. Grants and financial aid office
d. Intercollegiate basketball
e. Class time
f. Homework
g. School cafeteria
h. Bursar's office
i. Library
j. Career placement center

Exercise 14 Lack of Value. For each of the following items provide one product characteristic that does not add value.

a. Recently released movie
b. Car
c. Television set
d. College night course
e. Fast-food meal
f. Off-campus apartment
g. Dormitory room
h. Campus cafeteria
i. Business suit
j. CD player

Exercise 15 Product Versus Period Cost Classification. Classify each of the following costs as product (pro) or period costs (per).

a. Wages of material handlers
b. Wages for painters of cars working on an assembly line
c. Replacement bits for drilling machines used to manufacture products
d. Product advertising on television
e. Utility bill for management offices
f. Shipping clerk wages
g. Salary for vice president of production
h. Fire insurance for office building

i. Salaries for engineers that design new computer programs for a software manufacturing company
j. Ground meat patties in a fast-food restaurant

Exercise 16 Product Versus Period Cost Classification. Classify each of the following costs as product (pro) or period (per) costs.

a. Sales commissions
b. Setup labor wages
c. President's salary
d. Rent for factory
e. Utility bill for employee parking lot
f. Milk used to produce butter
g. Depreciation on the building wing that houses production
h. Salary for financial accountant who helps the company treasurer prepare financial statements
i. Paint for cars made on an assembly line
j. Inspector's wages

Exercise 17 Cost Classification. Classify each of the following costs as direct materials (dm), direct labor (dl), manufacturing overhead (moh), or not a product cost (n).

a. Sales commissions
b. Setup labor wages
c. Assembly line worker wages
d. Rent for factory
e. Utility bill for factory machines
f. Milk used to produce butter
g. Depreciation on the building wing that houses production
h. Paper to record cost accounting records for manufacturing
i. Paint for cars made on an assembly line
j. Inspector's wages

Exercise 18 Cost Classification. Classify each of the following costs as direct materials (dm), direct labor (dl), manufacturing overhead (moh), or not a product cost (n).

a. Wages of material handlers
b. Wages for painters of cars on assembly line
c. Replacement bits for drilling machines used to manufacture products
d. Bolts used in the assembly line to hold product steel plates together
e. Utility bill for management offices
f. Shipping clerk wages
g. Maintenance worker wages
h. Fire insurance for plant
i. Salaries for engineers that design new computer programs for a software manufacturing company
j. Ground meat patties in a fast-food restaurant

Exercise 19 Inventory Cost Classification. Classify each of the following costs as being part of materials inventory (m), work-in-process inventory (wip), finished goods inventory (fg), or not a product cost (n). You may have more than one answer for each item since costs may be part of one or more inventories depending upon the stated stage of completion.

a. Wages of material handlers who stock the warehouse with new parts
b. Wages for painters of unfinished cars on assembly line
c. Replacement bits for drilling machines used to manufacture products
d. Bolts used at the end of final assembly to hold a product's steel plates together
e. Utility bill for management offices for any stage of production
f. Shipping clerk wages
g. Metal charges for a partially completed car on an assembly line
h. Fire insurance for plant for any stage of production
i. Unused cartons for packaging the product at the end of production
j. Ground meat patties in a fast food restaurant for any stage of production

Exercise 20 Inventory Cost Classification. Classify each of the following costs as being part of materials inventory (m), work-in-process inventory (wip), finished goods inventory (fg), or not a product cost (n). You may have more than one answer for each item since costs may be part of one or more inventories depending upon the stated stage of completion.

a. Sales commissions
b. Setup labor wages for uncompleted units
c. Wages for production workers in the cutting department of a manufacturing plant for an uncompleted product
d. Rent for factory for any stage of production
e. Wages for workers who stock the warehouse that stores the product before it is shipped out to customers for any stage of production
f. Milk to produce butter before it is added to the process
g. Depreciation on the building wing that houses production for any stage of production
h. Paper to record cost accounting records for manufacturing for any stage of production
i. Unused paint for cars while it is stored in the warehouse
j. Inspector's wages when inspection occurs at the end of production

Problems

Problem 1 Top Management Positions. Select one of the four CCC top management positions (president, vice president of production, vice president of marketing, or vice president of finance). Fully describe the educational background of the person at CCC who fills that position and that officer's responsibilities.

Problem 2 Value Chain Activities. Cure-All Pharmaceuticals conducts extensive research in finding vaccines for newly detected viruses. After an effective vaccine is developed, Federal Drug Authority (FDA) approval is obtained, and then the company spends several months in selecting the proper containers, mode of delivery for the vaccine (injection or oral), and in designing packaging that is easy for medical professionals to store and open. Shortly before the vaccine is ready for distribution, the company begins a costly television and magazine campaign to arouse public awareness of the vaccine. The advertising continues after the product is first distributed. The antibodies for the vaccine are cultivated, produced in dispensable form, put into containers, packaged, and sent to the warehouse for shipment. A specially trained sales force provides medical offices with samples. Any incidences of vaccine imperfection result in an immediate recall of that lot of vaccines and a free replacement of product units to medical facilities. Draw a diagram for Cure-All Pharmaceuticals, similar to that in Exhibit 2-1.3, which depicts the process of manufacturing and selling vaccines starting with the initial research. Classify each activity as being upstream or downstream in the manufacturing value chain.

Case 2-1

CALIFORNIA CAR COMPANY BACKGROUND

Case Objectives

1. Introduce students to the products and financial statements of California Car Company.

INTRODUCTION TO CCC

California Car Company (CCC) is planning for its tenth year of business, year 2002. The company was formed in 1992 by a group of engineers and business people formerly associated with NUMMI.[1] The company manufactures two models of hybrid gas and electric vehicles. The company has one established model, a sedan-sized vehicle, and has developed a second, compact-sized model to fill the anticipated market demand for smaller vehicles. The compact model, which was introduced in 2000, incorporates solar panels (not included in the sedan) to lower its operating costs and increase miles per gallon. CCC's year 2002 capacity is 30 vehicles per day (single shift), or about 7,500 vehicles a year. CCC can increase its annual production through the use of overtime or by adding a second shift.

Bill of Materials

A list of the parts used in the manufacture of a product is called a **bill of materials**. It normally includes the quantity of each type of part used, as well as department or factory area in which the part is used. The price of each part is often included in the bill of materials so that the cost of materials for each product manufactured can be determined readily. The bill of materials for CCC is shown as Exhibit C2-1.1. The bill of material parts correspond to the toy blocks shown in Exhibit C2-2.2. If your school uses a different type of toy block, the bill of material will not match your blocks. Regardless of the type of blocks used at your school, use the number of parts and cost per sedan and compact shown in Exhibit C2-1.1 throughout the CCC case. To minimize assembly, CCC contracts with its suppliers to deliver large subassemblies. The sedan requires 25 subassemblies and the compact 20.

Financial Information

Balance sheets and income statements for CCC are presented in Exhibit C2-1.2 for 1999 through 2001 (actual results) and 2002 (projected). Note that three zeros have been dropped from all numbers in the financial statements, but not the computations below. For example, planned cash at the end of year 2002 is $1,462,000, not $1,462. The purpose for doing this is

[1] NUMMI is short for the New United Motor Manufacturing, Inc., a joint venture of Toyota and General Motors.

to make the statements easier to read. Financial statements for actual companies normally drop zeros. Ford Motor Company, for instance, drops six zeros from all dollar amounts in its financial statements. Note that CCC has been experiencing rapid growth and expects that to continue in 2002.

Exhibit C2-1.1
California Car Company
Bill of Materials

Sedan					
Part Code	**Part Name**	**Chassis Assembly**	**Final Assembly**	**Cost of Each**	**Total Cost**
811 Y	Batteries	2	0	$ 96	$ 192
943 B	Body base	1	0	324	324
720 B	Front wheel assembly	2	0	76	152
730 B	Rear wheel assembly	2	0	102	204
642 R	Floor panels	4	0	66	264
428 R	Axle Mounts	4	0	21	84
Chassis Assembly Total					$ 1,220
111 R	Taillight	0	1	$ 24	$ 24
214 R	Headlight	0	1	40	40
232 Y	Motor/Hood	0	2	573	1,146
212 Y	Windows	0	4	95	380
219 R	Roof panel	0	2	85	170
Final Assembly Total					$ 1,760
Sedan Totals		15	10		$ 2,980

Compact					
Part Code	**Part Name**	**Chassis Assembly**	**Final Assembly**	**Cost of Each**	**Total Cost**
201 R	Axle Mounts	4	0	$ 21	$ 84
811 Y	Battery	1	0	96	96
943 B	Body base	1	0	214	214
720 B	Front wheel assembly	2	0	76	152
730 B	Rear wheel assembly	2	0	102	204
Chassis Assembly Total					$ 750
111 R	Taillight	0	1	$ 24	$ 24
214 R	Headlight	0	1	40	40
212 Y	Windows	0	2	95	190
422 R	Motor	0	2	480	960
421 R	Rear panel	0	2	85	170
440 Y	Solar panel, small	0	1	418	418
441 R	Solar panel, large	0	1	808	808
Final Assembly Total					$ 2,610
Compact Totals		10	10		$ 3,360

Each Part is described by an alphanumeric code:
The first three digits are a unique part code
The last digit is the part color code (black, red, or yellow)

Exhibit C2-1.2

California Car Company
Financial Statements
(In Thousands of Dollars)

BALANCE SHEETS	**Planned 2002**	**Actual 2001**	**Actual 2000**	**Actual 1999**
Assets				
Cash	$ 1,462	$ 350	$ 400	$ 250
Accounts receivable—net	13,600	1,450	435	160
Direct material inventory	1,590	618	95	17
Work-in-process inventory	3,267	250	16	6
Finished goods inventory	2,238	2,238	111	111
Total current assets	22,157	4,906	1,057	544
Long-term assets—net	112,000	42,000	5,560	4,000
Total assets	$134,157	$46,906	$ 6,617	$4,544
Total liabilities	$ 44,868	$23,707	$ 819	$ 171
Shareholders' equity				
Contributed capital	80,000	22,000	7,000	5,750
Retained earnings	9,289	1,199	(1,202)	(1,377)
Total shareholders' equity	89,289	23,199	5,798	4,373
Total liabilities and shareholders' equity	$134,157	$46,906	$ 6,617	$4,544

INCOME STATEMENTS	**Planned 2002**	**Actual 2001**	**Actual 2000**	**Actual 1999**
Sales revenue*	$136,000	$31,800	$ 9,500	$ 1,600
Less: cost of goods sold	98,943	20,670	6,650	1,109
Gross margin	37,057	11,130	2,850	491
Less: Selling expenses	7,000	1,500	600	400
Administrative expenses	18,500	6,200	2,000	1,200
Income before tax	11,557	3,430	250	(1,109)
Less: income tax—30%	3,467	1,029	75	(333)
Net income	$ 8,090	$ 2,401	$ 175	$ (776)

*Sedan unit sales	5,100	900	225	100
Sedan selling price	21,000			
Total sedan sales	$107,100,000			
Compact unit sales	1,700	300	75	0
Compact selling price	17,000			
Total compact sales	$ 28,900,000			
Total CCC sales	$136,000,000			

Serial Cases

The California Car Company is a serial case that extends over a period of four years, as the timeline in Exhibit C2-1.3 shows. A serial case involves a sequence of decisions related to a single company over a period of time. During this course you will follow CCC as it progresses from a rather small automobile assembly firm to a sophisticated, global corporation. The rationale for using a serial case is that students should more fully understand and appreciate the processes and integrated nature of business if they follow one company through many decision situations. To maximize the learning experience, students must keep current with their case assignments and understand the progression and timing of CCC's decisions. You should, therefore, refer back to Exhibit C2-1.3 periodically during the course to better understand how each individual case relates to others.

Exhibit C2-1.3
California Car Company Timeline

Date	Case	Topic
Year 2001		
November:	Cases 2-1, 2-2, 2-3	Introduction to CCC
December:	Case 2-4	Estimating Manufacturing Costs
Year 2002		
March:	Case 2-5	Pricing and Profitability
March:	Case 2-6	Job-Order Costing
April:	Case 2-7	Performance Variances
May:	Case 3-1	Activity-Based Budgeting
June:	Case 3-2	Implementing a Quality Program
June:	Case 3-3, Part I	Cost of Quality
August:	Case 3-4	Implementing JIT
September:	Case 3-5	JIT Costing
November:	Cases 4-1, 4-2, 4-4	Budgeting
November:	Case 5-2	Opening a Foreign Subsidiary
Year 2003		
February:	Case 3-3, Part II	Cost of Quality
July:	Case 4-3	Ethical Decision
October:	Case 4-5	Balanced Scorecard
Year 2004		
January:	Case 5-3	The Foreign Subsidiary after One Year
January:	Cases 5-4 and 5-5	Financial Statement Analysis

Requirements

1. What specific products does CCC manufacture?
2. Why is the demand for CCC's products increasing so fast?
3. List the production departments through which CCC's products pass. In other words, which departments work directly on making cars or parts for the cars and thus add direct materials or direct labor to the cars? What are CCC's manufacturing overhead departments?
4. Are CCC's organizational structure and plant layout typical for a manufacturing organization? Answer this question the best you can based on your work experience and the course work you have completed.
5. What is the difference between product costs and period costs? List those CCC costs that are considered to be period costs. What are the three broad cost categories that comprise product costs at CCC? What cost categories at CCC can be included in inventory?
6. What are the three types of inventory in CCC's factory?
7. Based on the financial statements in Exhibit C2-1.2, what is CCC's total planned manufacturing costs for 2002?
8. Compute the following four ratios for CCC for both 2001 and 2002 (see Reading 1-1 for formulas):
   - Return on equity
   - Return on sales
   - Inventory turnover
   - Debt-to-equity
9. Compute CCC's projected return-on-equity ratio for 2003 assuming that the income statement and balance sheet for 2003 are identical to those shown for 2002. Why is the 2003 return on equity so much lower than in 2002?
10. Average ratios for the hybrid car industry are as follows:
    - Return on equity .212
    - Return on sales .065
    - Inventory turnover 20.400
    - Debt-to-equity 1.450

    Discuss CCC's performance compared to the industry average performance. Identify two actions CCC could take that would improve its return on equity.
11. What is a serial case? Why is a serial case used in this course?
12. Your instructor will arrange for you to be given the title of one of CCC's four senior managers: (1) president, (2) vice president of production, (3) vice president of marketing, or (4) vice president of finance.
    a. Describe the typical educational background and business experience of a manager with your title.
    b. What primary decision(s) would a manager with your title address? Explain.

Case 2-2

CALIFORNIA CAR COMPANY PRODUCTION LINE SIMULATION

Case Objectives

1. Introduce students to basic production concepts in a traditional plant setting
2. Demonstrate the linkage of cost accounting numbers to the operations of a firm

INTRODUCTION

To gain an understanding of the relationship between a physical production process and related cost information, you will participate in an in-class simulation of CCC's production process. CCC uses the same production process to produce both its sedan and compact models. CCC employs a traditional, departmentalized production layout. Activities in the plant are grouped by the type of work done. For example, all chassis assembly is done in the Chassis Assembly Department and all maintenance employees work in the Maintenance Department. Sedans and compacts pass through both production departments in batches. All overhead support is drawn from specialized overhead departments. Extensive setups are required on the equipment in the production departments to switch models. CCC believes that by specializing in a specific function, overall efficiency will be increased because all employees will be experts in their areas.

On the day of the simulation, small groups will be organized into independent production lines that mirror CCC's plant layout shown in Exhibit 2-1.2 in Reading 2-1. Two small groups normally will team up to form a production line. A simplified schematic showing the production flow for the simulation is presented as Exhibit C2-2.1. Each student will act out an assigned role during the simulation.

You will produce cars in lots of 5 compacts and 15 sedans. A lot is the number of units of one product that is manufactured before the equipment is switched over to make another product. The 15 sedans will be manufactured in batches of 5. Batch size is the number of units within a lot that are manufactured and moved through the plant at once. For the compact, lot size and batch size are the same. *For the sedan, however, the lot size is 15, but the batch size is only 5.*

A key measure in traditional manufacturing operations is the number of units produced. Similarly, the primary measure of your production line's performance is the number of cars produced. Therefore, the production line that produces the most *defect-free* units in a set period of time will be deemed the winner. A production line is disqualified from the competition if any one of its members violates the rules of the simulation.

Important Note

Some schools may be using sets of toy blocks that are different than those shown in this book. If so, your instructor will provide you with drawings of your set of blocks to replace Exhibit C2-2.2, a new bill of materials to replace Exhibit C2-1.1, and a new set of assembly instructions to replace Exhibit C2-2.3.

Exhibit C2-2.1

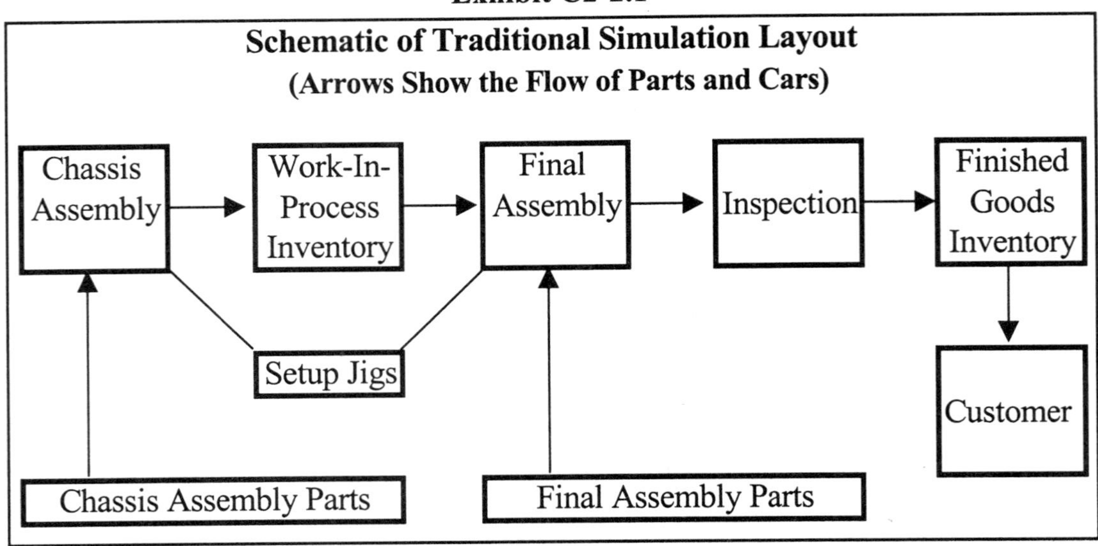

STUDENT ROLES IN THE PRODUCTION PROCESS

Students will be assigned one of ten different roles in the simulation. It is important that you study the responsibilities of your assigned role carefully so that your group can compete effectively against other groups. The simulation roles are listed below.

1. Setup person
2. Chassis material handler
3. Chassis assembler
4. Final assembly material handler
5. Final assembler
6. Inspector
7. Accountant
8. Plant manager
9. Customer
10. Union steward

Setup Person

A setup person puts in place the proper tooling jig for the assembly of a chassis in the Chassis Assembly Department or completion of a car in the Final Assembly Department. A jig is an apparatus used to help hold or align parts during assembly. Time and motion studies at the design stage prior to production have shown that utilizing a jig is the most cost-effective method of assembly.

Exhibit C2-2.2
California Car Company
Sedan and Compact Car Design

Chassis Assembly

1) Center the yellow "battery" under the black body panel.
2) Attach the four wheels under the black body panel placing them next to the yellow "battery".
3) Attach two small red mounts crosswise under each set of wheel "axles" to hold the wheels on.

Completed Chassis

COMPACT

Final Assembly

1) Stack two red panels and attach on top of the black body base placing them one peg in from the end. Repeat on the other end.
2) Attach one small red piece at each end of body base.
3) Attach the small yellow "solar panel/hood" on the front set of red panels.
4) Attach one window on each set of red panels.
5) Attach a large red "solar panel/roof" to the top of the windows.

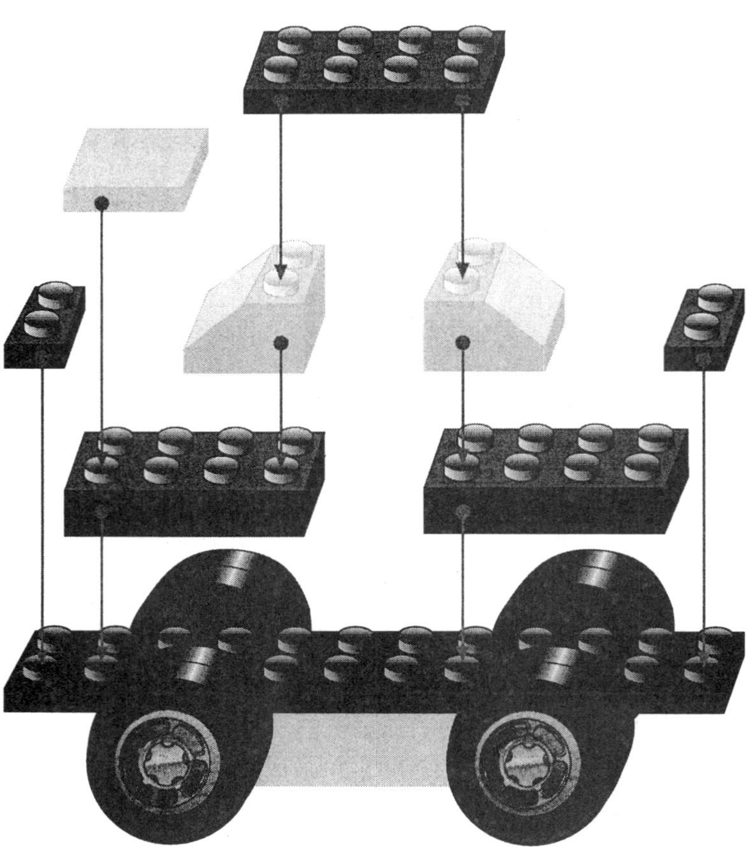

Completed Compact

SEDAN

Chassis Assembly

1) Underneath and at each end of the black body panel, attach one large red panel.
2) Attach two large red panels side by side across the top of the black body panel, placing them one peg away from the edge. Repeat at other end.
3) Center and attach two wheels under each pair of red panels.
4) Attach one red panel crosswise between each set of wheels to complete each axle.
5) Place the two large yellow "batteries" under the body panel between the axles.

Back

Completed Chassis

SEDAN

Final Assembly

1) Attach one large red panel on top of each inner large red panel already attached to the black body panel.
2) Attach one small red piece on top of the black body panel at each end.
3) Attach two flat yellow "hood" panels on the front large red panel.
4) Attach two windows on each inner large red panel.
5) Attach two large red panels to the top of each set of windows.

Back

Completed Sedan

Special Instructions

For purposes of the simulation, your instructor will provide the items to represent the jigs. These may be wooden devices or simply cardboard templates that need to be changed. Remember, however, that in a real factory changing jigs can be both difficult and time consuming. The chassis and final assemblers will call you for a setup when they are finished producing a lot. Your instructor also may tell you the minimum setup time to use. If so, it is your job to ensure that the assemblers do not begin work until the full setup time has expired. You should wait at a desk away from the assembly line until an assembler calls for a setup.

Chassis Material Handler

This person, when notified by the chassis assembler, selects parts from inventory storage bins and delivers a pallet of parts that contains sufficient quantities of each part to produce *five* chassis. A pallet is represented by a paper cup or some other container, into which the necessary parts are placed. You can place all parts for one batch in one cup. Use the bill of materials (Exhibit C2-1.1) and the drawings (Exhibit C2-2.2) to identify the parts used to assemble sedan and compact chassis. Just deliver the pallet (cup) of parts to the assembler, and the assembler will handle them from there. It is critical that you learn the parts you will deliver *before the simulation*, because slow delivery of parts will reduce the output of the entire line. The chassis assembler will begin the simulation by producing 15 sedans, 5 at a time.

Special Instructions

1. You are not allowed to fill cups from inventory before the assembler calls for parts.
2. The assembler cannot call for parts, and you are not allowed to retrieve parts, until that person begins assembling the last chassis in the batch.
3. If you grab or are given a defective part (wrong color) by your instructor, you must deliver it. You *cannot* exchange it for a correctly colored part.
4. If you deliver too few parts, you must make a special delivery of the missing parts before you deliver the next batch of parts.
5. If you deliver too many parts, you must retrieve those parts, plus you must wait 30 seconds before you deliver the parts for the next batch.

Chassis Assembler

Using the tooling jig for the appropriate vehicle, a chassis assembler assembles an individual chassis. The steps for chassis assembly of a sedan and a compact are listed in Exhibit C2-2.3. It is critical that you learn how to assemble the parts before the simulation, because slow assembly of parts will reduce the output of the entire line. It is your job to call for a setup at the completion of each lot and to tell the material handler to get parts when you are assembling the last chassis in a batch. *You will begin the simulation by assembling a lot of 15 sedan chassis, 5 at a time*. You will then assemble 5 compact chassis, followed by 15 sedan chassis, and so forth.

Upon completion of a batch, at CCC or at a real-life manufacturer, the assembler would call for a chassis material handler to move the assembled chassis to work-in-process (WIP) storage located between Buildings 1 and 2. In our in-class simulation, instead of relying on the material handler to move the completed chassis to the WIP area, the assembler will move the chassis. *You may not move any chassis to the WIP area until the full batch of five cars is complete.*

Exhibit C2-2.3
Step-By-Step Assembly Instructions

Sedan

Chassis Assembly

1. Underneath and at each end of the black body base, attach one large red panel.
2. Attach two large red panels side by side across the top of the black body panel, placing them one peg from the end. Repeat at the other end.
3. Center and attach two wheels under each pair of red panels.
4. Attach one large red panel crosswise between each set of wheels to complete each axle.
5. Place two large yellow "batteries" under the body base between the axles.

Final Assembly

1. Attach one large red panel on top of each inner large red panel already attached to the black body panel.
2. Attach one small red piece on top of the black body panel at each end.
3. Attach two flat yellow "hood" panels on the front large red panel.
4. Attach two windows on each inner large red panel.
5. Attach two large red panels to the top of each set of windows.

Compact

Chassis Assembly

1. Center the yellow "battery" under the black body panel.
2. Attach the four wheels under the black body panel placing them next to the yellow "battery."
3. Attach the two small red mounts crosswise under each set of wheel "axles" to hold the wheels on.

Final Assembly

1. Stack two red flat panels and attach them to the top of the black body base, placing them one peg in from the end. Repeat on the other end.
2. Attach one small red piece at each end of the body base.
3. Attach the small yellow "solar panel/hood" on the front set of red panels.
4. Attach one window on each set of red panels.
5. Attach the large red "solar panel/roof" to the top of the windows.

Special Instructions

1. You cannot call for more parts until you have started assembling the last car in a batch.
2. You cannot call for a setup until you have finished the current lot of 15 sedans or 5 compacts.
3. You must assemble defective (wrong colored) parts, even if you have extra good parts.

4. If the material handler delivers too many or too few parts, you must call the handler back to correct the situation before bringing parts for the next batch.

5. On a separate sheet of paper, keep track of the approximate amount of time you are idle while waiting for parts and setups.

Information You Must Collect for the Accountant

At the end of the simulation, estimate the percent of time you were idle while waiting for parts or setups. Record that percentage on Exhibit C2-2.4, item 8. The accountant will ask for this at the end of the simulation.

Final Assembly Material Handler

This person, when notified by the final assembler, selects parts from inventory storage bins and delivers a pallet of parts that contains sufficient quantities of each part to produce *five* completed vehicles. A pallet is represented by a paper cup or some other container, into which the necessary parts are placed. You can place all parts for one batch in one cup. Use the bill of materials (Exhibit C2-1.1) and the drawings (Exhibit C2-2.2) to identify the parts used in the final assembly of sedans and compacts. Just deliver the pallet (cup) of parts to the assembler, and the assembler will handle them from there. It is critical that you learn the parts you will deliver *before the simulation*, because slow delivery of parts will reduce the output of the entire line. When asked by the final assembler, you also move batches of five chassis from the WIP inventory to the final assembler. The final assembler will begin the simulation by performing final assembly on five compacts.

Special Instructions

1. You are not allowed to fill cups from inventory before the assembler calls for parts.

2. The assembler cannot call for parts until that person begins final assembly of the last car in the batch.

3. If you grab or are given a defective part (wrong color) by your instructor, you must deliver it. You cannot exchange it for a correctly colored part.

4. If you deliver too few parts, you must make a special delivery of the missing parts before you deliver the next batch of parts.

5. If you deliver too many parts, you must retrieve those parts, plus you must wait 30 seconds before you deliver the parts for the next batch.

Final Assembler

Using the tooling jig for the appropriate vehicle, a final assembler assembles an individual vehicle. The steps for the final assembly of a sedan and a compact are listed in Exhibit C2-2.3. It is critical that you learn how to assemble the parts *before the simulation*, because slow assembly of parts will reduce the output of the entire line. It is your job to call for a setup at the completion of each lot and to tell the material handler to get parts when you are assembling the last car in a batch. You also must tell the material handler to deliver a batch of five chassis from the WIP inventory (if five chassis are in inventory). When you have completed a batch of five cars, you can move them to the inspection area. *You will begin the simulation by finishing the assembly of five compacts*. You will then finish the assembly of 15 sedans, followed by 5 compacts, and so forth.

Special Instructions

1. You cannot call for more parts and chassis from work-in-process until you have started assembling the last car in a batch of five.
2. You cannot call for a setup until you have finished the current lot of 5 compacts or 15 sedans.
3. You must assemble defective (wrong colored) parts, even if you have extra good parts.
4. If the material handler delivers too many or too few parts, you must call the handler back to correct the situation before bringing parts for the next batch.
5. On a separate sheet of paper, keep track of the approximate time you are idle while waiting for parts and setups.

Information You Must Collect for the Accountant

At the end of the simulation, estimate the percent of time you were idle while waiting for parts or setups. Record that percentage on Exhibit C2-2.4, item 8. The accountant will ask for this at the end of the simulation.

Inspector

This person performs thorough inspections and parks each good vehicle in the finished goods storage area. Cars that do not pass final inspection are appropriately marked and are set aside for rework at a later time. Inspect the cars carefully. Wrong color parts, improper assembly, and poor fit are considered defects. The timing marker the accountant has attached to a car is not a defect. The inspector will be selected from another production line so that the inspector will have an incentive to perform a rigorous inspection.

Information You Must Collect for the Accountant

At the end of the simulation, count the number of defective cars. Record the number on Exhibit C2-2.4, item 5, and give that number to the accountant when asked.

Customer

The customer draws a playing card or some other sales marker at a fixed time interval determined by your instructor. If you use playing cards, a club represents a compact sale, and spades, hearts, and diamonds represent sedan sales. The customer removes the model indicated from finished goods inventory and places the car in a separate sold-car area. The card is then placed in the sold car stack. If a card is drawn and that model is not in finished goods inventory at the moment the card is drawn, then your line has a stockout. Place the card in a stockout pile that is separate from the sold-car pile. Once a stockout occurs the sale is lost forever. That is, the customer *does not* convert a stockout to a sale as soon as that model is available again.

You draw a card as soon as the instructor tells your group to start the simulation. At the end of the simulation, the number of cars placed in the sold-car area plus the number of stockouts should reconcile with the number of playing cards you have drawn. For example, if your instructor tells you to run the simulation for 15 minutes with sales occurring every 30 seconds, the total number of sold cars plus stockouts should equal 30. *You will need a watch or clock that indicates seconds to perform your role.*

Information You Must Collect for the Accountant

At the end of the simulation, you record the number of units sold and the total number of stockouts *by model* on Exhibit C2-2.4, items 2 and 3, respectively, and give this information to the accountant when asked.

Accountant

During the simulation the accountant is responsible for collecting the cycle time measurement. This is done by first marking any sedan chassis in the third batch of 5 sedans in the first lot of 15 sedan chassis produced and recording the time at which chassis assembly began. You then watch the marked chassis and record the time it takes for it to arrive in finished goods inventory (not in the sold-car area). Cycle time is the difference in the recorded times.

After the simulation has ended, the accountant is required to do the following in order to complete Exhibit C2-2.4:

1. Record the number of sedans and compacts in work-in-process and finished goods ending inventories.
2. Collect from the customer the number of sedans sold and the number of sedan stockouts. Collect the same information for the compacts.
3. Collect from the inspector the number of defective units needing rework.
4. Collect from the chassis and final assemblers their idle time estimates.
5. Calculate good units completed for both sedans and compacts, which equal:

   Sales + Ending inventory finished goods – Beginning inventory finished goods.
6. Compute average production time per unit. Average production is obtained by determining the number of seconds the simulation ran and dividing that number by the total number of good units produced (sedan and compact combined). For example, if the simulation ran for 15 minutes and 25 good units were produced, you divide 900 seconds (15 minutes × 60 seconds) by 25 cars, for an average production time of 36 seconds per car.
7. Record the cycle time for the marked sedan.

Finally, it is the accountant's responsibility to ensure that all members of the groups working on the production line have copied all of the information from the accountant's completed Exhibit C2-2.4 onto their own form. All students will need a completed Exhibit C2-2.4 in order to finish Part II of Case 2-2.

Plant Manager

The plant manager supervises the entire operation and troubleshoots during any unforeseen difficulties. It is the plant manager's job to learn the responsibilities of each job and to provide advice on how to improve operations, as long as the advice does not violate simulation rules. Some instructors may assign the plant manager the task of breaking down sold cars and returning the parts to the part bins.

Union Steward

The union steward observes the operation of the entire line and makes sure that all procedures are being followed. If a violation of procedure is detected, the line shuts down for 30 seconds while the union steward explains the violation. The union steward must be familiar with all procedures discussed in this case. This person will be selected from another assembly line so that there will be an incentive to enforce the rules.

Part I Requirements (Perform Prior to the Simulation)

In order for the simulation to proceed smoothly during the class session, each student must complete the following advance preparation steps outside of class.

1. Meet briefly with other members of your production line and review the steps needed to assemble both the sedan and compact models. See Exhibit C2-2.2 or drawings provided by your instructor and Exhibit C2-2.3 for the step-by-step sequence involved in the assembly of each car. See Exhibit C2-1.1 for a bill of materials for each car. Since CCC evaluates production line performance based on the number of good cars completed in a set time, your goal in the simulation is to produce as many defect-free cars as possible while following all stated procedures.

2. Become familiar with the schematic for the simulation in Exhibit C2-2.1. In addition, understand the following terms:

   - *Lot size*—the number of vehicles produced before a setup occurs. CCC's lot sizes are 15 sedans and 5 compacts,
   - *Batch size*—the number of vehicles produced from one delivery of material. CCC's batch size is five cars, the same for sedans and compacts,
   - *Production line*—the Chassis and Assembly Departments and all support services needed to produce completed cars. Your class probably will have multiple lines.

3. Become familiar with the roles and steps in CCC's production described in the case. Note that all steps are identical for each model, only the parts and time required to execute a step will differ depending on the model. Be sure to read and fully understand the instructions for your job.

Part II Requirements (Perform as Follow-Up to the Simulation)

Prepare a one-page, single-spaced, word-processed analysis of the simulation that provides the following:

1. A brief description of your tasks and how they relate to the tasks performed by others. Include a discussion of the following:

   a. How do your tasks affect the work done by others?

   b. How does the work performed by others affect your tasks?

   c. How much does your job add value to the car from the customers' perspective?

   d. Are the costs associated with your tasks direct or overhead costs? If they are overhead costs, how do accountants assign these costs to the cars?

2. A brief identification of any weaknesses/inefficiencies that you noticed involving your assigned tasks and the tasks that you observed being performed by others.

3. Complete the Accounting Data Sheet (Exhibit C2-2.4) and attach it to your answer. You will need to get much of the data from your group's accountant. Discuss why:

   a. The cycle time was so much higher than the average time to produce a car.

   b. The chassis and final assemblers were idle for as long as your accountant reported.

   c. Your group had stockouts.

Exhibit C2-2.4
California Car Company
Accounting Data Sheet for a Traditional Plant Layout

Assembly Line Number ______

	Recorded Value			CCC Total
	Sedan	Compact		
1. Inventory Levels:				
Beginning work-in-process	0	5		
Beginning finished goods	6	2		
Ending work-in-process	4	5		
Ending finished goods	5	2		
2. Sales	27	10		
3. Stockouts	3	0		
4. Good Units Completed	26	10	=	36
5. Defective Units	1	0		
6. Cycle Time (Sedan Only)	2.37			

	Both Models Combined
7. Average Production Time	164.4 sec
8. Assembler Idle Time Percentage	16.67%

Group Assignment 2-2

ASSEMBLING CARS AT CALIFORNIA CAR COMPANY

Group number __________ Signatures of group members participating:

____

____

Objectives

1. Introduce students to basic production concepts in a traditional plant setting
2. Demonstrate the linkage of cost accounting numbers to the operations of a firm
3. Familiarize students with the products and manufacturing processes of CCC

Requirements

Group Assignment 2-2 is a simulation of CCC's manufacturing process using a departmental production layout. Enter the required information below. You will receive credit for being prepared and actively participating. If anyone in your group did not prepare and/or did not actively participate, do not include that person's name above.

	Sedan	**Compact**
Total units sold	__________	__________
Total stockouts	__________	__________
Total good units completed	__________	__________
Defective units	__________	__________

Case 2-3

PRODUCTION PROBLEMS AT CALIFORNIA CAR COMPANY

Case Objectives

1. Reinforce production concepts developed in the simulation
2. Relate accounting costs to production activities

Decision: Is CCC's plant operating efficiently?

PROBLEMS EXPOSED BY THE SIMULATION

Sally Swanson, CCC's vice president of production, just viewed a production simulation video and was very interested to see that many features of the CCC production process were also evident in the video. Moreover, the video stimulated a number of questions in Sally's mind about the efficiency and effectiveness of CCC's assembly process. After circulating the video among her management group, Sally called a meeting of her plant manager, engineers, production line supervisors, and the head of inspection and raised the following questions:

1. "We (CCC) and the firm in the video both seem to keep adequate levels of raw materials and work-in-process inventories. Yet both companies experience frequent stockouts of finished products. Why does this happen? What do you think it really costs us to have a stockout of sedans or compacts?"

2. "In my walks around our plant, I frequently see workers who are idle. I noticed the same problem in the video. Why can't either company keep its workers busy throughout the workday? What does idle time really cost us? How can we reduce idle time?"

3. "Did you notice the disruption that occurred in the video when the template jig broke down at the second work station where the worker was drawing circles using the template jig? We frequently have breakdowns in our tooling that also cause disruptions. I wonder what these breakdowns are costing us. How can we avoid them?"

4. "I noticed that the firm in the video inspects its products just as we do at the end of its production process in order to prevent bad units from reaching the customer. Also, they seemed to have a defect problem just like we do. I wonder what defects are currently costing us. How can we reduce the defect problem?"

5. "Setups halted the production process in the video the same way they shut down our assembly line. I wonder whether we should increase the size of our production runs, say from 5 to 10 for compacts and possibly from 15 to 30 for our sedans, in order to reduce the number of setups. What costs per car do you think would change if we increased the size of our production runs?"
6. "As in the video, our cycle time is quite high. Many of our customers want 'special' extras such as sun roofs or built-in, high-quality sound systems, but they don't want to wait a long time for delivery. These specials are very profitable. How can we reduce our cycle time in order to attract more of this business?"

Requirements

For each of the above questions, write a one-paragraph word-processed response to Sally Swanson in which you present your interpretation and analysis of the problem that she has identified and your suggestions for addressing the problem.

Reading 2-4

ESTIMATING MANUFACTURING COSTS

INTRODUCTION

Providing management with information on the costs involved in operating an organization is the primary function of the management accountant. Although determining costs sounds easy in principle, providing management with cost information that is relevant to various decisions is a complex task. Management accountants must understand thoroughly the business, the decision involved, and how individual managers make decisions if they are to supply appropriate cost information. As you will see as the book progresses, different types of decisions require different types of cost information. In addition, you should learn why all managers should have a basic understanding of which costs are relevant to which decisions if they are to avoid making decisions based on inappropriate cost information.

Many decisions are based on planned future costs and levels of activity. These decisions include determining how much material to purchase, how many employees to hire, what price to charge for goods and services, and how much cash must be available to fund the organization. For some planning purposes total costs must be estimated for a department. For example, the receiving department must estimate the total cost of all employees required to receive the planned level of purchased goods as well as all other costs related to operating the department. Estimated future costs are collected in a **planning (static) budget**. Module 4 covers budgeting more comprehensively.

Other planning decisions require cost information on a per job or per unit of product basis. For example, if a firm is asked to bid on a job, it will need to estimate the cost of that one job. The estimate would include the labor, material, and overhead cost of that job. Case 2-4 provides an overview of how costs are estimated. Management can easily see the link between direct material and direct labor costs and the amount of material and workers they can afford to buy or hire to maintain competitive sales prices. If material or labor cost per unit increases then either the sales price will have to rise or the profit will decline. The role of overhead costs in making product decisions, however, is not as clear. The most difficult part of estimating costs in Case 2-4 is computing **predetermined overhead rates** used to approximate the overhead cost of a job. This topic is discussed later in this module.

ESTIMATING DIRECT COSTS

The following example, Quality Welding, illustrates how companies estimate costs. Quality Welding manufactures ornamental iron products, such as porch railings and support columns, to each customer's specifications. The firm has two production departments through which each job passes, Cutting and Welding. Quality also has the following three manufacturing **overhead (or service) departments**:

> *Equipment Management*, which prepares the cutting and welding equipment for each job and purchases and maintains all equipment and the factory building.

Material Handling, which receives all the incoming materials and loads the finished ornamental iron on trucks.

Inspection and Supervision, which inspects all completed jobs and is charged with the cost of production supervisors.

Estimating Costs for a Department

Estimating direct costs for the Cutting department, a production department, involves estimating total direct material and direct labor required to produce the projected volume for 2002. Assume that the Cutting Department estimates that it will require 16,000 direct labor hours (DLHs) and $1,400,000 in direct material. According to a labor contract, wages will remain stable at $20 per DLH. The Cutting department's estimated direct costs for 2002 are the following:

Direct materials	$1,400,000	
Direct labor	320,000	(16,000 DLHs × $20 per hour)
Total estimated direct costs	$1,720,000	

In December 2001, Quality Welding also estimates that the Material Handling Department's cost for 2002 will be as follows:

Hourly employees	$390,000
Supervisor	60,000
Supplies used	20,000
Total estimated costs	$470,000

All of Quality's departments, whether production or overhead, will prepare 2002 budget estimates similar to that produced by the Cutting and Material Handling Departments. Quality Welding charges depreciation for factory equipment and buildings to the Equipment Management Department, although many firms would show depreciation on departmental equipment as a department cost.

Estimating Costs for a Job

Each customer order is a job because the railings and columns must be cut and welded to the unique lengths and angles of each porch. In December 2001, Quality is asked to bid on a job, consisting of 50 packages of railings and columns, to be delivered in February 2002. The job will be labeled Job 101. It is estimated to take 540 DLHs and to require $39,500 in direct material. Quality is currently developing cost estimates, or budgets, for the year 2002. It estimates that the plant will use 30,000 DLHs for all of 2002. What are the estimated direct product costs of manufacturing this job? Remember that direct product costs consist of direct material and direct labor. The answer is:

Direct materials	$39,500	
Direct labor	10,800	(540 DLHs × $20 per hour)
Total estimated direct costs	$50,300	

ESTIMATING OVERHEAD COSTS

Manufacturing costs assigned to a job or unit of production include costs other than direct materials and direct labor that may not appear as obvious product costs. Called manufacturing overhead, they are categorized as indirect because they cannot be clearly associated or connected to specific jobs or units of production. Manufacturing overhead costs are accumulated in groups of similar costs, called **cost pools**. The **cost driver**, or activity that causes an indirect cost, often cannot be identified easily. The lack of direct connection of manufacturing overhead to the product does not mean that these costs are not important in making decisions that rely on product costs or that the underlying activities driving the costs are not essential to the successful production of a job. Cars could not be manufactured without electricity to run the machines used to lift parts. Although the electricity does not enter the car itself as a component part, the machines require electricity in order to operate and lift the heavy metal doors, engines, and other materials too large for a human to carry. Some examples of manufacturing overhead indirect costs include the following:

1. *Indirect material*—the cost of supplies and tangible items used for production that do not become part of the product and are not considered long-term assets. Examples are the costs of machine oil, soap and other cleaning supplies, repair parts, bolts to keep jigs in place, and nails, screwdrivers, and hammers to make repairs.

2. *Indirect labor*—the wages of employees who do not work, hands-on, to manufacture the product. Examples are the wages of supervisors, maintenance staff, inspectors, material handlers, inventory storage workers, and setup workers.

3. *Other indirect costs*—factory and equipment depreciation, or building rental costs, factory property taxes, insurance on factory and equipment, and electricity for air-conditioning, heat, light, and machine operation.

While studying Reading 2-4, keep in mind that CCC has five overhead departments: Inspection, Maintenance, Setup, Material Handling, and General Factory.

Reasons for Applying Manufacturing Overhead

Indirect costs become **applied overhead** after they are assigned or allocated to products through the use of predetermined rates. The application or allocation process involves a two-step method explained later in this section. One of the most confusing cost accounting concepts for many students is the notion of predetermined factory overhead rates. Much of the confusion arises because students do not understand why accountants apply factory overhead to products based on a predetermined rate rather than on the actual overhead costs incurred. The two main reasons for applying overhead rather than assigning actual overhead costs are timeliness of information for making decisions and the preparation of monthly or quarterly financial statements. First, if actual costing is used, management would have to wait until the overhead costs are known before making timely, relevant decisions, such as pricing. Consequently, management may miss achieving a competitive edge or may lose a contract if it is unable to price a product because essential, actual information on overhead costs, and thus profit, is unknown.

Second, the preparation of financial statements for an interval of less than a year requires the "smoothing" or "normalizing" of overhead over at least one year to prevent the erratic reporting of costs from one reporting period to the next. One frequently asked question is why businesses smooth overhead and net income over just one year when some industries have sales trends that fluctuate with economic cycles that last several years. In fact, many firms in cyclical industries, including auto companies, smooth overhead over a period of several years. How this is accomplished will be left to a cost accounting course.

Reasons Why the Occurrence of Overhead Costs Is Erratic

There are three primary reasons why actual overhead produces erratic and misleading costs per unit or job. First, some overhead expenditures tend to be "lumpy." For example, major equipment breakdowns may occur on average only once a year. If a company such as CCC uses actual monthly overhead to cost its cars, the cost per car would arbitrarily increase in a month of a production line breakdown. Maintenance costs would be higher than usual and car production would be lower. Reported profit for cars manufactured and sold during that period would decline. These overall annual or cyclical fluctuations in cost and income would be of little value to decision makers because they do not help predict future levels of costs and income.

Second, some overhead costs are seasonal. Suppose CCC is located in Florida or South Texas. Obviously air-conditioning expense, an overhead item, is much higher in the summer than in the winter. Unless the management decision makers are very sophisticated and can adjust reported costs and income for the seasonal effects, they may be misled by the fluctuating cost and income numbers reported during the hotter months.

Third, and often most important, a significant amount of overhead is a fixed cost, at least in the short run. As you have already learned in Reading 1-3, a key cost accounting concept is that fixed costs per unit change as the volume of activity changes. The production of cars represents the volume of activity for CCC. As a result, overhead cost per unit or job and hence cost per unit or job will vary from month to month as the volume of production activity varies. Suppose CCC stops production in its plant for two weeks every July to retool and engage in major equipment maintenance. As a result, CCC produces only 200 cars in July instead of the 400 or so they produce in other months. If fixed factory overhead is \$1,000,000 per month, fixed overhead cost per unit would go from \$2,500 per car (\$1,000,000 ÷ 400 cars) in a normal month to \$5,000 per car (\$1,000,000 ÷ 200 cars) in July. Obviously, this spike in cost per unit would not be useful for pricing decisions and the reduced income reported when the cars are sold would not predict future monthly income except for July of the following year.

If the idea of smoothing is still fuzzy, think of a landlord charging rent to students living in an apartment near campus. Utilities for heat and air-conditioning are seasonal due to climate variations, and the number of students living in the apartment building is probably less in the summer. The rent, however, is the same each month. The landlord has smoothed the rent to cover all overhead costs incurred during the entire year.

It now should be clear why virtually all companies use a predetermined overhead rate to apply costs to jobs and units produced. Use of a predetermined rate is the accountant's way of smoothing overhead for both relevant decision making and financial reporting. To assist you in computing and using predetermined overhead rates, a two-step process to assign, apply, or allocate overhead is presented next. Note that the terms *assign*, *apply*, and *allocate* all refer to the same procedure of connecting overhead costs to **cost objects**. Understanding how accountants use predetermined manufacturing overhead rates to cost products and make decisions is a key concept in this book.

Two-Step Process to Apply Overhead to Jobs or Departments

Traditional (or volume-based) overhead allocation is the application of manufacturing overhead based on one or more cost drivers, such as direct labor hours, machine hours, or material costs, that are closely linked to production volume. When applying overhead, most firms, including CCC, compute two predetermined **plantwide overhead rates**: one for variable manufacturing overhead and another for fixed. The process is the same, except that two overhead cost pools, one fixed and the other variable, are established. The process for allocating either type of overhead consists of the following two steps:

Step 1—Compute Predetermined Overhead Rate (Variable or Fixed)

To compute the predetermined overhead rate, divide estimated annual overhead (variable or fixed) by estimated annual volume of the cost driver, frequently DLHs.

To illustrate Step 1, assume that a company is computing predetermined overhead rates based on two different levels of production activity because sales predictions are rather uncertain. For a production level of 8,000 units the company estimates total annual variable overhead for 2002 will be $160,000 and fixed overhead for the same period to be $400,000. Overhead is applied using the cost driver of direct labor hours of 80,000. Predetermined overhead rates are:

Variable overhead rate = $160,000 ÷ 80,000 DLHs = $2 per DLH

Fixed overhead rate = $400,000 ÷ 80,000 DLHs = $5 per DLH

If production and sales increase to 10,000 units the total variable overhead will increase to $200,000. Total fixed overhead, by definition, will remain the same, and direct labor hours will increase to 100,000. The revised predetermined variable overhead predetermined rate remains at $2 per DLH ($200,000 ÷ 100,000 DLHs) since variable overhead costs increase in proportion to units produced. The revised fixed predetermined overhead rate, however, changes to $4 per DLH ($400,000 ÷ 100,000 DLHs).

The effect on the two predetermined overhead rates of changes in production and direct labor hour activity volume are different. Since variable overhead costs increase or decrease at the same rate as the volume of activity within a set range of production, the relevant range, the predetermined variable overhead rate stays the same. Total estimated fixed costs, however, remain the same within the relevant range. Consequently, the predetermined overhead rate for fixed costs fluctuates with the change in volume of activity. Because the cost driver is in the denominator of the fraction, the fixed overhead rate decreases with an increase in the level of production. Conversely, if production and direct labor hours decrease the predetermined fixed overhead rate will increase.

To smooth the costs over an entire year, a firm like CCC will compute only one predetermined rate for variable and one for fixed costs per year. If the predetermined rate is used for January costing purposes, it must be established before the year begins or at least before the end of January. Therefore, to compute a predetermined rate, divide *estimated* overhead for the coming year by the estimated annual volume of the cost driver, direct labor hours for CCC. Many of you will be uneasy using an estimated rate for the entire year as the basis for calculating overhead cost per unit for an actual job. On homework and exams you may have the incorrect tendency to use either an actual overhead rate for that job or a predetermined overhead rate based on data just for the month in question. However, if you understand that overhead must be smoothed over the entire year to avoid producing misleading cost numbers, you will not make these errors.

Step 2—Apply Overhead to Cost Object (Job or Unit of Production)

To apply overhead, multiply the predetermined overhead rate computed in Step 1 by the volume of the cost driver (e.g., direct labor hours) actually used or estimated to be used for each job or unit of product.

Step 2 applies or places the overhead costs onto the job or a single unit of production, such as a car in the case of CCC. When a company is in production, multiplying predetermined rates times actual activity levels enables overhead costs to be assigned to WIP and finished goods inventories as well as cost of goods sold when the cars are delivered to customers. Suppose that the company, discussed in Step 1, produced 500 units in Job 210 using 4,800 actual DLHs. Manufacturing overhead applied to job 210 is:

Variable applied overhead	= \$2 × 4,800 DLHs	= \$ 9,600
Fixed applied overhead	= \$5 × 4,800 DLHs	= 24,000
Total applied overhead	= \$7 × 4,800 DLHs	= \$33,600

Variable overhead per unit would be \$9,600 ÷ 500 units or \$19.20 per unit and fixed overhead unit costs would be much higher at \$48 (\$24,000 ÷ 500 units) per unit. The total overhead applied to each unit would be \$33,600 ÷ 500 units = \$67.20 per unit. As you can see fixed overhead makes up the greater portion of the total overhead cost per unit.

Quality Welding Example: Estimating Overhead Costs

To complete the estimated manufacturing costs for Job 101 described in the Quality Welding example discussed at the beginning of this reading, manufacturing overhead must be allocated to the departments and Job 101. Assume that in addition to the \$470,000 of variable costs in Material Handling shown earlier, fixed costs incurred by the Equipment Management Department are estimated to be \$580,000 for 2002. The costs for the Inspection and Supervision Department are variable and estimated to be \$300,000. Therefore, the plantwide variable predetermined manufacturing overhead rate per DLH is (\$470,000 + \$300,000) ÷ 30,000 DLH = \$25.67; the predetermined fixed overhead rate is \$580,000 ÷ 30,000 = \$19.33 and the total plantwide predetermined overhead rate per DLH is (\$470,000 + \$580,000 + \$300,000) ÷ 30,000 DLHs = \$45 per DLH. The sum of the variable and fixed rates (\$25.67 + \$19.33) also equals \$45.

Estimating Overhead Costs for a Department

Since Quality used allocates overhead department costs directly to the production departments, no overhead is allocated to the Material Handling Department and total costs remain \$470,000. The Cutting Department, however, is a production department, so overhead costs are added to its direct costs in order to determine its estimated total costs:

Direct materials		\$1,400,000	
Direct labor		320,000	(16,000 DLHs × \$20 per hour)
Variable manufacturing overhead	\$ 410,720		(16,000 DLHs × \$25.67 per hour)
Fixed manufacturing overhead	309,280		(16,000 DLHs × \$19.33 per hour)
Total manufacturing overhead		720,000	(16,000 DLHs × \$45 per hour)
Total estimated costs		\$2,440,000	

Estimating Overhead Costs for a Job

Total estimated manufacturing cost for Job 101 is:

Direct materials		$39,500	
Direct labor		10,800	(540 DLHs × $20 per hour)
Variable manufacturing overhead	$ 13,862		(540 DLHs × $25.67 per hour)
Fixed manufacturing overhead	10,438		(540 DLHs × $19.33 per hour)
Total manufacturing overhead		24,300	(540 DLHs × $45 per hour)
Total estimated costs		$74,600	

To determine the cost of one unit of production, divide the total estimated cost by the number of units produced. Job 101 is estimated to consist of 50 packages of railings and columns. One package equates to one unit of production. Total manufacturing overhead per package would be $486 ($24,300 ÷ 50 packages). Total estimated manufacturing cost per package would be $1,492 ($74,600 ÷ 50 packages).

SUMMARY

This reading provides the necessary procedural information to help you estimate manufacturing costs in Case 2-4. A two-step process illustrates an easy-to-understand method for computing predetermined overhead rates and for applying overhead to cost objects. The text gives reasons why firms apply overhead instead of using actual overhead numbers in their financial statements and explains why the occurrence of overhead is erratic. The example of Quality Welding is used to illustrate how to compute direct costs and to apply variable and fixed manufacturing overhead to a job, unit of production, and a department.

EXERCISES AND PROBLEMS

Exercises

Exercise 1 Types of Departments at CCC. Indicate which of the following CCC manufacturing departments are production (p) and which are overhead (o).

a. Inspection

b. Chassis Assembly

c. Maintenance

d. Setup

e. Final Assembly

f. Material Handling

g. General Factory

Exercise 2 Types of Costs at CCC. Indicate whether each of the following costs for CCC is a direct product (d), manufacturing overhead (mo), or nonmanufacturing cost (n).

a. Wages of trucker who delivers cars from WIP to final assembly
b. Chassis Assembly worker wages
c. Property taxes on the factory
d. Insurance on the office building
e. Screws that hold the battery in place on the sedan
f. Wages of janitor who mops the factory floor
g. Soap the janitor uses to clean the factory floor
h. Doors for the sedan model
i. Air-conditioning in Jena Butler's (CCC vice president) office
j. Line supervisor's salary
k. Heat in the factory
l. Wages of the person who checks for defects after assembly
m. Wages of employees who store and deliver raw materials
n. Equipment depreciation
o. Cost accountant working in the factory

Exercise 3 Types of Costs at CCC. Indicate whether each of the following costs for CCC is a direct product (d), manufacturing overhead (mo), or nonmanufacturing (n) cost.

a. Wages of material handler who delivers parts to WIP
b. Final Assembly worker wages
c. Property taxes on the office building
d. Insurance on the factory
e. Setup screws that hold the compact solar panel in place
f. Wages of product inspector
g. Soap the janitor uses to clean the office building
h. Headlights for the compact model
i. Air-conditioning in plant cost accountant's office
j. Plant manager's salary
k. Employee parking lot
l. Wages of the person who files invoices
m. Rear wheel assembly for compact
n. Depreciation of pc computers in the Marketing department
o. Union steward wages

Exercise 4 Types of Costs at CCC. Indicate whether each of the following costs for CCC is an indirect materials (im), indirect labor (il), other indirect (o), or not an indirect (n) cost.

a. Wages of trucker who delivers cars from WIP to assembly
b. Chassis Assembly worker wages
c. Property taxes on the factory
d. Insurance on the office building
e. Screws that hold the battery in place on the sedan
f. Wages of janitor who mops the factory floor
g. Soap the janitor uses to clean the factory floor
h. Doors for the sedan model
i. Air-conditioning in Jena Butler's (Vice President) office
j. Line supervisor's salary
k. Heat in the factory
l. Wages of the person who checks for defects after assembly
m. Wages of employees who store and deliver raw materials
n. Equipment depreciation
o. Cost accountant working in the factory

Exercise 5 Types of Costs at CCC. Indicate whether each of the following costs for CCC is an indirect materials (im), indirect labor (il), other indirect (o), or not an indirect (n) cost.

a. Wages of material handler who delivers parts to WIP
b. Final Assembly worker wages
c. Property taxes on the office building
d. Insurance on the factory
e. Setup screws that hold the compact solar panel in place
f. Wages of product inspector
g. Soap the janitor uses to clean the office building
h. Headlights for the compact model
i. Air-conditioning in plant cost accountant's office
j. Plant manager's salary
k. Employee parking lot
l. Wages of the person who files invoices and purchase orders
m. Rear wheel assembly for compact
n. Depreciation of pc computers in the Marketing department
o. Union steward wages

Exercise 6 Predetermined Overhead Rates. Discuss the reasons why firms use a predetermined overhead rate instead of actual overhead when computing the cost of manufacturing a job.

Exercise 7 Overhead Assignment. Explain how to apply overhead using the two-step process provided in Reading 2-4. Provide a numeric example illustrating how to assign overhead using this process.

Exercise 8 Variable versus Fixed Predetermined Overhead Rates. Explain the difference between variable and fixed overhead rates. State how each is computed and provide an example of both a variable and a fixed overhead cost.

Exercise 9 Predetermined Overhead Rates. Jensen Co. has estimated the following costs for next year. Each cost's behavior is indicated in parentheses. Jensen also estimates that 65,000 DLHs are required for next year's production. Jensen uses plantwide overhead rates with DLHs as the cost driver.

Direct materials (variable)	$3,500,000
Direct labor (variable)	1,250,000
General factory (fixed)	1,600,000
Maintenance (variable)	845,000
Inspection (fixed)	610,000

a. Compute both the variable and the fixed predetermined overhead rates for Jensen.
b. Compute both the variable and the fixed predetermined overhead rates for Jensen if the company estimates that 60,000 DLHs are required for next year's production.
c. Explain why the rates in b are different from those in a.

Exercise 10 Application of Overhead to Jobs. On July 8, 2002, Willows Corporation gives you the following accounting information for the year 2002 and the month of February 2002. Compute the manufacturing overhead costs allocated to Job 612, which will be started and completed during February 2002.

	Full Year 2002	February 2002
Estimated annual overhead	$10,000,000	$900,000
Estimated annual DLHs	500,000	40,000
Estimated DLHs, Job 612		4,500

Problems

Problem 1 Application of Overhead to Jobs. Garcia Products, Inc. estimates its manufacturing overhead to be $20,000 for the month of June and $217,000 for the year 2002. Garcia also estimates that DLHs for Job 1A will be 2,000, and for Job 6C, 3,500. Total DLHs are estimated to be 10,000 for June and 62,000 for the year 2002. Manufacturing overhead is applied to jobs based on DLHs. Estimate the overhead costs for Job 1A and Job 6C. Both jobs are to be started and completed in June 2002.

Problem 2 Application of Overhead to Jobs. Blanco Manufacturing produces batches of shutters for residence windows. The company estimates its variable manufacturing overhead to be $15,000 for the month of October and $120,000 for the year 2002. Fixed manufacturing overhead is expected to be $30,000 for the month of October and $360,000 for the year 2002. Blanco will work on three jobs during October and estimates that DLHs will be 12,000 for Job 203, 3,500 for Job 204, and 8,600 for Job 205. Total DLHs are estimated to be 26,000 for October, and 240,000 for the year 2002. Manufacturing overhead is applied to jobs based on DLHs. Estimate the variable, fixed, and total manufacturing overhead costs for Jobs 203, 204, and 205. All three jobs are to be started and completed in October 2002.

Problem 3 Application of Overhead to a Job and Units of Production. Portals, Inc. manufactures custom-ordered doors sold to building supply companies. Each job consists of a large batch of doors. Portals, Inc. uses DLHs as its overhead cost driver. The firm estimated the 2002 numbers below for its two overhead departments and one production department. Portals, Inc. is preparing to bid on a job of 2,000 doors that will be manufactured during January 2002 if they get the contract. Portals, Inc. estimates the job will take 8,500 DLHs and $277,000 in direct material to complete. Compute all estimated manufacturing costs for the Portals, Inc. job and the cost per door.

	January	Full Year
Maintenance	$280,000	$3,000,000
General factory	440,000	5,000,000
Total overhead	$720,000	$8,000,000
Direct material	$380,000	$4,500,000
Direct labor @ $22/hour	$363,000	$4,400,000
Direct labor hours	16,500	200,000

Problem 4 Application of Variable and Fixed Overhead to a Job and Units of Production. WrapAround manufactures bundles of custom-ordered fencing material suitable for enclosing small areas such as residential yards. Each job consists of sufficient fencing material to cover specified perimeters, fence posts, and gates. WrapAround uses DLHs as its overhead cost driver. The firm estimated the 2002 numbers below for its three overhead departments and one production department. WrapAround is preparing to bid on a job of 200 bundles ordered by a fence installation company. The job will be manufactured during November 2002 if they get the contract. WrapAround estimates the job will take 1,000 DLHs and $277,000 in direct material to complete. Compute all estimated manufacturing costs for the WrapAround job and the cost per fencing bundle.

	November	Full Year
Maintenance (variable)	$ 28,000	$ 300,000
Inspection (variable)	12,000	36,000
General factory (fixed)	40,000	500,000
Total overhead	$180,000	$ 836,000
Direct material	$380,000	$4,500,000
Direct labor @ $15/hour	$ 37,500	$ 420,000
Direct labor hours	2,500	28,000

Problem 5 Application of Overhead to Units of Production, Cost Per Unit. Manufacturing costs for Gazelle Autobike Makers, Inc. for the prior year follow. What was the total cost per unit to manufacture a motorbike last year? What are the predetermined variable, fixed, and total overhead rates for the coming year using last year's numbers as a basis? What is the expected total overhead per motorbike for the coming year if Gazelle estimates that production of one bike will take 18½ DLHs?

	Prior Year
Direct materials	$2,000,000
Direct labor wages	$2,250,000
Variable overhead	$ 225,000
Fixed overhead	$ 450,000
Direct labor hours	75,000
Number of bikes produced last year	4,000
Estimated number of bikes to be produced this year	4,054

Problem 6 Application of Overhead to Units of Production, Cost Per Unit. Manufacturing costs for Mighty Machine Works, Inc. for the prior year follow.

	Prior Year
Direct materials	$2,500,000
Direct labor wages	$2,160,000
Variable overhead	$ 320,000
Fixed overhead	$1,040,000
Direct labor hours	80,000
Number of machines produced last year	2,000
Estimated number of machines to be produced this year	2,150

a. What was the total cost per unit to manufacture a machine last year?
b. What are the predetermined variable, fixed, and total overhead rates for the coming year using last year's numbers as a basis?
c. What is the total expected overhead cost for the coming year using the predetermined rates computed in b above, assuming it takes Mighty workers the same amount of time as last year to make each machine, but that Mighty produces 2,150 instead of 2,000 machines? Why is total overhead different from last year?
d. Assume that Mighty estimates that production of one machine will take 38 DLHs this year instead of the amount of time it took them last year. Also assume that Mighty will use the same predetermined variable overhead rate as last year but will recompute the fixed overhead rate using the current year's total direct labor hours. What is the estimated variable, fixed, and total overhead per machine and the total estimated overhead for the current year for the production of 2,150 machines? Explain why the predetermined overhead rates and total estimated overhead are different than those in c above.

Case 2-4

DEVELOPMENT OF PRODUCT COST ESTIMATES FOR 2002

Case Objectives

1. Introduce the concept of predetermined overhead rates
2. Introduce product costing in a general way, using estimated costs for next year
3. Demonstrate the nature and flow of costs
4. Improve spreadsheet graphing skills

Decision (Planning): What costs of producing cars should be used in planning for 2002?

Note: In this case, CCC is preparing cost information for both planning and pricing purposes, which are addressed in more detail later in the course.

COST ESTIMATION

It is now December 2001, and you are assisting Mary Jones, head of accounting for CCC, in preparing manufacturing cost estimates for the company's sedan and compact vehicles. Mary needs product cost estimates in order to complete her preparation of projected financial statements for 2002. CCC plans to produce 5,100 sedans and 1,700 compacts in 2002. Mary explains: "I need you to figure out the amount of direct materials, direct labor, and manufacturing overhead that should be assigned to each car built next year based on our expected purchase costs, results of our recent labor wage negotiations, and expected overhead cost structure."

Direct Material and Direct Labor

Mary continues: "Direct materials for each car should be no problem. Our current bills of materials have been updated to reflect purchase prices that we expect to pay in 2002 for each part used in production." The bills of materials for sedan and compact models is presented in Exhibit C2-1.1. "Direct labor also is simple. Our production records show that it is presently taking about 108 hours of direct labor to produce a sedan, 52 hours in chassis assembly and 56 hours in final assembly. A compact requires 65 hours, 28 hours in chassis assembly and 37 hours in final assembly. We just completed negotiations for next year's wage and fringe package, and an average wage rate of $35 per direct labor hour will apply for 2002."

Manufacturing Overhead

Mary then tells you: "The development of overhead cost estimates for the sedan and compact, however, is not so simple. Our present cost system doesn't provide much detail on our overhead costs, and we don't yet have a good understanding of how overhead costs are influenced by changes in the ratio of sedans versus compacts produced each month."

"To get started on the overhead problem, let's take a look at this year's (2001) monthly data. Assume that overhead varies with the number of DLHs, so we can use direct labor as the measure of activity. Once we can come up with a reasonable formula for estimating total overhead for 2002, we can use that estimate to develop a predetermined overhead rate based on DLHs. That rate can then be used to assign a reasonable amount of estimated overhead to a sedan and to a compact. It is important for planning purposes, however, to develop the overhead rate in two components: fixed and variable."

Mary went back to her office and gathered all the overhead cost data for 2001 that she could find. She was able to develop data for variable manufacturing overhead for the first 10 months of 2001. Using the 10 months of variable manufacturing overhead data and discussions with production supervisors, Mary then estimated variable overhead for November and December. She presents you with a spreadsheet showing the total and variable overhead information she has developed (Exhibit C2-4.1).

Exhibit C2-4.1
California Car Company
Overhead Costs for 2001

Month	Direct Labor Hours	Manufacturing Overhead Total	Variable
January	3,475	$ 507,263	$ 137,263
February	3,265	497,335	127,335
March	4,430	542,770	172,770
April	5,400	577,900	207,900
May	8,470	683,390	313,390
June	7,920	667,000	297,000
July	8,910	696,106	326,106
August	9,360	706,960	336,960
September	9,900	726,400	356,400
October	13,180	818,120	448,120
November (Est.)	12,960	813,880	443,880
December (Est.)	12,730	802,876	432,876
Totals for 2001	**100,000**	**$ 8,040,000**	**$ 3,600,000**

Finally, Mary tells you: "Since we will not change the way we manufacture cars, and variable costs per unit remain constant as volume changes, the variable overhead rate per DLH should be about the same in 2002 as in 2001. Therefore, *you can get an estimated variable overhead rate for 2002 by taking the total variable overhead for 2001 (as shown in Exhibit C2-4.1) and dividing it by total DLHs for 2001.* Then you multiply this variable overhead rate by the total estimated DLHs for 2002 to get total estimated variable manufacturing overhead for the year 2002.

"With our major expansion this coming year, and with adding another building area for production, we have accumulated a large amount of fixed production costs. We have to incorporate these new fixed costs, as well as our variable overhead costs, into our manufacturing overhead cost estimates for the coming year. Therefore, we *cannot* use last year's actual fixed overhead as an estimate for this year." With the help of the production managers, Mary was able to determine that *fixed overhead* associated with production in 2002 is expected to total about $31,081,100.

You think to yourself, "What?" Luckily, you have written down exactly what Mary has said, so you go back to your office and attempt to develop formula relationships from her verbal instructions.

Requirements

Set up a computer spreadsheet in the format of Exhibit C2-4.2 to organize your work and to make the required calculations. Be sure to use formulas and cell references wherever possible so "what if" questions are easily answered. It is particularly important to use cell formulas in computing the predetermined variable and fixed overhead rates.

1. Develop a year 2002 estimate for direct labor for each car model assuming that (a) a sedan and compact require 108 and 65 hours of direct labor, respectively; and (b) direct labor employees will be paid $35 per hour. In other words, complete the outlined cells for three direct labor rows in Exhibit C2-4.2: Direct labor cost—sedan (cells C20–F20); Direct labor cost—compact (cells C29–F29); and Direct labor cost—total (cells D38–F38).
2. Determine if the data in Exhibit C2-4.1 indicate that DLHs is a good choice for a variable overhead activity measure. Use your spreadsheet software to graph the direct labor hour–variable overhead cost relationship. Instructions for using the Chart function in Excel are presented at the end of this case. In your chart, illustrate the relationship between DLHs and variable overhead and total overhead. Put DLH on the horizontal or X-axis and overhead costs on the vertical or Y-axis.
3. Regardless of your answer to requirement 2, assume that CCC allocates overhead on the basis of DLHs. Estimate the 2002 plantwide predetermined *variable* manufacturing overhead rate per hour based on the 2001 data presented in Exhibit C2-4.1. Enter your variable overhead estimate in the "Predetermined variable OH rate" cell (D13) on your spreadsheet. Then complete all three rows with a "Variable manufacturing overhead" label.
4. Enter the predetermined *fixed* manufacturing overhead in the "Predetermined fixed OH rate" cell (D14) on your spreadsheet. Estimate the plantwide predetermined fixed overhead rate per hour by using the formula below. The denominator must be entered by cell references only.

   $$\text{Predetermined Fixed overhead rate} = \frac{\text{Total estimated fixed overhead (\$31,081,100)}}{\text{Total 2002 estimated direct labor hours}}$$

   The total estimated direct labor hours for 2002 is found in Exhibit C2-4.1. You can now complete your spreadsheet by completing all three rows with a "Fixed manufacturing overhead" label and the three "Total" rows. At this point all of the blank cells in Exhibit C2-4.2 should be filled in. If your spreadsheet is missing has any blank cells, complete them now. Turn in a printout of your spreadsheet at this point and the spreadsheet formulas.
5. Sally Swanson believes that with some hard work and creative problem solving, the number of hours required to manufacture a sedan can be reduced to 103 DLHs in year 2002 instead of the 108 used in your estimates. The entire five-hour reduction would occur in final assembly. Prepare a new estimated 2002 product cost spreadsheet for CCC using 103 DLHs per sedan. Print out your new solution.

Exhibit C2-4.2
California Car Company
Estimated 2002 Product Costs

	A	B	C	D	E	F
5				**Per Unit**		
6				Chassis	Final	**Total**
7				Assembly	Assembly	
8	Direct materials—sedan			$ 1,220	$ 1,760	$ 2,980
9	Direct labor hours—sedan			52	56	108
10	Direct materials—compact			$ 750	$ 2,610	$ 3,360
11	Direct labor hours—compact			28	37	65
12	Direct labor wage rate =			$ 35.00		
13	Predetermined variable OH rate =					
14	Predetermined fixed OH rate =				(Use cell references for DLH)	
15				**TOTAL COSTS**		
16	**Sedan costs:**		Per	Chassis	Final	Total
17	Units produced:	5,100	Sedan	Assembly	Assembly	Sedan
18	Direct labor hours		108	265,200	285,600	550,800
19	Direct material		$ 2,980	$ 6,222,000	$ 8,976,000	$ 15,198,000
20	Direct labor cost					
21	Variable manufacturing overhead					
22	Fixed manufacturing overhead					
23	Total sedan costs					
24						
25	**Compact costs:**		Per	Chassis	Final	Total
26	Units produced:	1,700	Compact	Assembly	Assembly	Compact
27	Direct labor hours		65	47,600	62,900	110,500
28	Direct material		$ 3,360	$ 1,275,000	$ 4,437,000	$ 5,712,000
29	Direct labor cost					
30	Variable manufacturing overhead					
31	Fixed manufacturing overhead					
32	Total compact costs					
33						
34	**CCC Totals:**			Chassis	Final	CCC
35				Assembly	Assembly	Totals
36	Direct labor hours			312,800	348,500	661,300
37	Direct material			$ 7,497,000	$ 13,413,000	$ 20,910,000
38	Direct labor cost					
39	Variable manufacturing overhead					
40	Fixed manufacturing overhead					
41	Total manufacturing costs					

6. Explain why the cost per compact changes in Requirement 5 when the estimated DLHs to manufacture a sedan decreases.

7. George Olson believes that CCC can sell only 4,800 sedans instead of the 5,100 in the original cost estimate spreadsheet. For this question, assume that the estimated DLHs to manufacture a sedan are back to 108 hours. Prepare a new estimated 2002 product cost spreadsheet for CCC using a production level of 4,800 sedans instead of 5,100 sedans, with production of the compacts remaining the same. Print out your answer. Put 5,100 back in the sedan production cell.

8. Explain why the cost per compact changes in Requirement 7 when the estimated number of sedans sold decreases.

9. After reviewing the cost estimates, Sally Swanson, CCC's vice president of production, remarked: "Discussing all the costs mentioned above got me thinking about how we assign overhead costs to products. Currently, we assign overhead based on the direct labor hours used to produce a model. The sedan takes more than 1.5 times the direct labor hours to manufacture, so it is assigned 1.5 times the overhead cost. It appears to me, however, that some overhead costs such as the idle time due to setups or the time required to inspect and perform rework are about the same regardless of the model produced. Do you think our cost accounting system is accurately costing our cars?"

EXCEL CHART (GRAPH) INSTRUCTIONS

Spreadsheet graphical tools are powerful and effective ways to present numerical information. This case requires you to graph the relationship between manufacturing overhead costs and direct labor hours. In Excel spreadsheet software, graphing is done using the Chart function. The following are instructions for using the Excel 2000 Chart function on Case 2-4 data.

1. Create and save a spreadsheet with the DLHs and overhead cost data in Exhibit C2-4.1.
   a. Enter column headings in row 1 (e.g., enter direct labor hours in cell A1).
   b. Enter the direct labor hours, the X-axis data, in column A and overhead dollar amounts in columns B and C, formatting DLHs for commas (,) and costs for dollars ($).
2. Highlight the entire data area in columns A, B, and C, including the first row with column headings.
3. Select "Insert" from the top menu bar, and then go to the down arrow.
4. Select "Chart" from the pull-down menu.
5. Select "XY Scatter" on the next screen.
6. Select "Next" at the bottom of the next screen
7. Select "Series in: Columns" on the next screen (this should be the default setting).
8. Select "Next" at the bottom of the screen.
9. Type in titles for chart and axes.

(Chart instructions continued on the next page)

10. Select "Next" at the bottom of the screen.
11. Select "As Object in: Sheet 1" (or whatever you have named your sheet).
12. Select "Finish" at the bottom of the screen.
13. To have some fun customizing the graph, double click on any of the following areas:
    a. Axes numbers and titles (you probably will want to reduce the font size).
    b. The chart area (white area outside of plot and other writing).
    c. The plot area (colored area where the graph is).
    d. Experiment with "Borders, Area Colors, Fill Effects, Fonts, and Alignment."
    e. Click outside the chart area to delete the chart menu and return to the spreadsheet.
14. To print the graph, click on the graph area (you may want to remove the color background from the plot area first if you are printing in black and white).
    a. Select "File" from the top menu bar.
    b. Select "Page Setup" from the pull-down menu.
    c. Select "Chart" from the next pull-down menu.
    d. Select "Scale to Fit Page."
    e. Select "Print Preview" to view the graph as it will be printed or to change the format of the graph.
    f. Select "Print" from the pull-down menu.
    g. Select "OK" to print.
    h. *Note*: Some printers will not print a chart formatted in color.

Reading 2-5

PRICING AND PROFITABILITY DECISIONS

INTRODUCTION

Pricing decisions and related product or service profitability analyses are some of the most important issues faced by managers. Some companies face little or no competition and can set prices to build profits. Most businesses, however, must use discretion in determining prices so as not to lose sales to rivals. If firms facing competitive constraints set prices that are too high, they will lose sales, which in turn will result in decreased profits. For these same firms, prices that are set too low will not earn sufficient margins, which also will result in decreased profits. An example of a business that must use price discretion is a construction company or any other firm bidding on jobs. Pricing decisions are less important for firms that have little discretion in setting prices. Some companies are in such poor competitive positions that they are price takers and must accept the prices set by their rivals. Examples include most agricultural products and minerals, such as corn and gold. In these commodity industries, a seller must accept whatever price the market offers, and the only way to ensure a profit is to produce at a cost below the market price.

Product or service profitability analysis, commonly termed *product mix analysis*, is often critical. If a firm does not know which products are profitable, it will likely emphasize less profitable products at the expense of more profitable ones. Accurate product costing and relevant assignment of overhead is crucial for this analysis. This reading further illustrates the importance of using appropriate overhead application methods. Product costing, and its effect on pricing decisions for large corporations, also includes the study of internal, or transfer, pricing of units as they pass from one company division to another. Transfer pricing will be explained in more detail later in this reading.

Pricing and profitability decisions have two time horizons: long-term and special order, which is a short-term situation. Over the long term, a firm attempts to set prices so that sufficient revenue is earned to cover all costs and earn an acceptable profit. In some situations, however, a firm may be better off accepting a special order at a price that does not cover full product costs. This reading first explores long-term pricing and provides information and formulas that will help you solve the requirements of Case 2-5. The reading then discusses the conditions that should be present for firms taking advantage of short-term special orders. Group Assignment 2-5 requires you to be familiar with the content of this second discussion.

LONG-TERM PRICING

CCC and other firms that are in business to earn a profit must sell their goods and services at prices that ultimately cover all costs and leave a margin of profit. To establish selling prices, firms should consider the following factors:

- Competition
- Customers
- Constraints, both legal and political
- Costs

Competition

Consider the situation faced by CCC. Competition in the automobile industry is both domestic and foreign. As some car manufacturers have discovered, it may prove difficult to manufacture an automobile overseas, ship it over 10,000 miles to the United States, pay the appropriate import duties and taxes, and still sell it at a price that is lower than domestically manufactured cars.

If one competitor reduces the selling price on a vehicle, other firms may have to follow simply to retain their share of the market. However, no firm can lower its price to a point below cost for more than a short time and expect to remain in business.

As a means of reducing competition, many firms try to differentiate their products from those of their competitors. For example, both Ford and Toyota manufacture sport utility vehicles (SUVs). Some of Ford's SUVs are built on a truck chassis that rides high like a truck. In contrast, a Toyota SUV is built on a car chassis and rides lower like a car.

In setting its prices, CCC must carefully identify its competition. Does it compete with the major U.S. automakers? Are foreign-made vehicles also part of the competition? Must CCC match the price of its competitors or can it differentiate its vehicles and charge higher prices? CCC must consider both its competition and its customers in determining the prices of its cars.

Customers

The tastes and preferences of customers must be given careful consideration in bringing LEVs to market. CCC offers two models. The full-sized sedan is powered by a small gasoline engine, electric motor, and motor-rechargeable batteries. The compact runs with an even smaller gasoline engine, the same electric motor as the sedan, batteries, and solar energy. Will customers accept these LEVs? Customer compromises will be inherent with the hybrid. Is the American public willing to forgo the speed of high-powered engines and the capability to carry large loads of material possessions and people? If so, how much are they willing to pay for such vehicles?

Constraints

Legal and political constraints often limit a company's pricing practices. For example, U.S. laws prohibit companies from discriminating, without a cost justification, among customers in setting prices. Laws also prohibit collusion, in which several companies secretly agree upon the same price to be charged by all.

Political constraints are those favorable and unfavorable actions of governmental bodies that affect the marketing and/or pricing of products. In CCC's case, political constraints are positive and include the state government's policy to encourage LEV manufacture by giving favored tax status to companies producing LEVs and tax rebates to customers who purchase such cars. An undesirable action from other countries would be a deliberate increase in gasoline prices driven by government-restricted production in some oil-producing countries. A government may take such action to increase revenue or enhance its political or global market position. A worldwide increase in prices may make LEVs attractive to customers in all countries.

Costs

The previous discussion on competition mentioned that in the automotive industry, firms have some control over prices to be charged for goods and services. Although these companies are driven in pricing decisions by competition and customers, they have the opportunity and latitude to select **target prices,** or proposed prices, that hopefully customers will accept and rivals will not undercut. Target prices, once selected, drive the company to achieve estimated costs, called **target costs**, that permit a desired profit. These cost objectives usually are lower than existing production and selling costs. Target costing also promotes improved product design and production processes. Target costs are computed by subtracting a desired profit margin from the previously selected target price. In other words, management first determines the optimal target price and profit margin, then computes the target costs. The concept of target costing as a method to control product development costs is complex and is covered in depth in upper-level cost accounting classes.

Pricing policies as discussed in the previous section are part of a strategy called a market-based approach. A second and more traditional method takes an opposite stance by first computing product costs and then determining a price to cover costs and produce a profit. This second strategy, as you might have guessed, is called a cost-based approach and will be discussed next.

Traditional Approach to Long-Term Pricing Decisions

Economists have developed various models for selecting an appropriate price under varying market conditions. Such models make use of supply and demand functions, total revenue and total cost curves, and marginal revenue and marginal cost curves. Because it is difficult to apply economic concepts of supply and demand in practice, most companies make pricing and product profitability decisions using simplified, cost-based pricing formulas. These firms first determine price on the basis of the costs to produce and sell the product, then adjust the price to meet customer reaction to competitors' alternative prices. Cost-based or **cost-plus pricing** methods simply add a percentage of a product cost base to that cost base to cover other nonmanufacturing expenses and profit. Cost plus the addition, or **markup,** determines price. Cost-based pricing formulas can provide a quick method for setting prices if product costs are known. Indeed, lacking sophisticated market information, cost-based pricing formulas provide a good starting point for establishing prices. Ultimately, cost sets the bottom limit for prices; selling prices cannot remain indefinitely below cost if a firm intends to remain in business. The cost-plus procedures that will be discussed in this reading are labeled the *traditional approach* because, until recently, most firms used it to make computations that support pricing and profitability decisions.

Within the last decade many more sophisticated firms have begun using activity-based costing (ABC) to provide a more accurate cost basis for cost-plus pricing. ABC will be discussed in Module 3. One key difference between traditional and ABC approaches is the way in which selling and administrative expenses affect the pricing decision. In the traditional approach all selling and administrative costs, as well as profit, are covered in a markup percentage that is added on to product costs to arrive at a sales price. No effort is made to assign selling and administrative costs directly to the product. ABC, on the other hand, attempts to determine the level of selling and administrative costs a product uses, and assigns that cost to the product. Using an ABC approach is similar to the direct assignment of direct materials and direct labor dollars to products as described in Reading 2-4. In an ABC system, the markup percentage is used primarily to cover profit.

Why does the traditional approach make no effort to relate selling and administrative costs back to products? The answer is that traditional accounting systems, as discussed in this module, separate all operating costs into either *product costs* (direct materials, direct labor, and manufacturing overhead) or *period costs* (all other company costs). Therefore, a traditional accounting system does not contain the necessary information to assign selling and administrative costs more accurately.

Using Cost-Plus (Cost-Based) Pricing Formulas to Make Decisions

What if a firm has little discretion in setting prices? In such a situation do firms use cost-based calculations? The answer is that most firms use cost-plus analysis even if the market sets a selling price and the price does not cover their entire product cost plus markup. Why? Because firms need to know which product and service sales are covering costs and earning an acceptable profit and which ones are not. If a product is selling above its cost plus a markup, it is a product that probably should be pushed and likely should receive additional investment. Conversely, products that cannot consistently be sold at the computed cost-plus markup price require management's attention. Examples of management action triggered by profitability analysis include cost reduction efforts, product feature enhancement so the product can command a higher price, or discontinuance of the product.

In the actual business world firms use a wide variety of different cost-based pricing formulas. In some cases, a company may use only "direct materials" as the cost in developing prices. For example, a local grocery store might determine from trade journals that a normal markup is 25 percent above costs, and mark up its "produce" acquired from a wholesaler for a cost of $1.00 to a retail price of $1.25. In other cases, a company's cost-based pricing formula may be quite complex, taking into account a host of different cost factors. Major manufacturing industries, such as automobiles, household appliances, and retail gasoline stations, use such complex formulas.

Cost-based pricing formulas also are used by companies that are open to public inspection and criticism. For example, public utilities usually establish prices on a cost-plus basis. As a result, cost often is the major point of issue when companies, such as Pacific Gas & Electric or Bell South, appear before public utilities commissions to determine a fair measure of "cost" and a reasonable markup.

In this module, we will not attempt to consider the multitude of different cost-based pricing formulas found in practice. Our purpose is to introduce the concept of a cost-based pricing formula and show how it may be used as a first step in setting prices and analyzing product profitability. Do not forget that firms still consider the other factors of competition, customers, and legal and political constraints in determining prices.

Determining Prices Using Cost-Plus (Cost-Based) Formulas

A cost-plus pricing formula may be expressed in two equivalent formats: using total sales revenue and total cost base or using unit sales price and unit cost base. Both provide the same markup or sales revenue numbers. The two equations are:

1. Total sales revenue and total cost base format:
   Sales revenue = Cost + (Markup percentage × Cost)

   Restated: $\text{Markup percentage} = \dfrac{\text{Revenue} - \text{Cost base}}{\text{Cost base}}$

2. Unit price and unit cost base format:
   Unit sales price = Unit cost + (Markup percentage × Unit cost)

   Restated: $\text{Markup percentage} = \dfrac{\text{Unit sales price} - \text{Unit cost base}}{\text{Unit cost base}}$

Determining the Cost Base in Cost-Plus Pricing Formulas

We will examine four possible measures of cost bases that may be used in the above formulas. One possibility is to define the cost base in terms of only *variable manufacturing costs*. A second possibility is to define the cost base as all *variable and fixed manufacturing costs*, or *total manufacturing cost*. A third possibility is to define the cost base as only *total variable costs*. In this context, total means the sum of variable manufacturing and selling and administrative costs. Finally, a fourth possibility is to define the cost base *as total variable plus total fixed costs*, which is often referred to as *full product cost*. These possibilities are summarized in Exhibit 2-5.1 below and illustrated through the Almendia Example in Exhibit 2-5.2 later in this module.

Exhibit 2-5.1

Measures Used In Cost-Plus Pricing Formulas

- Variable product or manufacturing cost base
- Total manufacturing cost base (variable and fixed)
- Total variable cost base (manufacturing, selling and administrative)
- Full product cost base (fixed and variable manufacturing, selling and administrative)

Why are four different cost bases introduced? The answer is that all four bases are used in practice. A grocery store may use *acquisition cost* of goods, a variable product cost, as a base since it is readily available from purchase transaction information. A grocery store manager knows the exact cost per unit paid for produce and canned goods. In contrast, an automobile manufacturer might use total (variable and fixed) manufacturing cost as a base for its long-term pricing strategy and total variable cost for short-term special orders as will be discussed below. Although total manufacturing cost is the most common cost base used in practice, some manufacturing firms, as well as almost all retail firms, use only variable product or manufacturing cost because it does not require subjective allocations of fixed costs. Note that *total product line* or *firm costs* are normally used to determine markup percentage.

Answers Obtained Using Cost-Plus Computations

The objective of cost-plus pricing formulas can be twofold. The computations can be used to determine sales revenue, given a known markup percentage, or to determine the markup percentage given a desired dollar amount of profit, return on assets, or market position.

Frequently companies use revenue and cost numbers from prior income statements to determine a desired sales price or markup percentage. Typically, setting an individual product's markup percentage and price is a two-step process:

1. Determine a target markup percentage for all similar products based on desired profitability or industry norms. Frequently firms use revenue and cost numbers from prior income statements to determine a desired sales price or markup percentage. For example, a bookstore may establish a desired markup percentage for all textbooks.
2. Compute a selling price for each product based on the markup percentage determined in Step 1. For example, if a publisher sells a book for $30, the bookstore will try to price it at $39 [$30 + (.30 × $30)].

Determining the Markup Percentage

Given whatever cost base is used in a cost-plus formula, an appropriate markup percentage must be chosen in light of management's profit goal. In short, the markup percentage must be sufficient to cover all costs incurred by the firm and also provide the desired profit. As discussed earlier, a firm may be a price taker or at best have some price discretion. The company will look to the market average for markup percentages in deriving their own profit and sales prices. Data on industry markups appear in numerous sources, including information from government agencies, Dun & Bradstreet Key Business Ratios, Manufacturing USA, and Almanac of Business and Industrial Financial Ratios. If the firm has some price discretion, its desired return on total assets can serve as a tool to determine the profit goal in cost-plus pricing.

The following Almendia Corporation example will illustrate these ideas. Almendia desires a 20 percent return on total assets of $500,000. The cost structure for Almendia Co. is presented in Exhibit 2-5.2, where total manufacturing costs equal $180,000 and total selling and administrative costs are $64,000. In this case, desired profit is given by the following:

Desired profit = Average total assets × Desired return on total assets
= $500,000 × .2
= $100,000

Exhibit 2-5.2
Component Cost Items in Cost Bases
Almendia Example Cost Numbers

	Cost Bases			
	Variable Manufacturing Cost	**Total Manufacturing Cost**	**Total Variable Cost**	**Full Product Costs**
Direct materials	$ 48,000	$ 48,000	$ 48,000	$ 48,000
Direct labor	32,000	32,000	32,000	32,000
Variable overhead	20,000	20,000	20,000	20,000
Fixed manufacturing costs		80,000		80,000
Variable selling and administrative			24,000	24,000
Fixed selling and administrative				40,000
Total cost base	$ 100,000	$ 180,000	$ 124,000	$ 244,000

Note that desired revenue must be equal to the cost base (total manufacturing cost in this example) plus other costs, and plus desired profit as computed in the following equation:

$$\begin{aligned}\text{Revenue} &= \text{Total manufacturing cost} + \text{Selling and admin. costs} + \text{Desired profit}\\ &= \$180{,}000 + (\$24{,}000 + \$40{,}000) + \$100{,}000\\ &= \$344{,}000\end{aligned}$$

Recall that the markup percentage formula based on total sales revenue and total cost base is:

$$\text{Markup percentage} = \frac{\text{Total revenue} - \text{Total cost base}}{\text{Total cost base}}$$

In our example, the target markup percentage is computed as follows:

$$\text{Target markup} = \frac{\$344{,}000 - \$180{,}000}{\$180{,}000} = .9111$$

If, instead of using total manufacturing cost as a base, Almendia chose to use the variable manufacturing cost of $100,000 as the base, then the desired markup percentage would be determined as follows:

$$\text{Desired markup} = \frac{\text{Revenue} - \text{Variable manufacturing cost}}{\text{Variable manufacturing cost}}$$

$$= \frac{\$344{,}000 - \$100{,}000}{\$100{,}000} = 2.44$$

As you can see, the markup percentage is approximately 244 percent as applied to variable manufacturing cost. The percentage in this case is much higher because the markup now must be sufficiently large to cover all of Almendia's variable selling and administrative costs of $24,000 and its fixed costs of $120,000 plus its profit goal of $100,000.

Pricing an Individual Product. Information in Exhibit 2-5.3 is drawn from the accounting records of Almendia Corporation and relates to the production of its product.

Exhibit 2-5.3
Almendia Product Cost Information

Direct material	$ 12.00
Direct labor	8.00
Variable manufacturing overhead	5.00
Fixed manufacturing overhead	20.00
Total cost	$ 45.00

The markup percentage for Almendia based on total manufacturing costs is 91.11 per cent, as computed earlier. Therefore, the target selling price for each unit of product is:

$$\text{Target price} = \text{Cost base} + (\text{Markup percentage} \times \text{Cost base})$$

$$\text{Target price} = \$45 + (.9111 \times \$45)$$

$$\text{Target price} = \$86 \text{ (rounded)}$$

If Almendia can sell a unit for $86 or more, the product will be making its contribution to corporate profit. If Almendia cannot sell its product for $86, management will need to explore ways of improving the product's profitability.

Transfer Pricing

Large, divisionalized firms frequently establish multiple business units, or profit centers, that are evaluated, at least partially, on their reported income. These divsionalized firms face a second pricing problem in addition to the competition and customer pricing issues addressed earlier. They also must set prices on goods and services sold by one division to another. Pricing of internal sales is called **transfer pricing**. If there is a significant level of intra-company sales, how transfer prices are set may have a major impact on product pricing decisions for sales to external customers and will definitely affect how divisions operate and work with one another.

In general, if the goods and services being transferred have a readily determinable market price, then the market price should be the transfer price. However, goods and services transferred often have no clear market price, so one must be established arbitrarily. In practice, most transfer prices are based on one of the cost bases illustrated in Exhibit 2-5.1 and often include a percentage markup to cover other costs and profit. The organizational structure of CCC is not sufficiently large or complex to include profit centers. You should be familiar, however, with the term transfer pricing so that you will be prepared for more advanced courses, such as production management, that will expect you to have this knowledge base.

This section has discussed how firms to be successful in the long term must sell their goods and services at prices that ultimately cover all costs and leave a margin of profit. Also, four significant factors above and beyond profit influence pricing decisions: competition, customers, legal and political constraints, and costs. Next we will see that these are not the only elements of importance involved in short-term pricing decisions. Sometimes, a company may sell its product or service at a reduced price for a **special order**.

SPECIAL ORDER PRICING

The extent to which a firm should engage in special order pricing is controversial. Some experts recommend that special orders should be pursued aggressively any time a firm is operating below capacity. Proponents of a management philosophy known as the theory of constraints argue more specifically that any special order that does not pass through a bottleneck should be considered seriously. Others, including many who subscribe to the total quality management philosophy discussed in Module 3, argue that customer relations should be long term in nature and should not be focused primarily on price. They believe special order pricing diverts management from more important issues and use the example of airline pricing wars, explained later, as an example of what is wrong with special order pricing.

Required Conditions for Special Orders

Although a firm usually must cover all costs and earn an acceptable rate of return in the long term to remain in business, under certain conditions it may be profitable to accept special orders at a sales price well below the cost-plus target number. Conditions required for special order pricing normally include the following:

1. The firm is operating below full capacity,
2. The order will not affect current or future sales,
3. The order should represent only a small portion of total sales, and
4. The order does not violate pricing laws.

Some market and firm circumstances would not be conducive to special orders. For instance, special orders should not be filled if they displace other orders or increase fixed costs. They should be one-time-only sales. Other difficulties exist if the sale is to an existing customer who may purchase at the full price anyway, or if other current customers will demand a lower price when they find out about the special order. In these instances, the special order is unattractive. Also, if a lower price will harm the product's high-quality or exclusive image with customers, the special order can be harmful.

The ideal special order situation is to sell to a market segment that a firm does not currently serve. This can be a geographic location, distribution channel, or some other form of market segmentation. An example of an ideal market segment is a foreign market in which a firm does not ordinarily operate. If a firm does not sell its goods through discount stores, another way to segment a market is to relabel a product and sell it to chains such as Sam's Club.

One example of an attempt to segment a domestic market is the U.S. airline industry. Airlines try to create separate business traveler and casual traveler segments out of the total airline passenger market by instituting restrictions on purchasing discounted tickets that business travelers find difficult to meet. The idea is to apply special order pricing to the casual traveler segment to fill undercapacity flights, while charging business travelers full fare. During the 1980s and early 1990s, this pricing strategy led to devastating price wars, causing billions of dollars of losses for the major airlines. A big problem was the ability of many business travelers to modify travel plans in order to qualify for lower fares. In essence, the airlines allowed many of their full-fare business customers to fly on discounted rates, which violates condition 2 in the previous list.

The basic concept behind special order pricing is that a firm's total net income will increase if it can sell a special order at a price that is greater than its *incremental*, or *out-of-pocket*, costs for the order. Incremental describes those costs that will be added to total costs when at least one unit of the special order is produced. In most instances these additional costs include the variable costs of the special order plus any additional costs required to complete the sale. Variable costs, as you probably remember, include direct materials, direct labor, variable manufacturing overhead, and variable selling. Incremental variable costs could also include nonmanufacturing costs such as delivery charges. An example of an additional cost that usually is considered a fixed cost but occurs only because of the special order is a machine purchased to make the specified order. Previously incurred fixed costs of the firm remain the same whether the order is accepted or not and are not considered in computing the margin that the special order contributes to the company's net income.

Special Order Example

Reproduced in Exhibit 2-5.4 is the accounting information for Almendia Company that was presented earlier. Assume that Almendia is operating well below capacity and has the opportunity to sell a special order of 200 units of product to a customer in Italy at a price of $60 per unit. The customer will do the final assembly of the product, which will save Almendia $0.50 per unit in direct labor. However, Almendia must purchase a special stamping machine for $2,000 to print the customer's name and logo on the product. The stamping machine will be worthless to Almendia after the special order is complete. Almendia does not normally market its product in Italy, and the special order does not violate any of the other conditions listed previously. Should Almendia accept the special order and, if it is accepted, by how much would net income change? Note that the problem is simplified because Almendia sells only one product. A multiproduct firm normally would not know the amount of fixed selling and administrative costs associated with an individual product.

Exhibit 2-5.4
Full Product Cost
Almendia Company

	Per Unit	Total
Regular sales revenue	$ 86.00	$ 344,000
Direct material	$ 12.00	$ 48,000
Direct labor	8.00	32,000
Variable manufacturing overhead	5.00	20,000
Fixed manufacturing overhead	20.00	80,000
Total manufacturing costs	$ 45.00	$ 180,000
Variable selling and administrative costs	6.00	24,000
Fixed selling and administrative costs	10.00	40,000
Full product cost	$ 61.00	$ 244,000

The correct, short financial analysis for Almendia is as shown in Exhibit 2-5.5.

Exhibit 2-5.5
Special Order Total Incremental Costs and Revenue
Almendia Company

	Per Unit		Total (200 units)	
Sales revenue		$ 60.00		$ 12,000
Direct material	$ 12.00		$ 2,400	
Direct labor ($8.00 – $0.50 savings)	7.50		1,500	
Variable manufacturing overhead	5.00		1,000	
Variable selling and administrative costs	6.00		1,200	
Total incremental variable costs		30.50		6,100
Margin before incremental fixed cost		$ 29.50		$ 5,900
Incremental fixed cost (stamping machine)				2,000
Increase in Almendia's net income				$ 3,900

Notice that the incremental costs include only those costs that will change or be added because the special order is filled. Prior fixed manufacturing overhead and fixed selling and administrative costs are *not* included in the analysis. Only the fixed cost of the stamping machine is included and is added in its entirety since it cannot be used for any other purpose.

An even quicker method of computing the increase in net income is to compute the margin contributed by one unit of the special order, to multiply that margin by the number of units produced, and then subtract any incremental fixed costs, as shown in Exhibit 2-5.6.

To prove that the special order increases Almendia's net income by $3,900, before and after special order income statements are presented in Exhibit 2-5.7. As expected, Almendia's income after the special order is $3,900 greater than before. Although Almendia is better off financially, managers should consider many other factors before deciding to accept the special order. Customers may expect special orders to be repeated. Making a series of short-term decisions to accept special orders equates to a long-term decision in actuality, which results in lack of coverage of full product costs.

Exhibit 2-5.6
Calculation of Incremental Margin per Unit
Almendia Company

	Per Unit
Sales revenue	$ 60.00
Direct material	$ 12.00
Direct labor ($8.00 – $0.50 savings)	7.50
Variable manufacturing overhead	5.00
Variable selling and administrative costs	6.00
Total incremental variable costs	$ 30.50
Unit margin before incremental fixed cost	$ 29.50
Times the number of units produced	× 200
Total margin	$ 5,900
Less incremental fixed cost (stamping machine)	(2,000)
Increase in Almendia's net income	$ 3,900

Exhibit 2-5.7
Income Statements Before and After Special Order
Almendia Company

	Before Special Order	**After Special Order**
Sales revenue	$ 344,000	$ 356,000
Direct material	$ 48,000	$ 50,400
Direct labor	32,000	33,500
Variable manufacturing overhead	20,000	21,000
Fixed manufacturing overhead	80,000	82,000
Total manufacturing costs	$ 180,000	$ 186,900
Variable selling and administrative costs	24,000	25,200
Fixed selling and administrative costs	40,000	40,000
Full product cost	$ 244,000	$ 252,100
Net income	$ 100,000	$ 103,900

Make-or-Buy Decisions

Another use of incremental costing is the **make-or-buy** decision that, instead of being a sales decision, is a purchasing decision. Management makes the same analysis of out-of-pocket costs and contribution to profit as that performed with special orders. Let us suppose that Almendia is trying to decide whether to make the key component of its product, as it does currently, or to buy it from an outsider. Sometimes another firm can produce products more inexpensively because of expertise and larger production schedules that provide higher contributions to cover fixed costs and build profits.

Almendia's total manufacturing cost for the component is $13.60. Diaz Manufacturing has offered to make the component and sell it to Almendia at the special price of $10.00 per unit, which looks like a savings of $3.60. Almendia would be able to reduce its direct costs in material by $7.00 per unit and direct labor by $1.60 per unit. Variable overhead costs would decrease by $1.00 per unit. No savings in equipment or facilities, however, would occur. If management looks strictly at the component's total (fixed and variable) manufacturing cost, they may view buying the component as the lower-cost alternative.

Would fixed manufacturing overhead change or remain the same? You probably realize that since there are no changes in equipment or facilities, fixed costs will remain the same. The correct analysis for Almendia if they choose to buy the component instead of making it is presented in Exhibit 2-5.8. Note that the buy alternative is $0.40 per component more costly than the make alternative.

Exhibit 2-5.8
Full Product Cost of Make-or-Buy
Diaz Manufacturing

	Make Costs Per Unit	Buy Costs Per Unit
Regular sales revenue	$ 86.00	$ 86.00
Direct material	$ 12.00	$ 5.00
Direct labor	8.00	6.40
Variable manufacturing overhead	5.00	4.00
Purchase price from Diaz Manufacturing	0.00	10.00
Fixed manufacturing overhead	20.00	20.00
Total manufacturing costs	$ 45.00	$ 45.40
Variable selling and administrative costs	6.00	6.00
Fixed selling and administrative costs	10.00	10.00
Full product cost	$ 61.00	$ 61.40

A shorter analysis is to look only at the incremental costs, or those costs that change if one unit is purchased instead of made. The incremental analysis is presented as Exhibit 2-5.9.

Exhibit 2-5.9
Incremental Margin of Make-or-Buy
Diaz Company

	Make Costs Per Unit	Buy Costs Per Unit
Regular sales revenue	$ 86.00	$ 86.00
Direct material	$ 12.00	$ 5.00
Direct labor	8.00	6.40
Variable manufacturing overhead	5.00	4.00
Purchase price from Diaz Manufacturing	0.00	10.00
Total incremental costs	$ 25.00	$ 25.40
Incremental margin	$ 61.00	$ 60.60

SUMMARY

Firm managers must consider both competitive constraints and profit objectives in pricing their products. Some companies are forced to be price takers but others may use some discretion in setting prices both in the long term and for special orders in the short term. Reading 2-5 presents four primary factors—competition, customers, legal and political constraints, and costs—that managers must consider in establishing sales prices. The reading prepares the student for Case 2-5 by explaining the traditional, or cost-plus, method in detail and illustrates the computations involved in applying cost-based pricing formulas through an example, the Almendia Company. Almendia Company is also used to discuss how managers use incremental analysis in determining the profitability of special orders and make-or-buy decisions.

EXERCISES AND PROBLEMS

Exercises

Exercise 1 Cost Bases by Cost Components. Management accountants often classify a firm's operating expenses into six components: (1) direct materials, (2) direct labor, (3) variable manufacturing overhead, (4) fixed manufacturing overhead, (5) variable selling and administrative expenses, and (6) fixed selling and administrative expenses. For each of the following cost bases, provide the numbers for the cost components that constitute that base. More than one number may apply to each cost base.

a. Variable product or manufacturing cost
b. Total manufacturing costs
c. Total variable costs
d. Full product cost

Exercise 2 Markup and Sales Price. Cashmere Sweaters, Inc. is extremely concerned about the competition in their industry. The company wants to remain competitive, but also wants to make an annual sales revenue of at least $500,000. All sweaters are priced the same since there is little quality differentiation. Expected annual cost information follows. Assuming Cashmere uses full product cost to arrive at its sales price per sweater, compute its markup percentage and its desired sales price per sweater assuming that it sells at least 10,000 sweaters.

Variable manufacturing expenses	$200,000
Variable selling and administrative expenses	40,000
Fixed manufacturing expenses	100,000
Fixed selling and administrative expenses	80,000

Exercise 3 Sales Revenue and Profitability. Cashmere Sweaters, Inc. is extremely concerned about its profit margin. The company currently uses a markup percentage of 147 percent on variable manufacturing costs. The industry average sales price for a similar sweater is $50 and the firm wants to remain competitive. All sweaters are priced the same since there is little quality differentiation. Expected annual cost information is as follows:

Variable direct and indirect manufacturing expenses	$200,000
Variable selling and administrative expenses	40,000
Fixed manufacturing expenses	100,000
Fixed selling and administrative expenses	80,000

a. Compute Cashmere's expected sales revenue using its current markup percentage and assuming it expects to sell 10,000 sweaters. Will Cashmere remain competitive?
b. Will Cashmere remain profitable if it changes its sales price per sweater to $48?

Exercise 4 Markup and Sales Price. NoCrash Computers, Inc. is extremely concerned about the competition in its industry. The company has tried to manufacture a reliable but inexpensive line of computers. In order to focus on quality, the firm produces only one model. The target sales revenue for next year is $3,750,000. Expected cost information follows. Assuming NoCrash uses total manufacturing cost to arrive at its sales price per computer, calculate the markup percentage and desired sales price per unit assuming 2,500 computers are sold.

Variable direct and indirect manufacturing expenses	$1,500,000
Variable selling and administrative expenses	300,000
Fixed manufacturing expenses	750,000
Fixed selling and administrative expenses	600,000

Exercise 5 Sales Revenue and Profitability. NoCrash Computers, Inc. is extremely concerned about its profit margin. The company currently uses a markup percentage of 125 percent on total variable costs. The company has tried to manufacture a reliable but inexpensive line of computers. In order to focus on quality, the firm produces only one model. The industry average sales price for a similar computer is $1,450 and the firm wants to remain competitive. Expected annual cost information for the manufacture of 2,500 computers is as follows:

Variable direct and indirect manufacturing expenses	$1,500,000
Variable selling and administrative expenses	300,000
Fixed manufacturing expenses	750,000
Fixed selling and administrative expenses	600,000

a. Will NoCrash remain competitive at a sales price using the current markup percentage assuming it expects to sell 2,500 computers?

b. Compute NoCrash's expected profit using its current markup percentage and assuming it expects to sell 2,500 computers. Will NoCrash remain profitable if it adjusts its sales price to the industry average of $1,450?

Exercise 6 Relevant Costs. Mr. and Mrs. Rodriguez want to buy a larger home in expectation of an approaching increase in family, but money is tight. They are disgusted with their present house that has cost them many dollars in repairs and is in a poor school district. Two years ago they replaced the roof for $3,000. All rooms have been repainted and the carpeting has been replaced. These repairs cost the Rodriguez family approximately $4,000. Mrs. Rodriguez has found a newer home in an excellent school district and wants to place a down payment of $5,000 on the house. Mr. Rodriguez is hesitant to move since they have put so much into the old house due to all the repairs. House payments would remain about the same amount but the family would have to put another $1,000 into the old house to make it attractive to possible buyers. Real estate agents tell them that, due to current economic conditions, they can expect to receive only $4,000 in a down payment and that buyers would want to finance the rest of the purchase price. What are the relevant costs to the decision of buying the new house? Be sure to discuss the relevancy of all given costs and reasons why or why not such costs are relevant. What is your recommendation to Mr. and Mrs. Rodriguez?

Exercise 7 Relevant Costs. Your university has been considering a new computer lab system that will have faster modems, faster printers, and intelligent, helpful, and understanding student assistants to help students. Amazingly, the new lab may not result in increased costs due to the declining prices of computer hardware and the decrease in time that students will spend with faculty with their computer problems. Information regarding present university costs and those expected with the new system is as follows:

	Present System	New System
Original cost	$ 500,000	$ 300,000
Annual cash operating costs	50,000	65,000
Depreciation of computers and printers	100,000	100,000
Faculty salaries	13,000,000	13,500,000
Salvage value of equipment	1,000	500
Fixed utility expenses for lab	2,500	2,250

State which costs are relevant to the university in trying to decide whether to build the new computer lab. State why each listed cost is or is not relevant. Do not discuss non-monetary benefits such as the easing of student stress.

Exercise 8 Special Order Pricing with Incremental Fixed Costs. The per unit income statement for the production and sale of 20,000 units of mini refrigerators by Placido, Inc. follows. The production of the units is within Placido's relevant range.

Sales price	$ 1,100
Variable manufacturing expenses	380
Variable selling and administrative expenses	120
Contribution margin	$600
Fixed manufacturing expenses	200
Fixed selling and administrative expenses	300
Income	$100

A potential customer in Russia has offered to make a one-time purchase of 1,000 customized refrigerators at a price of $550 each. It costs Placido an average of $1,000 per unit to manufacture and sell a unit. If Placido accepts the special order, it will have to purchase a new customized paint machine for $55,000 that will be scrapped because it cannot be used for any other production. Placido currently does not sell any products abroad. The Russian customer is not likely to purchase from Placido on a regular basis and will not purchase a refrigerator for more than $550. Will Placido's net income increase or decrease if the special order is accepted?

Exercise 9 Make-or-Buy Decision. Multi-Plex Company is considering buying a major component for its product, Plexi-Plate, instead of making it in-house. The supplier of the component would sell the part to Multi-Plex for $44.36 per unit. Multi-Plex per-unit costs for producing the part are as follows:

Direct material	$ 22.66
Direct labor	15.95
Variable manufacturing overhead	12.75
Fixed manufacturing overhead (constant)	5.90
Total costs relating to component	$57.26

a. What are the relevant costs for the make-or-buy decision?

b. Should Multi-Plex buy the component from the supplier or make it in-house?

Problems

Problem 1 Markup on Cost. The 2002 contribution income statement for Dunsmuir Company is as follows:

Sales	$15,000,000
Variable manufacturing expenses	6,900,000
Variable selling and administrative expenses	1,350,000
Contribution margin	$ 6,750,000
Fixed manufacturing expenses	3,050,000
Fixed selling and administrative expenses	1,700,000
Net income	$ 2,000,000

Compute Dunsmuir's markup on cost for each of the following cost bases:

a. Total manufacturing cost
b. Total variable costs
c. Variable manufacturing costs
d. Full product cost

Problem 2 Markup on Cost. The 2002 sales and cost per unit information for Dunsmuir Company is as follows:

Sales price	$150.00
Variable manufacturing expenses	$ 70.00
Variable selling and administrative expenses	$ 13.50
Fixed manufacturing expenses	$ 31.00
Fixed selling and administrative expenses	$ 17.00

Compute Dunsmuir's markup on cost for each of the following cost bases:

a. Total manufacturing cost
b. Total variable costs
c. Variable manufacturing costs
d. Full product cost

Problem 3 Markup on Cost. Williamson Wire manufactures and sells cables to utility companies for use in laying electric and telephone lines. The company wants to submit a bid to a smaller utility company in the south of the state to supply 520,000 linear feet of cable. All contracts with utility entities are written as cost-plus using full product cost per foot. The utility has stated firmly that a bid in excess of $26 per foot of cable will be rejected. Williamson is used to making a return of 12 percent on full cost from contracts signed with large utilities. The cost accounting department at Williamson prepared information for the bid as follows:

Raw material	$1.75 per pound of cable fiber
Direct labor	$20 per DLH
Variable overhead	$5 per DLH
Fixed overhead	$12 per DLH
Incremental costs due to specialized service to the utility company	$2 per linear foot
Material useage	5 pounds of fiber per foot
Speed of production	3 feet of cable per DLH

a. Compute the minimum amount per linear foot that Williamson needs to bid to cover costs, make a desired profit, and still fall within the bid criteria set by the utility company.
b. Ignore your answer to requirement a. Assume that the minimum price per linear foot computed by Williamson is greater than the $26 per foot maximum bid set by the utility company. Discuss what Williamson could do to fall within the utility company's limits.

Problem 4 Special Order Pricing. Dunesberry Company makes air-conditioning units. Management estimates that Dunesberry's relevant range is 9,000 to 12,000 units. The sales price and cost per unit of producing and selling 10,000 units is as follows:

Sales price	$1,500
Variable manufacturing expenses	690
Variable selling and administrative expenses	135
Contribution margin	$ 675
Fixed manufacturing expenses	305
Fixed selling and administrative expenses	170
Income	$ 200

A potential customer in Argentina has offered to make a one-time purchase of 1,000 units at a price of $925. It costs Dunesberry an average of $1,300 per unit to manufacture and sell a unit. Dunesberry currently does not sell any products abroad. The Argentinean customer is not likely to purchase from Dunesberry on a regular basis and will not purchase any product for more than $925.

a. Will Dunesberry's net income increase or decrease if the special order is accepted at a unit price of $925?
b. Discuss noncost issues Dunesberry should consider before accepting the special order.

Problem 5 Special Order Pricing. ComputersPlus assembles and sells PC computer equipment. Frequently, the store puts together a custom-designed computer for a client. ComputersPlus often can beat the prices of other computer stores because they buy the parts at wholesale prices and keep labor wages to minimum. ComputersPlus is operating at approximately 85 percent of capacity, assembles approximately 1,000 computers annually, and specially designs each computer for a customer. No two PCs are the same. The quality of workmanship is excellent because the owner personally supervises each computer that leaves the facility. The average costs and sales price for computer models are as follows:

Sales price	$2,500
Direct materials	$1,200
Direct labor	$ 375
Variable manufacturing expenses	$ 250
Variable selling and administrative expenses	$ 125
Fixed expenses	$ 300

A local billing service has approached ComputersPlus to build a one-time order of 100 specially designed computers. The billing company wants a fairly substantial discount because it will pay cash on delivery. No variable selling and administrative costs will be incurred on the special order since the marketing representative is not responsible for this sale. The billing service has made a unique request. It wants each PC to be installed in a clear blue plastic case that matches the wallpaper on the office walls. The cost of the color cases is more than the regular grey shade and will cost an additional $75 per PC. Determine the lowest price that ComputersPlus can charge to the billing service without causing profits to decline. Should ComputersPlus accept the special order? Explain why or why not.

Problem 6 Markup Percentage and Special Order Profit. Pasture Purple Dairy manufactures three types of ice cream: 6 percent butterfat, 10 percent butterfat, and 12 percent butterfat. Projected cost information for 2002 is as follows:

	6 percent Butterfat	10 percent Butterfat	12 percent Butterfat
Sales revenue	$800,000	$700,000	$600,000
Gallons produced and sold	320,000	233,333	166,667
Direct material	$350,000	$220,000	$160,000
Direct labor	$175,000	$60,000	$45,000
Direct labor hours	8,000	4,000	3,000
Variable selling costs	$75,000	$35,000	$30,000

Pasture Purple's 2002 predetermined manufacturing overhead rates are as follows:

Variable manufacturing overhead rate	$ 6.50 per DLH
Fixed manufacturing overhead rate	$20.00 per DLH

Pasture Purple's estimated fixed selling and administrative costs are $350,000.

a. Compute Pasture Purple's projected markup percentage for each product based on a total manufacturing cost base.
b. Compute Pasture Purple's projected markup percentage for each product based on a total variable cost base.
c. An out-of-area customer has offered to purchase 10,000 gallons of 6 percent ice cream at $1.90 per gallon. The sale meets all of the special order conditions. By how much will Pasture Purple's net income change if it accepts the offer? Pasture Purple will incur all of its normal variable costs on the special order.

Problem 7 Make-or-Buy Decision. Wooster Manufacturing produces a major component for its primary product in its factory. The plant is operating below capacity, and Wooster expects this situation to continue for the foreseeable future. Wooster's accountant has presented you with the following incomplete cost information for one unit of the component:

Direct materials	$ 8.30
Direct labor (.7 hours)	14.40
Variable manufacturing overhead	?
Fixed manufacturing overhead	?
Total manufacturing costs	$?

The accountant also informs you that the total predetermined manufacturing overhead rate is $27 per direct labor hour, $15 for variable, and $12 for fixed. Wooster is to produce and use 10,000 units of the component in each of the next five years.

a. Compute Wooster's total cost to manufacture one unit of the component based on the information given.
b. A supplier has offered to provide Wooster with all of the components it requires for $35 per unit. By how much per year will income increase or decrease if Wooster accepts the supplier's offer?
c. A major piece of equipment used to manufacture the component is very near the end of its useful life. A new machine will cost $150,000 to purchase and will have a useful life of five years. Ignore the time value of money for this problem. Will the supplier's offer result in a savings or a loss under these circumstances?

Problem 8 Make-or-Buy Decision. Jiffy Production, Inc. manufactures car-washing machines and produces approximately 7,500 units per year of part X500, a bolt for these machines. Total expected annual costs for part X500 are as follows:

Direct materials	$2,200
Direct labor	1,650
Variable manufacturing expenses	150
Fixed expenses	100
Total	$4,100

Only $10 of the fixed expenses can be directly traced to Part X500. The rest is for the entire production facility and represents costs for all products manufactured. Jiffy has just learned that another company makes the same bolt and will sell it to Jiffy for $0.65 per bolt. The production manager believes this is a very good deal and is anxious to discontinue the production of the bolt.

a. Should Jiffy continue to make the bolt or buy it from the other company at $0.65?

b. What is the highest price that Jiffy should pay for part X500 if it buys the bolt from outside?

Case 2-5

PROFITABILITY ISSUES AT CALIFORNIA CAR COMPANY

Case Objectives

1. Introduce students to pricing decisions
2. Demonstrate the use of cost accounting information to support pricing decisions
3. Assess profitability of products and firms using financial data

Decision (Pricing): Does CCC need to adjust prices or reduce costs to remain competitive?

ASSESSING YEAR 2002 PRICES

It is now early March 2002. Jena Butler, Vice President of Finance, Sally Swanson, Vice President of Production, and George Olson, Vice President of Marketing, are presently working together on a project involving a review of the company's selling prices for its sedan and compact vehicles, which are currently set at $21,000 and $17,000, respectively. Up to now, the company has relied heavily on its assessment of customers' willingness to buy electric vehicles and on legal and political constraints in setting its prices (see Reading 2-5). The project team believes that it should reexamine its current prices in light of recent industry data that the team has just received (see Exhibit C2-5.1). Jena also has compiled recent cost and budget information provided by the company's accounting system (see Exhibits C2-5.2 and C2-5.3, Case 2-4, and your individual solution to Case 2-4).

Exhibit C2-5.1
2001 Hybrid Vehicle Industry Percentage Income Statement

	Percent	
Sales		100%
Cost of goods sold		
Direct materials	16%	
Direct labor	15%	
Manufacturing overhead	27%	
Total cost of goods sold		58%
Gross margin		42%
Selling and administrative expenses		
Selling expenses	10%	
Administrative expenses	19%	29%
Income before tax		13%
Income tax (30%)		4%
Net income		9%
Average industry sedan price		$ 20,000
Average industry compact price		$ 17,000

"Looking back, we've kept our prices constant at their current levels since 2000, and our budget for 2002 reflects those same prices," stated George. "I'm concerned that our prices are too high. If I'm right, we will miss both our 2002 sales volume targets and our profit targets. Our dealers tell me that they are losing sales to interested customers due to our prices. Can we be competitive in the long run by using our current prices? Let's reduce our profit on each car and cut the price of the sedan to $20,000 and the compact to $16,000. I wonder what our competitors are doing?" queried George.

"That's a good question," Sally responded. "When I look at our current prices in light of our estimated total manufacturing costs for 2002, those prices seem somewhat high. If our prices are too high, I'm worried about customers not buying our planned sales volume and the possibility of an inventory buildup during 2002 if they don't. However, we don't want to reduce our projected net income. Both our shareholders and creditors are demanding that level of profitability."

"I think you've both identified significant issues," said Jena. "I am concerned about the impact of a price reduction on our margins. Let me work up an analysis of the markups implied in our 2002 budget plan and a comparison of those markups with the competition. Let's plan to reconvene next Monday and go over the figures."

Exhibit C2-5.2
CCC Pricing and Cost Information
Based on 2002 Estimates in Case 2-4

	Sedan		Compact	
Sales price		$21,000		$17,000
Direct materials cost		$ 2,980		$ 3,360
Direct labor cost		3,780		2,275
Manufacturing overhead:				
Variable	$3,888		$ 2,340	
Fixed	5,076	8,964	3,055	5,395
Total manufacturing cost		$15,724		$11,030
Production volume (in units)		5,100		1,700

Requirements

1. Complete the costs in the table below. Assume that $2,000,000 of selling expenses and $1,000,000 of administrative expenses are variable. Fixed manufacturing costs are inserted in the table. Add the variable costs. Leave the shaded cells blank.

	One Sedan	One Compact	All Sedans	All Compacts	CCC Total
Variable manufacturing costs					
Fixed manufacturing costs	$ 5,076	$ 3,055	$25,887,600	$ 5,193,500	$31,081,100
Total manufacturing costs					
Total variable costs					

Exhibit C2-5.3

California Car Company
Financial Statements
(In Thousands of Dollars)

BALANCE SHEETS	Planned 2002	Actual 2001	Actual 2000	Actual 1999
Assets				
Cash	$ 1,462	$ 350	$ 400	$ 250
Accounts receivable—net	13,600	1,450	435	160
Direct material inventory	1,590	618	95	17
Work-in-process inventory	3,267	250	16	6
Finished goods inventory	2,238	2,238	111	111
Total current assets	22,157	4,906	1,057	544
Long-term assets—net	112,000	42,000	5,560	4,000
Total assets	$ 134,157	$ 46,906	$ 6,617	$ 4,544
Total liabilities	$ 44,868	$ 23,707	$ 819	$ 171
Shareholders' equity				
Contributed capital	80,000	22,000	7,000	5,750
Retained earnings	9,289	1,199	(1,202)	(1,377)
Total shareholders' equity	89,289	23,199	5,798	4,373
Total liabilities and shareholders' equity	$ 134,157	$ 46,906	$ 6,617	$ 4,544

INCOME STATEMENTS	Planned 2002	Actual 2001	Actual 2000	Actual 1999
Sales revenue	$ 136,000	$ 31,800	$ 9,500	$ 1,600
Less: cost of goods sold	98,943	20,670	6,650	1,109
Gross margin	37,057	11,130	2,850	491
Less: Selling expenses	7,000	1,500	600	400
Administrative expenses	18,500	6,200	2,000	1,200
Income before tax	11,557	3,430	250	(1,109)
Less: income tax—30%	3,467	1,029	75	(333)
Net income	$ 8,090	$ 2,401	$ 175	$ (776)

2. In response to George's and Sally's concerns, determine the following:

   a. CCC's estimated year 2002 markup percentages on estimated *variable manufacturing cost per unit* for each type of vehicle, sedan and compact. You need to calculate two separate markup percentages.

   b. CCC's estimated year 2002 markup percentage on estimated *total manufacturing cost per unit* for each type of vehicle, sedan and compact. You need to calculate two separate markup percentages.

(The requirements are continued on the next page)

c. CCC's total year 2002 corporate markup percentage on estimated *total manufacturing costs* reflected in its 2002 budgeted income statement in Exhibit C2-5.3. You need to calculate only one separate markup percentage for all of CCC.

d. The industry average markup percentage in 2001 on *total manufacturing cost*. Use Exhibit C2-5.1.

3. Assume that the industry markup percentage on *total manufacturing cost* you calculated above is 67 percent. How much would:

   a. Manufacturing costs per car have to go down on each model, sedan and compact, for CCC to match the industry markup? *Hint*: Either use algebra and the cost-plus pricing formula or trial and error with your spreadsheet solution to question 2b.

   b. Prices have to go up for each model, sedan and compact, to match the industry markup?

4. Prepare a *thorough* analysis, based on information in Case 2-5 and your answers above, to determine where CCC should focus its efforts. For example, should CCC reduce its profit on each car by lowering prices as George Olson suggests? Should it reduce material costs? Should it increase the price of each car? As part of your analysis, prepare a percentage income statement for CCC based on 2002 estimated figures in Exhibits C2-5.2 and C2-5.3. Use Exhibit C2-5.1 as a model.

5. Compute CCC's estimated 2002 contribution margin ratio. In Case 2-4 you calculated the variable manufacturing costs that are presented for you in Exhibit C2-5.2. Assume that $2,000,000 of selling expenses and $1,000,000 of administrative expenses are variable. *Hint*: Compute total sales revenue and total variable costs at CCC's budgeted 2002 level of production and sales.

6. Compute CCC's 2002 estimated breakeven sales level. Refer to Reading 1-3 for a review of breakeven analysis.

7. Discuss how likely it is that CCC will not attain a level of sales necessary to break even, if costs remain at the planned levels. In other words, will it take a large or small shortfall in projected sales to cause planned income to fall to zero?

Group Assignment 2-5

SAUDI GOLF CART ORDER

Group number __________ **Signatures of group members participating:**

____

____

Objectives

1. Introduce special order pricing concepts
2. Reinforce incremental cost concepts

A golf course developer in the Middle East, Saudi Sport, Inc., is proposing to purchase 1,000 compact units from CCC. Even though Saudi Sport is well aware of CCC's normal selling price of $17,000, it is offering to pay $8,500 per unit, half the normal selling price. Terms of this offer include (1) F.O.B. CCC's factory and (2) cash payments before shipment. F.O.B. stands for "free on board," which denotes where title and all risks and costs of shipping pass to the buyer. Therefore, title passes to Saudi Sport when the golf carts leave CCC's factory, and Saudi Sport assumes the shipping costs and risks at that time. Because the order is F.O.B. CCC's factory and there are no commissions, there are no variable selling and administrative costs associated with the order.

George Olson, vice president of marketing, is flabbergasted at the low offer price. "Why, the $8,500 selling price is below our production costs!" He suggests that the prospective customer "go fly a kite." Jena Butler, vice president of finance, advances a counter point. "George, we have more than enough production capacity to meet this special order and the growth in domestic sales for the foreseeable future. Perhaps we need to take a hard look at this proposal."

Sally Swanson, vice president of production, stated: "George, I can see your resistance to this proposal if these units were to somehow compete with our present dealer network. But these units would be exported to the Middle East to function as golf carts rather than as highway vehicles."

"It just occurred to me that our U.S. Federal Highway Standards need not apply to off-road vehicles. We can delete some parts!" added Jena. This will reduce CCC's material cost per compact by $300.

George responded, "You're making a persuasive case. We have excess capacity, no increased competition to our existing products, reduced material cost, and no legal problems on differential pricing for exports."

Requirements

1. Prepare an analysis of the impact that the Saudi Sports, Inc. order will have on CCC's planned year 2002 net income of $8,090,000 (see Exhibit C2-5.3). Show all your calculations. *Hint*: Initial computations may be done on a per-unit basis.

2. What four nonfinancial conditions should CCC explore before it makes its final decision? Does the Saudi order meet all of the conditions? Explain.

3. Recommend whether CCC should accept this special order. Explain.

Reading 2-6

JOB-ORDER COSTING

INTRODUCTION

Accountants compute product costs after manufacturing is completed in order to support pricing decisions, to report the firm's financial performance to outsiders, to evaluate the performance of departments and managers, and to improve operations. As discussed in Reading 2-5, actual product costs can be compared to pricing information to determine if markups are satisfactory. For instance, knowledge of why a bid differed from the completed cost can be used to improve the quality of bids on future jobs. Costs of completed products also are used to report profit or loss outcomes to shareholders, creditors, and other users of financial statements. More specifically, product costs are used to value inventory and to determine the cost of goods sold. Differences between estimated and completed costs can be investigated to encourage managers to implement better purchasing and manufacturing processes.

Reading 2-6 explains how manufacturing costs are accumulated and recorded as unit costs of production in inventories and cost of goods sold. Two methods of costing, job-order and process, are defined, but the reading emphasizes job-order costing so that you can apply these principles when completing Case 2-6. The discussion continues the Quality Welding Company example to illustrate the computation of job costs, including application of overhead costs to both jobs and units of product and the use of job-order cost sheets to gather information. The final section provides a brief summary of the uses of job cost data for pricing, financial reporting, planning, performance evaluation decisions, and operating decisions.

MANUFACTURING COST FLOWS

Two techniques can be used to cost completed goods as they flow through an assembly line: job-order costing and process costing. **Job-order costing** is used when a firm manufactures a unique, made-to-order product, or produces identifiable batches of different items. The single item or batch being manufactured is called a **job**. For example, commercial construction companies use job-order costing because each store or office building constructed is usually unique. Quality Welding, the example problem started in Reading 2-4, also uses job-order costing because each order must be cut to fit the customer's unique porch dimensions. In addition, companies that produce batches of different products using the same equipment normally employ a form of job-order costing. CCC is an example of this type of firm because it produces alternating batches of sedans and compacts.

Other firms use a **process costing** system where only one type of product, such as milk, or a family of closely related products is manufactured on one set of equipment. Each unit of product is indistinguishable from another. One quart of milk looks the same as another. Because all units are so similar, all of the manufacturing costs for a product in process costing are collected by time period, usually a month. These total costs for the period then are divided by the total units produced that period to arrive at an average or process cost per unit. CCC will switch to a form of process costing system in Case 3-5 after it has implemented a just-in-time system. The main difference between the two costing procedures is that job-order accumulates costs by the *job* and then divides that job cost by units produced to arrive at a cost per unit. Process costing collects costs by *time period* and then calculates cost per unit. Despite the somewhat different methods employed to arrive at unit cost, the basic concepts underlying the cost flow of the two methods are the same. The remainder of this section will illustrate only the use of job-order costing since that is the system employed by CCC in this module.

Accounting for manufacturing costs closely parallels the flow of goods through a factory. As employees begin work on a job and begin adding materials, accountants begin collecting direct material, direct labor, and manufacturing overhead costs on job-order cost sheets, described in the next section. Accountants treat costs for jobs being worked on in the factory as WIP inventory. Costs are added to a job *only* while it is in the WIP inventory. When jobs are completed, accountants move the cost of the completed jobs out of the WIP inventory and into the finished goods inventory. When the job is sold, the cost of the job is removed from the finished goods inventory and placed in the cost of goods sold account.

Normal Job-Order Costing

Jobs, or products, can be costed using actual costs, estimated costs, or a combination of actual and estimated costs. For reasons discussed in the estimating overhead section of Reading 2-4, almost no firms of any size use actual overhead when costing jobs. Many firms, particularly large industrial ones, cost jobs using estimated direct material, direct labor, and manufacturing overhead costs. When all costs assigned to jobs are estimated, firms are said to use a **standard cost system**. We will not work with a standard cost system in this course. Those of you advancing to upper-level accounting classes will receive detailed coverage of that topic in cost accounting.

CCC and Quality Welding use *actual* direct material and direct labor costs, but *estimated* overhead, by applying a predetermined overhead rate, to cost jobs. Use of actual direct costs, and estimated overhead is known as a **normal cost system**. All problems and examples in this book employ a normal cost system.

Costs for each job are collected on **job-order cost sheets**. The direct material and direct labor actually used on a job are recorded on these sheets as is the overhead applied to the job. Direct material costs initially are recorded on **material requisition forms** as material is removed from the warehouse. Data are then copied from the materials requisition form to the job-order cost sheet.

Direct labor time and costs initially are recorded on **time tickets** and then copied to the job-order cost sheet. You should note that time tickets are not the same as time cards used by many firms to clock in and clock out employees. Time cards record only the times employees arrived and left the site, not the jobs on which they worked. Examples of a material requisition form and time ticket for Quality Welding are presented in Exhibit 2-6.1.

Overhead is recorded on the job-order cost sheet periodically, usually once a month. The amount of overhead is computed by adding the DLHs recorded on the job-order cost sheet for the period and multiplying those hours by the predetermined overhead rate. Although calculating the overhead for a job-order cost sheet is easy, the record keeping required for direct material and direct labor costs is not. If a plant has 1,000 employees and each employee works on an average of three jobs per day, clerks in a manual accounting system must make 3,000 recordings per day just for direct labor costs! Today, however, most large firms have computerized systems that automatically record the data on the job-order cost sheet. Employees just enter the time worked on each job at a computer near their work.

Exhibit 2-6.1
Examples of Job-Order Data Collection Forms for Quality Welding Company

Materials Requisition Form		#9718
Job	*101*	
Date	*Feb. 7, 2002*	
Department	*Cutting*	
Item	**Quantity**	**Cost**
6' Tubular Steel	*6.100#*	*$ 14.945*

Time Ticket			#97386
Date		*Feb. 7, 2002*	
Department		*Cutting*	
Employee		*Baker*	
Job #	**Hours**	**Rate**	**Amount**
101	*6*	*$ 20.00*	*$120.00*
104	*2*	*$ 20.00*	*$ 40.00*

A job-order cost system is only as accurate as the direct material and direct labor data that employees record. Many firms, however, neglect to train employees about how important the job-order cost system is to the firm's success and why it is critical for employees to complete material requisition forms and time tickets accurately. Without proper training, many employees view completing forms a nuisance and make little effort to complete them correctly.

Quality Welding Example—Continued

Reading 2-4 illustrates how Quality Welding estimates costs for Job 101, consisting of 50 packages of porch railings with columns. The process by which Quality determines the completed cost of Job 101 is shown in this reading. The first step is to collect all direct material and direct labor costs on material requisition forms and time tickets. Examples of these forms were given in Exhibit 2-6.1. The italicized data is data provided by the employees. The next step is to copy data involving Job 101 direct costs to the job-order cost sheet shown in Exhibit 2-6.2. The final steps are to add the manufacturing overhead and sum the costs. Cost per product unit or railing package is determined by dividing total job costs by the number of railing packages manufactured ($74,020/50 units = $1,480 per package).

An example of how Quality Welding computes its predetermined overhead rates and allocates manufacturing overhead to actual jobs is illustrated in Exhibit 2-6.3. Job 101 applied overhead costs are shown as are overhead costs for two additional jobs. The budgeted costs for the three overhead departments and the estimated DLHs are those first presented in Reading 2-4. Notice that variable manufacturing overhead is applied at a predetermined rate of $25.67 and fixed manufacturing overhead at $19.33 per DLH as computed at the bottom of the exhibit. For convenience, the total manufacturing overhead rate of $45 per DLH is used to apply overhead to jobs. Also note on the job-order cost sheet in Exhibit 2-6.2 that only the total predetermined rate of $45 per DLH is used and that the date at which overhead is applied is February 28. Most firms apply overhead to jobs at the end of a month.

Exhibit 2-6.2
Quality Welding Company
Job-Order Cost Sheet—Job 101

Batch Size	50 pkgs. railings/columns			
Date Started	February 7, 2002	Date Finished	February 12, 2002	
Date Sold	March 4, 2002			

Cutting Department

	Hours	Date	Cost	Total
Direct Materials				
Tubular steel		2/7/02	$14,945	
Rolled steel		2/9/02	17,654	$32,599
Direct Labor				
Total from time tickets	82	2/7/02	$ 1,673	
Total from time tickets	164	2/10/02	3,362	
Total from time tickets	31	2/11/02	623	5,658
	277			
Overhead Applied				
Total overhead applied @ $45/DLH	277	2/28/02	$12,465	12,465
Total cutting department costs				$50,722

Welding Department

	Hours	Date	Cost	Total
Direct Materials				
Castings		2/14/02	$ 6,651	$ 6,651
Direct Labor				
Total from time tickets	67	2/11/02	$ 1,413	
Total from time tickets	186	2/12/02	3,849	5,262
	253			
Overhead Applied				
Total overhead applied @ $45/DLH	253	2/28/02	$11,385	11,385
Total welding department costs				$23,298
Job totals	530			$74,020
Average cost per package				$ 1,480

At this point, let's compare the estimated costs developed in Reading 2-4 with the completed job costs for Job 101.

	Estimated Costs			Actual Costs		
Direct materials		$ 39,500			$ 39,250	
Direct labor		10,800	(540 DLH)		10,920	(530 DLH)
Variable mfg. overhead	$ 13,860			$ 13,290		
Fixed mfg. overhead	10,440	24,300		10,560	23,850	
Total costs		$ 74,600			$ 74,020	

The direct material cost of Job 101 is slightly less than estimated. The direct labor cost is slightly higher than estimated even though 10 fewer hours were used. This means that the average labor rate must have been higher than predicted. The predetermined rates remained the same at $25.67 per DLH for variable overhead and $19.33 per DLH for fixed overhead because in a normal cost system the same rates used to estimate costs are used to cost completed jobs. Why is the total overhead different? The only cause of the $450 difference in total applied overhead ($24,300 – $23,850) is the use of 10 fewer hours times the predetermined rates as follows:

Variable overhead applied	$25.67	× 10 DLH	= $256.70
Fixed overhead applied	19.33	× 10 DLH	= 193.30
Total overhead applied	$45.00	× 10 DLH	= $450.00

Exhibit 2-6.3
Quality Welding Overhead Application to Jobs
Traditional Approach

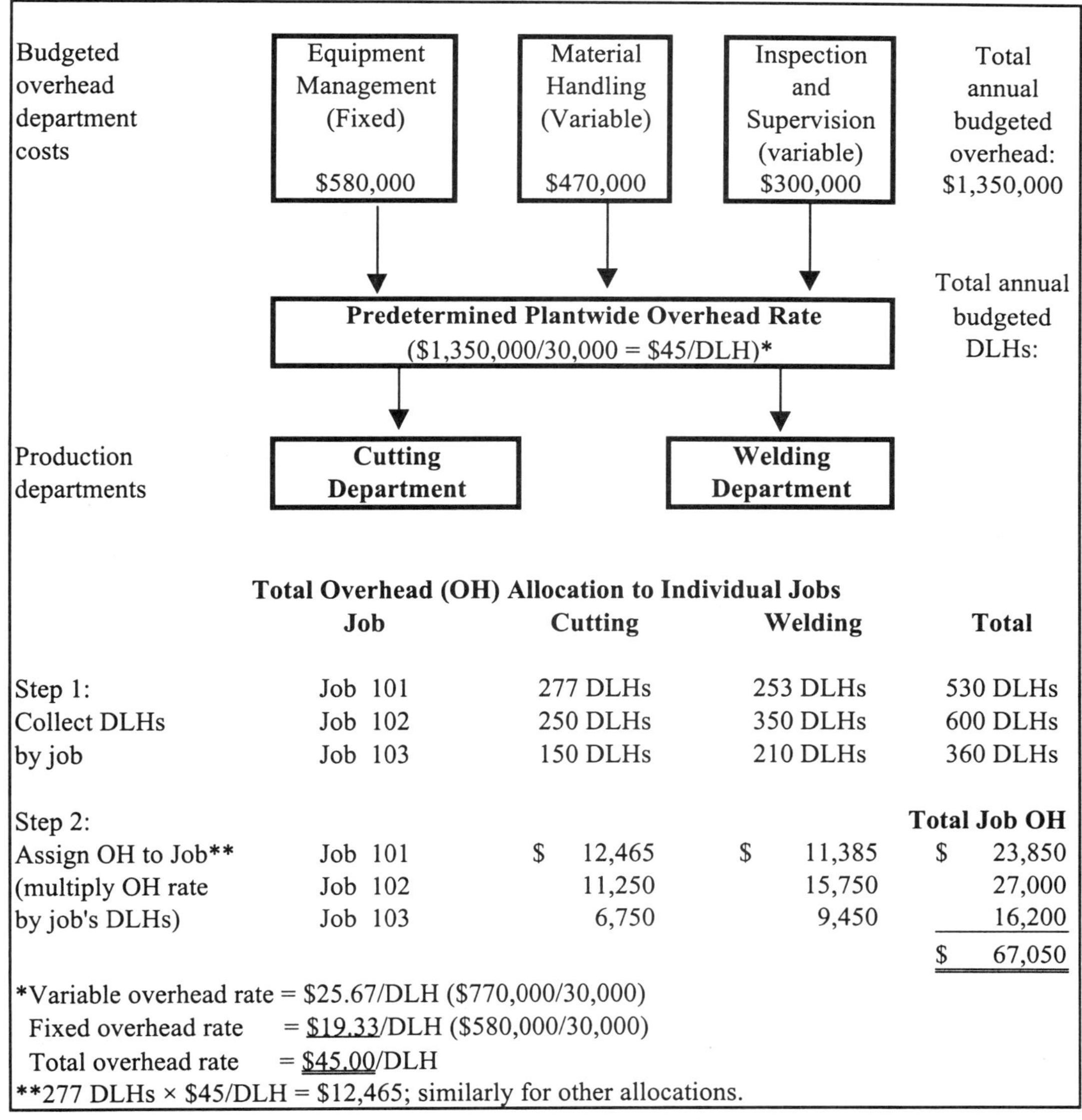

Total Overhead (OH) Allocation to Individual Jobs

	Job	Cutting	Welding	Total
Step 1: Collect DLHs by job	Job 101	277 DLHs	253 DLHs	530 DLHs
	Job 102	250 DLHs	350 DLHs	600 DLHs
	Job 103	150 DLHs	210 DLHs	360 DLHs
Step 2:				**Total Job OH**
Assign OH to Job** (multiply OH rate by job's DLHs)	Job 101	$ 12,465	$ 11,385	$ 23,850
	Job 102	11,250	15,750	27,000
	Job 103	6,750	9,450	16,200
				$ 67,050

*Variable overhead rate = $25.67/DLH ($770,000/30,000)
Fixed overhead rate = $19.33/DLH ($580,000/30,000)
Total overhead rate = $45.00/DLH
**277 DLHs × $45/DLH = $12,465; similarly for other allocations.

COST OF GOODS MANUFACTURED AND SOLD

Job-order cost information is used to cost ending WIP and finished goods (FG) inventories on the balance sheet and to determine the **cost of goods manufactured and sold** (CGMS) on the income statement. How is the cost of the ending WIP inventory determined? It is simple. The cost of all jobs that are started but not yet completed at the end of the month are added together. Job costs, of course, are those costs that have been recorded on the job-order cost sheets. For example, if Job 101 was not completed as of February 28, its job-order cost sheet would be collected and summed with the job-order cost sheets of all other jobs started, but not yet completed, to derive the WIP inventory balance.

The same procedure is used to determine ending finished goods inventory for all jobs that are completed but not yet shipped. The cost of all jobs that are completed at the end of the month are summed to derive the ending finished goods inventory. Job 101 falls into this category, so it is part of the ending February finished goods inventory. Cost of goods sold (CGS) is just as easy to determine because all that needs to be done is to total the job-order cost sheets for all jobs sold during the month. Recall that a sale is recorded only after title passes, which in most cases is after the goods are shipped.

Accountants usually compute cost of goods sold by walking through a CGMS schedule like the one presented in Exhibit 2-6.5. The CGMS schedule can be completed by summing cost information from all jobs being manufactured during a month, including those begun the previous month and finished by the end of the current month, and all units sold during the current reporting period. Information for the schedule can be obtained through the following steps:

1. Beginning FG inventory—use the cost information from the prior month's ending FG inventory records.

2. Cost of goods manufactured (CGM)—sum only the current costs from all job-order cost sheets for direct materials, direct labor, and applied manufacturing overhead.

3. Beginning WIP inventory—use the cost information from the prior month's ending WIP inventory records.

4. Ending WIP inventory—sum the cost of all jobs that have been started but not completed by the end of the current month.

5. Ending FG inventory—sum the cost of all jobs completed but unsold by the end of the current month.

6. CGS—add the beginning FG inventory plus CGM and subtract the ending FG inventory.

February manufacturing cost data for Quality Welding is given in Exhibit 2-6.4. Can you trace this information to the costs presented in Exhibit 2-6.5?

You should understand that the only jobs sold were those in the beginning inventory plus Job 102. You can tell that these jobs were sold because the only jobs left in inventory at the end of February are Job 101 in the FG inventory and Job 103 in the WIP inventory.

Exhibit 2-6.4
Quality Welding Company
February Manufacturing Cost Data

January ending FG inventory		$ 156,700
February direct material cost:		
Job 101	$ 39,250	
Job 102	25,700	
Job 103	15,650	$ 80,600
February direct labor cost:		
Job 101	$ 10,920	
Job 102	6,760	
Job 103	2,390	$ 20,070
Manufacturing overhead from Exhibit 2-6.3		
Job 101	$ 23,850	
Job 102	27,000	
Job 103	16,200	$ 67,050
Beginning WIP inventory		0
Ending WIP inventory: Job 103		$ 34,240
Ending FG inventory: Job 101		$ 74,020
Cost of goods sold:		
Beginning FG inventory	$ 156,700	
Job 102	59,460	$ 216,160

Exhibit 2-6.5
Quality Welding Company
Cost Of Goods Manufactured and Sold Schedule
February 2002

Beginning finished goods inventory		$ 156,700
Add: Cost of goods manufactured		
February direct material	$ 80,600	
February direct labor	20,070	
February applied manufacturing overhead	67,050	
Total February manufacturing costs	$167,720	
Add: Beginning inventory work-in-process	0	
Less: Ending inventory work-in-process	(34,240)	
Cost of goods manufactured		133,480
Total cost of goods available for sale		$ 290,180
Less: Ending inventory finished goods		(74,020)
Cost of goods sold		$ 216,160

Overapplied and Underapplied Overhead

Students often wonder what happens if the total amount of overhead applied to jobs is different from the actual overhead incurred by the firm during the year. The answer is that the total income for the year is usually adjusted to reflect the **underapplied or overapplied overhead**, which means that costs and income are adjusted to reflect actual overhead. Accountants are usually quite skilled at estimating annual overhead, therefore, the adjustment is usually small. Several accounting methods exist for recording the overapplied or underapplied overhead, which will not be used in this course. For our purposes we will just assume that the overapplied or underapplied amount is small and will be subtracted or added to cost of goods sold at the end of the year.

Let us assume that the actual manufacturing overhead for Quality Welding is $69,336. Total applied overhead for all three jobs from Exhibits 2-6.3 and 2-6.4 is $67,050. Quality does not apply enough overhead to jobs so overhead is underapplied for the month in the amount of $2,286 ($69,336 – $67,050). If Quality finished the reporting year with underapplied overhead, the amount underapplied would be added to cost of goods sold to increase the amount of applied overhead in cost of goods sold to the actual overhead incurred. Would overhead be over-or underapplied if actual February overhead was $65,925? The answer is it would be overapplied by $1,125 ($65,925 – $67,050). If at year end total overhead was overapplied, the amount overapplied would be subtracted from cost of goods sold to decrease the amount of applied overhead in cost of goods sold to match the actual amount.

These sections on manufacturing cost flows and cost of goods manufactured and sold have illustrated how costs are collected on job-order cost sheets during the production process and then summed on a CGMS schedule to derive cost of goods sold. The next section discusses how management uses this cost data in making decisions.

DECISION USES OF PREDETERMINED OVERHEAD RATES

Knowing when and how to use manufacturing overhead is important in making effective management decisions. You will have little trouble properly using predetermined variable overhead rates in future case assignments, but you will need an understanding of which overhead numbers and formats are relevant for different types of decisions. Manufacturing overhead cost numbers are used in five decision contexts: (1) pricing and profitability, (2) financial reporting, (3) planning, (4) performance evaluation, and (5) operating. Deciding when to use the variable overhead rate is easy: the predetermined rate per driver, DLHs in most cases, is used in all decision contexts.

Fixed overhead, however, is more confusing. Exhibit 2-6.6 presents all five decision cases and the proper usage of fixed overhead in making those decisions. For pricing and financial reporting purposes, a predetermined fixed overhead rate, which comprises most overhead in modern manufacturing settings, is used because the decisions require a cost per unit calculation. For planning and performance evaluation purposes, however, the decision focus is on *total* fixed overhead. The use of predetermined fixed overhead rates can lead to incorrect decisions. Reading 2-7 explains how to use fixed overhead for performance evaluation purposes. For operating decisions it is best to use an entirely different method, activity-based costing, for assigning overhead to products. That method will be illustrated in Module 3.

Exhibit 2-6.6
Accounting Treatment of Fixed Manufacturing Overhead

Decision	Focal Point for Decision	Required Accounting for Fixed Manufacturing Overhead
Pricing and profitability (C2-5)	Cost per job or unit (if relevant)	Predetermined OH rate per DLH
Financial reporting (COGS—C2-6)	Cost per job or unit	Predetermined OH rate per DLH
Planning Departmental Job or product (C2-4, C4-1)	 Total fixed OH cost Cost per job or unit	 Budgeted total fixed OH cost Predetermined OH rate per DLH
Performance evaluation (C2-7, C4-5)	Total fixed OH cost	Budgeted total fixed OH cost minus Actual total fixed OH cost (by department)
Operating (C3-1,C3-5)	Cost drivers	Activity-based costing

Why is the focus different for the different decisions that firms face? The reasons are discussed in the following sections.

Pricing

For most companies, customers need a quoted price for a unit they want to purchase or for the job on which they are obtaining bids from vendors. For example, when you purchase a textbook, you are interested only in how much the book will cost. You really do not care what South-Western's total fixed overhead costs are. Therefore, management must quote you a price per book if they hope to gain you as a customer. As a result, management's decision focus is on a per-unit and not a total cost basis. Similarly, if South-Western wants to know if a cost accounting book is profitable and its publication should be continued, it is not very useful to know only the total fixed overhead for the thousands of various books it publishes each year.

Financial Reporting

One key objective of financial reporting is to help external users, such as creditors and stockholders, predict how well the company will perform in the future. The theory is that historical results shown in the financial statements will give some useful information about the firm's future. In order to explain this thinking, the definitions of two terms need to be reviewed: product costing and period costing. *Product costing* refers to costs that are first inventoried when incurred and do not appear on the income statement until the product, with which they are associated, is sold. Accountants assign all manufacturing costs to jobs or products produced and match those costs to revenue as sales occur. *Period costing* refers to the assignment of costs to the income statement in the time period, month or year, in which they occur. In other words, they are not inventoried. Accountants match all selling and administrative costs to revenue by period.

The financial reporting emphasis on unit cost is the result of accountants choosing product costing as a means to match manufacturing costs to revenue. Accountants traditionally believed that assigning, or matching, fixed manufacturing costs to units or jobs presented the most relevant information for financial statement users. One reason for this position is that assignment of fixed manufacturing costs to products causes the reporting of manufacturing costs, as a percent of sales, to be stable during a year. Another way of saying this is that assignment of fixed costs leads to a stable gross margin percentage. Understand that actual

fixed manufacturing costs may not be even during the year and probably are seasonal and lumpy. Producing a consistent percentage of fixed costs to sales prevents users from having to work with possibly misleading information due to fluctuating fixed costs. Reading 2-4 discusses the effect of erratic overhead costs in greater detail. You may want to review this discussion to refresh your memory on the reasons for using predetermined fixed overhead rates.

Many users believe that period costing of fixed manufacturing costs provides more useful information because it highlights fluctuations in actual fixed costs from period to period. When fixed manufacturing costs are matched by period, the resulting financial statements are called *direct cost* or *variable cost* statements. The contribution income statements that you prepared in Case 1-3 are very similar to direct cost income statements. Although decision usefulness would be improved, and cost accounting would be much easier for students, direct cost statements are not allowed for external financial reporting purposes. Many firms do, however, use them for internal reporting purposes.

Planning

When a firm prepares formal plans, it does so by department because departments are the organization's basic responsibility units. Each department must plan or budget for how much material to acquire and how many people to employ. It would be of little value in planning purchasing and hiring needs to know that the cost per unit in the Welding Department will be $50 or that maintenance costs will be $5 per unit. You might think that unit costs would work, because all you would need to do is multiply the planned unit cost by planned units to arrive at the department's planned total costs. This would work for variable, but not fixed, costs. For example, would total planned fixed overhead be different in a month with a production volume of 1,000 units than for a month with a planned production volume of 1,500? Hopefully, you answered no to this question. Otherwise you would, for example, plan to pay more rent in a high-volume month than in a low-volume month.

Performance Evaluation

Since performance evaluation measures a manager's performance, and managers direct departments, the decision on how to use fixed costs in evaluating conduct must involve total department costs rather than unit costs. In addition, the performance evaluation decision focus must match that of planning because a difference, or **variance,** is computed by comparing actual and planned fixed costs.

Operating

Many operating decisions, such as deciding how to improve quality or on-time deliveries, do not involve fixed cost information. Other operating decisions, such as selecting batch size or evaluating the cost effectiveness of training production workers to perform some machine maintenance on their own, do require fixed cost information. For most operating decisions, however, neither unit nor total fixed cost information is very useful. The emphasis for operating decisions normally is on the cost drivers of the fixed overhead costs, because only by knowing these can the fixed cost implications of operating decisions be determined.

SUMMARY

Reading 2-6 first defines two manufacturing accounting methods, job-order and process costing. Then the reading illustrates how to account for manufacturing cost flows on job-order cost sheets and how to accumulate costs for financial reporting on a cost of goods manufactured and sold schedule. The reading concludes with a discussion on the correct usage of overhead rates for pricing, financial reporting, planning, performance evaluation, and operating decisions.

EXERCISES AND PROBLEMS

Exercises

Exercise 1 Use of Product Cost Information. Provide at least three specific examples of business decisions that require the use of product cost data.

Exercise 2 Use of Fixed Overhead Data in Company Decisions. Discuss how firms use job cost information in five different decision-making areas. Specifically, what are the five decision areas and how does the accounting for fixed overhead differ for each type of decision?

Exercise 3 Inventory Costs in a Job-Order Costing System. Biggs Company worked on only one job, Job 18, during July and August, 2002. All other jobs were sold by July 15. Job 18 was started on July 2, completed on August 29, and sold on September 3. The following costs are from the job-order cost sheet for Job 18.

	July	August
Direct materials	$22,560	$12,387
Direct labor	$16,980	$20,550
Direct labor hours	1,100	1,470

Biggs' predetermined total (variable plus fixed) manufacturing overhead rate for 2002 is $33 per direct labor hour.

a. Compute the July 31, 2002, ending inventory in work-in-process.
b. Compute the August 31, 2002, ending inventory in finished goods.

Exercise 4 Inventory Costs in a Job-Order Costing System. Small Company worked on only one job, Job 28, during July and August, 2002. All other jobs were sold by July 15. Job 28 was started on July 7, completed on August 19, and sold on September 8. The following costs are from the job-order cost sheet for Job 28.

	July	August
Direct materials	$32,460	$22,887
Direct labor	$36,980	$33,180
Direct labor hours	1,100	987

Small's predetermined variable manufacturing overhead rate for 2002 is $24 per direct labor hour and the fixed manufacturing overhead rate is $16.

a. Compute the July 31, 2002, ending inventory in work-in-process.
b. Compute the August 31, 2002, ending inventory in finished goods.

Exercise 5 Cost of Goods Manufactured and Sold Statement. BrightLight Company manufactures bedroom lamps. The plant cost accountant computed the following information as of April 1:

Raw materials inventory	$56,000
Work-in-process inventory	44,000
Finished goods inventory	35,000

April manufacturing costs were $84,000 for direct labor and $350,000 for raw materials purchases. Actual total overhead for the month was $215,700. Variable overhead was applied at $15 per DLH and fixed at $12 per DLH. Direct labor hours were 8,600. Inventories at the end of April were as follows:

Raw materials inventory	$58,500
Work-in-process inventory	34,000
Finished goods inventory	37,250

Prepare April's cost of goods sold statement. Did you use actual or applied overhead for the cost of goods sold statement? Explain why you used actual or applied.

Exercise 6 Overapplied or Underapplied Overhead. Maxim's produces custom-made suits for top business executives. The company applies overhead based on direct labor hours using a carefully computed predetermined overhead rate. In March 2002 the total applied overhead, variable and fixed, was $57,153, and the total actual overhead incurred was $56,192. The president of the firm was upset that the two amounts were not the same. He wants the accountant to bury the difference somewhere, anywhere, on the income statement.

a. Should the president be concerned about the discrepancy?
b. Is the overhead underapplied or overapplied? If so, by how much and in which direction?
c. Where should the accountant show the difference?

Exercise 7 Overapplied or Underapplied Overhead. Stevens Lighting, a lamp manufacturer, applies overhead to product cost at $15 per DLH for variable manufacturing overhead and $12 per DLH for fixed. Actual overhead for the month of April was $245,700 and direct labor hours were 8,600.

a. Was overhead overapplied or underapplied, and by how much?
b. Where should the difference be reported on the financial statements?
c. Should the company be concerned about the difference?

Problems

Problem 1 Costs of Production and Predetermined Overhead Rates in a Job-Order Costing System. The San Juan Bicycle Company produces one job per month, but produces a different number of bikes each month. San Juan has provided you with the following information for August 2002.

August actual production	150 bikes
August direct labor	2 hours per bike @ $20 per DLH
August direct material	$85 per bike
August variable manufacturing overhead	$8 per DLH
Budgeted August direct labor hours	200 hours
Budgeted August fixed manufacturing overhead	$2,500
Budgeted 2002 fixed manufacturing overhead	$35,000
Budgeted 2002 direct labor hours	2,500 hours

a. Compute the total cost of the August 2002 production of bikes.

b. Compute the August manufacturing cost per bike.

Problem 2 Predetermined Overhead Rates and Overapplied or Underapplied Overhead in a Job-Order Costing System. Wilmington manufactures batches of high-quality sweatshirts. The number of sweatshirts varies per job. During June 2002 manufacturing costs for Wilmington were as follows:

June actual production	2,000 sweatshirts
June direct labor	½ hour per sweatshirt @ $7 per DLH
June direct material	$10 per sweatshirt
June variable manufacturing overhead	$1 per DLH
Budgeted 2002 fixed manufacturing overhead	$60,000
Budgeted 2002 direct labor hours	15,000 hours

a. Compute the total cost of the June 2002 production of sweatshirts.

b. Compute the manufacturing cost of each sweatshirt.

c. Assume actual overhead incurred is $8,760. Has overhead been overapplied or underapplied? Should the management of Wilmington be concerned about this difference?

Problem 3 Cost of Goods Manufactured and Sold Statement and Income Statement. Delgado Manufacturing makes and sells inexpensive home furniture. The company prepares semiannual financial statements for its bank. The plant cost accountant computed the following information as of January 1.

Raw materials inventory	$256,000
Work-in-process inventory	144,000
Finished goods inventory	535,000

Manufacturing costs for the first half of the year are $884,000 for direct labor and $650,000 for raw materials purchases. Union contracts mandate that wages average $15 per DLH. Actual total overhead for the month is $215,700. Variable overhead is applied at $4 per DLH and fixed at $12 per DLH. Inventories at the end of June are as follows.

Raw materials inventory	$178,600
Work-in-process inventory	163,000
Finished goods inventory	338,250

Delgado had a business boom during the first half of the year. Assume that sales commissions were 2 percent of sales revenue, which was $3,045,000. Other selling and administrative expenses amounted to $240,000. Except for the sale commissions, these were all fixed expenses.

a. Prepare a cost of goods sold statement for the first half of the year.

b. Prepare an income statement for the first half of the year that will be included in the financial statements for the bank. You may ignore the effect of income tax.

c. Which of the above cost items will appear on the balance sheet as of June 30?

Problem 4 Cost of Goods Manufactured and Sold Statement. Top management is concerned about rising production costs. The vice president of production has asked you, the chief cost accountant, to prepare a cost of goods manufactured and sold statement for the previous month of July. You have obtained the following information concerning production during July.

Wages	$23 per DLH
Direct materials	$56 per unit
Variable manufacturing overhead	$15 per DLH
Fixed manufacturing overhead	$19 per DLH
Materials inventory, June 30	$ 38,760
Materials inventory, July 31	$ 49,600
Work-in-process inventory, June 30	$163,500
Work-in-process inventory, July 31	$176,400
Finished goods inventory, June 30	$ 89,765
Finished goods inventory, July 31	$101,922
Time worked	8,300 DLHs
Production	15,776 units

Prepare a cost of goods manufactured and sold statement for the month of July. Did you use actual or applied overhead for the statement? Explain why you used actual or applied.

Problem 5 Cost of Goods Manufactured and Sold Statement, Income Statement, and Overhead. The president of Lopez Company is concerned about rising production costs. The vice president of production has asked you, the chief cost accountant, to prepare a cost of goods manufactured and sold statement, income statement, and an analysis of overhead costs for the year 2002. You have obtained the following information concerning production and sales during 2002.

Sales price per unit	$120 per unit
Wages	$ 23 per DLH
Direct materials	$ 56 per unit
Variable manufacturing overhead	$ 15 per DLH
Fixed manufacturing overhead	$ 19 per DLH
Actual manufacturing overhead	$3,130,100
Sales commission	1% of sales price per unit
Fixed administrative expenses	$2,500,000
Materials inventory, January 1	$ 38,760
Materials inventory, January 31	$ 49,600
Work-in-process inventory, January 1	$163,500
Work-in-process inventory, January 31	$176,400
Finished goods inventory, January 1	$ 89,765
Finished goods inventory, January 31	$101,922
Time worked	105,600 DLHs
Production	206,315 units

a. Prepare a cost of goods manufactured and sold statement for the year.

b. Did you use actual or applied overhead for the cost of goods sold statement? Explain why you used actual or applied.

c. Compute the amount of overapplied or underapplied overhead. Should the president be concerned about this amount?

d. Prepare an income statement for the year.

Case 2-6

JOB-ORDER COSTING AT CALIFORNIA CAR COMPANY

Case Objectives

1. Introduce the specifics of job-order costing
2. Introduce students to the cost of goods manufactured statement
3. Demonstrate the linkage of product costing to the financial statements

Decision (Financial Reporting): What production costs will CCC report for March 2002?

THE PROFIT DISASTER

It is now early April 2002 and President David Gomez wants a ballpark estimate of CCC's March 2002 costs and gross margins. He has an assistant go into the accounting system and collect the March information in Exhibit C2-6.1. "This income is an absolute disaster!" was the response of David Gomez when his assistant handed him the March income statement. "When the bankers and board of directors see this they will take drastic action. We promised them a profit for March, not a huge loss. This loss is so large we will never come close to meeting our planned income of $8 million for 2002. We may have to close down the factory!"

Exhibit C2-6.1

Estimated March 2002 Net Income		
Sales (300 sedans and 100 compacts)		$ 8,000,000
March direct materials	1,539,159	
March direct labor	1,726,585	
March actual overhead (estimated)	4,094,473	7,360,217
Gross margin		639,783
March selling and administrative costs		1,940,000
Income (loss) before tax		$ (1,300,217)

Jena Butler, after talking to David Gomez, asks you to verify CCC's March income before tax. To do this you need to cost all March jobs and prepare a cost of goods sold schedule.

THE JOB ORDER COST SYSTEM

CCC uses a *normal job-order cost system* to determine the cost of manufacturing a sedan or compact car. This means that cars are costed by assigning *actual* labor and *actual* material costs to each car. Factory overhead, however, is assigned based on a *predetermined overhead rate* of $83 per DLH used, as shown in Exhibit C2-6.2. The computed costs of the cars are used to determine the cost of the ending WIP and ending finished goods inventories so that CCC's accountants can prepare monthly income statements and balance sheets. CCC also uses these costs to help set prices and evaluate performance.

Exhibit C2-6.2
Traditional Overhead Costing at CCC

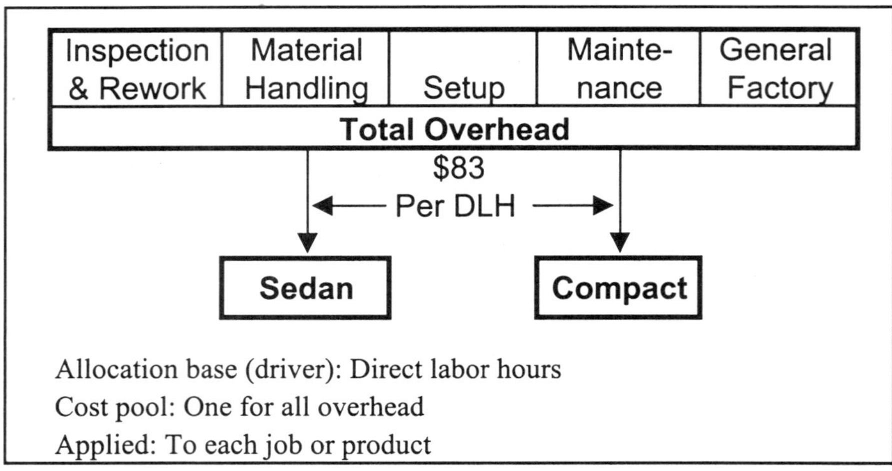

Allocation base (driver): Direct labor hours
Cost pool: One for all overhead
Applied: To each job or product

CCC chassis assemblers and final assemblers, who are classified as direct labor, carefully record the actual time spent working on each car model, sedan and compact, on forms called time tickets. Note that quite a few time tickets will be produced. If CCC has 200 direct labor employees and there are 20 work days during the month, then 4,000 time tickets will be created in that one month. A clerk must review each time ticket and copy the hours worked to the appropriate job cost sheet. The clerk then must look up the employee's wage rate and multiply the rate times the hours worked and enter that on the job cost sheet. This is a very tedious task.

Employees in material handling carefully record by model all direct material sent to assembly on material requisition forms. A clerk must copy these material costs to the appropriate job cost sheets. As a result, at the end of each month, CCC knows the actual direct labor and direct material costs for each model by simply adding up the labor and material costs that have been transferred to each job cost sheet.

CCC's controller has recommended that a networked microcomputer system be installed to replace the paper forms. In this system direct labor and material handling employees would simply enter the needed information into a computer. Total material and labor costs for each model would be determined each month by the computer without clerks completing all the forms and without transferring labor and material information to the job cost sheets.

To reduce the bookkeeping and computations required, CCC has simplified its cost accounting system so that it accounts for only four types of jobs per month:

1. The job that is in WIP at the beginning of the month,
2. All the sedan batches that are *both started and completed* during the month,
3. All the compact batches that are *both started and completed* during the month,
4. The job that is in WIP at the end of the month.

The four cost sheets for jobs that were worked on in March are presented as Exhibit C2-6.3a and b. Sedan Job 106 was in beginning WIP inventory on March 1, 2000. Sedan Job 107 and Compact Job 203 were started and completed during March; all work on these jobs was done in March. Sedan Job 108 was in ending WIP inventory on March 31. There were no compact jobs in March WIP beginning or ending inventories.

Exhibit C2-6.3a

CCC Summary Job Cost Sheet
Sedan Job 106

Batch size	15 Sedans			
Date started	2/26/2002	Date finished		3/3/2002
Date sold	3/14/2002			
Chassis Assembly Department				
	Hours	**Date**		**Cost**
Direct materials		2/26/2002	$	18,425
Direct labor	758	2/26 & 2/27/2002		26,530
Overhead applied		2/28/2002		
Total department costs				
Final Assembly Department				
Direct materials		3/2 & 3/3/2002	$	26,734
Direct labor	856	3/2 & 3/3/2002		29,960
Overhead applied		3/31/2002		
Total department costs				
Job totals	hours			
Average cost per sedan				

CCC Summary Job Cost Sheet
Compact Job 203

Batch size	125 Compacts			
Date started	3/2/2000	Date finished		3/30/2002
Date sold	(33 unsold on 3/31/2002)			
Chassis Assembly Department				
	Hours	**Date**		**Cost**
Direct materials		Various March	$	94,075
Direct labor	3,422	Various March	$	119,770
Overhead applied		3/31/2002		
Total department costs				
Final Assembly Department				
Direct materials		Various March	$	326,475
Direct labor	4,729	Various March	$	165,515
Overhead applied		3/31/2002		
Total department costs				
Job totals	hours			
Average cost per compact				

Exhibit C2-6.3b

CCC Summary Job Cost Sheet Sedan Job 107				
Batch size	360 Sedans			
Date started	3/3/2002	Date finished		3/25/2002
Date sold	(86 unsold on 3/31/2002)			
Chassis Assembly Department				
	Hours	**Date**		**Cost**
Direct materials		Various March	$	440,700
Direct labor	19,500	Various March	$	682,500
Overhead applied		3/31/2002		
Total department costs				
Final Assembly Department				
Direct materials		Various March	$	632,800
Direct labor	20,034	Various March	$	701,190
Overhead applied		3/31/2002		
Total department costs				
Job totals	hours			
Average cost per sedan				

CCC Summary Job Cost Sheet Sedan Job 108				
Batch size	15 Sedans			
Date started	3/30/2002	Date finished		4/2/2002
Date sold				
Chassis Assembly Department				
	Hours	**Date**		**Cost**
Direct materials		3/30/2002	$	18,375
Direct labor	790	3/30 & 3/31/2002	$	27,650
Overhead applied		3/31/2002		
Total department costs				
Final Assembly Department				
Direct materials		4/1/2002		(Next Month)
Direct labor		4/1 & 4/2/2002		(Next Month)
Overhead applied		4/30/2002		(Next Month)
Total department costs				(Next Month)
Job totals				(Next Month)
Average cost per sedan				(Next Month)

SUMMARY OF YEAR 2002 INFORMATION

You gather the following information useful in March job costs:

- The predetermined overhead rate for 2002 is $83 per DLH.
- All direct labor was paid $35 per hour in March.

Sales Information

CCC sold all cars completed except those in finished goods inventory. There were no sales returns or defective cars that were not repaired and shipped.

Finished Goods Inventory

CCC uses a first-in, first-out (FIFO) inventory flow assumption. This means that the car in inventory the longest is the first one sold. It also means that inventory is made up of the most recently completed units. Information on CCC's finished goods inventories is presented in Exhibit C2-6.4. Note that you must compute the March 31, 2002 ending finished goods inventory cost in order to complete the cost of goods sold statement.

Exhibit C2-6.4
Ending Finished Goods Inventory

	February 28, 2002	March 31, 2002
Sedans:		
Units	14	86
Cost	$221,200	You compute
Compacts:		
Units	9	33
Cost	$99,060	You compute

Requirements

1. Assume that sales revenue and selling and administrative cost numbers in Exhibit C2-6.1 are correct. What, if anything, is wrong with the March 2002 income calculation made for David Gomez showing a loss of about $1,300,000? You may want to come back to this question after you complete the other requirements.
2. Compute the costs for Jobs 106, 107, 108, and 203 as of March 31, 2002, by completing the outlined cells on the job cost sheets in Exhibit C2-6.3a and b.
3. Compute the cost of the March ending WIP inventory.
4. Compute the cost of the March ending finished goods inventory.
5. Prepare a cost of goods manufactured and sold (CGMS) schedule in the format given in Exhibit C2-6.5. *Be sure to link as many cells as possible in the statement to the job cost sheets* because it will make requirements 6 and 7 easier. See the Excel instructions for linking cells. Turn in this completed spreadsheet.

(Requirements are continued on the next page)

Exhibit C2-6.5

California Car Company **Cost of Goods Manufactured and Sold Schedule** **March 31, 2002**		
Beginning inventory, finished goods		
Cost of goods manufactured:		
March direct material		
March direct labor		
March manufacturing overhead applied		
Total March manufacturing costs		
Add: Beginning inventory work-in-process		
Less: Ending inventory work-in-process		
Cost of goods manufactured		
Total cost of goods available for sale		
Less: Ending inventory finished goods		
Cost of goods sold		

6. What is the impact on CCC's COGS and ending inventories in WIP and finished goods if CCC used 500 more Chassis Assembly DLHs (at $35 per hour) for Job 107 than are shown in Exhibit C2-6.3b? Show the impact by printing a new COGS schedule. Is the change in COGS merely $17,500 (500 DLHs × $35)?
7. Return your spreadsheet back to where it was in Requirement 4 by eliminating the 500 additional hours you added to Job 107 in Requirement 5. What is the impact on CCC's COGS and ending inventories in WIP and FG if CCC used 500 more Chassis Assembly DLHs (at $35 per hour) for Job 108 than are shown in Exhibit C2-6.3b? Show the impact by printing a new COGS schedule.
8. Explain why the COGS in your answers to Requirements 6 and 7 differ.

Reading 2-7

PERFORMANCE BUDGETS

INTRODUCTION

As Reading 2-4 discusses, most firms estimate costs and revenues for future periods. After production and sales have occurred, a natural reaction for organizations is to compare actual costs and revenues with the estimated ones. Differences between actual and estimated costs, which accountants call *variances*, are then used for future planning and as part of the departmental performance evaluation.[1] Variances are labeled favorable when actual costs are less than estimated and unfavorable when actual costs are greater than budgeted. It is much easier to use the definitions of favorable and unfavorable than to rely on the positive or negative sign of the computed variance when analyzing differences.

Most firms prepare both planning budgets and performance budgets as part of the planning and evaluation process. A *planning budget* looks forward in time to provide the estimated costs and revenues for the coming period. This budget is prepared in advance of the operating period in order to estimate resource needs as well as the other functions discussed in Reading 4-1. **Performance (flexible) budgets** and reports, conversely, look backward rather than forward. Performance reports compare actual costs to estimated costs based on the actual, not the planned, number of units produced and compute variances for use in performance evaluation.

The estimated cost portion of the report, based on current production levels, is the performance budget. Students may find the concept of a performance budget to be a difficult one. One reason is that, unlike most budgets, the performance budget is constructed after the period (month, year, etc.) is over, so use of the term budget appears to be odd. Accountants call it a budget because it contains all the same estimated per-unit variable cost numbers as does a planning budget. Only the *total* variable costs (unit variable cost times actual units produced) are different from the planning budget. To repeat, the key difference between planning budget costs and performance budget costs is that the planning budget is based on *planned* levels of production and the performance budget is based on *actual* levels of production.

In this reading you will receive information to help you construct performance budgets. The reading concludes with a brief discussion of how variances should be used and interpreted by management. The entire budgeting and performance evaluation system in an organization is termed its management control system. Important management control issues, including the setting of standards and the impact of performance systems on employee behavior, are discussed in Module 4. The purpose of this reading is to introduce you to the logic of a performance report as used in a traditional production environment.

---

[1] Those students who have taken statistics should note that accounting variances and statistical variances are completely different concepts. Accounting variances are not a measure of dispersion, but merely the difference between estimated and actual costs or revenues.

PREPARATION OF A PERFORMANCE REPORT FOR CALIFORNIA CAR COMPANY

To illustrate the concept of a performance budget, let us look at a firm like CCC that produces batches of standard products. The top part of Exhibit 2-7.1, CCC's manufacturing performance report, presents the planning budget, the performance budget, and actual February 2002 costs for the Chassis and Final Assembly production departments. Separate reports are prepared for each department, then the two department reports are added together. The February planning budget calls for the production of 330 sedans and 110 compacts. The following explanation only discusses the computations of costs for sedans, but similar steps will produce the cost data in Exhibit 2-7.1 for compacts.

Exhibit 2-7.1
California Car Company
Manufacturing Performance Report
February 2002

	Per Unit	Planning Budget	Performance Budget	Actual	Performance Variance	F or U
Combined Chassis and Final Assembly Departments:						
Units Produced						
Sedans		330	360	360	--	
Compacts		110	120	120	--	
Direct Labor Hours						
Sedan DLHs	108	35,640	38,880	38,965	(85)	U
Compact DLHs	65	7,150	7,800	7,721	79	F
Direct Materials						
Sedans	$ 2,980	$ 983,400	$ 1,072,800	$ 1,064,460	$ 8,340	F
Compacts	3,360	369,600	403,200	409,665	(6,465)	U
Direct Labor Cost						
Sedans	$ 3,780	1,247,400	1,360,800	1,363,765	(2,965)	U
Compacts	2,275	250,250	273,000	270,228	2,772	F
Combined OH Departments:						
Variable Mfg. OH (Inspection, Material Handling & Setup)						
Sedans	$ 3,888	1,283,040	1,399,680	(1)		
Compacts	2,340	257,400	280,800			
Total Variable Overhead		$ 1,540,440	$ 1,680,480	$ 1,677,268	3,212	F
Total Variable Costs		$ 4,391,090	$ 4,790,280	$ 4,785,386		
Fixed Manufacturing Overhead[2]**:** (Maintenance and General Factory)		2,590,092	2,590,092	2,593,521	(3,429)	U
February Totals		$ 6,981,182	$ 7,380,372	$ 7,378,907	$ 1,465	F

(1) CCC does not record the amount of actual variable OH by model, only in total.
(2) Budgeted 2002 annual fixed OH of $31,081,100 ÷ 12

Direct Costs

Direct material cost is $2,980 per sedan for a total planning budget direct material cost of $983,400 (330 × $2,980). Similarly, the planning budget calls for a direct labor cost of $3,780 per sedan producing a total direct labor cost of $1,247,400. CCC actually produced 360 sedans in February. Therefore, CCC needs to know how much should have been spent to produce 360 sedans. The performance budget in Exhibit 2-7.1 answers this question by multiplying 360 times either $2,980 to obtain $1,072,800 for direct materials or $3,780 to obtain $1,360,800 for direct labor. Then the schedule compares the performance budget amount to the actual costs to compute the performance variance. For sedan direct materials, the performance variance is a *favorable* $8,340 because the actual direct material costs of $1,064,460 are less than what was expected for the production of 360 sedans, $1,072,800. Note that the comparison of actual direct material costs with direct material costs in the planning budget of $983,400, based on 330 sedans, would yield an *unfavorable* variance of $81,060. Such a comparison would not be fair since 30 more sedans were produced than planned, and the increase in production should increase total variable costs proportionately.

Performance Budgets for Manufacturing Overhead

Performance budget amounts for variable overhead costs are computed in the same manner as performance budget quantities for direct material and direct labor costs. Total variable overhead in CCC's planning budget is estimated to be $36 per DLH (see Case 2-4). Since the sedan should use 108 DLHs, this translates into $3,888 per sedan. Therefore, the performance budget amount shown in Exhibit 2-7.1 for all three variable overhead departments combined is $1,399,680 (360 × $3,888).

The performance budget for fixed manufacturing overhead is completely different. To understand why, consider whether CCC should expect to incur higher total fixed manufacturing overhead in February given that the actual production was 360 sedans and 120 compacts instead of the planned production of 330 sedans and 110 compacts. Hopefully, you answered no because within the relevant range of production volume, total fixed costs should remain the same. Therefore, CCC should spend the *planning* budget amount on fixed manufacturing overhead, regardless of volume changes.

Performance Budget, Applied, and Actual Overhead Compared

Many students will enter the wrong number for fixed manufacturing overhead in the performance budget. If you are given a predetermined fixed overhead rate of $4,644 per sedan ($43 × 108 direct labor hours) many students will compute the fixed overhead in the performance budget to be $1,671,840 ($4,644 × 360). This is similar to the amount of fixed manufacturing overhead applied to the jobs during February, except that you applied overhead based on actual hours used rather than on the hours that should have been used. The diagrams in Exhibit 2-7.2 illustrate the differences between February performance budget and applied overhead for CCC. Applied overhead is not the same as the amount of overhead that appears in the performance budget.

Also, applied overhead is not used for the same purposes as the performance budget overhead. Recall that Exhibit 2-6.6 illustrated that fixed overhead is assigned to individual units by using a predetermined rate for the first two types of decisions: pricing and profitability and financial reporting. Readings 2-4 and 2-6 explained that financial reporting requires the use of applied overhead in order to produce a consistent percentage of fixed costs to sales and to shelter users from having to work with possibly misleading information due to fluctuating fixed costs.

Exhibit 2-6.6 also stated that budgets require the use of *total fixed* overhead, not applied. Although planning and performance evaluation decisions use predetermined variable overhead rates, they require the use of total fixed amounts. Total fixed overhead, planned or actual, will not change for a period when the production level varies. Consequently, total performance budget fixed overhead should be based on what was planned, not on production levels. Total fixed overhead is a more relevant number because firms plan future activity and costs by department, which are the organization's basic responsibility units. Since performance evaluation measures a manager's performance, and managers direct departments, the decision on how to use fixed costs in evaluating conduct must involve total department costs rather than unit costs. Remember this basic rule—the performance budget amount for total fixed manufacturing overhead is *always* the same as the planning budget amount within the relevant range.

Exhibit 2-7.2
Comparison of Performance Budget to Applied Overhead
(February 2002 CCC Numbers in Parentheses)

PERFORMANCE BUDGET OVERHEAD		
Sedan Variable Overhead		
Estimated variable OH cost per *sedan* : $3,888 ($36 x 108 DLH)	Actual Units → (360 Sedans)	Total sedan Performance Budget ($1,399,680)
CCC Fixed Overhead		
Total (sedan and compact) Planning Budget ($2,590,092)	Actual units → not used	Total CCC Performance Budget ($2,590,092)
APPLIED OVERHEAD		
Sedan Variable Overhead		
Total sedan actual DLHs used (38,965 DLHs)	Predetermined OH Rate → ($36 per DLH)	Total sedan Applied Overhead ($1,402,740)
CCC Fixed Overhead		
Total (sedan and compact) actual DLHs used (46,687 DLHs)	Predetermined OH Rate → ($47 per DLH)	Total CCC Applied Overhead ($2,194,219)

Actual overhead normally is not the same as either the performance budget amount or applied. Remember that both performance budgets and applied use rates based on estimated dollar numbers in the numerator. Actual overhead is the dollar amount of overhead that actually occurs and is known only after production has finished for the period. The following restates and reinforces the differences in terms between performance budget, applied, and actual overhead:

Performance budget—variable overhead, computed by multiplying a predetermined rate by the estimated amount of cost driver times the actual amount of produced units, plus budgeted total fixed overhead

Applied—applied overhead, computed by multiplying a predetermined rate times the actual amount of cost driver, is used for pricing and profitability decisions and financial reporting

Actual—compared to performance budget overhead for performance evaluations

Overhead Performance Variance versus Overapplied or UnderApplied Overhead

As previously described, actual overhead is compared to the performance budget overhead to evaluate performance. The difference between performance and actual overhead is not the same as the overapplied or underapplied overhead amount that is calculated at the end of the accounting period. The computations for and the use of the overhead performance variance and the overapplied or underapplied overhead amount are completely different. The underapplied or overapplied overhead amount only occurs when applied overhead is compared to actual. The amount is used to adjust financial statements to the correct amount spent for actual overhead not to evaluate people or departments. The following will help you to remember the difference between the two computations:

Underapplied or overapplied—the difference between applied and actual manufacturing overhead that is used in financial reporting

Performance variance—the difference between budgeted overhead and actual manufacturing overhead that is used for performance evaluation

USE OF PERFORMANCE BUDGET REPORT INFORMATION

Firms may begin using accounting information to evaluate performance by comparing the planning budget costs with actual cost outcomes. Shortly after calculating the accounting variances produced by comparing planning with actual figures, complaints of unfairness begin to arise. To understand why managers complain, let us revisit Quality Welding. In Reading 2-4, the year 2002 direct labor costs for the Cutting Department are estimated to be \$320,000, the estimated year 2002 DLHs are estimated to be 16,000, and the direct labor rate is estimated to be \$20 per hour. Assume that at the end of 2002, the actual direct labor costs and hours for Cutting total \$370,000 and 18,500 DLHs. Clearly, the Cutting Department spent \$50,000 more on direct labor than estimated. Should the Cutting Department manager be reprimanded for spending too much on direct labor?

Your answer should be that we cannot determine from the comparison of estimated and actual costs whether the manager's control of direct labor costs is good or poor. It is certainly unfair, however, to evaluate the manager negatively simply because actual direct labor costs are higher than estimated. What we really need to know is how many DLHs, as well as the cost of these hours, the Cutting Department should have used to complete work on its year 2002 jobs. Assume that the sum of all the estimated Cutting Department DLHs for all year 2002 jobs, actually produced, is 18,800. As a result, the Cutting Department's performance budget direct labor cost should have been \$376,000 (18,800 DLHs × \$20) for the actual work done in the year 2002. Comparison of the performance budget, not the planning budget, to the actual cost is the fair comparison. The resulting difference is a \$6,000 (\$370,000 actual less \$376,000 estimated) favorable year 2002 direct labor performance variance for the Cutting Department.

Preparation of the performance budget is just the first step in the performance evaluation decision process. An unfavorable variance does not necessarily mean that a manager or department has performed poorly. Variances merely signal that something has not occurred as planned. Each significant variance must be thoroughly investigated to determine its cause and the conditions surrounding its origin before a performance evaluation is made. In addition, numerical information such as variances should represent only a part of any evaluation. Subjective issues also must be considered.

At this point you may realize that the way in which estimates, called *standards* by accountants, are determined has a critical impact on the calculation for variances. If estimated costs per unit are set high, it will be much easier to attain favorable variances than if unit costs estimates are set lower. You also should realize that the way in which performance evaluation is done will impact employee morale and motivation.

SUMMARY

Case 2-7 will require you to complete a performance budget for CCC for the month of March and to analyze the computed variances in detail. This reading has provided you with an example that will help you prepare that performance budget. The reading also discusses differences in overhead terminology, appropriate usage of performance budget variances, and the effect that those variances may have on personnel.

EXERCISES AND PROBLEMS

Exercises

Exercise 1 Performance Budget Results. Specifically how should management use the variances determined in a performance budget when evaluating department performance?

Exercise 2 Performance Budget Results and Performance Evaluation. The management of Joyous Occasion Card Company is very cost conscious and focused on efficiency. Every year the accounting department prepares a planning budget and top management evaluates production and supervisory effectiveness using the numbers in the planning budget as criteria for performance. Mid-management, supervisors, and production employees are not very joyous and are complaining that the planning budget is unfair as a standard against which to measure performance. What would you recommend that the card company do to alleviate employee complaints about the budgetary and evaluation process?

Exercise 3 Performance Budget. Cool-Aire Company manufactures air conditioners. The year 2002 planning budget is based on the following information.

Direct materials cost	$200 per unit
Direct labor hours per unit	3 hours
Direct labor rate	$30 per hour
Predetermined variable overhead rate	$46 per direct labor hour
Predetermined fixed overhead rate	$75 per direct labor hour
Budgeted units of production	10,000 units

During 2002 12,000 units were actually produced. Prepare a year 2002 performance budget for Cool-Aire Company. Do not prepare a complete performance report since the accounting department has not finished collecting the information on actual production costs.

Exercise 4 Performance Budget. No-Freeze Company manufactures furnaces. The year 2002 planning budget is based on the following information.

Direct materials cost	$1,600 per unit
Direct labor hours per unit	5 hours
Direct labor rate	$20 per hour
Predetermined variable overhead rate	$12 per direct labor hour
Predetermined fixed overhead rate	$125 per direct labor hour
Budgeted units of production	10,000 units

During 2002 9,000 units were actually produced. Prepare a year 2002 performance budget for No-Freeze Company. Do not prepare a complete performance report since the accounting department has not finished collecting the information on actual production costs.

Exercise 5 Applied Overhead and Performance Budget Overhead. The vice president of production for the company where you work as chief cost accountant does not understand why you have to compute yet another overhead amount for the performance budget. To save time, he wants you to just copy and paste the applied overhead number from the financial cost of goods manufactured and sold schedule. Explain to the vice president why applied overhead should not be used for a performance budget and variance analysis.

Exercise 6 Overapplied or Underapplied Overhead and Performance Budget Overhead Variance. The vice president of production for the company where you work as chief cost accountant does not understand the difference between overapplied or underapplied overhead and the overhead variances found on a performance budget. He asks: "Aren't both of the differences between estimated and actual overhead? Don't both differences indicate that we are over or under budget for overhead?" Explain to the vice president the difference between overapplied or underapplied overhead and the performance budget variance for overhead and explain which is more appropriate for performance evaluations.

Exercise 7 Overhead Performance Budget. The cost accountant for your small manufacturing plant has finally finished the performance budget with a variance analysis for the year 2002. In order to save time, the accountant used applied overhead from the financial accounting computer system, combined the applied variable and fixed overhead numbers on the performance budget, and compared only this total applied overhead to total actual overhead. Even though you are not an accountant, you attended a university that used the California Car Company serial case in introductory accounting to teach you many useful managerial accounting tools. As vice president of production you suspect the accountant's method used to prepare the performance budget is not correct. How do you need to instruct the plant accountant so that a fairer, more useful, and correct performance budget that you can use to evaluate the performance of production employees is prepared?

Problems

Problem 1 Performance Budget with Variances. Orlando Company manufactures one product in one production department. The year 2002 planning budget is based on the following information.

Direct materials cost	$40 per unit
Direct labor hours per unit	½ hour
Direct labor rate	$20 per hour
Predetermined variable overhead rate	$6 per direct labor hour
Predetermined fixed overhead rate	$22 per direct labor hour
Budgeted units of production	10,000 units

Actual results for year 2002 units are as follows.

Total direct materials cost	$464,000
Total direct labor cost	$131,000
Total variable overhead	$42,000
Total fixed overhead	$116,000
Total units produced	12,000 units

Prepare a year 2002 full manufacturing performance report for Orlando Company. Use the format of Exhibit 2-7.1 in Reading 2-7.

Problem 2 Complex Performance Budget. Save-Your-Skin Lotion Company manufactures and bottles suntan lotion and body moisturizing lotion. Production costs for 5,000 12-ounce bottles during the month of May 2002 are as follows.

Direct materials cost	$2.35 per bottle
Direct labor hours per bottle	¼ hour
Direct labor rate	$4.60 per DLH
Variable overhead	$0.75 per bottle
Fixed overhead	$6,350

The planning budget for 5,200 12-ounce bottles during the month of May is as follows.

Direct materials cost	$2.30 per bottle
Direct labor hours per bottle	1/3 hour
Direct labor rate	$4.50 per DLH
Variable overhead	$0.80 per bottle
Fixed overhead	$1.25 per bottle
Budgeted fixed overhead	$6,500 (for May)

Prepare a thorough budget variance analysis that is fair to managers. Use the format of Exhibit 2-7.1 in Reading 2-7 to prepare your performance report. Then analyze those variances and suggest areas that need improvement. Be sure to provide the managers with information on the size or proportion of the variances needing attention.

Problem 3 Complex Performance Budget. Lopez Bottle Company is the manufacturer for several brands of soft drinks. Production costs for 25,000 6-packs of 16-ounce bottles during the month of October 2002 are as follows.

Direct materials cost	$1.35 per 6-pack
Direct labor hours per 6-pack	1/3 hour
Direct labor rate	$8.60 per DLH
Variable overhead	$1.75 per 6-pack
Fixed overhead	$3,350

The planning budget for 22,000 6-packs of 16-ounce bottles during the month of October is as follows.

Direct materials cost	$1.40 per 6-pack
Direct labor hours per 6-pack	¼ hour
Direct labor rate	$8.50 per DLH
Variable overhead	$1.70 per 6-pack
Fixed overhead	$0.147 per 6-pack
Budgeted fixed overhead	$3,250 (for October)

Prepare a thorough budget variance analysis that is fair to managers. Use the format of Exhibit 2-7.1 in Reading 2-7. Then analyze those variances and suggest areas that need improvement. Be sure to provide the managers with information on the size or proportion of the variances needing attention.

Problem 4 Complex Performance Budget. Nickle Manufacturing, Inc. produces metal plates as a component part for machines produced by another company. At the end of 2002 the cost accountants of Nickle meticulously prepared the company's planning budget for all 2003 production as follows:

Direct materials	$2,300,500
Direct labor	$5,600,250
Variable overhead	$1,775,300
Fixed overhead	$2,360,750
Estimated units to be produced	3,800 plates

Unfortunately, production for 2003 did not meet the expectations used for the planning budget and was only 3,500 plates. Actual costs for 2003 production were as follows.

Direct materials	$2,300,000
Direct labor	$5,300,250
Variable overhead	$1,775,300
Fixed overhead	$2,260,550
Units produced	3,500 plates

Prepare a performance budget with variances for Nickle, Inc. for the year 2003. Use the format of Exhibit 2-7.1 in Reading 2-7. What cost items, if any, would you recommend that Nickle management investigate?

Problem 5 Complex Performance Budget. Following the close of the 2002 calendar year, the management at Shutter, Inc. has asked you to prepare a performance analysis report for the year 2002. Shutter makes several products in its one factory, one of which is a digital camera for computers. Following is information you might find useful in your analysis.

Estimated production for year 2002	22,000 cameras
Estimated year 2002 costs (Used to prepare the budget):	
Direct materials	$20 per camera
Direct labor (3 hours @ $15)	$45 per camera
Variable manufacturing overhead	$24 per camera
Fixed manufacturing overhead	$21 per camera
(Both fixed and variable overhead are applied on the basis of DLHs.)	
Actual direct labor hours used	61,000 DLHs

a. Complete Shutter 's year 2002 performance report below. Show all calculations.

	Planning Budget	Performance Budget	Actual Results	Variance	F or U
Units	______	______	20,000	______	____
Direct materials	______	______	$420,000	______	____
Direct labor	______	______	$898,000	______	____

Variable OH	_______	_________	$472,000	________	_____
Fixed OH	_______	_________	$479,000	________	_____

b. What is the primary decision use of applied overhead?

c. How much overhead was applied in the year 2002?

d. Explain how both the variable and fixed components of applied overhead differs from variable and fixed overhead in the performance budget in a normal cost system.

Case 2-7

VARIANCE CONTROVERSY AT CALIFORNIA CAR COMPANY

Case Objectives

1. Introduce the concepts of performance (flexible) budgets and cost variances
2. Introduce the use of managerial accounting information in performance evaluation

Decision (Performance Evaluation): How have CCC and its departments performed in March?

THE CONTROVERSY

It is now the middle of April 2002. After reviewing the cost of goods manufactured numbers that you prepared in Case 2-6, Sally Swanson, vice president of production, and Jena Butler, vice president of finance, meet on April 14 to discuss cost control. Jena says: "After comparing the actual March manufacturing costs with the March planning budget for manufacturing costs (as shown in Exhibit C2-7.1), I am concerned that our manufacturing costs are much higher than planned. If CCC is to earn an acceptable profit this year, it is critical that we meet our 2002 cost estimates."

Sally responds: "I am surprised the cost of goods manufactured schedule indicates that our cost control in March is weak. The plant ran smoothly in March and I know of no reason why our costs should be too high. Both of my production department managers and a couple of my overhead department managers are fuming. They all feel accused of not controlling costs when they are convinced they have done a good job. We better get to the bottom of all this before I have an outright revolt on my hands." Sally and Jena have asked you to evaluate the cost control performance of the production area in March as quickly as possible.

The accountants have given you Exhibit C2-7.1, which contains CCC's planned March production level of 468 cars (351 sedans and 117 compacts) and planned cost of manufacturing 468 cars. Exhibit C2-7.1 also contains the actual March manufacturing costs, as reflected in the March cost of goods manufactured schedule you prepared in Case 2-6. You can trace the actual direct material and direct labor costs back to the job cost sheets for March. It also indicates that total March *actual* manufacturing overhead cost is $4,325,229, as opposed to the March *applied* overhead of $4,094,473 that you used in the cost of goods manufactured schedule for Case 2-6. CCC considers the Inspection, Setup, and the Material Handling Departments to be variable cost centers. Costs in the Maintenance and General Factory Departments are considered fixed.

Exhibit C2-7.1

California Car Company March 2002 Planning Budget Versus Actual Costs	Per Unit (Planned) (Case 2-4)	Planning Budget	Actual (Case 2-6)	Variance
Units Produced: (Same in each production dept.)				
Sedans		351	375	24 F
Compacts		117	125	8 F
Sedan direct labor hours		37,908	41,180	(3,272) U
Compact direct labor hours		7,605	8,151	(546) U
Production Departments				
Chassis Department:				
Direct material cost				
Sedans	$ 1,220	$ 428,220	$ 459,075	$ (30,855) U
Compacts	750	87,750	94,075	(6,325) U
Direct labor cost				
Sedans (52 hours)	1,820	638,820	710,150	(71,330) U
Compacts (28 hours)	980	114,660	119,770	(5,110) U
Total Chassis Department		$ 1,269,450	$ 1,383,070	$ (113,620) U
Final Assembly Department:				
Direct material cost				
Sedans	$ 1,760	$ 617,760	$ 659,534	$ (41,774) U
Compacts	2,610	305,370	326,475	(21,105) U
Direct labor cost				
Sedans (56 hours)	1,960	687,960	731,150	(43,190) U
Compacts (37 hours)	1,295	151,515	165,515	(14,000) U
Total Final Assembly		$ 1,762,605	$ 1,882,674	$ (120,069) U
Overhead Departments				
Inspection Dept. (@$16 per DLH):				
Sedans	$ 1,728	$ 606,528	(1)	
Compacts	1,040	121,680		
Totals		$ 728,208	$ 774,500	$ (46,292) U
Material Handling Dept. (@$9 per DLH):				
Sedans	$ 972	$ 341,172	(1)	
Compacts	585	68,445		
Totals		$ 409,617	$ 435,825	$ (26,208) U
Setup Department (@$11 per DLH):				
Sedans	$ 1,188	$ 416,988	(1)	
Compacts	715	83,655		
Totals		$ 500,643	$ 559,575	$ (58,932) U
Maintenance Dept. (fixed):		$ 510,667	$ 498,460	$ 12,207 F
General Factory Dept. (fixed):		2,079,425	2,056,869	22,556 F
Total overhead		$ 4,228,560	$ 4,325,229	$ (96,669) U
March total manufacturing costs		$ 7,260,615	$ 7,590,973	$ (330,358) U

(1) CCC does not record the amount of actual variable OH by model.

Total actual direct materials cost (from above)	$1,539,159
Total actual direct labor cost (from above)	1,726,585

Note that the first column of Exhibit C2-7.1 is information from Case 2-4. The material cost per sedan and per compact for each department is given at the top of Exhibit C2-4.2. The direct labor cost per car in each department is calculated by multiplying the hours shown in Exhibit C2-4.2 by $35 per hour. The 2002 predetermined variable overhead rate used in Case 2-4 is $36 per DLH. In Exhibit C2-7.1 the sum of the costs per DLH for the Inspection, Material Handling, and Setup departments is the same $36. The fixed overhead in Exhibit C2-7.1, the Maintenance and General Factory departments, total $2,590,092 for March. When this monthly total multiplied by 12 months, it equals (with rounding) the estimated 2002 fixed overhead of $31,081,100 used in Case 2-4.

In Case 2-6 you found that CCC produced the equivalent of 375 sedans during March. They started and completed all 360 sedans in Job 107, plus they did all final assembly work on the 15 sedans in Job 106 and completed all chassis assembly work on 15 sedans in Job 108. The combination of work done on Job 106 and Job 108 is exactly equal to the amount of work required to produce 15 completed sedans. CCC produced 125 compacts in Job 203, all started and completed in March. These numbers are in the actual column of Exhibit C2-7.1.

Other numbers in the actual column also come from your solution to Case 2-6. The total March cost of direct material cost for both the Chassis Assembly and Final Assembly Departments totals $1,539,159 (summed for you at the bottom of Exhibit C2-7.1), the same number shown in the cost of goods sold schedule in Case 2-6. Likewise, the total March direct labor cost of $1,726,585 (49,331 DLHs) is the number you computed in Case 2-6.

The estimated (budgeted) 2002 information from Case 2-4 follows:

Material costs per car:	
Sedan	2,980
Compact	3,360
Direct labor costs per car:	
Sedan	3,780 (108 hours)
Compact	2,275 (65 hours)

Planned and actual direct labor rate per hour:	$ 35
Predetermined overhead rates:	
Variable	$ 36 per direct labor hour
Fixed	47 per direct labor hour
Total	$ 83

Requirements

In answering the questions, refer back to your solution to Case 2-4 and to Reading 2-7.

1. Discuss whether you believe that the manufacturing cost analysis in Exhibit C2-7.1 is appropriate. Why are some department managers complaining?
2. Many numbers in Exhibit C2-7.1 are carried forward from previous cases. Identify which numbers are from other cases and which cases they are from.
3. Set up a spreadsheet in the format of Exhibit C2-7.1. Include a performance budget column and compute new variances so you have a complete cost performance report. Print your new spreadsheet.

(Requirements continued on the next page)

4. Prepare an analysis discussing:
   a. The overall cost control performance of the entire plant.
   b. The cost control performance of each manufacturing department:
      - Chassis Assembly
      - Final Assembly
      - Inspection and Rework
      - Material Handling
      - Setup
      - Maintenance
      - General Factory

5. If CCC actually produced 378 sedans and 126 compacts in March instead of the 375 sedans and 125 compacts shown in Exhibit C2-7.1 and *all actual costs remain the same*, by how much would the variances for each of the following departments change? *Hint*: you can copy your completed solution to a new sheet in your Excel workbook and change the actual number of sedans and compacts produced.
   - Chassis Assembly
   - Final Assembly
   - Inspection and Rework
   - Maintenance

6. On several different occasions in March, the production of compacts was halted because of stockouts of small solar panels. In each case the chassis and final assembly lines had to be changed over to sedan production temporarily until parts arrived from the outside vendor, at which time the lines were changed back to the production of compacts. As a result, more setups were required in March than expected. In the following table, indicate the impact of the extra setups on the March variances by placing a U for an unfavorable impact, an F for a favorable impact, and an N for no impact.

Variance	Impact (U, F, or N)	Explanation
Direct material		
Direct labor		
Setup overhead		

Group Assignment 2-7

OVERDONE OVERHEAD?

Group number __________ **Signatures of group members participating:**

____

____

Objectives

1. Understand overapplied and underapplied overhead
2. Emphasize the differences between applied overhead, planning budget overhead, and performance budget overhead numbers
3. Demonstrate the impact of operating events on variances

After reviewing the March 2002 performance report you completed in Case 2-7, David Gomez, president of CCC, is confused about March overhead costs. He notes that the planning budget for fixed and variable overhead combined is $4,228,560 while the actual overhead is $4,325,229. This is an unfavorable difference of $96,669, which David views as quite significant. Even more confusing is the $2,543,002 in overhead you reported on CCC's March cost of goods manufactured schedule in Case 2-6. Jena Butler has prepared the schedule shown in Exhibit G2-7.1 to summarize the situation.

Exhibit G2-7.1

California Car Company
Overhead Numbers for March 2002

Planning budget:			
Variable	Case 2-7	$ 1,638,468	
Fixed	Case 2-7	2,590,092	$ 4,228,560
Performance budget:			
Variable	Case 2-7	$ 1,750,500	
Fixed	Case 2-7	2,590,092	$ 4,340,592
Actual overhead:			
Variable	Case 2-7	$ 1,769,900	
Fixed	Case 2-7	2,555,329	$ 4,325,229
Applied overhead (from COGS schedule):			
Variable*	Case 2-6	$ 1,775,916	
Fixed†	Case 2-6	2,318,557	$ 4,094,473

*49,331 actual direct labor hours × $36

†49,331 actual direct labor hours × $47

Sally Swanson studies the March performance report and the cost of goods manufactured schedule and is a bit confused. She asks for your help in understanding the various March 2002 overhead numbers.

Recall that the planned production for March was 351 sedans and 117 compacts, while the actual production was 375 sedans and 125 compacts. Average planned monthly production for 2002 is 425 sedans (5,100 ÷ 12 months) and about 142 compacts.

Requirements

1. Module 2 explores four important management decisions: Planning (Case 2-4), pricing (Case 2-5), financial reporting (Case 2-6), and performance evaluation (Case 2-7). Show Sally the primary decision purpose(s) for each of the three March overhead measures (planning budget, applied, and actual) mentioned by David Gomez by placing an "X" in the appropriate boxes (you can check more than one box in each row or column).

	Decisions			
	Planning	**Pricing**	**Financial Reporting**	**Performance Evaluation**
Planning Budget OH				
Applied Overhead				
Actual Overhead				
Performance Budget OH				

2. Explain why the March planning budget overhead differs from the March applied overhead for:

   Variable overhead:

   Fixed overhead:

3. Explain why the March applied overhead differs from the March actual overhead for:

   Variable overhead:

   Fixed overhead:

4. By how much is CCC's March overhead overapplied or underapplied? Explain.

5. Sally is aware of a production problem that occurred during March that caused fewer cars to be produced than scheduled. Four times during March production of compacts was halted when inspection discovered defects in the solar panels. Each time a solar panel was found to be defective, the line was shut down, to see whether other defective solar panels were in the process of being installed or were on the pallet in the final assembly area ready to be installed. As a result, CCC used more labor hours than planned for March production. Fortunately, CCC received credit from its supplier for all defective panels discovered. Indicate how this event would have affected the March labor, material, and overhead manufacturing variances and the amount of overhead applied during March by completing the following table. The question is not asking for any calculations.

Variance	Impact (U, F, or N)	Explanation
Direct material		
Direct labor		
Variable manufacturing OH		
Fixed manufacturing OH		
I (Increase) or D (Decrease) for applied OH only		
Total applied OH		

Module 2

Peer Evaluation of Group Members	Class Section	Group No.

Evaluator's Name ____________________________________

Module 2

In the table below, please indicate your estimate, in percentage terms, of the contributions that individual group members made to each of the group assignments listed. Each column should add to 100 percent. For example, if there are five members in your group and all were present for Group Assignment 2-2, you would divide the 100 percent among the five members, including yourself. If you felt that all group members were prepared to discuss the assignment and contributed equally to the solution, you would give each person 20 percent. If only four members were present and you felt that one particular member contributed twice as much as the other three, you would give the heavy contributor 40 percent and the other three members 20 percent. Any group member who was absent should be listed and given a zero percent.

	Group Assignment Number		
Group Members (List)	**2-2**	**2-5**	**2-7**
Myself			
Totals	**100**	**100**	**100**

Fill in this sheet after each group assignment is completed and turn in at the completion of Group Assignment 2-7.

MODULE 2 REVIEW

REVIEW QUESTIONS

1. Identify and define the basic elements of manufacturing costs and how to identify which company costs are assigned to products and which are assigned to periods.

2. How do accountants determine the amount of overhead assigned to a unit of product and to a job?

3. Describe how a traditional factory is organized and how products physically pass through a traditional factory.

4. Identify problems and nonvalue-added activities, or waste, which arise in a traditional factory.

5. Discuss the accounting issues associated with problems found in a traditional factory.

6. How is short-term and long-term analysis of a firm's pricing and profitability decisions done in a traditional firm? Also, what did CCC discover when it analyzed its pricing and profitability policies?

7. How are costs in a job-order cost system collected? How are job costs used to prepare a cost of goods manufactured and sold (CGMS) schedule?

8. What does manufacturing overhead mean on a CGMS schedule, and how is underapplied or overapplied overhead calculated?

9. Describe how a manufacturing performance report is prepared and interpreted.

10. Describe the impact of a line shutdown on a firm's performance variances and the amount of overhead applied.

REVIEW PROBLEM

The Peach Computer Company manufactures two models of personal computers, the standard model and the multimedia model, in one factory. The factory has two production departments, the Motherboard (MB) Department and the Final Assembly (FA) Department. There also are two overhead departments, the Inspection and Maintenance (I&M) Department and the General Factory (GF) Department. Cost analyses indicate that I&M is a variable overhead department and that the GF is a fixed overhead department. The standard model sells for $2,100, and the multimedia model sells for $2,800. The October 2002 planned and actual production information, as well as planned 2002 full year information, follows.

PEACH COMPUTER COMPANY
COST PERFORMANCE REPORT
OCTOBER 2002

	Per Unit	October Planned	October Performance Budget	October Actual	October Performance Variance	U or F	Full Year Planned
Units							
Standard		1,000		900			15,000
Multimedia		600		700			8,000
Direct materials							
Standard	$ 900	$ 900,000		$ 817,000			$ 13,500,000
Multimedia	$1,250	$ 750,000		$ 864,000			$ 10,000,000
Direct labor hours							
Standard	5	5,000		4,600			75,000
Multimedia	8	4,800		5,520			64,000
Direct labor cost							
Standard	$ 110	$ 110,000		$ 101,200			$ 1,650,000
Multimedia	$ 176	$ 105,600		$ 121,440			$ 1,408,000
Variable mfg. OH							
Standard				- - -	- - -		
Multimedia				- - -	- - -		
Total Variable OH				$ 175,000			
Fixed mfg. OH		$ 474,917		$ 486,800			$ 5,699,000
Total mfg. Costs				$ 2,565,440			

Requirements

1. Compute Peach's 2002 predetermined overhead rate. Peach expects the predetermined variable overhead rate for 2002 to be the same $18 per DLH as it was in 2001.

2. Compute Peach's 2002 estimated cost to manufacture a) one standard computer and b) one multimedia computer.

3. Compute Peach's markup percentage on a total manufacturing cost base for the *entire* firm, *not* by model. Use corporate *planned* costs and volume for the entire year. Selling prices are listed on the previous page.

4. Based on the corporate markup percentage computed in requirement 3, what price should Peach charge for each product in order to earn the corporate markup percentage in requirement 3?

5. Explain how Peach can use its cost information to assess its profitability and to detect problem areas.

6. Prepare an October 2002 cost of goods manufactured schedule for Peach. October WIP inventories are beginning inventory—$62,000 and ending inventory—$76,000. FG inventories are beginning inventory—0 and ending inventory—$25,568.

7. Complete Peach's October 2002 cost performance report by computing the numbers that are missing in the report. Items that you need to calculate are box-outlined on the performance report.

8. Is manufacturing overhead overapplied or underapplied in October?

9. Based on the performance report, discuss how well each of Peach's departments controlled costs.

10. Assume that during October Peach received some defective computer chips from its supplier. These faulty chips fortunately were used only for the multimedia model. Unfortunately, production for that model had to be stopped for five days to wait for delivery of good quality chips. The defective chips were discarded, and any computers found to have defective chips during inspection were rebuilt with the proper chip component installed. Discuss how the delivery and use of the defective chips would affect October labor, material, and overhead manufacturing variances.

11. Assume Peach has excess production capacity and can sell an additional 500 multimedia units to a new U.S./Mexican private joint marketing venture in Nuevo Laredo. If the contract is executed, Peach will sell the units at $2,000 U.S. dollars each and will incur additional distribution costs of $150 per unit. The contract is for a one-time only sale and would not violate any federal or state regulations. Should Peach enter into the contract? Why? Show support for your answer with cost and profit data.

MODULE THREE

COST MANAGEMENT

Systems

Module 3 Introduction

COST MANAGEMENT SYSTEMS

MODULE OVERVIEW

Cost management systems are information systems used to support managers in their efforts to improve efficiency and to better meet customer needs. Module 3 begins with a discussion of activity-based costing (ABC), followed by coverage of activity-based management (ABM). Issues of quality and continuous improvement and the accounting implications of implementing quality programs are covered next. The module concludes by exploring just-in-time (JIT) production and the accounting impacts of this philosophy. Also included in this module is an introduction to many accounting-related careers.

An important objective of Module 3 is to demonstrate that the accounting and management control system used by an organization must change when a process-based management system is adopted. The traditional accounting and control system presented in Module 2 supports the department-based organization of a traditional firm, but often work counter to the goals of a process management.

The California Car Company (CCC) case continues in Module 3. In Module 2 CCC management discovered that CCC is less profitable than the industry. They found that very high manufacturing overhead is the primary cause for CCC's poor profitability. To better understand their overhead problems, CCC completes an ABC study. Based on the results of this study, CCC implements a quality program and adopts the JIT philosophy. By the end of Module 3 CCC improves the quality of its processes and products and the efficiency of its operations. The three decision contexts used in this module are the following:

- What manufacturing overhead activities are creating high overhead costs?
- How can CCC improve its quality and reduce its costs created by poor quality?
- How can CCC reduce its costs for setup, maintenance, inspection and rework, and purchasing and material handling?

Learning Objectives

After completing Module 3, the student should be able to:

1. Understand the basic approach of ABC; compute activity-based costs, understand how activity-based costs differ from traditional costs, and understand how activity-based costs can be used by management to improve operations.

- Reading 3-1	Activity-Based Costing
- Case 3-1	Activity-Based Costing at California Car Company
- Group Assignment 3-1	A Cost by Any Other Name
- Exercises and Problems	Exercises and Problems at the end of Reading 3-1

2. Understand process management and how it differs from traditional departmental control. Understand the concepts of quality and continuous improvement, including a basic understanding of variability and quality; understand the accounting and management control changes that occur when a quality program is implemented; and understand cost of quality and how cost of quality can be used to improve performance.

- Reading 3-2	Process Management and Accounting
- Case 3-2	Implementing a Quality Program at CCC
- Case 3-3	Cost of Quality at California Car Company
- Exercises and Problems	Exercises and Problems at the end of Reading 3-2

3. Understand basic JIT production concepts, including demand pull and cellular manufacturing; understand the impact of a JIT operating philosophy on the accounting and management control system; and introduce basic concepts of process costing.

- Reading 3-4	JIT and Process Improvement
- Case 3-4	Implementing JIT at California Car Company
- Group Assignment 3-4	JIT Simulation at California Car Company
- Case 3-5	JIT Costing at California Car Company
- Group Assignment 3-5	A Cost Is a Cost Is a Cost?
- Exercises and Problems	Exercises and Problems at the end of Reading 3-4

4. Understand the roles accountants play in business and government, explain the projected demand for accounting and related professionals, and be aware of some of the varied career paths open to accounting graduates.

- Reading 3-6	Careers in Accounting
- Exercises and Problems	Exercises and Problems at the end of Reading 3-6

TERMINOLOGY LIST FOR MODULE 3

Activity
Activity-based costing
Activity-based management
Activity improvement measures
Appraisal costs
Benchmarking
Continuous improvement
Control chart
Core processes
Corporate performance measures
Cost management systems
Cost of quality
Cost pool
Demand pull
Enterprise resource planning software
External failure costs
Internal failure costs
Just-in-time system
Kanban system
Key success factors
Lean production
Management control system
Operations management
Paradigm
Prevention costs
Preventive maintenance
Process
Process output measures
Process quality improvement
Six Sigma
Special cause events
Statistical quality control
Suboptimization
Supply chain management
Support processes
Tampering
Total quality management
Work cell

Reading 3-1

ACTIVITY-BASED COSTING

INTRODUCTION

Activity-based costing (ABC) is a technique used to assign costs of related overhead activities (both manufacturing and selling and administrative overhead) to jobs, products, customers, and other cost objectives more accurately than the traditional method discussed in Module 2. Note that direct material and direct labor costs are not affected by a change to ABC. An **activity** is a unit of work within a process. Preparing a customer invoice, repairing equipment, or preparing a midterm examination are examples of activities. Reading 3-1 compares ABC with the traditional approach, explains how to compute activity-based costs, and provides examples of uses in industry.

TRADITIONAL VERSUS ABC APPROACHES

In traditional overhead allocation, manufacturing overhead is assigned to jobs based on the direct labor hours (DLHs) used on each job or on some other measure that varies in proportion to the volume of production. Examples of other measures include machine hours and direct labor costs. Exhibit 3-1.1 reproduces traditional overhead allocation for the Quality Welding example presented in Module 2. ABC, by contrast, uses additional, nonvolume allocation bases or cost drivers to assign overhead. In most situations ABC yields more accurate cost estimates because more cost drivers are used. ABC usually is extended to selling and administrative costs as well as manufacturing costs. This difference is illustrated below.

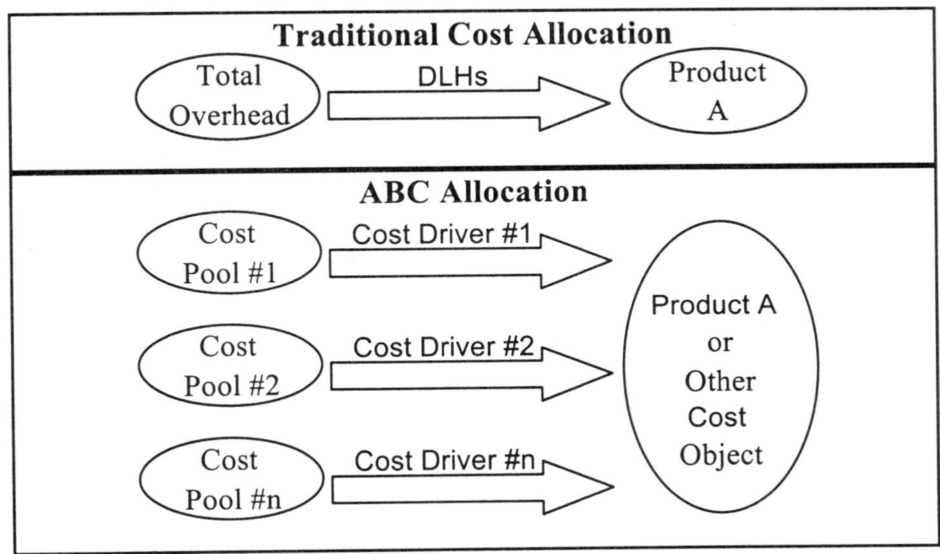

Exhibit 3-1.1

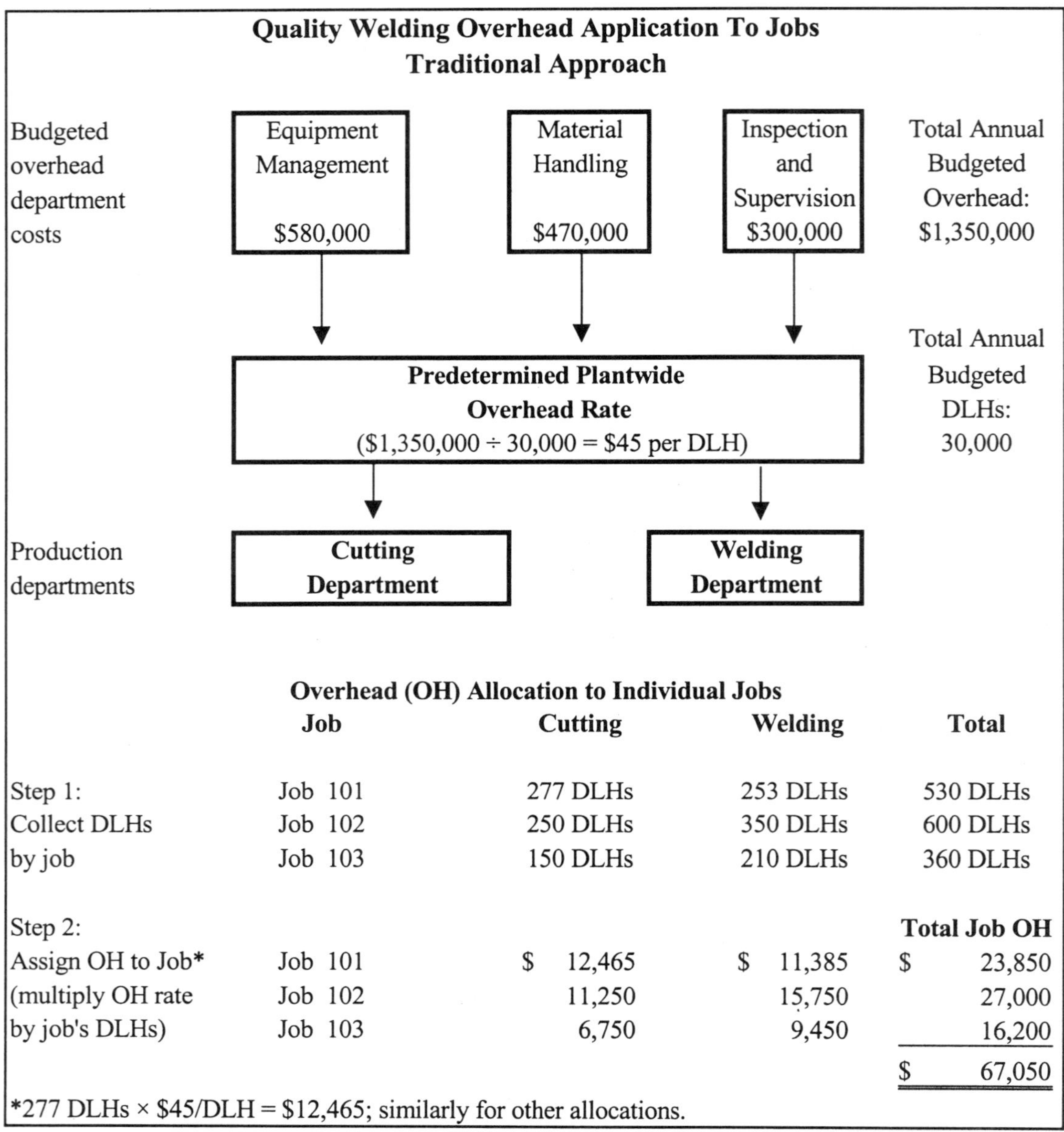

Overhead (OH) Allocation to Individual Jobs

	Job	Cutting	Welding	Total
Step 1:	Job 101	277 DLHs	253 DLHs	530 DLHs
Collect DLHs	Job 102	250 DLHs	350 DLHs	600 DLHs
by job	Job 103	150 DLHs	210 DLHs	360 DLHs
Step 2:				**Total Job OH**
Assign OH to Job*	Job 101	$ 12,465	$ 11,385	$ 23,850
(multiply OH rate	Job 102	11,250	15,750	27,000
by job's DLHs)	Job 103	6,750	9,450	16,200
				$ 67,050

*277 DLHs × $45/DLH = $12,465; similarly for other allocations.

Use of Additional Cost Drivers

ABC usually creates more accurate costs because the cost driver (or cause of each type of overhead cost) is examined carefully. Overhead costs are then assigned based on different cost drivers for different types of overhead costs. Note that traditional costing assumes that all overhead costs are driven by direct labor hours (DLHs) or some other volume-based measure. To illustrate the difference, consider the setup overhead cost pool for CCC. Traditional costing assigns setup costs to jobs based on DLHs used. Total setup costs aren't caused by the use of DLHs and don't vary in proportion to them. Therefore, assigning setup costs based on DLHs is both arbitrary and inaccurate.

ABC, on the other hand, searches for the cause of setup costs. One possible cause is the number of setups that must be made. The more setups a firm must perform, the higher its total setup cost. In fact, it is likely that a large job requiring 2,000 DLHs but only one setup will cause the same setup cost as a small job that uses only 20 DLHs and one setup. When

ABC is used, each job will be assigned the same setup costs because each job has the same driver usage (one setup). In contrast, traditional costing would assign the large job 100 times as much setup cost because it uses 100 times as many DLHs—2,000 compared to 20 DLHs.

Allocation of Selling and Administrative Costs

ABC also is more accurate because of the way in which selling and administrative (S&A) costs are handled. Recall from Case 2-5 that most traditional costing systems address S&A costs by adding a percentage markup based on the total manufacturing costs (or some other manufacturing cost base). In effect, traditional costing systems assign S&A costs based on the cost of manufacturing each job. Manufacturing cost, however, is not the cause or driver for many S&A costs. Therefore, allocating S&A costs based on manufacturing costs is again arbitrary and inaccurate. For example, although a new, electronic version of a product might take a large research and development effort (classified by accountants as an administrative expense), it may be fairly inexpensive to manufacture. On the other hand, the firm's existing, mechanical product requires little research and development effort but is much more expensive to manufacture. As a result, the mechanical product is likely to be marked up the same percentage, thus absorbing far more development cost than it causes. The costing error that results will lead to incorrect pricing and a potential loss of market share.

ABC extends the search for cost drivers beyond manufacturing costs to selling and administrative costs. By assigning sales, delivery, development, and accounting costs based on the causes or drivers of these costs, a much more accurate picture of product profitability can be obtained. In addition, many firms perform ABC analysis on customers, sales territories, vendors, and other cost objects that cannot be addressed using traditional costing techniques. Although the CCC case focuses on manufacturing costs, ABC also is a powerful tool for analyzing other costs and cost objects.

Using ABC to Determine Customer Profitability

ABC is frequently used to cost objects other than products, an application for which traditional costing is not suitable because volume-based drivers are not relevant. The most common nonproduct application of ABC is to determine the profitability of individual customers or classes of customers. Customer characteristics and behavior can create significant cost differences, even for customers that purchase similar quantity and types of goods or services. For example, Customer A may make many small purchases, pay its invoices late, demand refunds for problems it creates, and require a large number of service calls. Customer B purchases the same volume of the same goods and services, but it does so in a few large orders, pays invoices before they are due, and never asks for refunds or service. Customer B obviously is more profitable, but traditional accounting systems are unable to report this to managers. Even if managers know from observation that Customer B is more desirable, they don't know if Customer A is too costly to keep or how much of a discount to give to Customer B if another supplier is threatening to take their business.[1]

A typical result of an ABC customer profitability study is that about 20 percent of customers produce most of a firm's profit. This means that the other 80 percent are either marginally profitable or unprofitable. One example is Kanthal, which undertook an ABC analysis to determine the individual profitability of each of their customers in order to improve return

---

[1] For further information, see J. A. Ness, M. J. Schroeck, R. A. Letendre, and W. J. Douglas, "The Role of ABM in Measuring Customer Value," *Strategic Finance*, March 2001, pp. 32–37.

on equity.[2] Using ABC to determine the true order and setup costs caused by individual customers, Kanthal found that the actual costs it incurred exceeded sales revenue for 50 percent of its customers. This was a complete surprise. In addition, they found that 5 percent of customers caused most of this dollar loss. These hidden losses went undetected by the traditional accounting system.

COMPUTING ACTIVITY-BASED COSTS

Before continuing with this section, review the traditional approach to overhead allocation presented in Exhibit 3-1.1. Quality Welding has three overhead departments with budgets that total $1,350,000. DLHs are used to allocate or assign all of this manufacturing overhead to each job, even though Quality knows that most overhead is not caused by DLHs. Quality's predetermined overhead rate is $45 per DLH. As a result, Quality assigns $45 of overhead to a job each time a job uses one DLH.

ABC Cost per Driver

Determination of the overhead rate per unit of driver is at the heart of any costing system. In a traditional system, this is the predetermined overhead rate per DLH, which is $45 for Quality Welding. The following six–step approach can make the calculation of costs per driver easier in an ABC system.

Step 1 *Identify cost drivers*. What drives or causes overhead costs to happen?

Step 2 *Create overhead cost pools*. What is the total dollar amount of overhead that needs to be allocated?

Step 3 *Determine* total *usage of each driver for the entire organization*. How much of each cost driver is used for all cost objects annually?

Step 4 *Compute driver rate*. How much overhead cost will be allocated to costs objects for each unit of driver used? (Step 1 divided by step 3)

Step 5 *Determine Cost Object and Related Driver Use*. To what am I trying to allocate overhead and how much of the driver does my cost object use?

Step 6 *Assign Overhead Costs to Cost Object*. What is the total amount of overhead assigned to my cost object? (Step 4 multiplied by step 5)

Each step is illustrated using the Quality Welding example presented in ABC format in Exhibit 3-1.2. In the example, assume that each job requires one setup (Equipment Management costs) in each production department; material is added only in the Cutting Department, and all jobs are inspected in the Welding Department.

1. Identify Cost Drivers

Potential cost drivers are identified by talking to the people involved in an organization's support activities (overhead areas). These employees should have a good idea of what causes the overhead costs in their areas. Overhead costs are then compared to driver activity to verify the relationship between the proposed drivers and the overhead costs. Quality Welding determines that the number of setups is the best driver for Equipment Management Department costs. An example of how Quality Welding might verify that the number of setups is an accurate driver is presented in Exhibit 3-1.3, where both actual DLHs (in thousands of hours) and number of setups are plotted against the Equipment Management

[2] R. Kaplan, Kanthal (A) Case, Boston: Harvard Business School, 1990.

actual overhead costs. Note that the relationship is better for the number of setups because overhead costs are more directly related (correlated) to the number of setups than to DLHs.

Exhibit 3-1.2

Quality Welding Overhead Application to Jobs
Activity-Based Approach

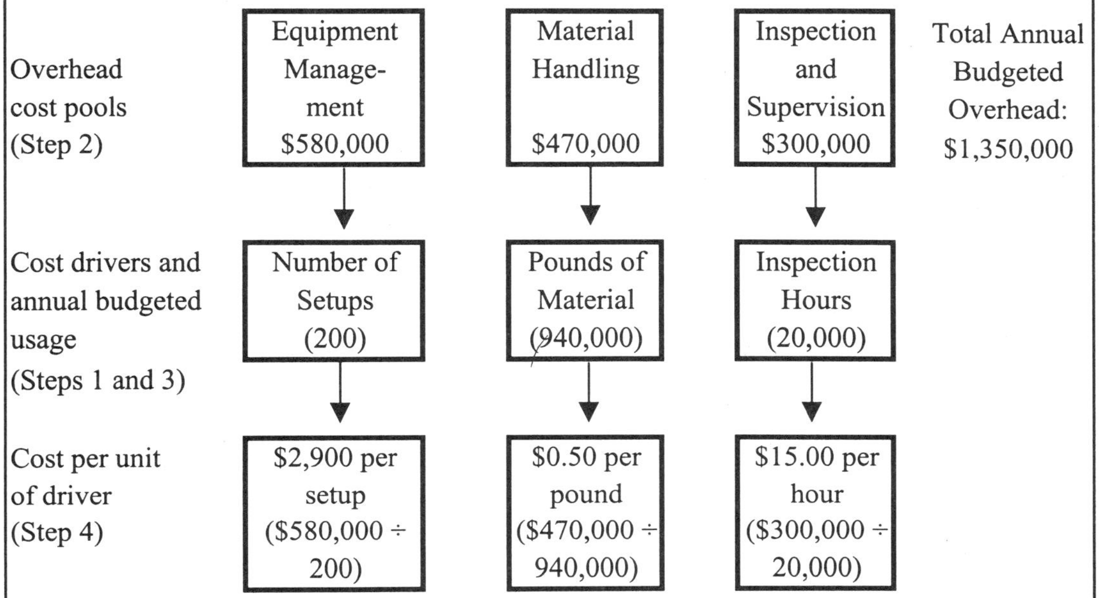

Overhead cost pools (Step 2)	Equipment Manage-ment $580,000	Material Handling $470,000	Inspection and Supervision $300,000	Total Annual Budgeted Overhead: $1,350,000
Cost drivers and annual budgeted usage (Steps 1 and 3)	Number of Setups (200)	Pounds of Material (940,000)	Inspection Hours (20,000)	
Cost per unit of driver (Step 4)	$2,900 per setup ($580,000 ÷ 200)	$0.50 per pound ($470,000 ÷ 940,000)	$15.00 per hour ($300,000 ÷ 20,000)	

Overhead Assignment to Cost Object (Jobs)

		Job 101	Job 102	Job 103
Driver usage by job (Step 5)	Number of Setups	2	2	2
	Pounds of Material	18,000	9,000	10,000
	Inspection Hours	200	600	450
Cost to job (Step 6)	Setup Cost	$ 5,800	$ 5,800	$ 5,800
	Material Hand. Cost	9,000	4,500	5,000
	Inspection Cost	3,000	9,000	6,750
Activity-based overhead costs		$ 17,800	$ 19,300	$ 17,550
Total traditional overhead costs		$ 23,850	$ 27,000	$ 16,200

Note: Total overhead for the three jobs using ABC is $54,650.

Quality Welding also determines that pounds of material used is the best driver of Material Handling Department costs, and number of hours used to inspect the ornamental iron is the best driver of Inspection and Supervision Department costs. A cost driver is identified in traditional costing, but the task is a trivial exercise because it is automatically assumed to be DLHs or some similar volume-based driver.

The number of cost drivers an organization decides to select results from a trade-off between the accuracy of cost computations (more drivers equals more accuracy) and the cost of collecting and using more drivers. Many ABC systems begin with relatively few drivers, but become more sophisticated over time by adding additional drivers. A further issue that must be addressed once drivers are identified is the cost of collecting driver usage data. This also involves a trade-off between accuracy (collecting detailed data) versus low cost (collecting easily acquired data). Setup costs provide a good example. If different types of setups require varying amounts of time to perform, using the *setup hours* it takes technicians to perform each setup would be more accurate, but more expensive to collect, than simply using the *number of setups* as the driver.

Exhibit 3-1.3

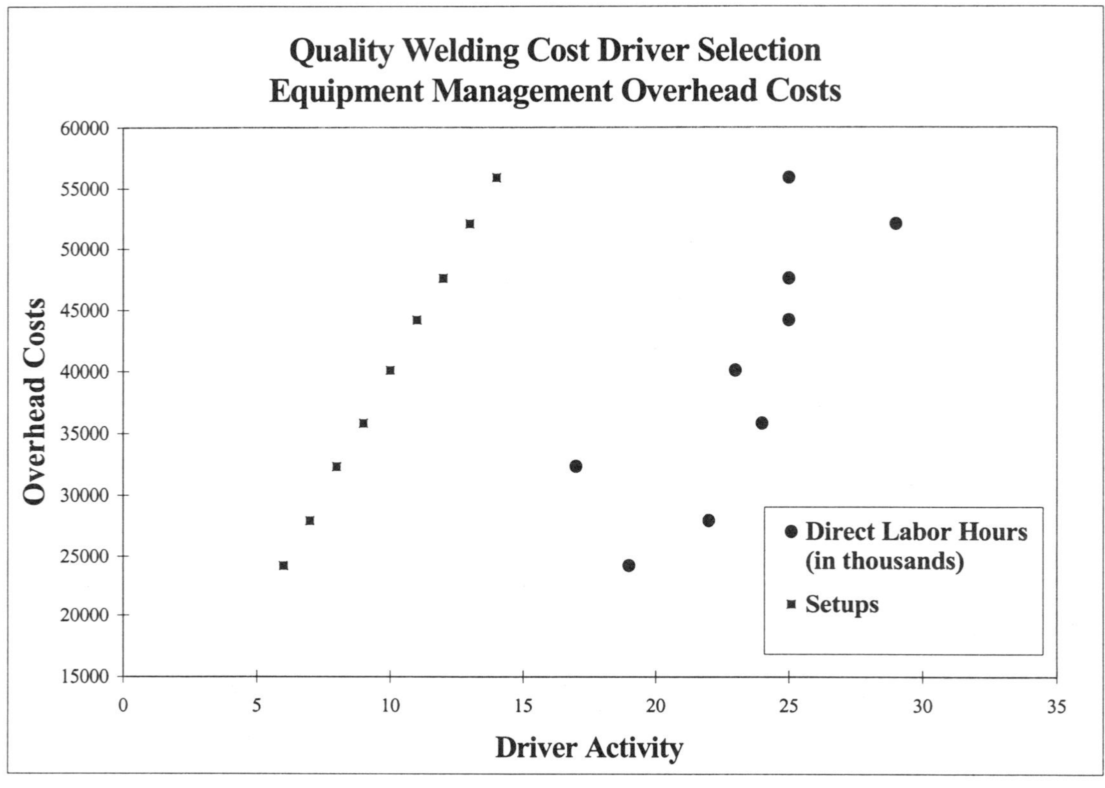

2. Create Overhead Cost Pools

Once the cost drivers have been identified in step 1, all overhead costs caused by each driver for a specified time period (usually one year) are aggregated into a **cost pool**. In traditional costing covered in Module 2, only one cost pool exists—all manufacturing overhead costs. Cost pools may be the planned overhead costs for the coming year, in which case *predetermined* ABC overhead rates are computed in step 4, explained later. Alternatively, cost pools may be the past year's overhead actual costs, in which case historical overhead rates are calculated. Predetermined ABC rates are used to cost jobs and products during the coming year instead of the one traditional predetermined rate used in Cases 2-4 and 2-6. Historical ABC costs are used to make product profitability and pricing decisions in place of the traditional costs used in Case 2-5.

In the Quality Welding example and in the CCC case, one driver is identified for each overhead department. For Quality Welding, the cost pool caused by the number of setups driver is the Equipment Management Department with a cost of $580,000. The cost pool caused by the pounds of material driver is the Material Handling Department cost of $470,000, and the cost pool caused by the inspection hour driver is the Inspection and Supervision Department cost of $300,000. In reality, two or more drivers may best explain why one department's costs occur. In this situation the department's costs may be broken up and different drivers selected for different cost pools in that department. In addition, activities in several departments may have the same driver. Costs that have the same driver, even if incurred in different departments, are usually combined into one large cost pool. For example, employee medical expenses and payroll may be different departments, but if number of employees is the driver selected for both, one large cost pool containing both costs can be created.

3. Determine *Total* Usage of Each Driver for the Entire Organization

In this step the level of *total* usage of each driver for the specified time period is collected. If the cost object is a product or job, then step 3 is the driver usage for all products or all jobs, not just the product being costed. For example, if one cost driver identified is the number of setups, the cost object is Job 103, and the specified time period is one year, then the driver usage would be the *total* number of setups performed during the year for *all* jobs. In the Quality Welding example, the factory's estimated driver usage for the entire year is the estimated number of setups for all jobs—200; pounds of material used for all jobs—940,000; and inspection hours for all jobs—20,000. In a traditional system, driver usage is just the number of planned DLHs (or other volume-based measure), which is 30,000 DLHs as shown in Exhibit 3-1.1.

Warning: For most students step 3 will be the most confusing step. If you remember that step 3 requires the usage for *all* products, jobs, or other cost objects, you will probably solve ABC problems correctly.

4. Compute Driver Rate

This step involves dividing the cost pool created in step 2 by the total usage of its driver determined in step 3. Note that this step results in a cost *per unit of driver*, not a cost *per unit of product*. In the Quality Welding ABC example the cost per setup is $2,900, the cost per pound of material is $0.50, and the cost per inspection hour is $15. Costs per unit of driver frequently will vary greatly in magnitude as they do for Quality Welding. For a traditional system, this step results in computing the predetermined overhead rate per DLH. Step 4 in the traditional approach is simply the total estimated overhead divided by the total estimated DLHs, which is $45 per DLH for Quality.

5. Determine Cost Object and Related Driver Use

A cost object is the item that the organization wishes to cost. Products or jobs are the objects most frequently costed, but customers or sales territories are other examples of cost objects. If the product or job is the cost object as is the case in Quality Welding and Case 3-1, this step calculates how much of each driver each product uses. For a traditional system this is the number of DLHs a product or job uses. In the Quality Welding ABC example in Exhibit 3-1.2, Job 101 uses 2 setups, 18,000 pounds of material, and 200 inspection hours.

For firms such as CCC that produce standard products, the cost object often is one unit, a sedan or compact in CCC's case. As shown in Exhibit C3-1.3 in Case 3-1 at the end of this reading, step 5 for sedan inspection and rework (I&R) costs is the number of I&R hours one sedan requires, which is 25. Alternatively, the cost object can be defined as all sedans produced in a year, which total 5,100 in the CCC case. Step 5 sedan I&R hours would then be 127,500 (5,100 sedans × 25 I&R hours). Cost objects also could be departments, customers, or divisions.

6. Assign Overhead Costs to Cost Object

In this final step the cost per driver computed in step 4 is multiplied by the cost object's driver usage calculated in step 5. For a traditional system this involves multiplying the predetermined overhead rate by the number of DLHs used in a job. In the Quality Welding ABC example, Job 101 is assigned $5,800 in setup costs by multiplying the $2,900 cost per setup by the job's use of 2 setups. Similar calculations are made for the other two drivers.

In Exhibit C3-1.3 of Case 3-1, each sedan is assigned $1,244.80 (25 × $49.792) in I&R cost. Some students find it easier to identify the cost object in step 5 as all units produced for a year. For CCC's I&R costs, sedan step 5 will now be the total I&R hours for all sedans: 127,500 (5,100 × 25). Step 6 is then the $6,348,480 (127,500 × $49.792) I&R costs assigned to all 5,100 sedans. Finally, to compute I&R cost for one sedan, divide the $6,348,480 I&R cost for all sedans by the 5,100 sedans produced to get the $1,244.80.

The "Big Picture"

Although the six ABC steps require several calculations, the purpose of ABC is simple: Cut the overhead pie more accurately. Exhibit 3-1.2 showed that ABC and traditional approaches assign quite different total overhead costs to each job. Can you explain why Jobs 101 and 102 receive somewhat less overhead under ABC, but Job 103 receives considerably more? The key is that Job 103 is a smaller job using only 360 direct labor hours, while Jobs 101 and 102 use 530 and 600 hours, respectively. As a result, Job 103 is allocated much less overhead in the traditional approach, even though we discover using ABC that it uses about the same amount of overhead resources as do the other two jobs. Note that in this example the total overhead assigned to the three jobs using the traditional and ABC methods is different. However, total overhead assigned to all jobs for the entire year will be about the same.

CCC's I&R cost pool is $10,580,800 and total driver usage is 212,500 I&R hours (see Exhibits C3-1.2 and C3-1.3). The goal of ABC is to allocate part of the I&R cost pool to the sedans based on the sedan's percentage use of the driver. The sedan is expected to use 127,500 I&R hours (5,100 × 25), or 60 percent of the total CCC I&R hours. The sedan should then be allocated 60 percent of the total I&R cost pool, or $6,348,480. Note that this is the same amount we calculated in the last sentence of the step 6 section above. The difference in how ABC cuts the overhead pie for I&R costs in presented in Exhibit 3-1.4.

ABC Proof

For many ABC calculations, including Case 3-1, the final answer can be checked against the total overhead pool allocated to see if an error has been made. For I&R cost the sum of the total sedan and total compact allocations should equal the I&R cost pool because there are only two products involved. From Exhibit C3-1.3 the total I&R cost allocated can be computed as follows:

	I&R Cost Per Car	Number of Cars	Total I&R Allocated
Sedan	$1,244.80	5,100	$ 6,348,480
Compact	2,489.60	1,700	4,232,320
Total			$10,580,800

The calculations show that the total ABC allocation equals the original I&R cost pool. A graphical representation of the difference between traditional and ABC I&R overhead allocation for CCC is presented in Exhibit 3-1.4.

Exhibit 3-1.4
Traditional and ABC Overhead Allocation

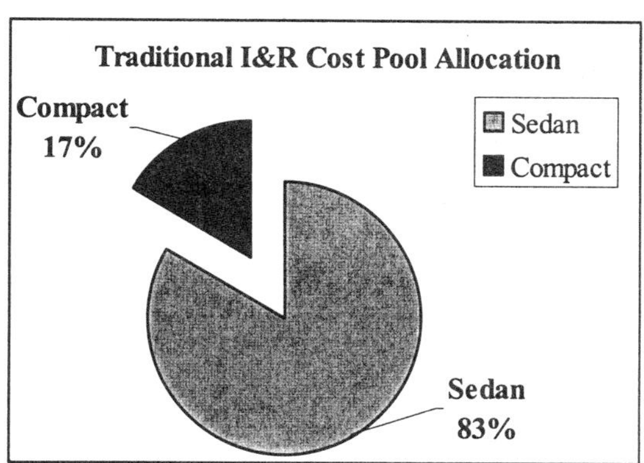

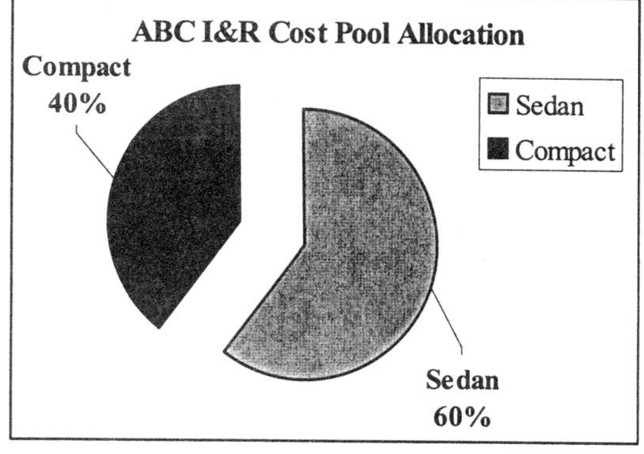

ACTIVITY-BASED COSTING IN PRACTICE

ABC has been used extensively by organizations of all types. Dozens of seminars have been held, training thousands of accountants and other users of cost information. Several software packages are on the market to help organizations set up ABC systems. Hundreds of case studies of ABC implementations have been published. Some firms, including Chrysler Corporation, have created separate positions with titles such as Manager, Activity-Based Costing. ABC has, among other uses, been employed to improve the cost of manufactured products, to better identify the cost of patient services in hospitals, to better evaluate the drivers of accounting costs, to determine the profitability of individual customers, and to assess the profits generated by sales personnel. In short, ABC is a popular accounting technique that has a broad range of applications.

Unlike traditional costing, ABC usually requires the involvement of many business employees, whether they work in marketing, production, finance, or other areas. This is because identifying appropriate cost drivers is best done by the people who work in the areas that generate overhead costs, not by accountants. In addition, because costs computed using ABC are so much more useful in helping to manage operations, employees in all areas use them more extensively than traditional costs, thus they must understand and improve ABC information. As a result, it is critical that all managers in an organization have a good understanding of ABC.

Organizational Fit

Is ABC equally applicable to all organizations? The answer is no. The more the following four attributes apply to an organization, the more likely it is that ABC will help managers make better decisions. If none of these attributes is applicable, then a simple, traditional cost system will probably serve the organization adequately.

1. The organization offers a large number of different products or services at one location.
2. The operation is relatively complex; that is, products or services pass through several departments or steps.
3. The percent of costs classified as overhead is relatively large.
4. The organization's industry is becoming more competitive.

Do you believe that organizations in general are finding that these attributes apply more or less in today's global environment? Most managers believe that the current economy causes these attributes to be more descriptive of their organizations. First, customers are demanding more variety and customization in the products and services received, creating pressure to increase the number of options offered. Second, increased automation is causing the percent of total costs classified as overhead to increase, making accurate overhead allocations more critical. Third, the economy is widely perceived to be more competitive because of increased foreign competition, deregulation, and technology's role in breaking down barriers between industries. Based on these trends, most analysts expect the significance of ABC to increase in the future.

Students often ask why cost accountants developed an overhead allocation procedure based on DLHs, or other volume-based measures, when DLH-based drivers create inaccurate allocations for many overhead costs. There are two reasons for this historical development. First, at one time, direct labor made up a very large proportion of manufacturing costs, up to 70 percent in many organizations, and manufacturing costs represented most of the firm's total cost. Today, however, direct labor is often less than 10 percent of manufacturing costs, and manufacturing costs are often less than half the total costs of the firm. The situation is most extreme for advanced, highly automated manufacturing systems in which direct labor often doesn't exist at all, but overhead is quite high. Therefore, although crude overhead allocations did not distort costs much in the past, inaccurate allocation now can create large distortions. Second, until recently it was quite costly to collect and process all the data necessary to implement an ABC system, so a simple, low-cost method made sense. The recent decline in information processing costs, however, has made ABC systems much more cost effective.

Service Application of ABC: University Costs

Is ABC applicable only to manufacturing operations that handle physical products? No. Many service organization, including banks, insurance companies, and hospitals, have implemented ABC. Consider the severe budget reductions imposed on many universities where state funding has been reduced by as much as 30 percent. The first step in determining the value of ABC to universities is to ask whether the campus environment is conducive to an ABC application. The four attributes of organizations that tend to make implementation of ABC attractive are as follows:

1. The organization offers a large number of different products or services at one location.
2. The organization is relatively complex.
3. The percent of costs classified as overhead is large.
4. The organization's industry is becoming more competitive.

How would your campus rate on these attributes? Most colleges offer 100 or more majors, minors, and other programs that are their "products," so criterion 1 is met. Colleges have a complex production process by which students can select from thousands of combinations of courses that lead to a degree, so criterion 2 is met. Direct material cost for colleges is negligible, although students incur a significant cost for books. The only large cost that might be classified as direct is instructor salaries, although this would imply that each professor has approximately the same number of students. This is seldom true even in the same department. Nevertheless, since faculty costs represent about 35 percent of total costs, overhead amounts to at least 65 percent of total costs, meeting criterion 3. Finally, the education industry is becoming much more competitive, with many schools expanding and corporate, proprietary, and distance education institutions on the rise.

Although cost certainly should not be the sole criterion for determining budget reductions, campus administrators definitely need accurate cost estimates. Unless true costs are known, administrators will not know if proposed reductions will really balance the budget. In addition, administrators need good cost information if they want to improve the operations of the overhead departments. To illustrate, the costs of operating four academic areas are compared below. This comparison is based on fictitious data since most universities don't collect activity-based costs.

	Accounting	**Art**	**Biology**	**Computer Science**
Faculty	11	15	17	14
Full-time equivalent students	285	160	255	224
Clerical staff	1	2	2	2
Technicians	0	2	1	1
Supply budget	$20,000	$100,000	$200,000	$50,000
Occupied space (square footage)	2,500	20,000	25,000	15,000
Annual library cost	$20,000	$15,000	$200,000	$75,000
Annual computer cost	$5,000	0	$20,000	$300,000

Hypothesized ABC information for the four departments and related cost drivers include the following:

Driver	**Activity Cost Per Driver**
Faculty positions	$60,000 (includes benefits)
Clerical positions	$40,000 (includes benefits)
Technician positions	$50,000 (includes benefits)
Supplies	Actual cost
Square feet	$40
Library cost	Actual cost
Computer cost	Actual cost

Supplies, library, and computer costs can be allocated on a basis other than actual costs. For example, computer costs could be allocated on the number of students enrolled in courses using computer facilities. This example assumes that the actual costs of these items are collected, but in practice these data might prove to be too expensive to collect.

Universities frequently use full-time equivalent students (FTES) as a volume measure of the number of students served. Based on the ABC and departmental information presented, the cost per department and per FTES is as follows:

	Accounting	Art	Biology	Computer Science
Faculty	$660,000	$ 900,000	$1,020,000	$ 840,000
Clerical staff	40,000	80,000	80,000	80,000
Technicians	0	100,000	50,000	50,000
Supply budget	20,000	100,000	200,000	50,000
Occupied space	100,000	800,000	1,000,000	600,000
Annual library cost	20,000	15,000	200,000	75,000
Annual computer cost	5,000	0	20,000	300,000
Total ABC cost	$845,000	$1,995,000	$2,570,000	$1,995,000
FTES	285	160	255	224
Cost per FTES	$2,965	$12,469	$10,078	$8,906

Key questions facing administrators the past few years include where and by how much services should be cut. If a campus is facing a 10 percent cut in funding and the impossibility of cutting salaries, is it a sensible approach to cut faculty positions in all areas by 10 percent? If not, how would you, if you were the president, reduce the budget? Note how a 10 percent cut in faculty costs impacts the total costs caused by different departments:

	Accounting	Art	Biology	Computer Science
10% Faculty reduction	$66,000	$90,000	$102,000	$84,000
Percent of total ABC cost	7.8%	4.5%	4.0%	4.2%

University Example Summary

These numbers are not meant to represent actual costs. And, just because a department has a higher cost per FTES does not mean that the department should be singled out for special reductions or elimination. Instead, the purpose of this illustration is to demonstrate the following points:

1. Service costs, like manufacturing costs, are often used differently by different operating departments.
2. The true cost of products, services, and departments is hidden by traditional accounting systems.
3. Managing a complex organization effectively without the knowledge of true costs is very difficult.

ACTIVITY-BASED MANAGEMENT

Activity-based management (ABM) is the use of activity information obtained by performing an ABC analysis to improve the operations of an organization. ABM can be implemented using aggregated data with easy-to-collect cost driver information. It can be used to help identify overhead cost problems, aid in more cost-effective product design, support pricing and profitability analyses, and identify nonvalue-added activities. CCC uses ABC information for all of these purposes except improvement of product design.

In the university example, better knowledge of the true academic area operating costs is important information for administrators. ABC information can be used to support management decisions such as eliminating an academic department. It also can be used to help manage the costs of an overhead department such as the library. Suppose that administrators want to reduce the library's budget, but for good reason do not want to impose an across-the-board 10 percent cut in the acquisition of all books and periodicals, because this will weaken all academic areas on campus.

With the ABC information collected in the example above, administrators notice that the Biology area's annual acquisition cost of $200,000 represents 20 percent of the total for the entire library budget of $1,000,000. Based on this information, the campus administrators may want to work with the Biology Department and explore less expensive ways to meet the Biology curriculum's needs. By better managing this one department's library needs, much of the 10 percent cut might be met by reviewing just that one area and finding a better way to fulfill its needs. Both of these uses of ABC information are examples of ABM.

Another use of ABM involves first breaking an organization into processes. A process is a set of interrelated activities that lead to an important output. Examples of processes are manufacturing, new product development, and sales order and shipping. Most firms today realize the importance of process management to their success and are reorganizing to focus on processes. Each process is then examined to identify all the activities that make up the process. ABM uses activity cost information to improve the process by eliminating nonvalue-added activities and waste. This form of ABM can be a powerful tool to improve organizational performance, but it requires a sophisticated accounting system and a major commitment to change the way work is done.

In summary, ABM is widely used in industry, and there is a large employment demand for managers and accountants with ABM expertise. In fact, much of the corporate downsizing and reengineering that you read about is accomplished through the use of ABM analysis.

Activity-Based Management at Hewlett-Packard

An example of how accountants can help a process team improve operations through the use of ABC is provided by Hewlett-Packard's Roseville Division.[3] Engineers involved in the printed-circuit board design process are required to design boards that can be manufactured at a cost that makes them competitive in the market. To know if their design is cost-effective, the engineers must know the exact cost of each manufacturing step through which boards pass. The engineers were concerned that the traditional product cost measurements being provided by their accountants were inaccurate, causing design to be less cost-effective than it should be. Working together, the accountants, production managers, and engineers developed an ABC costing approach for the circuit boards. The more accurate cost information allowed the engineers to develop much more cost-effective designs.

SUMMARY

ABC is a powerful cost management tool used by thousands of organizations for a number of different purposes. It creates separate cost pools of overhead costs that have the same cost driver, and assigns these costs to cost objects based on the objects' driver usage. ABC is used by both manufacturing and service organizations and is applied to both manufacturing

---

[3] D. Berlant, R. Browning, and G. Foster, "How Hewlett-Packard Gets Numbers It Can Trust," _Harvard Business Review_, Jan.–Feb. 1990, pp. 178–183.

and selling and administrative costs. The increased accuracy of ABC over traditional costing is one reason for its rapid growth over the past decade. The ability of ABC to give managers better insights into the operation of business processes is a second reason for its widespread use in business. As a result, employees in almost all areas of business will encounter ABC in their work.

EXERCISES AND PROBLEMS

Exercises

Exercise 1 Organizational Fit of ABC. What are the four attributes that indicate whether an organization can benefit from the use of ABC?

Exercise 2 Universities and ABC. Is a university a good candidate for the use of ABC? Explain why or why not.

Exercise 3 Hospitals and ABC. Is a hospital a good candidate for the use of ABC? Explain why or why not.

Exercise 4 Cost Driver Selection. Identify a reasonable driver for each of the following activities:

a. Material handling
b. Equipment setup
c. Equipment maintenance
d. Inspection
e. Factory occupancy (rent, insurance, etc.)
f. Human resource administration
g. Information systems
h. Customer billing
i. Delivery

Exercise 5 Steps in ABC. Place the following six steps in computing activity-based costs in the order in which they occur.

a. Determine cost object and related driver use
b. Identify cost drivers
c. Compute driver rate
d. Assign overhead costs to cost object
e. Determine *total* usage of each driver for the entire organization.
f. Create overhead cost pools

Exercise 6 Cost Drivers and Cost Pools. Aragon Inc. has two manufacturing overhead departments, Maintenance and General Factory. Maintenance costs for 2002 totaled \$3,000,000 and General Factory costs totaled \$5,000,000. Based on studies performed by the accountants, it was determined that maintenance costs change in proportion to machine hours, and general factory costs are related to how long a job takes to manufacture (cycle time). Aragon used a total of 600,000 machine hours for the entire year of 2002 and had a total cycle time for all of its 2002 jobs of 2,000 days. Identify Aragon's cost drivers and overhead cost pools.

Exercise 7 Overhead Costs Per Driver and Per Job. Refer to the Aragon Inc. data in Exercise 6. Assume that Aragon is performing a historical ABC analysis by recalculating job costs for last year (2002). Compute the following:

a. Aragon's 2002 maintenance cost per machine hour.
b. Aragon's 2002 general factory cost per day of cycle time.
c. The ABC overhead Aragon would assign to Job 862 that uses 800 machine hours and takes four days to manufacture.

Exercise 8 Selecting a Driver. Corrine Co. is implementing an activity-based cost system. Making setups on complex equipment is a major manufacturing overhead cost. Corrine is trying to decide whether the driver for these costs should be the number of setups or the hours used to set up each job. Discuss an advantage and a disadvantage of using each driver.

Exercise 9 ABC Calculations. Schwartz Inc. manufactures two products, Akron and Summit, in one factory. Budgeted information for its two manufacturing overhead cost pools for 2002 follows:

Cost Pool	2002 Cost	Cost Driver	Driver Activity
General factory	$490,000	Square feet	70,000 square feet
Maintenance	280,000	Machine hours	80,000 machine hours

Production of 5,000 units of Akron during 2002 is expected to take 30,000 square feet of factory space and 50,000 machine hours. Production of 10,000 units of Summit is expected to take 40,000 square feet of factory space and 30,000 machine hours. How much overhead per unit of each product does Schwartz expect for 2002?

Exercise 10 Customer Profitability. The sales manager at Excel Corp. just read an article that discussed how the profitability of customers may differ even when the customers purchase a similar quantity of the same products. You learn that delivery and service are Excel's largest selling and administrative costs. You also decide that the number of deliveries is a good driver for delivery cost and that the number of service calls is a good driver for service cost. Excel's 2002 information as follows:

Cost Pool	2002 Cost	Cost Driver	Driver Activity
Delivery	$4,000,000	Number of deliveries	20,000 deliveries
Service	6,000,000	Number of service calls	10,000 calls

Customer A purchased $100,000 of one product and required 12 deliveries and 5 service calls. Customer B also purchased $100,000 of the same product, but required 33 deliveries and 17 service calls. Compute the service and delivery cost for each customer. Would each customer look equally profitable using traditional costing? Why or why not?

Exercise 11 Completing ABC Steps. Amavisca Co. wants to determine how much equipment maintenance overhead cost should be charged to its X32 product. X32 requires 3 DLHs per unit, 1.5 machine hours per unit, and 30 setups to produce 5,000 units during the year. Budgeted equipment maintenance for Amavisca in 2002 is $600,000, which changes in proportion to the number of machine hours used. Amavisca's entire factory plans to use 72,000 DLHs, 30,000 machine hours, and 700 setups. Determine the correct answer for each ABC step listed below. Note that the steps are not listed in the correct order.

a. Determine cost object and related driver use
b. Identify cost drivers
c. Compute driver rate
d. Assign overhead costs to cost object
e. Determine *total* usage of each driver for the entire organization
f. Create overhead cost pools

Problems

Problem 1 ABC and Job Costing. Waldsmith Co. uses an ABC system with three manufacturing overhead cost pools. Budgeted 2002 information for these overhead costs are as follows:

Total 2002 Budgeted Manufacturing Overhead

Cost Pool	2002 Cost	Cost Driver	Driver Activity
General factory	$3,000,000	Production days	600 days
Setup	600,000	Number of setups	1,000 setups
Maintenance	270,000	Machine hours	9,000 machine hours

During March 2000, job 126 was completed. It used $15,000 in direct materials, $8,500 in direct labor, 4 production days, 3 setups, and 150 machine hours. Using ABC, how much cost did this job add to Waldsmith's March cost of goods manufactured?

Problem 2 Basic Activity-Based Costing. SpringCrest Co. manufactures two products, Theta and Beta, in one factory. All manufacturing overhead is collected in two departments: Setup and General Factory. SpringCrest has identified the number of setups as the best cost driver for Setup Department costs and machine hours as the best cost driver for General Factory Department costs. Planned information for 2003 follows:

Planned 2003 Setup costs	$280,000
Planned 2003 General Factory costs	$480,000

Estimated yearly usage per product:	Theta	Beta
Direct labor hours	60,000	40,000
Direct materials	$50,000	$20,000
Setups	250	450
Machine hours	32,000	28,000
Units produced	10,000	7,000

a. Assume that SpringCrest uses traditional costing and allocates all overhead based on direct labor hours. Calculate both the total and per-unit amount of overhead that would be allocated to Theta and to Beta.

b. Compute the estimated 2003 ABC total and per-unit manufacturing overhead cost assigned to Theta and to Beta.

Problem 3 Traditional Versus ABC Costing. Planned 2002 cost information for Frederick Co. is presented below. Frederick produces two products, A and B, in one plant.

Cost Pool	Planned 2002 Cost	Cost Driver	Planned 2002 Driver Activity
Material handling	$2,400,000	Pounds of material	600,000 pounds
Maintenance	5,000,000	Maintenance hours	40,000 hours
General factory	2,000,000	Number of units	8,000 units
Total overhead	$9,400,000		

	Product A	Product B	Total
Units produced	6,000 units	2,000 units	8,000 units
DLHs	180,000 DLHs	70,000 DLHs	250,000 DLHs
Material handling	400,000 pounds	200,000 pounds	600,000 pounds
Maintenance hours (MHs)	18,000 MHs	22,000 MHs	40,000 MHs

a. Determine the predetermined overhead rate(s) for both traditional costing and ABC.

b. Determine the cost driver usage for one unit of each product for both traditional costing and ABC.

c. Calculate the total overhead cost per product for both traditional costing and ABC.

Problem 4 Traditional Versus ABC Product Costs. MBI Corp. manufactures three electronic products in one plant: Delta, Gamma, and Iota. The following actual data for 2002 have been provided for you:

Total 2002 Manufacturing Overhead Costs

	Dollars	Driver
Machinery cost pool	$9,600,000	Machine hours
Inspection cost pool	4,380,000	Number of inspections
Material handling cost pool	6,000,000	Direct material costs

	Product		
	Delta	**Gamma**	**Iota**
Machine hours (all of 2002)	10,000	24,000	16,000
Number of inspections (all of 2002)	300	900	800
Units produced in 2002	80,000	150,000	37,500
Direct labor hours per unit	1 hour	.6 hour	.4 hour
Direct material costs (all of 2002)	$ 2,000,000	$ 7,800,000	$ 1,125,000
Direct material cost per unit	25.00	52.00	30.00
Labor cost per unit	20.00	12.00	8.00
Current MBI selling price	190.00	210.00	175.00

Competitors seem uninterested in entering the market for Iota, while other producers sell Delta for $180 in a very competitive market. Gamma seems to be priced about right.

a. Compute the total manufacturing cost per unit for each product using DLHs as the cost driver for all overhead costs. MBI's direct labor wage rate is $20 per hour. Note that MBI's actual overhead rate is not $20 per DLH. You must compute the actual rate from the information above.

b. MBI sets a target price, the price it hopes to obtain in the market, for each product based on total manufacturing costs plus a 55 percent markup on total manufacturing costs. Compute MBI's target price for each product.

c. Compute the total manufacturing cost per unit for each of MBI's products using ABC and the cost drivers listed above. Use the six-step method presented in the reading.

d. Recompute the target selling prices for each of MBI's products using the ABC manufacturing costs computed in part c and the same 55 percent markup used in part b.

e. Explain why traditional product costing procedures used in part a produced such different cost per unit numbers than the ABC procedures used in part c. Refer specifically to the costs of each of MBI's three products in your answer. Explain which costing method enables MBI to set more competitive prices.

Problem 5 Service application of ABC. Great State University (GSU) is interested in better understanding the true cost of its various programs. Major overhead costs for GSU include the library, the computer labs, plant operations (building occupancy costs), and advising. Budgeted 2003 costs and the driver selected for each cost pool are as follows:

Cost Pool	Planned 2003 Cost	Cost Driver	Budgeted Total GSU Usage
Library	$2,400,000	Number of book checkouts	800,000 checkouts
Computer labs	3,720,000	Hours of computer use	310,000 hours
Plant operations	1,640,000	Square feet	820,000 sq. feet
Advising	1,920,000	Number of majors	16,000 majors
	$9,680,000		

a. Compute the total overhead and overhead per major from the four cost pools assigned to the accounting program, which has 10,000 books checked out per year, 25,000 hours of computer time, 8,000 square feet of space occupied, and 400 majors.

b. Compute the total overhead and overhead per major from the four cost pools assigned to the art program, which has 20,000 books checked out per year, 5,000 hours of computer time, 28,000 square feet of space occupied, and 100 majors.

c. The current cost system at GSU assigns costs based on student credit units (SCUs) in the program. For 2003, the accounting program is expected to have 24,000 SCUs and the art program 6,000. The entire campus is expected to have 484,000 SCUs. Compute the total overhead and overhead per major from the four cost pools that assigned to both the accounting and art programs under the current system.

d. Discuss how the administration of GSU can use this information.

Problem 6 ABC for Selling and Administrative Costs. Sunshine Dairy Co. manufactures ice cream mix sold to restaurants and ice cream stands. The product sells for $2.50 per gallon. It successfully implemented ABC for its manufacturing cost pools two years ago. Sunshine's marketing manager is impressed with the ABC manufacturing information and is wondering if ABC could help her better understand customer profitability. Sunshine's controller reports that, on average, it costs about $0.25 per gallon to take customer orders, bill the customer, and deliver the product. It is possible, however, that some customers may cost much more than this and others much less. The controller has provided the following information on last year's costs for two departments:

Ordering and Billing (O&B)	$ 864,000
Delivery	4,200,000

The controller tells you that order and billing costs are driven by the number of orders received. The delivery manager estimates that each delivery stop adds about $10 in cost. The remaining delivery cost varies in proportion to the number of gallons delivered. Last year 20,000,000 gallons of product were delivered. Sunshine received 160,000 orders and made 160,000 deliveries.

a. Compute the ABC O&B and delivery costs per gallon for each of the following customer orders.

Customer A	300 gallons
Customer B	40 gallons
Customer C	5 gallons

b. Suggest actions that Sunshine could take to address the high O&B and delivery costs of Customer C.

Case 3-1

ACTIVITY-BASED COSTING AT CALIFORNIA CAR COMPANY

Case Objectives

1. Introduce the concept of activity-based costing
2. Demonstrate the use of activity-based management
3. Contrast ABC with traditional costing

Decision (Operating, pricing): Which overhead costs are too high?

This problem builds on two cases completed in Module 2: Cases 2-4 and 2-7. You should review those cases and your solution notes before completing this case. Exhibit C3-1.1 presents CCC's 2002 planning budget overhead costs first shown in Case 2-7. Note that in Module 2, CCC classified Inspection, Material Handling, and Setup Department costs as variable. Predetermined overhead rates per DLH used in Module 2 are shown in Exhibit C3-1.1. Although these costs last year varied roughly in proportion to DLHs, this does not necessarily mean that the appropriate cost driver is DLHs, particularly since the ratio of sedans to compacts produced last year remained constant.

THE PROBLEM

It is now May 2002. Mary Jones, head of accounting for CCC, is concerned that the traditional costing method used in Module 2 does not adequately reflect the true costs of making each model. In addition, Jones wants to produce data that will help focus efforts to reduce manufacturing overhead so that CCC's profitability can be brought up to industry norms. Therefore, she is considering the possibility of converting to an ABC approach for assigning various overhead costs to the company's sedans and compacts.

Overhead Costs Details

The first step in implementing the ABC approach is to perform a detailed analysis of each overhead activity in the company. Although not all costs associated with an overhead cost pool will vary with a single cost driver, CCC decides to select the one driver for each cost pool that it believes best causes the cost to occur. The five manufacturing overhead cost pools used by CCC are described in Case 2-1. The following information for each cost pool is the result of extensive discussions among the production, sales, administrative, and accounting employees. It is based on their knowledge of how work is done at CCC. Note that cost pools assumed to vary directly with DLHs (variable overhead) in traditional costing used in Module 2 are found to have drivers other than DLHs.

Exhibit C3-1.1

California Car Company Traditional Overhead Planning Budget for 2002	
Units produced	
Sedans	5,100
Compacts	1,700
Direct labor hours*	661,300
Overhead departments	
Inspection and rework department†	$ 10,580,800
Material handling department†	5,951,700
Setup department†	7,274,300
Total Variable Manufacturing Overhead	$ 23,806,800
Maintenance department	$6,128,000
General factory department	24,953,100
Total Fixed Manufacturing Overhead‡	$ 31,081,100
Selling and administrative costs	
Compact redesign	$ 4,500,000
Other selling and administrative costs	21,000,000
Total S&A Overhead	$ 25,500,000

*Total budgeted DLHs computed as follows:

5,100 sedans × 108 DLH per sedan =	550,800	DLHs
1,700 compacts × 65 DLH per compact =	110,500	DLHs
Total Budgeted DLHs	661,300	DLHs

†In Module 2, Inspection Dept. costs were applied to jobs at the rate of $16 per DLH, Material Handling Dept. costs were applied at the rate of $9 per DLH, and Setup Dept. costs were applied at $11 per DLH, which resulted in the predetermined variable overhead rate of $36 you used in Module 2. Although these costs were classified as variable in Module 2, for this case you should determine whether DLHs are in fact the best driver.

‡The total fixed manufacturing overhead presented in Case 2-4 was $31,081,100. The amounts shown for the two departments are 12 times the monthly estimated overhead costs presented in Exhibit C2-7.1.

Inspection and Rework (I&R)

Defects are found in almost all cars completed at CCC. Many cars require a minimum amount of rework, but some require many hours to disassemble and repair. Due to poor design and the delicacies of assembling the solar panels, the compact car has many more quality problems than does the sedan. As a result it takes twice as many hours on average to inspect and correct each compact (50 hours) than each sedan (25 hours). Therefore, CCC estimates that the sedans will require 127,500 inspection and rework hours (25 × 5,100) and the compacts will require 85,000 inspection and rework hours (50 × 1,700).

Material Handling

CCC employees found that material handling costs vary with the total number of parts used. Each sedan requires 25 parts, 15 in Chassis Assembly and 10 in Final Assembly (see bill of materials in Exhibit C2-1.1). Each compact requires 20 parts, 10 in Chassis Assembly and 10 in Final Assembly. Use these numbers even if the models you assembled in the simulation used a different number of parts.

Setup

Due to the complexity of the design, management believes that the compact requires more setup hours than the sedan, but setup hours are not recorded by model. CCC's production schedule requires one setup for each batch of 15 sedans and one setup for each batch of 5 compacts. CCC plans to manufacture 5,100 sedans and 1,700 compacts.

Maintenance

This cost is most closely related to the age and usage of the machines. Both the sedan and compact use approximately the same number of machine hours (30 machine hours) per car on the same machines. Do not confuse machine hours with direct labor hours.

General Factory

This cost is fixed for a wide range of production volumes. It also does not have one activity that drives the cost. In ABC applications there is usually one cost pool like this that does not have a good driver, so the situation with the general factory costs is normal. Since this cost is not caused by any single activity in the short run, you should allocate this cost on a basis that you believe is most reasonable to CCC's situation.

Selling and Administrative

CCC budgeted $2,550,000 of its year 2002 administrative expenses exclusively for the redesign of the compact chassis and solar panels. Compact development costs at this level are expected to continue for several years. All development costs for the sedan are funded by grants from the government and electric utilities, so there are no separate development costs for the sedan. Management believes that the driver for the remaining $22,950,000 of selling and administrative costs is the number of cars produced.

Requirements

1. Complete the unshaded, outlined cells in Exhibit C3-1.2 using the traditional, plantwide overhead allocation used in Case 2-4. The I&R cost pool allocation has been completed for you. Use it as a model. Note that the total manufacturing cost for the sedan and compact models should be the same as computed in Case 2-4.

2. Complete the unshaded, outlined cells in columns marked as steps 1, 3, and 4 in the top part of Exhibit C3-1.3. Select cost drivers for each of the five manufacturing and two selling and administrative overhead cost pools. Determine estimated driver usage for the year 2002, and compute year 2002 estimated cost per driver.

3. Complete an ABC analysis by computing cost per car in Exhibit C3-1.3 using year 2002 budgeted full-year data for the compact and sedan. Also, complete the target selling prices for each model based on a 67 percent markup on total manufacturing costs. This should complete your worksheet. Print the spreadsheet and cell formulas if you completed the assignment on a spreadsheet.

4. Complete the following ABC proof by using your solution to requirement 3 in the cost per car column. Multiply the cost per car by the number of cars to compute the total allocation. The total cost pool for each overhead cost calculated in the proof should equal the cost pool shown in Exhibit C3-1.3.

Proof:		**Cost per Car**	**Number of Cars**	**Total Allocation**
Manufacturing overhead:				
Inspection and rework (I&R):	Sedan	$ 1,244.80	5,100	$ 6,348,480
	Compact	2,489.60	1,700	4,232,320
	Total Cost Pool			$ 10,580,800
Material handling:	Sedan		5,100	
	Compact		1,700	
	Total Cost Pool			
Setup:	Sedan		5,100	
	Compact		1,700	
	Total Cost Pool			
Maintenance:	Sedan		5,100	
	Compact		1,700	
	Total Cost Pool			
General factory:	Sedan		5,100	
	Compact		1,700	
	Total Cost Pool			

5. Explain the major reasons why the cost per sedan and compact computed in requirements 1 and 3 differ so much.

6. Discuss what, if any, pricing or product deletion actions you would recommend based on your ABC analysis.

7. Are any operating problems highlighted by your ABC analysis? Briefly discuss each overhead cost that you believe looks out of line at CCC.

Exhibit C3-1.2

California Car Company
Traditional Costing Worksheet

ABC Calculation Steps:	(1)	(2)	(3)	(4)	(5)	(6)	(5)	(6)
					Sedan		Compact	
Title	Cost Driver	Cost Pool	Total Driver Usage	Driver Rate	Driver Usage Per Car	Cost Per Sedan	Driver Usage Per Car	Cost Per Compact
Direct material	- - -	$ 20,910,000	- - -	- - -	- - -	$ 2,980	- - -	$ 3,360
Direct labor	Direct labor hours	23,145,500	661,300	$ 35.00	108	3,780	65	2,275
Manufacturing overhead:								
Inspection and rework	Direct labor hours	10,580,800	661,300	16.00	108	1,728	65	1,040
Material handling		5,951,700						
Setups		7,274,300						
Maintenance		6,128,000						
General factory		24,953,100						
Total manufacturing cost		$ 98,943,400						
Desired markup (67%)								
Target selling price								

Exhibit C3-1.3

California Car Company ABC Worksheet								
ABC Calculation Steps	**(1)**	**(2)**	**(3)**	**(4)**	**(5)**	**(6)**	**(5)**	**(6)**
					Sedan		**Compact**	
Title	**Cost Driver**	**Cost Pool**	**Total Driver Usage**	**Driver Rate**	**Driver Usage Per Car**	**Cost Per Sedan**	**Driver Usage Per Car**	**Cost Per Compact**
Direct material	---	$ 20,910,000	---	---	---	$ 2,980.00	---	$ 3,360.00
Direct labor	Direct labor hours	23,145,500	661,300	$ 35.00	108	3,780.00	65	2,275.00
Manufacturing overhead:								
Inspection and rework (I&R)	I&R hours	10,580,800	212,500	49.792	25	1,244.80	50	2,489.60
Material handling		5,951,700						
Setups		7,274,300						
Maintenance		6,128,000						
General factory		24,953,100						
Total manufacturing cost	---	$ 98,943,400	---	---	---		---	
Selling and administrative:								
Special development		$ 2,550,000						
Remaining $28 million		22,950,000						
Full cost per car	---	---	---	---	---		---	
Total mfg. cost (above)	---	$ 98,943,400	---	---	---		---	
Desired markup (67%)	---	---	---	---	---		---	
Target selling price	---	---	---	---	---		---	

Group Assignment 3-1

A COST BY ANY OTHER NAME

Group number __________ **Signatures of group members participating:**

____

____

Group Assignment Objectives

1. Contrast ABC with traditional costing.
2. Develop a better understanding of the impact of ABC on cost numbers.
3. Explore the use of cost numbers in a discontinue product decision.

George Olson, vice president—marketing at CCC, comes to your office with the new ABC data you prepared in Case 3-1. "I can't believe you accountants! You just finished your cost estimates for year 2002 last December (in Case 2-4) that produced the traditional costs in Exhibit G3-1.1. Now, just four months later, you give me new ABC manufacturing cost numbers (computed in Case 3-1) also shown in Exhibit G3-1.1. When I apply the industry average markup on full manufacturing cost of 67 percent to the ABC costs, I get the target prices shown. I do not understand how costs can change so much! I need some explanation!"

Exhibit G3-1.1

CCC 2002 Manufacturing Costs		
	Sedan	**Compact**
Traditional costs (Case 2-4)	$ 15,724	$ 11,030
Activity costs (Case 3-1)*	14,210	15,572
ABC target selling prices (67% markup)	23,731	26,005

* Your ABC numbers may differ based on the drivers you selected.

Requirements

Help George Olson out by addressing the following issues:

1. Did the cost estimates change because CCC changed the way it manufactured a car? In other words, was the factory rearranged, more productive equipment purchased, or other changes made? Explain.

Yes ☐ No ☐

2. If total manufacturing costs for CCC stayed the same ($98,943,400 as computed in Case 2-4), explain to George how the manufacturing cost of the compact model increased by more than $3,000, but the manufacturing cost of the sedan model decreased only by about $1,000. Use your solutions to Case 3-1 as the basis for your answer. Your answer must go beyond just saying that the cost drivers changed.

3. After reviewing the ABC information, David Gomez, president of CCC, is considering dropping the compact model because its manufacturing plus selling and administrative costs total about $20,447 ($15,572 manufacturing costs plus $4,875 S&A—see your solution to Case 3-1). This is about $3,447 more than the compact's $17,000 selling price. David asks Jena Butler for her recommendation.

   As a result, Jena Butler asks you to estimate the year 2002 manufacturing cost per sedan and the total cost of each overhead department if the compact is eliminated. Please help Jena out by completing the following schedule. Note that Jena expects total General Factory costs will decrease to only $20,400,000 because many of these costs such as depreciation will not decrease if the compact is eliminated. Use the costs computed in your solution to Case 3-1.

Annual Costs if Compact Is Eliminated

	New Cost per Sedan	New Total Cost
Direct materials	$2,980	$15,198,000
Direct labor	3,790	19,329,000
Inspection and rework cost		
Material handling cost		
Setup cost		
Maintenance cost		
General factory cost		20,400,000
Total manufacturing costs		

Note: CCC plans to produce 5,100 sedans in 2002

4. Should CCC eliminate the compact? Justify your answer.

Reading 3-2

PROCESS MANAGEMENT AND ACCOUNTING

INTRODUCTION

Organizations throughout the world are striving to focus more on managing processes and improving the quality of these processes.[1] Reading 3-1 discussed how ABM looks at the activities that make up processes and uses ABC analysis to manage these processes better. A **process** is a series of related activities focused on accomplishing a specified output. Most firms find that they have between 10 and 15 large processes. Examples of processes in a typical company include:

- *Product or Service Development*. Researching, designing, and launching new products and services.
- *Order Fulfillment*. Manufacturing the product or performing the service and delivering it to the customer.
- *Customer Service*. Supporting customers after delivery.
- *Billing and Collection*. Preparing invoices and receiving payment for goods and services.
- *Planning*. Planning for the future and deciding how funds will be allocated.
- *Information Systems*. Providing data and information to support business decisions.
- *Human Resource Support*. Hiring skilled people and training employees.

The first three processes listed are key processes in the value chain (see Exhibit 2-1.3) and are referred to as **core processes**. The final four processes support the value chain, but are not part of it. Therefore, they are known as **support processes**. The alternative to managing processes is to manage departments, which is how organizations have been traditionally managed. In a traditional organization, the accounting department is an independent operation that performs certain activities in the order fulfillment process (cost accounting), billing and collection process (preparing invoices and recording cash receipts), planning (preparing budgets), and information systems (providing data and information for decision making). In process management, accountants become members of process teams rather than staying together in a separate department. For example, some accountants will become members of the order fulfillment team to provide cost accounting support.

Process quality improvement (PQI) is a generic term used to describe any methodology used to improve process quality. This reading presents an overview of how organizations implement PQI programs. Several specific PQI methodologies are used to improve quality, but this reading focuses on elements common to all. In addition, the accountant's role in establishing a management control system for process quality, as well as in determining the cost of quality, is discussed.

---

[1] See for example, P. S. Pande, R. P. Neuman, and R. R. Cavanagh, *The Six Sigma Way* (New York: McGraw-Hill, 2000).

WHAT IS QUALITY MANAGEMENT?

Total quality management (TQM) was the original PQI methodology and most others borrow its key tenets. It can be described as a management *philosophy* emphasizing the development of processes that consistently deliver to *customers* products and services that exceed their expectations. The key words in this definition are "philosophy" and "customers." Many experts view continuous improvement as the key to TQM and often use the term continuous improvement as synonymous with TQM. **Continuous improvement** is the concept that every employee is at all times responsible for managing and measuring ongoing process improvements. **Six Sigma**, a more recent PQI methodology, is a system to build quality into processes to the extent that each activity will have a defect rate of less than 3.4 defects per million. For many of you, these process management terms are new. However, for those of you who either have work experience, particularly in larger organizations, or have read the general business press (an excellent idea for all students serious about a career in business), these are familiar concepts.

Managing process quality represents a different philosophy. It is not a technique, not a quick fix, and not purely a statistical tool. Instead, it is a comprehensive and different way to look at organizations and the problems they face in today's highly competitive global economy. Many experts believe that this change in philosophy is so great that it represents a paradigm shift. A **paradigm** is the way you look at the world. For example, moving from a "flat earth" to a "global earth" perspective represented a paradigm shift.

The other key word in the definition is customers. In PQI all employees must focus their attention on their customers. All actions are motivated by the desire to meet and exceed customer expectations. To many students this may appear to be a simplistic truism. However, for those of you with business experience, you may recall that much of your time was spent focused on issues other than customer needs, such as meeting a numerical standard or pleasing your boss or your boss's boss. Similarly, for a university, consider how much staff and administrator time is spent centered on you, one of the university's major customers. The notion of placing the customer first is a very difficult idea for many organizations to accept. Exhibit 3-2.1 compares the traditional paradigm with the PQI paradigm.

History of Quality Management

The history of TQM can be traced back more than 70 years to a statistician at Bell Labs by the name of Walter Shewhart who developed statistical measures for controlling manufacturing operations. During World War II, the now famous disciples of Shewhart, W. Edwards Deming and J. M. Juran, were called upon by the United States government to assist manufacturers in producing quality military equipment. Although very successful with their ideas during the war, American industry quickly reverted to its prewar management philosophy, discarding Deming's and Juran's ideas of statistical quality control. **Statistical quality control** (SQC) is the use of statistics to improve the quality of products and services. After the war Deming joined the business faculty at New York University and engaged in private consulting.

The Allied forces under General Douglas McArthur, who oversaw the rebuilding of Japan after the war, were familiar with the work of Deming. As a result, in 1947 Deming was invited to Japan to help organize a census. After completing this task, he returned to the United States. In 1950, based on recommendations and contacts made in 1947, a group of Japanese businessmen intent on rebuilding Japan invited Deming to return, which he did. His charge was to teach statistical quality control and its relation to Western management concepts. The irony, of course, is that Deming did not teach the Japanese postwar American business practices, but instead taught them quality control ideas. A little later the Japanese learned of Juran and also invited him to Japan. Deming and Juran were ultimately credited in large part for the postwar economic miracle that took place in Japan. In fact, the most prestigious commercial award in Japan today is the Deming Quality Award.

Exhibit 3-2.1
Comparisons of the Traditional and PQI Paradigms

	Traditional View	**PQI View**
Primary focus	Cost—Assumption: In a competitive market a firm sells homogeneous goods. Since price is set by the market, cost is the key.	Quality—Assumption: Almost all products or services are differentiable on service, quality, design, etc. Key to throughput is customer satisfaction.
Typical measures	Manufacturing cost, standard cost variances	Customer satisfaction, cycle time, quality (defect rates, etc.)
Inventory	Viewed as an asset (WIP, finished goods inventory, increased income)	Viewed as a liability, which should be eliminated
Typical measures	Traditional (absorption) cost	Inventory turnover
Pricing	Stimulate sales with marginal cost pricing; rely on contribution margin (CM)	Establish partnerships with customers based largely on nonprice variables
Typical measures	Favorable CVP, increase in CM, market share, marketing variances	Percent of partners' needs you meet, number of partnerships
Management approach	Experts and management design an optimum (static) system and give employees operating rules	Empower workers to find root causes of problems, conduct continuous improvement
Typical tools	Economic order quantity (EOQ), production scheduling, linear programming	Statistical quality control (SQC), just-in-time (JIT)

Oddly enough, American business first became interested in the work of Deming and Juran through a 1980 NBC television documentary entitled "If Japan Can . . ., Why Can't We?" U.S. managers were at first skeptical of these radical new ideas. In addition, most managers had great difficulty in fully understanding them. Nevertheless, some persevered with these ideas, driven by the demonstrated prowess of Japanese manufacturing capabilities and the quality of their products. By the mid-1980s a large number of managers at leading and successful firms, such as Motorola, Ford, Texas Instruments, Harley-Davidson, and Hewlett-Packard, had implemented the Deming/Juran ideas with startling results.

Many managers are now convinced that their organizations must commit to the TQM philosophy if they are to survive in the future. Since firms are implementing quality improvement ideas at a rapid pace, a sound understanding of TQM concepts will soon be required of any new employee. For example, the American Hospital Association found that 69 percent of hospitals report that they have launched "sophisticated quality improvement campaigns," 75 percent of which have been started since 1991. Also, Ford Motor Company management reports that they have taken $40 billion out of their operating budget because they have adopted quality principles and have begun to change their culture.[2] Therefore, while in school, students are well-advised to learn as much about process management and quality as possible.

Today, quality is a crucial issue worldwide. In Europe the International Organization for Standardization (ISO) in 1987 issued the 9000 series of standards covering quality. Organizations that apply to be ISO 9000 certified must go through a rigorous review process that audits conformance to the standards. Most large and many smaller firms outside of Europe have been awarded ISO 9000 certification.

PRINCIPAL ELEMENTS OF QUALITY

There are four common elements to PQI systems:

- Customer orientation.
- System of interrelated processes.
- Emphasis on measures.
- Continuous improvement and process variation.

Customer Orientation

The first step of a quality program is to define quality. The answer in PQI systems is simple: Quality is what the customer values. Customers are defined as those who use the output of a process. Note that the customer can be external or internal to the firm, but all employees must be responsive to their customers. The first step in process improvement is to focus the organization on the customer, so that everything a company does is driven by the desire to exceed customer expectations. In contrast, traditional manufacturing departments center not on customer needs, but rather on cost control and efficient plant scheduling. Traditional accounting departments concentrate on processing invoices, preparing financial statements, and issuing factory cost reports. With PQI, all employees, not just the marketing department, extensively interact with either external or internal customers.

System of Interrelated Processes

Traditional companies are organized by function. For example, production employees work for the production department, accountants work for the accounting department, and salespeople work for the marketing department. In adopting PQI, a company becomes organized by processes, with the customer(s) of each process determining whether the process is functioning appropriately.

For example, the customer service process normally has one customer, the purchaser of the product. The primary supplier for customer service is the order fulfillment process, but customer service is concerned with the product development process because good design is normally critical to reduced product defects and breakdowns that customer service must deal with. Conversely, the direct customer of the product development process is order fulfillment, but customer service and the final purchaser are also critical customers. In PQI, the needs of multiple internal and external customers are met through the use of cross-functional teams.

---

[2] *The Wall Street Journal*, November 3, 1993, p. 1.

To illustrate, in a traditional automobile firm the design department designs a new model based on some sales and market research information obtained from the marketing department and what the designers think is "good design." The design team is composed strictly of engineers from the design department. In PQI, a cross-functional design team is organized and made up of employees trained in design, manufacturing, marketing, accounting, and often supplier and customer representatives as well. The result is a car design that more effectively meets customer needs, has quality which is designed in, can be manufactured efficiently and at low cost, and can meet the firm's financial constraints. Note that meeting customer requirements means involving all processes downstream from an activity, not just meeting the needs of the final customer.

The role of top management in implementing PQI is to structure the organization around processes staffed by employees from the appropriate functional areas and to ensure that such groups are working in the organization's overall interest. The role of employee groups is to manage the various processes. A key notion is that company demands, such as improving quality, reducing cost, increasing sales, or meeting other numerical goals, are worthless unless management also explains how processes should be restructured to meet these demands. A traditionally managed firm typically sets short-term goals for each functional area, which are often unattainable because the firm is not organized in such a way that process improvement is possible. The most extreme of traditional management style is found in television and movie portrayals of business. Typically, the media portrays top managers who ruthlessly give commands to subordinates to increase profits or sales. However, businesses of even moderate size are far too complex to be managed this way, and such a management approach would certainly be unsuccessful when competing against a company utilizing PQI.

Emphasis on Measures

An absolutely critical component of the PQI philosophy is the centrality of measures in achieving organizational focus and in fostering continuous improvement. In fact, a favorite saying is, "You can't manage what you can't measure." Many observers of PQI companies in America and Japan are struck by the employees' fixation with measures. As Deming states, "In God we trust. All others bring data." A focus on process measures forces employees to think *specifically* about what customers want and how they are going to tell if they are making progress. Specific measures can create cohesion by giving workers a relatively unambiguous, commonly shared goal over which they have significant control. Many participative sports use shared goals to build cohesive teams. One way of setting process goals is to employ benchmarking. **Benchmarking** is evaluating a process by comparing it to the best similar process in the world.

Traditional firms, in contrast, often use only the most recent financial data for monitoring progress. This causes several problems. First, it may lead to tampering by management. **Tampering** is the attempt to correct or improve a process based on differences between a standard and actual measures that are caused by random events. Tampering is attractive because there are normally too few relevant financial observations to perform statistical quality control analysis. Second, financial measures generally involve broad aggregations and, hence, do not relate to the work done by individuals or small groups of workers. Third, the financial performance of one department or area is heavily influenced by actions of other departments. As a result, variation in a department's financial measures may be unrelated to its own actions. Finally, the traditional firm is departmentally organized making it nearly impossible for managers to improve underlying processes that are responsible for the reported financial numbers.

Continuous Improvement and Process Variation

The emphasis on continuous improvement forces firms to define what it is they need to make better, a decision that leads directly to a customer orientation. Soon firms realize that to determine whether they are continuously improving in relation to customer needs, they must carefully measure what they do. Once an appropriate measurement system is in place, firms realize that to achieve significant improvements they must focus on processes rather than functions. Hence, pursuit of continuous improvement leads directly to the other elements of PQI.

An employee group manages its process through continuous improvement activities, with improvement defined by the group's customers. Continuous improvement is the opposite of the old adage "if it ain't broke, don't fix it." Instead, quality proponents believe that improvement of processes is a never-ending quest orchestrated by the employees themselves. By contrast, in traditional firms management attempts to design and implement optimal systems (often with the help of outside consultants) and employees are instructed to operate those systems. The systems remain static in design until years later when management decides to design and impose a new optimal system on the employees.

Continuous improvement is accomplished by first obtaining an in-depth understanding of all the activities in a process. Each activity is then examined to determine if it is in control. If possible, this is done statistically using control charts. If the activity is out of control, action must be taken to bring it into control. If the activity is in control, quality improvements are tested that reduce the variation of the activity and move it closer to its target. The effectiveness of quality improvement ideas is then tested statistically. In short, variability and an understanding of statistics are at the heart of continuous improvement.

The Quality Program at General Electric

In 2000, General Electric (GE) won *Fortune* magazine's "Most Admired Company in America" award for the fourth straight year.[3] Shortly before receipt of the first award, GE launched the largest corporate quality initiative ever.[4] It was called the Six Sigma program and with it GE hoped to reduce defects to less than 3.4 per million process operations. Six Sigma undertook 6,000 team-based projects in 1997 and resulted in $320 million in productivity gains in 1997. It has trained 100,000 people in Six Sigma methodology. The program was expected to increase GE's net income by up to $5 billion through the year 2000. Improvements reported by GE and attributed largely to the Six Sigma initiative between 1995 and 2000 are:[5]

	1995	2000
Annual productivity gain	1.5%	4.0%
Operating margin	14.5%	18.4%
Inventory turnover	5.8	9.2

GE reports that "Six Sigma has turned the Company's focus from inside to outside, changed the way we think and train our future leaders and moved us toward becoming a truly customer-focused organization."[6] GE is applying Six Sigma not only to its manufacturing

---

[3] *General Electric 2000 Annual Report*, p. 1.

[4] "Jack: a Close-up Look at How America's #1 Manager Runs GE," *Business Week*, June 8, 1998, pp. 90–106.

[5] G. T. Lucier and S. Seshadri, "GE Takes Six Sigma Beyond the Bottom Line," *Strategic Finance*, May 2001, pp. 41-46.

[6] *General Electric 2000 Annual Report*, p. 2.

operations, but also to its huge services business, which include the NBC television network and financial and insurance subsidiaries.

ROLE OF ACCOUNTING IN QUALITY IMPROVEMENT

Accountants can play a critical role in the implementation and operation of PQI. Indeed, accounting firms are probably the largest and most active group of quality consultants. Why? Because accountants have always had primary responsibility for designing and operating a firm's management control system and have historically been the principal information experts in an organization. This latter role, however, is shared more and more with management information systems professionals. A **management control system** (MCS) determines (1) how management communicates to employees what ought to be done, and (2) how employee and business unit performance is measured. Exhibit 3-2.2 illustrates the structure of an MCS. Since PQI can be viewed as a new and more sophisticated MCS, it is only natural that accountants will be heavily involved. In addition, many firms use cost of (poor) quality analyses to help implement improvement efforts. As you might expect, accountants are involved in determining cost of quality information.

Exhibit 3-2.2

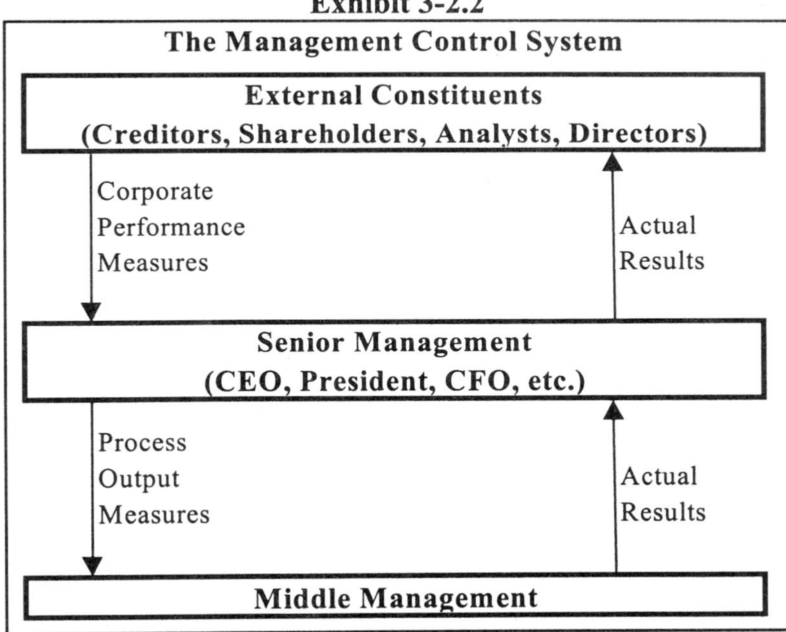

Quality Measures in a Management Control System

A major theme of Module 3 is that when a firm changes the way it operates, it must change its MCS. If a firm adopts a new process management system but retains a traditional MCS, employees will continue to do those things that improve traditional performance measures rather than taking actions consistent with the new system. Two changes in the MCS must be made when a PQI program in implemented: (1) quality measures need to be included in the process output measures and (2) the focus is placed on process performance rather than departmental performance. Firms use three levels of measures for different purposes: (1) corporate performance, (2) process output, and 3) activity improvement. These three levels are summarized in Exhibit 3-2.3 and discussed next. The first two are part of the MCS.

Exhibit 3-2.3

PQI Measurement Levels			
Measurement Levels	**Responsibility**	**Traditional Measures**	**PQI Measures**
Corporate Performance	Top management	Return on investment, market share, stock price, income	Return on investment, market share, stock price, income
Process Output	Middle management	Cost, volume of production	Defect rate, cycle time, late deliveries, cost of quality
Activity Improvement	Lower management, process employees	Production quotas and standards	Control charts, preventive maintenance logs

Corporate Performance Measures

Corporate performance measures are those that reflect performance toward critical goals of the entire organization. Since these performance outcomes affect the entire firm, individual employees and process teams have limited impact on them. Typical corporate performance measures include external customer satisfaction, income, return on equity, stock price, and market share. It is the accountant's role to work with senior management to develop a corporate strategy that will meet the organization's critical goals. An example of a strategy is management's decision that the firm is going to compete only in the high-quality, technologically advanced part of the market and forego other market opportunities. Note that a PQI program does not change these measures but, if successful, will improve performance based on these measures.

Process Output Measures

Management and accountants next identify key success factors that relate to the strategy selected. **Key success factors** are those few things that the firm must do well for its strategy to succeed. Examples of key success factors are quality and rapid commercialization of technological developments.

Process output measures are developed from key success factors and are used to monitor how each process, in its limited way, contributes to meeting the key success factors. The process output measures are developed by accountants and the process team as part of the budgeting system. It is crucial to a firm's success that accountants select output measures that are clearly linked to key success factors. Examples of process output measures for a manufacturing process are the number of quality defects and cost of quality.

Accountants periodically collect data for the output measures and prepare performance reports for middle and upper management. It is important to understand that if process output measures are improperly linked to key success factors, PQI will fail because process teams will focus their continuous improvement efforts on factors that are not closely related to the firm's overall success.

Most traditional organizations use cost and production volume as the overriding process output measures. You can see this in the operation of most universities where cost and the number of students enrolled are the typical measures of performance for academic departments. The problem with selecting traditional process output measures for all organizations is that these no longer reflect the key success factors for most businesses. For instance, does the number of students graduated each year measure the quality of those graduates or their ability to gain professional employment in their fields? In fact, quality proponents argue that improper and outdated process output measures are perhaps the major cause of poor quality in traditionally run American firms.

Activity Improvement Measures

Although process output measures will tell the process team what to concentrate on, they are of little value in telling the team *how* to improve the process, and, hence, the process output measures. It is the role of **activity improvement measures** to provide guidance on how to improve activities within a process. Activity improvement measures are critical, but they are not part of the MCS because these measures are not used to evaluate manager performance.

Firms use both statistical and non-statistical activity measures. One important statistical quality control technique is a control chart. SQC and preventive maintenance logs are examples of activity improvement measures. A **control chart** is simply a graph of recent observations involving some measurable characteristic of the process. The graph also includes lower and upper control limit lines. The appendix to this reading explains control charts in more detail. An example of a nonstatistical activity measure is a preventive maintenance log that shows when and what preventive maintenance was performed on a piece of equipment. Accountants help process teams identify the SQC data as well as other information they need to collect. Accountants then help design the system to actually collect and report the data for the team.

MCS Focus on Processes Rather than Departments

A second MCS change that accountants need to make is to evaluate the performance of processes rather than departments. A key part of a traditional MCS is the computation of detailed cost variances by department and even by each activity in a department. CCC employed this type of performance evaluation in Case 2-7. Use of cost variances to measure performance is antithetical to the philosophy of PQI because the process must be evaluated as a system. To do otherwise will cause individual activities and departments to take actions that will improve their performance at the expense of the entire process. This phenomenon is termed **suboptimization**. In addition, it encourages managers to try to improve the department based on this inadequate accounting information. Deming termed such departmental corrections tampering and demonstrated how it only makes a process worse. It is critical that accountants move away from detailed cost variances when a quality program is initiated.

As an example, look at what the direct labor variance calculation encourages production managers at CCC to do. If the lot size is increased, direct labor idle time will be decreased. This means that more cars can be built for a given amount of direct labor. More production increases the performance budget for direct labor, but since actual direct labor cost remain constant, the labor variance will be favorably impacted. CCC's direct labor variances will improve, but this may not be optimal to CCC because we know from the simulation that stockouts and inventory will increase.

The Power of Measures: Global Airlines Example

Global Airlines (GA) is a passenger airline that runs a cargo operation that utilizes the excess capacity of the luggage area on scheduled passenger flights. Given the large fixed costs associated with putting an aircraft into the air, generation of additional revenues through cargo operations is critical to airline profitability. Based on your knowledge of cost behavior, can you explain why this is so? Historically, performance of the cargo division was measured by the volume of freight carried and by the utilization of available capacity in the cargo holds of scheduled passenger flights. Performance of individual cargo handlers was measured by the quantity of cargo handled. These measures of efficiency and volume made good sense when viewed from an internal economic perspective. However, they have nothing to do with what the customer wants—*the customer does not ship air cargo to enhance the profits of the airlines.* The GA cargo measures naturally encouraged the employees to offer low prices and to schedule shipping to match available cargo space.

Although the cargo division was perceived to be performing well with performance improving on all measures, in the spirit of PQI, the division decided to ask customers what they wanted. Perhaps not surprisingly, the customers said that the most important factor to them was prompt service, which usually meant next day delivery. Note that the capacity utilization measurement provides a disincentive to prompt delivery because utilization can be maximized by building an "inventory" of orders to a given city and then drawing from this backlog to fill up available cargo space on a flight. By accepting only those orders for which GA could guarantee space and thus next day delivery, some cargo space would be empty on those flights on which the passenger luggage did not take up its maximum allowed space or weight. As a test, GA tracked a large number of its cargo packages and discovered that it took four days to get a package to the destination airport.

The test indicated that GA clearly was not meeting customer expectations. Cargo division performance measures were redirected to emphasize customer satisfaction and revenue generation. The cargo handlers were asked to participate in developing measures of their performance that would enhance customer satisfaction.

The process output measures agreed upon were the following:

- Conformance to promised deadlines.
- Arrival of cargo on intended flight.
- Length of time from landing to customer availability.

Monthly measures for each of these items were calculated so that employees at each cargo terminal could compare their performance over time and against other terminals. Note how customer satisfaction was defined in a very clear way so that the cargo employees could easily take actions to improve.

Emphasis on these new measures caused procedures and employee assignments to be changed. As a result, GA was able to reduce late shipments greatly, lower the average arrival time, and improve customer satisfaction. Improved customer relations will eventually increase GA's competitive position, which will be reflected by improved financial results. Previous attempts by GA to improve financial results by using efficiency measures of performance actually degraded customer satisfaction, which impaired its financial performance.

Enterprise Resource Planning (ERP) Software

Software that integrates accounting and other information from most functional areas of the firm is known as **enterprise resource planning software**. These enormous and complex packages can cost tens of millions or even hundreds of millions of dollars to install. They are, nevertheless, hugely popular because they allow firms to access information to manage processes. Without ERP software, it is not feasible for larger organizations to manage processes. Traditional software, built around functional departments, cannot do this. At the heart of ERP software are the accounting modules, but they also contain marketing, human resource, production, and several other components. Popular ERP packages include SAP and Oracle for large organizations, and Great Plains for the mid-range market.

COST OF QUALITY

Many organizations prepare cost of quality (COQ) information in order to fix employees' attention on the importance of good quality and to help direct continuous quality improvement efforts. Although most firms use the term **cost of quality**, it is more appropriately labeled the cost of *poor* quality, because the computations emphasize how much a firm is losing due to the poor quality of its products and services. J. M. Juran is COQ's best know proponent. COQ analyses have been performed by hundreds of firms, and the results show that the cost of poor quality is consistently around 25 percent or more of sales. This percentage holds true for both manufacturing and service firms. To appreciate the magnitude of this percentage, profit for most successful firms averages between 5 and 10 percent of sales. Therefore, most firms could earn several times their current profit if poor quality could be either reduced significantly or eliminated.

Cost of quality information usually is presented in the following four categories:

1. **Prevention costs** are costs incurred to prevent defects. These include costs related to product design reviews, statistical quality control, preventive maintenance, employee quality training, and vendor planning and production reviews.
2. **Appraisal costs** are costs incurred to check that products, processes, and services conform to specifications. These include all costs necessary to inspect incoming parts and goods produced. Appraisal costs include quality audit and testing costs.
3. **Internal failure costs** are costs incurred to correct problems detected by inspection, testing, etc. These include the cost to correct defects (rework), the cost of scrap, and cost of downtime due to quality problems.
4. **External failure costs** are costs incurred due to the discovery of defects by customers. These include warranty, legal liability, and time involved in handling customer complaints. The largest external failure costs, the loss of existing and future customers due to loss of goodwill and reputation, are difficult to measure and often are not formally reported as costs of poor quality.

Notice that the first category, prevention costs, are "good" costs in that activities supported by these costs should reduce the level of defects. The other three categories are "bad" costs because they are the costs of not doing it right the first time. As a firm improves quality, it should reduce the last three categories of cost because failures will decrease and the need for appraisal should be reduced. Prevention costs, however, may increase as a firm invests more in training, vendor relations, preventive maintenance, and product design. Many firms not adopting a quality program are motivated to cut prevention costs, because these are discretionary in the short term and because the impact of these cuts is not clearly visible if the firm does not prepare COQ information.

Limitations of Traditional Accounting Systems

The reason that so many firms have found COQ information to be so important to their continuous improvement efforts is that traditional accounting information is limited in its ability to report quality costs. Traditional accounting does not collect information in a format that allows managers to support quality decisions. Although traditional accounting systems collect some quality costs, they often combine quality costs with other costs. For example, most firms collect training costs, but do not separate training that is designed to improve quality from other training. Most firms also record customer service costs, but do not separate costs related to addressing complaints from those relating to product inquiries. Traditional systems do not recognize some costs at all. For example, preventive maintenance usually is buried in direct labor costs, and the cost of losing a customer due to poor quality is not recorded at all. Finally, traditional accounting systems do not classify costs into the four categories discussed earlier.

Since existing accounting systems are inadequate, a new cost of quality accounting system must be developed. Most firms do this by assembling a team of accounting, engineering, and operations people; having the team identify and categorize quality costs; and designing a collection and reporting system. Most quality accounting systems are simple and use microcomputer spreadsheets. Teams tend to rely heavily on estimates and easy-to-collect data so information can be collected quickly and reported promptly. For example, 20 percent of engineering design costs may be classified as internal failure costs related to the redesign of products to correct quality problems. Lost sales due to poor quality, if collected at all, are often set at some multiple of internal failure and other external failure costs. The reasoning is that lost sales are a large and critical quality cost that should be communicated to employees, even if it is difficult to measure accurately. Managers believe that if other failure costs are decreasing, then the cost of lost sales also will decrease.

Uses of Cost of Quality Information

Organizations use COQ information for many purposes and decisions, including the following:

- Serve as a wake-up call.
- Put quality into the language of business.
- Identify quality problems and prioritize projects.
- Serve as a process output measure for business units.

<u>Serve as a Wake-Up Call</u>

The initial use of COQ information often is to demonstrate to everyone—managers, staff and operating employees—how critical it is to improve quality. The magnitude of the cost of poor quality "knocks the socks" off most people. COQ information can get people's attention and place an emphasis on quality because of the huge magnitude of the cost of poor quality for most firms. Very few other actions that a company can take have the potential to double net income like a quality program can.

<u>Put Quality into the Language of Business</u>

Accounting is referred to as "the language of business" because managers typically discuss problems and opportunities in terms of quantifiable costs and revenues. Most quality programs talk about statistical variation, defect rates, preventive maintenance, and other nonfinancial terms, which are new to most employees. Without the kind of "hard" financial data to support continuous improvement, most organizations find it is very difficult to communicate the importance of quality to managers and other employees. COQ information addresses this problem by translating quality into terms that everyone can understand.

Identify Quality Problems and Prioritize Projects

COQ information helps managers decide where to focus quality efforts because the data collected to create the four COQ categories listed at the beginning of this section can be used to find the root cause of quality problems. Once a root cause has been determined, a quality project can be proposed, and the potential savings associated with each quality project can be quantified. The magnitude of cost savings can be an important factor in selecting which quality projects to pursue. For example, if the cost of quality information indicates that a large portion of appraisal and internal failure costs are due to poor vendor quality, the first quality effort may be working with vendors to help them improve quality.

Serve as a Process Output Measure for Business Units

Defect rates and other nonfinancial measures can be important process output measures, but the most important measurement is whether quality efforts are having a positive financial impact. It is difficult to maintain continuous improvement efforts over time if progress in financial terms cannot be demonstrated. COQ provides a measurement that can clearly show if the quality program is having the expected financial impact.

In summary, COQ information plays a critical role in the successful implementation of continuous improvement or quality initiatives. Accountants play an important role in designing and maintaining a cost of quality system because they are familiar with the existing accounting system, possess broad understanding of the firm, and have knowledge of costs and cost measurement. All employees should have a basic understanding of COQ information because this is how firms implementing continuous improvement "keep score."

Cost of Quality Example

The managers of Quality Welding decided to perform a COQ analysis in order to focus their quality efforts. The first step in the analysis was to collect quality costs by category. In practice this was a time-consuming task that required good knowledge of Quality Welding's processes and considerable judgment. Some of the costs came from Quality Welding's accounting system, but many others were collected elsewhere or estimated. The results of their categorization efforts are as follows:

Prevention costs	$ 730,000
Appraisal costs	1,220,000
Internal failure costs	6,720,000
External failure costs	9,810,000
Total cost of quality	$18,480,000

The next step is to use the COQ information to improve operations at Quality Welding. As soon as top management saw the magnitude of total COQ for a company with only $50 million in sales, they were ready to take action. When top management distributed these numbers to other managers and employees, they all agreed that a quality program was necessary. Everyone understood the significance of $18,480,000, whereas not everyone understood the magnitude of the problem based on defect rates and late delivery numbers.

Once Quality Welding was galvanized for action, management created several teams whose charge was to identify quality projects with the potential to make the largest reductions in total COQ. One of the projects identified and selected was the implementation of a preventive maintenance program. This program was estimated to increase prevention costs by $200,000 per year. However, better machine reliability would reduce the level of defects and reduce the plant's downtime. As a result, it is estimated that appraisal costs would be reduced by $300,000 per year because fewer defective products means that fewer inspections are required. Internal failure costs would decrease by about $1,200,000 because of fewer defective products manufactured and a reduction in downtime. Finally, external failure costs would be reduced by an estimated $1,800,000 because fewer defects and better on-time delivery (due to less downtime) means increased customer goodwill. COQ has demonstrated to Quality Welding that a $200,000 annual investment in preventive maintenance creates a $3,300,000 annual reduction in COQ. Top management at Quality Welding had no idea the payoff from a preventive maintenance program could be so large.

SUMMARY

There is a global effort to manage organizations' processes for the benefit of customers and away from managing departments for the good of the departments. One indication of this movement is the spectacular increase in the use of integrated enterprise software. At the heart of this movement are process quality improvement techniques such as TQM and Six Sigma. Four key elements of PQI methodologies are (1) a customer orientation, (2) a view of the organization as a system of interrelated processes, (3) an emphasis on measures, and (4) a focus on continuous improvement and process variation. The major accounting implications of this movement are (1) a need to redesign management control systems in general and process output measures in particular, and (2), a need to redesign cost systems to collect COQ information to support quality initiatives.

APPENDIX TO READING 3-2: CONTROL CHARTS

One basic tool employed in TQM to improve processes continuously is the study of process variation using control charts. All observations that fall within the control limits are considered to be random results of the process, while any observations beyond the limits are considered to have one or more special causes that reflect factors that are *not* a normal part of the process. An event that impacts the operation of an activity, but is external to the normal operation of that activity, is termed a **special cause event**. In short, a control chart is used to distinguish between special causes of variation and random fluctuations. As we will see, these two types of variation have important management implications.

For example, a machine operator can periodically take measurements of how full a machine is filling bottles of juice. If one set of data show that the juice is above or below the control limits, the operator knows to stop the process and find the special cause of the improperly filled bottles. The operator can also use SQC to test whether a change in how the bottles are filled lowers the variability of the juice in the bottles. If it does, the quality of the process has been improved.

Exhibit 3-2.4 shows a hypothetical distribution of exam scores along with calculations to compute control limits. A simplified control chart of this data is shown in Exhibit 3-2.5. Note that the mean score is 74.43 with a high score of 108 and a low score of 21. Is this examination process, and the underlying learning process, in control? To answer this, a teacher would check to see if all observations fall between the upper and lower control limits. From Exhibit 3-2.5 it is clear that the score of 21 lies below the lower control limit. The teacher would conclude that the score of 21 occurred due to a "special cause" that is not a normal part of the examination and learning process. The teacher's first step would be to investigate the cause of the 21 score. Before looking at the control chart analysis, how many of you thought that the 108 score was also due to a special cause?

Exhibit 3-2.4

Simplified Statistical Quality Control Exam Score Example

Test Score	(Test Score – Mean)	(Test Score – Mean)^2
108	33.57	1,126.72
98	23.57	555.39
90	15.57	242.32
88	13.57	184.05
88	13.57	184.05
87	12.57	157.92
85	10.57	111.65
82	7.57	57.25
80	5.57	30.99
79	4.57	20.85
78	3.57	12.72
77	2.57	6.59
77	2.57	6.59
76	1.57	2.45
75	0.57	0.32
75	0.57	0.32
75	0.57	0.32
74	(0.43)	0.19
73	(1.43)	2.05
72	(2.43)	5.92
71	(3.43)	11.79
69	(5.43)	29.52
68	(6.43)	41.39
66	(8.43)	71.12
65	(9.43)	88.99
64	(10.43)	108.85
61	(13.43)	180.45
57	(17.43)	303.92
54	(20.43)	417.52
21	(53.43)	2,855.12
2,233		6,817.37

The following statistics can be calculated as shown below or can be obtained directly by using the Excel commands also shown below, assuming data begin in row 4.

Test mean = 74.43 [2,233/30 or =average(b4:b33)]

Variance = 235.07 [6,817/29 or =var(b4:b33)]

Standard deviation = 15.33 [Square root of 235.08 or =stdev(b4:b33)]

Upper control limit (UCL) = 74.43 plus (3 × 15.33) = 120.42

Lower control limit (LCL) = 74.43 minus (3 × 15.33) = 28.44

Exhibit 3-2.5

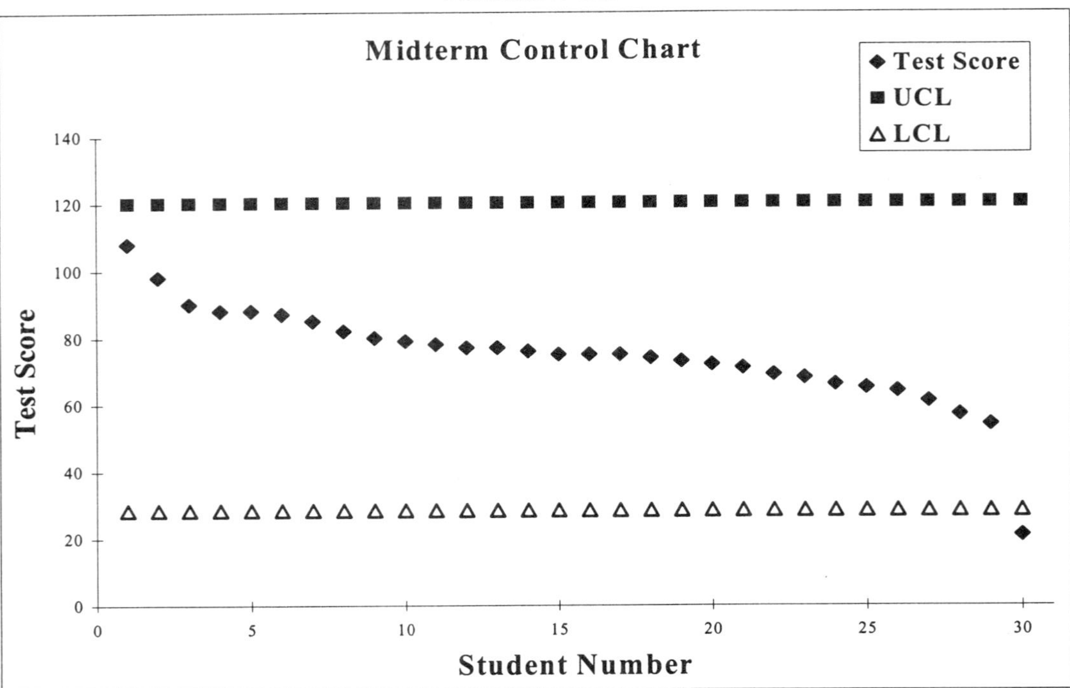

Note: For this control chart, the order in which the scores are placed on the chart is irrelevant. However, for many SQC applications, particularly those done over time, the order of the observations is critical. For example, if the performance for a group of students was measured several times over the semester, the observations must be kept in chronological order.

Let's assume that the teacher asked Bill, the student with the score of 21, why he performed so poorly on the test. Suppose Bill responded that his alarm failed to ring, causing him to be 30 minutes late for the 50-minute exam. To improve the examination process, the teacher will want to eliminate this special cause from happening again.

What can the teacher do? Several actions can be taken to avoid having a student sleep through part of the test. All exams could be given at night, or perhaps a phone tree could be initiated by the teacher so that all students would be called 30 minutes before the exam to ensure that they are up. Notice from Exhibit 3-2.4 that the special cause creates a disproportionate share of the process variance (i.e., of the total of 6,817.37 shown in the last column, 2,855.12 was caused by the score of 21 alone). Since control limits are based on the process variance, elimination of special causes will cause the upper and lower control limits to move considerably closer to the mean.

After correcting the special cause problem of oversleeping, is the examination and related learning process a quality process? Probably not. The customers of the process (students, employers, society) probably would be unhappy with the large variation in the level of students' knowledge as reflected by the exam scores. If so, the instructor has not met the customers' expectations. In short, the class is not a quality learning experience.

What would it mean if the calculated control limits for the exam fell outside the range of possible scores? Note that this has happened with the upper control limit in the example. The answer is that although statistically no special causes can be identified, because the system exhibits so much variability, it indicates that the learning process is of low quality.

What should the instructor do? The instructor could study, modify, and then test modifications to the learning process. The goal would be to *increase* the average level of learning in the class and to *reduce* the variability of the process. New ideas for process improvement would be tried, and virtually 100 percent of the students would learn what is expected. At this point, the instructor would have created a "total quality learning" process. TQM, however, requires that the instructor still continue actions to improve the average test scores and reduce the variation between student scores. The learning process would soon exceed customer expectations, and the instructor would have delighted customers.

In summary, the selection of appropriate measures is the means by which an organization translates overall corporate goals into meaningful objectives for individual process teams. Hence, the design of an MCS is critical to the ultimate success of the firm and the work satisfaction of its employees. Accountants, as the MCS experts, are therefore absolutely essential to the successful implementation of TQM.

EXERCISES AND PROBLEMS

Exercises

Exercise 1 Elements of PQI. Identify the four elements of process quality improvement. Explain each element and how each element interrelates with the other elements.

Exercise 2 Management Control System. Explain what a management control system is. Why do accountants have the primary responsibility for designing and operating the MCS?

Exercise 3 Processes Versus Departments. What is a process? How does a process differ from a department?

Exercise 4 Types of Processes. Indicate for each item below whether it is a core process, a support process, or not a process at all.

a. Planning
b. Chassis assembly
c. Product development
d. Accounting
e. Human resources
f. Order fulfillment
g. Equipment maintenance
h. Customer service
i. Billing and collection

Exercise 5 History of Quality Management. Trace the history of the quality movement. Include in your answer three quality pioneers.

Exercise 6 Management Control System Changes for PQI. How does the management control system change when an organization implements a PQI program?

Exercise 7 PQI at Global Airlines. From the example in the text, describe how the traditional performance measures used to control performance at Global Airlines caused the airline to take actions that were contrary to customer preferences. How did the quality measures align customers' needs with the performance measures at Global Airlines?

Exercise 8 Measurement Levels. Identify the three levels of measurement used to control a PQI organization. Give two examples of measures at all levels for both a PQI firm and a traditional firm. You need to give a total of 12 examples.

Exercise 9 Matching Actions with the Principal Elements of PQI. Match each of the following actions with one principal element of PQI and explain you reasoning.

a. Formation of teams composed of employees from different disciplines
b. Identification of organizations to serve as benchmarks
c. Identification of all users of an output from a process
d. Movement of accountants from the accounting department to manufacturing
e. Refusal to accept "if it ain't broke, don't fix it" excuses
f. Realization that tampering is a real danger
g. Require product designers to spend two weeks per year with a salesperson

Exercise 10 Traditional and PQI Measures. Indicate whether the following measures are Traditional or PQI:

a. Detailed cost variances
b. Cycle time
c. Number of late deliveries
d. Control charts
e. Idle labor time
f. Supplier defect rate
g. Department cost variances

Exercise 11 Interpretation of Control Charts (Appendix). Discuss the management implications of the following control chart that plots the percentage of items that have paint defects and must be repainted. Be sure to include a discussion of any "special cause" effects and variability contained in your answer.

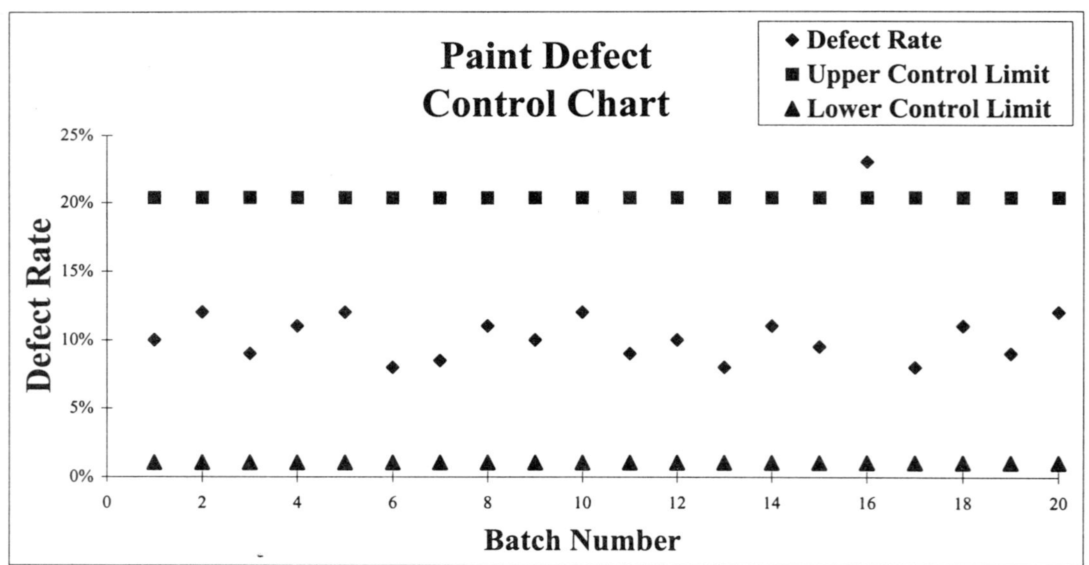

Exercise 12 Cost of Quality Categories. Identify the four cost of quality categories and give one example of a cost for each category.

Exercise 13 Uses of Cost of Quality Information. Discuss three ways in which organizations can use cost of quality information to support a successful quality program.

Problems

Problem 1 Cost of Quality Calculations. The controller at Collins, Inc. has provided you with the following costs for 2002:

Scrap	$ 57,000
Equipment depreciation	262,000
Inspection of finished units	92,000
Warranty claims	124,000
Setup costs	203,000
Employee quality training	77,000
Rework	194,000
Preventive maintenance	43,000
Inspection of incoming parts	62,000
Material handling	139,000
Downtime due to quality problems	81,000
Lost customer goodwill due to quality	199,000

a. Place the costs in the correct cost of quality category. Total the costs in each category. Not all costs fit in a cost of quality category.

b. How much, if any, of the quality costs are considered to be "good" quality costs?

Problem 2 Are You Receiving a Total Quality Education? The purpose of this individual exercise is for you to demonstrate your knowledge of PQI concepts by applying those concepts to your campus' educational system. You should begin this exercise by reviewing the section on the Accountant's Role in PQI earlier in this reading.

Prepare a three-page (word processed, double spaced, and carefully edited using a spellchecker) PQI analysis of your educational system that addresses the six questions below. Structure your answer so that each question is addressed sequentially. That is, address question a. first, question b. next, and so forth. Your paper should, however, flow smoothly and should not move abruptly from one question to the next.

a. Who is (are) the customer(s) of the college's education system? Explain your answer.

b. Describe two process output measures that would be appropriate for each of the following two processes. Be specific with your suggested measures.
   - The class registration process
   - The introductory accounting curriculum process

c. Briefly describe two activity improvement measures that would be appropriate for the following two processes. Be sure you understand how these measures differ from process output measures. Be specific with your suggested measures.
   - The class registration process
   - The introductory accounting curriculum process

d. Focusing just on business education, how might the business faculty use PQI concepts to improve the business education process? Link your answer to Reading 3-2.

e. As a student, what do you see as your role in the development of a total quality education?

f. In summary, are you presently receiving a total quality education? Explain by addressing each element of PQI discussed in Reading 3-2.

Problem 3 Midterm Grade Control Chart (Appendix). After the class has taken a midterm, your instructor will give each member of your group a list of the class's actual test scores for one question on the midterm. Each group will receive scores for a different test question. Reading 3-2 explains how to construct a control chart.

a. On a spreadsheet create a table of the individual exam question scores given to you by your instructor. This table should be in the format of Exhibit 3-2.4. The first step is to list all of the test scores in column 1. The next step is to have the computer calculate the mean. Show the computed mean below the table as illustrated in Exhibit 3-2.4. Once you have the mean, the second and third columns can be constructed.

b. Sum the third column, i.e., the column headed (Test Score-Test Mean)^2. Divide the third column sum by the number of test scores you have *minus* 1. For example, if you are given 34 test scores, divide the third column by 33. The result of this division is called the *variance*. You can instead use the spreadsheet variance command. Show the computed variance below the table.

c. Find the square root of the variance number you computed in b. This is called the *standard deviation*. You can instead use the spreadsheet standard deviation command. Show the computed standard deviation below the table. In Works and Excel, the square root is found by typing =SQRT followed by the variance in parentheses. To find the square root of 81, you would enter =SQRT(81).

d. Compute the upper and lower control limits by multiplying the standard deviation by three, and adding and subtracting this amount from the mean. TQM practitioners have arbitrarily selected three standard deviations for control limit purposes. Show the computed upper and lower control limits below the table.

e. Prepare a control chart for the test scores in the same format as shown in Exhibit 3-2.5. You can either draw in the UCL and LCL lines or you can have the computer show the control limits by including two additional dependent variables (columns) with the value of the UCL and LCL for each student. This means you should highlight three columns: test score, UCL, and LCL. When asked by Excel, enter zero for the column containing the X data.

f. Interpret what it means if the maximum points possible on the question, zero points, or both fall within the control limits.

g. Is the examination activity for your question under control?

h. In your judgment, is the learning activity reflected by the test scores for the question you analyzed a high-quality activity?

i. Based on your answer to h. and your considerable knowledge of the specific learning activity evaluated by your test question, list three factors you believe were at least partially responsible for the quality or lack of quality you observed.

Case 3-2

IMPLEMENTING A QUALITY PROGRAM AT CCC

Case Objectives

1. Introduce the concepts of continuous improvement and quality
2. Demonstrate the accounting changes that occur when a quality program is implemented
3. Develop a broader understanding of management control systems

Decision (Operating): How can CCC improve quality and reduce the costs?

David Gomez calls a meeting of CCC's top managers. David states: "I have read quality books by Deming and Juran as well as *The Six Sigma Way*.[1] I am convinced that CCC can improve its quality and reduce its cost of poor quality if we implement a quality program. What do you think about beginning a quality journey?"

Jena Butler, vice president—finance, replies: "Based on the ABC analysis performed in Case 3-1, I have concluded that poor quality is a major reason that CCC's profitability is below the industry average. I also read quality books and I believe that a quality program can really help CCC." "Great," says President Gomez, "Why don't you and your staff develop a report outlining changes CCC would need to make if a quality program is initiated. Let's meet again in a couple of weeks once it is completed." As a result of this discussion, Jena asked you to prepare the part of that report that relates to the manufacturing process.

Requirements

1. Who are the customers of the order fulfillment (primarily manufacturing) process? How should manufacturing decide what constitutes quality so that they will know specifically what to measure?

2. Identify the areas outside of manufacturing from which representatives should be recruited to serve on the order fulfillment continuous improvement oversight committee. For example, marketing should have a representative.

3. Identify at least three actions that Jena Butler and the accounting department at CCC should take to support the quality program.

4. Develop at least four process output measures for the manufacturing process that you think might be reasonable. Be very specific in defining these measures, and be sure you link them to CCC's strategy and key success factors: (a) product reliability, (b) cost, (c) customer service, and (d) product innovation.

[1] P. S. Pande, R. P. Neuman, and R. R. Cavanagh, The Six Sigma Way (New York: McGraw-Hill, 2000).

5. Performance budgets have been a key element of CCC's management control system since the company was founded because the variances play a critical part in evaluating the performance of each department and its manager. In Case 2-7 you completed a performance budget for CCC that included variances for each of CCC's seven manufacturing departments (Chassis Assembly, Final Assembly, and five overhead departments). In reality, hundreds of variances are calculated for each activity in each department. These detailed variances are used to evaluate individual worker performance. Jena Butler was wondering if the quality program would change this. Should this change? Explain why or why not.

6. (Appendix) You have collected data for two areas in the factory: the inspection of the incoming solar panels and the one-quarter inch drilling operation. Based on this data you have prepared control charts, shown in Exhibits C3-2.1 and C3-2.2, for each area. What conclusions can you draw from each control chart? What actions should management take based on each chart?

Exhibit C3-2.1

Exhibit C3-2.2

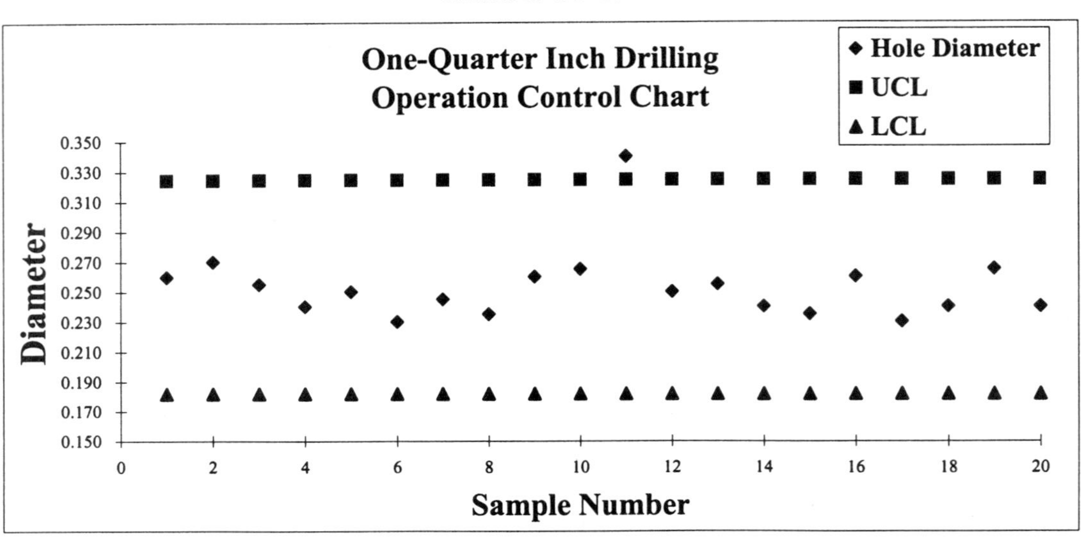

Case 3-3

COST OF QUALITY AT CALIFORNIA CAR COMPANY

Case Objectives

1. Introduce students to the basics of COQ
2. Demonstrate the diagnostic and control uses of COQ information

Decisions (Operating): Where should CCC focus its quality efforts? Is the quality program successful?

Part I

It is now June 2002. David Gomez has reviewed the report on the impact of a quality program prepared under the supervision of Jena Butler. He calls an all day meeting of CCC's top managers to discuss the proposal. Sally Swanson, vice president—production, says, "Quality is very important at CCC, but with our rapid increase in production, the level of commitment and time required to implement the changes in Jena's report is beyond what we can do. Besides, we produce quality vehicles now and all of our workers already are committed to quality. We won't be able to show the magnitude of improvement some other companies have. Finally, this program is going to be very costly and CCC just can't afford it at this time. For the next two years, let's instead concentrate on expanding our capacity."

At the end of the meeting David concludes, "I believe that implementing a quality program at CCC is critical. However, everyone must be convinced that this is of the highest priority or it will never succeed. A quality program is a major undertaking and I am also concerned about our ability to select projects that will have the greatest payoff. Jena, can you provide more evidence about the possible benefits of a quality program, as well as some guidance as to where we should begin, if we decide to go forward?"

After the meeting Jena returns to her office with David. Jena says, "The only idea I have to address your request is to undertake a cost of quality (COQ) analysis. This will tie up my staff for several weeks and also will require the cooperation and time of many other managers. We will have to let the installation of the accounts payable slip by another month to do the COQ analysis. What do you think?" David responds, "I really want to get the quality program launched, and if COQ can persuade others, it's worth it. Go for it!"

Jena assembles a team of 11 people, consisting of a management accountant, an engineer, a purchasing agent, one person from each production department, a person from marketing, and one person from each of the five overhead departments. She also assigns three accountants from her staff as support people. A month later the team has developed estimated COQ information for 2002 assuming no quality improvements are made. This analysis is presented in Exhibit C3-3.1.

Exhibit C3-3.1

CCC Year 2002 Cost of Quality Worksheet
(Traditional Accounting Classification in Parentheses)

		Supplier Quality		Assembly Quality		Equip. Reliability	
		%	$	%	$	%	$
Prevention Costs							
Design reviews (S&A)*	$ 68,000						
Preventive maintenance (Manufacturing)	163,000						
Vendor production specification review (Mfg.)	114,000						
	$ 345,000						
Appraisal Costs							
Inspection and testing of assembled vehicles (Mfg.)	$ 926,000						
Inspection and testing of purchased parts (Mfg.)	157,000						
	$ 1,083,000						
Internal Failure Costs							
Rework (Mfg.)	$ 9,497,800						
Scrap (Mfg.)	208,000	20%	41,600	25%	52,000	55%	114,400
Downtime due to quality problems (Mfg., partially)	1,538,000						
Safety stock to cover quality problems (Mfg.)	412,000						
Machine repair costs due to poor maintenance (Mfg.)	2,418,000						
	$ 14,073,800						
External Failure Costs							
Warranty claims (S&A)	$ 5,859,000						
Customer quality-related complaints (S&A)	258,000						
Profits on sales lost due to poor quality (Not collected)	17,577,000						
	$ 23,694,000						
Total Cost of Quality	$ 39,195,800						

* This cost is not related to any of the three initiatives.

How the Cost of Quality Estimates Were Collected

The team had to collect data from departments throughout CCC. Some data came from recorded manufacturing costs, some from recorded selling and administrative costs, and a few costs were not recorded at all. A description of how information on each type of cost was collected is presented, following the underlined label for each category. The costs of each category are the costs shown in Exhibit C3-3.1.

Design review costs are estimates of engineering time spent to review and modify product design to reduce defects in the manufacturing process. Vendor production specification review costs are estimated by purchasing agents in the Material Handling Department with the help of engineers. Preventive maintenance is the cost of performing routine cleaning and adjustment of equipment, as well as replacement of parts that show significant wear and tear. Both inspection and testing of assembled vehicles and inspection and testing of purchased parts are performed by inspectors in the Inspection Department and comes straight from the accounting records.

Rework is done by mechanics in the Inspection Department, and scrap is part of direct material cost, both of which are recorded in the current accounting system. Workers estimate that about 38 percent of rework is due to defective material used in assembling the car with the remaining 62 percent due to assembly errors. About 55 percent of scrap is caused by improperly maintained machines, 20 percent by defective parts, and 25 percent due to assembly errors.

Cost of labor idled by downtime due to quality problems is estimated by the percentage of time that direct labor is idle. Production supervisors estimate that about 42 percent of production downtime due to quality problems is the result of defective parts, 20 percent is due to assembly errors, and 38 percent is due to machine maintenance. The cost of safety stock to cover quality problems is an estimate made by the Material Handling Department. The need for safety stock is caused 45 percent by defective parts and 55 percent by assembly errors. The Maintenance Department estimates the machine repair costs due to poor maintenance.

Warranty claims are recorded by the current accounting system, and the costs of responding to customer quality-related complaints are estimated by the Marketing Department. The Marketing Department estimates that about 48 percent of warranty claims and customer complaints are the result of defective parts used in manufacturing the cars. The other 52 percent are due to assembly errors. Profits on sales lost due to poor quality is the "softest" and largest number in the analysis. This number is a rough estimate arrived at by tripling the warranty costs. George Olson believes that this is a conservative number because a reputation for quality problems will cause a large percentage of customers not to purchase cars from CCC.

The top managers at CCC are shocked when they see the COQ information. Gomez comments: "Our quality costs are over 30 percent of sales. This is about five times our projected profit. We can double net income if we can reduce our quality costs by only 20 percent. Even if the profits from lost sales due to poor quality is excluded, quality costs are about 16 percent of sales and more than five times estimated 2002 net income! We need a plan for reducing the quality costs."

Requirements

1. Based on the COQ analysis Jena's staff performed, presented in column 1 of Exhibit C3-3.1, prepare a one-paragraph memo to David Gomez discussing whether David can justify a quality program based on potential cost savings.

2. You have been assigned the task of evaluating the potential cost savings from three quality initiatives that various CCC managers have identified as potential high priority projects: (a) improved supplier quality, (b) building quality into the product the first time, and (c) improved equipment reliability. Compute the quality costs related to each project. Use the cost numbers from Exhibit C3-3.1 and the description of each of these costs presented earlier. The cost of scrap that can be impacted by each of the initiatives has been entered into the solution template as an example of how to approach this requirement. *Hint*: Not every quality cost is related to one of the three initiatives. If no percentages are given for breakdown of a quality cost between categories, the entire cost should be assigned to one category.

3. Do you recommend that CCC spend more in any COQ areas? Identify the areas and explain why you would increase spending. How can costs in one category affect the level of costs in other categories?

4. David Gomez has reviewed your analysis and believes that one quality initiative that CCC should undertake is improving the quality of incoming parts from suppliers. The Purchasing Department estimates that it will cost $500,000 to set up a vendor review and certification (VR&C) program and $100,000 per year to administer it each year thereafter. It is estimated that the VR&C program will eliminate 80 percent of the defective parts CCC is now receiving. This in turn will allow the inspection and testing of incoming parts to be reduced by 80 percent. Although Gomez believes that improving vendor quality is important, he is concerned about the costs versus the benefits of the Purchasing Department's proposal. To save $117,750 (75% of $157,000) in annual material inspection costs, CCC must spend $500,000 this year and $130,000 each year thereafter. Should CCC pursue the VR&C program? Prepare an analysis showing why or why not.

Part II[1]

It is now February 2003. CCC has been working on the three quality projects described in Part I for almost one year. Sally Swanson and David Gomez questioned whether the efforts of management and employees to improve their products and processes were actually cost effective and resulted in improved reported net income. Jena Butler suggested that CCC estimate the *actual* cost of quality for 2002 and compare it to the estimated costs shown in Exhibit C3-3.1. In short, she suggested that CCC use cost of quality as a *process output measure* for the manufacturing process. As a result, the Accounting Department prepared this COQ information, which is presented in Exhibit C3-3.2.

Requirements (Continued from Part I)

5. Using the data in Exhibit C3-3.2, prepare a bar graph of the costs of quality, by category, both with and without a quality program. For example, your bar graph should show the prevention costs *without* the quality program next to the prevention costs *with* the quality

[1] This portion of the case was originally prepared by Matt Mouritsen.

program so it is easy to compare the two. Use the instructions in Case 2-4 for making an Excel chart (graph), but select *Column* instead of *XY Scatter*.

6. Analyze Exhibit C3-3.2 and the column graph made for requirement 5 and assess the impact of the quality program on CCC's costs during 2002. Is the quality program at CCC showing results? Based on the category information in Exhibit C3-3.2, discuss specific activities that you believe have contributed or not contributed to the improvement of quality at CCC.

Exhibit C3-3.2

2002 Cost of Quality for CCC
With and Without Quality Program

	Estimated Without Program	Actual With Program
Prevention costs		
Design reviews	$ 68,000	$ 347,000
Preventive maintenance	163,000	473,000
Vendor production specification review	114,000	644,000
	$ 345,000	$ 1,464,000
Appraisal costs		
Inspection and testing of assembled vehicles	$ 926,000	$ 691,000
Inspection and testing of purchased parts	157,000	101,000
	$ 1,083,000	$ 792,000
Internal failure costs		
Rework	$ 9,497,800	$ 5,287,000
Scrap	208,000	173,000
Downtime due to quality problems	1,538,000	887,000
Safety stock to cover quality problems	412,000	314,000
Machine repair costs due to poor maintenance	2,418,000	1,733,000
	$ 14,073,800	$ 8,394,000
External failure costs		
Warranty claims	$ 5,859,000	$ 3,744,000
Customer quality-related complaints	258,000	146,000
Profits on sales lost due to poor quality	17,577,000	11,232,000
	$ 23,694,000	$ 15,122,000
Total cost of quality	$ 39,195,800	$ 25,772,000

Reading 3-4

JIT AND PROCESS IMPROVEMENT

INTRODUCTION

Reading 3-2 discussed a widespread management approach of business process quality improvement (PQI) often termed Six Sigma or total quality management. The **just-in-time system** (JIT), also known as **lean production**, is another process-improvement methodology that is used by thousands of organizations throughout the world. JIT shares many ideas with PQI, but differs in two crucial aspects: the way work is organized and the overriding emphasis placed on cycle time. JIT also necessitates significant changes in a firm's accounting system, beyond the changes required by PQI.

HISTORY OF JUST-IN-TIME

Operations management is the study of how work is organized to meet the goals of an organization. Three individuals stand out as major contributors to the discipline of operations management. Frederick Taylor is known as the "father of scientific management" because he was one of the first to break down production tasks systematically. He then analyzed each step for possible improvements and restructured the production process to incorporate these improvements.

The second major contributor was Henry Ford, who developed the first complete system of what is now called "traditional mass production." Prior to Ford's time, production was done mostly by individual craftsmen who completed entire products or components themselves, including all production tasks. Each component was crafted individually to fit a particular unit of a product. Ford exploited the notion of interchangeable parts. His mass production ideas spread throughout the industrialized nations, causing the real prices of manufactured goods to drop dramatically, thus creating enormously wealthy, by historical standards, societies.

A third major contributor to operations management is Taiichi Ohno, the Toyota engineer who developed the JIT production management philosophy in the 1950s. Although Ohno's system is often referred to as the JIT *inventory* system, he intended it to be a complete production management system or paradigm and not merely a way to manage inventories. The stunning success of Japanese firms in capturing huge, worldwide market shares for numerous manufactured products is partly attributable to the widespread implementation of JIT. It is, of course, the Japanese success in manufacturing that led to the Japanese economic miracle.

It is now clear that Ohno's production system is far superior to traditional mass production. Consequently, many United States and European manufacturers have adopted the JIT approach. The problem is that the Japanese have 40 years of experience, while the U.S. and European manufacturers have only recently begun their own implementation of this method.

WHAT IS JUST-IN-TIME?

JIT is an operating philosophy whereby goods and services are produced only when customers demand them and in which short cycle times are the critical process output measurements. JIT systems produce products that (1) are less costly, (2) are of higher quality, (3) use radically shorter cycle times, and (4) result in higher worker satisfaction. An indication of the superior results achieved by JIT are provided by the following comparison. In a recent year, Toyota employed 37,000 employees and produced 4 million vehicles, while General Motors (GM) employed 850,000 employees and produced 8 million vehicles.[1] Some of the difference in the number of employees reflects the fact that JIT producers rely much more heavily on suppliers. Thus, Toyota itself is responsible for adding only 27 percent of a car's cost while GM adds about 70 percent of a car's cost. In spite of these vendor differences, however, efficiency clearly explains much of the difference between Toyota's and GM's results. Since Toyota's cost percentage of 27 percent is a bit more than 33 percent of GM's 70 percent, Toyota's employee total can be tripled to 111,000 to roughly adjust for the percentage difference. Also, to adjust Toyota's volume of vehicles produced to GM's volume, the employment figure of 111,000 can be doubled to 222,000. This adjusted number is still only about one fourth of GM's 850,000 employees.

As you study JIT systems, it is important to understand that JIT is *not* a unique part of Japanese culture. Recently constructed Japanese auto plants in the United States have quickly matched the performance of those in Japan. Also, many United States firms, including Ford, have successfully implemented JIT. In addition, Ford has been very successful with JIT in Mexico. In fact, JIT really has its roots in the United States because Ohno developed many of his ideas based on the writings of Henry Ford and Edwards Deming.

Impact of Just-In-Time

Many companies, including Harley-Davidison, Hewlett-Packard, and Xerox, have adopted JIT and reported impressive results. One study of several manufacturing firms adopting JIT found the range of improvements shown in Exhibit 3-4.1[2] Note the huge reduction in manufacturing cycle time, which is a key measure in JIT. Also note the large reduction in all types of manufacturing inventories, once again a focus of JIT. Manufacturing space was reduced by between 40 and 80 percent. Much of this was achieved by using space previously dedicated to storing inventory. The cost of quality control decreased significantly because in JIT quality is built in during manufacture rather than being inspected in later. Finally, material cost decreased even though vendors were required to make more frequent deliveries and become involved in designing parts. This result is due to the benefits of working together as partners. All of the measures in Exhibit 3-4.1 represent substantial cost savings for the firms adopting JIT.

Relationship Between Just-In-Time and PQI

Before we explore JIT in more depth, it is useful to compare and contrast JIT and PQI. Remember from Reading 3-2 that while Ohno was developing JIT, Deming was in Japan teaching Japanese managers the principles of quality. As a result, Ohno became familiar with Deming's ideas and incorporated many of them into JIT. In particular, Ohno included

---

[1] J. P. Womack, T. J. Daniel, and D. Roos, *The Machine That Changed the World: The Story of Lean Production* (New York: HarperCollins, 1990), p. 155.

[2] G. W. Plossl, *Just-In-Time: A Special Roundtable* (Atlanta: George Plossl Educational Services, Inc., 1985).

statistical quality control, process orientation, and empowerment of worker groups into his JIT philosophy.

Exhibit 3-4.1

Reported Benefits of JIT Study of Five Firms Adopting JIT	
Benefit	**Range of Improvement**
Manufacturing cycle time reduction	80%–90%
Inventory reductions:	
Materials	35%–70%
Work-in-process	70%–90%
Finished goods	60%–90%
Labor cost reductions:	
Direct	10%–50%
Indirect (overhead)	20%–60%
Space requirement reduction	40%–80%
Quality cost reduction	25%–60%
Material cost reduction	5%–25%

Today, JIT is generally considered to be a production or operations management system, while PQI is viewed more broadly as a complete corporate management philosophy involving all activities in the value chain from product development to after-sale service. Given these differing perspectives, a firm could, and some do, implement JIT without committing to PQI. Conversely, a firm could, and many do, commit to PQI without implementing a JIT production system. Finally, many of the most successful firms, including Toyota and Xerox, have implemented both concepts simultaneously.

PRINCIPAL ELEMENTS OF JUST-IN-TIME

The key components of JIT are the following:

- Reorganization of operations into work cells.
- Inventory reduction and production to meet customer orders.
- Employee involvement in group problem solving.
- Total preventive maintenance.
- Supplier partnerships.

Reorganization of Operations into Work Cells

In a JIT system, specialized departments that work on several dissimilar products or jobs are eliminated, at least to the extent that it is economically feasible. Instead, each product (or closely related group of products) is manufactured in a separate, compact area called a **work cell**. This type of plant layout is know as *cellular manufacturing*. For example, consider a firm that manufactures four significantly different models of ornamental iron railings. If organized in the traditional manner, this firm would cut the steel for all models in a cutting department, weld all four models in a welding department, deburr and polish all models in a finishing department, and paint and bundle all models in a paint department. Each of these departments would require a significant setup time to change from the production of one model to another. In contrast, if this firm adopted the JIT approach, it would physically rearrange the factory to create four work cells, one for each model. Each work cell would contain cutting, welding, deburring, polishing, painting, and banding equipment. The JIT approach greatly simplifies the plant's operations and increases its ability to react to demand changes. A schematic of CCC's plant after it was reorganized into work cells is shown in Case 3-4.

Inventory Reduction and Production to Meet Customer Orders

In JIT systems, inventories are considered to be wasteful and undesirable. Conversely, traditional accounting considers inventories to be an asset. JIT recognizes that inventories are costly to hold because they occupy expensive space, are costly to move around, tend to spoil or become obsolete, and tie up cash that results in interest expense or foregone interest revenues. Given this view, production is started only if there is a customer order for the product. In short, production is triggered by **demand pull**, rather than production push. Unlike traditional manufacturing, no production is scheduled simply to build up inventory. The JIT view is that it is better to have workers sit idle than to produce for inventory. Further, to avoid idle time, JIT proposes that management and the workers find useful activities to perform during slack periods, such as maintenance and training.

JIT firms often use a **Kanban** system, developed in Japan, to implement demand pull. A Kanban is a card or ticket that directs production workers on what to produce and how many to produce. A Kanban is created when more completed units are required because sales have occurred. The Kanban is routed back through production and eventually to suppliers telling them how many parts to ship. The paramount rule in a JIT factory is that no worker will produce anything without a Kanban. In short, the Kanban system is a very simple production scheduling system. CCC uses a Kanban system in Case 3-4.

Inventory Reduction and Quality

JIT proponents believe that inventories cause other problems in addition to incurring holding costs mentioned earlier. Specifically, inventories tend to hide serious quality problems. A traditional production environment puts no pressure on either management or workers to identify and solve production quality problems quickly. Because of large stocks of inventory, defective units can be scrapped, and additional units can be pulled from inventory to keep production flowing. Under JIT, however, there are no excess inventories at any stage of production, so a production quality problem brings the entire production process to a halt. Shutting down the entire production line quickly focuses everyone's attention toward a permanent solution for the problem. In other words, because JIT systems are so vulnerable to quality problems, everyone is much more motivated to identify and correct these problems quickly.

A simple example of the importance of production quality in JIT systems is the operation of an office copier. In a traditional system, since there is a large inventory of blank paper, an occasional torn or smeared copy is no problem. The user simply takes another copy to replace the unusable one. In a JIT system, however, there would be just enough blank paper to run the number of copies needed. A torn or smeared copy would halt the copy job until more paper was ordered from the supplier and delivered to the copy room. The JIT environment will obviously create more interest on the part of the entire office staff to solve copier quality problems quickly and permanently.

Employee Involvement in Group Problem Solving

JIT incorporates the same notion of continuous improvement that was discussed in Reading 3-2. That is, it is everyone's job to improve at all times the process in which they are involved. In JIT, the manufacturing process is divided into work cells and the workers in a cell become a problem-solving team. Extensive cross-functional training is required so that the team can effectively solve problems, smooth the flow through bottlenecks, and fill in for absent team members. JIT firms often spend up to ten times as much money on training production workers as do traditional firms.

Total Preventive Maintenance

Production employees in JIT environments are expected to perform **preventive maintenance** on their own equipment on a regular basis. In traditional firms, production employees usually do not know how to maintain their equipment and are not expected to do so. Maintenance is the responsibility of a separate group of skilled mechanics. In practice, these separate groups often repair machines only after breakdowns occur rather than perform extensive preventive maintenance.

Preventive maintenance is a critical aspect of JIT because, with no inventory buffer, the firm must have the maximum amount of machine availability if it is to meet demand. Because of effective preventive maintenance, many Japanese JIT firms have been able to keep equipment operating at least twice as long as American firms using identical equipment.

Supplier Partnerships

Traditionally, U.S. manufacturers and suppliers had an adversarial relationship characterized by a lack of trust, providing each party with an incentive to disclose the minimum amount of information possible in order to gain an upper hand in price negotiations. Naturally, without a relationship based on trust, manufacturers were hesitant to contract out important work. Thus, suppliers never had a chance to use their specialized expertise to improve the manufacturer's final product.

JIT firms consider suppliers to be "family" and treat them as such. JIT recognizes that the establishment of proper supplier relationships is very time-consuming, so the number of partnerships must be kept small if the firm is to establish trusting relationships. Thus, JIT firms have far fewer suppliers than do traditional companies, often only about one tenth as many. Because suppliers are considered full partners, JIT firms rely more heavily on supplier expertise in design and manufacturing. This reliance requires an open relationship in which both the JIT firm and the supplier are willing to disclose all relevant financial and design information. As a result, prices for components are based upon true supplier costs, with an incentive for both the supplier and manufacturer to cooperate to reduce total system costs.

The integration of suppliers, producers, and distributors of goods or services to minimize cost and optimize service is called **supply chain management**, a "hot" topic in business today. The essence of supply chain management is to have independent companies integrate their information systems to improve decision making. A well-known example is the Proctor & Gamble–Wal-Mart relationship. Wal-Mart's online inventory system for each store is linked directly to Proctor & Gamble's order entry and inventory systems, which in turn are linked to its production scheduling system. In this way Proctor & Gamble knows exactly what customers have purchased so it can produce the proper products and ship them to the correct stores in a timely manner.

Because of the trust developed in the supplier partnership, the JIT manufacturer feels more confident in contracting out more work, which means specialist suppliers are responsible for a much higher percentage of the design and manufacture of the final product. The reliance on specialists reduces the management complexity for the JIT manufacturer and creates a higher level of innovation and quality in the total system. JIT firms also feel more comfortable integrating information systems with suppliers. In addition, for a firm to sell its products on a JIT basis, there must be a very close relationship between JIT firms and their customers. In short, by its very nature of JIT, firms must implement effective supply chain management.

Toyota Expands in North America

As it expanded production operations in North America in the 1990s, Toyota began purchasing components from local suppliers who never worked with Toyota before. For most suppliers the initial experience was quite traumatic. Typical was a Michigan supplier who believed it had fully implemented lean production. Toyota sent specialists from its Toyota Supplier Support Center in Kentucky to review the supplier's operations. After an extensive tour, Toyota informed the supplier that it needed to make major changes before it could become a Toyota supplier. Toyota suggested changes that greatly improved both quality and productivity, while decreasing floor space and cost. As a result, Toyota receives high-quality, low-cost components and the supplier is enjoying record profits.

JUST-IN-TIME AND ACCOUNTING

The radical changes in operations that have been brought about by JIT have also led to radical changes in accounting for operations. Taiichi Ohno discovered that JIT called for such a major change in accounting that he reassigned all of Toyota's cost accountants to other jobs. He then proceeded to develop a new manufacturing cost system staffed by engineers untrained in traditional cost accounting.

Major accounting changes brought about by JIT include the following:

1. Change in cost flows.
2. Change in overhead allocations.
3. Change in accounting-based performance measures.

Change in Cost Flows

Exhibit 3-4.2 presents an overview of cost flows for one job, or batch, in a traditional job-order cost system. The job moves through two work-in-process (WIP) departments, WIP-1 and WIP-2, that represent production departments similar to the Chassis and Assembly Departments for CCC. Detailed job cost records are maintained in each department so that WIP inventories can be accurately costed. Recall that in a traditional cost system, overhead is normally applied on the basis of DLHs.

There are four reasons that cost flows change in JIT firms:

1. All labor is considered a fixed cost in the short run and is treated as fixed overhead.
2. Work cells replace specialized production departments and, consequently, become the cost focus.

3. WIP inventories are reduced greatly or even eliminated. This means that WIP inventory valuation is no longer a major goal of cost accounting.
4. Finished goods inventories are greatly reduced, if possible.

Exhibit 3-4.2

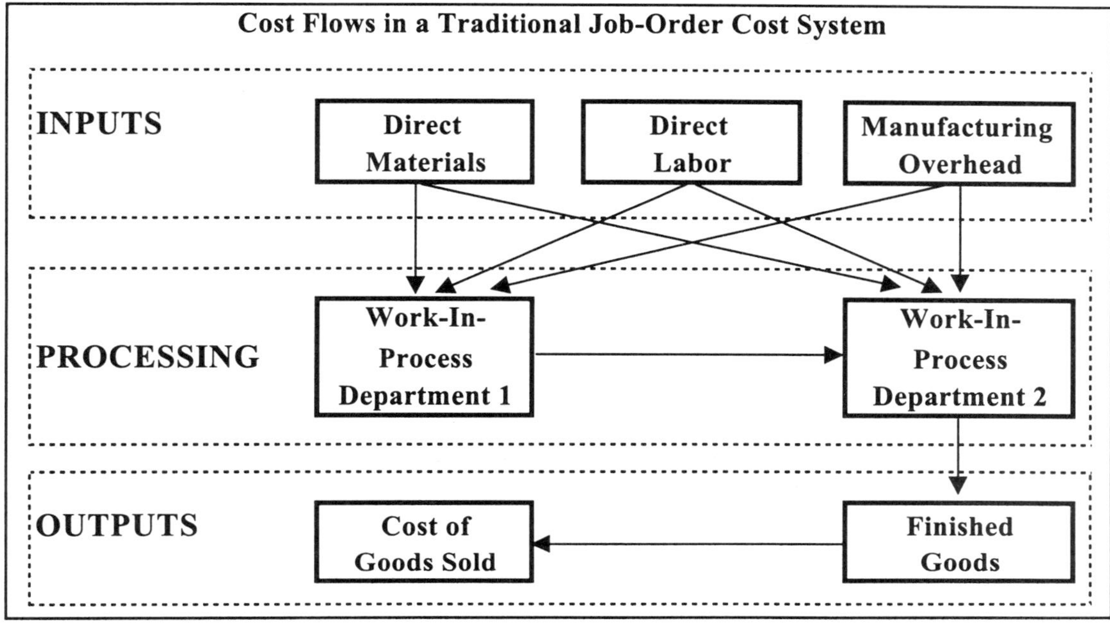

The cost flow implications of these JIT changes are reflected in Exhibit 3-4.3. Note how simple the cost flows have become under JIT. There are no longer any batches because each work cell manufactures only one product, or a family of very similar products. Therefore, each work cell must keep track only of its direct costs for the month. These direct work cell costs usually consist of materials, work cell labor, and directly incurred overhead such as work cell equipment depreciation, electricity costs, etc. To compute cost per unit, factory overhead incurred outside of work cells must be allocated to each work cell. If there is little or no WIP inventory in the work cell, the cost per unit can be computed as follows: direct work cell costs plus allocated overhead divided by the number of completed units. This system is a form of *process or average costing*, rather than the job-order costing used by CCC in Module 2.

If the JIT system has finished units in ending inventory, those units can be costed by multiplying the computed cost per unit for the work cell by the number of units in finished goods inventory. If the firm maintains no finished goods inventory, then the sum of costs from all work cells becomes the firm's cost of goods sold. To illustrate, assume that accounting records related to a particular work cell show the following costs for the month:

Direct materials	$ 66,000
Total work cell labor	53,000
Directly incurred manufacturing overhead	16,000
Total direct work cell costs	$135,000
Allocated general manufacturing overhead	35,000
Total work cell manufacturing costs	$170,000
Material cost in beginning WIP	$ 500
Material cost in ending WIP	$ 490
Units completed	1,700 units

Exhibit 3-4.3

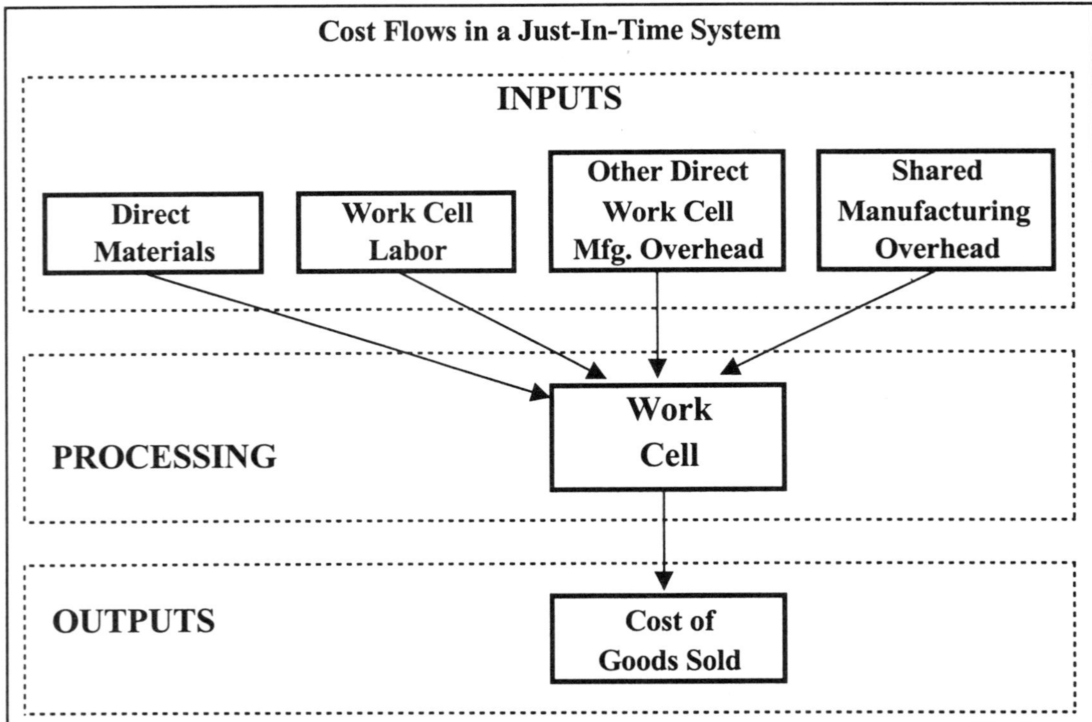

If the firm ignores the cost of materials in WIP, the work cell's cost per unit for the month is \$100 (\$170,000 ÷ 1,700 units). If the firm has 250 units in ending finished goods inventory, the cost of the finished goods inventory (under FIFO) is \$25,000 (250 units × \$100). The firm could cost the beginning and ending WIP inventories, but if WIP inventories are small, most JIT firms consider the costs to be immaterial and ignore them. Compare the complexity of this costing system with CCC's traditional system that must cost two jobs per day for the entire month. Which system do you think produces more accurate, or less distorted, costs? Why?

Flexible Manufacturing Systems

JIT is not the only production innovation that changes cost flows. Flexible manufacturing systems (FMS) have sophisticated production equipment that can perform the function of several different machines in one operation and can switch from the manufacture of one product to another with little setup time. For example, a FMS might cut, lathe, and drill an aluminum part in one operation and switch to making a different part simply by changing its preprogrammed computer instructions. From an accounting perspective, FMSs and JIT systems have a similar impact on cost flows and overhead allocations.

Change in Overhead Allocations

Allocating overhead to a unit of production in JIT requires three steps:

1. Allocate estimated shared overhead to the work cells.
2. Estimate direct work cell overhead.
3. Compute predetermined overhead rate per unit.

Allocation of Estimated Shared Overhead to Work Cells

One part of a JIT costing process that is similar to the traditional method is the allocation of several common manufacturing overhead cost pools to work cells. A JIT predetermined overhead rate for general factory overhead is computed *per unit of driver*. Since the final overhead allocation objective is to compute a predetermined overhead rate, the calculations are made before the year begins using estimate cost pools and driver usage. For example, at CCC the predetermined maintenance overhead rate is based on the *estimated* annual usage of maintenance hours by each work cell. Note that maintenance costs are "lumpy" and do not occur evenly throughout the year. If maintenance costs are allocated to the work cells on the basis of *actual maintenance hours* used during the month, cost per car will be high in months with high maintenance costs and low in months with low maintenance costs. For pricing, profitability, and financial decision purposes, manufacturers do not want their cost per unit calculations to vary from month to month because such variability would only confuse the decision process.

Because JIT overhead costing is similar to using activity-based costing, the three JIT overhead costing steps are ABC steps 4, 5, and 6 (see Reading 3-1 for ABC steps). The three steps used to assign common overhead to work cells are:

1. The estimated cost per driver of a plantwide overhead cost pool is computed (ABC step 4).
2. The driver usage for each work cell (cost object), sedans and compacts for CCC, is determined (ABC step 5).
3. Each work cell is assigned its share of the overhead cost pool (ABC step 6)

For example, assume that Sparta, Inc. manufactures two products, Sigma and Tau, in two separate work cells in the same factory. *Estimated* Maintenance Department overhead costs (a common cost used by both work cells) for 2002 are $1,000,000. Sparta uses maintenance hours (MHs) as the cost driver for maintenance costs. It is *estimated* that Sparta will use a total of 20,000 MHs, with 12,000 MHs used in the Sigma work cell and 8,000 in the Tau work cell. Sparta plans to produce 15,000 Sigma units and 25,000 Tau units in 2002.

Sparta first computes the cost per driver (MHs), by dividing total estimated Maintenance Department costs ($1,000,000) by the total 2002 estimated cost driver usage (20,000 MHs). This step yields a $50 cost per MH (ABC step 4). In the second step, Sparta computes the estimated driver usage for each cost object, which is the work cell. From the given information, this is 12,000 MHs for Sigma and 8,000 MHs for Tau (ABC step 5). Finally, total *estimated* cost allocated to each work cell (cost object) is calculated. For Sigma, the cost is $600,000 (12,000 MHs × $50). For Tau, the cost is $400,000 (8,000 MHs × $50).

Estimation of Direct Work Cell Overhead

Some overhead costs are incurred directly by the work cell and are not shared with other work cells. These costs include depreciation on the equipment in the work cell, utilities and indirect materials used by the work cell, and work cell supervision costs. They also include work cell labor. For these costs, ABC allocations are not required. All that is needed is the total *estimated* cost pool for the year. To continue the Sparta, Inc. example, assume that Sparta estimated the following 2002 direct overhead cost pools for each work cell:

	Sigma	Tau
Work cell labor	$1,100,000	$850,000
Work cell depreciation	270,000	160,000
Other work cell overhead	130,000	90,000

Computation of Predetermined Overhead Rate per Unit

The final step is to compute a predetermined overhead rate for each work cell. During the year, each time a unit is completed in a work cell this amount of overhead will be added to the direct material cost to determine manufacturing cost per unit. The predetermined rate in computed by summing all common overhead allocated to the work cell and the direct overhead and dividing by the estimated units. For Sigma, the predetermined overhead rate is calculated as follows:

	Sigma	Tau
Common overhead allocated	$ 600,000	$ 400,000
Work cell labor	1,100,000	850,000
Work cell depreciation	270,000	160,000
Other work cell overhead	130,000	90,000
Total overhead	$2,100,000	$1,500,000
Estimated 2002 units produced	÷ 15,000	÷ 25,000
Predetermined overhead rate	$140	$60

If the April 2002 direct material cost per Sigma is $70 and per Tau is $40, then the April cost per unit for each product is as follows:

	Sigma	Tau
Direct material	$ 70	$ 40
Predetermined overhead applied	140	60
April manufacturing cost per unit	$210	$100

If, during April, Sparta manufactured 1,000 units of Sigma and 2,000 units of Tau, then the cost of good manufactured for April is $210,000 for Sigma ($210 × 1,000 units) and $200,000 for Tau ($100 × 2,000) for a total of $410,000.

Implications

In traditional costing the critical costing step is allocating overhead costs collected in production departments to units produced. This is accomplished by selecting some basis, such as DLHs, that is common to all units. In JIT allocating manufacturing overhead to units is much simpler. Manufacturing overhead in JIT normally is allocated to a product using a predetermined rate per unit of production, cars in CCC's case. But allocating overhead directly to the products is exactly what ABC accomplishes. Therefore, JIT costing results are similar to ABC product costing numbers. In fact, JIT firms tend to have very accurate unit costs, which give them a competitive advantage against firms still using traditional costing methods.

Another implication of a JIT system on overhead cost allocation is that far less overhead must be allocated from overhead departments to work cells than from overhead departments to production departments in a traditional system. This occurs for two reasons. First, many traditional overhead activities are considered waste and are eliminated or significantly reduced in JIT. Frequently decreased activities include material handling, inspection, inventory storage, and most cost accounting. Second, work cell employees in a JIT environment do many of the functions previously performed by separate overhead groups in a traditional manufacturing environment. These functions include maintenance, setup, quality control, and line management. Overhead incurred within the work cell requires no allocation from an overhead department to the work cell.

Change in Accounting-Based Performance Measures

Traditional firms rely heavily on performance (flexible) budget variances, computed on a department-by-department basis, to measure the performance of manufacturing employees, particularly that of lower-level managers. The notion of departmental performance budget variances, however, is contrary to the JIT philosophy for several reasons.

First, performance budget variances make sense only if significant amounts of manufacturing costs are variable and controllable by manufacturing employees. Since JIT firms believe that all labor is a fixed cost, the bulk of manufacturing costs are fixed for most firms. In addition, JIT firms view the price of materials as fixed, because long-term material and component contracts are negotiated with their partner-vendors. Prices therefore are changed infrequently. Also, because JIT firms place emphasis on quality and on the elimination of waste, they have very little scrap or wasted material. Thus, JIT firms rarely, if ever, have a significant performance budget variance for material or components. Thus, performance budget variances for labor, materials, and overhead have no real value as performance measures.

Second, the calculation of individual department variances violates the JIT systems or process orientation because it leads to suboptimization and the accumulation of inventory. For example, to achieve a favorable performance budget material variance, a traditional purchasing department has the incentive to buy less expensive, but lower quality, steel. Although this saves money at the time of purchase, production departments will use more labor and machine hours to work the low-quality steel, as well as creating more scrap. Thus, the calculation of variances provides an incentive for the purchasing department to work against the interests of the firm.

Finally, and perhaps most importantly, the easiest way to create favorable performance budget variances for labor and overhead is to have long production runs that create excessive amounts of inventory that may never be sold. How does producing more units, even if they are not sold, improve performance variances? For labor, keeping existing employees busy manufacturing products means that the total labor costs *allowed* in the performance budget increase as the units produced increase. Remember that performance budget costs are computed by multiplying planned direct labor cost per unit by the actual number of units produced. Since employees will be paid whether they are producing or not, the actual labor costs don't increase. Increasing costs allowed in the performance budget while holding the actual labor costs constant will have a favorable effect on the variance. JIT proponents recognize this problem as a major flaw in traditional performance measures.

Just-In-Time Process Output Measures

How do JIT firms measure performance? As with PQI, JIT uses *process output* measures to evaluate work cell employees. JIT process output measures are mostly nonfinancial and include cycle time, quality, machine reliability, and worker training measures. The only cost measures normally used are *total* directly incurred work cell costs and *total* overhead costs allocated to the work cell. Since the work cell performs all or almost all production steps, total directly incurred costs represent a broad production process measure. Total allocated overhead costs are important because management wants work cell employees to be aware of the plantwide overhead they are causing and to take actions that will minimize these costs.

The critical difference in JIT, however, is the extreme importance placed on cycle time as a measure of performance. Many JIT firms focus intensely on reducing WIP inventory. WIP inventory is used as a process output measure because it is a good, easy-to-collect surrogate measure of cycle time. JIT proponents believe that a reduction in cycle time will simultaneously cause many good things to happen. First, quality will increase because quality *problems* will cause cycle time to increase, particularly if production stops when quality problems arise. Second, cost per unit will decrease because more units can be produced over a given time period in the same facility with the same employees if cycle time decreases. Third, the company becomes more flexible and better able to respond quickly to market demand. Speed and flexibility have become keys to success for many companies, which is why cycle time reduction is so critical.

SUMMARY

JIT, like PQI, is a method for improving the management of processes. Toyota developed the JIT system in the 1950s, but is now used by firms throughout the world. Although it began as a manufacturing philosophy, many service firms, including insurance companies and banks, have adopted it. JIT impacts the accounting system because it changes the cost flows, overhead allocations, and the process output measures a firm uses. The net effect of JIT costing is a much simpler and far more accurate cost accounting system, which has provided Japanese and other firms adopting JIT with a significant competitive advantage. With more accurate cost numbers than their competitors, firms have been able to enter markets in which existing firms overpriced products, while avoiding nasty price competition in other markets in which products are underpriced.

EXERCISES AND PROBLEMS

Exercises

Exercise 1 PQI Versus JIT. Discuss the three similarities and three differences between PQI and JIT.

Exercise 2 History of JIT. Trace the development of JIT from Henry Ford to today.

Exercise 3 Principal Elements of JIT. List and briefly describe the five principle elements of JIT.

Exercise 4 Principal Elements of JIT. Indicate which principal element of JIT is related to each of the following events. Explain your reasoning.

a. All employees are given JIT training.
b. JIT operations experts are sent to evaluate firms' operations before purchasing contracts are signed.
c. Functional departments such as welding are eliminated.
d. Each worker is given 30 minutes each day to work on equipment.
e. A Kanban system is implemented.
f. A continuous improvement program is instituted.
g. Production is scheduled only to meet demand.

Exercise 5 JIT Accounting Changes. Describe three accounting changes caused by the implementation of JIT in a traditional organization, as well as the significance of each change.

Exercise 6 Traditional and JIT Accounting. Indicate whether each of the following items is consistent with traditional or JIT operations, or both. Explain your answer.

a. Costs collected in departments
b. Labor accounted for as a fixed cost
c. ABC often used to allocate shared overhead
d. Costing of WIP inventory very important
e. Predetermined overhead rates are used
f. One plantwide overhead rate used
g. Cycle time a critical performance measure
h. Departments are the focus of performance evaluation

Exercise 7 Impact of JIT on Costs. Explain how the switch from a traditional to a JIT production system will impact each of the following manufacturing costs.

a. Direct material cost
b. Direct or work cell labor cost
c. Machine repair and maintenance cost
d. Material handling costs
e. Inspection and rework costs
f. Inventory holding costs
g. Purchasing transaction costs (not the cost of purchasing materials)

Exercise 8 JIT Predetermined Overhead Rates. Green Bay Company has one cost pool for all shared overhead not directly incurred by its work cells, which it calls the factory support overhead pool. Green Bay estimates that its factory support overhead will be $1,000,000 in 2002. It allocates the factory overhead pool to work cells on the basis of machine hours. Green Bay estimates 2002 machine hours for the entire plant to be 200,000. The Omega work cell plans to use 40,000 machine hours in 2002. It also plans to produce 4,000 units and incur $320,000 in overhead within the work cell (in addition to its allocation of factory support overhead). Compute the predetermined overhead rate per unit for the Omega work cell. This rate should include both the factory support and overhead incurred within the cell.

Problems

Problem 1 JIT Costing. Westfield Company produces two products, Amber and Crimson, in one production facility. Amber and Crimson are manufactured in separate work cells each dedicated to that one product. The October 2002 production information for the two work cells is as follows:

October Costs and Units	Amber Work Cell	Crimson Work Cell
Direct materials	$51,000	$45,000
Work cell labor*	56,000	52,500
Work cell depreciation*	28,800	61,500
Work cell utilities*	14,000	36,250
Units produced	1,000	750

* This amount was computed based on a predetermined labor cost per unit, depreciation cost per unit, or utility cost per unit for each work cell times the units produced in October.

Westfield also has one overhead pool for costs not incurred directly by the work cells, which it calls general factory overhead. General factory overhead is allocated to the work cells based on square footage occupied. The Amber work cell occupied 12,000 square feet while the Crimson work cell occupied 20,000 square feet. General factory overhead is budgeted for $80,000 in 2002. Westfield planned to manufacture 15,000 units of Amber and 10,000 units of Crimson in 2002.

a. Using JIT costing, determine the total October general factory overhead allocated to the Amber and Crimson work cells.

b. Using JIT costing, calculate the predetermined manufacturing overhead rate for the Amber work cell and for the Crimson work cell.

c. Using JIT costing, compute the October cost of manufacturing one unit of Amber and one unit of Crimson.

Problem 2 Cost of Goods Manufactured and Sold Schedule. Refer to the information for Westfield Company in Problem 1. Westfield's accounting records show the following October inventory information:

October Inventory Values	Amber	Crimson
Beginning inventory, work-in-process	$ 0	$ 0
Ending inventory, work-in-process	0	0
Beginning inventory, finished goods	7,500	11,000
Ending inventory, finished goods	8,400	10,700

Prepare the October 2002 cost of goods manufactured and sold schedule for Westfield.

Problem 3 JIT Cost Flow Changes. Just as the physical flow of goods or services changes when a firm adopts JIT, significant changes also occur in the accounting cost flows.

a. Complete the following two flowcharts.
b. Explain the important accounting differences illustrated by the two flowcharts.

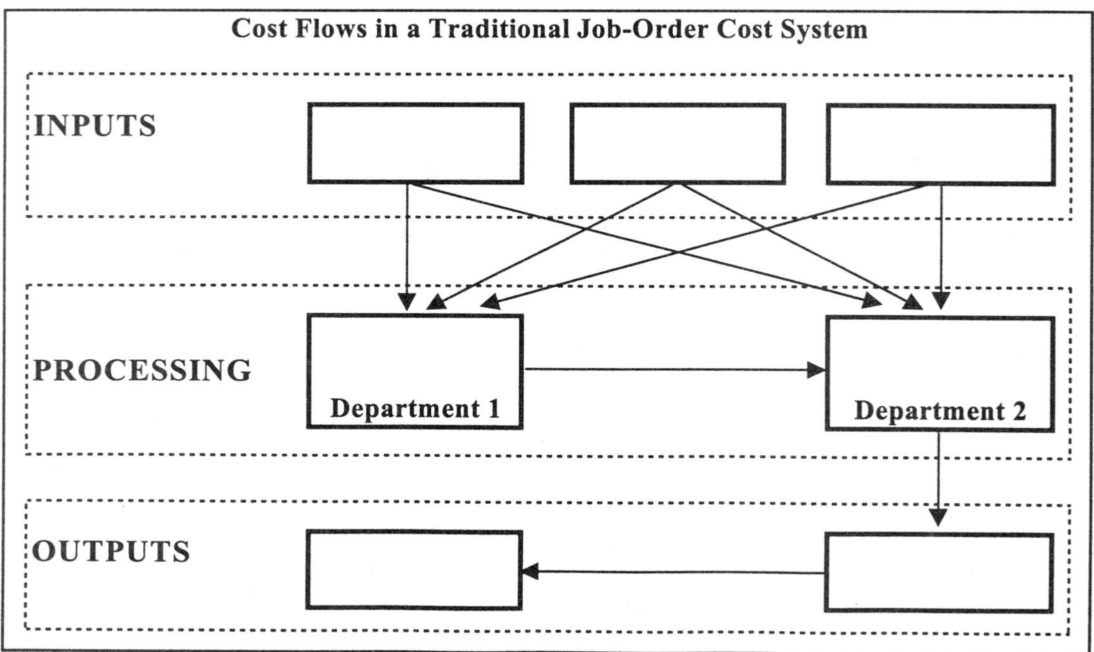

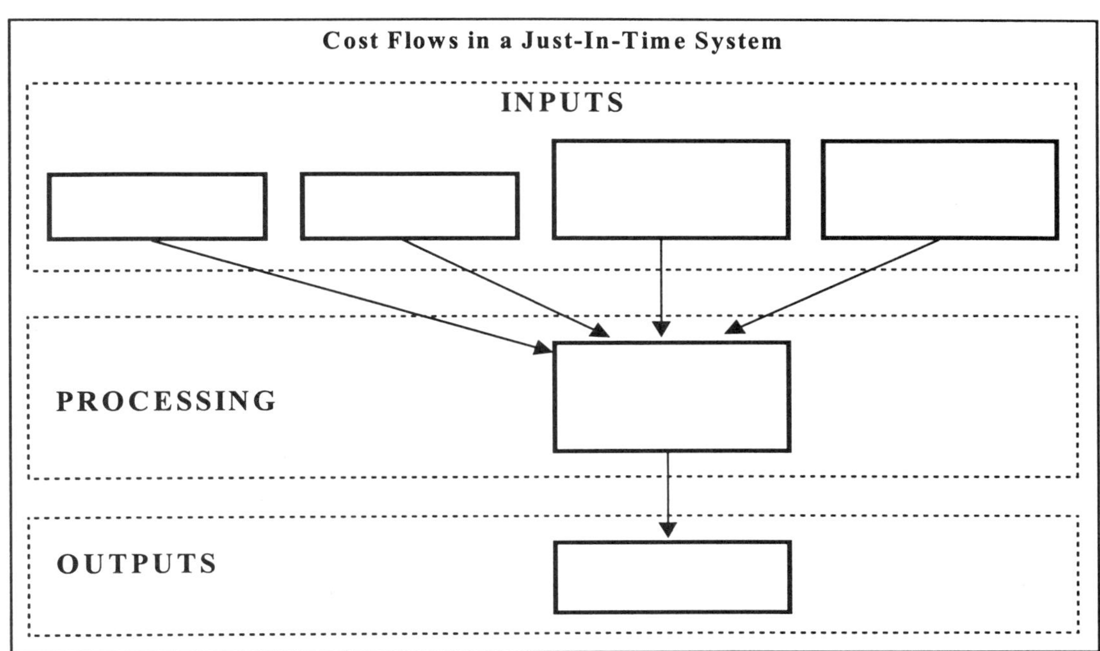

Problem 4 JIT in a Service Industry. Until recently Plymouth Life Insurance Company has been organized by department. The Sales Department sent customer information to the Actuarial Department, who sent the information to the Legal Department, who sent it to the Policy Department where the final policy was drafted and mailed to the customer. Plymouth restructured to create work cells by product lines. Information on shared corporate overhead and costs for the Term Life work cell follows. Plymouth uses square footage occupied as the cost driver for corporate overhead costs.

a. Discuss how the restructure can improve customer satisfaction.

b. What process output measures do you suggest Plymouth use for the Term Life work cell?

	Actual July 2002	Estimated Year 2002
Total corporate overhead	$ 198,000	$ 2,400,000
Total corporate square footage	200,000	200,000
Term life work cell:		
Square footage	29,000	30,000
Salaries cost	$ 275,000	$ 3,276,000
Depreciation cost	$ 6,800	$ 84,000
Other costs	$ 5,500	$ 60,000
Policies processed	42,000	500,000

c. Prepare a July performance report for the Term Life work cell comparing the July performance budget with the actual July costs. Assume that all work cell costs are fixed and occur evenly throughout the year.

d. Compute the estimated full cost (including corporate overhead) of processing a term life insurance policy in 2002.

Problem 5 JIT Cost of Goods Manufactured. Paskenta Inc. manufactures two products, lawn mowers and snow blowers, in two separate work cells in the same factory. Estimated general factory overhead costs (a common cost used by both work cells) for 2002 are $2,000,000. Paskenta uses square feet (SF) occupied as the cost driver for general factory costs. It is estimated that Paskenta will use a total of 25,000 SF, with 15,000 SF used in the mower work cell and 10,000 SF in the blower work cell. Paskenta plans to produce 21,000 mowers and 16,000 blowers units in 2002. Actual May 2002 and estimated total year 2002 information is presented below.

	Mower Work Cell		Blower Work Cell	
	Actual	**Estimated**	**Actual**	**Estimated**
	May 2002	**All 2002**	**May 2002**	**All 2002**
Work cell labor	$ 170,000	$ 1,995,000	$ 103,000	$ 1,250,000
Work cell depreciation	$ 35,000	$ 420,000	$ 20,000	$ 240,000
Other work cell overhead	$ 15,500	$ 180,600	$ 11,200	$ 140,000
Direct material	$ 162,500	$ 1,680,000	$ 63,700	$ 1,040,000
Units	2,000	21,000	1,000	16,000

a. Compute the May 2002 JIT cost per mower and cost per blower used to calculate cost of goods manufactured.

b. Calculate the May 2002 JIT cost of goods manufactured.

c. Prepare a May 2002 performance report that includes a performance budget and variances for each work cell. Paskenta budgets all monthly direct work cell overhead as 1/12 of the annual estimate.

Case 3-4

IMPLEMENTING JUST-IN-TIME AT CALIFORNIA CAR COMPANY

Case Objectives

1. Introduce students to basic production concepts in a JIT plant setting
2. Demonstrate the impact of JIT on accounting numbers
3. Introduce the basics of process costing

Decision (Operating): Does JIT improve manufacturing effectiveness?

INTRODUCTION

Toyota's Prius and Honda's Insight hybrid vehicles are priced less than similar CCC cars, while receiving high-quality ratings. As a result, CCC's management accepted the recommendation of Sally Swanson to adopt JIT ideas as soon as possible to compete successfully with Toyota.

In August 2002, during the two-week period in which most employees take vacation, CCC drastically modified its plant layout to the format shown in Exhibit C3-4.1. In addition, the company developed and introduced a Kanban system for scheduling production according to customer demand.

A Kanban is simply a card that authorizes a work cell to produce a unit or batch of units. A series of Kanban cards will be used in CCC as follows. Every time a sedan or compact is sold, a Kanban card will be passed from the customer to the final assembly person for the model sold. The card informs the worker to begin final assembly of another car. *The final assembly worker will not begin production until a Kanban is received*. At the time the final assembler begins work on the next car, the worker also passes the Kanban card to the chassis assembly person who then begins production of a chassis. See Exhibit C3-4.2 for Kanban instructions. Note that CCC's Kanban system is set up for the production of one car at a time rather than for a batch of two or more cars. Therefore, in the simulation there should never be more than one sedan and one compact in the finished goods area.

To illustrate how these JIT concepts are carried out at CCC, a second, in-class simulation will be carried out to illustrate ideas. During this simulation, your group will once again assemble sedans and compacts. This time, however, CCC's production facility will be arranged in the work cell format similar to that shown in Exhibit C3-4.1. A schematic of the simulation layout is presented in Exhibit C3-4.3.

Exhibit C3-4.1
California Car Company
JIT Plant Layout

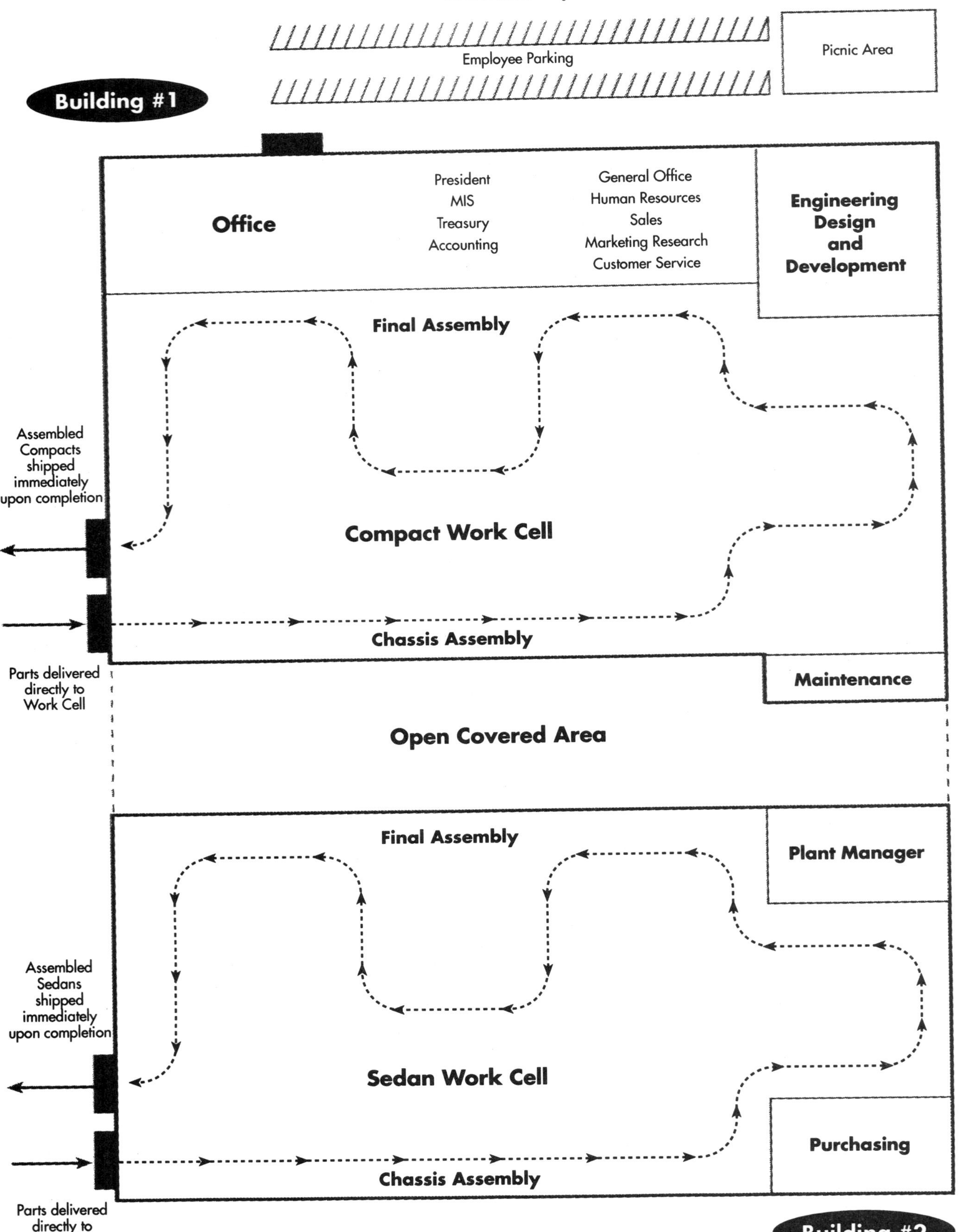

Exhibit C3-4.2
Kanban (Demand Pull) Instructions

1. The sales person, or customer if there is no salesperson, passes the Kanban card to the final assembler.
2. The final assembler takes the chassis from WIP and passes the Kanban card to the chassis assembler.
3. The chassis assembler takes the Kanban from the final assembler and gives it to the supplier when requesting more parts.
4. The supplier receives the Kanban from the chassis assembler, carefully files it, and delivers both final assembly and chassis parts for *one car only*. At the end of the simulation the Kanbans collected are given to the customer. The number of Kanbans given to the customer should equal the number of cars of that model sold plus defects.

Exhibit C3-4.3

Schematic of JIT Simulation Layout
(Arrows show the flow of parts and cars)

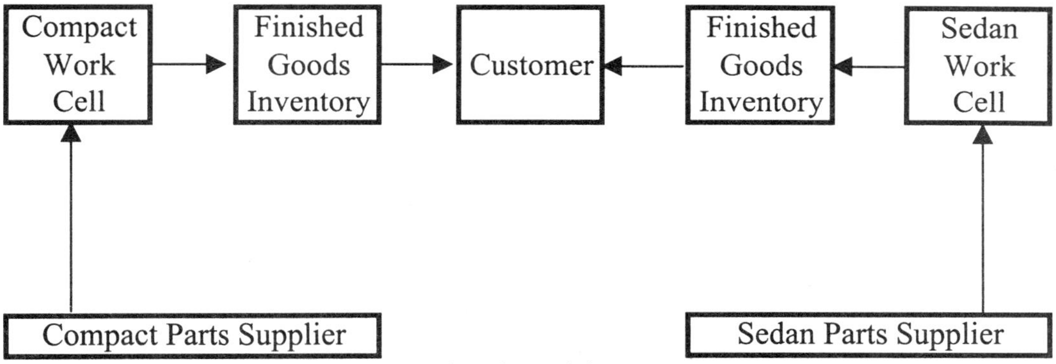

Note: Kanbans flow in the opposite direction of the arrows.

On the day of the CCC JIT simulation, each small group will assemble either sedans or compacts in a JIT work cell. For example, your small group may assemble compacts and the other small group you worked with on the first simulation will then assemble sedans. For assembly purposes, your small group is confined to a work cell and does not interact with the other work cell producing the other model.

If your instructor showed your class the Styro, Inc. video, you were able to see the positive impact a move to JIT can have. The statistics collected during the video are recreated in Exhibit C3-4.4. If you did not view the video, the statistics presented in Exhibit C3-4.4 will give you a sense of the impact JIT had on Styro, Inc.

STUDENT ROLES IN THE JUST-IN-TIME SIMULATION

Each student may be assigned one of up to ten different roles in the simulation. It is important that you study the responsibilities of your assigned role carefully so that your group can compete effectively against other groups. The simulation roles are listed on the next page.

1. Sedan parts supplier
2. Sedan chassis assembler
3. Sedan final assembler
4. Sedan salesperson
5. Accountant
6. Compact parts supplier
7. Compact chassis assembler
8. Compact final assembler
9. Compact salesperson
10. Customer

Exhibit C3-4.4

Summary of Styro, Inc. Video

Numerical Results of Lot Size Reductions

	Lot Sizes		
	8	**4**	**1**
Lead time or cycle time in minutes	5.1	2.4	0.5
Unfinished work-in-process inventory	43	19	4
Finished goods inventory	6	10	16
Quantity of potential rework	40	16	0
Space used (number of tables)	4	3	2
Average length of stockouts	2.4	1.2	0
Total units produced	36	26	22
Total production time (in minutes)	10	6	4
Average seconds per piece	16.7	13.8	10.9

Actions Taken to Reduce Lot Sizes

1. Rearrange the factory by reducing the number of tables.
2. Apply statistical quality control.
3. Reduce material handling by eliminating trucker.
4. Install universal die to eliminate setups.
5. Perform value-added analysis to eliminate waste.
6. Redistribute work among workers.
7. Implement preventive maintenance.

During the simulation, each student will act out one of the designated roles described below. The assembly of sedans and compacts will involve the same parts and the same assembly instructions as in the earlier simulation. See Case 2-2 for the bill of materials and assembly diagrams.

Important Note

Some schools may be using sets of toy blocks that are different than those shown in this book. If so, your instructor will provide you with drawings for your set of blocks to replace Exhibit C2-2.2 and a new bill of materials to replace Exhibit C2-2.3.

Suppliers

Each work cell in a production line has a supplier. Therefore, each line will have two suppliers, one for the sedan work cell and one for the compact work cell. The chassis assembly worker in each work cell will inform the supplier when the parts for a model have been used and more parts are needed by passing a Kanban to the supplier. The supplier will then deliver more parts to the appropriate workers in the work cell. For example, when the chassis assembler in the sedan work cell receives a Kanban card to initiate assembly of a chassis, he notifies the supplier by giving him the Kanban. The supplier promptly delivers parts for one chassis to the chassis assembler and parts to complete one sedan to the final assembler. The supplier should keep one set of parts for one chassis and one set of parts for final assembly in inventory to allow for prompt delivery to the work cell.

Each supplier must keep all Kanbans received during the simulation and give them to the customer at the end of the simulation. The number of Kanbans received by the customer must equal the number of cars sold from the work cell. If sales and Kanbans are not equal, it indicates that the line has not maintained JIT discipline, and is disqualified.

Chassis Assemblers

Each work cell in a production line has a chassis assembler. Therefore each company will have two chassis assemblers, one for the sedan work cell and one for the compact work cell. The chassis assembler will assemble the chassis for the work cell's model when a Kanban is received from the final assembler. *Assembly will not begin without the Kanban.* The chassis assembler will notify the supplier when work begins on a chassis by giving the supplier the Kanban so more parts will be delivered. This chassis assembler *carefully inspects* incoming parts and the assembled chassis.

Information You Must Collect for the Accountant

At the end of the simulation, estimate the percent of time you were idle while waiting for parts or a Kanban and record that percentage on Exhibit C3-4.5, item 8. The accountant will ask for this information at the end of the simulation.

Final Assemblers

Each work cell in a production line has a final assembler. Therefore, each company will have two final assemblers, one for the sedan work cell and one for the compact work cell. The final assembler will convert a chassis into a finished car for the work cell's model when a Kanban is received from the salesperson or customer. *Final assembly on a car will not begin without the Kanban card.* The final assembler *carefully inspects* incoming parts, the chassis, and the completed cars.

Information You Must Collect for the Accountant

At the end of the simulation, estimate the percent of time you were idle while waiting for parts or a Kanban and record that percentage on Exhibit C3-4.5, item 8. The accountant will ask for this information at the end of the simulation.

Accountant

During the simulation the accountant is responsible for collecting the cycle time measurement. Cycle time is computed by marking any sedan chassis, recording the time the chassis is marked, recording the time the marked chassis is moved from final assembly to finished goods inventory, and calculating the difference in recorded times. After the simulation has ended, the accountant is required to perform the following duties to complete Exhibit C3-4.5:

1. Record the number of sedan and compacts in work-in-process and finished goods inventories.
2. Collect from the customer the number of units sold by model, the number of stockouts by model, the number of defective cars by model, and the number of Kanbans received from the suppliers.
3. Collect from the chassis and final assemblers "idle time" estimates for the assemblers.
4. Calculate good units completed for both sedans and compacts. Good units completed = sales + cars in ending finished goods inventory – cars in beginning finished goods inventory.
5. Compute average production time per unit. To compute the average, determine the number of seconds the simulation ran, then divide that number by the total number of good units produced, sedan and compact combined. For example, if the simulation ran for 15 minutes and 25 good units were produced, divide 900 seconds (15 minutes × 60 seconds) by 25 cars, for an average production time of 36 seconds per car.

Finally, it is the accountant's responsibility to ensure that all members of the groups working on the production line have copied all of the information from the accountant's completed Exhibit C3-4.5 onto their own form. All students will need a completed Exhibit C3-4.5 to finish Part II of Case 3-4.

Salespersons

When informed of a sale, the salesperson physically gives the one sedan or one compact in finished goods inventory to the customer and initiates the Kanban system by passing a Kanban to the final assembler. This person should help collect sales and stockout data for the accountant. If your work cell has only four members, you will operate without this person. In this case the final assembly person will pass a car to the customer.

Customer

The customer draws a playing card (or some other sales marker) every 30 seconds. If you use playing cards, a club represents a compact sale, while spades, hearts and diamonds represent sedan sales. If there is a salesperson, the customer requests the proper model from that person. If not, the customer removes the model indicated from finished goods inventory and places the car in a separate sold-car area. At the same time he passes a Kanban to the final assembly person in that model's work cell. The customer next inspects the vehicle. If it is defect free, the playing card is then placed in the sold car stack. If the car is defective, place the card in a separate defect pile.

If a card is drawn and that model is not in finished goods inventory at the moment the card is drawn, then your line has a stockout. Place the card in a stockout pile that is separate from the sold car and defect piles. Once a stockout occurs the sale is lost forever. The customer *does not* convert a stockout to a sale as soon as that model is available again.

Drawing a playing card or sales marker begins as soon as the instructor tells your group to start the simulation. At the end of the simulation, the number of cards placed in the sold-car area plus the number of defects should equal the number of Kanbans received from the supplier. In addition, if the simulation runs for 15 minutes with sales occurring every 30 seconds, the total number of sold cars plus defective cars plus stockouts should equal 30. For your role *you will need a watch or clock that indicates seconds.* Customers should be selected from a competing production line so that customers have an incentive to enforce the JIT discipline and control quality.

Information You Must Collect for the Accountant

At the end of the simulation, you record the number of units sold *by model*, the total number of stockouts *by model*, and the number of Kanbans you receive from the suppliers on Exhibit C3-4.5. You give this information to the accountant when asked.

Part I Requirements (Complete Prior to the Simulation)

1. Review CCC's revised plant layout (Exhibit C3-4.1) and briefly identify major changes from the original plant layout in Exhibit C2-1.2. For each major change noted, briefly explain *why* you think CCC made the change. Refer to Reading 3-4, the Styro, Inc. video if shown, and Exhibit C3-4.4.

2. Meet briefly inside or outside of class with your group to assign simulation roles to each member of your group. Briefly describe the role that you will be playing in the simulation.

Part II Requirements (Complete After the Simulation)

Prepare a one-page, single-spaced, typewritten analysis of the simulation that addresses the following:

1. A description of how the Kanban system actually worked for your job, within your work cell, and between your work cell and outside suppliers. Did sales equal the number of Kanbans collected by the supplier?

2. A brief identification of any weaknesses/inefficiencies in CCC's JIT operation.

3. A brief comparison of the JIT results with the results of the traditional manufacturing approach that you witnessed in carrying out the simulation in Case 2-2. Make comparisons using Exhibit C3-4.5.

4. An analysis of whether the JIT system has made CCC more competitive with Toyota. Identify specific improvements reflected in the JIT operation.

5. A brief identification of "process output measures" that you would recommend to CCC for use in evaluating work cell performance.

6. Complete Exhibit C3-4.5 and attach to your write-up. Data can be obtained from your group's accountant.

Exhibit C3-4.5

CCC Accounting Data Sheet
Comparison of Traditional and JIT Simulations

Student Group Numbers: Sedan [ ] Compact [ ]

	Results (1) Typical Traditional	(2) Your JIT	Percent Change*
1. Ending Inventory Levels:			
Work-in-Process:			
Sedan	8	—	
Compact	5	1	
Finished Goods:			
Sedan	8	1	
Compact	2	—	
2. Sales[1]			
Sedan	22	18	
Compact	7	7	
3. Stockouts[1]			
Sedan	3	3	
Compact	2	2	
4. Good Units Completed[1] (sales + finished − ending)			
Sedan	24	18	
Compact	7	6	
Total	31	24	
5. Defective Units[1]			
Sedan	4	—	
Compact	2	—	
6. Cycle Time (Sedan Only)	300 seconds	90 sec.	
7. Average Production Time			
Both models combined	38.7 seconds	20 sec.	
8. Assembler Idle Time Percentage			
Sedan	30%	18%	
Compact	30%	75%	
9. Kanbans Received from Supplier	N/A	25	N/A

*Difference between traditional and JIT results divided by traditional results:

(Column 1 – Column 2) / Column 1

[1] Based on running the simulation for 20 minutes

Group Assignment 3-4

JUST-IN-TIME SIMULATION AT CALIFORNIA CAR COMPANY

Group number __________ **Signatures of group members participating:**

____

____

Group Assignment Objectives

1. Demonstrate the changes in production in a JIT setting
2. Link accounting information to changes in the production environment

Requirement

Group Assignment 3-4 is to perform the simulation for CCC using a JIT production layout. You will receive points for preparation and active participation. If anyone in your group did not prepare and/or did not actively participate, do not include his or her name above.

Have the accountant for your production line provide the information requested below collected in Exhibit C3-4.5.

Total good units sold (both sedan and compact): ____________________

Total defective cars (both sedan and compact): ____________________

Total stockouts (both sedan and compact): ____________________

Total Kanbans held by the suppliers (both sedan and compact): ____________

Case 3-5

JUST-IN-TIME COSTING AT CALIFORNIA CAR COMPANY

Case Objectives

1. Demonstrate the differences in product costing between JIT and traditional environments
2. Reinforce product costing and ABC concepts
3. Demonstrate with accounting data how JIT can improve manufacturing performance

Decision (Operating, financial reporting): Should CCC continue with its JIT initiative?

Assume that it is now early October 2002 and that CCC has fully implemented its JIT production approach. President David Gomez comes to Jena Butler and you very concerned.

> "I promised the Board of Directors and the bank that the September markup on total manufacturing costs would be at least 70 percent. My calculations show that we only had a 58 percent markup. This time I checked for changes in finished goods inventory, but units in finished good inventory remained unchanged during September. You reported that our quality program in conjunction with JIT has reduced our costs, but you were wrong! Our shareholders will not be happy."

David gives you the following calculations he prepared. Most of the numbers come from Exhibit C3-5.1.

September Markup Percentage Calculations			
	Sedan	Compact	CCC
Unit sales	360	120	480
Sales revenue	$ 7,560,000	$ 2,040,000	$ 9,600,000
Material costs	$ 1,067,040	$ 411,000	$ 1,478,040
Maintenance			124,000
General factory			400,000
Depreciation	425,000	170,000	595,000
Labor	2,800,000	591,500	3,391,500
Other overhead	51,000	21,250	72,250
Total manufacturing costs			$ 6,060,790
Markup percentage			58.40%

Jena asks you to get back to David ASAP either confirming or correcting his calculations. She also asks you to compute the cost of goods sold for CCC for the month of September 2002 in which 480 cars were produced: 360 sedans and 120 compacts. There were 60 sedans and 20 compacts in both the beginning and ending finished goods inventory. Cost of the beginning finished goods inventory was: sedans, $702,000; compacts, $200,000.

Exhibit C3-5.1

California Car Company JIT Cost and Production Data September and Estimated Full Year 2002		
Production Information	**Actual Sept. 2002**	**Revised Estimated Full Year 2002**
Units		
Sedan	360	5,100
Compact	120	1,700
Direct materials cost (per car)		
Sedan	$ 2,964	$ 2,980
Compact	3,425	3,360
Work cell labor hours		
Sedan	80,000	969,000
Compact	16,900	204,000
Total work cell labor cost		
Sedan	$ 2,800,000	$ 33,915,000
Compact	591,500	7,140,000
	$ 3,391,500	$ 41,055,000
Work cell labor rate	$ 35	$ 35
Maintenance costs	$ 124,000	$ 1,463,700
Maintenance department hours:		
Devoted to sedan work cell	2,200	22,440
Devoted to compact work cell	900	12,410
Total maintenance hours	3,100	34,850
Depreciation costs		
Sedan work cell	$ 425,000	$ 5,100,000
Compact work cell	170,000	2,040,000
Total depreciation costs	$ 595,000	$ 7,140,000
Other work cell overhead		
Sedan work cell	$ 51,000	$ 612,000
Compact work cell	21,250	255,000
Total other overhead costs	$ 72,250	$ 867,000
General factory overhead	$ 400,000	$ 4,998,000

CCC still uses a FIFO inventory flow assumption. There was no *WIP inventory* in either work cell at the start or the end of the month. Both work cells had just enough parts in the *raw material* beginning and ending inventories to manufacture one car.

CCC now considers all work cell labor costs to be fixed (within the relevant range of expected 2002 production) and for managerial purposes treats labor costs like manufacturing overhead. Because CCC switched to JIT in the year 2002, the company has estimated how much overhead it would have incurred for all of 2002 if JIT had been implemented for the entire year. This estimate is based on the annual production of 6,800 cars for 2002—5,100 sedans and 1,700 compacts. The revised 2002 *estimated* data and the *actual* September 2002 data are presented in Exhibit C3-5.1. CCC is still asking $21,000 for the sedan and $17,000 for the compact.

Shared plantwide overhead consists of the Maintenance and General Factory departments. Since the implementation of JIT, CCC has installed a new maintenance information system that separately records and accumulates the number of maintenance hours spent repairing sedan work cell machines and compact work cell machines. General factory overhead includes all other manufacturing overhead not directly incurred by the work cells. CCC has elected to use total cars produced as the driver for the general factory overhead cost pool. Three types of overhead occur completely within the work cell itself: equipment depreciation, work cell labor, and other overhead, which includes indirect materials, and the work cell manager's salary.

Requirements

1. Is the analysis that David Gomez presented to you correct? Explain why or why not.

2. Select a cost driver for each of the shared manufacturing overhead costs in Exhibit C3-5.2 and compute the total shared overhead ABC cost assigned to each work cell.

3. Calculate the predetermined manufacturing overhead rate per car for the sedan and compact. Complete the September 2002 manufacturing cost per sedan and compact by completing Exhibit C3-5.2.

4. Compute CCC's September 2002 cost of goods sold (COGS) as well as the markup percentage based on COGS by completing the schedule in Exhibit C3-5.3. Be sure to link all of the September manufacturing costs and WIP inventory amounts in Exhibit C3-5.3 with the appropriate cells in Exhibit C3-5.2.

5. Why is the markup percentage you calculated different than David Gomez's? Write an explanation for David.

6. On average, CCC needs to produce and sell about 420 sedans and 140 compacts per month to meet its annual goal of 5,100 sedans and 1,700 compacts. Compute the markup percentage the way David Gomez calculated it, but use average monthly sales and production numbers of 420 sedans and 140 compacts. Why has it changed from David's original calculation?

7. If the September markup percentage in the cost of goods manufactured and sold schedule is actually on target, what issue related to your analysis should David Gomez be concerned with?

8. In Case 2-6 you costed sedans and compacts using a traditional job-order cost system. Describe two differences in how you costed the sedans and compacts in Case 3-5 compared to how you costed them in Case 2-6.

Exhibit C3-5.2

California Car Company
2002 JIT Costing Spreadsheet

	Cost Driver	Cost Pool	Estimated Total 2002 Driver Usage	Estimated Cost per Driver	Total 2002 Cost for Sedan Work Cell	Total 2002 Cost for Compact Work Cell	Total CCC Costs
Shared overhead:							
Maintenance							
General factory							
Direct work cell overhead:							
Work cell labor							
Work cell depreciation							
Other work cell overhead							
Total 2002 estimated overhead cost							
Predetermined OH Rate							

	Sedan	Compact	Total
Scheduled 2002 production	5,100	1,700	6,800
September units produced	360	120	480
September materials used **per car**			
September overhead applied **per car**			
Sept. mfg. cost **per car**			

Exhibit C3-5.3

CCC Cost of Goods Manufactured and Sold Schedule September 2002		
Beginning finished goods inventory		
Add: Cost of goods manufactured:		
September direct material		
September manufacturing overhead applied		
Total September manufacturing costs		
Add: Beginning inventory work-in-process		
Less: Ending inventory work-in-process		
Cost of goods manufactured		
Total cost of goods available for sale		
Less: Ending inventory finished goods		
Cost of goods sold		
Markup percentage on total manufacturing costs		

Group Assignment 3-5

A COST IS A COST IS A COST?

Group number: ___________ **Signatures of group members participating:**

____

____

Group Assignment Objectives

1. Reinforce an understanding of how and why costs changed at CCC
2. Reassess CCC's new competitive position based on its markup percentages

The top management team at CCC is delighted with the JIT costs for the sedan and compact you computed in Case 3-5. David Gomez states: "Our JIT and continuous improvement efforts have really paid off. Our costs are now at the level that will allow us to earn industry-average profits and attract capital needed to expand. However, I think we all need to fully understand why our costs per car changed so that we all have confidence in the numbers." Jena Butler's staff has prepared the following schedule to help you review these changes.

Exhibit G3-5.1

Summary of Different CCC Cost Calculations

	Sedan			Compact		
Cost	**Traditional Est. Cost Case 2-4[1]**	**ABC Est. Cost Case 3-1[2]**	**JIT Cost Case 3-5**	**Traditional Est. Cost Case 2-4**	**ABC Est. Cost Case 3-1**	**JIT Cost Case 3-5**
Direct materials	$ 2,980	$ 2,980	$ 2,964	$ 3,360	$ 3,360	$ 3,425
Labor	3,780	3,780	6,650	2,275	2,275	4,200
Inspection	1,728	1,245	-	1,040	2,490	-
Material handling	972	921	-	585	737	-
Setup	1,188	713	-	715	2,140	-
Maintenance	1,001	901	185	602	901	307
General factory	4,075	3,670	735	2,453	3,669	735
Work cell depreciation	-	-	1,000	-	-	1,200
Other work cell overhead	-	-	120	-	-	150
Total manufacturing cost	$ 15,724	$ 14,210	$ 11,653.8	$ 11,030	$ 15,572	$ 10,016.6

[1]The total traditional cost comes from the *planned* costs in Case 2-4, but the detailed breakdown of overhead costs was completed as part of Case 3-1 requirements.

[2]ABC costs are one of many reasonable solutions to Case 3-1. Also, ABC and traditional costs are estimates for all of 2002, while JIT costs are based on monthly production and costs.

Requirements

1. Compare the traditional and ABC columns in Exhibit G3-5.1 and explain why there are differences in manufacturing overhead costs per car. For example, are the differences due to changes in how the cars are manufactured?

2. Compare the ABC and JIT columns in Exhibit G3-5.1 and explain why there are differences in:
   a. The material cost per car.

   b. The labor cost per car.

   c. The overhead cost per car.

3. With selling prices of $21,000 for the sedan and $17,000 for the compact, calculate CCC's markup percentage based on total JIT manufacturing costs for the sedan and compact models. See Case 2-5 for a review of how to compute markup percentages.

4. Compute the overall markup percentage for *the entire CCC firm* based on JIT costs. CCC plans to produce 5,100 sedans and 1,700 compacts in 2002. Is CCC now earning the industry average of 67 percent markup on full manufacturing costs on each model and for the company in total?

5. Now that its profitability is above average, discuss three initiatives that CCC can undertake that would have been difficult for it to do previously. For example, CCC could begin paying dividends because its future profitability and cash flows are more assured.

Module 3

Peer Evaluation of Group Members	Class Section	Group No.

Evaluator's Name

Module 3

In the table below, please indicate your estimate, in percentage terms, of the contributions that individual group members made to each of the group assignments listed. Each column should add to 100 percent. For example, if there are five members in your group and all were present for Group Assignment 3-1, you would divide the 100 percent among the five members, including yourself. If you felt that all group members were prepared to discuss the assignment and contributed equally to the solution, you would give each person 20 percent. If only four members were present and you felt that one particular member contributed twice as much as the other three, you would give the heavy contributor 40 percent and the other three members 20 percent. Any group member who was absent should be listed and given zero percent.

	Group Assignment Number		
Group Members (List)	**3-1**	**3-4**	**3-5**
Myself			
Totals	**100%**	**100%**	**100%**

Fill in this sheet after each group assignment is completed and turn in at the completion of Group Assignment 3-5.

Reading 3-6

CAREERS IN ACCOUNTING

INTRODUCTION

Accountants have been termed business physicians because they are often asked to diagnose business problems and prescribe remedies to these problems. The most common student misconception about accounting is that the job requires hours upon hours of solitary number crunching and little or no human interaction. To the contrary, accounting is intensively people-oriented and requires excellent communication and team skills. The misconception arises because the jobs of bookkeepers and accounting clerks, often called accountants in many organizations, tend to be solitary, number-crunching positions, but professionals with degrees in accounting do not perform these tasks. Accountants perform a wide variety of services to almost all organizations, so it is possible to find positions that fit your interests and permit you to combine knowledge in accounting with disciplines. In fact, accounting graduates can enhance their marketability by combining an accounting degree with other course work in areas such as management information systems, real estate, small business, or a foreign language.

ACCOUNTING EMPLOYMENT OUTLOOK

Employment prospects for accountants are excellent. The U.S. Bureau of Labor Statistics, in its 2000–2001 update, predicts that accounting and financial management will have one of the largest increases in employment of any profession between 1998 and 2008, as shown in Exhibit 3-6.1. Most accounting graduates are offered an accounting or related job either before or shortly after they graduate.

Exhibit 3-6.1

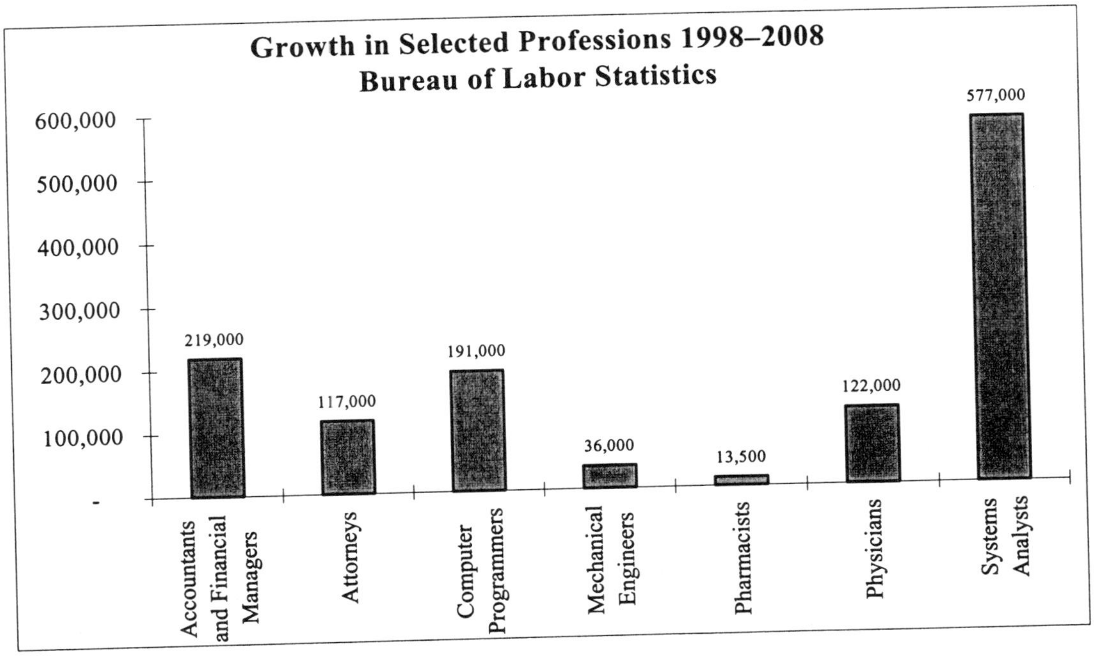

Growth in Selected Professions 1998–2008
Bureau of Labor Statistics

600,000
500,000
400,000
300,000
200,000
100,000
-

219,000 Accountants and Financial Managers
117,000 Attorneys
191,000 Computer Programmers
36,000 Mechanical Engineers
13,500 Pharmacists
122,000 Physicians
577,000 Systems Analysts

In addition, many accountants, particularly those with some computer training, are employed as systems analysts. As Exhibit 3-6.1 indicates, system analysis is projected to be the fastest growing of all professions. Accountants often are employed as systems analysts because the accounting system is by far the largest system in most companies. Although the Bureau of Labor Statistics does not make a projection, college placement officers confirm that a combination of accounting and computer information course work results in some of the hottest recruiting efforts and highest-paying job offers.

More than 1,770,000 people were employed in the area of accounting and financial management in 1998 (a number that does not include bookkeepers and accounting clerks). Each year many of these people will move to jobs outside the area, largely into management positions and opening their own businesses. In addition, significant retirements occur each year. Therefore, the total job openings are much larger than the growth numbers. Exhibit 3-6.2 shows the total job openings through 2008 if a four percent exit rate per year is assumed. Note that total accounting and financial management openings are over 900,000, larger than any other occupation shown. A major in accounting is the preferred undergraduate background for most of these jobs.

Exhibit 3-6.2

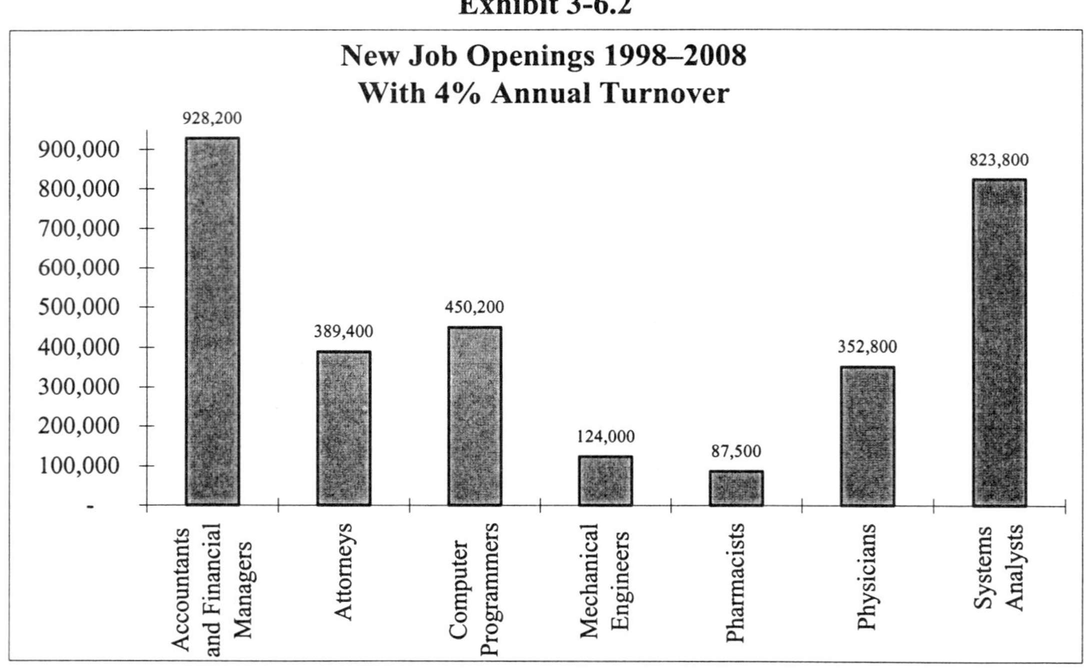

TYPES OF ACCOUNTING POSITIONS

Every organization in every country requires the services of accountants. The variety of employment includes the management of a firm's financial systems, external auditing, corporate accounting, tax accounting, and governmental accounting. Many of these areas of opportunity are described in the following section. If some of these areas sound like an attractive career path, you should talk to your instructor and search the library and World Wide Web for additional information. There are several good accounting career information Web sites, many of which can be accessed through the Web site for this course.

Accounting Information Systems (AIS)

The area of AIS involves the design and operation of a firm's computerized accounting information systems. This is the most rapidly growing area in accounting and also one of the highest paying. Organizations are rushing to restructure around processes and need integrated accounting, production, marketing, and human resource software to support process management. The enterprise resource planning (ERP) software, such as SAP or Great Plains, used to achieve this integration requires the employment of highly trained technical and content specialists to install and operate the system. Since accounting is by far the largest information subsystem in most firms, accountants with a knowledge of process management and information systems are in great demand. Graduates with accounting systems background also are employed by corporations, consulting firms, and governmental agencies. Students need to combine a major in accounting with substantial course work in information systems areas such as database management, systems analysis and design, and network systems.

Typical salary range:

Entry level:	\$45,000–\$70,000
Manager	\$120,000 and up

External Auditing

Certified public accountants (CPAs) perform audits of an organization's financial statements and render an opinion as to whether the statements fairly present the financial position of the organization. Auditors spend much of their time at their clients' premises and have the opportunity to work with a number of different organizations. Auditors also frequently serve as business consultants, particularly to smaller clients.

Auditing is a demanding profession. Firms are looking for graduates with the following traits:

1. Good oral and written communication skills;
2. Excellent analytical abilities, including the ability to analyze complex, unstructured problems;
3. Ability to learn independently (have learned how to learn); and
4. Broad business knowledge.

Many CPA firms specialize in certain industries or areas such as real estate, small business, high technology, or international trade. For example, one CPA firm has offices in Los Angeles, Palm Springs, New York, and Nashville. Their specialty is providing accounting services for musical performers ranging from Barbra Streisand to rap groups. Since organizations in all industries and throughout the world require accounting services, auditing (as well as corporate accounting) provides students with the opportunity to combine an interest in accounting with another outside interest.

Typical salary range:

Entry level:	\$30,000–\$55,000
Senior partner at a large firm:	\$250,000 and up

Assurance Services

A new extension of external auditing is *assurance services*. The purpose of assurance services is to improve the quality, in terms of reliability and relevance, of information used by decision makers. Assurance providers are independent professionals who add value by decreasing the risk of material bias in information. For instance, assurance can be provided that information obtained from Internet sources, health care organizations, and governments is reliable. Assurance also can be given that both financial and nonfinancial performance measures used by an organization are relevant and effective. As you can see, many decision makers in society, beyond those involved in business, would find such a service beneficial to their decision needs.

Corporate Accounting

The majority of degreed accountants work for corporations. The top financial person in a company is usually called the chief financial officer (CFO). The CFO is normally one of the four of five officers that make up senior management and is critical to a firm's success. Corporate (or management) accountants perform a variety of specialized tasks, including those listed below. Some typical advertisements for corporate accounting positions are presented in Exhibit 3-6.3.

1. *Managerial accounting* is the preparation of information that helps management operate a firm more effectively. This course focuses on this area of corporate accounting. Additional course work in operations management and MIS will enhance your career opportunities.
2. *Internal auditing* is similar to the work done by external auditors. Internal auditors place particular emphasis on the design and operation of internal controls. One major difference is the increased emphasis on the audits of operations and management that assess the efficiency and effectiveness of processes and managers.
3. *Accounting information systems*, which was described previously.
4. *Financial and tax accounting* involves the management of the accounting data collection process and the preparation of financial statements and tax reports. The controller, also spelled comptroller, is the person in an organization who oversees the financial records and is responsible for tax and other reporting responsibilities. The controller usually reports to the vice president of finance, CFO.
5. *Financial management* involves the planning and physical control of cash and other assets. Financial managers are responsible for budgeting, including capital budgeting, control of cash, inventory and fixed assets, and investing and obtaining cash for the organization.

The role of the corporate accountant has changed significantly over the past decade. A recent study of practicing corporate accountants by the Institute of Management Accountants found that there is "a sea change in the role of management accountants. Their work has become more analytical and less transactional, more decision orientated and less compliance oriented. Management accountants are more involved in running the business. Their new role is more exciting and more challenging ..."[1]

---

[1] G. Siegel, "Where the Profession is Headed," *Strategic Finance*, March 2001, pp. 71–72.

Exhibit 3-6.3
Sample Corporate Accounting Position Announcements

Corporate Accounting Manager The position will oversee the integrity of various accounting systems. The candidate will facilitate communication with zone management regarding financial issues and coordinate financial information provided to external auditors. A financial degree required, as well as Peoplesoft or SAP and Microsoft Office skills. Strong working knowledge of GAAP preferred. Must have strong problem-solving and people skills. Salary to $75,000.

International Controller International manufacturing company is seeking a Controller to oversee the accounting/financial department. Position will be responsible for development and tracking of annual budgets and analysis of new product, capital expenditures, and other strategic investments. Bachelor's degree in accounting or finance is required. Ideal candidate will be a CPA. Salary to $90,000.

VP of Finance A leading manufacturer is seeking a VP Finance for a subsidiary. This position will report directly to the CEO and oversee the Controller, HR Manager, and the Senior Accountant. Financial MBA a necessity; CPA and CMA are pluses. Salary and benefits to $100K.

Assistant Controller A 40-million dollar manufacturing company seeks an individual with 3+ years of accounting experience. Individual will be responsible for local Southern California office and a maquilladora in Ensenada, Mexico, in addition to supporting other international divisions. A bachelor's degree in accounting is preferred. Experience with ERP systems and very strong PC skills, especially Excel, are required. Salary to $60K.

Controller Inventive, established company is seeking a Controller. This exciting growth opportunity requires an individual who can be a team player and leader. Position will be involved with charting, graphing, and planning, and will report directly to the CEO and President, as well as the Board of Directors. The company uses an MRP/ERP system, and requires a manufacturing background with cost accounting, budgeting, and cash management. CPA is required. Salary to $80K.

Financial Analyst E-commerce company is looking for a self-motivated Financial Analyst. Responsibilities include monthly report generation, capital expense, participation in annual planning/budgeting process, and periodic ad hoc analysis and projects. Position requires a strong working knowledge of GAAP and Excel expertise. Salary $50-55K.

Source: Adapted and included with permission from *Strategic Finance*, June 2001 and July 2001, published by Institute of Management Accountants.

The changing role of management accountants requires a changing skill set. In a recent study by Robert Half International (complete results at www.nextgenaccountant.com), chief financial officers surveyed said that in addition to financial expertise technology skills are mandatory. Also important are general business knowledge, as well as communication and interpersonal skills.[2]

Typical salary range:

Entry level	$25,000–$65,000
Vice president—finance at a sizable firm	$200,000 and up

[2] K. Williams, "Are You a Next-Generation Accountant?," Strategic Finance, July 2001, p. 17 and 75.

Tax Accounting

Taxes play a major role in our society. Private sector tax accountants are client advocates, who use financial accounting data as well as state, federal, and international laws to minimize individual and business costs. All large companies have a tax staff, and tax accounting is often the major area of practice in a CPA firm. Tax accounting also is a growing area of employment in the governmental sector, as the Internal Revenue Service and state agencies increase their sophistication.

Management

Accounting has traditionally been an excellent path to middle and upper management positions. Numerous chief executive officers (CEOs) and chief operating officers (COOs) of major companies were trained as accountants. One example of a manager with an accounting background is the first woman president of an operating division at a major oil company. Other examples include Phillip Knight, CEO and founder of Nike, and Hiroshi Okuda, CEO of Toyota Motors.

Why is accounting good training for management positions? Obviously, accounting develops strong analytical skills and excellent data analysis abilities that are invaluable to managers. Less obvious to students is the broad exposure to all areas of an organization many accountants receive early in their careers. Accountants routinely work with marketing people to help solve marketing problems, production people to help solve production problems, human resource people to help solve human resource problems, and so forth. It is this unique opportunity to learn how the different areas of a company operate and the extensive professional contacts developed in the process that give accountants an edge when management positions open up.

Governmental Accounting

Federal, state, and local governments, as well as not-for-profit organizations, hire an enormous number of accountants for a wide variety of positions. All organizations have a need for financial and systems accountants. A General Accounting Office (GAO) study estimates that about 15 percent of all federal expenditures, over $200 billion, cannot be accounted for. Naturally, there is a big push to hire accountants and thus to increase governmental accountability. Government agencies at all levels also hire tax accountants.

Several interesting government agencies hire accountants. The GAO needs accountants to prepare, at the request of Congress, reports evaluating the costs and effectiveness of federal programs. The Federal Bureau of Investigation (FBI), which primarily recruits accountants and lawyers, aggressively pursues accounting majors at most campuses. The reason for the FBI's interest in accountants is the investigation of white collar crime. You may not realize that it was the FBI who nailed Al Capone on income tax evasion charges.

Specialty Areas

A number of more specialized areas of accounting are growing quickly and provide exciting career opportunities. One is *environmental accounting*. This rapidly growing area involves computing the costs and benefits of environmental protection programs and estimating firms' potential environmental legal liabilities.

A second specialty area is *forensic accounting*. This involves the investigation of financial fraud and abuse and the presentation of results in a court of law. This is a booming area that has been fueled by fraudulent real estate, securities, and savings and loan cases.

A third rapidly growing specialty area is *quality auditing*. The International Standards Organization (ISO) has a rigorous quality certification program known as ISO 9000. Most European and many Japanese and American companies require that all products purchased be from an ISO 9000-certified vendor. As a result, virtually all major U.S. companies plan to become ISO 9000-certified in the near future. A key requirement of certification is an ongoing quality audit of all major processes within a firm. Accountants with extensive training in quality management have the ideal background to become quality auditors.

SUMMARY

Accounting is a people-oriented profession that requires excellent communication and team skills. An accounting degree, particularly when combined with supporting course work, provides an enormous variety of career opportunities. You are encouraged to schedule an appointment with your instructor to discuss accounting career opportunities.

EXERCISES

Exercise 1 Accounting Job Prospects. Discuss the employment prospects for accountants through the year 2008. Include in your discussion an analysis of any professional positions beyond accounting and financial management jobs for which accountants can be qualified.

Exercise 2 Accounting Areas. Describe each of the accounting areas listed below. In which area would you prefer to work? Why?

a. External auditing

b. Corporate accounting

c. Tax accounting

d. Quality auditing

Exercise 3 Accounting Job Web Sites. Go to the World Wide Web page for this course. Then go to the career section shown on that page where you will find a list of linked Web sites. Based on the first letter of your last name, link to the corresponding Web site shown below. Prepare a one-page summary, based on this content, of what you believe is the most useful and interesting career information.

Last Name Begins With	Web Site
A–G	KPMG Peat Marwick
H–O	Institute of Management Accountants (IMA)
P–Z	Robert Half

Exercise 4 Supporting Areas. The demand for graduates with a standard accounting major is strong. However, if a major in accounting is combined with course work in other areas, opportunities and salaries increase significantly. Discuss three supporting areas that, when combined with an accounting major, provide increased career opportunities.

Exercise 5 Requirements for a CPA. Go to the Web and collect information about the requirements for becoming a Certified Public Accountant in your state. Prepare a one-page, word-processed paper that includes the following aspects of certification:

a. Educational requirements including accounting course work required
b. Experience requirements
c. Nature and grading of the CPA exam

Exercise 6 Requirements for a CMA. Go to the Web and collect information about the requirements for becoming a Certified Management Accountant. *Hint*: www.imanet.org is a good site to start your research. Prepare a one-page, word-processed paper that includes the following aspects of certification:

a. Educational requirements including accounting coursework required
b. Experience requirements
c. Nature and grading of the CMA exam

Exercise 7 Role of Accountants. Richard Halpenny, CFO at a publishing company, is quoted as saying what most managers believe, particularly about Internet businesses: "You can have a really creative person in charge of the Internet project, but you have to put a good financial accountant behind him."[3] Discuss why you think accountants are critical to a company's success.

---

[3] R. Banham, "Malice in Wonderland," *ECFO*, Fall 2000, p. 36.

MODULE 3 REVIEW

REVIEW QUESTIONS

After you have completed Module 3, you should be able to answer the following questions. If you are unable to answer these questions in a reasonable manner, you should go back and review the readings and/or go over the Module 3 cases and readings again.

1. Activity-based costing (ABC) caused CCC's cost per sedan and compact to change from the costs calculated in Module 2. Why did the costs change? Did ABC by itself cause CCC to be more competitive?

2. How did the implementation of PQI and JIT make CCC more competitive?

3. How did the adoption of PQI and JIT impact CCC's accounting procedures?

4. Are CCC's computed costs per car using JIT more accurate than the costs computed in Module 2? Explain why or why not.

REVIEW PROBLEM

Peach Computer Company manufactures two models of personal computers, the standard model and the multimedia model, in one factory. The factory has two production departments, the Motherboard (MB) Department and the Final Assembly (FA) Department. There also are two overhead departments, the Inspection and Maintenance (I&M) Department and the General Factory (GF) Department. Cost and production information for 2002 is presented in Exhibit R3-1. The cost information in Exhibit R3-1 is computed by applying overhead on the basis of DLHs.

Requirements

1. Peach has determined that the number of machine hours is the best cost driver for inspection and maintenance costs and that the number of units of production is the best driver for general factory costs. Based on these cost drivers, compute the 2002 estimated ABC cost per standard and multimedia computer by completing a new table like the top part of Exhibit R3-1. *Hint*: Only those cells highlighted will change. The total predetermined overhead cell will not be meaningful in ABC.

2. Explain why the ABC and traditional costs are different.

3. A cost of quality analysis of Peach's manufacturing costs shows the following:

   a. About 15 percent of inspection and maintenance costs relate to the physical inspection of materials and computers.

   b. About 40 percent of inspection and maintenance costs relate to rework and repair of defective computers.

   c. About 10 percent of inspection and maintenance costs relate to equipment repair caused by poor preventive maintenance.

d. About 2 percent of general factory cost relates to vendor certification and inspection work.

e. Scrapped materials are about 5 percent of total material cost.

f. About 10 percent of labor time is idle due to equipment breakdowns.

Place Peach's manufacturing costs of quality in the appropriate categories (prevention, appraisal, internal failure, and external failure). Compute the cost of quality for each category.

Exhibit R3-1

Peach Computer Company
Estimated 2002 Cost and Production Data
Based on Traditional Costing

	Per Standard Unit	Per Multimedia Unit	Predetermined Overhead Rate (Per DLH)	2002 Totals
2002 Budget:				
Units produced	20,000	10,000		30,000
Direct labor hours	5	10		200,000
Machine hours	3	4		100,000
Direct material cost	$ 900.00	$ 1,240.00		$ 30,400,000
Direct labor cost	110.00	220.00		4,400,000
Inspection & maintenance cost	86.40	172.80	$ 17.28	3,456,000
General factory cost	165.00	330.00	33.00	6,600,000
Total costs	$ 1,261.40	$ 1,962.80	$ 50.28	$ 44,856,000

JIT Costing Estimates

	Total Factory	Standard Work Cell	Multimedia Work Cell
Estimated 2002 labor cost		$3,600,000	$ 2,100,000
Work cell depreciation cost	- - -	600,000	400,000
Maintenance cost	$ 1,400,000	- - -	- - -
General factory cost	4,500,000	- - -	- - -

4. Peach is considering switching to a JIT production environment and would like an estimate of proposed JIT costs. Material costs per unit will remain unchanged. Cost drivers for maintenance and general factory costs also remain unchanged (machine hours and units). Under JIT, Peach will incur the work cell labor costs shown even if they end up producing fewer units. Compute the cost of a standard and a multimedia computer if JIT is implemented.

MODULE FOUR

PLANNING AND PERFORMANCE

Evaluation

Module 4 Introduction

PLANNING AND PERFORMANCE EVALUATION

MODULE OVERVIEW

The management planning and control functions are very closely related and have a strong foundation in accounting. This module begins by looking at the comprehensive budgeting and control process and ends with standard setting, performance evaluation, and the balanced scorecard. Also contained in this module is a reading on ethical considerations in decision making, a topic often underemphasized in business curricula. Long-term decision making using capital budgeting analysis with emphasis on discounted cash flow techniques is presented as a major component of the planning process.

The California Car Company (CCC) case continues in Module 4. In cases 4-1 and 4-2 CCC prepares a financial budget as part of its planning process for 2003. Case 4-3 contains a CCC ethical decision situation in which you will propose a solution. Case 4-4 requires you to evaluate a ten-year capital budgeting decision concerning the purchase of one of two different machines. In the last case, Case 4-5, 2003 work cell performance is assessed by comparing actual 2003 results to budgeted performance using a balanced scorecard approach.

Learning Objectives

After completing Module 4, you should be able to:

1. Understand the basic purpose served by financial and nonfinancial plans in organizations

- Reading 4-1	Budgeting and Control
- Reading 4-5	Standard Setting, Performance Evaluation and Balanced Scorecard
- Case 4-1	California Car Company: Plans for 2003
- Case 4-2	California Car Company: Plans for 2003 (Continued)
- Exercises and Problems	Reading 4-1

2. Understand the basic "building blocks" (for example, sales volumes, prices, production volumes, costs, and so on) that must be predicted in the course of preparing a comprehensive plan and be able to organize those building blocks into an integrated set of financial statements and supporting budget schedules

- Reading 4-1	Budgeting and Control
- Reading 4-5	Standard Setting, Performance Evaluation, and Balanced Scorecard
- Case 4-1	California Car Company: Plans for 2003
- Case 4-2	California Car Company: Plans for 2003 (Continued)

- Case 4-5	The Balanced Scorecard at California Car Company
- Group Assignment 4-2	The Best Laid Plans
- Exercises and Problems	Readings 4-1 and 4-5

3. Understand the role of nonfinancial measures of performance in the development of a comprehensive plan and how such measures may be linked to financial measures of performance

- Reading 4-5	Standard Setting, Performance Evaluation, and Balanced Scorecard
- Case 4-5	The Balanced Scorecard at California Car Company
- Group Assignment 4-5	Setting Standards for 2004
- Exercises and Problems	Reading 4-5

4. Understand how budget information (both financial and nonfinancial) may be used to evaluate actual results and be able to identify variances between plan and actual results

- Reading 4-5	Standard Setting, Performance Evaluation, and Balanced Scorecard
- Case 4-5	The Balanced Scorecard at California Car Company
- Group Assignment 4-5	Setting Standards for 2004
- Exercises and Problems	Reading 4-5

5. Become familiar with the ethical issues facing management accountants

- Reading 4-3	Ethical Considerations in Decision Making
- Case 4-3	Ethical Decision at California Car Company
- Exercises and Problems	Reading 4-3

6. Understand the basics of capital budgeting, including income tax impacts and the strategic nature of capital budgeting

- Reading 4-4	Capital Budgeting
- Case 4-4	Capital Budgeting at California Car Company
- Exercises and Problems	Reading 4-4

TERMINOLOGY LIST FOR MODULE 4

Accounting rate of return
Activity-based budgeting
Attainable standards
Balanced scorecard
Benchmark standard
Budgeted balance sheet
Budgeted statement of cash flow
Budgeted income statement
Budgeting
Capital budget
Comprehensive budget
Control
Cost of goods sold budget
Critical success factors
Direct labor budget
Direct labor efficiency variance
Direct labor rate variance
Direct material price variance
Direct material usage variance
Discretionary cost center
Ethics
Financial budget
Future value
Future value factor
General and administrative expense budget
Internal rate of return
Manufacturing overhead budget
Multiple (performance) measures
Net present value
Nonfinancial measures of performance
Operating budget
Ordinary annuity
Participative (budgeting)
Payback period
Performance (control) budget
Performance report
Planning
Planning budget
Present value
Present value factor
Production budget
Purchases budget
Sales budget
Selling and distribution expense budget
Standards
Strategic planning
Time value of money

Reading 4-1

BUDGETING AND CONTROL

INTRODUCTION

The planning and control functions of management are very closely related and have a strong foundation in accounting. All organizations, regardless of type or size, need to develop sound plans. In this reading we cover the planning function as it applies to organizations, especially as it relates to operational and financial planning. The reading contains an extensive illustration of an operating and financial budget for a small manufacturing company. The reading concludes with a discussion of how activity-based costing can be used to improve the budgeting process.

WHY ORGANIZATIONS BUDGET

Planning is one of the most important functions of management. It is a necessary prerequisite to management control. All organizations must plan if they are to avoid shortages, oversupply, and general disorganization. In fact, all individuals, including students, must plan in order to be successful. Students must budget their cash inflows and outflows to ensure that they have the resources to pay for tuition, books, and living expenses. Students must budget their time so that they can complete assignments on time while meeting all of their other commitments. We all know students who are poor planners; they always appear to be disorganized and are perpetually short of cash.

As organizations grow in size, budgeting becomes more critical. Large organizations cannot rely on a couple of managers to plan everything in their heads. Neither can large organizations expect effective planning to occur simply by casual face-to-face discussions among employees. Instead, large firms, government entities, and not-for-profit organizations must formalize the planning process. This formalized, detailed planning process is called **budgeting**. For large organizations, the planning process is part of a comprehensive profit planning and control system needed to plan and control activities. Without planning there can be no effective control or performance reporting. Organizations prepare budgets for several different, but related, reasons. Some of the more important reasons for budgeting are presented in the following sections.

Coordination

The reason most firms begin budgeting is to coordinate activities so that the required people, materials, and money are available at the right place and time to meet customer demand. It is not a trivial task, particularly in large manufacturing firms, to ensure that thousands of parts and hundreds of workers come together to produce the mix of products that customers want when they want them. In fact, production planning, which includes the preparation of a production budget, is a major function in manufacturing firms. This area provides good job opportunities for production and operations management majors.

Communication

The budgeting process provides the primary formal means of communicating to all employees the priorities top management established in the strategic planning process. **Strategic planning** is the process that top management uses to establish the long-term goals and objectives of the organization. The long-term objectives must be communicated to employees throughout the organization in understandable bites. Of course, top management can issue memos or give speeches telling employees to cut costs, improve quality, or improve cycle times, but these demands will have little impact unless they are reflected in the firm's budgeting system. J. M. Juran, one of the best known quality "gurus," strongly believes that quality improvement programs cannot succeed unless quality objectives are communicated to employees through the formal budgeting system. It is, therefore, critical that firms move beyond traditional financial budgeting procedures to comprehensive budgeting systems. Comprehensive budgeting systems include both financial measures and nonfinancial measures such as quality, which are essential to the success of the firm. An effective communication loop is a critical component of any well-run organization.

Motivation

Continuous improvement requires that employee work groups be motivated to improve. The formal budgeting process, with the help of accountants and participation of work groups, can facilitate the development of the required motivation by setting continuous improvement standards that the group believes are attainable. The key words are participation and attainable. In order to achieve buy-in by the group, the group must feel itself a part of the standard-setting process. In addition, the group must view the standards as attainable if they are going to be motivated to achieve them.

Many firms are moving to benchmark standards as a way to provide the motivation to continuously improve. A **benchmark standard** is set by the performance of the best firm in the world at a specific task. For example, many firms benchmark their order taking and shipping processes against the L. L. Bean Co. Benchmarks have the advantage of eliminating arguments about whether large process improvements are possible. Questioning the feasibility of meeting goals is a typical first reaction of a work group asked to pursue continuous improvement. Benchmarks quickly move the budgeting negotiations toward how to improve and how much improvement should be made in the coming year rather than whether major improvements are possible at all. Benchmark standards also are motivational because they focus the firm's efforts on an external goal and away from internal turf battles.

Resource Allocation

Financial budgets frequently are used to allocate resources to departments, divisions, and other areas of an organization. Budgets often set the maximum spending level an area is allowed. This is particularly true in governmental and not-for-profit organizations, and is also true for discretionary cost centers in firms. A **discretionary cost center** is one that is budgeted at a certain level for the period and whose activities are not tied directly to a level of input or output. Discretionary cost center activities include research and development, advertising, and maintenance. When a budget for a discretionary cost center sets the maximum an area can spend during the year, then a budget does not form the basis for performance measurement (see next section). Instead it can lead to a "spend-it-or-lose-it" mentality, because funds not spent will revert back to the organization. In addition, failure to spend a budget usually means that the area will be in a weak position to negotiate its budget the next year. Capital budgets discussed in Reading 4-4 also are used to allocate resources.

Performance Measurement

Recall the quality philosophy that a firm cannot manage what it cannot measure. Measurements are, therefore, a key component of any successful implementation of a quality program. Budgets lay out the critical, measurable factors necessary for a firm's success. The management control system collects actual performance data during the year, or other reasonable period, on these critical factors. Then accountants, in consultation with the group under review, prepare performance reports based on the comparison of budgeted versus actual performance measures of these critical factors. Management and work group members review how factors beyond the control of the work group impacted actual performance.

Financial budgets are most useful in establishing a basis for comparison with actual results for areas directly involved in the production of goods and services. For production activities, measuring performance based, at least partially, on the costs incurred to produce quality output is very useful. For discretionary cost centers financial budget control is not very useful, and is often dysfunctional. The reason for the dysfunctionality is that managers of discretionary cost centers can, with little difficulty, reduce the budget and/or spending without affecting current output, thus demonstrating good cost control. Budget reductions in these areas, however, usually have a negative impact on future results of the firm. The solution is to rely on nonfinancial budget measures as a basis for performance measurement for discretionary cost centers.

TYPES OF BUDGETS

Operating Budgets

The **operating budget** outlines what various areas of the firm plan to achieve during the coming year. For example, the **sales budget** projects the level of sales for every product in every market. The **production budget** is a detailed plan of how many units of each product will be produced and when they will be produced. This budget includes the planned level of work-in-process and finished goods inventories. The **purchases budget** is a detailed plan of how many of each part will be purchased and when the purchases will occur. The employee development budget is a detailed plan of how many employees will be hired for what positions, and the training that the firm plans during the year. An operating budget for a manufacturing firm would include, at a minimum, the following budget schedules:

- Sales budget
- Production budget
- Purchases budget
- Direct labor budget
- Manufacturing overhead budget
- Cost of goods sold budget
- Selling and distribution expense budget
- General and administrative expense budget

This course does not focus on operating budgets, but a relatively simple illustration of an operating budget for Micro Manufacturing Company is detailed in the next few pages. Preparation of operating budgets is probably the most important step in the budgeting process. You will prepare simple sales and production estimates in Case 4-1, but you will not prepare a full operating budget.

Capital Budgets

The list of approved projects that will impact operations for more than one year is termed the **capital budget**. Items in a capital budget include expenditures for plant and equipment, new product development, new computer information systems, and other long-term investments. Many people consider the capital budgets to be part of the operating budget, but since they typically follows a different approval process, cover time periods greater than one year, and involve discounting projected cash flows they are discussed separately in Reading 4-4.

Financial Budgets

The **financial budget** takes the plans developed in the operating and capital budgets and converts them into projected (often called pro forma) financial statements. These projected statements include the budgeted income statement, budgeted cash receipts and disbursements, budgeted balance sheet, and the budgeted statement of cash flows. You already have prepared a partial, simplified financial budget in Case 2-4. Recall that you estimated cost per car and total manufacturing costs for the coming year. This cost information is a major part of the budgeted income statement.

Financial budgets are a critical part of the overall budgeting process for at least two reasons. First, financial budgets provide a reality check as to the financial feasibility of an organization's plans. For example, each department and area within a firm may propose operating budgets that are reasonable, but when all the plans are aggregated into a financial budget, the firm may not have access to the amount of cash required to fund all of the plans.

Second, the financial budget helps highlight the interrelationships among the various departments and areas in the firm. For example, the marketing department may propose a major promotional effort featuring reduced selling prices that result in a sales budget with a large increase in unit sales. The full impact of the marketing plan on the production and personnel departments may not be clear until the costs of expanding the factory and hiring new employees are reflected in the financial budget.

For most large organizations the budgeting process is not a simple, once-a-year effort. A common scenario is for the budgeting process for the coming calendar year to begin in August. Each department and area within a firm will begin preparing rough estimates of their operating budgets based on organizational goals and objectives. These budget drafts are reviewed by higher management, and, after adjustments, are given to accountants to prepare a financial budget.

When senior management reviews the first draft of the financial budget, they typically make comments like, "Total income is not high enough," or "Total cash requirements are too high." These remarks lead to revisions of the operating budgets by the originating departments and areas. The operating budgets may be passed up and down the organization several times before they are finally approved.

The introduction of computers, particularly computer spreadsheets, has had an enormous impact on the budgeting process. Good managers want to ask “what if” questions in order to better understand the risks and the impacts of alternate courses of action. For example, the sales manager may want to know the operating and financial implications of a reduction in the promotional budget of $1,000,000 that reduces sales by 200,000 units. If the operating and financial budgets are linked spreadsheets, all the sales manager needs to do is change the promotion and sales volume numbers and new budgets will be produced. You will get a chance to sample the power of spreadsheets in Cases 4-1 and 4-2.

Accounting and finance professionals are responsible for creating the budgeting process in most organizations. As you probably can tell, the budgeting staff must work closely with, and provide guidance to, managers in all areas of the firm. Since almost all managers participate in the preparation of operating budgets and must understand how operating budgets impact the financial budget, basic knowledge of financial budgeting should better prepare students in all majors to be more effective managers.

OPERATING AND FINANCIAL BUDGET EXAMPLE

By their nature, budgets contain many schedules and detailed financial and production data. Simplified operating and financial budgets are provided for Micro Manufacturing Company for the year 2002 so that you can focus on the process instead of the preparation of numerous schedules and details. The illustration includes the following budget schedules:

1. Sales budget
2. Production budget
3. Purchases budget
4. Direct labor budget
5. Manufacturing overhead budget
6. Cost of goods sold budget
7. Selling and distribution expense budget
8. General and administrative expense budget
9. Budgeted income statement
10. Budgeted cash receipts and cash disbursements
11. Budgeted balance sheet
12. Budgeted statement of cash flows—Indirect method

Micro Manufacturing Company ended 2001 with the balance sheet shown in Exhibit 4-1.1.

In planning for 2002, Micro's managers believe there will be very few changes from 2001 other than their planned continuous improvement goals. Planning information for their one product includes the following (You should be able to trace this planning information through to Exhibits 4-1.2 through 4-1.13):

- Sales are estimated to be 100,000 units of Kid Stuff at $10 per unit. All sales are on account and it is estimated that the amount of accounts receivable at December 31, 2002 will equal 10 percent of sales.
- Variable product costs are expected to be as follows:
  Material Cee, 1 lb. @ $1.00 per pound = $1.00 per finished unit
  Material Em, 2 items @ $0.50 each = $1.00 per finished unit
  Direct labor I, $16.00 per hour @ .10 hour per unit = $1.60 per finished unit
  Direct labor II, $10.00 per hour @ .05 hour per unit = $0.50 per finished unit
  Variable manufacturing overhead is incurred at $0.80 per finished unit

Exhibit 4-1.1

Micro Manufacturing Company Balance Sheet December 31, 2001						
Assets			**Liabilities and Stockholders' Equity**			
Current Assets			Current Liabilities			
Cash		$ 40,000	Accounts Payable		$ 15,000	
Accounts Receivable		80,000	Taxes and Other		30,000	
Inventory			Total Current Liabilities		45,000	
Raw Materials	$ 11,000					
Finished Goods	48,000	59,000	Stockholders' Equity			
Total Current Assets		$ 179,000	Common Stock	$ 200,000		
			Retained Earnings	234,000	434,000	
Fixed Assets - Net		300,000				
			Total Liabilities and			
Total Assets		$ 479,000	Stockholders' Equity		$ 479,000	

- Fixed manufacturing overhead, including $20,000 of depreciation, is planned at $106,700 for the year for 97,000 units = $1.10 per finished unit.
- Selling and distribution expenses are planned at 10 percent of sales plus $40,000 (includes $5,000 of depreciation for the year).
- General and administrative expenses are planned at $160,000, all fixed.
- Inventory quantities and estimated costs are planned as follows:

	Quantity	**Estimated Cost**
Raw materials—Cee (1/1/2002)	4,000	$4,000
Raw materials—Em (1/1/2002)	14,000	7,000
Raw materials—Cee (12/31/2002)	7,000	7,000
Raw materials—Em (12/31/2002)	10,000	5,000
Finished goods (1/1/2002)	8,000	48,000
Finished goods (12/31/2002)	5,000	30,000

- Micro has no work-in-process inventories at either the beginning or end of the budget period.
- Micro expects that its combined federal and state income tax rates will approximate 40 percent of earnings before taxes.
- The company expects to pay dividends of $20,000 to stockholders during 2002.
- The capital budget indicates that $75,000 of equipment will be purchased for cash near the end of the year.
- Accounts payable are expected to increase from $15,000 at January 1, 2002 to $20,000 at December 31, 2002. All accounts payable relate to the purchase of raw materials.
- Taxes and other current liabilities are expected to be at $30,000 at both the beginning and end of 2002.

Example Solution

The first schedule to prepare in an operating budget is the sales budget. It is often called the cornerstone of budgeting. The sales budget will contain planned sales by product, by territory, by other desired segments, and by expected sales price. The sales budget drives (directly affects) most of the other schedules in the operating budget process. The sales budget for Micro by territory is presented in Exhibit 4-1.2. Because Micro has only one product, only one line of data is included in the exhibit.

The next budget schedule to prepare is the production budget. The production budget contains information from the sales budget regarding expected sales by product and takes into consideration the finished goods inventories at the beginning and end of the budget period. The production budget schedule becomes the basis for all the other manufacturing budget schedules, and results in the planned production target for the year. See Exhibit 4-1.3 for Micro's production budget for the year 2002.

Exhibit 4-1.2

Micro Manufacturing Company
Sales Budget
Year Ended December 31, 2002

Product	Territory	Quantity	Price	Total Amount
Kid Stuff	East	30,000	$ 10.00	$ 300,000
	Midwest	22,000	10.00	220,000
	South	27,000	10.00	270,000
	West	21,000	10.00	210,000
Totals		100,000		$ 1,000,000

Exhibit 4-1.3

Micro Manufacturing Company
Production Budget
Year Ended December 31, 2002

	Product Units
Budgeted sales	100,000
Add: Planned ending finished goods inventory	5,000
Total units required	105,000
Less: Beginning finished goods inventory	8,000
Planned production for year	97,000

The next schedule to be prepared is the raw materials purchases budget. This schedule will be the most complex one to illustrate because we have two raw materials for each unit that is produced. The raw materials purchases budget contains the quantities Micro needs for each material including the effects of both the beginning and ending raw materials inventories. Units to be purchased are then multiplied by the cost per unit of raw material to determine the total dollar cost of purchases. See Exhibit 4-1.4 for details of the purchases budget.

The direct labor budget is illustrated next. Micro has two classes of direct laborers, class I workers who earn $16 per hour and class II workers who earn $10 per hour. Carefully note how each class of laborer is identified and how much time each class spends working on a unit of product. The **direct labor budget** is illustrated in Exhibit 4-1.5 with details concerning the different direct labor classes.

Exhibit 4-1.4

Micro Manufacturing Company
Purchases Budget
Year Ended December 31, 2002

	Raw Material			
	Cee		Em	
Raw material per finished unit	1 pound		2 items	
Total material required for production	97,000	pounds	194,000	items
Add: Planned ending inventory	7,000	pounds	10,000	items
Total material required	104,000	pounds	204,000	items
Less: Planned beginning inventory	4,000	pounds	14,000	items
Total material to be purchased	100,000	pounds	190,000	items
Planned material purchase price	$ 1.00		$ 0.50	
Total cost of purchases	$100,000		$95,000	
Total cost of Cee and Em to be purchased		$195,000		

Exhibit 4-1.5

Micro Manufacturing Company
Direct Labor Budget
Year Ended December 31, 2002

Labor Class	Units to Produce	Standard Time per Unit	Total Hours Planned	Wage Rate	Direct Labor Cost
DL - Class I	97,000	.10 hour	9,700	$ 16.00	$155,200
DL - Class II	97,000	.05 hour	4,850	10.00	48,500
Total direct labor budgeted					$203,700

The manufacturing overhead budget is typically made up of many schedules because overhead is incurred in each of the production departments and each factory service department. Thus, the **manufacturing overhead budget** contains all the planned costs in the factory area other than direct materials and direct labor. All this data must be planned, collected, and summarized. In our illustration we have assumed a very simple manufacturing overhead budget as illustrated in Exhibit 4-1.6. All factory overhead costs have been summarized and identified as fixed or variable. Detailed supporting overhead schedules are not shown for Micro Manufacturing.

Exhibit 4-1.6

Micro Manufacturing Company
Manufacturing Overhead Budget
Year Ended December 31, 2002

Overhead Item	Behavior	Computation	Amount
Total variable overhead	$0.80 per unit produced	$.80 x 97,000	$ 77,600
Total fixed overhead	Planned fixed expense*	Budgeted in each department	106,700
Total planned factory overhead			$184,300

*Includes depreciation expense of $20,000 for year.

The last budget to be illustrated for manufacturing activities will be a cost of goods sold budget. The **cost of goods sold budget** summarizes all the factory cost information regarding the cost of units produced and sold. This budget, illustrated in Exhibit 4-1.7, will use information from Exhibits 4-1.1 and 4-1.3 through 4-1.6. The format of Exhibit 4-1.7 closely resembles that in Reading 2-6 and Case 2-6.

Exhibit 4-1.7

Micro Manufacturing Company
Cost of Goods Sold Budget
Year Ended December 31, 2002

	Exhibit Reference		
Raw materials used:			
Beginning inventory	Given	$ 11,000	
Purchases of raw materials	4-1.4	195,000	
Materials available for use		$ 206,000	
Less: Ending inventory*	Given	12,000	
Cost of raw materials used			$ 194,000
Direct labor	4-1.5		203,700
Manufacturing overhead	4-1.6		184,300
Total manufacturing costs (also cost of goods manufactured)			$ 582,000
Add: Beginning finished goods inventory	4-1.1		48,000
Cost of goods available for sale			$ 630,000
Less: Ending finished goods inventory*	Given		30,000
Cost of goods sold			$ 600,000

* Inventory data are given in the introductory information.

The last two detailed operating budget schedules are for nonmanufacturing activities. They are the selling and distribution expense budget and the general and administrative expense budget. The **selling and distribution expense budget** illustrated in Exhibit 4-1.8 contains all the planned costs of marketing, selling, and distributing the product to customers. The **general and administrative expense budget** illustrated in Exhibit 4-1.9 contains all planned costs other than manufacturing and selling and distribution costs. Expenses in both of these schedules are highly condensed and are period costs, not product costs.

Exhibit 4-1.8

Micro Manufacturing Company Selling and Distribution Expense Budget Year Ended December 31, 2002	
Variable selling and distribution expenses (estimated at 10 percent of budgeted sales)	$ 100,000
Fixed selling and distribution expenses (planned in total, as a fixed cost)*	40,000
Total budgeted selling and distribution expenses	$ 140,000

* Includes $5,000 depreciation expense.

Exhibit 4-1.9

Micro Manufacturing Company
General and Administrative Expense Budget
Year Ended December 31, 2002

Expense	Amount
Salaries and benefits	$ 105,000
Telephone and communications	25,000
Insurance	12,000
Other	18,000
Total budgeted G&A expenses	$ 160,000

The last step in preparing the operating budget is to prepare the budgeted income statement. The **budgeted income statement** summarizes all of the information in the other operating budget schedules, Exhibits 4-1.2 through 4-1.9. The budgeted income statement illustrated in Exhibit 4-1.10 contains an extra column for percentages for each item in the statement. This feature is often used for internal budget documents because it makes it very easy to compare current and historical percentage relationships for each income statement item.

Once the operating budget, including the budgeted income statement, is complete, the capital budget and three other financial budget schedules would be prepared next. The capital budget is discussed in Reading 4-4. The cash receipts and disbursements budget, budgeted balance sheet, and budgeted statement of cash flows needed are illustrated below as Exhibits 4-1.11, 4-1.12, and 4-1.13, followed by explanations as to how the amounts were determined in each.

Exhibit 4-1.10

Micro Manufacturing Company
Budgeted Income Statement
For the Year Ended December 31, 2002

	Amount	Percent of Sales
Sales	$ 1,000,000	100.0%
Cost of goods sold	600,000	60.0%
Gross margin on sales	$ 400,000	40.0%
Less:		
Selling and distribution expenses	$ 140,000	14.0%
General and administrative expenses	160,000	16.0%
Total operating expenses	$ 300,000	30.0%
Earnings before income taxes	$ 100,000	10.0%
Estimated income taxes (40%)	40,000	4.0%
Budgeted net income	$ 60,000	6.0%

The amounts in the budgeted cash receipts and disbursements schedule shown in Exhibit 4-1.11 were determined as follows:

- The beginning cash balance came from the opening balance sheet, Exhibit 4-1.1.
- Collections from accounts receivable were determined by adding the beginning balance of accounts receivable (Exhibit 4-1.1) and sales (Exhibit 4-1.2) and then deducting the ending accounts receivable calculated to be 10 percent of sales ($100,000 from Exhibit 4-1.12) [$80,000 + $1,000,000 – $100,000 = $980,000].
- Cash payments for purchases of raw materials are determined by adding the beginning balance of accounts payable (Exhibit 4-1.1) and purchases of raw materials (Exhibit 4-1.4) and then deducting the ending accounts payable given in the introductory information ($15,000 + $195,000 – $20,000 = $190,000).
- Cash payments for direct labor came from Exhibit 4-1.5.
- Cash payments for manufacturing overhead came from Exhibit 4-1.6 ($184,300 less $20,000 depreciation = $164,300).
- Cash payments for selling and distribution expenses came from Exhibit 4-1.8 ($140,000 less $5,000 depreciation = $135,000).
- Cash payments for general and administrative expenses came from Exhibit 4-1.9.
- Cash payments for income taxes came from Exhibit 4-1.10, the income statement.
- The cash payment for equipment purchased was given in the introductory information as $75,000.
- Cash payments of $20,000 for dividends, as stated in the introductory information.

Exhibit 4-1.11

Micro Manufacturing Company
Budgeted Cash Receipts and Disbursements
Year Ended December 31, 2002

Beginning cash, 1/1/2002		$ 40,000
Budgeted sources of cash:		
Collection of accounts receivable		980,000
Estimated available cash		$ 1,020,000
Budgeted uses of cash:		
Purchase materials	$ 190,000	
Direct labor	203,700	
Manufacturing overhead	164,300	
Selling and distribution	135,000	
General and administrative	160,000	
Income taxes	40,000	
Equipment purchase	75,000	
Dividends paid	20,000	
Total budgeted uses of cash		988,000
Budgeted ending cash balance		$ 32,000

- Lastly, if our budgeted cash flow statement is correct, the ending amount should agree with the balance of cash on the December 31, 2002 budgeted balance sheet. It agrees.
- Micro expects the December 31, 2002 balance for taxes and other current liabilities on the balance sheet to be the same as it was at the end of 2001.

Amounts in the December 31, 2002 budgeted balance sheet shown in Exhibit 4-1.12 were determined as follows:

- The cash amount came from the budgeted cash receipts and disbursements, Exhibit 4-1.11.
- The ending accounts receivable balance was estimated to be 10 percent of year 2002 sales (10 percent of $1,000,000 = $100,000) as stated in the introductory information.
- Raw materials and finished goods inventories were given in the introductory information and can also be determined from the ending balance shown on Exhibits 4-1.3 and 4-1.4 multiplied by the average cost for each. The raw materials inventory is derived from (7,000 x $1 = $7,000) + (10,000 x $0.50 = $5,000) = $12,000 total raw materials inventory; finished goods inventory is 5,000 units x $6 per unit cost = $30,000.
- Fixed assets—net were determined as follows: Equipment, net of depreciation, increased $50,000 from the January 1 to the December 31, 2002 balance sheet. The $75,000 purchase minus the $25,000 depreciation for the year would explain the $50,000 increase in fixed assets—net.
- Accounts payable were planned at $20,000.

Exhibit 4-1.12

Micro Manufacturing Company
Budgeted Balance Sheet
December 31, 2002

Assets			**Liabilities and Stockholders' Equity**		
Current Assets			Current Liabilities		
Cash		$ 32,000	Accounts Payable		$ 20,000
Accounts Receivable		100,000	Taxes and Other		30,000
Inventory			Total Current Liabilities		$ 50,000
Raw Materials	$ 12,000				
Finished Goods	30,000	42,000	Stockholders' Equity		
Total Current Assets		$ 174,000	Common Stock	$ 200,000	
			Retained Earnings	274,000	474,000
Fixed Assets - Net		350,000	Total Liabilities and		
Total Assets		$ 524,000	Stockholders' Equity		$ 524,000

- As stated in the introductory materials, taxes and other current liabilities did not change in total. This simplified some of the computations in the budgeted cash flow schedule.
- Common stock did not change from the amount in the beginning balance sheet.
- Retained earnings is comprised of the beginning balance of $234,000 plus net income of $60,000, minus $20,000 dividends = $274,000.

The amounts in the budgeted statement of cash flows shown in Exhibit 4-1.13 were determined as follows:

- Net income is from Exhibit 4-1.10, the income statement.
- Depreciation expense is taken from Exhibits 4-1.6 and 4-1.8.
- The increase in accounts receivable is the difference in the balances in accounts receivable in Exhibits 4-1.1 and 4-1.12.
- The decrease in inventories is the difference in the balances in inventories in Exhibits 4-1.1 and 4-1.12.
- The increase in accounts payable is the difference in the balances in accounts payable in Exhibits 4-1.1 and 4-1.12.
- Both the equipment purchase and the payment of dividends were given in the introductory information.
- The beginning balance of cash on hand was taken from the balance sheet at January 1, 2002 as given in Exhibit 4-1.1.
- The ending balance of cash agrees with the December 31, 2002 cash balance in the balance sheet shown in Exhibit 4-1.12.

Exhibit 4-1.13

Micro Manufacturing Company Budgeted Statement of Cash Flows - Indirect Method Year Ended December 31, 2002		
Operating activities:		
Net income		$ 60,000
Add (deduct) adjustments to cash basis:		
Depreciation expense	$ 25,000	
Increase in accounts receivable	(20,000)	
Decrease in inventories	17,000	
Increase in accounts payable	5,000	
Total adjustments		27,000
Net cash flows from operations		$ 87,000
Investing activities:		
Equipment purchase		(75,000)
Financing activities:		
Dividends paid		(20,000)
Net cash outflow for the year		$ (8,000)
Add cash on hand on January 1, 2002		40,000
Budgeted ending cash balance		$ 32,000

Now that you have completed reading this operating and financial budget example, we strongly encourage you to go back through the example to make sure you understand how the numbers and schedules relate to (articulate with) each other. As was stated in the beginning of this illustration, it was greatly simplified to help you understand the operating and financial budgeting process. In a real-life business situation, you would have computer software to help you enter data and direct the information to the many other budget schedules.

COMPREHENSIVE BUDGETING

In the past, traditional budgeting ended with completion of the financial budget process similar to the preceding illustration. The operating and financial budgets were then used as the basis for a major component of performance evaluation. Managers usually considered some nonfinancial items when evaluating performance, but nonfinancial measures were often not included in the budgeting process. Today, many firms explicitly include nonfinancial measures in the budgeting process. In other words, **nonfinancial measures of performance** such as cycle time or defect rates, as well as financial measures, are negotiated during the budgeting process. The nonfinancial measures are aggregated, along with the financial data, to form the completed comprehensive budget. When this occurs, the budget is sometimes termed a comprehensive budget because it includes financial and nonfinancial targets. The relationship of comprehensive budgeting, control systems, and a technique called the balanced scorecard will be discussed in Reading 4-5 as part of performance reporting.

THE NEW MANUFACTURING ENVIRONMENT

During the last 20 years many changes have taken place in manufacturing companies: their processes, structure, control systems, and the economic climate in which they operate. Enterprise resource planning and activity-based budgeting are two concepts that have had a significant influence on budgeting in many companies. **Enterprise resource planning** (ERP) systems have evolved to help companies integrate their operations to be consistent with business strategies in a seamless operating system. It is costly to implement an ERP system that often takes up to four years to be fully operational. An ERP system should integrate all business processes and provide real-time information to all appropriate users worldwide. The ERP system is like a giant database in which users can retrieve and/or update data as needed by the end user. [1]

With increasing interest in activity-based costing (see Reading 3-1 for details), many firms have taken the next logical step to implement activity-based budgeting. **Activity-based budgeting** (ABB) is budgeting costs by activity, with the intent to use the different activity costs to determine the cost of producing a product or providing a service. Thus, the focus of ABB is on budgeting costs for activities, not by departments or other business segments. Generally, ABB is much more detailed than traditional budgeting because of the use of many cost drivers, one for each significant activity.

We will use Micro Manufacturing Company to briefly illustrate the use of ABB. Assume that Micro randomly quality tests 5 percent of its manufactured products. Each product requires 3 minutes to test. Therefore, 4,850 units (97,000 x 5%) will be tested during the year, at a total time commitment of 14,450 minutes (4,850 x 3 minutes). A total of 242.5 man-hours (14,450 minutes/60 minutes) of testing time will be required. Also, testing equipment and supplies will be used in the testing process. The budgeted cost of this activity for 2002 would be as follows:

Labor (242.5 hours @ $15 per hour)	$ 3,637.50	Variable cost
Depreciation (on testing equipment)	1,000.00	Fixed cost
Supplies, power, other	250.00	Variable cost
Total budgeted activity cost	$ 4,887.50	

The $4,887.50 total budget activity cost is included, but not identified, in the variable and fixed costs summarized in Exhibit 4-1.6, the manufacturing overhead budget. Based on this information, Micro will budget $4,887.50 for product random testing, which would be $20.15 per test hour ($4,887.50/242.5 hours). This cost per hour could be used to compare to baseline data from other companies for similar test operations to see how efficiently Micro is performing this operation.

The use of ABB typically requires more detailed data than traditional budgeting. However, the added detail can aid in understanding the cost structure better and in making more informed management decisions.[2]

---

[1] See, for example, Kip P. Krumwiede and Win G. Jorday, "Enterprise Resource Systems, Strategic Finance, October 2000, pp. 49-52, and Brian Jarzynski "Thriving on Uncertainty with an MPC System," Strategic Finance, July 2001, p. 62.

[2] R. S. Kaplan and R. Cooper, "Using ABC for Budgeting and Transfer Pricing," *Cost and Effect* (Boston: HBS Press, 1998) Chapter 15, and Katheryn Jehle "Budgeting as a Competitive Advantage," Strategic Finance, October 1999, pp. 54–57.

SUMMARY

In this reading we have presented material concerning the planning function as it applied to organizations, especially as it related to operating and financial planning. Details concerning the process of operating and financial budgeting were discussed and illustrated to lay a foundation for the control process to be discussed in Reading 4-5.

EXERCISES AND PROBLEMS

Exercises

Exercise 1 Reasons Organizations Budget. List and briefly explain the reasons organizations budget.

Exercise 2 Planning and Control. How are planning and control related? Explain briefly.

Exercise 3 Budgets and Responsibility. Discuss the three types of budgets and explain who within an organization is primarily responsible for preparing each type.

Exercise 4 Sales Budgets. Explain why the sales budget is often called the "cornerstone" of budgeting.

Exercise 5 Production Budget Effects. In the Micro Manufacturing Company operating budget example in this reading, which budgets' schedules were _not_ directly affected by the production budget? Why were these schedules not affected?

Exercise 6 Performance Measurement. How is performance measurement related to budgeting?

Exercise 7 Comprehensive Budgeting. How does comprehensive budgeting differ from traditional budgeting illustrated in this reading?

Exercise 8 Enterprise Resource Planning. What is enterprise resource planning and how has it impacted budgeting in many companies?

Exercise 9 Activity-Based Budgeting. What is the major advantage of activity-based budgeting? What is its major disadvantage?

Problems

Problem 1 Sales Budget and Production Budget. Quick Company is planning its operating budget for 2002. It sells two products, Fast and Swift, for $12 and $19, respectively. Expected sales and inventory quantities planned for 2002 are as follows:

	Fast	**Swift**
Sales	15,000	12,000
Beginning finished goods inventory	800	1,000
Ending finished goods inventory	900	600

Use the information presented to prepare a sales budget and a production budget for Quick Company for 2002. Use Exhibits 4-1.2 and 4-1.3 as guidelines for your budget schedules.

Problem 2 Production Budget. Duffy Company has just completed its sales budget for 2002. Expected planned unit sales and finished goods inventories for its two products, Gass and Ragg, are as follows:

	Gass	Ragg
Budgeted sales in units	50,000	80,000
Finished goods inventory, 1/1/02	5,000	2,000
Finished goods inventory, 12/31/02	3,000	6,000

Prepare a production budget for Duffy Company for 2002; use Exhibit 4-1.3 as a guideline for your budget schedule.

Problem 3 Raw Materials Purchases Budget. Prepare a raw materials purchases budget similar to Exhibit 4-1.4 using the following information for Donler Company for August 2002:

- Planned sales of 22,000 units at $20 each.
- Planned production of 20,000 units.
- Raw materials to produce one unit of product:
  - 2 square feet of fleece at $3 per square foot
  - 1 kit of bungles at $2 per kit
- Raw materials inventories planned are as follows:

	Beginning	Ending
Fleece	3,000 square feet	4,000 square feet
Bungles	4,000 kits	2,000 kits

Problem 4 Raw Materials Purchases Budget. Alpha Company makes one product, Numerals that contains three raw materials, A, B, and C. For 2002 Alpha has budgeted 100,000 units to be sold at $40 each. Information concerning raw materials is as follows:

	A	B	C
Raw material per unit of product	2 gallons	3 pounds	1 each
Cost of raw materials	$2.50/gal.	$2.00/lb.	$4.00 each
Beginning raw material inventory	3,000 gals.	6,000 lbs.	4,000
Planned ending raw material inventory	5,000 gals.	7,000 lbs.	3,000

Use the information presented to prepare a raw materials purchases budget for Alpha Company for the year 2002. Use Exhibit 4-1.4 as a guide for your raw materials purchases schedule.

Problem 5 Direct Labor Budget. Use the following information to prepare a direct labor budget similar to Exhibit 4-1.5 for Mersay Company for the year 2002. Production for the coming year is scheduled at 30,000 units.

Direct labor information:

Class A, 1.5 hours per unit, paid $20 per hour

Class B, 3 hours per unit, paid $18 per hour

Class C, 1 hour per unit, paid $16 per hour

Class D, 2 hours per unit, paid $12 per hour

Problem 6 Direct Labor Budget. Kimber Kompany makes two products, Leens and Reahs. For July 2002 is has planned the following production in units and direct labor needs:

		Leens	Reahs
Budgeted unit sales		12,000	7,000
Direct labor needed per unit:	Class I	2 hours	3 hours
	Class II	3 hours	1 hour

Class I labor cost is $22 per hour and Class II labor cost is $17 per hour. Use the given information to prepare a direct labor budget similar to Exhibit 4-1.5 for Kimber Kompany for 2002.

Problem 7 Budgeted Cash Receipts and Disbursements. Prepare a budgeted cash receipts and disbursements schedule similar to Exhibit 4-1.11 for Micro Manufacturing Company for the year 2002 assuming the following three changes in the information:

- It is estimated that the amount of accounts receivable at December 31, 2002 will equal 9 percent of sales (not 10 percent as used in the reading).
- Assume that $8,000 of depreciation expense is included in the $160,000 general and administrative expense budget for 2002 (there was no depreciation used in the reading).
- Dividends paid in 2002 will increase to 50 percent of the budgeted net income for the year.

Case 4-1

CALIFORNIA CAR COMPANY: PLANS FOR 2003

Case Objectives

1. Introduce the concepts of financial budgeting
2. Review the income statement
3. Develop spreadsheet skills

Decision (Planning): How should CCC prepare for next year? How much income do we plan to earn in 2003?

INTRODUCTION

In late October 2002, CCC's president, David Gomez, called a meeting of the company's Executive Committee: Dennis Madison, vice president–engineering, George Olson, vice president–marketing, Sally Swanson, vice president–production, and Jena Butler, vice president–finance. The purpose was to begin the development of plans for 2003. David began the meeting by asking Jena Butler to give the group a brief presentation on the expected financial results for the year ending December 31, 2002.

Jena began by passing out the financial information contained in Exhibit C4-1.1. She explained: "Net income for 2002 will be approximately $6.020 million, which is well below our budgeted amount of $8.090 million. Several factors account for this disappointing performance.

- Although sales prices of $21,000 for the sedan and $17,000 for the compact and a sales mix of 3 sedans sold for each compact sold have remained on target, sales volume fell short of our targeted amounts for both the sedan and compact. Competition from Toyota certainly appears to have hurt us here.

- Our production operations experienced numerous difficulties during the first half of the year, which resulted in significant cost overruns on units produced through July 31, 2002. Fortunately, our change to JIT in August led to improved efficiency, which prevented our income from being even lower.

- As our ending balance sheet is expected to show, the move to JIT will have a major impact on levels of ending inventories. Consequently, total assets will not be as high as budgeted. However, even with the significant reduction in inventories, we still fell short of our budgeted return on total assets (net income ÷ average assets)."

David turned next to George Olson and asked: "George, where do we stand with our competitors at the end of this year?"

George responded: "Jena correctly noted that we managed to maintain our sales mix at 25 percent compacts and 75 percent sedans, and kept selling prices constant at $17,000 for the compact and $21,000 for the sedan. Our problem is that our competition is beating us both on prices and on delivery times. In addition, we are still having problems with customer-reported defects that are hurting the sales of both models, but particularly the compact with its solar panel problems."

Exhibit C4-1.1

CCC Income Statements
For Year Ended December 31, 2002

	Budgeted*	Actual†
Sales revenue	$ 136,000,000	$120,000,000
Cost of goods sold	98,943,400	86,400,000
Gross margin	$ 37,056,600	$ 33,600,000
Operating expenses:		
Selling expenses	7,000,000	6,800,000
Administrative expenses	18,500,000	18,200,000
Income before taxes	$ 11,556,600	$ 8,600,000
Income tax	3,466,980	2,580,000
Net income	$ 8,089,620	$ 6,020,000

* From Exhibit C2-5.3
† Nine months actual plus Oct.–Dec. estimated

Sally Swanson responded, "George, we're going to be able to help you on all three counts next year. Our JIT approach is leading to significant reductions in production costs per unit, particularly for the sedan. This means that you will be able to be more competitive in pricing both models next year. Additionally, our cycle time has improved, and we are gradually solving some of our defect problems in both models. We are continuing to train our work cell personnel to become better inspectors at both the chassis and final assembly stages. Our vendor review and certification program should start showing results in 2003 also. Nevertheless, the solar panels on the compact may continue to be troublesome."

"I have been working closely with Solar Products, Inc., our supplier of solar panels," stated Dennis. "Based on our suggestions, they will alter the design of their panels next year in the hopes of reducing the number of defects that eventually show up in our completed compacts."

David Gomez concluded the meeting by observing, "Based on this discussion, I think we've got a pretty fair idea of where we will be at the end of 2002. We have also identified some good ideas to be considered in developing plans for 2003. Let's plan to reconvene in early December to complete our strategy for 2003. I want you to come to the December meeting with specific recommendations improving the following two items."

- Planned sales and production volumes in units and planned selling prices for both models for the year 2003. See Exhibit C4-1.2 for the results of a market research study recently completed for CCC by Accurate Market Research Company.
- Planned production costs per unit for each model.

Exhibit C4-1.2

Accurate Market Research Study Results Projected Market Shares for Year 2003			
LEV Industry Sales Forecasts:			
Sedans	90,000 vehicles		
Compacts	40,000 vehicles		
CCC Sedan Market Shares			
	Level of Advertising Expenditures		
Sales Prices	High ($70M)	Medium ($40M)	Low ($15M)
$ 21,000	11%	8%	5%
20,000	15%	11%	9%
19,000	21%	17%	13%
CCC Compact Market Shares			
	Level of Advertising Expenditures		
Sales Prices	High ($70M)	Medium ($40M)	Low ($15M)
$ 17,000	13%	10%	7%
16,000	15%	12%	10%
15,000	24%	18%	16%

DETAILED BUDGET INFORMATION

All managers at CCC identified the cost drivers for their department's costs and prepared an activity-based operating budget based on those drivers. The marketing department also developed CCC's sales drivers. The results of this operating budget effort follow. Some key drivers used in the budgeting process are:

Cost or Revenue	Driver
Work cell labor cost	Number of sedans or compacts
Maintenance cost	Maintenance hours
General factory cost	Number of shifts
Marketing cost	Level of advertising
Sales revenue	Selling price and advertising

Market Research

Accurate Market Research Company (AMRC) has determined that the 2003 demand for the entire LEV industry is 90,000 sedans and 40,000 compacts. AMRC then estimated the percent of total LEV industry demand CCC will achieve given various selling prices and advertising levels CCC can select.

To determine the number of sedans and compacts CCC can sell in 2003, first select CCC's advertising level, then select a selling price for the sedan and selling price for the compact. CCC can select only *one* advertising level for the entire firm. Therefore, if you select a medium advertising level for the sedan, you must also select a medium level for the compact. You can, however, select a $21,000 sedan price and a $15,000 compact price. The percentages in Exhibit C4-1.2 represent the share of each car market that CCC can expect to achieve. For example, if you select a low advertising level for CCC and a $20,000 selling price for the sedan, CCC would expect to capture a 9 percent share of the total sedan market, which is forecasted to be 90,000 vehicles. Thus, the estimated sales for sedans would be 8,100 cars.

Material and Labor Costs

The following information on work cell capacities, labor hours, labor rates, and material costs has been compiled for preparation of the 2003 budget. Material costs in 2003 are estimated to be the same as 2002 material costs: sedan, $2,980, and compact, $3,360. All labor is expected to cost $35 per hour. The sedan and compact labor requirements are summarized in Exhibits C4-1.3 and C4-1.4 respectively. Note that since CCC has adopted JIT, labor is now considered a step fixed cost rather than a variable cost.

Sedan Labor

As shown in Exhibit C4-1.3, the sedan work cell can produce up to 6,000 sedans per year with the current work cell labor force of 969,000 work cell labor hours (WCLHs) per year. The work cell output can be increased from 6,001 to 7,500 sedans per year by employing an additional 281,000 WCLHs per year. However, production levels of more than 6,000 sedans require implementation of a second shift in the sedan work cell. Note that the WCLHs required to produce 5,100 sedans is more than the 550,800 DLH computed in Case 2-4 because CCC has moved workers from support areas to the work cells after JIT was implemented. CCC's maximum two-shift sedan capacity is 12,000 sedans. You cannot produce or sell more than 12,000 sedans in 2003.

Exhibit C4-1.3
Sedan Work Cell Labor Hours

Annual Production Level	Number of Shifts Required	Annual Work Cell Hours Required
0 - 3,000	1	580,000
3,001 - 4,500	1	775,000
4,501 - 6,000	1	969,000
6,001 - 7,500	2	1,250,000
7,501 - 9,000	2	1,510,000
9,001 - 10,500	2	1,790,000
10,501 - 12,000	2	2,070,000
Note: 12,000 sedans are CCC's maximum two-shift capacity in 2003.		

Compact Labor

The compact work cell can produce 9,000 compacts per year with its current equipment and square footage of space. The compact labor requirements are summarized in Exhibit C4-1.4. CCC does not plan to operate a second compact shift.

Overhead Costs

Total overhead costs include manufacturing overhead as well as the period costs of selling, administrative, and income tax expense. Specific information regarding overhead costs follows.

Exhibit C4-1.4
Compact Work Cell Labor Hours

Annual Production Level	Number of Shifts Required	Annual Work Cell Hours Required
0 - 1,000	1	115,000
1,001 - 2,000	1	204,000
2,001 - 3,000	1	323,000
3,001 - 4,000	1	429,000
4,001 - 5,000	1	525,000
5,001 - 6,000	1	640,000
6,001 - 7,000	1	750,000
7,001 - 8,000	1	860,000
8,001 - 9,000	1	970,000
Note: 9,000 compacts are CCC's maximum capacity in 2003.		

Maintenance

Maintenance is expected to be $42 per maintenance hour, which is CCC's maintenance cost driver. CCC estimates that in 2003 they will use 4.4 maintenance hours per sedan and 7.3 maintenance hours per compact, which is a reduction from the hours per car used in 2002. The compact work cell requires more maintenance because it employs older, less reliable equipment.

General Factory Overhead

Plantwide overhead costs are expected to be $7,000,000 per year for a one-shift operation. Increased plantwide fixed overhead costs to add the second sedan shift are $3,000,000 per year due to the addition of a second shift plant manager and support staff.

Equipment, Depreciation, and Interest

To improve quality and reduce breakdowns, CCC plans to purchase and install, early in 2003, $108,000,000 of new equipment for the sedan work cell, which will be depreciated over 10 years with no salvage value. All existing equipment will be kept to improve the compact work cell and to reduce bottlenecks throughout the plant. Therefore, the current annual depreciation charges of $5,100,000 for sedan work cell equipment and $2,040,000 for the compact work cell will continue.

CCC and the equipment vendor have agreed that CCC will pay $108,000,000 plus $8,640,000 in interest expense on December 31, 2003. On December 31, 2003, CCC will obtain $64,000,000 from the bank in exchange for a note payable of that amount payable to the bank on December 31, 2006.

Marketing, Administrative, and Income Tax Expenses

Advertising expenses are based on your selection of a high, medium, or low level in Exhibit C4-1.2. Non-advertising selling expenses are expected to be $6,000,000 per year. In other words, the total marketing costs for 2003 are the sum of the $6,000,000 in non-advertising selling costs plus the level of advertising expenditures you select.

Due to continued major research and development efforts and general expansion, administrative expenses are expected to increase to $46,000,000 in 2003. CCC must pay a corporate income tax of 30 percent of reported net income before taxes in 2003.

Requirements

1. On a computer spreadsheet, prepare a budgeted income statement in the format shown in Exhibit C4-1.5. Save your spreadsheet electronically, because you will use it to answer Case 4-2. Make two copies of your printout so you will have one on which to write any corrections. The following detailed instructions should help you complete the budgeted income statement:

   a. Go to Exhibit C4-1.2 and first select an advertising level and then select selling prices for the sedan and compact. Enter these in the data table in Exhibit C4-1.5. The choice is yours, but try to select combinations that yield a high net income.

   b. Based on your selections, enter the market share percentages from Exhibit C4-1.2 in the data table.

   c. The industry sales forecasts are entered into the data table. Your instructor may have you change these numbers, however. Enter formulas in cells G8 and G9 to multiply the industry sales forecast by the market share percentage. This will produce CCC's demand for sedans and compacts, although it is possible that CCC may not be able to produce sufficient cars to meet that demand.

   d. If projected sedan sales in cell G8 are greater than 6,000, enter a 1 in the "shift =" cell (D9). If sedan sales are less than 6,000 units, enter a 0. You can make this happen with this IF statement: =IF(G8>6000,1,0)

   e. Enter Excel IF statements in the unit sales cells (C17 and C18) for the sedan and the compact. For example, cell C17 is: =IF(G8>12000,12000,G8). The IF statement will prevent your projected sedan sales from exceeding CCC's plant capacity of 12,000 units. The second IF statement should limit compact sales to 9,000 units.

   f. Go to Exhibit C4-1.3 and determine the number of work cell labor hours required to manufacture the projected sedan production in cell C17. Enter this number of hours in the "step labor hour: sedan" cell (D10). Do the same for projected compact sales, but use Exhibit C4-1.4 to find the work cell hours and enter them in cell D11. Note that work cell labor now is a (step) fixed cost. You can automatically enter the correct work cell hours for different projected sales levels in cells D10 and D11 if you build VLOOKUP tables in Excel, but it is not required. See the Excel help function for instructions.

   g. Complete the material, maintenance, and step work cell labor rows. All entries you make in columns C and D should have a cell reference to the data input table or to cells C17 and C18. If you don't enter cell references, Case 4-2 will be very time consuming.

(Requirements are continued after Exhibit C4-1.5)

Exhibit C4-1.5

	A	B	C	D	E	F	G
2	**California Car Company**						
3	**Budgeted 2003 Income Statement**						
4							
5	**Data Input Table:**						
6	Advertising level in dollars:				Market	Sedan =	%
7	Selling Prices:		Sedan =		Share %:	Compact =	%
8			Compact =		Unit	Sedan =	
9	Shift = (1 if second shift needed)*				demand:	Compact =	
10	Step Labor Hours:		Sedan =		Industry Sales	Sedan =	90,000
11			Compact =		Forecast:	Compact =	40,000
12			Tax rate =				
14			**Units**	**Price or**	**Subtotal**	**Income**	
15				**Cost**	**(Extension)**	**Statement**	
16	Sales:		Cars				
17	Sedan*						
18	Compact*						
19	Total Sales						
20	Variable Costs:		Cars				
21	Material:	Sedan		$ 2,980			
22		Compact		3,360			
23	Maintenance:		Maintenance hours				
24	Sedan			$ 42			
25	Compact			42			
26	**Contribution Margin**						
27	Step Costs:		Labor hours				
28	Work Cell	Sedan		$ 35			
29	Labor:	Compact		35			
30	General Factory Overhead:						
31	First Shift						
32	Second Shift						
33	Other Fixed Costs:						
34	Depreciation:						
35	Sedan, Existing Equipment						
36	Sedan, New Equipment						
37	Compact						
38	Marketing and Advertising						
39	Administrative						
40	Interest Expense						
41	**Total Fixed Costs**						
42	Income before Tax						
43	Less: Income Tax						
44	Budgeted Net Income						

* Enter an Excel IF statement in cells surrounded by dashed boxes.

h. For general factory overhead, in the second shift cell, you want to multiply the additional cost of the second shift by cell D9 in the data input table. By doing this, the cost of the second shift will appear in your budget if cell D9 =1. If D9 =0, then your budget will show no second-shift cost. Cell D9 is called a binary variable, which is useful in constructing many types of spreadsheets.

i. If your income before tax is negative, then your income tax should be positive, which will reduce the amount of the loss. In other words, cell F43 should have the formula =(–D12*F42) and cell F44 should have =F42+F43.

2. Compute CCC's breakeven level of sales based on budgeted 2003 figures.

3. Compute CCC's 2003 budgeted markup percentage based on total manufacturing costs.

Case 4-2

CALIFORNIA CAR COMPANY: PLANS FOR 2003 (CONTINUED)

Case Objectives

1. Further develop budgeting concepts
2. Demonstrate how the financial statements are interrelated
3. Reinforce an understanding of balance sheets and cash flow statements

Decision (Planning): Can CCC finance its aggressive growth strategy?

THE PRICING DISAGREEMENT

At a weekly executive meeting George Olson, vice president of marketing, states, "Let's reduce the sedan selling price to $19,000 and the compact price to $15,000 and bump our advertising budget up to $70,000,000. Our sales force can really kick *&# at these prices and with that advertising exposure." "You will be giving up $2,000 per car based on our current prices," responds Jena Butler, vice president of finance. If we sell 20,000 cars next year, that is a loss of $40,000,000 in sales revenue. Since no costs will be avoided, net income before tax will decrease by $40,000,000! In addition, we will be forced to issue so much stock that we could lose control of CCC to outside investors. Let's keep our prices where they are and set advertising at $40,000,000." President David Gomez interrupts the disagreement: "Before we make any decision to lower prices dramatically, let's fully explore the financial implications."

President Gomez asks you to gather information about the financial impact of reduced prices. You have collected the following additional budget information.

Assets

Because CCC plans to increase sales significantly in 2003, it needs to make major asset acquisitions. The specific budgeted needs are presented in this section.

Accounts Receivable

To encourage dealers to stock more cars, CCC is not going to require payment on shipped cars for either 90 days or until the cars are sold, whichever is shorter. Therefore, CCC expects accounts receivable at the end of 2003 to be 20 percent of total 2003 sales.

Inventory

Inventory is expected to total $840,000 at the end of 2003.

Long-Term Assets

No long-term assets will be purchased or sold during 2003 except for the $108 million purchase of equipment described in Case 4-1.

Liabilities and Shareholders' Equity

The buildup in CCC's assets will need to be financed. As a result, liabilities and shareholders' equity are budgeted to increase greatly in 2003, as described in this section.

Current Liabilities

Total current liabilities are not expected to change during 2003, except for an increase due to income taxes payable. Each month's estimated tax expense is paid to the government by the fifteenth day of the following month. Therefore, on December 31, 2003, CCC expects to owe the government its December estimated taxes, or 1/12 of its total 2003 income tax expense. CCC will have no taxes payable at the beginning of 2003.

Long-Term Liabilities

Long-term liabilities at the end of 2003 will be the $64 million owed on the bank note.

Shareholder's Equity

CCC plans to declare and pay a $2,600,000 dividend in 2003. CCC plans to issue stock in increments of $1,000,000 to cover any cash shortage during the year. For example, if cash flow from operations, investing activities, and financing activities other than issuance of stock plus the beginning balance is a negative $2,450,000, CCC would issue $3,000,000 in stock.

Requirements

1. Correct the budgeted income statement spreadsheet you prepared for Case 4-1 and resubmit it.

2. Extend the Case 4-1 spreadsheet by including a budgeted 2003 cash flow statement in the format shown in Exhibit C4-2.1. Also complete a comparative projected balance sheet for 2003 in the format given in Exhibit C4-2.2. Note that the 2003 budgeted balance sheet and cash flow statement draw information from your income statement. Be sure that you link all three statements. In other words, some formulas in the cash flow statement and balance sheet should refer back to cells in the income statement. Thus, if you change one number, for example depreciation expense, all three statements should automatically be updated. Refer to Case 4-1 because you will need some of its information. Detailed instructions are presented below.

   a. Since they are interrelated, you can start with either the statement of cash flows or the balance sheet, but you can't complete one independent of the other. These instructions assume that you start with the balance sheet.

   b. You can't complete the ending 2003 cash balance until you complete the statement of cash flows, so skip to the 2003 accounts receivable balance and complete the cells for it and inventory.

Exhibit C4-2.1
California Car Company
2003 Budgeted Statement of Cash Flows

	A	B	C	D	E	F
5	**Cash Flow from Operating Activities**					
6	Budgeted income - 2003					
7	Add (deduct) adjustments to cash basis:					
8	Depreciation					
9	Change in accounts receivable					
10	Change in inventory					
11	Change in current liabilities					
12	Net cash flow provided by operations					
13	**Cash Flow from Investing Activities**					
14	Purchase of equipment					
15	**Cash Flow From Financing Activities**					
16	Sale of stock					
17						
18						
19	Cash flow provided by financing activities					
20	Net increase in cash and equivalents					
21	Cash at beginning of the year					
22	Cash at the end of the year					

c. When completing the ending 2003 balance in Long-term assets—net, think about what events increase or decrease this account during the year.

d. The ending current liabilities balance is simply the beginning balance plus 1/12 the income tax payable from your income statement. Be careful with the sign because a negative amount in income tax expense cell on your income statement is a positive expense and will result in an increase in current liabilities. If you should happen to have a negative income before tax on your income statement, the ending 2003 current liability balance should be less than the beginning balance.

e. The ending 2003 balance in contributed capital cannot be determined until you complete the cash flow from financing activities in the statement of cash flows. Leave the contributed capital cell blank for now.

f. Complete all blank cells in the statement of cash flows except sale of stock. Note that you need to identify two of the three cash flow from financing activities. Enter all formulas for subtotals and calculation of cash at the end of the year. At this point you should have a large negative balance in cash at the end of the year. You now need to enter in the sale of stock cell an amount, in increments of $1,000,000, that brings the cash at the end of the year to a positive number, but less than $1,000,000.

(Requirements are continued on the next page)

Exhibit C4-2.2
California Car Company
Comparative Balance Sheets

	A	B	C	D	E	F
29					**Budgeted**	**Projected**
30					**2003**	**2002**
31	Assets					
32	Cash					$ 1,462,000
33	Accounts receivable					13,600,000
34	Inventory					840,000
35	Long-term assets—net of depreciation					90,000,000
36	Total Assets					$ 105,902,000
37						
38	Current liabilities					$ 8,853,000
39	Long-term liabilities					10,000,000
40	Total Liabilities					$ 18,853,000
41	Shareholders' Equity					
42	Contributed capital					80,000,000
43	Retained earnings					7,049,000
44	Total Liabilities and Shareholders' Equity					$ 105,902,000

3. Create new budgeted income, balance sheet, and cash flow statements based on George Olson's recommendation of a $70,000,000 level of advertising and a selling price of $19,000 for the sedan and $15,000 for the compact. Use the market share percentages for this combination found in Exhibit C4-1.2, which is 21 percent for the sedan and 24 percent for the compact. Print your new set of financial statements. If you have built your spreadsheet correctly, this should involve changing only the following items:
   a. CCC's market shares for sedans and compacts: 21 and 24 percent,
   b. The selling price for sedans and compacts: $19,000 and $15,000,
   c. The level of advertising: $70,000,000,
   d. The number of labor hours, and
   e. The amount of stock that must be issued on the budgeted cash flow statement.

4. Create new budgeted income, balance sheet, and cash flow statements based on Jena Butler's recommendation of a $40,000,000 level of advertising and a selling price of $21,000 for the sedan and $17,000 for the compact. Use the market share percentages for this combination found in Exhibit C4-1.2, which is 8 percent for the sedan and 10 percent for the compact. Print your new set of financial statements.

Group Assignment 4-2

THE BEST LAID PLANS

Group number ___________ **Signatures of group members participating:**

____

____

Objectives

1. Demonstrate the linkage of financial budgets to the operations of a firm
2. Reinforce financial statement articulation

Assume that your budgeted financial statements for 2003 produced the following numbers:

Budgeted net income (after tax):	$21,000,000 (The income tax rate is 30%)
Cash at end of year:	437,000
Total assets:	252,000,000
Total liabilities and owners' equity:	252,000,000

Assume that CCC's contribution margin ratio is 80 percent.

Each requirement is independent. Use the original numbers given for each question.

1. Compute the new amounts for each of the following if CCC decides that it will declare and pay an additional $1,000,000 dividend in 2003.

   Budgeted net income: No Change

   Cash at end of year: —$1,000,000

   Total assets: —$1,000,000

   Total liabilities and OE: —$1,000,000

2. Compute the new 2003 amounts for each of the following if CCC sells 10 more sedans at $20,000 per sedan. Use the original numbers as a starting point. Assume that accounts receivable and accounts payable do not change.

   Budgeted net income: + 12,000

   Cash at end of year: + 12,000

Total assets: + 12,000

Total liabilities and OE: + 12,000

3. Compute the new 2003 amounts for each of the following if CCC decides to depreciate the $108,000,000 over 8 years instead of 10 years. Assume that this reduction in useful life does not change CCC's tax expense. In other words, the change in pretax income equals the change in net income after tax. Use the original numbers as a starting point.

Budgeted net income: No Change

Cash at end of year: No Change

Total assets: − 2,700,000

Total liabilities and OE: − 2,700,000

4. At a meeting to review the budget, David Gomez states: "The shareholders and bankers demand that we earn at least a $20,000,000 net income in 2003 and issue a maximum of $50,000,000 in new stock. Let's work on a budget that meets these requirements"

   a. Should CCC reduce prices to $19,000 for the sedan and $15,000 for the compact, while increasing advertising to $70,000,000 as George Olsen suggests? Refer to your solution to requirement 3 in Case 4-2.

      Yes.

   b. Should CCC keep the current prices for the sedan and compact and spend $40,000,000 on advertising in 2003? How can CCC meet David's constraints? Refer to your solution to requirement 4 in Case 4-2.

      No.

5. Discuss the advantages and disadvantages related to CCC's issuance of common stock versus borrowing all the cash needed to meet the 2003 budget.

Reading 4-3

Ethical Considerations in Decision Making

INTRODUCTION

Ethics, values, morals, character, and the golden rule all have much in common. What you do affects others and what others do affects you. Discussing ethical considerations in decision making is a challenging and somewhat illusive topic but is very important for everyone. In this reading you are presented with some background on ethical concepts and a practical way to approach ethical dilemmas.

Ethical Decision Making

Ethics can be defined as the moral principles that determine the "rightness" or "wrongness" of human behavior. Even though thoughtful, caring individuals may disagree about the details of ethical behavior, everyone seems to recognize ethical failure when it appears in the media. Ultimately each individual must decide and is responsible for what is right or just.

We all know that information is not necessarily "neutral" or "unbiased." Information can be slanted or distorted by the preparer in order to mislead or deceive others. Financial information is no different. Although numbers may appear to be "objective" because they are quantified measures, numbers—just like any information—may be manipulated by preparers to serve their own purposes. Thus, ethical aspects involved in the preparation and uses of accounting information in decision making are of significance both to the preparers (accountants) and users (internal and external decision makers) of that information.

Management accountants are in a particularly sensitive position in most firms. They have the dual roles of being part of the management team and also have the responsibility to report to top management. In addition, management accountants must be technically competent and follow rules and regulations of the Securities and Exchange Commission, Foreign Corrupt Practices Act, and many others. Although difficult, it is essential that management accountants be fair and objective in fulfilling all of their roles within an organization.

A provocative article in *Management Accounting* reported the results of a recently published study by James Collins and Jerry Porras of Stanford University entitled, "Built to Last: Successful Habits of Visionary Companies." The article reported the Collins and Porras study as stating:

> . . . supports the wisdom of companies becoming more focused on their values and less on the bottom line. The authors studied 18 companies that have an average age of nearly 100 years and that have outperformed the stock market by a factor of 15 since 1926. They studied each company in direct comparison to one of its top competitors. Many of the companies are well known for their excellent ethics programs—Johnson & Johnson, Merck, Motorola, and GE.[1]

---

[1] Susan Jayson, "Ethics Programs: Make Them Real," *Management Accounting*, July 1997, p. 14.

What makes these companies visionary, say Collins and Porras, is that while they seek profits, they are equally guided by a core ideology—core values and a sense of purpose beyond just making money. According to the authors, the key to creating such an organization is to make the core values and ethics of an organization real to the employees and to demonstrate that corporate leadership truly is committed to the program.

The article went on to list and discuss the following recommendations for an effective ethics program:

- Make ethics training real for employees through the use of cases and dilemmas based on situations relevant to the organization.
- Provide employees with on-site support.
- Visually demonstrate leadership's commitment to ethics.
- Make sure integrity and ethical conduct are part of employee performance appraisal.
- Communicate to every employee why ethical behavior is an individual responsibility and should not be delegated to others.
- Harmonize the ethics initiatives throughout the organization.

Top management must support ethics, like any other program or system in an organization, or it will not be effective. An old adage states that the fruit does not fall far from the tree.

According to Michael Josephson of the Josephson Institute of Ethics, surveys of politicians, journalists, lawyers, accountants, students, and others reveal that our society suffers from a lack of ethical behavior. For example, of 8,600 teenagers surveyed across the country during the last 12 months, 71 percent admitted to cheating on an examination, 91 percent said they had lied to their parents, and 27 percent said they would lie to get a job. This, in Michael Josephson's opinion, shows "shocking levels of moral illiteracy."[2] This lack of morality is too often displayed by politicians, businessmen, teachers, and parents based on what is reported in the popular press.

Michael Josephson believes that character is ethics in action. In this regard, he believes that character contains six pillars: trustworthiness, respect, responsibility, fairness, caring, and citizenship. These six pillars are the foundation for his "Character Counts" program that he is presenting throughout the country to businessmen, teachers, coaches, parents, and others. The essence of his concept is that character is how you would act if no one were looking.[3]

Ethical Decision-Making Model

Everyone has ethical dilemmas that they will face in both personal and business situations. A brief description of a "decision model" for dealing with ethical problems that arise is presented below.

The facts: What are the significant facts in the decision problem faced by the decision maker? Get the facts straight before worrying about ethical considerations.

---

[2] Michael Josephson, "In Times of Plenty, Survey Finds U.S. Youth Wanting," *Ethics in Action*, Fall 2000, p. 1 and p. 7.

[3] Based on Michael Josephson, "Ethics Across the Curriculum Workshop," University of San Diego, January 25–26, 2001.

The stakeholders: Identify all parties that may be affected by the alternative courses of action under consideration by the decision maker. Again, try to think broadly about all parties that may potentially be affected by the decision maker's choice of action.

The ethical issue(s): An ethical dilemma is simply a situation involving a choice among two or more alternatives that have significant—often adverse—impacts on others. What is the ethical "dilemma" faced by the decision maker? State the major ethical issues from the decision maker's point of view as possible conflicts: for example, personal benefit vs. compliance with company policy, self esteem vs. loyalty to supervisor, personal financial gain versus honesty and integrity, and so on.

The alternatives: Identify alternative courses of action available to the decision maker. Try to think broadly and creatively about alternatives. Problems are rarely of the "either/or" variety. For example, a narrow view of a problem may suggest that the decision maker must either comply with his or her supervisor or must quit. Viewed more broadly, however, other alternatives might be to refuse to comply and point out to the supervisor your reservations about the request, go around the supervisor and gain necessary support from others, or "blow the whistle" (i.e., go outside the organization and report your supervisor's questionable request).

The consequences: Each alternative should be examined in terms of its positive and negative consequences to all of the identified stakeholders. Consequences should include consideration of economic costs and benefits, basic human rights, and matters of justice, fairness, and equity.

The decision: The decision should reflect an explicit "balancing" of consequences that reflects the decision maker's principles and values.

These steps are summarized in Exhibit 4-3.1.

Exhibit 4-3.1

Six Steps in Ethical Decision Making	
1.	Determine the facts
2.	Identify the stakeholders
3.	Specify the ethical issues involved
4.	Determine the alternatives
5.	Identify the consequences
6.	Make the decision

The ethical decision-making model outlined in Exhibit 4-3.1 is simple, yet very useful when trying to work your way through an ethical dilemma. Following is the complete standard of ethical conduct for management accounting and financial managers as prescribed by the Institute of Management Accountants.

STANDARDS OF ETHICAL CONDUCT FOR MANAGEMENT ACCOUNTING AND FINANCIAL MANAGEMENT

Practitioners of management accounting and financial management have an obligation to the public, their profession, organizations they serve, and themselves to maintain the highest standards of ethical conduct. In recognition of this obligation, the Institute of Management

Accountants (IMA) has promulgated the following standards of ethical conduct for practitioners of management accounting and financial management. Adherence to these standards, both domestically and internationally, is integral to achieving the *Objectives of Management Accounting*. Practitioners of management accounting and financial management shall not commit acts contrary to these standards nor shall they condone the commission of such acts by others within their organizations.[4]

COMPETENCE Practitioners of management accounting and financial management have a responsibility to:

- Maintain an appropriate level of professional competence by ongoing development of their knowledge and skills.
- Perform their professional duties in accordance with relevant laws, regulations, and technical standards.
- Prepare complete and clear reports and recommendations after appropriate analyses of relevant and reliable information.

CONFIDENTIALITY Practitioners of management accounting and financial management have a responsibility to:

- Refrain from disclosing confidential information acquired in the course of their work except when authorized, unless legally obligated to do so.
- Inform subordinates as appropriate regarding the confidentiality of information acquired in the course of their work and monitor their activities to assure the maintenance of that confidentiality.
- Refrain from using or appearing to use confidential information acquired in the course of their work for unethical or illegal advantage either personally or through third parties.

INTEGRITY Practitioners of management accounting and financial management have a responsibility to:

- Avoid actual or apparent conflicts of interest and advise all appropriate parties of any potential conflict.
- Refrain from engaging in any activity that would prejudice their ability to carry out their duties ethically.
- Refuse any gift, favor, or hospitality that would influence or would appear to influence their actions.
- Refrain from either actively or passively subverting the attainment of the organization's legitimate and ethical objectives.
- Recognize and communicate professional limitations or other constraints that would preclude responsible judgment or successful performance of an activity.
- Communicate unfavorable as well as favorable information and professional judgments or opinions.
- Refrain from engaging in or supporting any activity that would discredit the profession.

---

[4] Institute of Management Accountants, "Standards of Ethical Conduct for Practitioners of Management Accounting and Financial Management," *Statement 1C Revised*, April 30, 1997. Reprinted with permission from IMA.

OBJECTIVITY Practitioners of management accounting and financial management have a responsibility to:

- Communicate information fairly and objectively.
- Disclose fully all relevant information that could reasonably be expected to influence an intended user's understanding of the reports, comments, and recommendations presented.

RESOLUTION OF ETHICAL CONFLICT In applying the standards of ethical conduct, practitioners of management accounting and financial management may encounter problems in identifying unethical behavior or in resolving an ethical conflict. When faced with significant ethical issues, practitioners of management accounting and financial management should follow the established policies of the organization bearing on the resolution of such conflict. If these policies do not resolve the ethical conflict, such practitioners of management accounting and financial management should consider the following course of action:

- Discuss such problems with the immediate superior except when it appears that the superior is involved, in which case the problem should be presented initially to the next higher managerial level. If satisfactory resolution cannot be achieved when the problem is initially presented, submit the issues to the next higher managerial level.
- If the immediate superior is the chief executive officer, or equivalent, the acceptable reviewing authority may be a group such as the audit committee, executive committee, board of directors, board of trustees, or owners. Contact with levels above the immediate superior should be initiated only with the superior's knowledge, assuming the superior is not involved. Except where legally prescribed, communication of such problems to authorities or individuals not employed or engaged by the organization is not considered appropriate.
- Clarify relevant issues by confidential discussion with an objective advisor (e.g., IMA Ethics Counseling Service) to obtain an understanding of possible courses of action.
- Consult your own attorney as to legal obligations and rights concerning the ethical conflict.
- If the ethical conflict still exists after exhausting all levels of internal review, there may be no other recourse on significant matters than to resign from the organization and to submit an informative memorandum to an appropriate representative of the organization. After resigning, depending on the nature of the ethical conflict, it may also be appropriate to notify other parties.

MAKING AN ETHICAL DECISION

Sally Potter, controller of Dark Side Industries, has recently encountered an ethical dilemma in regard to how a transaction is to be recorded in the company financial statements. The company president, Mr. Dark, has requested that she make changes in the financial statements so that the company will meet one of its bond indenture conditions.

What Mr. Dark has requested is that Sally Potter include $60,000 of inventory that had been received on the last day of the fiscal year as a current asset in the balance sheet, one day ahead of its scheduled delivery. This is proper accounting. However, he also requested that she *not* include the account payable, a current liability, on the same balance sheet. His reasoning is that the bonds require a current ratio of 2 to 1 and without this "change" the company will be in violation of its bond indenture. This will allow the bondholders to call for full payment of the bonds now.

The current ratio would be 1.5 to 1 ($150,000 current assets and $100,000 current liabilities) without any effect from the inventory purchase. If only the asset side of the transaction is recorded (part of the periodic inventory count), then the current ratio would be 2.1 to 1 ($210,000 current assets and $100,000 current liabilities). Mr. Dark's reasoning is that this may not be proper accounting but it is good for the future of the company and for Sally's future with the company. Also, prospects for next year are very good, as a very lucrative contract has been signed with a large, established company. Sally does not want to make this change because it is improper accounting and is unethical, but she does not want to lose her well-paying job with Dark Side Industries either.

Six Step Ethical Decision

Step 1. Determine the Facts. The facts include: inventory arrived in the current accounting period, proper accounting requires that the payable be set up and shown as a liability on the year-end balance sheet, Mr. Dark does not want the payable to be recorded as required, and the current ratio will be higher than the bonds allow. She should talk with Mr. Dark to make sure that she has the facts correct. Assume that Mr. Dark again made the same request of Sally as outlined above.

Step 2. Identify the Stakeholders. The primary stakeholders would be Sally Potter, Mr. Dark, bondholders, company stockholders, company employees, Sally's family, and Dark's family.

Step 3. Specify the Ethical Issues Involved. The primary dilemma is personal gain (be loyal to the company president and continue to earn a good salary) versus honesty. The short-term personal gain will be weighed against the long-term benefits of honesty.

Step 4. Determine the Alternatives. Sally Potter has four primary alternatives: (1) Refuse to make the change and report the inventory transaction correctly, (2) Discuss the matter further with the president and persuade him to change his mind and report the inventory transaction correctly, (3) Make the change as requested by the president, or (4) Resign her position.

Step 5. Identify the Consequences. The likely consequence of alternative (1) would be for Mr. Dark to fire her. Sally and her family would be the primary stakeholders affected. The likely consequence of alternative (2) is that all stakeholders would benefit in the long run assuming that the bondholders don't request the immediate payment of the bonds. Sally may earn the respect of her superiors.

The likely consequence of alternative (3) is that the incorrect recording will be picked up by either the internal or external auditors and the corrected financial statements will have to be issued. Both Sally Potter and Mr. Dark will, at a minimum, be embarrassed or, at worst, be fired with the possibility of other legal ramifications. If the mistake is not discovered Sally may win the favor of Mr. Dark. The likely consequence of alternative (4) is that Sally is unemployed for a short time and Mr. Dark now has to present the same request to Sally's replacement.

Step 6. Make the Decision. The final decision will be made by Sally Potter based on her personal ethical composition and the consequences of those decisions. The least risky decision is to try alternative (2) first, and if not successful do either (1) or (4) depending on her personal situation and the effect on stakeholders.

Decision Following Professional Standards

If Sally Potter is either a Certified Management Accountant or a Certified Public Accountant, her decision should be guided by the ethical standards of these certification bodies. Both would require full and correct disclosure of the inventory purchase. If she is a CMA, not recording the inventory transaction properly would be in violation of the standards of competency, integrity, and objectivity as presented above in the Standards of Ethical Conduct for Management Accounting and Financial Management. If she were a CPA, not recording the inventory transaction would be a violation of the state law in which her certificate is issued. She will lose both her CMA and CPA certificates if she records the transaction improperly and it is uncovered later.

SUMMARY

There is no substitute for ethical behavior in defining an organization's character. This reading outlined an ethical decision-making model that can be used to help solve ethical dilemmas. Standards of ethical conduct for management accounting and financial managers outlined characteristics for resolution of ethical conflict by practitioners. The reading concluded with an example illustrating how an ethical decision could be made.

EXERCISES AND PROBLEMS

Exercises

Exercise 1 Ethical vs. Economic Dilemma. How does an ethical dilemma differ from an economic dilemma (decision)? Give a simple example of each.

Exercise 2 Ethics in Practice. The Collins and Porras study drew some interesting conclusions. List three reasons why ethical companies also seem to be quite profitable (in their study many times more profitable than the stock market average).

Exercise 3 Facts in Ethical Decision Making. Why are facts so important in making ethical decisions? Explain.

Exercise 4 Conflict of Interest. One of the tenets of the Standards of Ethical Conduct for Practitioners of Management Accounting and Financial Management states, "Avoid actual or apparent conflicts of interest and advise all appropriate parties of any potential conflict." Why is this tenet necessary? And what is meant by "advise all appropriate parties of any potential conflict"?

Exercise 5 Resolution of Ethical Conflict. What is the first step that a CMA should take in resolving an ethical conflict? If this step does not succeed, what should be the second step?

Exercise 6 Objectivity. What does objectivity mean as used in the Standards of Ethical Conduct presented in this reading? Explain briefly.

Exercise 7 Confidentiality. In the IMA Standards of Ethical Conduct under the Confidentiality Standard the third bulleted item states "Refrain from using or appearing to use confidential information acquired in the course of their work for unethical or illegal advantage either personally or through third parties." Why do you think this standard is necessary? Explain briefly.

Problems

Problem 1 Library Research on an Ethical Dilemma. Use your library to find a recent article in a business periodical, for example, *The Wall Street Journal, Business Week,* or other publication, reporting an ethical failure and write a summary of the article. Also include in your summary a listing of the five most significant stakeholders affected by the ethical failure.

Problem 2 Personal Ethical Dilemma. Select a personal situation that you have been involved in that contained an ethical dilemma. Explain in step-by-step fashion (use Exhibit 4-3.1 as a guide) how you made your decision. Explain how your decision-making process could have been improved.

Problem 3 Receiving a Gift. John Sportsmind is controller of Glossy Printing, a large commercial printing and duplicating firm. Glossy Printing is in the process of negotiating a one-year paper contract with three potential suppliers. One potential supplier salesman, Oscar Rodriguez, gave John two tickets to the sixth game of the World Series a few days before the selection was to be made on the paper contract. Based on this information, if John is a CMA, has he violated the Standards of Ethical Conduct? If so, which one?

Problem 4 Friendly Times. Professor Hugh Greene is an avid golfer. A student in one of his classes plays on the university golf team. The professor and the student play golf together at least once per week during the semester. The student performs well in class and receives a high grade. Is there an ethical problem here? If Professor Greene is a CMA, has he violated any standards of ethical conduct? If so, which one(s)?

Problem 5 Good Deal. Jane Highnote, CPA, was auditing the records of an electronics manufacturing firm. The firm's policy is to sell products to employees at "the cost to make." Jane is an avid classical music buff. One of the products of the electronics firm is a DVD player. During the course of the audit, Jane casually mentioned to the company controller her interest in music and the desire to eventually purchase a DVD player. Upon hearing this, the controller stated that he would be willing to extend the company policy to her and to sell a DVD player to her at the discounted employee rate.

Use the six-step ethical decision-making model and the IMA Standards of Ethical Conduct to decide whether Jane should purchase the DVD player from the company she is auditing.

Case 4-3

ETHICAL DECISION AT CALIFORNIA CAR COMPANY

Case Objectives:

1. Review the steps in ethical decision making
2. Illustrate that management accountants are placed in a special ethical position

Decision (Financial reporting): Should the management accountant overreport the number of cars produced?

ETHICAL PROBLEM

It is now July 1, 2003. Assume that you are CCC's manager of cost management, an accounting position within the factory. Your department is responsible primarily for supporting the production management team headed by Sally Swanson, the vice president–production, who is your boss. You and the production people have been working together particularly hard for the past year. First you were involved with establishing an activity-based costing system that was instrumental in focusing attention on CCC's critical problems: setup costs and quality. You then were involved in designing the TQM and JIT systems that brought CCC's costs under control, greatly improving CCC's competitive position. Finally, you are working 60-hour weeks to implement a new balanced scorecard budgeting and performance evaluation system based on both financial and nonfinancial measures.

You purchased an expensive new home one year ago. The purchase stretches your family's finances to the limit, but CCC's bonuses give you a cushion. Unfortunately, your spouse was laid off last month and has no immediate prospects of landing another job. You are already one payment behind on the mortgage and without the bonus you may lose your house.

Over the past couple of years you have become very good friends with Sally Swanson and the other production people. You also have shared in the recognition and praise that the production team has received for the enormous improvements that have been made. Not insignificantly, you also have participated in sizeable performance bonuses that CCC has given the production group.

The six-month performance review is very important at CCC. Overall the JIT and TQM initiatives are working great. Demand for both the sedan and the compact has been strong. Due to supplier problems with the compact's solar panel and May parts shortages for the sedan, the production group was working feverishly to meet their demanding six-month vehicle shipment targets on June 30. After working overtime for two weeks, everyone thought that the production targets would be met. However, CCC's automated paint room broke down on June 30. As a result, the June 30 production runs of both sedans and compacts were not completed on schedule, but will be finished on July 1.

Missing the six-month production targets is very detrimental to morale and means that the production group will not receive a bonus. Since it is your job to report production figures to Jena Butler, vice president–finance, Sally Swanson calls you into her office. Sally explains how close production has come to meeting its targets. She also points out that the paint room problem is not major and that today, July 1, it will again be operative. As a result, CCC will be able to complete twice the normal daily production on July 1. Sally asks that you report the June 30 production as completed even though the cars were not painted until July 1. She argues that CCC will be better off because employee morale will be much higher, resulting in increased production and higher quality in the second half of 2003. She also points out that the overreporting is just a temporary, self-correcting issue, because total production numbers will be accurate after the doubled July 1 production. Finally, Sally appeals to you as a friend and dedicated production team member to help the group.

Requirements

Prepare a word-processed, single-spaced paper of at least one page in length that answers the following questions.

1. Address the following considerations you face in making your decision on whether to overreport June production:
   a. Relevant, significant facts
   b. Stakeholders
   c. Ethical issues involved
   d. Alternatives
   e. Consequences
2. Assuming that you are not a Certified Management Accountant (CMA) or Certified Public Accountant (CPA), would you report the higher production numbers that Sally Swanson requests? Explain.
3. Would your decision change if Sally threatened to fire you if you did not report the higher numbers?
4. Assuming that you are a CMA, would you have any additional professional ethical responsibilities in this situation? Cite any CMA professional code sections (the specific bullets) that apply.
5. Explain why management accountants are placed in a particularly sensitive ethical position compared to production, marketing, and many other employees.

Reading 4-4

CAPITAL BUDGETING

INTRODUCTION

This reading covers two important aspects of long-term decision making. The first part of the reading discusses discounted cash flow concepts, including present value, future value, net present value, and internal rate of return. The second part of the reading covers long-term decision making where discounted cash flow concepts are important aspects of the capital budgeting decision-making process.

STRATEGIC NATURE OF CAPITAL INVESTMENTS

Most management experts believe that making effective long-term investments is absolutely critical to the success of organizations. Firms that make poor investment decisions usually will perform poorly, regardless of how well they manage other aspects of business. Long-term investments include more than the property, plant, and equipment shown on the balance sheet. Other important long-term investments include research and development, employee development, and product and brand market development. Case 4-4 involves an equipment investment decision, but the concepts discussed also apply to other forms of long-term investments.

Long-term investments impact the organization for several years into the future. As a result, one special concern in these types of decisions is the time value of money. The **time value of money** states that the dollar cost of a current investment decision cannot be compared to the dollar benefits received five years from now unless the time value of money is considered. Material is presented in the next few pages to make sure you understand discounted cash flow analysis, net present value, and the internal rate of return before these concepts are used in capital budgeting analysis.

USING PRESENT VALUE CONCEPTS

Present value is the value today of an amount to be received or paid at some future date given a specified interest or discount rate. **Future value** is the value at some future date of an amount invested or borrowed today given a specified interest rate. If someone gave you $100 today, you could invest it for one year at a certain interest rate, 5 percent for example, and at the end of one year it would have grown or "compounded" to $105. If you keep that $105 invested for another year, it will grow to $110.25 at the end of the second year. Not only is the original $100 earning 5 percent in the second year, but the $5 interest you earned in the first year is also earning interest at 5 percent in the second year.

We can generalize this relationship between the present value of a $1 and its future value ($1.05 at n=1, $1.1025 at n=2) as follows:

FV = future value
PV = present value
n = the number of compounding periods
i = the periodic interest rate

$FV_n = PV_0 (1 + i)^n$

e.g., $FV_1 = \$1 (1 + .05)^1 = \$1.05$
$FV_2 = \$1 (1 + .05)^2 = \$1.1025$

$(1 + i)^n$ is what we call the **future value factor.** Factors are always stated in terms of \$1, which can be converted to any number of dollars by multiplying the factor by the number of dollars we are trying to value.

This relationship can be graphically illustrated on the following future value timeline:

i = 5%			
n =	0	1	2
	PV_0	FV_1	FV_2
	\$100	\$105	\$110.25

The amounts in the timeline should be interpreted as follows: The \$100 represents the value now, the present value, of the investment. Next, the \$105 represents the future value of the \$100 one year later (\$100 plus \$5 interest at 5 percent on the \$100). And, the \$110.25 represents the future value of the \$105 one additional year later (\$105 plus \$5.25 interest at 5 percent on the \$105).

Suppose you wanted to know how much you would have to invest at 5 percent at time 0 (today) to get \$105 at time period 1 (one year from now)? In this case you know the future value (\$105) and need to solve for the present value. We can rearrange the future value equation to isolate the PV variable by inverting the present value factor as follows:

$PV_0 = FV_n [1 \div (1 + i)^n]$

e.g., $PV_1 = \$105 (1 \div 1.05) = \$100$
$PV_2 = \$110.25 [1 \div (1.05^2)] = \$100$

$\frac{1}{(1+ i)^n}$ is what we call the **present value factor.**

Notice that the relationship between the present value and the future value is *inverse.* We "compound" the present value at a certain interest rate to arrive at the future value. We "discount" the future value at the same interest rate to arrive at the present value.

What if we want to find out what our \$100 is worth at the end of year 5? If we have a calculator that has an exponential function we can input $(1 + .05)^5$, or alternatively, we could multiply (1.05 × 1.05 × 1.05 × 1.05 × 1.05). Since neither of these solutions may be practical, we suggest using a computer spreadsheet to calculate the present value or future value factors. A computer spreadsheet is a far superior method in "real" business practice because it allows the decision maker to perform sensitivity analysis (answer "what if" questions) much more easily.

Raising a number to a certain power on the computer is usually done by using the ^ sign. So the future value factor formula for year 5 in a computer spreadsheet would be:

Future value factor: =(1 + .05)^5, which equals 1.2763

As shown, our \$100 investment will have grown to \$127.63 (\$100 × 1.2763) after five years assuming interest at 5 percent per year. Please note that the future value factor above was preceded by an equal sign. This must be done when using Excel or the computer thinks the cell formula is a label.

The five-year computation can also be shown by the following future value timeline:

i = 5%						
n =	0	1	2	3	4	5
	PV_0	FV_1	FV_2	FV_3	FV_4	FV_5
	\$100	\$105	\$110.25	\$115.76	\$121.55	\$127.63

The timeline should be interpreted as follows: The \$100 now will grow at 5 percent for one year and equal the future value at the end of the first year of \$105. Then, the \$105 will earn interest at 5 percent for the second year and will have a total future value of \$110.25 (\$105 plus \$5.25 interest earned during the second year). This happens each year so that in the fifth year the \$121.55 balance at the end of year 4 earns interest at 5 percent (\$121.55 × 5% = \$6.08 interest) so the final balance in the account at the end of the fifth year would be \$127.63 (\$121.55 plus interest for year 5 of \$6.08 = \$127.63).

Now let's look at the opposite situation. That is, how do we determine the present value of an investment if we know its future value? We need to compute its present value, as follows:

Present value factor (for computer): =1/((1.05)^5), which equals .7835

Therefore, if we wanted to know how much we would have to invest today at 5 percent annual interest to accumulate to \$127.63 at the end of five years, we can multiply the \$127.63 by the present value factor of .7835. We find that we would have to invest \$100 today (\$127.639 × .7835) at 5 percent to end up with \$127.63 at the end of year 5, just as we expected.

Present Value of an Annuity

An **ordinary annuity** is a series of equal cash flows that are received or paid at the end of each time period in the series. Cash flows occurring at the beginning of each period constitute an "annuity due" and require different applications of these principles. These will not be discussed here.

An example of an annuity is a series of cash flows that you would receive upon your retirement as a result of making a lump-sum payment to a retirement plan today. As an example, suppose you want to determine what amount of cash to invest today at 5 percent annual interest so that you will receive equal annual cash flows of \$10,000 for five years, starting one year from today when you retire. How much will you have to invest today (a cash outflow) to receive all of these future cash inflows and have nothing left in the fund at the end of the five years? It is helpful to plot these cash flows on a present value timeline as follows:

i = 5% 0	1	2	3	4	5
(outflow?)	\$10,000	\$10,000	\$10,000	\$10,000	\$10,000

To find the amount of the lump sum we must invest, you must discount each of the five \$10,000 cash receipts back to the present time (time 0). You will have to use a different present value factor for each year. These factors can be calculated using a computer spreadsheet as illustrated before.

Year	Factor Formula	Factor	Cash Received	PV of Receipt
1	1/(1.05)^1	0.952381	\$10,000	\$ 9,524
2	1/(1.05)^2	0.907030	10,000	9,070
3	1/(1.05)^3	0.863838	10,000	8,638
4	1/(1.05)^4	0.822702	10,000	8,227
5	1/(1.05)^5	0.783526	10,000	7,835
		4.329477		\$ 43,295

In other words, if we invest a sum of \$43,294.77 today at 5 percent, we will be able to receive \$10,000 at the end of each of the next five years, leaving a zero balance in the account at the end of the fifth year. Notice that the same figure could be arrived at by adding up all of the present value factors and multiplying the sum by the annual cash inflow of \$10,000 as follows:

$$4.329477 \times \$10{,}000 = \$43{,}294.77 \text{ rounded to } \$43{,}295$$

We will show a simpler way to determine the present value of these amounts in the following section.

Net Present Value

Net present value (NPV) is defined as the difference between the sum of future cash flows discounted to the present time at the required rate of return and the initial cash outflow made at time 0. The purpose of determining present value is to better understand the financial effects of transactions in today's dollars. We will illustrate the calculation of net present value by using an Excel spreadsheet with a timeline for the cash flows.

Exhibit 4-4.1 illustrates the computer spreadsheet approach to this problem by using mathematical calculations to determine the discount factor for each year. Cell C5 shows the discount rate as 5 percent and cell C6 shows the net present value of the cash inflows and outflows as \$0 by algebraically adding cells B4 through G4. The formulas used to construct the worksheet are presented at the bottom of Exhibit 4-4.1.

There is an easier way to calculate the net present value of these cash flows. The results of this, as well as the formulas used, are shown in Exhibit 4-4.2. We do this by using the NPV formula provided in our spreadsheet program. We show this in cell C4 of Exhibit 4-4.2. As you can see, the computer calculated a zero NPV by this method. In the spreadsheet formula, we give the computer the cell address for the interest rate per period, C3 in our example, the cell address for the annual cash inflows C2 to G2, and then we add the cell address for the initial cash outflow, cell B2, at the end of the formula. The computer does all the calculations for us. This is the simplest way to compute net present value. Please note that when you put =NPV in the beginning of the cell formula you are telling the computer you want it to do a net present value computation. It is very important that the cell references in the rest of the cell formula are entered correctly.

Exhibit 4-4.1

Ordinary Annuity Example – NPV With Discount Factors
Initial Investment of $43,295

	A	B	C	D	E	F	G
1	Year	0	1	2	3	4	5
2	Cash flow	$ (43,295)	$ 10,000	$ 10,000	$ 10,000	$ 10,000	$ 10,000
3	P.V. factor	1.00000	0.95238	0.90703	0.86384	0.82270	0.78353
4	Discounted C.F.	(43,295)	9,524	9,070	8,638	8,227	7,835
5	Discount rate		5%				
6	Net present value		$ (0)				

Selected Formulas

	A	B	C	D	E
1	Year	0	1	2	3
2	Cash flow	-43295	10000	10000	10000
3	P.V. factor	=1/((1+$C$5)^B1)	=1/((1+$C$5)^C1)	=1/((1+$C$5)^D1)	=1/((1+$C$5)^E1)
4	Discounted C.F.	=B2*B3	=C2*C3	=D2*D3	=E2*E3
5	Discount rate		0.05		
6	Net present value		=SUM(B4:G4)		

Exhibit 4-4.2

Ordinary Annuity Example – NPV Using Excel
Initial Investment of $43,295

	A	B	C	D	E	F	G
1	Year	0	1	2	3	4	5
2	Cash flow	$ (43,295)	$ 10,000	$ 10,000	$ 10,000	$ 10,000	$ 10,000
3	Discount rate		5%				
4	Net present value		$ (0)				

Formulas

	A	B	C	D	E	F	G
1	Year	0	1	2	3	4	5
2	Cash flow	-43295	10000	10000	10000	10000	10000
3	Discount rate		0.05				
4	Net present value		=NPV(C3,C2:G2)+B2				

Internal Rate of Return

Internal rate of return (IRR) is the interest rate that will cause the net present value of an investment to equal zero. Thus, the IRR is the rate at which the present value of cash outflows exactly equals the present value of the cash inflows. In the previous retirement annuity example, the interest rate used to compute discounted cash flows was the IRR. By definition, a series of cash flows discounted at the IRR will have a net present value equal to zero. Note that the retirement fund would have a zero balance after the fifth annuity payment is made at the end of year 5. Also, the $43,295 present value of the future cash inflows exactly equaled the $43,295 period 0 cash outflow, thus giving a net present value of zero for the investment.

The computer calculates the IRR (See cell B3 of Exhibit 4-4.3) when we provide the necessary information including the cell addresses for all the cash flows. See cell B3 at the bottom of Exhibit 4-4.3 for the IRR formula.

Exhibit 4-4.3

Ordinary Annuity Example – IRR
Initial Investment of $43,295

	A	B	C	D	E	F	G
1	Year	0	1	2	3	4	5
2	Cash flow	$ (43,295)	$ 10,000	$ 10,000	$ 10,000	$ 10,000	$ 10,000
3	Internal rate of return	5.00%					

Formulas

	A	B	C	D	E	F	G
1	Year	0	1	2	3	4	5
2	Cash flow	-43295	10000	10000	10000	10000	10000
3	Internal rate of return	= IRR(B2:G2)					

To prove that the NPV is indeed equal to zero when the cash flows are discounted at the IRR, we must compute the NPV as shown in Exhibits 4-4.1 and 4-4.2.

Changed Initial Investment

What if our investment advisor had told us that we could receive the same series of $10,000 inflows, but that we would have to invest only $42,000 today? Do you think the actual return on our investment is still 5 percent? Or is it higher or lower than 5 percent? Let's find out. Exhibit 4-4.4 illustrates the spreadsheet approach to solving this problem, with the formulas shown in the lower part of the exhibit.

Using the same timeline as above, but changing the required initial investment to $42,000 (see cell B2), we find that our retirement investment actually has a positive net present value of $1,295 (cell B4) when the future cash flows are discounted at a rate of 5 percent (cell B3). The fact that we have a positive net present value (greater than zero) indicates that we have received a return on our $42,000 investment that is greater than our required 5 percent.

Exhibit 4-4.4

Ordinary Annuity Example – NPV
Initial Investment of $42,000 with a 5 Percent Discount Rate

	A	B	C	D	E	F	G
1	Year	0	1	2	3	4	5
2	Cash flow	$ (42,000)	$ 10,000	$ 10,000	$ 10,000	$ 10,000	$ 10,000
3	Discount rate	5%					
4	Net present value	$ 1,295					

Formulas

	A	B	C	D	E	F	G
1	Year	0	1	2	3	4	5
2	Cash flow	-42000	10000	10000	10000	10000	10000
3	Discount rate	0.05					
4	Net present value	=NPV(5%,C2:G2)+B2					

We still have not answered the question as to what is the actual rate of return on this $42,000 investment. In other words, what is the IRR actually generated by this investment? We must determine what rate of interest would cause the net present value to equal zero when we invest $42,000 and receive five annual cash inflows of $10,000.

One way to solve this is to start guessing at rates above 5 percent until we find the one that results in an NPV of zero. This can be very time consuming. A much faster way to do this is to use a computer spreadsheet. In fact, the computer will "guess" for you. Exhibit 4-4.5 illustrates this approach to solving this problem, with the formulas shown below.

Exhibit 4-4.5
Ordinary Annuity Example – IRR
Initial Investment of $42,000

	A	B	C	D	E	F	G
1	Year	0	1	2	3	4	5
2	Cash flow	$ (42,000)	$ 10,000	$ 10,000	$ 10,000	$ 10,000	$ 10,000
3	Internal rate of return	6.11%					
4	Net present value	$ 0					

Formulas

	A	B	C	D	E	F	G
1	Year	0	1	2	3	4	5
2	Cash flow	-42000	10000	10000	10000	10000	10000
3	Internal rate of return	=IRR(B2:G2)					
4	Net present value	=NPV(B3,C2:G2)+B2					

The actual internal rate of return of this $42,000 investment, which has inflows of $10,000 per year for five years beginning one year from today, is 6.11 percent (see cell B3). At this rate of return (IRR), the net present value of the investment is zero.

To recap what we have done, in Exhibit 4-4.3 the IRR calculated by the computer is 5 percent (see the formula in cell B3 at the bottom). In Exhibit 4-4.4, we have held the 5 percent return constant to calculate what the net present value of a $42,000 investment would be at this required 5 percent rate (see cell B4 at the bottom). Since it has a positive NPV, we know its actual return must be higher than 5 percent. To find the actual return on the $42,000 investment, we let the computer calculate the IRR (see cell B3 of Exhibit 4-4.5).

The present value concepts presented above are very important and are used extensively in the analysis that follows. Before you continue with the capital budgeting materials presented below, be sure you understand the present value concepts presented above.

CAPITAL BUDGETING TECHNIQUES

The capital budgeting process in an organization normally is coordinated with all the other comprehensive budgeting activities. The capital budget most closely aligns with the cash budget and the pro forma financial statements that are part of comprehensive budgeting. Also, the capital budget must fit closely with the organization's long-range strategic plans and operating goals.

Our focus in this text is on discounted cash flow techniques used in the capital budgeting process. Other capital budgeting techniques sometimes used and discussed later include the payback period and the accounting method (sometimes called the finance method). The payback method is often used as a preliminary screen for potential capital budgeting investments to quickly eliminate those with no chance of funding and to provide a measure of risk.

Discounted Cash Flow Analysis

Although understanding discounted cash flow analysis is important, the numerical analysis should be used only as a "reality check" on proposed capital expenditures. Because capital expenditures are critical strategic actions, proposed capital investments first should be evaluated as to whether they advance the strategic interests of the firm. For example, if a firm's strategy is to compete on quality and flexibility, investments in high-speed, but inflexible, equipment that produces highly variable (low quality) products should not be made, regardless of the return on investment shown in the discounted cash flow analysis.

A common practice, at least in the United States, is for a firm to rank its investment opportunities and then fund those with the highest return. This is sometimes referred to as the portfolio approach to investment decisions. Many experts believe that this approach has led to a loss of manufacturing competitiveness and short-term profit maximization behavior at the expense of long-term growth of the firm. There are at least three critical deficiencies with the portfolio approach. First, it is almost impossible to demonstrate high returns on incremental, annual investments that increase the flexibility or quality of a factory. Only when the entire plant is operating on a quality management or JIT basis are the full financial benefits of these approaches realized. If, however, a firm can never justify initial quality or JIT investments, it will never realize the benefits of these approaches.

Second, the portfolio approach tends to under-invest in projects that are more difficult to quantify because they don't fit nicely into discounted cash flow analyses. Benefits of investments in quality and flexibility are often difficult to measure, so firms tend to under-invest in these. More significantly, investments like research and development and employee development are very difficult to quantify objectively, often putting them at a disadvantage when compared to projects that have easily quantifiable benefits and show a high net present value or internal rate of return.

Third, a portfolio approach typically looks only at the cash flows of the proposed project. This assumes that if the investment is not made, nothing negative will happen. In today's competitive environment, however, a failure to make investments that improve quality and flexibility will almost certainly cause a firm to be less competitive and lose income. Therefore, investments in quality and flexibility often must be made just to stay in business.

Impact of Income Taxes

Income taxes are significant cash outflows for most firms, and should be considered when assessing the profitability of proposed investments. The easiest way for most students to include income taxes in a discounted cash flow analysis is to compute taxable income and income tax for each year of a proposed investment. The key to converting the net cash flows laid out in your analysis to taxable income is to: (1) include items in taxable income that are expenses for income purposes, but are not cash flow items (primarily depreciation); and (2) exclude items that are cash flows, but are not expenses for income tax purposes (purchase of equipment or increase in accounts receivable are examples).

Assets at the End of the Analysis

Some assets related to a capital budgeting analysis frequently remain at the end of the analysis time period, and the firm does not intend to sell them at that time. Accounts receivable and inventory are typical examples when a firm is exploring whether to expand production with a purchase of new equipment. Even though these assets are not sold at the end of the analysis period, they should be included as a cash inflow at the end of the period.

Interest Costs

Accountants include interest as an expense on the income statement. Cash payments of interest during the year also are recorded as a cash outflow from operations on the statement of cash flows. When performing capital budgeting analyses, however, interest should not be shown as a cash outflow associated with the project. To do so would be "double counting" because the cost of the funds used in the project is captured by the rate used to discount the cash flows. In addition, how a firm raises the funds for the project and whether any interest is paid should be an independent financing decision. Therefore, even though interest expense is deductible for income tax purposes, *do not* include it as an expense when computing the income tax outflow of a project. You will address these issues in more depth in a finance course.

LITTLE TRAVERSE EXAMPLE

Little Traverse, Inc. (LTI) is considering an investment in a new machine that will produce a new type of boat part used by an LTI customer. The customer will make a three-year commitment to purchase 25,000 parts per year at $30 per part. LTI does not believe that it can sell the product after three years, and does not believe that the machine used to manufacture the part will be of any value in three years. The machine will occupy empty space in the factory building that won't be needed for the next three years. The machine will cost $600,000 to purchase and install, and LTI uses straight-line depreciation. Incremental annual operating expenses, other than depreciation, related to the contract will be $450,000. The customer will pay for the parts as they are delivered, so there will be no increase in accounts receivable. LTI will, however, need to create a $100,000 inventory of material and finished parts to ensure that it can deliver on time. The inventory will be liquidated for its cost of purchase at the end of the contract.

Required: Lay out the cash flows in a timeline on a spreadsheet and compute the net present value and the internal rate of return for the contract. LTI uses a 14 percent discount rate. LTI's income tax rate is 35 percent.

Solution Ignoring Income Taxes

The solution in presented in Exhibit 4-4.6. Note that the inventory is shown as a $100,000 cash outflow in year 0, and a cash inflow in year 3. Why bother to include the inventory cash flows at all since the net effect is zero? Because the $100,000 inflow in year three after being discounted is not equal to the $100,000 outflow in year 0. Also note that the Excel formulas for net present value and internal rate of return (IRR) are shown below the respective headings.

Solution Including Income Taxes

One way to include taxes in the analysis is to compute the net income of the project and include the income tax effect in the analysis. Exhibit 4-4.7 presents the computation of net income and income taxes for the LTI project. Income for each year is computed by subtracting the annual operating cash outflows plus depreciation from the sales revenue. Depreciation is $200,000 ($600,000 ÷ 3). Taxable income, therefore, is $100,000 ($750,000 – $450,000 – $200,000). After deducting tax at 35 percent, net income is $65,000. Notice that the inventory is not an expense (or revenue) for income tax purposes, so it has no tax impact in any year.

Exhibit 4-4.6
Little Traverse, Inc.
Discounted Cash Flow Analysis for the Contract
Income Tax Ignored

	A	B	C	D	E
1		**Year 0**	**Year 1**	**Year 2**	**Year 3**
2	Sales		$ 750,000	$ 750,000	$ 750,000
3	Operating costs		(450,000)	(450,000)	(450,000)
4	Inventory	$ (100,000)			100,000
5	Purchase of machine	(600,000)			
6	**Total Cash Flows**	$ (700,000)	$ 300,000	$ 300,000	$ 400,000
7	**Net present value**	$ 63,987	**Internal rate of return**		19.11%
8	=NPV(.14,C6:E6)+B6		=IRR(B6:E6)		

Exhibit 4-4.7

Little Traverse, Inc.
Income Statement of Proposed Investment
For Each Year, 1, 2, and 3

Added sales revenues		$750,000
Less added costs:		
Operating expenses	$450,000	
Depreciation	200,000	
Total added costs		650,000
Added operating income		$100,000
Less income taxes (35%)		35,000
Added net income		$ 65,000

For larger problems with many more operating expenses, it is often easier to enter the net income related to the project into the discounted cash flow spreadsheet. Adjustments required to move from the accrual-based net income to cash flows are then made. This is the same approach used in the preparation of the indirect approach to the statement of cash flows. For many capital budgeting problems the only adjustment will be for depreciation. Recall that net income is always a positive adjustment. The template for Case 4-4 uses this approach that starts with net income. Exhibit 4-4.8 presents this approach for the LTI example.

Salvage Value

Salvage (or residual or economic) value is the amount received (or estimated to be received at a future date) when a long-lived asset is sold or scrapped. If taxes are ignored, the amount expected to be received is entered into the analysis as a cash inflow in the year it occurs. For example, if the machine purchased by LTI is expected to be sold for $16,000 at the end of year 3, then a cash inflow of $16,000 would be entered in year 3 for salvage. With income tax, if the salvage value used to compute depreciation is the same as the actual salvage value expected at the end of a machine's life, there is no tax to consider in the analysis.

Exhibit 4-4.8
Little Traverse, Inc.
Discounted Cash Flow Analysis for the Contract
Income Tax Included

	A	B	C	D	E
1		**Year 0**	**Year 1**	**Year 2**	**Year 3**
2	Net income		$ 65,000	$ 65,000	$ 65,000
3	Depreciation		200,000	200,000	200,000
4	Inventory	$ (100,000)			100,000
5	Purchase of machine	(600,000)			
6	**Total cash flows**	$ (700,000)	$ 265,000	$ 265,000	$ 365,000
7	**Net present value**	$ (17,270)			
8	**Internal rate of return**	12.60%			

A problem arises, however, when the salvage value used to compute annual depreciation is different from the amount a firm expects to receive when the equipment is sold. The difference between the two salvage values becomes a taxable gain or loss. Note that LTI does not use a salvage value when annual depreciation of $200,000 is computed (see Exhibit 4-4.7). If LTI actually plans to sell the machine for $16,000 at the end of year 3, then the $16,000 will be a taxable gain because the machine will be fully depreciated and have no book value at the end of year 3. In this case, a cash inflow of $16,000 and a cash outflow in the amount of the $5,600 income tax owed (.35 × $16,000) must be entered in year 3.

Alternate Solution Including Income Tax

Although this method is often more confusing for students, many accounting and finance texts show the income tax effects of each cash flow, rather than compute one income tax cash outflow. The notion is that each taxable cash inflow (like sales revenue) increases taxable income, so it is offset by the increase in taxes caused by the cash inflow. Note on the spreadsheet below that the tax on sales revenue row is simply 35 percent of the sales revenue row. Likewise, all tax-deductible cash outflows are offset by the tax savings that these expenses create because they reduce taxable income. Again, the tax savings row is simply 35 percent of the operating cash outflow row. The tax savings on depreciation line is simply 35 percent of the amount of depreciation, $200,000, which is $70,000 ($200,000 × 35%). Some presentations shortcut the analysis by showing all taxable cash inflows and outflows in one row, that is (1-tax rate) times the cash flow. You should see that this is equivalent to adding the cash flows and the tax effects in Exhibit 4-4.9.

Payback Period

Payback is a simple cash flow method of evaluating capital budgeting projects. The **payback period** is the time it takes to get your investment back. For example, if we look at the LTI investment proposal the payback period would be computed as follows:

Payback period = Investment ($600,000 + $100,000) / annual cash inflow ($265,000) = 2.64

This should be interpreted as a payback period of 2.64 years. A payback period of 2.64 years for a project with a three-year life is a very poor payback period. Many companies will not invest in any project if the payback period is more than one-half of the life of the project. This rule of thumb is adopted to eliminate more risky projects. If a project can return its initial investment in less than half its life, unfavorable future economic events are less likely to make the investment unprofitable.

Exhibit 4-4.9
Little Traverse, Inc.
Discounted Cash Flow Analysis for the Contract
Alternate Analysis

	A	B	C	D	E
1		**Year 0**	**Year 1**	**Year 2**	**Year 3**
2	Sales revenue		$ 750,000	$ 750,000	$ 750,000
3	Tax on sales revenue		(262,500)	(262,500)	(262,500)
4	Operating costs		(450,000)	(450,000)	(450,000)
5	Tax savings on operating costs		157,500	157,500	157,500
6	Inventory	$ (100,000)			100,000
7	Purchase of machine	(600,000)			
8	Tax savings on depreciation		70,000	70,000	70,000
9	**Total cash flows**	$ (700,000)	$ 265,000	$ 265,000	$ 365,000
10	**Net present value**	$ (17,270)			
11	**Internal rate of return**	12.60%			

Accounting Rate of Return

The accounting rate of return (often called the finance method) is not a cash flow method. The **accounting rate of return** (ARR) is based on the net income of the proposed project (see Exhibit 4-4.7) divided by the net investment at the beginning of the project. For the LTI project, the ARR would be computed as follows:

Accounting rate of return:
Net income ($65,000)/Investment ($600,000 + $100,000) = .0929

This should be interpreted as a 9.29 percent return on the investment. This is not a good rate of return on an investment and would be an indication that the company should not invest in the new machine. The ARR method is not based on discounted cash flows and is the least used of the capital budgeting techniques discussed in this reading.

CHOOSING BETWEEN ALTERNATIVE INVESTMENTS

Many long-term decisions involve choosing between two or more competing alternatives. The general approach to analyzing these types of problems is to find the NPV of each alternative first. The NPVs for all alternatives are then compared, and the alternative with the highest NPV is the best from a pure financial perspective. An example is presented below.

Decision: Should Amy, a second-semester sophomore majoring in accounting, take out a loan and finish her degree in two years or should she work 30 hours a week and finish her degree part-time in four years?

Information:

Pay rate at part-time job:	$8 per hour/$240 per week
Number of weeks worked:	35 per school year (Amy will work summers at $8 per hour under either option)

Discount rate:	Amy feels that she could earn about 5 percent with low risk.
Professional accounting pay:	Beginning salary of $40,000 with an 8 percent average salary increase.
Student loan:	$9,000 per year for two years. First $9,000 will arrive at the beginning of junior year. Loan will have a 6 percent interest rate and Amy will pay it back over 5 years once she starts working.
Analysis time horizon:	7 years

Although there are other cash inflows and outflows faced by Amy (e.g., living expenses and summer earnings), we don't have to worry about including them in the analysis because they are approximately the same under either alternative. Including them would change the numbers for each option separately, but the difference between the two options (what Amy really cares about) would remain the same. Accountants would say these inflows and outflows are not relevant to Amy's decision. In this example we will assume (to simplify computations) that any cash flows that occur anytime during the year are discounted from the end of the year.

Note that there are other nonquantitative advantages to going to school full-time. One is that Amy will have more time to participate in student activities and interact with faculty and other students, including study groups (all studies show that students who work extensively in peer groups find college more rewarding than those who do not). Amy would also be in a better position to take a summer internship position because she would not have to give up her part-time job to do so.

Solution

The solution to Amy's analysis is presented in Exhibit 4-4.10. Note that if Amy were a second semester sophomore in the spring, the analysis would begin the following August, which is labeled now on the solution (remember that she is going to work this coming summer under either alternative). Year 1 in the solution will represent her junior year if she attends school full-time. Year 2 will represent her senior year, Year 3 her first year at work, and so on. Also note that the years in the solution don't have to correspond to calendar years, but can begin and end in August. As can be seen in the last line of Exhibit 4-4.10, Amy will be $54,558 better off if she goes to school full-time and borrows money than if she goes to school part-time and works part time. This solution ignores the impact of income taxes.

SUMMARY

Capital budgeting is a significant component of successful long-range planning that is needed for organizations to prosper. The most useful technique to measure potential success of a proposed capital investment is to use discounted cash flow analysis, such as net present value and internal rate of return. In this reading we introduced many of the common capital budgeting cash flow analysis techniques used in business today.

Exhibit 4-4.10
Solution to Student Loan Decision

BORROW ALTERNATIVE

	Year 0	Year 1	Year 2	Year 3	Year 4	Year 5	Year 6	Year 7
Cash Inflows:								
Accounting pay	$0	$0	$0	$40,000	$43,200	$46,656	$50,388	$54,420
Student loan	9,000	9,000	0	0	0	0	0	0
Cash Outflows:								
Repay loan	0	0	0	(4,945)	(4,945)	(4,945)	(4,945)	(4,945)
Net cash flows	$9,000	$9,000	$0	$35,055	$38,255	$41,711	$45,443	$49,475

NPV = $181,079

Note: The $18,000 loan plus accrued interest will total $20,832 in year 3. A five-year amortization of the $20,832 at 6% is $4,945 per year.

PART-TIME WORK ALTERNATIVE

	Year 0	Year 1	Year 2	Year 3	Year 4	Year 5	Year 6	Year 7
Cash Inflows:								
Accounting pay	$0	$0	$0	$0	$0	$40,000	$43,200	$46,656
Part-time work	0	8,400	8,400	8,400	8,400	0	0	0
Cash Outflows:								
None	0	0	0	0	0	0	0	0
Net cash flows	$0	$8,400	$8,400	$8,400	$8,400	$40,000	$43,200	$46,656

NPV = $126,521

Advantage of taking out the loan: $181,079 – $126,521 = $54,558

EXERCISES AND PROBLEMS

Exercises

Exercise 1 Present Value and Future Value. Explain how present value and future value are related; that is, how you get from one to the other.

Exercise 2 Present Value Factor. The present value factor for 6 percent for 10 periods is .558. Explain how you could use the .558 present value factor.

Exercise 3 Annuity. Define annuity. Distinguish between an ordinary annuity and an annuity due.

Exercise 4 Net Present Value. Define net present value. If an investment has a positive net present value, what does that signify?

Exercise 5 Internal Rate of Return. Define internal rate of return. Why is the net present value of an investment always zero when discounting at the internal rate of return?

Exercise 6 Cash Flow Timeline. You can purchase today a machine for $18,000 that will increase your annual net cash inflow for each of the next four years by $5,500. The machine will have a salvage value of $3,000 at the end of year 4. Prepare a cash flow timeline similar to Exhibit 4-4.2 by using this information. Do not try to determine the net present value or internal rate of return on this investment.

Exercise 7 Net Present Value. Max's father put enough money in the bank today so that he will have $12,000 when he turns 21 in five years. The bank pays interest at 5 percent, compounded annually. How much money did Max's father put in the bank today? Show computations.

Exercise 8 Present Value of Annuity. Determine the present value of an annuity of $3,000 per year for 10 years at 6 percent interest. Explain whether the present value would be larger or smaller if the interest rate was 8 percent for 10 years.

Exercise 9 Cash Flow from Net Income. Tom Company had the following items, among others, on its income statement for 2002: Sales revenues, $600,000; operating expenses, $400,000 (including $30,000 of depreciation); income tax expense, $80,000; and net income, $120,000. Based on this information, determine the amount of cash flow from operations for 2002 that could be used in capital budgeting analysis.

Exercise 10 Depreciation and Cash Flows. When performing discounted cash flow analysis, how is depreciation included in the analysis when income taxes are included? Explain briefly.

Exercise 11 Payback Period. How is the payback period determined for an investment? What is its major advantage?

Exercise 12 Accounting Rate of Return. How is the accounting rate of return determined for an investment? What is its major disadvantage?

Problems

Problem 1 Net Present Value Calculation. Alcala Candy Company is considering the purchase of a new candy processing machine. The machine would cost $27,000 to purchase and install. It is estimated that it would last six years and that it would reduce operating costs (mostly labor and utility costs) by $6,400 per year. The machine would have a salvage value of $3,000 at the end of its six-year life. Alcala requires a 12 percent return on all investments. Determine the net present value of the machine. Ignore income taxes and use Exhibit 4-4.4 as an example for your solution. Would you recommend that Alcala Candy Company purchase the new candy processing machine?

Problem 2 Net Present Value and Income Taxes. This is an extension of Problem 1. Assume the same facts as in Problem 1 and in addition that Alcala Candy Company pays 40 percent in federal and state income taxes. Also assume that the machine will be depreciated over the six-year life without considering salvage value, that is, that the full $27,000 will be written off over the six-year life of the machine. This will then cause the $3,000 salvage value to be a taxable gain in year 6. Your solution should look similar in layout to Exhibit 4-4.8 or 4-4.9.

Problem 3 Net Present Value and Internal Rate of Return. Cho Industries is considering the addition of a new product to its operations. The new product would produce net cash benefits, before income taxes, of $22,000 per year. The investment in equipment, inventory, and other items would be $110,000. The investment will be evaluated over a seven-year period. At the end of the seventh year, the recoverable value of the equipment and inventory is expected to be $18,000. Assuming Cho Industries requires a 16 percent return on all investments, should it invest in the new product? Prepare a solution similar to Exhibit 4-4.5 for Cho Industries to determine the net present value and the internal rate of return on the proposed investment.

Problem 4 Payback Period and the Accounting Rate of Return. Bumble Chip Company is a large computer chip maker. Bumble has recently received a large, special order from a Canadian company that would have the following income implication each year for the life of the contract:

Added sales revenues		$400,000
Added expenses:		
Cash operating expense	$300,000	
Depreciation	40,000	
Total added expenses		340,000
Added operating income		$ 60,000
Less income taxes (40%)		24,000
Added net income		$ 36,000

The Canadian company is willing to enter into a five-year, non-cancelable contract with Bumble Chip Company. The added cost of equipment and working capital to Bumble would be $240,000. Bumble requires a 14 percent return on all investments and a payback period of less than 60 percent of the life of the equipment (contract). Determine the payback period and the accounting rate of return for Bumble Chip Company. Should Bumble accept the order? Why?

Problem 5 Net Present Value and IRR Computations. Juan's Tortilla Factory would like to automate its facilities. Juan has found a machine that would cost $33,000 to purchase, has a useful life of 10 years, has no salvage value, and would save him $6,000 in cash operating costs per year. His desired rate of return is 12 percent.

Show supporting computations when answering the following.

a. Ignore income taxes. What is the net present value of the machine investment?

b. Ignore income taxes. What is the internal rate of return on the machine investment?

c. Assume a 30 percent income tax rate for Juan. What is the net present value of the machine investment?

d. Based on the information in c, should Juan purchase the machine for his business? Explain briefly.

Problem 6 Net Present Value Concepts. Donna Debit has just completed her accounting major at Anywhere University. She has accepted a position with a large public accounting firm for $45,000 a year. She would like to purchase a home to live in and has talked to a mortgage broker to evaluate her options. He told her that in addition to the $25,000 she has for a down payment, she would have to pay 7 percent interest on a 30-year mortgage loan. The maximum loan payment would be limited to one-third of her gross salary. Assume that Donna would make only one annual payment on the loan each year.

Use this information to determine the maximum amount that Donna could pay for a house. *Hint:* Remember that Donna has $25,000 for a down payment on the house.

Case 4-4

CAPITAL BUDGETING AT CALIFORNIA CAR COMPANY

Case Objectives

1. Introduce the basics of capital budgeting
2. Review time value of money and present value concepts

Decision (Planning): Should CCC invest $108,000,000, $74,000,000, or nothing in new equipment?

David Gomez, president of CCC, has been reviewing the 2003 financial budget and is concerned about the $108,000,000 investment in new equipment that is part of the budget. He states to Jena Butler, vice president–finance: "The $108,000,000 investment in new equipment is quite a commitment for CCC. Our net long-term assets at the end of 2002 are expected to total only $134,000,000. The new equipment is almost equal to our current investment in all of our assets! Are we sure that the benefits of the new equipment justify the investment? If purchase of the equipment turns out to be a major mistake, it could jeopardize CCC's financial stability. Can you have someone on your staff prepare a more detailed analysis of the new equipment purchase?"

Jena Butler has asked you to prepare an analysis of the new equipment purchase. Jena suggests that your first step is to talk to Sally Swanson, vice president–production, about the purchase. You schedule a meeting with Sally and ask her what the new equipment will do for CCC and if there are any other alternatives. Sally states:

> The new equipment will be installed during our end-of-year shutdown and will begin producing sedans on January 15, 2003. The equipment will make CCC a formidable competitor in the hybrid vehicle industry. The equipment is specially designed to be flexible, to be reliable, and to produce high-quality cars. By flexible, I mean that it will be very easy to manufacture cars with features that are special-ordered by individual customers. For example, if a customer orders a green convertible sedan with air conditioning and a CD player, we can economically build that car so the customer doesn't have to wait until we can produce a large run of similar cars.
>
> With respect to alternatives, we could purchase less flexible, less reliable equipment similar to our current machinery for about $74,000,000. This equipment, however, will seriously impair our efforts to implement a JIT system that is on a par with Toyota's current system or the capabilities of the other U.S. auto manufacturers. Both equipment purchases will increase CCC's production capacity to 12,000 sedans and 9,000 compacts per year. Without any new equipment, our production capacity will remain capped at its current level of 6,000 sedans (working two shifts) and 3,000 compacts per year.

After receiving this useful information from Sally, you decide to touch base with Jena to get a better feel for the parameters you should use in your analysis. In response to your question, Jena states:

> Since the new $108,000,000 equipment has an estimated useful life of 10 years, I suggest that you use a 10-year time period in your analysis. In addition, assume that the equipment will have a $4,000,000 economic (salvage) value at the end of 10 years, even though we will have fully depreciated it for financial statement purposes. When considering the $74,000,000 equipment, assume no economic value at the end of 10 years.
>
> Also assume that if no new equipment is purchased, annual cash flows from operations will be $8,090,000. If we purchase the new equipment, we will manufacture and sell 12,000 sedans and 7,200 compacts at a selling price of $19,000 and $15,000, respectively. This was management's final decision after reviewing the planning budget in Case 4-2. Assume this level of sales revenue for all 10 years.

The easiest way to compute the net increase in operating cash flows from the new investment is to:

a. Start with the estimated net income for each year. For your analysis use the budgeted net income for 2003 shown in Exhibit C4-4.2 for each of the 10 years for the $108 million alternative. Compute the $74 million alternative income by reducing the depreciation and increasing poor quality costs by $4,000,000.

b. Make the same adjustments to net income you do in an indirect statement of cash flows. For this analysis assume that inventories, prepaid assets, and current liabilities are unaffected by the equipment purchase. This means you don't have to make any adjustments for capital budgeting purposes. Assume that all expenses are paid for in the year incurred.

c. Accounts receivable is the odd account. It will increase by $46,000,000 at the beginning of the first year (year zero in the analysis), but there will be no other changes in the balance for the rest of the 10 years. Assume that there are no uncollectable accounts. At the end of 10 years, however, we will have $46,000,000 more accounts receivable than if we don't expand, so the correct way to handle this is to show on your spreadsheet a cash *inflow* of $46,000,000 in year 10 for accounts receivable.

d. A good way to show the incremental impact of the new investment is to enter CCC's $8,090,000 net cash flow if no new machines are purchased as a negative cash flow for each alternative. By including this, you have shown the net effect of the new equipment on the operations of CCC.

Your first reaction is that this is too much to absorb. Jena, however, helps you set up the format in Exhibit C4-4.1 and enters some numbers for you.

Requirements

1. On a spreadsheet, lay out the 10-year cash flows for the two alternatives: (a) purchase the $108,000,000 new equipment, or (b) purchase the $74,000,000 new equipment. Use the format presented in Exhibit C4-4.1. Note that years 2 through 9 are shown in one column to save space, but you will need to create in your spreadsheet a separate column for each year. CCC's income tax rate is 30 percent. Recall that the equipment will be

purchased by giving the vendor a note payable in the amount of $108M. Interest on this note *should not* be included in the cash flow analysis because how the equipment is financed is a separate decision.

2. Compute the net present value and internal rate of return for each alternative in Requirement 1. CCC uses a 17 percent discount rate in calculating net present value.

Exhibit C4-4.1
California Car Company
Discounted Cash Flow Analysis Format

	A	B	C	D	E	G
5	**Alternative: $108,000,000 Equipment**					
6			**Year 0**	**Year 1**	**Years 2-9**	**Year 10**
7		**Cash Flows:**				
8	Equipment purchase		$ (108,000,000)			
9	**Operating cash flow:**					
10		Net income				
11						
12	Increase in accounts receivable					
13	No purchase cash flows			(8,090,000)	(8,090,000)	(8,090,000)
14	Residual value					
15	Tax on salvage value					
16	**Total net cash flows:**					
17						
18			**NPV =**		**IRR =**	
19						
20	**Alternative: $74,000,000 Equipment**					
21			**Year 0**	**Year 1**	**Years 2-9**	**Year 10**
22		**Cash Flows:**				
23	Equipment purchase		$ (108,000,000)			
24	**Operating cash flow:**					
25		Net income				
26						
27	Increase in accounts receivable					
28	No purchase cash flows			(8,090,000)	(8,090,000)	(8,090,000)
29	Residual value					
30	Tax on salvage value					
31	**Total net cash flows:**					
32						
33			**NPV =**		**IRR =**	

3. Because of the significance of the investment, David Gomez has discussed the two options with the board of directors. The board strongly supports the $74,000,000 alternative because of its higher NPV. Prepare a one-page, word-processed analysis reporting your equipment purchase recommendation to David Gomez. Be sure to conclude whether CCC should (1) buy the $108,000,000 equipment, (2) buy the $74,000,000 equipment, or (3) buy no equipment at all.

(Requirements continue on the next page)

4. George Olsen believes that, based on CCC's improved quality and reputation and resulting ability to offer less generous terms, the level of accounts receivable can be reduced by $10,000,000 per year in each of the first four years of the project. This will reduce the year 10 inflow from accounts receivable to just $6,000,000. This reduction in accounts receivable will not happen if the $74,000,000 alternative is selected. Compute a new NPV and IRR for both alternatives under George's new assumption. Why did the NPV and IRR change so much when the total amount of the cash inflow for inventory in years 1 through 10 remain the same as before?

Exhibit C4-4.2
Budgeted 2003 Income Statement

	A	B	C	D	E	F
14			**Units**	**Price or**	**Subtotal**	**Income**
15				**Cost**	**(Extension)**	**Statement**
16	Sales:		Cars			
17	Sedan		12,000	$ 19,000	228,000,000	
18	Compact		7,200	15,000	108,000,000	
19	Total sales					$ 336,000,000
20	Variable costs:		Cars			
21	Material:	Sedan	12,000	$ 2,980	35,760,000	
22		Compact	7,200	3,360	24,192,000	59,952,000
23	Maintenance:		Maint. hours			
24		Sedan	52,800	$ 42	2,217,600	
25		Compact	52,560	42	2,207,520	4,425,120
26	Contribution margin					$ 271,622,880
27	Step costs:		Labor hours			
28	Labor:	Sedan	2,070,000	$ 35.00	72,450,000	
29		Compact	860,000	35.00	30,100,000	102,550,000
30	General factory overhead:					
31	First shift				7,000,000	
32	Second shift				3,000,000	10,000,000
33	Other fixed costs:					
34	Depreciation:					
35	Sedan, existing equipment				5,100,000	
36	Sedan, new equipment				10,800,000	
37	Compact				2,040,000	17,940,000
38	Selling					46,000,000
39	Administrative					46,000,000
40	Interest expense					8,640,000
41	Total fixed costs					231,130,000
42	Income before tax					40,492,880
43	Less: income tax					(12,147,864)
44	Budgeted net income					$ 28,345,016

Reading 4-5

STANDARD SETTING, PERFORMANCE EVALUATION, AND THE BALANCED SCORECARD

INTRODUCTION

Reading 4-1 introduced the topic of performance evaluation and briefly described how CCC uses accounting information for performance evaluation purposes. Performance budgets were introduced in Reading 2-7, and you prepared a performance budget in Case 2-7. Therefore, the purpose of this reading is to expand on the previous performance evaluation coverage and discuss behavioral implications of standard setting and performance evaluation. The concluding materials discuss and illustrate how CCC uses the balanced scorecard in performance planning and evaluation.

EVOLUTION OF PLANNING AND CONTROL SYSTEMS

Planning is the management function of selecting goals, predicting results of specified plans, and deciding how to attain the selected goals. **Control** is the management function that seeks to ensure that plans are being followed and appropriately modified as circumstances change. Most organizations progress step-by-step over time through the following four levels of planning and control (or management control) sophistication:

1. Prepare operating and financial planning budgets for communication, coordination, and resource allocation purposes.

2. Compare the *planning budget* with actual results for performance evaluation purposes.

3. Compare the *performance budget* with actual results for performance evaluation purposes and analyze variances.

4. Integrate nonfinancial measures into the process to create a balanced scorecard for communication and performance evaluation purposes.

While organizations of all sizes prepare planning budgets, and most compare planning budgets with actual results, many never advance to level four. You should note that the terminology that organizations use is not consistent in the planning and control area. For example, a firm may use nonfinancial measures linked to key success factors, but may have managers who have never heard of the term " balanced scorecard." The **balanced scorecard** contains performance evaluations based on a variety of operating (internal), customer (external), learning and growth, and financial measures.

THE MANAGEMENT CONTROL CYCLE

Our focus will be on the management control cycle that is part of an overall management control system of an organization. A management control system is the total process of gathering information to help in coordinating the decision-making process in an organization. Organizations go through a periodic (usually once a year) management control cycle. Exhibit 4-5.1 presents a schematic of the management control cycle. The first step is to set standards for variable and step costs and some nonfinancial items. Examples of **standards** are material cost per completed unit and defect rate. Some standards, including those for labor and material cost per unit, are broken down into a rate and price standard as illustrated later in this reading. The standard labor cost per unit (if labor is considered to be a variable rather than a step cost) is determined by setting a standard number of labor hours per unit and a standard labor rate per hour.

Exhibit 4-5.1

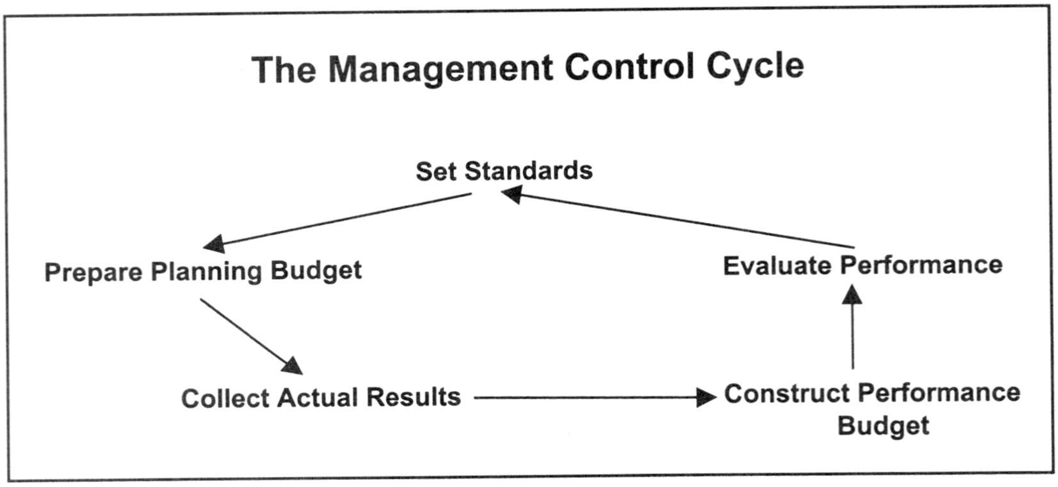

Although you have prepared budgets earlier in the course (Cases 2-4, 4-1, and 4-2), the standards were given to you. Setting standards is, however, the most critical part of the cycle. Improperly set standards can reduce employees' motivation and, in extreme cases, impair their productivity and effectiveness. These issues are discussed later in this reading. Key input into the standard-setting process is the performance evaluation report from the previous period, because previous results will help determine what is reasonably attainable in the next period. Also, benchmarking will help form the basis for setting standards. For example, the benchmark performance of the best firm in the world helps move the focus toward how to improve and how much improvement should be made in the coming year. For example, recent data show that the average cost (costs included labor and outsourcing) to process an accounts payable transaction is $3.55, whereas the best practices of companies that have reengineered this process have a cost of $0.54. If you are a company with average accounts payable transaction costs, there is considerable room for reducing costs in future budget cycles.

The second step of the management control cycle is to prepare the planning budget (operating and financial budgets). The budgeting process was explained and illustrated in Reading 4-1. The planning budget is constructed by first determining the planned level of unit sales and production for the coming period. Using the standards set in the first step, the total variable and step costs plus variable nonfinancial measures are determined. The planning budget is completed by estimating the level of fixed costs and "fixed" nonfinancial measures that are expected for the coming period.

The third step is to collect actual results. Most of the revenue and cost data are collected by the organization's accounting information system. Some of the nonfinancial data and a few cost items (particularly ABC information) are collected by ad hoc (or informal) information systems. The accounting information system is by far the largest system in most organizations. A large number of accounting and management information systems people are employed to design, maintain, and operate these systems.

The fourth step is to construct the **performance (control) budget** and collect other relevant performance information. You constructed a performance budget in Case 2-7, and you will construct another one in Case 4-5. By this point you should have little trouble in constructing a performance budget. In order to prepare a fair evaluation, you must also collect all other information, both quantitative and qualitative, that is available and relevant.

The final step in the management control cycle is to evaluate either the manager or the business unit performance, or both, based on the performance budget and other information collected. This, along with setting standards, is the most important part of the cycle. Evaluating performance is a subjective process that requires the manager to synthesize all the information, to subjectively weigh various bits of information, and to produce a holistic judgment on performance that is summarized in a **performance report.**

Balanced Scorecard Performance Report Example

An example of a balanced scorecard performance report for a small company that has recently implemented a continuous quality improvement program is illustrated in Exhibit 4-5.2. The company, Maryanne's Machine Shop, Inc. (MMS), is a relatively small family-owned business that specializes in machining steel, aluminum, and similar metals for industrial customers. Presented in Exhibit 4-5.2 is a condensed performance report for MMS for 2002. Will MMS be happy with the performance of its employees?

Exhibit 4-5.2

Maryanne's Machine Shop, Inc.
Balanced Scorecard Performance Report
Year Ended December 31, 2002

Item	**Performance Budget**	**Actual**	**Variance**	**F/U**
Direct labor	$ 100,000	$ 102,000	$ (2,000)	U
Supplies	18,000	18,500	(500)	U
Setups	33,000	32,000	1,000	F
Maintenance	14,000	14,000	0	-
Power	9,500	9,800	(300)	U
Others	20,000	21,000	(1,000)	U
Totals	$ 194,500	$ 197,300	$ (2,800)	U
Nonfinancial Items				
Percent on-time deliveries	90%	88%	-2%	U
Customer reported defects	1%	3%	-2%	U
Percent rework cost (of total job budgeted variable cost)	5%	6%	-1%	U
Supplier defect rate	2%	5%	-3%	U

You may have noticed that there are no direct materials listed in the report. MMS has its industrial customers furnish all materials so there is no variance for material costs. Next, in interpreting the financial data, the overall variance of $2,800, unfavorable, is only 1.44 percent of total costs ($2,800 ÷ $194,500). This reflects reasonably good performance for the year. However, it would be desirable to look at the details behind the direct labor and setup variances. Could some setup costs be misclassified as direct labor costs, thus causing a favorable setup cost variance and part of the unfavorable direct labor cost variance?

All the nonfinancial measures of performance are unfavorable. This should be of some concern. The two most troublesome variances are the customer-reported defect rate at 3 times the budgeted rate of 1 percent and the supplier defect rate at 2.5 times the budgeted rate of 2 percent. These two variances could be related. The accounting staff and the operating personnel should look behind the numbers to see what the problem is and to plan how they can perform better in 2003.

A Closer Look at Variances

A variance is the difference between a planned amount, a standard or budget, and the cost incurred. The variance can be based on aggregated data or it can be the result of a single cost item. In the following section we will illustrate how variances can be broken down into more detail.

Direct Labor Variances

Direct labor and direct material variances are often broken down into more detailed variances. For example, the direct labor variance can be separated into a direct labor rate variance and a direct labor efficiency variance. The **direct labor rate variance** represents the difference between the actual labor rate paid to employees and the budgeted rate (or standard rate) that was planned, multiplied by the actual hours. The direct labor rate variance can be computed as follows:

(Actual direct labor rate – Budgeted direct labor rate) × Actual direct labor hours

For MMS the direct labor rate variance can be computed as follows (using assumed actual hours and the budgeted rate of pay):

($9.9029 – $10.00) × 10,300 = $1,000 favorable variance

In the preceding computation, we assumed that 10,300 actual direct labor hours were worked during the year and that the budgeted labor rate for the year was $10 per direct labor hour. The actual direct labor rate paid employees during the year is approximately $9.9029 ($102,000 cost divided by 10,300 direct labor hours). Thus, the variance is favorable as indicated in the computation because the actual rate paid was less than the planned rate of pay.

The **direct labor efficiency variance** represents the difference between the actual direct labor hours worked and the hours that should have been worked to produce the output for the period, multiplied by the budgeted (or standard) direct labor pay rate. The direct labor efficiency variance can be computed as follows:

Budgeted rate of pay × (Actual direct labor hours worked – Direct labor hours allowed)

Since the budgeted rate of pay is known, \$10 per hour, and the actual hours worked are known, 10,300, the only component of the computation that is unknown is the direct labor hours needed. Direct labor hours needed is an output measure, and is the number of hours that *should have been worked* to produce the output for the period. In the case of MMS, the number of hours that should have been worked is 10,000, based on the units produced. Using this information, we can now compute the direct labor efficiency variance as follows:

$$\$10 \times (10{,}300 - 10{,}000) = \$10 \times 300 = \$3{,}000 \text{ unfavorable labor efficiency variance}$$

The direct labor efficiency variance computed is unfavorable because the actual direct labor hours worked is 300 hours more than what should have been worked to attain the output for the period. The 10,000 hours are normally referred to as control budget hours allowed or standard hours allowed for production attained.

The sum of the two direct labor variances equals the \$2,000 unfavorable variance shown in Exhibit 4-5.2 (\$1,000 favorable less \$3,000 unfavorable = \$2,000 unfavorable variance). The purpose of determining the direct labor rate and efficiency variances is to break down into smaller parts the total variance for direct labor shown in the performance report and to help in determining the causes of the variances.

Direct Material Variances

Similar variances to those illustrated for direct labor can be computed for direct materials. Since MMS does not purchase direct materials (customers furnish the direct materials), the material variance computations will be illustrated by using amounts for another company. The **direct material price variance** can be computed as follows:

> Actual direct material cost – (Actual quantity of direct material purchased × Budgeted direct material cost per unit)

NowCo produces a single product from a single raw material. Each unit of product uses one pound of raw material, goral, that has a standard cost (planning budget cost) of \$3.00 per pound. During the year, NowCo purchased 30,000 pounds of goral for \$91,500 and used all of the material to produce 29,000 units of product. Using this information, we can compute the direct material price variance as follows:

$$\$91{,}500 - (30{,}000 \times \$3.00) = \$91{,}500 - \$90{,}000 = \$1{,}500 \text{ unfavorable variance}$$

The direct material price variance is unfavorable because NowCo paid more than \$3.00 per pound for goral. Apparently they paid \$3.05 per pound (\$91,500 ÷ 30,000 pounds purchased). The direct material price variance computation is parallel to the direct labor rate variance computation. The resulting variance represents the difference between the actual cost per unit and the budgeted (or standard) cost per unit paid for direct material. Sometimes this variance is called the materials spending variance. If the actual cost per unit of purchased direct material is higher than the budgeted cost per unit, then the price variance is unfavorable, as it was for NowCo. The variance is favorable if the actual cost per unit of purchased direct material is lower than the budgeted cost per unit.

The **direct material usage variance** represents the difference between the direct material used in production and the direct material that *should have been used* to produce the output for the period, multiplied by the budgeted material cost per unit. As with the direct labor efficiency variance, the direct material that should have been used to produce the products is an output measure. The direct material usage variance can be computed as follows:

Budgeted direct material cost per unit × (Actual quantity of direct material used – Direct material allowed for output)

For NowCo, the direct material usage variance is computed as follows:

$3.00 × (30,000 pounds – 29,000 pounds) = $3.00 × 1,000 =
$3,000 unfavorable variance

The direct material usage variance is unfavorable because the quantity of material used, 30,000 pounds, exceeded the quantity allowed based on units produced, 29,000 pounds (1 pound per unit).

If the actual quantity of direct material used was more than what was budgeted (or standard) for the output attained, then the direct material usage variance will be unfavorable, as it was for NowCo. It is important to remember that the direct material needed for output is based on the actual quantity of units produced for the period.

Total variances for fixed and variable factory overhead can be broken down into variances similar to those illustrated for direct labor and direct material. Discussion of these variances is beyond the scope of this text.

Evaluating Business Units and Business Unit Managers

Students should note that two, sometimes separate, evaluations take place: (1) the evaluation of a unit manager's performance, and (2) the evaluation of the business unit's performance (department, product, etc.). For example, it is possible to have an effective manager of a business unit that is performing poorly due to poor location or declining market. A possible outcome in such a situation is to close the unit, but promote the manager to a higher position in another unit. Conversely, it is possible to have an ineffective manager at a business unit that is performing well.

In a performance report for a manager of a cost center, the report would contain actual costs, planning budget costs and performance budget costs for all costs *controllable* by the manager. The evaluation of a unit manager's performance should not include any noncontrollable costs. In the evaluation of a business unit, all costs of the business unit are included in the report. The business unit performance report would include all the costs controllable by the business unit manager plus any other noncontrollable costs of the business unit. In evaluating a business unit cost center, you need to know the total cost of the unit regardless of who has control of the costs.

A performance report for Zona Manufacturing Company and its two products is presented in Exhibit 4-5.3 for 2002. This is a highly condensed report illustrating how the two product managers can be evaluated separately from the products. Each manager is evaluated on the revenues and costs he or she controls. Typical fixed costs controlled by a product manager would be product advertising, product development, product insurance, and certain facilities costs. Fixed costs incurred for the product but controlled by someone outside the product segment would include the product manager's salary, property taxes, and casualty insurance. Examples of unallocated other fixed costs would include the company president's salary, corporate headquarters costs, and general company advertising or promotions for the benefit of all products.

The information in Exhibit 4-5.3 needs to be evaluated. The product contribution for Shakers of $25,000 is five times greater than that for Movers; it is 12.5 percent of sales ($25,000/$200,000) for Shakers versus only 3.3 percent of sales ($5,000/$150,000) for Movers. So, Shakers as a product is doing much better than Movers. However, both product managers are doing about the same in performance if we look at the product manager's margin, 22.5 percent ($45,000 ÷ $200,000) for the Shakers' manager and 20 percent ($30,000 ÷ $150,000) for the Movers manager. The major problem seems to be the relatively high direct fixed costs controllable outside the product line. The question to be asked and answered is, "Why are fixed costs controllable outside the product segment so large for Movers?"

There are other measures of performance that can be used to evaluate the performance of a business or business unit. These other measures include return on assets, return on investment, residual income, and economic value added. Return on assets is covered in Module 1 of this text; see other accounting and finance texts for explanations of the other measures.

Exhibit 4-5.3

Zona Manufacturing Company
Segment Report--Actual Revenues & Costs
Year Ended December 31, 2002

	Movers	**Shakers**	**Total**
Sales	$ 150,000	$ 200,000	$350,000
Less variable costs	100,000	130,000	230,000
Contribution margin	$ 50,000	$ 70,000	$ 120,000
Fixed costs controllable by product manager	20,000	25,000	45,000
Manager controllable margin	$ 30,000	$ 45,000	$ 75,000
Fixed costs controllable outside the product line	25,000	20,000	45,000
Traceable product margin	$ 5,000	$ 25,000	$ 30,000
Other fixed costs--unallocated			20,000
Operating income			$ 10,000

Behavioral Aspects of the Management Control System

Any system that supports the performance evaluation of people is going to have significant behavioral implications. This means that the design and operation of the management control system will impact how people in the organization behave. The power of a system to impact behavior is best summed up in a paraphrase of the French philosopher René Descartes' quote: "I am as I am measured." Although this is a common sense idea that has been well understood for some time, many organizations do a poor job of considering the behavioral implications of their management control systems.

One typical problem organizations have is that employees focus on the performance measures rather than on the activity that is imperfectly being measured. For example, grades are meant to be a measure of how well students are learning the subject matter. As we all know, grades are at best an imperfect measure of learning, particularly as the subject matter becomes more sophisticated. As a result, we all know students (hopefully just a few) who focus their efforts on receiving a good grade (the performance measure) rather than on learning the material (the activity). To the extent that the performance measure is imperfect, students may spend considerable time trying to maximize their grade (memorizing, cramming, begging the instructor for more points, etc.) at the expense of learning and retaining the subject matter.

The less perfectly a measure captures all dimensions of an activity, the more likely it is to cause employees to maximize the measure rather than the activity. Net income is a comprehensive measure that captures most dimensions of performance for firms or major divisions of firms. However, even income does not adequately measure the performance of a firm. Performance based on net income alone tends to cause managers to maximize the measure (currently reported net income) at the expense of the activity (long-term well-being of stakeholders). A typical problem, particularly in the United States, is that managers make decisions to maximize current income at the expense of long-term profitability. This is the problem that the balanced scorecard addresses.

In the mid-1970s U.S. Industries, Inc. recognized the short-term and narrow focus of using one or two factors to measure division managers' performance.[1] Their approach to the problem was to measure each division manager on twelve different factors broken down into the following three major groups:

- Doing better than last year
- Planning realistically
- Managing cash and capital

The three factors that division managers were evaluated on in the "planning realistically" area included (1) return on average capital employed, (2) pre-tax dollar profit for the period, and (3) pre-tax percentage profit on sales for the period. In this evaluation scheme it was almost impossible for a manager to do well on more than three or four evaluation items unless his or her performance was well planned and executed.

When more comprehensive measures aren't available, behavioral problems increase. This happens as measures are developed for areas of the firm such as cost centers that do not have control over all components of net income. This was also an issue in the former Soviet Union. Under communism, income is not a meaningful measure of performance because prices (and hence costs to firm) are set bureaucratically rather than by the market. As a result, other performance measures must be developed that less perfectly capture all dimensions of the activity.

The story of a Soviet chandelier factory is widely told. Since net income was not meaningful and the factory produced many sizes of chandeliers, performance was measured by the weight of the chandeliers produced during the year. As a result, managers kept making heavier and heavier chandeliers so that they could meet budgeted performance. Over time, chandeliers became so heavy that ceilings were being pulled down all over Moscow. Note that if the number of chandeliers had been chosen as the factory's performance measure, the factory would have produced small, easy-to-manufacture chandeliers rather than what was needed.

---

[1] Frank J. Tanzola, "Performance Rating for Divisional Control," *The Financial Executive,* March 1975.

Key Components of a Behaviorally Sound System

A management control system should include the following four components in order to reduce the behavioral problems created by measuring employee behavior.

1. The system must be **participative**. This means that the employees being evaluated must be fully involved with their managers in setting standards and developing the budget. In addition, the employees must "buy in" to the standards and budget, meaning that they think they are reasonable, and they are willing to be held accountable for them. In short, standards and budgets should be the result of a negotiation process.

2. The standards must be viewed as challenging, but reasonably **attainable standards**. Standards set too low do not provide an incentive to excel, while standards set too high often cause employees to give up and refuse to be held accountable.

3. **Multiple measures** of performance should be used so that the measures taken together better capture all dimensions of the activity being evaluated.

4. Employees should only be evaluated by measures over which they have control. If department managers do not have control over underlying activities that are reflected in their departments' cost reports, the costs of these activities should be excluded from their performance reports. For example, since the Sedan Work Cell manager does not control the plant depreciation cost allocated to her, this cost should not be included in her performance report.

COMPREHENSIVE BUDGETING

In the past, the traditional budgeting process often ended with completion of the financial budgets described in Reading 4-1. The financial budgets were then used as the basis for a major component of performance evaluation. Managers considered some nonfinancial items when evaluating performance, but nonfinancial measures were not included in the budging process. Today, many firms explicitly include nonfinancial measures in the budgeting process. When this occurs, the financial budget is sometimes termed a **comprehensive budget** because it includes financial and nonfinancial targets.

Comprehensive budgeting is a major component of the balanced scorecard performance measurement concept. The balanced scorecard evaluates performance based on a combination of operating, customer, learning and growth, and financial measures. CCC uses a form of the balanced scorecard as its management control system.

Balanced Scorecard Concepts

The balanced scorecard is a relatively new concept that has evolved in the business community. It better meets the critical information needs of management than other planning and control systems. Typically, financial accounting measures do not stress the current environment, as they are historical in nature. That is, they look backward, not forward, to activities that have already happened. Thus, the financial accounting measures alone are not sufficient if management is looking for information to guide them to improve current and future operations. The strength of the balanced scorecard is its ability to focus management's attention on the direction the organization should pursue in the future and its ability to link strategy to operations.

Much credit goes to Robert Kaplan and David Norton for writing a classic article on the nature and operation of the balanced scorecard.[2] The overall concept of the balanced scorecard is that it should create learning; communicate; provide feedback; and align organizational strategy, objectives, and performance measures with daily operational control. The balanced scorecard approach can be outlined with the following four perspectives with metrics for each category to track performance for both the short term and long term:

1. Customer satisfaction/loyalty perspective
    - Customer profitability
    - Customer loyalty
    - Customer satisfaction
2. Organizational learning and growth
    - Employee training
    - Number of new products
    - Time-to-market new products
3. Internal business processes perspective
    - Cycle time
    - Process quality control
    - Reduction in waste
4. Financial perspective
    - Revenue growth
    - Product profitability
        - Cash flow ROE
        - Cost

An in-depth look at the balanced scorecard approach is beyond the scope of this text. However, the important concept is that there has to be a linkage that ties together operating control to management control through metrics that are tied to organizational objectives.[3] CCC management has subscribed to this philosophy and is beginning to use it as discussed later in this module.

Three-Step Procedure for Determining Budget Measures

Measures used to prepare a comprehensive budget and to subsequently assess performance using a balanced scorecard are determined in a three-step process that links the strategic plans for the organization with the performance measures for individual work groups. The three steps are as follows:

1. Determine the corporate strategy (how the firm plans to gain a competitive advantage in the market);
2. Identify **critical success factors** (a few things that the firm must do well to successfully implement its strategy); and
3. Develop measures that will help the work groups continuously improve critical success factor performance.

---

[2] Robert S. Kaplan and David P. Norton, "The Balanced Scorecard—Measures That Drive Performance," *Harvard Business Review,* January/February 1992, pp. 71–79.

[3] See for example, Marc Epstein and Jean-Francois Manzoni, "The Balanced Scorecard and the Tableau de Bord: Translating Strategy into Action," *Management Accounting,* August 1997, pp. 28–36, and Russ Kershaw and Susan Kershaw, "Developing a Balanced Scorecard to Implement Strategy at St. Elsewhere Hospital," *Management Accounting Quarterly,* Winter 2001, pp. 28–35.

Example: The Balanced Scorecard at CCC

In 2002, the top managers of CCC and a management-consulting group developed a strategic plan for CCC in consultation with the other managers and the work groups. Since the major auto manufacturers have entered the LEV market, CCC has developed a strategy that focuses on the high-quality, technologically advanced segment of the LEV market. Based on this strategy, CCC determined that its critical success factors are:

1. Low defect rate;
2. Excellent customer service (no stockouts, prompt delivery of special orders);
3. Cost competitiveness; and
4. Product development, including new features for existing models.

Since the fourth success factor does not relate directly to the sedan and compact work cells, the focus of the discussion will be on the first three factors. Two important process output measures that CCC selected to reflect the low defect success factor are percent of customers reporting defects and percent of defective parts from suppliers. Important process output measures related to the second success factor are percent of on-time deliveries to customers and cycle time (CCC realizes that on-time delivery and prompt delivery of special orders improves as cycle time is reduced). CCC also understands that to continuously improve on all of the first three success factor measures, it must extensively train its employees. CCC has selected percent of labor hours spent in training as a process output measure supporting the first three critical success factors.

Finally, total work cell cost will be CCC's measure of cost control. Note that CCC is not computing the cost effectiveness (variances) of each station in the work cell as a traditional budgeting and control system would. The reason is that CCC wants the work team to work together to reduce total work cell costs, rather than focus their energies on minimizing costs at one station at the expense of the entire process. For example, in a traditional system, the body paint work station may be more efficient if it runs large batches of one color before it changes paint color. This behavior, however, is likely to cause stations further down the line to be idle while they wait for the proper color of body ordered by the customer to arrive.

To summarize, the process output measures that CCC has identified are as follows:

1. Percent of on-time deliveries to customers.
2. Supplier defective parts rate.
3. Customer-reported defect rate.
4. Cycle time.
5. Percent of labor time spent in training.
6. Total work cell cost.

Although work cell employees will use statistical quality control and other techniques to help them improve performance, it is the process output measures that are included in comprehensive budgets that are used to evaluate performance.

Developing the Comprehensive Budget at CCC

In October 2002, CCC decided to begin developing benchmark standards. In order to speed up the process, CCC decided to use Toyota as a benchmark for all six of their process output measures. CCC was able to obtain the following Toyota performance standards for LEV sedans and compacts:

1. Percent of on-time deliveries: 98 percent.
2. Supplier defective parts rate: .5 percent, or 1/2 of 1 percent.
3. Customer-reported defect rate: 1 percent.
4. Cycle time: 3 days.
5. Percent of labor time spent on training: 6 percent.
6. Total work cell cost: unavailable, but Toyota uses 100 hours of labor to assemble a sedan and 70 hours for a compact.

With the benchmark information at hand, Jena Butler, vice president of finance, meets with Sally Swanson, vice president of production, and each of the two work cell teams separately. CCC's historical process output measures (see Exhibit C4-5.2) are also available to all parties. After two long and often heated meetings, all parties agree that the following standards are attainable during 2003:

	Sedan	**Compact**
1. Percent of on-time deliveries	92%	84%
2. Customer-reported defect rate	2%	6%
3. Cycle time	5 days	8 days
4. Supplier defect rate	3%	7%
5. Percent of time spent on training	5%	5%
6. Total direct work cell costs	see budget	see budget

Work Cell Performance Evaluation at CCC

During the year Jena Butler and her staff collect monthly data on the six process output measures and report them to Sally Swanson and the work cell teams. The work cells also are evaluated on whether they meet the production schedule for the month (that is, if the sedan work cell is scheduled to assemble 500 compacts in June, did they actually produce 500?). Any actual results that are significantly out of line are discussed with Sally and the appropriate work cell team immediately. It is very embarrassing for the work cell team to perform below standard, because they believe that they are world-class auto assemblers.

In early October, Jena's staff accountants prepare an interim performance review report for each work cell. In this report the cause of all significant variations to date are discussed. Each work cell receives a copy of its report and prepares a response. Copies of the reports also are distributed to David Gomez, CCC's president, and Sally Swanson. Finally, an extended meeting is held with each work group in which the report is discussed and ideas to prevent similar problems in the future are presented. These meetings are quite positive and forward-looking because the work cell group has already addressed causes for most of the past nine months' problems. Most of the discussion centers on work cell employees' suggestions for major changes beyond their control that can improve performance. Significant time is also spent discussing why certain standards turned out to be unrealistic.

Results of the performance meeting are used as valuable input in developing revised standards for the coming year's budget. A similar process occurs in January, except standards are seldom changed at this time.

SUMMARY

The focus of this reading is to finish coverage of performance evaluation and to take a closer look at behavioral aspects of standard setting and performance evaluation. When looking at performance evaluation it is very important to keep in mind the managerial level within the organization targeted in the report and whether the report evaluates the unit manager or the business unit. This reading also concludes our discussion of the balanced scorecard as a significant component of the management control system and how it is implemented at CCC.

EXERCISES AND PROBLEMS

Exercises

Exercise 1 Planning Budget and Performance Budget. Distinguish between a planning budget and a performance budget. How is each budget used in business?

Exercise 2 Performance Reporting with Balanced Scorecard. How does a performance report using a balanced scorecard differ from a performance report using a traditional performance budget only? Explain.

Exercise 3 Setting Standards in a Management Control Cycle. Explain why setting standards is such an important step in the management control cycle.

Exercise 4 Performance Budget. In preparing a performance budget, what activity level is used and why is that activity level used?

Exercise 5 Direct Labor Variances. Explain how the direct labor rate variance and the direct labor efficiency variance are computed. What does the sum of the two variances represent, that is, what should the total of the two variances equal?

Exercise 6 Direct Material Variances. Explain how the direct material price variance and the direct material usage variance are determined.

Exercise 7 Manager versus Business Unit Performance. Why do business people distinguish between evaluating the performance of a business unit manager and evaluating the performance of a business unit?

Exercise 8 Motivation and Grades. Why are grades (performance in a course) sometimes not good measures of student performance? Give an example to illustrate your answer.

Exercise 9 Behaviorally Sound Systems. Select one of the four components of a behaviorally sound evaluation system and explain why you think it is the most important component for a business.

Exercise 10 Comprehensive Budgeting. Explain the concept of comprehensive budgeting.

Exercise 11 Characteristics of the Balanced Scorecard. What are the four characteristics of the balanced scorecard? Select one and explain how CCC uses it.

Exercise 12 Balanced Scorecard System. In establishing a balanced scorecard system, what is the first step in the process, that is, where does management begin? Why does it begin there?

Problems

Problem 1 Direct Labor Variances. For the year 2002 Angelica Company had the following budgeted and actual data concerning its direct labor cost and activity.

Budgeted direct labor cost per unit of product: 2.2 hours at $15 per hour
Actual cost and activity:

Direct labor cost for the year	$331,000
Direct labor hours worked	222,000
Units of product produced	100,000

Use the information to determine (1) the direct labor rate variance and (2) the direct labor efficiency variance. Be sure to indicate whether the variances are favorable or unfavorable.

Problem 2 Balanced Scorecard Performance Report. The following is a changed version of Exhibit 4-5.2 for Maryanne's Machine Shop for 2002. Use the information in this exhibit to answer the questions that follow.

Maryanne's Machine Shop, Inc.
Balanced Scorecard Performance Report
Year Ended December 31, 2002

Item	Performance Budget	Actual	Variance	F/U
Direct labor	$ 100,000	$ 102,000	$ (2,000)	U
Supplies	18,000	18,500	(500)	U
Setups	33,000	33,100	(100)	U
Maintenance	14,000	14,000	0	-
Power	9,500	9,800	(300)	U
Others	20,000	20,100	(100)	U
Totals	$ 194,500	$ 197,500	$ (3,000)	U
Nonfinancial Items				
Percent on-time deliveries	90%	92%	2%	F
Customer reported defects	1%	3%	-2%	U
Percent rework cost (of total job budgeted variable cost)	5%	6%	-1%	U
Supplier defect rate	2%	2%	0%	-

Using the information given, explain what two things seem to be going best for Maryanne's Machine Shop. Also, what seems to be the primary problem it is having? Explain briefly.

Problem 3 Direct Material Variances. Gabriel Company makes a plastic decorative gate from recycled plastics. The gate has become very popular because of its strength and durability. During the year Gabriel Company purchased 70,000 pounds of plastic at a total cost of $76,600. Gabriel Company budgets 14 pounds of plastic to make each gate. The budgeted cost of plastic is $1.10 per pound. The company made 4,900 gates from the 70,000 pounds of plastic it purchased.

Determine for Gabriel Company (1) the direct material price variance and (2) the direct material usage variance. Be sure to indicate whether the variances are favorable or unfavorable.

Problem 4 Segment Report. Dumble, Ltd., wants to evaluate its territory managers and the performance of its territories. You have been given the following to help you prepare an evaluation of the managers' performance and the territory performance. Selected data for the year 2002 follows:

	Territory	
	South	West
Sales	$400,000	$600,000
Variable costs (% of sales)	60%	62%
Fixed costs controllable by manager	100,000	110,000
Fixed costs controlled by top management, but traceable directly to territory	40,000	50,000

Other fixed costs, common to both territories, but not allocated: $35,000

Use the information to prepare a segment report for Dumble, Ltd., for 2002, similar to Exhibit 4-5.3. When you have completed the report, comment on the performance of each manager.

Problem 5 CCC Balanced Scorecard. Illustrate the use of a balanced scorecard management control system by explaining how CCC has implemented the balanced scorecard.

Problem 6 Performance Report. Refer to the Micro Manufacturing Company planning budget for the year 2002 in Reading 4-1. Assume that the company results for 2002 are as follows:

- Sales were 99,000 units of Kid Stuff at $10 per unit
- Units produced for the year were 96,000
- Costs incurred for production were:
  Material Cee purchased, 100,000 pounds at $1.00 per pound
  Material Em purchased, 190,000 kits at $0.50 per kit
  Direct labor I, $16 per hour for 9,700 hours worked
  Direct labor II, $10 per hour for 4,800 hours worked
  Variable manufacturing overhead, $77,000
  Fixed manufacturing overhead, $106,000
- Other costs incurred were:
  Variable selling and distribution expenses, $101,000
  Fixed selling and distribution expenses, $40,000
  Fixed general and administrative expenses, $158,000

- Ending 12/31/2002 inventory levels were:

	Quantity	Cost
Finished goods inventory	5,000	$30,000
Raw material Cee	8,000	8,000
Raw material Em	12,000	6,000

- All other budgeted costs and activities were the same as planned.

Based on this information, prepare a performance report for Micro Manufacturing Company for 2002 similar to the one illustrated in Exhibit 2-7.1. Note that your performance report will contain all the income statement items, not just manufacturing costs.

Problem 7 Direct Labor and Direct Materials Variances. DeGonia Unlimited is a producer of men's swimsuits. The company uses a comprehensive budgeting system. The following are budgeted costs and actual costs for a recent month.

	Budgeted Cost (Per Unit)	Actual Cost (Total)
Direct labor:		
Budgeted: 1 hour at $12 per hour	$12.00	
Actual hours worked: 5,000		$60,500
Direct materials:		
Budgeted: 2 yards at $4 per yard	$ 8.00	
Actual yards purchased: 10,400		$ 40,560

During the month DeGonia Unlimited produced 5,000 swimsuits. There was no inventory of materials on hand to start the month. During the month all 10,400 yards of materials were used in production.

Based on the information, determine the direct labor rate variance, direct labor efficiency variance, direct material price variance, and the direct material usage variance. Be sure to state whether the variance is favorable or unfavorable.

Case 4-5

THE BALANCED SCORECARD AT CALIFORNIA CAR COMPANY

Case Objectives:

1. Reinforce the concept of performance (flexible) budgets
2. Extend financial control concepts to include nonfinancial measures
3. Demonstrate the subjective nature of performance evaluation
4. Demonstrate the importance and dynamics of standard setting

Decision (Performance evaluation): How well did the work cells perform in 2003?

PERFORMANCE BUDGET INFORMATION

It is now mid-October, 2003 and Jena Butler's staff has gathered performance information for each of the work cells for the first nine months of the year. A summary of the actual performance information for each work cell is presented in Exhibit C4-5.2. In order to keep everyone working with the same numbers, use the sales and production data in Exhibit C4-5.2 rather than the figures you used for your Case 4-1 budget. You should, however, use the same unit costs per car that you used for your budget (see Cases 4-1 and 4-2).

Sedan Work Cell

Three significant budget events impacted the sedan work cell during the first nine months of 2003.

- A critical machine broke down in May, and all assembly had to stop for four production days until a replacement part could be obtained. The machine is rather old and heavily used. The cause of the part failure was a buildup of dirt from the routine operation of the machine.

- A supplier sent a batch of parts that had so many defects that the entire delivery was rejected, causing the work cell to shut down for two days until additional parts could be delivered.

- About 40 of the customer-reported defects involved a wiring problem that caused the headlights and taillights to suddenly stop working. Engineers redesigned the wiring in February, and no customer reports of electrical problems have been filed on sedans manufactured after this redesign.

Compact Work Cell

Two significant budget events impacted the compact work cell during the first nine months:

- The supplier of solar panels continued to ship many defective parts. Production was maintained only by having the supplier deliver far more solar panels than needed so that enough acceptable panels were always available in inventory. Nevertheless, approximately 25 percent of customer-reported defects for the compact involve faulty solar panels. The rest are due to assembly problems.

- In April the compact work cell adopted a "minimum line shutdown" policy whereby the line stopped only for absolute emergencies. The line was no longer shut down while a defect was corrected. Instead, a group of employees inspected and repaired the defective compacts after the compacts were completed. This change greatly improved cycle time and helped the compact work cell meet and exceed its production schedule.

Nonfinancial Performance Measures

CCC's actual performance on nonfinancial measures in 2001 and 2002 is presented in Exhibit C4-5.1. Based on the TQM and JIT changes implemented during 2002, the historical results presented in Exhibit C4-5.1, and extensive negotiations with the work cell employees, CCC has established the nonfinancial standards for 2003, also shown in Exhibit C4-5.1.

Exhibit C4-5.1
California Car Company
Nonfinancial Measures of Performance

	2001 Standards		2002 Standards		Budgeted 2003 Standards	
	Sedan	Compact	Sedan	Compact	Sedan	Compact
Percent late deliveries	30%	38%	19%	32%	8%	16%
Supplier defective part rate	4%	13%	6%	12%	3%	7%
Customer defect rate	5%	16%	4%	12%	2%	6%
Cycle time	11 days	14 days	6 days	12 days	5 days	8 days
Training hours percentage	3%	3%	3%	3%	5%	5%

Production and Sales

CCC is scheduled to produce 11,700 sedans and 6,400 compacts in 2003. By the end of September CCC is scheduled to have produced 75 percent of 2003's production. Therefore, production of 8,775 sedans and 4,800 compacts is scheduled through September 30, 2003. Projected cars sold through September 30, 2003 are equal to the projected production.

Actual production of sedans and compacts through September 30, 2003, totaled 8,446 and 4,930 cars, respectively. Actual sales through September 30, 2003, were 8,446 sedans and 4,816 compacts, as shown in Exhibit C4-5.2. Demand for sedans totaled 9,100 units through September.

Exhibit C4-5.2

California Car Company
Balanced Scorecard
For Nine Months Ended September 30, 2003

	Budgeted Unit Amount	Planning Budget	Performance Budget	Actual	Variance	
Sedan Work Cell						
Units produced	---	8,775		8,446		
Units sold	---	8,775		8,446		
Material costs	$ 2,980			$ 25,216,842		
Number of parts	25			212,678		parts
Labor hours	---	1,552,500		1,551,462		hours
Labor costs	$35/hr.			$ 54,611,462		
Late deliveries	8%			649		cars
Supplier defects	3%			6,394		parts
Customer defects	2%			148		cars
Cycle time	5 days	5 days		5.3 days		days
Training hours	5%			76,480		hours
Compact Work Cell						
Units produced	---	4,800		4,930		
Units sold	---	4,800		4,816		
Material costs	$ 3,360			$ 17,245,972		
Number of parts	20			99,834		parts
Labor hours	---	562,500		541,934		hours
Labor costs	$35/hr.			$ 19,130,270		
Late deliveries	16%			746		cars
Supplier defects	7%			7,772		parts
Customer defects	6%			386		cars
Cycle time	8 days	8 days		6.7 days		days
Training hours	5%			9,672		hours

Work Cell Labor

From Case 4-2, an estimated 2,070,000 work cell labor hours are required to produce 11,700 sedans, and an estimated 750,000 work cell labor hours are required to produce 4,800 compacts. As shown in Exhibit C4-5.2, projected work cell labor hours through September 30, 2003, are 75 percent of these annual estimates. The planned and actual work cell labor rates for a 40 hour week are $35 per hour. CCC pays time and a half for overtime, which is included as part of total actual work cell labor cost.

Requirements

1. Complete the following table by computing the full year 2003 budgeted level for each nonfinancial measure. Use production and sales of 11,700 sedans and 4,800 compacts as a basis for your answer. For example, the total budgeted number of late sedan deliveries is 936 (8% × 11,700). Sedans require 25 parts per car, and compacts require 20 parts. Note the units used for each measure in the last column. Some are cars, but others are parts, days, and hours. Within a reasonable range, will cycle time change as production varies?

Measure	Standard Rate		Planning Budget Full Year Amount		Unit of Measure
	Sedan	Compact	Sedan	Compact	
Percent late deliveries	8%	16%	936		Cars
Percent of supplier Defective parts	3%	7%			Parts
Customer-reported defect percentage	2%	6%			Defective cars
Cycle time	5 days	8 days			Days
Training hours	5%	5%			Labor hours

2. Is CCC using a balanced scorecard approach to performance measurement? Explain. Indicate to which of the four balanced scorecard perspectives each measure in the table is most closely related.

   For the remaining requirements, each group will be assigned a model (sedan or compact) and a perspective (work cell labor or management).

3. Complete the portion of CCC's nine-month balanced scorecard for the model assigned to your group in the format of Exhibit C4-5.2. For example, if your group is assigned the compact model, you need only fill out the compact (lower) portion of the performance budget. Use the 2003 standards shown in Exhibit C4-5.1.

4. Compute the work cell labor rate variance and the work cell labor efficiency variance for your assigned model.

5. Prepare a one-page, word-processed performance report from your assigned perspective (work cell labor or management) for your model. For example, if you are assigned the sedan model from the work cell labor's perspective, you will write the report to reflect as favorably as possible on your group, within the constraints provided by the available information. The management perspective group will try to hold the work cell accountable for results to the extent that the information permits. The case provides plenty of information on which to write a full-page performance analysis. Discuss each performance measure and the significance that you placed on each in arriving at an overall performance evaluation.

Group Assignment 4-5

SETTING STANDARDS FOR 2004

Group number ___3___ **Signatures of group members participating:**

____

____

Your group's model (sedan or compact): ___compact___

Your group's perspective (management or labor): ___labor___

It is now early November 2003. CCC must set new standards for 2004 so that the 2004 planning budget can be constructed. Jena Butler explains that the new standards should be set by having the work cell employee representatives negotiate with CCC's production managers. The negotiations should use the following quantitative information: (1) Year 2003 nine-month variances computed in Case 4-5, (2) Toyota benchmarks, and (3) standards from last year (2003). Non-quantitative factors will also enter into the negotiations.

Jena Butler has collected the following 2002 benchmark information for Toyota hybrid cars:

1. Percent of on-time deliveries to customers: 98 percent
2. Defective part rate from suppliers: .5 percent, or ½ of 1 percent
3. Customer-reported defect rate: 1 percent
4. Cycle time: 3 days
5. Percent of labor time spent in training: 6 percent
6. Total work cell cost: Unavailable, but Toyota used 100 work cell hours of labor to assemble a sedan and 70 hours for a compact

Requirements

1. Complete column 3 in Exhibit G4-5.1 before meeting with the opposing group. Use your answer to Case 4-5, particularly your evaluation of performance in 2003, as one input in setting the new standards. At the start of negotiations, obtain the opposing group's starting position for each standard record these figures in column 4. After the negotiations, complete column 5, the standards you agreed upon with your opposing group. Note that the numbers you offer as your first bargaining position often impact the final negotiated amount.

Exhibit G4-5.1
Your Negotiation Record

(1) Standards	(2) 2003 Standards	(3) Your Group's Consensus 2004 Standards	(4) Opposing Group's 2004 Standards	(5) Negotiated 2004 Standards
Labor hours per car	Sedan: 177 hours Compact: 117 hours	115 hours	115 hours	115 hours
Late deliveries	Sedan: 8% Compact: 16%	10 %	12 %	11 %
Supplier defects	Sedan: 3% Compact: 7%	2 %	4 %	3 %
Customer defects	Sedan: 2% Compact: 6%	1 %	4 %	2.5 %
Cycle time	Sedan: 5 days Compact: 8 days	8 days	7 days	7.5 days
Training time	Sedan: 5% Compact: 5%	6 %	4 %	5 %
Wage rate	$35 per hour	$ 35/hr.	$ 32/hr.	$ 33.5/hr

2. Summarize your team's justification for the year 2004 standards you proposed in column 3 of Exhibit G4-5.1 for the following standards:

   a. Labor hours per car

   We need to meet our standards before we work to decrease them. If we want to compete w/ Toyota, our standards should still be set lower than 2003's.

   b. Customer defect rate

   Reapplying JIT Production will greatly reduce Customer defect rate.

   c. Cycle time

   The cycle time may not be easy to reduce because production will stop to fix defects and problems.

Module 4

Peer Evaluation of Group Members	Class Section	Group No.

Evaluator's Name ______________________________

Module 4

In the table below, please indicate your estimate, in percentage terms, of the contributions that individual group members made to each of the group assignments listed. Each column should add to 100 percent. For example, if there are five members in your group and all were present for Group Assignment 4-2, you would divide up 100 percent among the five members, including yourself. If you felt that all group members were prepared to discuss the assignment and contributed equally to the solution, you would give each person 20 percent. If only four members were present and you felt that one particular member contributed twice as much as the other three, you would give the heavy contributor 40 percent and the other three members 20 percent. Any group member who was absent should be listed and given a zero percent.

	Group Assignment Number	
Group Members (List)	**4-2**	**4-5**
Myself		
Totals	**100**	**100**

Fill in this sheet after each group assignment is completed and turn in at the completion of Group Assignment 4-5.

Module 4

REVIEW PROBLEM

INTRODUCTION

This review problem contains four parts designed to cover all of the Module 4 materials. Requirements 1, 2, 3 and 4 are for the same company, Micro Manufacturing Company, and are based on the same or updated data given in Reading 4-1.

MICRO MANUFACTURING INFORMATION

This review problem is a continuation of the Micro Manufacturing Company (Micro) illustration in Reading 4-1. Use the information in the "Operating and Financial Budget Example" as a basis for this review problem. Following is the actual operating information for the year 2002. (This is the same data as used in Problem 6 from Reading 4-5.) In addition, the income statement and balance sheet for Micro containing actual data for 2002 is given.

Assume that the company results for 2002 are as follows:

- Sales were 99,000 units of Kid Stuff at $10 per unit
- Units produced for the year were 96,000
- Costs incurred for production were:
  Material Cee purchased, 101,000 pounds at $1.00 per pound
  Material Em purchased, 190,000 kits at $0.50 per kit
  Direct labor I, $16 per hour for 9,700 hours worked
  Direct labor II, $10 per hour for 4,800 hours worked
  Variable manufacturing overhead, $77,000
  Fixed manufacturing overhead, $106,000
- Other costs incurred were:
  Variable selling and distribution expenses, $101,000
  Fixed selling and distribution expense, $40,000
  Fixed general and administrative expenses, $158,000
- Ending 12/31/2002 inventory levels were:

	Quantity	Cost
Finished goods inventory	5,000	$30,000
Raw material Cee	8,000	8,000
Raw material Em	12,000	6,000

- All other budgeted costs and activities were the same as planned.

Micro Manufacturing Company
Income Statement
Year Ended December 31, 2002

	Amount	Percent of Sales
Sales	$ 990,000	100.0%
Cost of goods sold	597,200	60.3%
Gross margin on sales	$ 392,800	39.7%
Less:		
Selling and distribution expenses	141,000	14.2%
General and administrative expenses	158,000	16.0%
Total operating expenses	$ 299,000	30.2%
Earnings before income taxes	$ 93,800	9.5%
Extimated income taxes (40%)	37,520	3.8%
Net income	$ 56,280	5.7%

Micro Manufacturing Company
Balance Sheet
December 31, 2002

Assets			Liabilities and Stockholders' Equity		
Current Assets			Current Liabilities		
Cash		$ 27,280	Accounts Payable		$ 20,000
Accounts Receivable		99,000	Taxes and Other		30,000
Inventory			Total Current Liabilities		$ 50,000
Raw Materials	$ 14,000				
Finished Goods	30,000	44,000	Stockholders' Equity		
Total Current Assets		$ 170,280	Common Stock	$ 200,000	
			Retained Earnings	270,280	470,280
Fixed Assets - Net		350,000			
Total Assets		$ 520,280	Total Liabilities and Stockholders' Equity		$ 520,280

Requirements:

1. Based on the information provided here and in Reading 4-1, prepare a statement of cost of goods sold for Micro for the year 2002. Your statement should look similar to Exhibit 4-1.7, except leave out the exhibit reference column and the footnote. Your ending cost of goods sold amount should agree with the amount in the income statement above for the year 2002.

2. Use the information in Part I plus the data in the example in Reading 4-1 to determine the direct labor rate variance and the direct labor efficiency variance for Direct Labor I for year 2002.

3. Using the information in Reading 4-1 and the material in Part I, prepare a segment report similar to Exhibit 4-5.3 measuring the performance of the production manager separately from total production. Assume that fixed manufacturing overhead for the year 2002 was controlled as follows:

	Actual	**Control Budget**
Production manager	$ 48,000	$ 47,000
Others outside of production department	58,000	59,700
Total	$106,000	$106,700

In preparing the segment report note that (1) there will be only one column in the report since there is only one product, and (2) remember that selling and distribution expenses, and general and administrative expenses are not production expenses.

4. Now we are going to budget for the year 2003. Assume the following changes from the year 2002 plan:

- Sales are estimated to be 110,000 units of Kid Stuff at $10 per unit.
- Material Cee cost per unit is expected to increase to $1.05 per pound, which equals $1.05 per finished unit
- Beginning and ending inventory quantities for 2003 are planned as follows:

	January 1	**December 31**
Raw material—Cee	8,000	6,000
Raw material—Em	12,000	11,000
Finished goods	3,000	4,000

Based on the information above and in Reading 4-1 operating and financial budget example, prepare for the year 2003:

a. A sales budget
b. A production budget
c. A raw materials purchases budget

5. For a review of ethical considerations in decision making, review the discussion of "Ethical Decision-Making Model" detailed on pages 362 and 363 of Reading 4-3.

6. For a review of capital budgeting concepts and computations, solve Problem 5 at the end of Reading 4-4.

MODULE FIVE

ANALYSIS OF FINANCIAL STATEMENTS IN A

Global Economy

Module 5 Introduction

ANALYSIS OF FINANCIAL STATEMENTS IN A GLOBAL ECONOMY

MODULE OVERVIEW

Transacting business on a global basis requires companies to consider the added risk that is present when revenues or expenses are received or paid in the form of a foreign currency. The price of one currency in terms of another currency is called the exchange rate. Because each country's economy has different strengths and weaknesses, the exchange rate reflects the underlying supply and demand for the currency that is the result of the worldwide perceptions of the health of the economy.

This module will introduce you to exchange rates and the impact that they can have on financial statements. It will also introduce you to the content of an annual report of a major corporation and allow you to make comparisons of its financial performance and that of CCC.

The module exposes you to profitability analysis in a global setting by augmenting the breakeven calculation when foreign currencies make up part of the cost structure of a company. This module emphasizes three major decisions:

- Will the exchange rate risk impact profitability?
- Should a U.S. corporation open a subsidiary in a foreign country based on consolidated financial statements?
- Which company's financial statements depict better performance?

Learning Objectives

After completing Module 5, you should be able to:

1. Understand the concept of a foreign exchange rate and the factors that determine the day-by-day currency values in a global market economy.

- Reading 5-1	Global Business and Foreign Exchange Rates
- Exercises and Problems	Exercises and Problems at the end of Reading 5-1

2. Understand how transactions may be measured in a variety of foreign currencies, how sales or purchases on credit involving two currencies can cause gains or losses due to exchange rate fluctuations, and how changes in exchange rates can affect profitability.

- Case 5-1	RF Circuit's Contract with Osaka Components
- Group Assignment 5-1	"Exchanging" Thoughts
- Exercises and Problems	Exercises and Problems at the end of Reading 5-1

3. Understand the accounting process of consolidating foreign financial statements into parent company financial statements.

- Reading 5-2	Translation and Consolidation of Foreign Subsidiaries
- Case 5-2	Opening a Foreign Subsidiary at California Car Company
- Case 5-3	The Mexico Subsidiary After One Year
- Exercises and Problems	Exercises and Problems at the end of Reading 5-2

4. Understand how to use financial statements to analyze financial performance.

- Reading 5-4	Reading and Interpreting Annual Reports
- Case 5-4	Analysis of Ford Motor Company Annual Report
- Exercises and Problems	Exercises and Problems at the end of Reading 5-4

5. Understand how to compare financial statistics of companies to estimate the range of possible stock prices.

- Case 5-5	Comparison of Ford and CCC Financial Statements
- Group Assignment 5-5	Financial Horsepower

TERMINOLOGY LIST FOR MODULE 5

Additional paid-in capital
Basic earnings per share
Consolidated financial statements
Consolidation
Cross exchange rate
Cumulative translation adjustment
Currency devaluation
Diluted earnings per share
Earnings per share ratio
Earnings/price ratio
Exchange gain or loss
Exchange rate
Forward exchange contract
Hedge
Historical exchange rate
Inflation
Intercompany accounts receivable
Joint venture
Multinational corporation
Par value of stock
Preferred stock
Price/earnings ratio
Settlement date
Stock option
Trade balance of payments surplus (deficit)
Translation
Treasury stock

Reading 5-1

GLOBAL BUSINESS AND FOREIGN EXCHANGE RATES

INTRODUCTION

For a business to sustain its growth and sales revenue, it is often compelled to seek new markets for its goods and services. When McDonald's began to saturate the U.S. market with its fast-food restaurants, it pursued a growth strategy that involved opening restaurants in foreign countries. McDonald's 2000 annual report to shareholders reported that over 50 percent of its sales revenue and income were derived from operations outside the United States. McDonald's generates revenues in 119 foreign countries. Its non-U.S. revenue grew faster than that of its U.S. stores.

U.S. corporations have been engaging in international business for quite some time. Ford Motor Company built its first overseas factory in England in 1911. In 1999, Ford purchased the auto manufacturing division of Volvo. Ford now operates in over 25 foreign countries. Some of these operations are in the form of joint ventures. A **joint venture** is a partnership of two or more entities that pool a part of their resources to pursue a new business opportunity. Some of Ford's joint ventures include establishing the production systems for the Chinese auto industry and partnering with Volkswagen to design and build a sport utility vehicle for the European market.

In 1998 the German auto manufacturer Daimler-Benz acquired Chrysler Corporation for $42 billion. Although both companies were transacting business on a global basis at the time of the merger, their respective shareholders agreed to consolidate the two companies to better compete in various world markets.

GLOBAL BUSINESS RISKS

Tariffs, trade restrictions, and cultural differences can make it very difficult for a company to engage in profitable commerce in a foreign country. Recently there has been much criticism by U.S. government officials of Japan's unwillingness to allow U.S. products to be sold in Japan. Complex political issues such as free trade and reduced tariffs heighten the risks associated with international business. Moreover, economies of foreign countries often are not as stable as the U.S. economy. During the 1980s Japan's economy was one of the world's strongest. Beginning in the 1990's and continuing through the next decade, Japan's economy has become stagnant. Its stock market has declined 60 percent from the highs attained in 1990. Its banking system is in crisis due to huge loan losses, which are estimated to approach $1 trillion.

An example of foreign business risk is the 1994 devaluation of Mexico's peso and the 1999 devaluation of Brazil's real as shown in Exhibit 5-1.1. The **currency devaluation** left both country's currencies worth only half of their previous value in U.S. dollars or other currencies. For investors holding assets in either of these countries, the losses were large. The value of their investments depreciated in proportion to the drop in the value of the currency. For the Mexican or Brazilian consumer, the devaluation meant that imported foreign goods cost much more than before. Conversely, consumers in importing countries found that Mexican and Brazilian goods were considerably less costly than before the devaluations. The abrupt devaluations created uncertainty. Participants in international trade need additional time to assess the new economic environment posed by devaluation.

Exhibit 5-1.1
Devaluations of Brazil and Mexico Currencies

Daily Exchange Rates: Brazilian Reals per U.S. Dollar

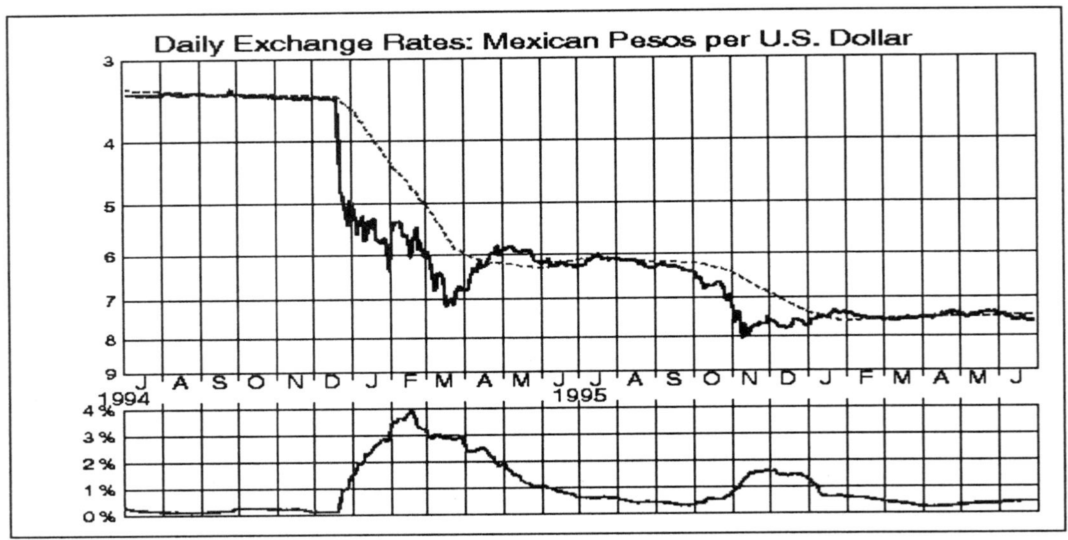

Source: Courtesy of Professor Werner Antweiler, University of British Columbia, Vancouver, British Columbia, Canada. http://pacific.commerce.ubc.ca/xr/

In 1997 and 1998 a domino pattern of currency devaluations was triggered by the collapse of Thailand's currency, the bhat. As illustrated in Exhibit 5-1.2, neighboring countries in Southeast Asia, as well as Korea and Japan, saw their currencies drop in value relative to the world's strongest currencies, the U.S. dollar, the German deutsche mark, and the Swiss franc. For residents of these countries, the price of imported goods soared. Foreign banks lending money to businesses in these countries experienced huge losses because of the reduced value of the loan portfolio they held. The stock markets of these emerging industrialized countries also collapsed, leaving foreign investors fearful of making further investments.

Exhibit 5-1.2
The Collapse of Southeast Asian Currencies

Comparative Daily Exchange Rates: Relative to U.S. Dollar

120 110 100 90 80 70 60 50 40 30 20 10

Philippines Pesos
Thai Baht
Malaysian Ringgit
Indonesian Rupiah

Apr 97 May 97 Jun 97 Jul 97 Aug 97 Sep 97 Oct 97 Nov 97 Dec 97 Jan 98 Feb 98 Mar 98 Apr 98 May 98 Jun 98 Jul 98 Aug 98 Sep 98

Source: Courtesy of Professor Werner Antweiler, University of British Columbia, Vancouver, British Columbia, Canada. http://pacific.commerce.ubc.ca/xr/

Toward the end of 1998, the devaluations spread to other countries. Russia was particularly hard hit. Because Russia is an exporter of natural resource commodities, the devaluations of other countries that export the same commodities lowered the prices Russia could get for its exports. Russia's inability to acquire adequate foreign exchange from exports, along with other structural problems in its economy, caused many to sell the Russian ruble in favor of owning other stronger currencies. The effect of these actions are shown in Exhibit 5-1.3. The crisis did not stop at Russia's borders. A large U.S. investment fund, Long-Term Capital Corporation, was forced to liquidate as a result of trading losses precipitated by Russia's economic problems.

Exhibit 5-1.3
The Devaluation of the Russian Ruble

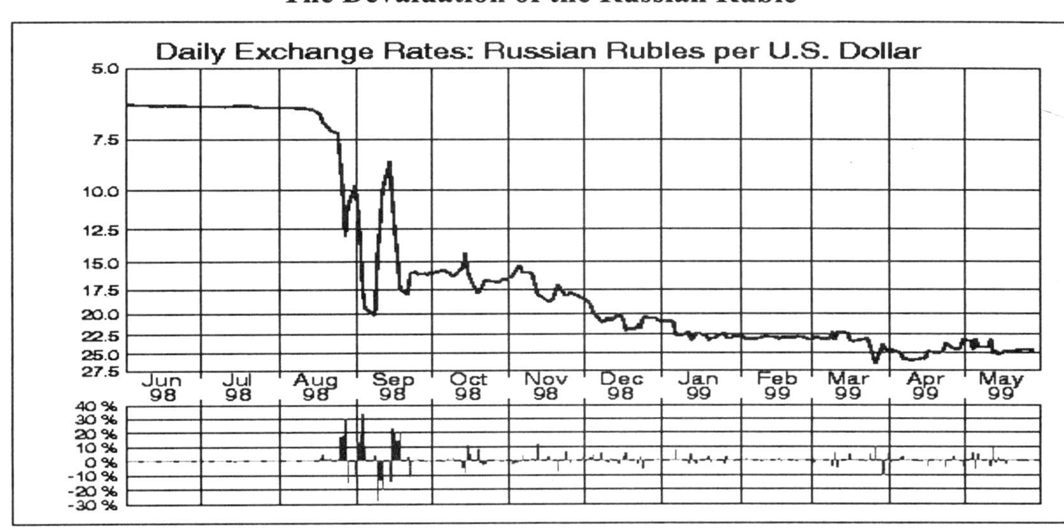

Source: Courtesy of Professor Werner Antweiler, University of British Columbia, Vancouver, B.C, Canada.

In the United States, the ripple effect of currency devaluations around the world was manifested in decreased corporate profits. Year-to-year comparisons of some of the largest corporations' earnings showed a decline from 1997 to 1998. Many companies experienced "pricing pressures," meaning that competitors exporting to the United States made products available to consumers at lower prices. For example, if an electronic component made in Malaysia cost $10 before the devaluation of that country's currency, it might have cost only $6 afterward. Thus, for example, the U.S. manufacturer competing with the Malaysian manufacturer would consider lowering prices even though its costs would not decline. This would put a severe squeeze on profits.

Assuming that companies know the risks involved in international business, why do increasing numbers pursue a global business strategy? The most likely reason is that many areas of the world are experiencing strong economic growth that is resulting in greater disposable income for their citizens. This increased purchasing power creates a rapidly growing demand for consumer products and the prospect of increased sales and profits for companies based in advanced, but mature, economies such as the United States, Japan, and Europe. Emerging economies in Asia, particularly China, are viewed by many industries as important new markets because of the large population of the regions.

Recent developments in telecommunications technology have enhanced companies' abilities to transact business on an international scale. Nearly instantaneous access to information permits managers to be cognizant of the ever-changing global business environment. As conditions in a foreign market change, quick decisions must be made to stay competitive.

Paralleling the advances in information technology is the evolution of a growing list of financial instruments that can be used to manage risk. For example, if a U.S. company wishes to sell products in France, a member country of the European Union, it would increase its success rate if it quoted its prices in euros, the new currency of Western Europe. Buyers in France would like this because they would not have to worry about the possible drop in the value of the euro versus the dollar between the time they placed an order and the time they had to pay for it. Instead the U.S. company would assume this risk. However, it is possible to mitigate the risk of a loss on the transaction by entering into a **forward exchange contract** by selling euros for delivery at a later date. This is called a **hedge** and is intended to reduce the exposure to losses arising out of fluctuating exchange rates. It can be thought of as insurance to reimburse losses. Details of how forward exchange contracts and risk management instruments work are covered in international finance classes.

Beginning in 2002, twelve European countries will transact business using the euro. Citizens and companies holding country currencies will be able to convert them to the euro. Instead of twelve different currencies needed to carry on commerce throughout much of Western Europe, there will be only one. One can think of how complicated it might have been to take a road trip across the United States if each state had its own currency, the value of which changed constantly. That is what travelers in Europe experienced.

From a career standpoint, business professionals will find that an increasing number of positions involve a significant international dimension. Most new job descriptions will include a global component. Exciting career opportunities in international business include logistics and distribution, export and import management, sales and advertising, and finance and accounting. For example, export marketing managers are in charge of selling goods for their firms in a particular part of the world. Their jobs include supervising sales personnel, coordinating contractual and legal matters, arranging for custom agents, and working with financial institutions to obtain letters of credit (financing) and insurance.

EXCHANGE RATES

An **exchange rate** is the price of one foreign currency in terms of another. Changes in exchange rates result from the trading of currencies in open markets around the world. The supply of and demand for a country's currency can change abruptly, causing its exchange rate in relation to other currencies to change dramatically. Following are some of the factors that influence the supply and demand for a particular currency.

1. **Trade balance of payments surpluses (deficits)**. A good example of this is China's present trade surplus with the United States. China currently exports more goods and services to the United States than we export to China. This imbalance is growing rapidly. The aggregate U.S. trade deficit with all countries is forecast to be over $150 billion in 2001. The combination of a U.S. trade deficit and China's trade surplus is the most important factor in the drop in the value of the dollar relative to the renmimbi, China's currency unit. In 1994 the cost of one unit of the Chinese currency in U.S. dollars was $.115. At the start of 1998, the U.S. dollar cost was almost $.12, a 5 percent increase in the value of the renmimbi. See Exhibit 5-1.4.

Exhibit 5-1.4

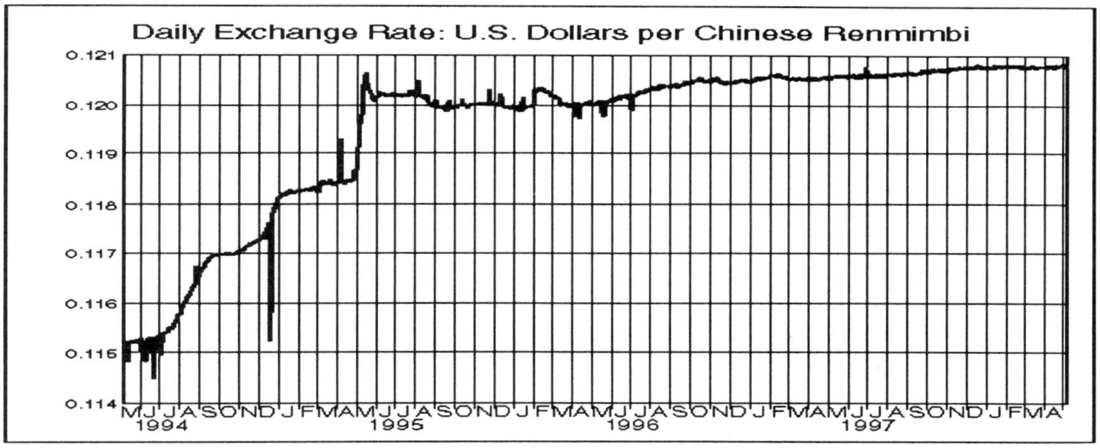

Daily Exchange Rate: U.S. Dollars per Chinese Renmimbi

Source: Courtesy of Professor Werner Antweiler, University of British Columbia, Vancouver, B.C, Canada.

2. Relative rates of **inflation**. A country experiencing high inflation will see its exchange rate fall relative to a country with low inflation. Brazil's inflation has been much higher than that of the United States, causing massive devaluation of the real (name of Brazil's currency, pronounced ree-'el) in recent years relative to the dollar. In January 1999, Brazil abandoned its policy to maintain the real exchange rate by letting it float to whatever equilibrium level the market found. This action resulted in a 25 per cent devaluation of the real.

3. Relative *real* interest rates. Central banks, like the U.S. Federal Reserve, set monetary policy and interest rates. Money flows to wherever real returns are maximized. Therefore, if the United Kingdom issued government bonds at yield rates materially higher than another country's government bonds, the pound's exchange rate would rise relative to the other country's currency because of increased investor demand for the British currency needed to buy the higher-yield UK bonds.

4. Political instability or government intervention. If investors fear that a country may be vulnerable to anarchy or civil war, they will be disinclined to own that currency.

The Impact of Changes in Exchange Rates: An Example

To illustrate how one's wealth could be impacted by fluctuating exchange rates, assume that you won a contest for which the prize was a trip around the world. Your itinerary specifies that you will visit the following places:

Week 1	London (England)
Week 2	Geneva (Switzerland)
Week 3	Johannesburg (South Africa)
Week 4	Tokyo (Japan)

Your prize pays for airfare, ground transportation, food, lodging, and miscellaneous items. In spite of this all-expense-paid vacation, you decide to take along some money in case of unforeseen events. Let us assume that you leave the United States with exactly $1,000. Also assume that the moment you arrive in a new country, you plan to convert your dollars into the local currency.

Week 1

You have just arrived at London's Heathrow Airport and wish to convert your dollars into the British currency called pounds (£). There are also smaller currency denominations in the United Kingdom like our quarter, dime, and so forth, but these are not relevant unless you purchase items with a price that is not an even number of pounds. The question that is extremely important to you is, "How many British pounds will I get for my $1,000?" To answer this question, we must determine the exchange rate. Suppose that the currency exchange booth at the airport has a sign that says the following:[1]

Pound per dollar rate = .588 pounds per dollar

This means that for each U.S. dollar converted, you will receive .588 British pounds, that is, if you convert your dollars within the next few minutes. The exchange rate could change at any moment. Your $1,000 is thus converted to 588 British pounds ($1,000 × .588). Another way of stating this is that a pound is worth $1.701 ($1 ÷ .588), which is the dollar per pound exchange rate. You can also use this rate to compute how many pounds $1,000 will purchase as follows: $1,000 ÷ 1.701 = 588 pounds.

End of Week 1

Assume that at the end of a magnificent week in London, you decide that you want to convert your pounds back to dollars before departing. You have been a frugal traveler and you have not spent any of your British pounds. The sign at the currency exchange booth now says:

Pound (£) per dollar rate = .597

---

[1] Almost all international airports have a foreign currency exchange service. In reality, the service charges a commission when buying or selling foreign currency. Often the "commission" is the spread between the buy rate and the sell rate. To simplify the illustrations, we ignore the buy/sell rate spread; gains and losses are solely the result of exchange rate fluctuations.

You are, of course, aware that the exchange rate has changed but you are not sure if the change was in your favor. Let's analyze the data. If each dollar is currently worth .597£, it means that you will get fewer dollars for 588 pounds than at the beginning of the week.

When you arrived in London, you paid \$1.701 per pound, as calculated previously. Now, when leaving, you will redeem pounds at \$1.675 (\$1 ÷ .597)—a loss of 2.6 cents per pound. But we still haven't determined how much your 588 pounds are worth in total U.S. dollars. Using the new exchange rate your 588 pounds will convert into:

\$1.675 × 588 £ = \$984.90 (\$985 rounded)

Your plane to Geneva, Switzerland, is on final boarding call. You have no choice but to exchange your pounds for dollars and accept the \$15 loss (about 1.5 per cent for the week).

Week 2

You deplane in Geneva, Switzerland, anticipating an exciting week in this beautiful country. As you proceed to baggage claim, you pass a currency exchange desk similar to the one in London. There is an electronic bulletin board that reads:

Swiss francs per U.S. dollar = 1.500

After being burned by the exchange rate fluctuation in London, you decide to keep your 985 U.S. dollars (the original \$1,000 less the \$15 exchange loss) to avoid the risk of another loss. You realize, however, that if you converted your \$985 upon arrival, you would receive 1,477.5 Swiss francs (\$985 × 1.500).

End of Week 2

Your week in Switzerland was spectacular; perfect weather to go along with stunning sights. But now it's time to move on to Johannesburg, South Africa. As you begin your trek to your boarding gate, your curiosity begins to build. You wonder how the value of the Swiss franc has changed, if at all, during the week. As it turned out, you spent no U.S. dollars while in Switzerland, and you still have \$985. You wonder whether you could have experienced a gain in the value of your currency if you had exchanged your dollars for Swiss francs.

As you approach the currency exchange desk, the bulletin board now reads:

Swiss francs per U.S. dollar = 1.455

You recall the rate at the beginning of week 2 was 1.500, which made your \$985 worth 1,477.5 Swiss francs. With the current exchange rate of 1.455, the 1,477.5 Swiss francs would now be worth the francs held divided by the current exchange rate, or

1477.5 ÷ 1.455 = \$1,015.50

Dismayed that you chickened out at the beginning of the week and missed out on the \$30.50 gain, you pledge to yourself that your \$985 will be converted into South African rands. We assume that our traveler is deciding to "invest" in another foreign currency for reasons other than the lost opportunity just experienced. The factors influencing South Africa's future exchange rate may be different from those in Switzerland in the previous week.

Week 3

Arriving in Johannesburg, you make a beeline for the foreign exchange desk, where the sign reads:

South African rand per U.S. dollar = 5.000

You convert your \$985 into rands. The number of rands acquired is \$985 × 5.000 = 4,925. On the second day in Johannesburg, you find yourself in the financial district. The pulse of business activity is high, and you find yourself being caught up in the excitement. You stroll past the Krugger Central Bank. A sign showing interest rates catches your eye. You are astonished to learn that investing money in South African government bonds is extremely attractive. If you buy a one-year government bond, the sign says you will receive 18 percent interest! You recall that back in the "good ole USA," a one-year government bond currently pays only 4 percent.

You approach the bond counter in the bank. You learn that South African banks are authorized to sell government bonds much like U.S. banks are allowed to sell savings bonds. You ask the clerk at the counter: "How will I redeem my bonds when they mature after I return to the United States?" The clerk is delighted to say:

> That will be absolutely no problem. All banks of any size can convert your bond into U.S. dollars. Very likely they will charge a small fee to handle the transaction. I've heard the fee is usually \$5, mainly to pay for the telex wire transfer.

You start to think: "If I invest the equivalent of \$500 in South African bonds, I will earn an interest return of \$90 in one year (.18 × 500). This compares to the \$20 that I would earn at the going rate of 4 percent in the United States." You make the decision—you are going to invest. You buy a South African 18 percent bond, paying the face value of 2,500 rand.[2]

End of Week 3

Assuming you continue your frugal habits and avoid spending any of your local currency holding, you would have 2,425 rand (4,925 – 2,500) to convert back to dollars when departing Johannesburg. However, an unforeseen situation faces you at the airport—the foreign exchange desk is closed. You have no choice but to take your South African currency with you to Tokyo.

Week 4

During your flight to Tokyo, you become preoccupied with the uncertainty about what the South African rand will be worth in Tokyo. You would have preferred to have left South Africa with U.S. dollars left over after your purchase of the 18 percent South African bond.

Very soon after landing in Japan, your fears are allayed when you learn that the Bank of Tokyo is willing to convert the rand into yen. You happen to see a *Wall Street Journal*. You find buried deep in Section C a table showing all the foreign exchange rates. Below is an excerpt:

---

[2] The difference between the two so-called nominal rates (4% and 18%) suggests a relatively high expected inflation rate in South Africa. If the expected inflation becomes a reality, the exchange rate of rand will devalue against other currencies. Thus, our world traveler may later find that the apparent high return will be offset by an exchange rate loss when the bond is redeemed.

Foreign Currency per U.S. Dollar	
South African rand	4.945
Japanese yen	134.5

Recall that you have 2,425 rand. You are anxious to determine the number of yen you will receive upon conversion. Since both of the rates reported above are foreign currency units per U.S. dollar, you must compute the cross exchange rate (in this case the number of yen per rand). The **cross exchange rate** for two currencies is the rate that is computed based on these two currencies' exchange rates with a third currency. The yen (¥) per rand cross exchange rate can be found as follows:

(134.5¥ ÷ $1) ÷ (4.945 rand ÷ $1) = 134.5 ÷ 4.945 = 27.20 yen per rand

Note that the currency you want to convert to is always in the numerator and the currency you are converting from is in the denominator. You decide that converting rand into yen is a good idea. The currency exchange clerk gives you your yen and the receipt shown below:

2,425 rand × 27.20 = 65,960¥

You are immediately amazed at the large quantity of Japanese currency that you receive. You experience a momentary sense of wealth. But you reflect on the yen per dollar exchange rate of 134.5 and realize that each yen is worth less than one U.S. cent. You quickly come to the conclusion that the dollar value of your yen is only or about $490 (65,960¥ ÷ 134.5).

Without making precise calculations, you now recognize that your original $1,000 is presently made up of a South African government bond worth about $500 and a seemingly large quantity of Japanese currency worth about $490. After experiencing a loss in London from a small exchange rate fluctuation, you are aware that you face another risk of loss because your assets are once again held in currencies other than U.S. dollars. On the other hand, it is also possible to realize a gain from your portfolio of international assets. The conclusion you come to is that the dollar value of your foreign assets will constantly change as the various exchange rates fluctuate. At times you may be in a gain position, at other times a loss position.

Your travels through Tokyo and the countryside immersed you in the contrasts of ancient culture in a complex society. The blend of samurai traditions and world-class technology creates a certain mystique for every visitor. The apparent inconsistencies are amplified when you come across an artist who is working on an oil painting of a quaint fishing village while listening to Matchbox 20 on a Walkman. Stacked next to the painting are other works of various landscapes. You are drawn to one painting and want to have it as a lasting memento of your world travels. You also think it may appreciate in value after a few years. You ask the price; the artist indicates 70,000 yen. Disappointed, you start to rationalize that this unique painting wasn't that important after all. Just then the artist, being able to see your gloom, asks if there is a problem. You tell him that the amount of money you have is 65,960 yen. He pauses for a moment, and then decides to sell the painting for 65,960 yen. You have your memento.

End of Week 4

On the return flight to the States, you again ponder the valuation problem created by holding the two foreign assets. How should you combine the two assets?

Assets

South African bond @ cost	2,500 rand
1 Japanese painting @ cost	65,960 yen
Total assets	?

You realize that adding two or more foreign currencies together would be like adding the number of acres a farmer owns to his quantity of sheep to measure his wealth. In either case, the sums are meaningless because they do not reflect a common measuring unit (i.e., common denominator, such as dollars). In our case, we need to convert our foreign assets into a common medium of exchange—the U.S. dollar. If our traveler were from Sweden, then in his or her home country the Swedish krona would be the medium of exchange.

The valuation of the world traveler's assets is based upon which exchange rates are used to translate the foreign assets into U.S. dollars. Should the traveler use the rates that existed at the time the asset was purchased? Or should the traveler use the rates now, at the time the valuation is made, often referred to as the current rate? For the sake of comparison, let's calculate the U.S. dollar value of the South African bond and the Japanese painting both at the historical and the current rates for these assets.

	Purchase Cost	Historical Rate	Current Rate*	Historical Rate	Current Rate
South African bond	2,500 rand	5	4.9	$ 500.00	$ 510.20
Japanese painting	65,960 yen	134.5	136	490.41	485.00
Total				$ 990.41	$ 995.20

*Assumed Week 5 exchange rate

The difference in the U.S. dollar value of the assets is, of course, the result of fluctuating exchange rates. The traveler who has invested in these two assets will probably view the current rate approach as a better measurement of economic wealth because one cannot sell the assets at the past exchange rates. However, assuming that the assets can be sold for the same price as the traveler paid for them, 2,500 rand for the bond and 65,690 yen for the painting, the traveler's wealth is $995.20, as shown earlier. If the two assets were valued at the historical rates, the value would be $990.41. Since the time the assets were purchased, the exchange rates have slightly benefited the traveler. Many argue that historical exchange rates are not relevant in determining the value of assets today. As you will see in the next section, in most situations accounting rules require that assets and liabilities be translated at current rates.

GAINS AND LOSSES FROM SALES AND PURCHASES

Most companies do not buy and sell foreign currencies in order to make a profit, but nevertheless face a risk of suffering a loss due to changes in exchange rates. The risk arises when a company buys or sells goods or services from or to a foreign firm if (1) the transaction is denominated in a foreign currency, and (2) if the date at which cash is transferred, know as the **settlement date**, is different from the date the transaction is recorded in the accounting records.

For example, assume that a U.S. firm purchased 2,000,000 yen of product from a Japanese supplier on January 1, 2000, when the exchange rate was 106 yen per dollar. The U.S. firm recorded an increase in inventory and an increase in accounts payable on January 1, 2000. The U.S. firm settled the liability by paying the Japanese firm 2,000,000 yen on January 30,

2003, when the exchange rate was 104 yen per dollar. The **exchange gain or loss** (also called transaction gain or loss) is computed as follows:

January 1, 2003	Inventory and liability recorded (2,000,000 yen ÷ 106)	$18,868
January 30, 2003	Debt settled (2,000,000 yen ÷ 104)	19,231
Loss		$ 363

The U.S. firm could avoid this risk by paying the vendor in full on January 1, 2003, or it could have hedged the risk by purchasing a forward exchange contract. The firm would show a loss of $363 if they did not hedge. This loss would be included as an operating expense on the income statement. Of course, the firm would have a gain if the yen per dollar exchange rate had increased over the period. Would the Japanese firm report a gain of $363 (or 37,752 yen) on the transaction? No, because the sale, payment, and records of the Japanese vendor were all dominated in yen.

SUMMARY

Transacting business on a global basis is becoming part of the competitive fabric of today's commerce. The opportunities to expand market scope come with the added complexity and financial risk of dealing in various currencies. Profitability analyses must also include the consideration of currency values when such currencies may be later received or paid in settlement of sales or purchase transactions, respectively. Case 5-1 is an example of a company whose costs are not only determined by its managerial effectiveness but by the dollar cost of a foreign currency.

EXERCISES AND PROBLEMS

Exercises

Exercise 1 Exchange Rates. Which translates into more U.S. dollars—ten Swedish krona when the krona per dollar rate is 1.7 or five British pounds when the rate is .65 pounds per dollar?

Exercise 2 Exchange Rates. If you are holding 10,000 Swiss francs and the exchange rate changes from 7.2 to 6.9 francs to the dollar. How much gain or loss will you have?

Exercise 3 Exchange Rates. A U.S. company purchases inventory from a manufacturer in China on credit and is billed 1,000,000 in Chinese currency, the yuan, when the exchange rate is 7 yuan to the dollar. In which direction would the exchange rate need to change in order to create a gain on the settlement (payoff) of this account payable? Prove your answer by showing calculations.

Exercise 4 Fluctuating Currency Rates. If a company is either to receive or to send foreign currency to settle a transaction, the fluctuating currency rates pose an additional risk. To experiment with this concept, use the Antweiler web site (you can link to it through the web site for this book) described in this Reading 5-1 to determine the gain or loss you would experience by holding one million units of two foreign currencies of your choice for a one-year period. The form on the Antweiler web site will permit you to select various time periods for virtually any currency around the world.

Exercise 5 Foreign Asset Valuation. Worldly Investments Inc. is contemplating purchasing a portfolio of assets located in several countries. Calculate the cost in U.S. dollars of these investments using the exchange rates of Monday of the week before this exercise is assigned. The investments, at their cost, are:

South African government bonds	10,000,000	rand
Factory building in Canada	5,000,000	Canadian dollars
Hotel in Hong Kong	25,000,000	H.K. dollars
Oil Tanker registered in Greece	95,000,000	drachmae

Problems

Problem 1 Cross Exchange Rates. Global International Inc. is a corporation headquartered in San Francisco. It has operating divisions worldwide. Its French division transacts its business in euros (€) because France is a member of the European Union. Britain has not adopted the euro and therefore Global's London division continues to transact its business in pounds (£).

Global's policy is to assign exchange losses (or gains) to division managers as part of a system of performance evaluation and bonus awards. It is up to division managers to negotiate and/or structure transactions in such a way as to neutralize the effects of possible exchange rate fluctuations. A related policy is that managers must not speculate on currency movements. A major transaction involving the French and British divisions is as follows:

The British division purchased equipment manufactured by the French division having a value of 1,000,000 £ on December 5, 2002.

a. What is the cross exchange rate £ per € if the exchange rates are:

On December 5, 2002	$ per £:	1.42
	$ per €:	.89

b. On January 5, 2003, the British division will settle its open invoice by paying the French division in €. Using the data above and the following estimated exchange rates, what is the gain or loss to the British division from the settlement of the open invoice? Give your answer in £ and $.

On January 5, 2003	$ per £:	1.40
	$ per €:	.95

Problem 2 Exchange Rate Scenario. Use the data from problem 1, part b. The manager of the French division is anxious to meet a sales goal for the final quarter of 2002. Given that the sale to the British Division is valued at 1,000,000 £, what would the cross exchange rate need to be in order for the French division to record a sale of 1,750,000 € if the $ per £ rate remains stable at 1.40?

Problem 3 Cross Exchange Rates and Exchange Gains and Losses. You have been assigned by Megatronics to manage a new foreign subsidiary involving an assembly plant in a foreign country. Your particular country assignment corresponds to your group number (see Exhibit 5-1.5). The U.S. parent corporation, Megatronics, Inc., has decided to open the foreign subsidiary with the transfer of $1,500,000.

Note: You can use the actual current exchange rates instead of those shown in Exhibit 5-1.5 (settlement date column) by going to the web site for this book and linking to a currency site.

a. Using the exchange rates in the first column of Exhibit 5-1.5, complete the balance sheet as of the opening date (first column of Exhibit 5-1.6) as it would appear denominated in the local currency of your assigned country and currency. If you are group 1, you are in Western Europe and the euro is your currency. You only need to use Cash and Parent's Equity balance sheet captions on the template.

b. As manager of the subsidiary, you are authorized to invest the $1,500,000 in other assets as follows:

   1. You are to purchase inventories of parts from suppliers located in China, Hong Kong, and Sweden as follows:

	Purchase Amount	**Currency Symbol**
China	R5,000,000	R
Hong Kong	D2,500,000	D
Sweden	K3,750,000	K

   These purchases are all on credit and are billed to you in the currency of the supplier country; for example, renmimbi for China.

   2. You also are to purchase manufacturing equipment on credit from Kyomitsu Tool Company in Japan in the amount of 35,000,000 ¥ (yen). You are billed in yen for this purchase. Complete the balance sheet as of the purchase date (second column of Exhibit 5-1.6) denominated in your local currency reflecting the assets purchased and the liabilities to the suppliers of those assets. Is there any gain or loss from the purchase of inventory and equipment?

c. As indicated above, your credit purchases are billed in terms of supplier currencies. Thus, settlement of your accounts payable requires you to purchase the appropriate quantity of foreign currency. Assume you do this at the exchange rates shown in Exhibit 5-1.5 under "At Settlement Date." *Note*: The actual cost of completing the purchase transactions may be more or less than that recorded in b above.

   First determine the invoice amounts fixed at the purchase date, June 15. Then determine your local currency cost of acquiring those amounts of foreign currency in order to settle the account payable on July 15 (column 3 of Exhibit 5-1.6). From these calculations, complete a balance sheet as of the settlement date (column 5 of Exhibit 5-1.6) showing the full settlement of liabilities to foreign suppliers. The adjustment for the net gain or loss from the transactions (column 4 of Exhibit 5-1.6) will be shown on the income statement. Since there are no other events that affect the income statement, net income for the period will be equal to the exchange rate gain or loss. Therefore, the gain or loss, if any, should be shown in the balance sheet below retained earnings as an "exchange gain (loss)" as of the settlement date, July 15.

Requirement 2 and 3 Example: Netherlands subsidiary owes 35,000,000 ¥ to Japanese supplier (*Note*: Netherlands is a euro country). Calculations necessary for this problem are illustrated below.

- What is the account payable stated in euros? To determine this, you must compute the cross exchange rate at the June 15 purchase date, the euro/yen exchange rate. From Exhibit 5-1.5, the euro/dollar exchange rate is 1.0830 and the yen/dollar rate is 134.0. To obtain the cross exchange rate of euro per yen, use the following relationship:

  Euro per dollar ÷ yen per dollar = 1.083 ÷ 134.0 = .0082

  The cross exchange rate is .0082 euro/yen and the 35,000,000 payable in yen is 287,000 euros (.0082 × 35,000,000). This amount would be reflected on the Netherlands subsidiary balance sheet as equipment and as accounts payable.

Exhibit 5-1.5
Units of Foreign Currency Per U.S. Dollar

Group Number	Country	Symbol	At Opening Date (June 1)	At Purchase Date (June 15)	At Settlement Date (July 15)
1	Euro(one of 12 € countries)	€	1.0760	1.0830	1.0920
2	China (renmimbi)	R	8.7190	8.3450	8.6570
3	Australia (dollar)	A	1.9800	1.9200	1.9000
4	New Zealand (dollar)	Z	1.9900	1.9500	1.9000
5	Hong Kong (dollar)	D	7.9900	7.8500	7.9500
6	Japan (yen)	¥	139.0000	134.0000	128.0000
7	Mexico (peso)	P	9.3100	9.1000	9.1000
8	Israel (shekel)	S	4.3500	4.2500	4.3500
9	Sweden (krona)	K	10.8500	10.6000	10.1000
*Assume that the average rate and the reporting rate are the same.					

- What is the amount of euros needed to pay off the account payable at the July 15 settlement date assuming the rates per dollar are 1.092 and 128.0?

$$\frac{1.092\ €}{128.000\ ¥} = .008531 \times 35{,}000{,}000\ ¥ = 298{,}585\ €$$

- The Netherlands subsidiary owes the Japanese supplier 35,000,000¥. In the interval between the time of purchase and the time of settlement (payoff), exchange rates changed. This cost the purchaser more euros (287,000 – 298,585) to satisfy the debt, resulting in an exchange loss of 11,585 euros.

Exhibit 5-1.6

Megatronic, Inc.
Foreign Subsidiary
Balance Sheets

Your Country: ____________ Domestic Currency: ____________

	(1) **Opening Date** **June 1**	(2) **Purchase Date** **June 15**	(3) **Cost to Settle** **July 15**	(4) **Loss (Gain)**	(5) **Settlement Date** **July 15**
Assets					
Cash					
Inventory:					
China supplier					
Hong Kong supplier					
Sweden supplier					
Equipment					
Total Assets					
Liabilities and Equity					
Accounts Payable:					
China supplier					Columns 2,3,4 should sum to zero for all payables
Hong Kong supplier					
Sweden supplier					
Japan supplier					
Total Liabilities					
Parent's Equity					
Retained Earnings					
Exchange Gain (Loss)					
Total Liabilities and Parent's Equity					

Note: Only those cells outlined need to be completed in your spreadsheet.

Case 5-1

RF CIRCUIT'S CONTRACT WITH OSAKA COMPONENTS

Case Objectives

1. Understand the effect of fluctuating exchange rates on manufacturing costs
2. Become acquainted with risk management in foreign exchange transactions
3. Reinforce your understanding of contribution margin analysis, present value analysis, and internal rate of return

Decision: Should RF Circuits have entered into the purchase commitment to buy components from Osaka?

RF Circuits manufactures computer high-speed wireless modems for other companies that market a full line of computer system components. Northwestern Digital, Inc. has agreed to purchase 1,000,000 completed modems annually that are specially manufactured for Northwestern by RF Circuits. Under the terms of the contract, Northwestern Digital, Inc. will take delivery of 1,000,000 units per year, at the following unit prices:

2002	2003	2004
$25	$20	$15

RF Circuits has agreed to the declining prices of its product because it believes new technology will render the existing product design somewhat obsolete.

In response to its deal with Northwestern Digital, RF Circuits, Inc. entered into a purchase commitment contract with Osaka (Japan) Components Corporation on January 1, 2002. The contract specified that Osaka will supply RF Circuits with 1,000,000 each of the fiberboard and chip set assemblies annually for three years commencing January 1, 2002. These assemblies are two of six subassemblies comprising the modem. The contract further stated that the prices per unit are fixed for the three-year term. Prices and engineering specifications are subject to renegotiation after the three-year contract has expired.

It is April of 2002. RF Circuits is heavily engaged in manufacturing to meet its 1,000,000 unit order for 2002. Management has asked you to project the manufacturing contribution margin for each of the three years.

Note: (¥ = yen, Japan's currency unit)

The following cost projections are provided:

Subassembly Costs	2002	2003	2004
Composite fiber board	300 ¥	300 ¥	300 ¥
Radio frequency transmitter	900 ¥	900 ¥	900 ¥
Cable	$ 2.00	$ 2.00	$ 2.00
Speaker/ringer assembly	2.00	2.00	2.00
Port connector assembly	3.00	3.00	3.00
Software and packaging	1.00	1.00	1.00

Because of its highly automated factories, RF Circuits has no direct labor costs. Direct variable overhead per unit is $2 for each of the three years.

U.S. economic policies have resulted in a strong dollar on currency markets. This, combined with Japan's persistent recession, caused the yen to decline in value relative to the dollar. For 2002, RF Circuit's management is projecting 150 yen to the dollar. However, it believes that Japan's long-awaited stimulative economic policies will strengthen Japan's currency to 125 yen in 2003 and 100 Yen in 2004 as the Japanese economy returns to a healthy growth rate.

Requirements

1. Using the data supplied, prepare an analysis of the sales revenue less the variable manufacturing cost for each of the three years. Compute the resulting manufacturing contribution margins for the three years. Using a computer spreadsheet will facilitate this assignment.

2. For a one-time $1,000,000 fee in addition to the cost of the two components, Osaka will guarantee an exchange rate of 128 yen per dollar. That is, if the exchange rate falls below 128 yen, Osaka will exchange yen for dollars at that rate for the amount RF Circuits owes them. If the exchange rate is above 128 yen per dollar, U.S. Circuits loses the benefit of the more favorable rate. In other words, for the $1,000,000 fee, Osaka will insulate RF Circuits from any risk (or benefit) of exchange rate fluctuations. Compare the contribution margin determined in Requirement 1 with the contribution margin resulting from the guaranteed exchange rate for the three-year project.

3. Using present value and internal rate of return functions on an electronic spreadsheet, advise the management of RF Circuits on whether it should accept the offer of a fixed exchange rate for three years from Osaka in return for the extra fee of $1,000,000. RF Circuits uses a 15 percent discount rate to evaluate potential investments.

Group Assignment 5-1

"EXCHANGING" THOUGHTS

Group Number __________ **Signature of group members participating:**

____

____

Objectives

1. Understand the effect of exchange rate change on contribution margin
2. Evaluate the financial risk of alternative scenarios

Requirements

1. Suppose that after the completion of the first year of the purchase and sales contracts with Osaka and Northwestern, respectively, RF Circuits can terminate its agreement with Northwestern to deliver 1,000,000 modems per year. The penalty for voiding the contract with Northwestern is $1,000,000. The amount is, coincidentally, the same as the one-time fee to Osaka, but the nature of the two supplementary payments is different. Contemplating this alternative, RF Circuits has negotiated a draft agreement (unsigned at this point) with Kompac Systems Corporation of Germany wherein Kompac will commit to the purchase of 1,000,000 wireless modems for the remaining two years of the original project. Determine the modem unit price and the aggregate sales revenue in dollars that RF Circuits would need to earn from Kompac to break even. Assume that the Osaka guarantee is not accepted.

2. You have determined that Kompac will enter into a fixed price contract with RF Circuits only if the price per modem is 20 euro. Kompac further demands that its settlement payment be in euro since it does not want to assume the risk that the European currency will depreciate against the dollar. Recently the exchange rate has hovered around $0.90 per euro. Evaluate this scenario and recommend a course of action to RF Circuit's management.

Reading 5-2

TRANSLATION AND CONSOLIDATION OF FOREIGN SUBSIDIARIES

INTRODUCTION

When a U.S. company has operations in foreign countries, the balance sheets, income statements, and statements of cash flows for majority-owned subsidiaries must be combined with the financial statements for its U.S. operations. The results are called the **consolidated financial statements** for that company. The process of combining parent and subsidiary financial statements is termed **consolidation**. The reason for consolidating all owned segments of the enterprise is to give shareholders a full disclosure of all activities over which the parent company has control. If a consolidated financial statement were not required, gains or losses experienced by a firm's subsidiaries would go unreported, possibly creating misperceptions about the financial health of the corporation.

TRANSLATION OF FOREIGN FINANCIAL STATEMENTS

Translation is the process of converting the financial statements of a foreign subsidiary into the currency used by the parent company. Recent changes in U.S. accounting rules specify that financial statements for most foreign subsidiaries be translated to U.S. dollars using the following rules:

1. All income statement accounts are translated at the average exchange rates for the year.

2. All balance sheet items except stockholders' equity accounts are translated at the current (or reporting date) exchange rate even though the assets remain on the books of the subsidiary at the original cost of acquisition in that country's currency. Translation is at a current rate for the sole purpose of published financial statements.

3. Stockholders' equity accounts are translated at their historical exchange rates. The exchange rate existing at the time a balance sheet item was set up is called the **historical exchange rate**. For example, if the initial investment in the foreign subsidiary occurred in 1980, then the 1980 exchange rate will be used to translate that amount of the parent's equity despite subsequent devaluations and other economic calamities. An **intercompany account receivable**, often called "due from subsidiary" and "due to parent", is also translated at the historical rate.

4. The amount required to balance the balance sheet is called the **cumulative translation adjustment**, or some similar title, and appears below Retained Earnings in the equity section of the balance sheet. It is called a "foreign currency translation" adjustment by Ford Motor Company, whose annual report is analyzed in Cases 5-4 and 5-5.

5. A footnote to the financial statements disclosing "comprehensive income" discloses gain and loss items that are not included in the income statement due to special accounting rules governing those transactions.

Translation and Consolidation Example

The following example illustrates the application of the basic translation rules that most U.S. multinational corporations use in their financial reports. A **multinational corporation** is a firm with subsidiaries located in more than one country. Let us begin by focusing on the opening balance sheet of a 100 percent owned subsidiary located in Great Britain. The opening date on the balance sheet is the date on which the U.S. parent corporation acquired or started the subsidiary, in our example December 31, 2002. The opening date balance sheet is presented as Exhibit 5-2.1. Note that the balance sheet is stated in British pounds (£) and that we will assume that the pound/dollar rate is .66667 at the close of business on December 31, 2002. The dollar/pound rate is the reciprocal, or 1.5, which is the multiplier when going from pounds to dollars.

Exhibit 5-2.1

British Subsidiary
Opening Balance Sheet
December 31, 2002

Assets	In Pounds	Exchange Rate	Translation (In Dollars)
Cash	£ 900	1.5	$ 1,350
Accounts Receivable	1,200	1.5	1,800
Inventory	1,500	1.5	2,250
Long-term Assets (net)	3,000	1.5	4,500
Total Assets	£ 6,600		$ 9,900
Liabilities and Stockholders' Equity			
Accounts Payable	£ 1,050	1.5	$ 1,575
Long-Term Debt	3,000	1.5	4,500
Total Liabilities	£ 4,050		$ 6,075
Stockholders' Equity			
Parent Equity	2,550	1.5	3,825
Retained Earnings	0		0
Total Stockholders' Equity	£ 2,550		$ 3,825
Total Liabilities and Stockholders' Equity	£ 6,600		$ 9,900

A summary of the different exchange rates used in this example is presented on the next page. The reciprocal rates state the dollar cost to buy one pound at the three dates. The cost to purchase the British currency increased by almost $.17 (rounded up) in 2003. This means that the value of the pound increased relative to the dollar. Now consider a U.S. company that has invested in Britain. The value of its investment would have increased, other factors being equal, because the value of the British currency has increased.

	December 31, 2002	**Year 2003 Average**	**December 31, 2003**
Pound per dollar rate	.66667	.64000	.60000
Dollar per pound rate (reciprocal)	$1.50000	1.56250	$1.66667

Recall that at the date of acquisition the pound/dollar rate was .66667. Translating stockholders' equity to U.S. dollars (2,550 × 1.5) gives $3,825, which is the amount paid in U.S. currency to acquire the net assets of the British subsidiary. The translation of the opening balance sheet to U.S. dollars would be completed using the current rate (December 31, 2002 rate), namely .66667 pounds per dollar.

Translation of the balance sheet as of the opening date is simply restating the assets, liabilities, and stockholders' equity accounts in another currency. Because all items in the balance sheet are translated at the same rate, no complications occur. However, as you will see in the next series of exhibits, the fluctuation in exchange rates coupled with the earning of revenue and incurring of expenses will require the inclusion of a translation adjustment.

Translation of the Income Statement

Exhibit 5-2.2 presents the British subsidiary's income statement for 2003. Note that the subsidiary earned 100 pounds from operations during 2003. Recall that the revenue and expenses are translated at the *average* rate for 2003, which we have assumed to be .64 pounds/dollar; the reciprocal rate is 1.5625 (1 ÷ .64) dollars/pound. This yields a net income figure of $156 in U.S. dollars.

Exhibit 5-2.2

British Subsidiary
Income Statement
Year Ended December 31, 2003

	In Pounds	Exchange Rate	Translation (In Dollars)
Sales	£ 9,000	1.5625	$ 14,062
Cost of goods sold	6,000	1.5625	9,375
Gross margin	3,000		4,687
Operating expenses:			
Selling and administrative	2,000	1.5625	3,125
Depreciation	500	1.5625	781
Interest	300	1.5625	469
Income before taxes	200		312
Income taxes (50%)	100	1.5625	156
Net income	£ 100		$ 156

Translation of the Balance Sheet

As indicated above, the assumed December 31, 2003 exchange rate is .6000 pounds/dollar, the reciprocal of which is 1.66667 dollars/pound. Exhibit 5-2.3 shows the translation of the year-end balance sheet at December 31, 2003. Note that all balance sheet items are restated at the current rate except that Parent Equity is translated at the historical rate and retained earnings is brought forward from Exhibit 5-2.2 in the amount of $156.

Exhibit 5-2.3

British Subsidiary
Balance Sheet
December 31, 2003

	In Pounds	Exchange Rate	Translation (In Dollars)
Assets			
Cash	£ 1,050	1.6667	$ 1,750
Accounts Receivable	1,600	1.6667	2,667
Inventory	2,000	1.6667	3,333
Due from Parent	1,000	1.5	1,500
Long-term Assets (net)	2,500	1.6667	4,167
Total Assets	£ 8,150		$ 13,417
Liabilities and Shareholders' Equity			
Accounts Payable	£ 3,100	1.6667	$ 5,167
Long-term Debt	2,400	1.6667	4,000
Total Liabilities	5,500		9,167
Shareholders' Equity			
Parent Equity	2,550	1.5	3,825
Retained Earnings	100		156
Cumulative Translation Adjustment	0		269
Total Shareholders' Equity	2,650		4,250
Total Liabilities and Shareholders' Equity	£ 8,150		$ 13,417

The intercompany account receivable resulted from the shipment of inventory to the parent having a cost of 1,000 pounds. This transaction is assumed to have occurred when the exchange rate was $1.50 per pound.

Translating the balance sheet items at different rates than at the beginning of the year rate is bound to cause an imbalance because the mix of assets and liabilities invariably changes over the year. In addition, depreciation expense is translated at the average rate of 1.5623 but the book value of long-term assets is translated at the current rate of 1.66667, another cause of a translation adjustment.

The translation adjustment of $269 results from changes in exchange rates when the net assets of the foreign operations are increasing or decreasing. To obtain insight into what caused the $269 addition to stockholders' equity, let us focus on the direction of change in the exchange rates.

Note that the parent corporation began its investment with $3,825. Even though that investment went into assets like receivables, inventory, and long-term items such as equipment, the translation process values the net assets as if the investment were held in currency instead of operational assets. Recall that had our world traveler in the previous reading converted dollars into Swiss francs, a gain would have been realized. Similarly, assets held in a country whose currency is appreciating relative to the parent country currency will report a translation adjustment in the parent balance sheet. In our example, the increase in value of the pound relative to the dollar caused a "gain" or increase in the cumulative translation adjustment of $269 in 2003.

The increase in value of the pound was approximately 11 percent in 2003. The translation adjustment of $269 is due to using a non-current exchange rate to translate the equity and intercompany receivable accounts, while using the current rate for the other assets and liabilities.

While the above may seem complicated and inconsistent, extensive debates surrounding the translation of foreign operations culminated in the consensus view that investors are best served if they see the assets, liabilities, revenues, and expenses translated at the current and average rates, as illustrated.

Consolidation

Exhibit 5-2.4 illustrates the consolidation of the parent and subsidiary balance sheets. Note that the British subsidiary balance sheet was translated to U.S. dollars in Exhibit 5-2.3. Also note that the Parent Corporation balance sheet shows the original investment of $3,825.

Consolidation is basically adding like balance sheet items together, with two exceptions. First, if there are intra-entity (within the same entity) receivables and payables, these are eliminated against each other to show the summarized financial position of the entire set of controlled corporations. An analogy might be a family in which one sibling owes another $100. If individual balance sheets were prepared, the creditor sibling would report a receivable of $100 and the debtor sibling would report a payable of $100. Now if it were deemed important to prepare a *family* balance sheet that consolidates all of the individual balance sheets, the intra-family receivable/payable would be eliminated since the transaction did not involve any other entity *outside* the family economic unit.

In Exhibit 5-2.4, the amount of the intercompany receivable/payable was £1,000 when the transaction took place. Intercompany items are not subject to exchange rate fluctuations so this item is translated at the exchange rate that existed at the time of the transaction, $1.50 per pound or $1,500.

The second exception is the Investment in subsidiary account on the parent's balance sheet and the Parent Equity account on the subsidiary's balance sheet. Because the objective of consolidated financial statements is to provide a report of the entire economic family of companies, the intra-entity investment and contributed capital cancel each other out. The elimination entry of $3,825 avoids the overstatement of assets and equities that would occur if we simply added across all balance sheet items.

Exhibit 5-2.4

Consolidation of Parent and Subsidiary
Balance Sheets
December 31, 2003

Assets	Parent	Subsidiary	Elimination Entry	Consolidation
Cash	$ 9,000	$ 1,750		$ 10,750
Accounts Receivable	15,000	2,667		17,667
Inventory	24,000	3,333		27,333
Due from Parent		1,500	(1,500)	
Long-Term Assets (net)	46,000	4,167		50,167
Investment in Subsidiary	3,825		(3,825)	0
Total Assets	$97,825	$ 13,417	$ (5,325)	$ 105,917
Liabilities and Shareholders' Equity				
Accounts Payable	$ 8,500	$ 5,167		$ 13,667
Due to British Subsidiary	1,500		$ (1,500)	
Long-Term Debt	40,000	4,000		44,000
Total Liabilities	$50,000	$ 9,167	$ (1,500)	$ 57,667
Shareholders' Equity				
Contributed Capital/Parent Equity	40,000	3,825	(3,825)	40,000
Retained Earnings	7,825	156		7,981
Cumulative Translation Adjustment		269		269
Total Shareholders' Equity	$47,825	$ 4,250	$ (3,825)	$ 48,250
Total Liabilities and Shareholders' Equity	$97,825	$ 13,417	$ (5,325)	$ 105,917

Exchange Rates and Profitability Analysis

Recall in Module 1 the discussion of profitability analysis. Module 1 explored the breakeven, target sales, and contribution margin components of profitability analysis. Also in Case 5-1, RF Circuits experienced a reversal from a highly positive contribution margin to a negative one due to the disadvantageous movement of a foreign currency exchange rate over a three-year period. Hopefully, you gained some insight into the impact of exchange rates on profitability. This section extends these related readings and cases to illustrate a model that can be used to better analyze profitability in a global business context.

Increasing global competition is the impetus for a new currency in Europe aptly called the euro. To improve the ability of Europe's countries to engage in commerce with one another the European Union (EU) decided to eliminate the barriers to trade created by those 12 different currencies. The euro is the currency unit that 12 countries, making up the majority of the European Union (EU), adopted in 1999 to replace the previous separate country currencies. Three countries, Great Britain, Sweden, and Denmark, are not adopting the euro.

Consider Renaud Import Company, an importer of champagne from the Epernay District in France. France is one of the countries that has adopted the euro. For illustrative purposes assume that champagne is the only product it markets. Renaud sells champagne to distributors in 12-bottle case lots for $120 per case. It pays the French winery 100 euro for each case. The variable costs are $5 per case and cover ocean shipping, insurance, agent fees, and import duties. These variable costs are paid in the United States. Renaud's annual fixed costs are $250,000. Jacques, Renaud's corporate controller, wants to know the company's breakeven point in case units at the current exchange rate of $0.90 per euro. Jacques is also concerned about the dollar declining against the franc, thereby increasing the variable cost of the imported champagne. If his company is currently selling 12,000 cases, Jacques wants to know what exchange rate would eliminate the current net income.

The basic breakeven formula presented in Module 1 is expanded to include the exchange rate:

Breakeven (units) = Fixed cost ÷ (Selling price – Variable cost)
Variable cost = Variable cost (domestic) + Variable cost (import)
Variable cost (import) = Variable cost (stated in foreign currency) × Exchange rate

Placing the various values in the adapted equation gives the following:

Breakeven = $250,000 ÷ (120 – [5 + (100 × .90)]) = 10,000 cases

The proof of this result can be shown in Renaud's income statement shown in Exhibit 5-2.5.

Exhibit 5-2.5

Renaud Import Company
Contribution Income Statement
Proof of Breakeven Point
For Any Year Ended December 31

Sales (10,000 cases @ $ 120)	$ 1,200,000
Variable costs:	
Import costs (10,000 @ $5)	50,000
Champagne cost (10,000 cases @ (100 euro at $.90)	900,000
Total variable costs	$ 950,000
Contribution margin	$ 250,000
Less: Fixed costs	250,000
Net income	$ 0

Note that the variable cost of imported champagne is shown parenthetically at the price of the product in terms of the foreign currency and its current exchange rate, $0.90 per euro. Because Renaud is selling 12,000 cases of champagne per year, 2,000 above breakeven, the net income is $50,000. Jacques is concerned that a fairly small movement in the exchange rate could wipe out the small profit of $50,000. The equation to determine the dollar price of a euro that would eliminate the profit is based upon the income statement equation:

Sales = Variable cost + Fixed cost + Net income

Because Jacques is worried about an exchange rate change wiping out the profit, the equation can set net income to zero because he wants to assess the likelihood that sales to the U.S. will not earn a profit. By setting the current revenue from the sales of 12,000 cases of champagne to the variable costs, we can compute the exchange rate, R.

$$\$1{,}440{,}000 = (12{,}000 \times \$5 + 12{,}000 \times [100 \times R]) + \$250{,}000 + 0 \text{ (net income)}$$

The two terms inside the parentheses are the import costs of \$5 per case and the expression that defines the dollar cost of champagne. The $[100 \times R]$ term is the price of the case of champagne in euro. Solving for R:

$$\begin{aligned}
\$1{,}440{,}000 &= \$60{,}000 + 1{,}200{,}000 \times R + \$250{,}000 + 0 \text{ (net income)}\\
\$1{,}130{,}000 &= 1{,}200{,}000 \times R\\
R &= \$1{,}130{,}000 \div 1{,}200{,}000\\
R &= \$\ .94167
\end{aligned}$$

If the euro appreciated relative to the U.S. dollar by moving from \$0.90 to \$0.94167, a case of champagne would now cost Renaud \$94.167 instead of \$90. A fairly small rise in the cost of euros of slightly more than 4½ percent was enough to wipe out the net income that Renaud was earning. The effect of the rise in the exchange rate is the same as if domestic variable costs rose by the same dollar amount. The increased variable cost reduces contribution margin and, therefore, net income.

Companies whose cost structure is largely determined by international currency rates take steps to insulate costs from fluctuations in exchange rates. There are many risk management strategies that financial managers use to, in effect, buy insurance against unforeseen losses due to unfavorable exchange rate shifts. Strategies such as hedge contracts, interest rate swaps, and financial derivatives are becoming a normal part of corporate financial management. These topics are typically covered in advanced international financial management courses.

SUMMARY

Many companies seek growth by expanding the scope of their business, seeking customers on other continents. Advances in transportation and information technology have facilitated the movement toward a global business strategy for many companies. With this global strategy comes greater complexity in dealing with many different customs and cultures but also the financial risk associated with fluctuating exchange rates. You were introduced to the impact of changing values of currencies and how businesses report their operations in foreign countries. Two accounting processes are involved when a U.S. company has a foreign subsidiary—translation and consolidation. Translation converts the accounting information stated in the foreign currency into dollars. Consolidation combines the accounting measurements to show the assets and liabilities of the entire economic family.

It was shown that profit volume analysis can help companies impacted by exchange rate movement assess their exposure to risk. A breakeven model can be developed to produce the range of exchange rate fluctuations that will test the company's ability to reach its financial goals.

EXERCISES AND PROBLEMS

Exercises

Exercise 1 Translation. A U.S. company established a subsidiary in Sweden on December 31, 2002, when the value of the krona was $0.44. The net assets at this date (assets minus liabilities) were 500,000 krona. A year later the net assets have not changed but the value of the krona is now $0.45. In the translation of the subsidiary's net assets, would a gain or a loss result? Provide your calculation.

Exercise 2 Consolidation. In a parent/subsidiary affiliation of two separate entities where the parent owns 100 percent of the subsidiary, how is the subsidiary's payable to the parent handled on the consolidation?

Exercise 3 Consolidation. How is the investment account on the parent company's books related to the shareholder equity account on the subsidiary's book? What is the treatment on the consolidation worksheet?

Exercise 4 Consolidated Statements. If a U.S. corporation consolidates the financial statements of subsidiaries in Japan and Brazil, what combined amount will be reported on the consolidated balance sheet if the amounts for inventory are $1,500,000, ¥27,000,000, and 14,000,000 real, and if the foreign exchange to dollar rates are 125 and 2.5 for Japan and Brazil, respectively?

Exercise 5 Intercompany Receivables. A U.S. parent company has transferred equipment costing $1,000,000 to its subsidiary in Canada. Its balance sheet reports a total of $40,000,000 in accounts receivable, including the $1 million receivable from the subsidiary. The Canadian subsidiary balance sheet reports 6,000,000 C (Canadian dollars) at the same date. On a consolidated balance sheet, what will be the total amount reported for accounts receivable assuming the $ per C exchange rate is .67?

Exercise 6 Intercompany Payables. Use the data from Exercise 5. If the U.S. parent reports $8,000,000 and the subsidiary reports 4,000,000 C in accounts payable, including the $1 million due the parent for the new equipment, what will the consolidated balance sheet show for accounts payable assuming the $ to C exchange rate is .65?

Problems

Problem 1 Translation of a Balance Sheet. Suppose the opening balance sheet of a subsidiary operating in Mexico is as follows (all amounts in pesos):

Cash	5,000	Accounts Payable	6,500
Inventory	7,000	Contributed Capital	16,500
Equipment	11,000	Retained Earnings	-0-

Translate the balance sheet items, assuming that the exchange rate at the opening balance sheet date is 9.5 pesos to the dollar. The parent's original investment in the subsidiary was $1,737.

Problem 2 Translation of Income Statement. The income statement of the Mexican company in Problem 1 for Year 1 is as follows:

Sales	25,000
Cost of goods sold	10,000
Gross profit	15,000
Operating expenses	2,000
Net income	13,000

Translate this income statement from pesos to dollars, assuming that the average exchange rate for Year 1 was 10.2 pesos to the dollar.

Problem 3 Translation of Balance Sheet at End of Year. Assume that the balance sheet of the Mexican subsidiary at the end of Year 1 is as follows:

Cash	$15,000	Accounts Payable	$30,500
Inventory	17,000	Contributed Capital	16,500
Equipment	18,000	Retained Earnings	3,000
Total	$50,000	Total	$50,000

If at the end of Year 1 the exchange rate is 11.2 pesos to the dollar, what are the dollar values of Contributed Capital, Retained Earnings, and the cumulative translation adjustment that would be used in consolidating the parent and subsidiary balance sheets? The exchange rate at the opening of the subsidiary was 9.5 peso per $ and the average rate was 10.2. The contributed capital was 16,500 pesos.

Problem 4 Profit Volume Analysis. Vancouver Software in British Columbia imports U.S. made software for resale in western Canada. Vancouver entered into an agreement to be the sole distributor of the software and to pay $100 per unit of product imported. Other pertinent information:

Projected unit sales	1,000
Selling price	240 Canadian
Current exchange rate	1.4 C per $
Fixed costs	100,000 C

Determine the dollar breakeven point for Vancouver Software.

Problem 5 Return on Sales. Assume Vancouver Software sells 1,500 units of the imported software at the projected price of 240 C. If the cost is 150 C per unit and fixed costs are 100,000 C, what is the return on sales?

Problem 6 Target Exchange Rate. By how much and in what direction would the exchange rate have to change for Vancouver to have net income of 25,000 if 1,000 units are sold? Use data from Problem 4 for this question.

Problem 7 Contribution Margin Ratio. Use data from Problem 4 for this question. Assume that the exchange rate suddenly changes from 1.4 C/$ to 1.2 C/$. What is the Vancouver's CMR before and after the change?

Case 5-2

OPENING A FOREIGN SUBSIDIARY AT CALIFORNIA CAR COMPANY

Case Objectives

1. Understand foreign currency concepts
2. Become familiar with issues involved in operating a foreign subsidiary
3. Demonstrate a simple balance sheet consolidation of a foreign subsidiary

Decision (Investment): Should CCC open a subsidiary in Mexico?

PRELIMINARY ANALYSES

CCC's president, David Gomez, is a member of the board of trustees of the state university located near the company's headquarters. At an October 1, 2002, meeting, the dean of the College of Business, Catherine Collinsworth, proposed to Gomez that the university's international business students do a market research study to determine the sales potential of low emission vehicles (LEV) in various foreign countries.

In response, David Gomez stated: "Your proposal is timely, Dean Collinsworth, for two reasons. First, our new manufacturing process utilizing a JIT work cell approach has significantly enlarged our unit capacity, so we are looking to increase our sales. The other reason is that the rising value of the U.S. dollar in currency markets has allowed foreign competition to lower their prices. This is hindering our strategy to appreciably improve domestic market share. We have been contemplating a global market strategy but, frankly, we have not done sufficient research to make a final decision."

Dean Collinsworth replied: "David, let me suggest that our students do the research for CCC. The university's Internet access as well as substantial library resources should enable the team to assess the export potential for CCC's products. I will put Jeremy Schiller, professor of International Marketing, in touch with you. He is always looking for good projects for his students."

David responded: "There's one hitch, timing. We will need their report in 30 days if we are going to launch an export initiative in this budget cycle. We will need to forecast foreign sales so that manpower and material needs can be formulated. We will also need to get together with our banking and legal folks to determine policies and procedures to operate in foreign countries."

"Understood, David. I will present this deadline to Professor Schiller. I am confident that his students will deliver an excellent report within that time frame," said Dean Collinsworth.

Excerpts From the Student Export Report

Thirty days later the students presented their report to CCC. Excerpts from the report are presented here.

Factors creating demand for LEVs in foreign countries:

* Tax credits exist for persons buying a LEV.
* Highway infrastructure is sufficiently well developed.
* There is growing preference for auto transport over rail or bus.
* Auto purchase is affordable for over 25 percent of households.

Screening criteria for CCC's products:

* Average trip length is less than LEV's range—150 miles.
* Cost is less than half of annual household income.
* The banking system is well developed to facilitate auto financing.
* A one percent market share is equal to 1,000 or more units.
* LEVs are less than one percent of autos in the country.

The top three countries meeting the criteria:

Based on the study performed, sales projections for the three countries with the predicted demand are as follows:

	Sedan Demand Forecast		
	India	Mexico	Brazil
High	5,000	3,000	2,000
Most Likely	4,500	2,400	1,500
Low	3,400	1,600	1,200

Limitations of the Study

The scope of the study did not include the differential variable and fixed costs that may be encountered in the various countries. Therefore, a ranking based solely upon demand criteria may not be the same ranking of profit potential in the three countries. Import duties, export licenses, commissions, freight, insurance, and sales costs may vary significantly in these countries. We recommend that these costs be determined and a comparative profit projection be made.

Management Meeting of November 10, 2002

David Gomez began the management meeting of November 10, 2002, by stating: "Last week Professor Schiller provided us the market research report authored by a team of his international marketing students. I trust all have studied the report and its recommendation. Let's go around the table for comments. George, let's hear marketing's input on this."

George Olson, vice president of marketing, responded: "The conclusions of the report appear to be backed up by solid data. There appears to be an unmet demand for cars like ours in the various foreign markets. However, I note that household income levels are considerably higher in Mexico than in Brazil or India. The government is achieving much-improved fiscal and monetary policies with the result that the economy has never been stronger. I recommend that Mexico be our initial foreign market to pursue."

Jena Butler, vice president of finance, interjected: "Let me second that. My staff researched shipping and insurance costs. From this analysis, Mexico is a market where we can deliver our products at very competitive prices. I estimate that it is going to take $1,000,000 to establish a sales subsidiary in Mexico. However, Mexico is encouraging foreign investment and is willing to arrange local financing of 70 percent of the initial investment required. That means our cash requirement is $300,000. There is one catch. Mexico, like so many countries, has serious limits on how much currency can leave the country. We may not be able to pull profits out of Mexico for several years."

Dennis Madison, vice president of engineering, stated: "Multinational companies repatriate (bring cash back to the parent company) the return on their foreign investments by forming a vendor alliance in the country where they sell products. Our Mexican subsidiary could pay for certain components and ship them back here for assembly into our LEVs. We need to locate ISO certified suppliers in Mexico."

Sally Swanson, vice president of manufacturing, interrupted, "I have studied the demand forecast for Mexico provided by the student team. The expected market share means a production requirement of 2,400 units per year. In 2003 we are planning to run at 80 per cent of absolute maximum capacity of 12,000 sedans, or 9,600 sedans. To add production requirements beyond that is really impossible for 2003. I agree that we need to open new markets. The projected Mexican sale of 2,400 sedans brings us right to capacity. My recommendation is that we adjust our planned production to 12,000 sedans and try to meet both domestic and Mexican demand."

David Gomez said: "It appears we have a plan. We will enter the Mexican market with our sedan LEV, provided the projected financial results meet our goal of a 20 percent return on equity. Jena, please crunch the numbers to see if we can meet that criterion in Mexico. I need that report at 8:00 a.m. tomorrow."

Requirements

1. Prepare a spreadsheet showing an opening balance sheet for the proposed CCC–Mexico subsidiary based upon the following transactions. Use the format shown in Exhibit C5-2.1. Requirement 1 asks you to complete columns 2, 3, and 4. Make sure your balance sheets balance.

    a. CCC–U.S. transfers $300,000 to CCC–Mexico as of January 1, 2003. Assume Jorg Hachenberger, CCC–Mexico's manager, converts the dollars into pesos using an exchange rate of 9.5 pesos/dollar.

    b. Jorg signs the necessary papers on January 1, 2003 to obtain a loan from the Bank of Cortez in the amount of 6,650,000 pesos.

2. Consolidate the effects of the above transaction with the balance sheet of CCC–US utilizing Exhibit C5-2.1. This requirement asks you to complete columns 5, 6, and 7.

Exhibit C5-2.1

California Car Company
Consolidated Balance Sheets for CCC–U.S. and CCC–Mexico
At January 1, 2003 (Planned)

	U.S. Parent			Mexican Subsidiary		CCC Consolidated	
	(1) CCC - U.S. Before Investment	(2) Investment Impact On CCC-U.S.	(3) CCC-U.S. After Investment	(4) CCC-Mex. After Loan & Investment	(5) CCC-Mex. Translation To Dollars	(6) Eliminations	(7) CCC Combined Balance Sheets
	$	$	$	Peso	$	$	$
Assets							
Cash	$ 1,462,000						
Accounts Receivable	13,600,000						
Inventory	840,000						
Long-Term Assets–net	90,000,000						
Investment in CCC–Mexico	0						
Total Assets	$105,902,000						
Liabilities and Shareholders' Equity							
Current Liabilities	$ 8,853,000						
Bank Loan to CCC–Mexico	0						
Long-Term Liabilities	10,000,000						
Total Liabilities	$ 18,853,000						
Shareholders' Equity							
Contributed Capital/Parent Equity	80,000,000						
Retained Earnings	7,049,000						
Total Liabilities & Equity	$105,902,000						

3. Jena Butler asks you to prepare a projected income statement for 2003 to estimate income of the Mexican sales subsidiary. In preparing the projection, several assumptions were given and are listed below. Use the format of Exhibit C5-2.2 to prepare the income statements.

Exhibit C5-2.2

California Car Company–Mexico
Budgeted Income Statement
Year Ended December 31, 2003

	Units	Unit Price (In Pesos)	Income in Pesos	Exchange Rate	Income in $
Sales	1,800	200,000	360,000,000		
Cost of sales	1,800				
Contribution margin					
Operating expenses			45,000,000		
Interest					
Income before tax					
Tax on income					
Net income					

a. Sale of sedan units will be less than the 2,400 originally forecasted. The development of effective advertising will take longer than anticipated, as is also true of prospective customer trust in the new product. Consequently, 1,800 units are forecasted to be sold in 2003, and 600 units will be in inventory at December 31, 2003.

b. CCC management decided to set the 2003 sedan price at 200,000 pesos. They plan an aggressive promotional campaign to introduce the LEV in the new market.

c. CCC–U.S. will ship CCC–Mexico sedan units using a transfer price of $14,000 each during 2003. The exchange rate used to record the intra-entity sales will be the forecasted average pesos/dollar rate for 2003. CCC–U.S. will ship 200 units to Mexico each month starting in January, 2003.

d. Forecasted 2003 exchange rates:

Beginning of year	9.5 pesos per dollar
Average for the year	10.2 pesos per dollar
End of year	11.0 pesos per dollar

e. Operating expenses are expected to be 45,000,000 pesos. Tax on income is 35 percent.

f. Interest on the loan from the Bank of Cortez is 13 percent per year.

4. Prepare a second income statement with the same information as in Requirement 3, except that the projected average exchange rate for 2003 is 11.2 pesos per dollar.

Case 5-3

THE MEXICO SUBSIDIARY AFTER ONE YEAR

Case Objectives

1. Understand concepts of translation gains and losses
2. Demonstrate year-end consolidation of a foreign subsidiary
3. Explore currency risk issues

Decision (Investment): Are the exchange rate risks associated with the Mexican subsidiary acceptable?

In Case 5-2 you began the financial analysis of opening a sales subsidiary in Mexico. This case looks at CCC's venture into foreign markets by combining the parent and subsidiary projected balance sheets at the end of 2003, after the first year of the Mexico operation. The purpose of this case is to complete the financial analysis and explore the risks involved in opening the subsidiary.

The Mexican peso per U.S. dollar exchange rates for 2003 are expected to be:

January 1, 2003	9.5 pesos per dollar
Average for 2003	10.2 pesos per dollar
December 31, 2003	11.0 pesos per dollar

Requirements

1. Make corrections to your solution to Case 5-2 based on the class discussion of that case. You must be sure that your projected income statement for CCC–Mexico for 2003 is correct. The retained earnings for CCC–Mexico is equal to the net income from the projected income statement

2. The balance sheets for CCC–U.S. and CCC–Mexico as of December 31, 2003 have been mostly completed for you in columns 1 and 2 of Exhibit C5-3.1. Using the information that follows, explain how the accounts receivable, inventory, and CCC–Mexico payable to parent amounts were determined for CCC–Mexico.

    a. Accounts receivable will be equal to the sales price of 50 sedan units at the selling price of 200,000 pesos each.

    b. Inventory is 600 units at the unit transfer price of $14,000 from the parent CCC–U.S. All units shipped to CCC–Mexico in 2003 were valued using the average exchange rate of 10.2 pesos per dollar.

c. The loan from the Bank of Cortez will be continued for another year at 6,650,000 pesos.

d. The 600 units in ending inventory have not been paid for and are a liability of CCC–Mexico called "Payable to U.S. parent."

e. There have been no changes in contributed capital, and no dividends have been paid by CCC–Mexico to the U.S. parent.

f. Current liabilities of CCC–Mexico at December 31, 2003 are 2,805,050 pesos. Included in this amount are payables for interest, salaries and wages, and supplies and services purchased locally.

3. Complete the balance sheet (column 2) for the Mexican subsidiary by computing the payable and retained earnings amounts and the total liabilities and total liabilities and shareholders' equity boxes.

4. Translate and consolidate the balance sheets of CCC–Mexico with CCC–U.S. In other words, complete the spreadsheet template shown in Exhibit C5-3.1. *Hint*: The cumulative translation adjustment will be the amount that makes the Mexican subsidiary's assets, after they are translated, equal to liabilities plus shareholders' equity.

5. Suppose that CCC–Mexico pays off the December 31, 2003, payable to CCC–U.S. for the 600 sedans on January 15, 2004, when the exchange rate is 11.35 pesos per dollar. CCC–U.S. demands to be paid in U.S. dollars, which amounts to $8,400,000 (600 sedans × $14,000). How many pesos does CCC–Mexico need on January 15 to convert to $8,400,000? Would CCC–Mexico have an exchange gain or loss on settlement of the payable?

6. If everything else remains as planned, to what level must the peso per dollar exchange rate change for CCC–Mexico to break even (earn zero income) in 2003? *Hint*: The only CCC–Mexico transactions that are not in pesos are the purchase of sedans from CCC–U.S. Use the income statement in Case 5-2. What is your assessment of the currency risk faced by CCC–Mexico?

7. Compute the projected 2003 return on investment for the Mexican subsidiary. CCC's investment in the Mexico subsidiary at the end of 2003 is expected to be $8,700,000 ($8,400,000 in receivables due from the subsidiary and the $300,000 initial investment).

8. David Gomez is concerned about the impact of political instability on the peso per dollar exchange rate. Is the projected income sufficient to earn an after-tax 20 percent return on investment if the peso per dollar exchange rate averages 12 instead of the projected 10.2? *Hint*: Recompute the 2003 income at an exchange rate of 12 pesos per dollar.

9. Based on your first-year calculations and analysis of risk, should CCC open the Mexican subsidiary?

Exhibit C5-3.1
California Car Company
Planned Consolidated Balance Sheet for CCC–U.S. and CCC–Mexico
December 31, 2003

	(1) CCC–U.S.	(2) CCC–Mex.	(3) Trans.	(4) CCC–Mex.	(5) Elimination	(6) Consolidated
	$	Peso	Rate	$	$	$
Assets						
Cash	$ 259,338	32,697,125				
Accounts Receivable	67,200,000	10,000,000				
Inventory	840,000	92,400,000				
Long-Term Assets–Net	180,060,000	0	N/A			
Investment in CCC–Mexico	300,000	0	N/A			
Receivable from CCC–Mexico	8,400,000	0	N/A			
Total Assets	$ 257,059,338	135,097,125	N/A			
Liabilities and Shareholders' Equity						
Current Liabilities	$ 18,265,322	2,805,050				
Bank Loan to CCC–Mexico	0	6,650,000				
CCC–Mexico Payable to Parent	0		10.2*			
Long-Term Liabilities	74,000,000	0	N/A			
Total Liabilities	$ 92,265,322		N/A			
Shareholders' Equity						
Contributed Capital/Parent Equity	132,000,000	2,850,000				
Retained Earnings	32,794,016					
Cumulative Translation Adjustment	0	0	N/A			
Total liabilities & Share. Equity	$ 257,059,338		N/A			

* For technical accounting reasons, use the average exchange rate of 10.2.

Reading 5-4

READING AND INTERPRETING ANNUAL REPORTS

INTRODUCTION

When corporations sell shares to the public, federal regulations require that they communicate with their shareholders on a prescribed periodic basis. The annual report is the most important means of accomplishing this requirement. Other important tools include Form 10K filings with the Securities and Exchange Commission (SEC), which are available to the public, meetings with securities analysts and reporters, and quarterly reports. Annual reports also are used to communicate with other corporate stakeholders, including prospective shareholders, employees, creditors and customers. In addition, competitive firms in the same industry may find annual reports of interest. We use Ford Motor Company's annual report as a model to compare its performance with the much smaller California Car Company.

THE CORPORATE ANNUAL REPORT

There is no universal style that annual reports follow. However, most annual reports include, in the following order:

1. A public relations section presenting the achievements of the firm,
2. A management discussion and analysis of operations,
3. The auditor's report,
4. The current year's financial statements and at least the previous year's statements for comparison purposes,
5. Footnotes to the financial statements, and
6. Supplementary data and a listing of the board of directors and top management.

Public Relations Section

The beginning section of most annual reports presents a positive view of the company and its prospects for the future. This section typically has numerous glossy pictures and highlights the firm's achievements during the year. This section is not audited so managers feel less constrained about painting a rosy picture here then in the management discussion and analysis of operations section.

Despite the optimistic slant, this section is very useful to investors. Readers can discover management's strategies, perceived progress toward implementing these strategies, and goals for the future. This section often discusses new product developments, programs to modernize production facilities, progress toward total quality management and just-in-time initiatives, and global issues. All this information helps investors better predict the firm's future performance.

Management Discussion and Analysis of Operations

In this section management presents its interpretation of the events that have occurred during the year that affect the financial statements. Financial results for the current and prior year are normally compared, and causes of differences in performance explained. Changes in accounting standards that impacted the financial statements are presented. Production problems, addition of new plant capacity, the economic environment facing the firm, and problems with individual products are usually discussed here. Finally, events related to investing and financing activities, as well as events that caused accounting write-offs, are explained.

Knowledge of these underlying events is important if an investor is trying to estimate future profitability and cash flows for the firm. For example, if some unusual and nonrecurring events significantly impacted the financial statements, then the investor will want to take these into consideration when using current statements to estimate future results. Although not audited, this section is reviewed by the auditors to ensure that no material misstatements are made.

Auditor's Report

The SEC, a U.S. government agency that regulates the financial investment industry, requires all publicly traded corporations to have their annual financial records audited by a certified public accounting (CPA) firm. The auditor's report expresses the CPA firm's opinion as to whether the financial statements present fairly the financial position, the results of operations, and the cash flows of the company audited.

The phrase "present fairly" means that the informed reader of the statements can rely on the statements to make investment decisions. It doesn't mean that they are accurate to the penny. Rather, present fairly means that the financial statements accurately portray the financial health of the firm. The auditor will report any uncorrected problems and material misstatements discovered. The report gives investors increased confidence that the financial statements and footnotes.

Although the auditor renders an opinion on the fairness of the financial statements, the statements are the product of the company's record keeping and thus are the responsibility of management. There has much litigation about whether the auditor or the management is responsible for the financial statements appearing in annual reports. Regulations now specify that management is responsible for preparing the financial statements and developing the internal controls needed to create accurate financial information. In Ford's annual report there is a section entitled "Management Report on Responsibility for Financial Reporting."

What, then, is the auditor's role? Auditors assess the adequacy of the company's internal control system and test transactions to see if the control system is operating properly. Because modern accounting systems operate using sophisticated computer systems, the CPA must be able to evaluate the integrity, security, and reliability of the data entering and exiting the system. The auditors also test the reasonableness of financial information given the economic environment and the company's level of sales and production. For large companies like Ford, CPA firms will perform such tests throughout of the year and have a large team working on the audit after the fiscal year has ended (December 31 for Ford). The auditor for Ford Motor Company is PricewaterhouseCoopers, L.L.P., a very large international CPA firm that is one of the so-called "Big Five" accounting firms. "L.L.P." is an abbreviation for limited liability partnership.

Although the vast majority of auditor's reports state that the financial statements fairly present the financial position of the companies being audited, you should not conclude that the auditors do not add value to their clients. First, most audits generate a list of recommended adjustments to the financial statements and footnotes to the financial statements. Companies are anxious to avoid having the auditors report anything negative because it may cause investors to lose confidence in the management and negatively impact the market price of its stock. Therefore, most companies agree to adjust their financial statements to reflect the work of the auditors.

Second, because management knows that the financial statements will be audited, they have a strong incentive to develop adequate internal control systems and to avoid reporting inaccurate results. In other words, simply knowing that an audit will occur helps keep management honest and careful. This is perhaps the most important role of the audit.

Because CPAs have a diverse set of clients in many industries, they are in a position to observe business trends and the evolution of the best management practices. Thus, another value perceived by many clients is the ability of the auditor to be an advisor. Managements often seek the CPA's advice about business strategy. Frequently the CPA who managed the audit of a company is hired by that company to be its chief financial officer (CFO). This is just one indication of both the financial and overall business expertise that the CPA brings to the client.

Footnotes to the Financial Statements

The footnotes to the financial statements (often referred to simply as notes, as Ford does) are an integral part of the financial statements. They are audited just as the financial statements themselves are. Footnotes address three main types of issues. The first type, Footnote 1, presents a summary of significant accounting policies. This footnote is important because GAAP allows alternate methods of accounting for similar business events. For example, companies are allowed to use straight-line depreciation or one of several accelerated depreciation methods. Footnote 1 tells the reader what alternate method(s) the company uses. A user of financial statements should always read these footnotes because a fair comparison of two companies may require reconciling different accounting policies.

A second use of footnotes is to present detailed information about key numbers shown in the financial statements. These footnotes usually provide readers with information explaining events that occurred during the year that affect items such as inventories, receivables, property and equipment, liabilities, income tax expense and accruals, stock options and other management compensation plans, shareholders' equity, pension costs and accruals, and changes in accounting methods. For diversified global companies, a footnote discloses detailed information on revenues and income from product or geographic segments of the company. The reader of Ford's annual report could determine the sales in the U.S. versus Asia, South America, and Europe. These footnotes provide the reader with sufficient information to spot problems at the company which are not apparent in the more summarized financial statements.

The third type of information in footnotes describes events that may have a significant impact on the company, but are difficult to quantify and to put in the financial statements. These footnotes address commitments made by the company, contingent liabilities, and special risks faced by the company. Items reported in these footnotes can have a catastrophic impact on a company. For example, the possibility of large losses arising from asbestos lawsuits was disclosed in the footnotes of Johns-Manville Corporation and several other asbestos producers years before actual losses caused these firms to declare bankruptcy. More recently, in 2001, a Florida court ruled against a large tobacco company and ordered it to compensate a long-term smoker who contracted lung cancer. This exposure to liability will appear in the footnotes well before it directly impacts the financial statements.

IMPORTANCE OF FINANCIAL INFORMATION

Does the disclosure of audited financial information in annual reports and SEC Form 10K filings benefit you? Does it benefit society? The answer is yes and yes. The information benefits both you and society because it helps to expand the economy. An improved economy raises our standard of living, causes the creation of good, high-paying jobs, and provides the resources to address societal problems such as pollution and crime.

To understand how audited financial information can improve economic performance, let's review the strengths of a market economic system. If people have an increased desire for a product or service, they will be willing to pay enough that an attractive profit is made by producers. When producers see that it is profitable to create the goods or services demanded, they will shift resources into the production of the profitable items. For example, when demand for in-line skates exploded, companies realized that a good profit could be made at the current price. Based on the profit potential, more manufacturers entered the industry to meet the huge increase in demand. The addition of more producers meant more competition. For producers of in-line skates to survive, they had to find ways to be as efficient as possible, thereby lowering the price to consumers. Note that no government official or anyone else ordered companies to manufacture more skates. Firms simply responded to market signals.

How do companies acquire capital to expand production when the market signals a profit opportunity? Two of the most important ways are the issuance of stock and the borrowing of money. How do stock and bond purchasers and other lenders such as banks decide if and at what rate of return they will provide funds to firms? They estimate how the firm will perform financially in the future. A company's financial statements are key pieces of information most investors and creditors use to make these decisions.

As a result of decisions made worldwide by millions of firms and millions of investors, firms with high future income and cash flow potential attract funding and grow. An example of this phenomenon is Microsoft Corporation. In 1998 it received the distinction of being the world's most valuable publicly owned corporation. This happened because investors bid up the price of Microsoft's stock. Conversely, firms with poor potential cannot attract capital. They stagnate. Once again, the market has signaled where funds should be invested. No one orders banks, pension funds, and other investors to provide capital for certain firms or industries. The alternative to a market system is to let the government and politicians pick winners and losers. Most economists attribute the collapse of the Soviet and other Eastern European "planned" economies to woefully inefficient allocation of resources by politicians and bureaucrats making the investment decisions.

What role does *audited* financial information play? The ability to focus investments toward firms that show high potential is limited by the quality of information to which investors have access. Investors cannot, of course, acquire perfect information, but the better the information that investors have, the more funding high potential firms will receive. If high potential firms receive better funding, the economy will grow faster and consumer wants will be better satisfied. Audited financial information gives investors more accurate, complete, and unbiased financial information than firms might give in the absence of an audit. Thus, the improved quality of audited information used by investors creates a more efficient allocation of resources in the economy and increases the standard of living.

RATIO ANALYSIS

Users of financial information typically employ ratio analysis to better assess a company's performance. Several key ratios were discussed in Reading 1-1 and that discussion is reproduced here for your convenience. Three additional ratios are introduced in this section so that you can expand the scope of your analysis. You may also want to go back and review Reading 1-2, which discusses how the cash flow statement can be used to analyze financial performance.

Shareholders' Equity Section of the Balance sheet

The shareholders' (or stockholders') equity section of the balance sheet (also termed the *book value* of the firm) is the accounting valuation accruing to the preferred and common shareholders. It is composed primarily of the following six components of total shareholders' equity:

1. *Preferred stock* is the par value assigned to the preferred shares outstanding at the balance sheet date. **Par value of stock** is an arbitrary valuation assigned to the stock at the time the stock is initially authorized (created). CCC has no preferred stock. Ford has almost no preferred stock in 2000. **Preferred stock** is a stock that has the first claim on dividends and priority over common stock in the event of a liquidation of the company.

2. *Common stock* is the par value assigned to the common shares outstanding at the balance sheet date. Ford's common stock has a par value of $0.01. More than a billion common shares were outstanding at the end of 2000.

3. **Additional paid-in capital** (also referred to as contributed capital in excess of par) is the difference between the par values of the preferred and common shares issued and the actual amount received by the firm when the shares were issued (exchanged for cash or other assets).

4. The *retained earnings* balance is the sum of all net income reported by the firm over the period of its existence, less dividends and other distributions, less adjustments (discussed separately in the next item). Ford is a corporation with a long history of profitable operations. Its retained earnings were over $17 billion at the end of 2000 as reported on its balance sheet.

5. *Adjustments to retained earnings* are accounting entries that adjust retained earnings for special events. The most important adjustment for most global firms is the cumulative translation adjustment (CTA). Many firms show the CTA as a separate line item in the shareholders' equity section of the balance sheet. For example, Ford reported a CTA (termed *foreign currency translation adjustment* by Ford) of more than negative $1.5 billion on its December 31, 2000 consolidated balance sheet. CCC has no adjustments to retained earnings (but it will when and if the Mexico subsidiary is operational).

6. **Treasury stock** is the cost paid to buy back shares in the corporation from shareholders. These shares are not part of the shares outstanding number, so they are not used to compute earnings per share (EPS) and book value per share.

Current Ratio

The *current ratio* (CR) is a measure of a company's ability to meet its short-term debt obligations. A value of 1.0 would result if current assets were equal to current liabilities. A CR equal to one is considered marginal; the company would possibly have difficulty meeting scheduled payments to creditors. A CR of 4 means that there are four dollars of current assets for every dollar of current liabilities reported on the balance sheet. This favorable ratio gives the company much flexibility to manage its current assets and still have sufficient cash resources to pay short-term debts when due. In equation form:

$$\text{CR} = \frac{\text{Total current assets}}{\text{Total current liabilities}}$$

For many companies, a long-standing rule of thumb is that the current ratio should be no less than 2. For every dollar of current liabilities, there should be at least two dollars of current assets. However, there needs to be a careful assessment of the liquidity needs of the business. For example, in a highly seasonal business such as a holiday ornaments or fireworks manufacturer, it may be more prudent to have a significantly greater ratio than 2 because of the time it will take to manufacture the product, sell the product on credit, and collect the resulting accounts receivable. Conversely, an airline, which collects much of its revenue in advance of service, may not require a robust CR since it does not manufacture a product, thus precluding the need for inventory investments. Many electric and water utilities similarly have a CR of less than 2.

The best approach to determining the range of CR that is appropriate is to compare the CR of the company being researched with its counterparts in the same industry. Because the financial characteristics of an industry will impact all companies in essentially the same way, a study of the CR exhibited by competitors will provide a good guide to the appropriate CR level.

Return on Equity Ratio

The *return on equity ratio* (ROE) is computed by dividing net income by average shareholders' (or stockholders') equity. Average equity is the sum of the beginning equity balance and ending equity balance divided by 2. In equation form,

$$\text{ROE} = \frac{\text{Net income}}{(\text{Beginning equity} + \text{Ending equity}) \div 2}$$

ROE is usually considered to be the primary measure of overall firm performance. A high ROE compared to previous years and to firms that face similar risks is an indication of good performance.

Return on Sales Ratio

The *return on sales ratio* (ROS), often referred to as profit margin percentage, is computed by dividing net income by sales revenue. In equation form:

$$\text{ROS} = \frac{\text{Net income}}{\text{Sales revenue}}$$

ROS is a measure of the profit earned on each sales dollar. Increasing ROS or a high ROS relative to other firms in the same industry is usually an indication of efficient operations and good cost control. It is important to compare ROS only with firms in the same industry because ROS will vary greatly from industry to industry. For example, a reasonable ROS might be .02 for a supermarket, but might be .08 for a jewelry store. One reason for the difference in the example ROS is that supermarkets may generate several times the level of sales per dollar of investment than do jewelry stores. As a result, supermarkets need only have an ROS that is a fraction of the jewelry business in order to earn the same ROE.

In Ford's 1997 Annual Report to shareholders, its chairman of the board writes:

> In 1997, for the first time ever, we announced financial goals for our automotive business. In North America, we targeted a return on sales (ROS) of 4 percent. We exceeded (that goal) . . . Our North American return on sales was 5.1 percent.

Inventory Turnover Ratio

The *inventory turnover ratio* (ITR) is computed by dividing cost of goods sold by the average inventory. In equation form:

$$\text{ITR} = \frac{\text{Cost of goods sold}}{(\text{Beginning inventory} + \text{Ending inventory}) \div 2}$$

ITR is a measure of how efficiently inventory is managed. Increasing ITR or a high ITR relative to other firms in the same industry is an indication of efficient inventory management. All other factors held constant, the higher a firm's ITR, the better able it is to charge lower prices than the competition. The ROS can be lower to earn the same ROE because less investment is needed when inventories are efficiently managed. In Module 3 you learned that ITR is also an important measure of flexibility and ability to meet customer needs effectively. Just-in-time inventory policies have increased ITR in recent years because less investment in inventory is required for the same level of output.

Debt-to-Equity Ratio

The *debt-to-equity ratio* (DER) is computed by dividing total debt by total equity. In equation form:

$$\text{DER} = \frac{\text{Total liabilities}}{\text{Total shareholders' equity}}$$

DER is a measure of a firm's financial risk (likelihood of going bankrupt) and the extent to which a firm is taking advantage of cheaper debt financing. Both a relatively high DER and a relatively low DER are undesirable. Therefore, firms strive to achieve an optimum DER. An increase in a firm's DER or a high DER relative to the industry indicates higher financial risk and greater use of debt financing. DER varies greatly from industry to industry. For example, utilities, with a stable demand in a monopoly market, normally have a much higher DER than electronics firms, which face intense competition and short, risky product life cycles. DER is particularly important to bankers, bondholders, and other creditors.

Earnings per Share Ratio

The **earnings per share ratio** (EPS) is computed by dividing net income less preferred stock dividends by the average number of common stock shares outstanding during the year. In equation form:

$$\text{EPS ratio} = \frac{\text{Net income} - \text{Preferred stock dividends}}{\text{Average number of common stock shares}}$$

Although this equation is somewhat complicated, this does not present a problem in analyzing financial statements because EPS is computed for you. At the bottom of the income statement, two earnings per share numbers are computed: basic EPS and diluted EPS. **Basic EPS**, as the name implies, is the number most analysts focus on. It uses the weighted average number of shares outstanding for the year as the denominator. **Diluted EPS** includes in the denominator all potential new shares that could be issued to fulfill contractual arrangements. An example of the additional shares in diluted EPS arises from stock options. A **stock option** is a right to purchase shares at a fixed price for several years into the future. Another example is contingent shares based upon future profitability arising from an acquisition of another company.

Earnings/Price Ratio and Price/Earnings Ratio

The **earnings/price ratio** (E/P) is computed by dividing the EPS (normally basic EPS) by the stock price. Although the E/P ratio is not commonly used in business, it often is more understandable to students. The E/P ratio shows the current "rate of return" on the purchase of a share of common stock. That is, an E/P ratio of .10 means that a firm's EPS is 10 percent of the stock's market price. You can think of E/P as similar to interest received on a bond or a bank certificate of deposit. The E/P ratio is not, however, a true rate of return because (1) the return has not been realized, since shareholders seldom receive cash dividends equal to EPS; and (2) it ignores the impact of personal income taxes.

The **price/earnings ratio** (P/E) is much more commonly used in business. It is simply the reciprocal of the E/P ratio and in equation form is:

$$\text{P/E ratio} = \frac{\text{Common stock price}}{\text{Basic earnings per share}}$$

All other things being equal, a high P/E ratio means that investors have a favorable opinion of a firm's growth potential compared to other firms, particularly in the same industry. A firm with a high P/E ratio is also considered "expensive" because a high price is being paid for the stock compared to the firm's earnings. Conversely, a low P/E ratio often occurs when a firm is out of favor with investors. Thus the P/E ratio can be viewed as an indicator of investor sentiment about the prospects for growth in income and cash flows.

EPS is used by financial analysts instead of total income because it adjusts a firm's income for an increasing or decreasing number of shares. For example, assume that a firm's net income increases from $1,000,000 in 2002 to $1,200,000 in 2003. During the same period common stock and equivalents increase from 500,000 shares to 1,000,000 shares because the firm issued more shares. Does this increase in income represent good performance from a common stockholders' perspective? Not necessarily, because EPS declined from $2.00 in 2002 to $1.20 in 2003. In response to this issue of more shares, the market price of this company's stock price would probably fall because investors would anticipate the effect on

EPS. EPS is the denominator of the price/earnings ratio. A PE ratio of 20 applied to the EPS given above would suggest that the market price would be $40 per share in 2002 and $24 in 2003.

However, if the 20 percent growth in earnings is a sustainable pattern for the company in our example, the stock price decline might not be so severe. PE ratios are correlated with growth rates of sales and income. High growth rate companies tend to have high PE ratios and low growth rate companies tend to have low PE ratios.

Book Value per Share

The *book value per share ratio* (BV/S) is computed by dividing total shareholders' equity (if no preferred stock exists) by the number of common stock shares outstanding *at the balance sheet date*. In equation form,

$$BV/S = \frac{\text{Total shareholders' equity}}{\text{Common stock shares outstanding}}$$

BV/S is a number frequently used by analysts. A BV/S that is near or above the stock price indicates that investors are not enthused by the firm's performance. The stock price is reflecting the net assets per share rather than future income potential. It could mean that the firm's earnings are weak, that there is little confidence in management's ability, that the firm has created little goodwill or value through product and personnel development, or that uncertainties exist that could have a negative impact on the firm. Conversely, when the stock price is way above the BV/S, it means that investors have favorable expectations that are not yet reflected by the financial statements.

Ratio Analysis Example

The following financial information relates to Walnut Woods Company. Walnut Woods has no preferred stock and no convertible bonds or stock options.

	2003	2002
Net income	$1,200,000	$ 800,000
Shareholders' equity, December 31	$8,000,000	$6,000,000
Weighted average shares outstanding	100,000	90,000
Shares outstanding, December 31	110,000	95,000
Stock price, December 31	$100.00	$90.00

Key Walnut Woods ratios for 2003 and 2002 are computed below.

	2003	2002
Earnings per share	$12.00	$8.89
	[$1,200,000 ÷ 100,000]	[$800,000 ÷ 90,000]
Earnings/Price ratio	.120	.099
	[$12 ÷ $100]	[$8.89 ÷ $90]
Price/Earnings ratio	8.33	10.12
	[$100 ÷ $12]	[$90 ÷ $8.89]

Book value per share	$72.73	$63.16
	[$8,000,000 ÷ 110,000]	[$6,000,000 ÷ 95,000]

The EPS for Walnut Woods increased from 2002 to 2003, indicating that earnings are increasing faster than the number of common shares, which is a positive result. The E/P ratio shows that EPS as a percent of common share price increased from 2002 to 2003. The P/E ratio declined from 2002 to 2003. The interpretation of changes in the E/P and P/E ratios suggest several scenarios. The changes could mean that the earnings for Walnut Woods are just catching up to investors' expectations, or it could mean that investors see problems ahead and are unwilling to pay a higher multiple of earnings for Walnut Woods' stock.

The increase in BV/S indicates that total shareholders' equity is increasing faster than the number of shares of common stock, which is positive. In addition, the book value is well below the market price of the stock in both years, possibly indicating that investors view the operations of the company favorably.

Of the total increase in shareholders' equity, $800,000 is explained by the issuance of 15,000 additional shares, and $1,200,000 is explained by net income (no dividends were paid). On average the new shares were issued for $53.33 each ($800,000 ÷ 15,000). Issuing stock below market price often occurs in companies that give a stock option to employees. This is because the option price is frequently below the market price at the time an employee is permitted to exercise the option. If an employee exercised an option to purchase 1,000 shares at $53.33 when the market price was $100, the unrealized gain for the employee on the transaction would be $46.67 per share ($100 – $53.33). The employee could realize the gain by selling the shares on the open market providing there were no restrictions imposed by the stock option contract or SEC rules.

Assessing Market Price of Shares

Top management of publicly-held corporations are concerned about the stock price of the corporation because they are expected to consistently increase shareholder value. At any point in time, shareholder value can be measured by the number of outstanding shares times the market price per share. When a company reports increased income compared to the previous year, the investing public may perceive that the company and its management have the ability to sustain growth. This in turn causes greater relative demand for the stock of that company. More people wanting to own the stock of a growing company and fewer willing to sell the stock will normally result in a higher stock price. An increase in stock price may also result from a new product announcement, which means higher future revenues and income. When these favorable developments occur, the management is deemed to be successful at attaining the goal of increasing shareholder value.

The various financial ratios presented in this reading can be used to make a rudimentary assessment or estimate of the market price of a company's shares. It often happens that a privately-held corporation may wish to consider an initial public offering. It uses the market price of other public companies together with their financial statements to estimate the probable market value of its shares. However, a word of caution is appropriate here. There are many factors that can influence the value of a company. You should not infer that the following hypothetical example is a definitive valuation model. The goal of this section is to illustrate how the financial ratios can be used to interpret financial statement information.

Suppose you are given the following comparison data for Public Corporation and Private Company, the latter being interested in selling shares to the public and wanting to get an estimate of what its stock might sell for.

	Public Corp.	Private Co.
Return on equity (ROE)	22.4%	36.8%
Return on sales (ROS)	4.5%	6.0%
Inventory turnover ratio (ITR)	10	12
Debt to equity ratio (DER)	30.5%	65.0%
Earnings per share (EPS)	$1.50	$2.21
Book value per share (BV/S)	$6.70	$6.00
Price earnings ratio (P/E)	20	unknown
Market price of a share	$30	?

If Public's P/E ratio were applied to the EPS of the Private Co., the estimated stock price would be $44.20 (20 × $2.21). Comparing Public's market price per share ($30) to its BV/S of $6.70, the stock is trading at 4.478 (30 ÷ $6.7) times its book value per share. If Private's stock also trades at 4.478 times its book value, the estimated stock price would be $26.87 (4.478 × $6).

The significant difference ($44.20 versus $26.87) illustrates the valuation of a company stock based upon its income versus a valuation based upon book value. In many industries, the expectation of investors focuses on future net income because income predicts future cash flows. Investors are interested in future cash flows because they are the source of dividends and the ability of the corporation to expand with internally generated resources.

Even though the book value of Private Company is lower than Public, its stock price could be higher if the evidence points to a better-managed company. Private has a better ITR, a better ROS, and a better ROE. However, its much higher DER means that Private has a much greater proportion of its assets financed by creditors than by shareholders (more risk). The interest cost associated with the borrowing is a fixed cost and could cause net income to drop quickly if sales revenue falls. Therefore, Private is a more risky company than Public.

If Private is in an industry typified by low DER companies, its market price would probably be somewhat below the $44.20 because investors would discount the normal P/E due to the higher DER. Based upon the limited information, a reasonable estimate for the Private Company's stock price would be about $40 per share, still considerably above the BV/S valuation above.

SUMMARY

The annual report to shareholders is a primary source of information to investors and discloses the financial state of the corporation. Two parts of the report are the auditor's opinion and the financial statements. Investors rely on the opinion of the CPA firm that audits the financial statements. Investors want to see an opinion that states that the financial statements present fairly the financial position, income, and cash flow of the company in accordance with generally accepted accounting principles.

Audited financial statements provide a basis on which investors can analyze the performance of a company. Various ratios were presented to facilitate a comparison of one company's performance with its ratios in prior years or with ratios of another company in the same industry. Both small and large companies can be compared using ratios because the magnitude differences are eliminated. The ratio values can be compared to industry statistics to determine if the company is performing better, worse, or equal to other companies in the same industry. A comprehensive analysis using these ratios can provide insights into the proper valuation of companies.

EXERCISES AND PROBLEMS

Exercises

Exercise 1 Debt to Equity Ratio. The Mission Corporation balance sheets for 2002 and 2003 report total liabilities of $2 million and $4 million respectively. If the DER changed from 1.0 in 2002 to 1.5 in 2003, explain the changes that must have occurred in 2003 on Mission's balance sheet.

Exercise 2 Inventory Turnover Ratio. A shipbuilder has an ITR of 1 while a supermarket chain has an ITR of 18. Discuss the industry characteristics that explain this contrast.

Exercise 3 Book Value per Share Ratio. Using the 2000 Ford Motor Company annual report, http://www.ford.com/2000annualreport/default.html, calculate the BV/S of Ford common stock. Show your computation. Ignore preferred stock. The number of shares is given in the caption "Common Stock."

Exercise 4 Book Value and Earnings per Share. At the end of 2002, Verve Company had a BV/S of common stock of $22 based on one million shares outstanding. Retained earnings was zero. For the entire year 2003 the EPS was $5 and Verve paid a $1 dividend to shareholders owning the total of one million shares. What is the BV/S at the end of 2003?

Exercise 5 Return on Equity and Return on Sales. Stamp Incorporated reported sales of $15 million, net income of $2 million, and average shareholders' equity of $6 million for 2003. What is Stamps' ROE and ROS? If the industry norms for these ratios are .20 and .15 respectively, comment on the performance of Stamp.

Exercise 6 Ford's Current Ratio. Use the Ford web site to access the balance sheet: (http://www.ford.com/2000annualreport/default.html). Calculate the current ratio for 1999 and 2000. Because Ford has a financing as well as a manufacturing division, it is necessary to add the current assets and current liabilities for automotive to the financing current assets and current liabilities. Comment on the direction of change. What is your opinion of Ford's current ratio?

Exercise 7 Earnings per Share. Tahoma Corp reported net income of $15,000,000 for both 2002 and 2003. The average shares outstanding for 2002 was 3,000,000 and Tahoma issued no shares in 2002. Tahoma issued 500,000 new shares at the beginning of 2003. What is the earnings per share for both years?

Exercise 8 P/E Ratio and Stock Price. Use the data in Exercise 7. If Tahoma shares were selling for $100 at the end of 2002, what is your estimate of its stock price at the end of 2003 if the PE ratio does not change?

Exercise 9 Return on Equity. Atlas Corp. currently has an ROE of .25 on an average stockholders' equity of $10,000,000. It plans to acquire another company by issuing more stock. This will make the average stockholders equity next year $15,000,000. What consolidated net income must Atlas attain to maintain its ROE?

Exercise 10 Ford's Debt to Equity Ratio. Using the 2000 annual report, determine whether Ford's DER improved or worsened during 2000. Combine the liabilities of automotive and financing to make this calculation. Comment on the change if any. http://www.ford.com/2000annualreport/default.html

Problems

Problem 1 Interpreting Financial Statements from Different Industries. The income statements and balance sheets of three companies are reproduced at the end of the problem section. Hard Rock Industries is a producer of cement. Michaelangelo Foods, Inc. is a processor of food products such as potatoes, eggs and dairy items. Second Street Cafes is an operator of franchise restaurants. These three companies represent very different industries.

All three companies are publicly traded, meaning that investors have purchased shares in these corporations. Federal law requires that publicly traded corporations have an independent auditor—a certified public accountant—render an opinion on their financial statements each year. In all three companies, the CPA firms performing the audit services reported that the "statements present fairly, in all material respects, the income and financial position ... in conformity with generally accepted accounting principles."

a. What is a major difference in the industries represented by these three companies?

b. Which company has had the greatest increase in revenues from 2001 to 2002?

c. Because the three companies are in different industries, the expense classifications on the income statements are different. Comment on the differences you observe and relate it to the industry each company is in.

d. Which company has the largest income (earnings) before income tax in dollar terms? In terms of a percentage of revenues? What is the ROS of each company?

e. Calculate the ITR of each company. Present your theory of why the industries differ and help explain varying inventory turnover ratios.

Problem 2. Analyzing Balance Sheet Information. Use the financial statements for Hard Rock Industries, Michaelangelo Foods, Inc., and Second Street Cafes to complete the requirements. Problem 1 describes the industries in which these companies operate.

a. Calculate the DER for each company. Use all items on the balance sheets that are listed under the liability heading. For stockholders' equity use all items under that heading. Which company has the highest DER?

b. Calculate the ROE for each company.

c. In which company would you prefer to invest based solely upon these two ratios? Explain your rationale.

Problem 3. Comparing Financial Results and Stock Prices. Assume that the stock prices for the three companies listed in Problem 1 are:

	Ending 2002 Stock Price
Hard Rock Industries	$ 76.00
Michaelangelo Foods	26.00
Second Street Cafes	5.00

a. Calculate the P/E ratio for each company at the end of 2002. Do the different P/E ratios correlate with any of the ratios in Reading 5-4? For example, did the company with the highest ROS also have the highest P/E ratio? Explain.

b. Compare the book value per share of each company with its market price per share. If price per share exceeds the book value per share does the excess correlate with any of the financial performance ratios presented in Reading 5-4?

Hard Rock Industries, Inc.
Consolidated Statement of Income

(In thousands except per share amounts)	For the Year Ended December 31, 2002	For the Year Ended December 31, 2001	For the Year Ended December 31, 2000
Revenues	$ 374,059	$ 378,058	$ 333,776
Deductions from revenues:			
Cost of sales	219,290	237,114	217,942
Selling, general and admin. expenses	28,857	28,508	29,734
Depreciation and depletion	23,591	24,060	23,628
Interest expense	3,585	6,606	9,096
	$ 275,323	$ 296,288	$ 280,400
Income before income taxes	$ 98,736	$ 81,770	$ 53,376
Provision for income taxes	33,323	27,610	17,614
Net income applicable to common stock	$ 65,413	$ 54,160	$ 35,762
Weighted average common shares outstanding:			
Basic	10,941	11,290	11,990
Earnings per common share:			
Basic	$ 5.98	$ 4.80	$ 2.98

Hard Rock Industries, Inc.
Consolidated Balance Sheets

(Dollars In thousands)	December 31 2002	December 31 2001
Assets		
Current Assets		
Cash and equivalents	$ 154,080	$ 71,215
Accounts and notes receivable, net	28,217	33,336
Inventories	43,103	53,869
Other current assets	7,576	6,794
Total current assets	$ 232,976	$ 165,214
Property, plant and equipment, net	299,255	322,982
Other assets and deferred charges	66,746	73,955
Total assets	$ 598,977	$ 562,151
Liabilities and Shareholders' Equity		
Current Liabilities	$ 63,382	88,236
Long-term liabilities	201,961	209,633
Total liabilities	$ 265,343	$ 297,869
Common stock, $1 par value.		
Shares issued: 2002—12,091,866; 2001—12,086,510	12,092	12,087
Warrants to purchase common stock	15,554	15,574
Additional paid-in capital	174,915	163,664
Retained earnings	178,444	115,228
Treasury stock, shares: 2002—1,366,009;2001—1,373,509	(47,371)	(42,271)
Total shareholders' equity	$ 333,634	$ 264,282
Total liabilities and shareholders' equity	$ 598,977	$ 562,151

Michaelangelo Foods, Inc.
Consolidated Statement of Income

YEARS ENDED DECEMBER 31	*2002*	*2001*	*2000*
Net sales	$ 956,223,000	$ 616,395,000	$ 536,627,000
Cost of sales	813,771,000	545,055,000	454,652,000
Product line inventory markdown	-	12,225,000	-
Gross profit	$ 142,452,000	$ 59,115,000	$ 81,975,000
Selling and administrative expenses	76,173,000	44,822,000	45,729,000
Product line asset impairment	-	10,472,000	-
Operating profit	$ 66,279,000	$ 3,821,000	$ 36,246,000
Interest expense, net	10,830,000	7,264,000	7,635,000
Earnings (loss) before income taxes	$ 55,449,000	$ (3,443,000)	$ 28,611,000
Income tax expense (benefit)	23,010,000	(370,000)	11,020,000
Net Earnings (loss)	$ 32,439,000	$ (3,073,000)	$ 17,591,000
Net Earnings (loss) per share			
Basic	$ 1.53	$ (0.16)	$ 0.91
Weighted average shares outstanding -	21,181,000	19,386,000	19,328,000

Michaelangelo Foods, Inc.
Consolidated Balance Sheets

DECEMBER 31,		*2002*		*2001*
ASSETS				
Current Assets				
Cash and equivalents	$	4,038,000	$	2,585,000
Accounts receivable, less allowances		83,495,000		51,394,000
Inventories		68,929,000		58,976,000
Prepaid expenses and other		1,676,000		2,976,000
Total current assets	$	158,138,000	$	115,931,000
Property, Plant and Equipment - At Cost				
Land		4,336,000		4,317,000
Buildings and improvements		99,023,000		99,133,000
Machinery and equipment		274,980,000		230,725,000
	$	378,339,000	$	334,175,000
Less accumulated depreciation		160,800,000		149,014,000
	$	217,539,000	$	185,161,000
Goodwill and Other Assets		127,978,000		63,567,000
	$	503,655,000	$	364,659,000
LIABILITIES AND SHAREHOLDERS' EQUITY				
Current Liabilities				
Current maturities of long-term debt	$	8,509,000	$	8,410,000
Accounts payable		46,910,000		28,412,000
Accrued liabilities		47,931,000		22,432,000
Total current liabilities	$	103,350,000	$	59,254,000
Long-Term debt, less current maturities		137,519,000		104,491,000
Deferred Income Taxes		33,540,000		26,872,000
Total liabilities	$	274,409,000	$	190,617,000
Shareholders' Equity				
Common stock, $.01 par, shares issued: 21,816,098 in 2002; 19,459,731 in 2001		218,000		195,000
Additional paid-in capital		140,188,000		113,268,000
Retained earnings		88,840,000		60,579,000
Total shareholders' equity	$	229,246,000	$	174,042,000
	$	503,655,000	$	364,659,000

Second Street Cafes
Consolidated Statement of Income
(In Thousands, Except Per Share Amounts)

	Year Ended		
	2002	2001	2000
Revenue	$ 107,997	$ 122,563	$ 119,508
Restaurant Operating Expenses			
Cost of sales	30,995	35,089	34,005
Payroll and benefits	32,469	38,858	36,769
Depreciation and amortization	3,552	4,586	4,353
Other operating expenses	30,589	36,944	35,250
Total restaurant operating expenses	$ 97,605	$ 115,477	$ 110,377
Income from restaurant operations	$ 10,392	$ 7,086	$ 9,131
Depreciation and amortization	953	1,450	1,331
General and administrative expenses	4,559	4,388	4,410
Restructuring and reorganization	(2,390)	20,208	-
Operating income (loss)	$ 7,270	$ (18,960)	$ 3,390
Interest expense, net	2,466	3,206	4,424
Net income (loss) before income taxes and extraordinary item	$ 4,804	$ (22,166)	$ (1,034)
Provision for income taxes	-	-	-
Income (loss) before extraordinary item	4,804	(22,166)	(1,034)
Extraordinary loss	1,638	-	-
Net income (loss)	$ 3,166	$ (22,166)	$ (1,034)
Basic earnings per share			
Income (loss) before extraordinary item	$ 0.48	$ (2.73)	$ (0.22)
Extraordinary item	(0.16)	-	-
Net income (loss)	$ 0.32	$ (2.73)	$ (0.22)
Diluted earnings per share			
Income (loss) before extraordinary item	$ 0.47	$ (2.73)	$ (0.22)
Extraordinary item	(0.16)	-	-
Net income (loss)	$ 0.31	$ (2.73)	$ (0.22)
Weighted average number of shares outstanding:			
Basic	9,918	8,110	4,621
Diluted	10,098	8,110	4,621

Second Street Cafes
Consolidated Balance Sheets
(In Thousands)

	2002	2001
ASSETS		
Current Assets		
Cash and cash equivalents	$ 8,424	$ 2,613
Accounts receivable, net	3,293	1,248
Inventories	1,043	1,275
Prepaid expenses	289	173
Assets held for disposal, net	363	10,929
Total current assets	$ 13,412	$ 16,238
Property and equipment, net	30,194	32,162
Other assets, net	3,091	4,780
Franchise costs, net	15,288	16,418
Note receivable	757	1,250
	$ 62,742	$ 70,848
LIABILITIES AND STOCKHOLDERS' EQUITY		
Current Liabilities		
Current portion of long-term debt	$ 1,233	$ 2,523
Accounts payable	3,890	3,750
Other accrued liabilities	9,619	11,308
Total current liabilities	$ 14,742	$ 17,581
Long-term debt, net of current portion	24,308	33,809
Other liabilities and deferred credits	1,489	2,873
Total liabilities	$ 40,539	$ 54,263
Stockholders' Equity		
Common stock, $.001 par value, 25,000,000 shares authorized; 9,970,691and 8,718,491 shares issued and outstanding in 2002 and 2001, respectively	10	9
Additional paid-in capital	44,145	41,694
Accumulated deficit	(21,952)	(25,118)
	$ 22,203	$ 16,585
	$ 62,742	$ 70,848

Case 5-4

ANALYSIS OF FORD MOTOR COMPANY'S ANNUAL REPORT

Case Objectives

1. Become familiar with real financial statements and annual reports
2. Review how financial statements articulate with each other
3. Demonstrate the wealth of information found in annual reports

Decision: How is Ford Motor Company performing?

INTRODUCTION

The purpose of this assignment is to analyze the annual report of Ford Motor Company. The years covered by CCC's financial statements have been assigned arbitrarily and do not reflect the economic environment of any particular time. Therefore, for purposes of Cases 5-4 and 5-5, assume that Ford's statements are for the same years as CCC's 2003 and 2002 statements.

Requirements

Carefully read the most current Ford Annual Report and prepare a word-processed answer to each question below. The full annual report can be found under the investor's section of the Ford web site: www.ford.com. The abbreviated 2000 financial statements for Ford Motor Company are presented in Exhibits C5-4.1, C5-4.2, and C5-4.3 for your convenience. The most recent abbreviated Ford statements can be downloaded from this book's web site (adams.swcollege.com). Note that the boxed items in Exhibit C5-4.3 are not part of this case, but will be completed in Case 5-5.

1. Is Ford a global company? Explain and give specific examples from the first two sections of the annual report. What percent of Ford's external sales, income from continuing operations, and net property are due to activities outside of the United States? Hint: The segment information footnote (Note 21 in 2000) may be helpful.

2. Has Ford adopted quality, JIT, and value chain concepts? Give three examples from the annual report to support your answer. Hint: This type of information is not found in the financial statements or the footnotes to the financial statements (although it probably should be). Instead, it is usually found in the "Management's Discussion and Analysis of Financial Results and Operations" and the "Public Relations" sections of the annual report.

Exhibit C5-4.1
Income Statements

Income Statements:	Ford Motor Company* (In Millions) 2000	1999	CCC (In Thousands) 2003	2002
Revenues (Autimotive only)[1]	$ 141,230	$ 135,073	$ 336,000	$ 120,000
Cost of goods sold (note 1 and 15)	126,120	118,985	194,867	86,400
Selling, admin. and other expenses	9,884	8,874	92,000	25,000
Net expenses-Financial services	(6)	45	0	0
Loss (gain) from affiliates	70	(35)	0	0
Net interest expense (income)	(105)	(71)	8,640	0
Earnings before taxes–Auto	5,267	7,275	40,493	8,600
Earnings before taxes–Financial	2,967	2,579	0	0
Provision for income taxes	2,705	3,248	12,148	2,580
Earnings before minority interest	5,529	6,606	28,345	6,020
Minority interest	(119)	(104)	0	0
Income (loss) from discontinued operations	(1,943)	735		
Net profit (loss)	$ 3,467	$ 7,237	$ 28,345	$ 6,020
Basic earnings per share:				
From continuing operations	$ 3.66	$ 5.38		
Net income	2.34	5.99		
* As reported in the 2000 Ford Annual Report				
[1] Ford total revenues	$ 170,064	$ 160,658		

3. Did Ford have a foreign currency translation adjustment? If so, how much was it for the most current year? Was it a gain or a loss? Provide details from the financial statement you used to answer this question. Hint: Review Note 1—Foreign Currency Translation, the consolidated balance sheet, and the consolidated statement of stockholders' equity.

4. Based on your knowledge of the causes of translation gains and losses, what do you think is the primary reason for Ford's current year foreign currency adjustment?

5. How much cash did Ford generate from operating activities in both the automotive and financial services divisions? That is, what was Ford's total cash flow from all operating activities? See Ford's cash flows footnote (Note 20 in 2000). Explain the four major differences between Ford's net income and the cash flow from automotive operations for the most current year.

6. Compute Ford's book value per share at the end of the most current year (ignore Ford's preferred stock; add Class A stock and Class B stock to determine the total common shares outstanding). Use Ford shares issued (rather than shares outstanding) found in the capital stock footnote (Note 14 in 2000) to compute book value per share. What reasons might explain why the book value differs from the average common stock price at the end of the year?

7. Explain what caused Ford's retained earnings to increase or decrease in the current year. Hint: What are the two main events that normally affect the retained earnings account during the year?

Exhibit C5-4.2
Balance Sheets

Balance Sheets:	Ford Motor Company (In Millions) 2000	1999	CCC (In Thousands) 2003	2002
Assets:				
Cash and short-term investments	$ 4,851	$ 4,381	$ 559	$ 1,462
Marketable securities	13,933	19,676	0	0
Accounts receivable-net	129,849	118,565	67,200	13,600
Inventories	7,514	5,684	840	840
Other current assets	9,144	9,897		
Equity in affiliated companies	2,949	2,539		
Property, equip. and tools-net	37,508	38,094	180,060	90,000
Deferred taxes	3,342	2,454	0	0
Operating leases - Financial Services	46,593	42,471		
Other	28,738	26,488	0	0
Total assets	$ 284,421	$ 270,249	$ 248,659	$ 105,902
Liabilities:				
Accounts payable (current)	$24,383	$21,620	$8,001	$7,722
Short-term debt (current)	277	1,338	0	0
Accrued liabilities (current)	23,964	20,197	1,864	1,131
Long-term debt	165,279	150,317	74,000	10,000
Other noncurrent liabilities	51,908	49,173	0	0
Total liabilities	265,811	242,645	83,865	18,853
Shareholders' equity				
Common stock (Class A and B)	19	1,222	20,000	15,000
(Ford shares outstanding: 1,908,000,000 in 2000; 1,222,000,000 in 1999)				
(CCC: $1.00 par value in all years)				
Additional paid-in capital	6,174	5,049	112,000	65,000
Retained earnings	13,955	21,906	32,794	7,049
Foreign currency translation	(1,538)	(573)	0	0
Total stockholders' equity	$ 18,610	$ 27,604	$ 164,794	$ 87,049
Total liabilities and equity	$ 284,421	$ 270,249	$ 248,659	$ 105,902
Automotive assets	95,343	99,201		
Automotive liabilities	88,581	82,344		
Capital expenditures for CCC are: 2003: $108,000,000; 2002: $15,100,000				

8. Which company's inventory asset (Ford or CCC) most closely reflects current market value? <u>Hint</u>: CCC uses a FIFO inventory flow assumption. See Ford's inventory footnote (Note 8 in 2000).

9. By law, the annual financial statements for all U.S. companies with stock that is publicly traded must be audited by certified public accountants (CPAs). CPAs issue an opinion on the fairness of the financial statements. The CPA's opinion is presented just prior to Ford's financial statements. Based on Ford's audit opinion:

   a. Who are the auditors for Ford? What was the auditors' opinion regarding the information in the financial statements?

   b. Why do you think it is a legal requirement that Ford have a CPA firm audit its records? You will need at least a paragraph to answer this question.

10. A key financial measure is the price/earnings (P/E) ratio, which is the stock price per share divided by the earnings per share (EPS). What is Ford's basic earnings per share for the most current year? What was Ford's P/E ratio at the end of the most current year? Use the average fourth quarter high and low prices for Ford's stock price. Ford's stock price can be found near the end of the annual report shortly after the footnotes.
11. What is your overall assessment of Ford's performance in the most current year? Use the ratios you computed to help support your assessment. Consider the fact that high-quality corporate bonds at the end of 2001 yielded approximately 8.5 percent.

Exhibit C5-4.3
Statements of Cash Flows

	Ford Motor Company (In Millions)		CCC (In Thousands)	
Statement of Cash Flows:	2000	1999	2003	2002
From Operating Activities:			(Completed in Case 5-5)	
Net profit (loss)	$ 5,410	$ 6,502	$28,345	$ 6,020
Add (subtract):				
Depreciation and amortization	15,949	14,542	17,940	7,140
Securities sales	6,406	2,159	----	----
Change in receivables*	(1,204)	(1,153)	(53,600)	(12,150)
Change in inventories	(1,369)	955	----	2,266
Change in current liabilities	3,953	(59)	1,012	(4,760)
Other	4,619	4,445	----	----
Cash provided by operations	$ 33,764	$ 27,391	$ (6,303)	$ (1,484)
From investing activities				
Acquisitions of other companies	(2,774)	(5,907)	----	----
Marketable security transactions	18,975	8,874	----	----
Leased asset transactions	(42,222)	(33,776)	----	----
Capital expenditures	(8,348)	(7,659)	(108,000)	(60,140)
Other	(1,782)	(361)	----	----
Provided by investing activities	$ (36,151)	$ (38,829)	$ -	$ (60,140)
From financing activities				
Change in long-term debt	14,482	15,952	64,000	4,736
Issuance of common stock	592	274	52,000	58,000
Purchase of treasury stock	(7,376)	(707)	----	----
Cash dividends	(2,751)	(2,290)	(2,600)	----
Other	(1,176)	(1,368)	----	----
Provided by financing activities	$ 3,771	$ 11,861	113,400	$ 62,736
Effect of exchange rate on cash	(914)	(336)	----	----
Change in cash	470	87	(903)	1,112
Cash at beginning of year	4,381	4,294	1,462	350
Cash at end of year	$ 4,851	$ 4,381	559	$ 1,462

*Due to the complexity of Ford's transactions, changes in its balance sheet amounts cannot be traced to the amount reported on the cash flow statement.

Case 5-5

COMPARISON OF FORD AND CCC FINANCIAL STATEMENTS

Case Objectives

1. Enhance financial analysis skills
2. Increase understanding of the statement of cash flows
3. Demonstrate how financial information provides a picture of a firm's performance

Decision: Is CCC's financial performance competitive with Ford's?

The purpose of this case is to compare Ford's performance and future prospects with that of CCC. Note: The years covered by CCC's financial statements have been assigned arbitrarily and do not reflect the economic environment of any particular time. Therefore, for purposes of comparisons in Case 5-5, assume that Ford's statements are for the same years as CCC's 2003 and 2002 statements. The abbreviated 2000 financial statements for Ford Motor Company are presented in Exhibits C5-4.1, C5-4.2, and C5-4.3 for your convenience. The most recent abbreviated Ford statements can be downloaded from this book's web site (adams.swcollege.com).

Requirements

1. Complete CCC's statement of cash flows shown in Exhibit C5-4.3 for 2003 by entering numbers in the outlined areas. Use the indirect method described in Reading 1-2. Additional CCC accounting information for 2003 includes the following: depreciation and amortization, \$17,940,000; capital expenditures, \$108,000,000; and dividends \$2,600,000.

2. Using CCC's income statements and balance sheets shown in Exhibits C5-4.1 and C5-4.2, respectively, explain a second way (other than completing the statement of cash flows) to determine the \$559,000 cash at end of the year 2003.

3. Compute the ratios (see Reading 5-4) in the table provided. Use the condensed financial statements in Exhibits C5-4.1, C5-4.2, and C5-4.3 and the Ford statements at their web site (www.ford.com) to compute the ratios. Add Ford's Class A and Class B common shares outstanding to determine total common shares issued. Use shares issued rather than shares outstanding to compute book value per share. Use pretax auto sales and auto income in computing the return on sales ratio for Ford. Use pretax income to compute CCC's return on sales ratio. Use the average Ford stock price for the fourth quarter to compute the P/E ratio. Weighted average shares outstanding for CCC are year 2003, 18,000,000 shares; year 2002, 13,000,000 shares.

	FORD		CCC	
	Current Year	Previous Year	2003	2002
Book value per share				
Basic earnings per share				
Basic EPS - Continuing oper.				
Price/earnings ratio[1]				
P/E ratio - Continuing operations[1]				
Pretax return on sales - Auto				
Inventory turnover[2]		18.82		43.80
Debt-to-equity				
Debt-to-equity - Auto				
Return on stockholders' equity[2]		0.311		0.109
ROE - Continuing operations[2]		0.280		0.109

[1] Since there is no a stock price, a PE ratio cannot be computed for CCC.

[2] Since these ratios require an average balance sheet amount, the first year has been given to you.

4. The payment of dividends has an impact on the financial statements. Both Ford and CCC paid dividends in the current year. Explain specifically two impacts that the payment of dividends had on the financial statements of Ford and CCC. That is, what lines in the financial statements changed because dividends were paid? Be sure to consider the impact on all three financial statements.

5. In the current year for Ford and 2003 for CCC, which firm (Ford or CCC) had the higher inventory turnover? Compare the turnover ratios. How does inventory turnover relate to JIT? Is Ford improving its inventory turnover?

6. If you were a banker, which firm would be a less risky loan customer? Base your answer to this question strictly on the current year financial statements and ratios (2003 for CCC). Explain your answer.

7. Base your answer to this question on (1) Ford's book value per share compared to its stock price, and (2) Ford's EPS compared to its stock price. Approximate what a share of CCC would sell for if its relationships (1) between book value and stock price and (2) EPS and stock price were the same as Ford's. You will calculate two different prices for CCC stock. Remember, for purposes of this case assume that Ford's statements are for the same time period as CCC's. Ford's stock prices can be found near the end of the annual report shortly after the footnotes. Use the average of the fourth quarter high and low prices for Ford's stock price at the end of the year. Hint: Reading 5-4 presents an example on estimating stock price for a firm whose stock is not traded.

Group Assignment 5-5

FINANCIAL HORSEPOWER

Group Number ___________ **Signatures of group members participating:**

____

____

Objectives

1. Enhance financial analysis skills
2. Demonstrate how financial information provides a picture of a firm's performance

Requirements

1. Enter your group's consensus values for the ratios you computed individually in Case 5-5 in the table below.

	FORD		CCC	
	Current Year	**Previous Year**	**2003**	**2002**
Book value per share				
Basic earnings per share				
Basic EPS - Continuing oper.				
Price/earnings ratio				
P/E ratio - Continuing operations				
Pretax return on sales - Auto				
Inventory turnover		18.82		43.80
Debt-to-equity				
Debt-to-equity - Auto				
Return on stockholders' equity		0.311		0.109
ROE - Continuing operations		0.280		0.109

2. *Based entirely on your analysis of the comparative financial statements* (including your ratio analysis) for CCC and Ford performed in Case 5-5, the financial statements for Ford and CCC, and the following additional information, estimate the market value of one share of CCC stock on December 31, 2003. You must support your answer with a detailed financial comparison of Ford and CCC. Do not consider the nonfinancial issues that might impact either firm's stock price.

CCC has 20,000,000 shares of $1 par common stock outstanding at December 31, 2003. Remember, for purposes of this exercise, assume that Ford's statements are for the same time period as CCC's.

Both CCC and Ford are in the auto assembly business. Therefore, use Ford's current midrange fourth quarter stock price ($24.35 for 2000) as a benchmark for estimating CCC's stock price.

Note: Estimating the value of a firm's stock is a complex process that involves many nonfinancial variables. The *only* purpose of this question is to demonstrate your ability to interpret financial statements. This question is *not* meant to be a comprehensive market valuation exercise.

What is your group's December 31, 2003 estimated value for one share of CCC common stock?

$ ____________________

3. Present your analysis to support the stock price you listed in Requirement 2. The points you receive on this assignment will be based on the *quality* of your answer to this question.

Module 5

Peer Evaluation of Group Members	Class Section	Group No.

Evaluator's Name ______________________________

Module 5

In the table below, please indicate your estimate, in percentage terms, of the contributions that individual group members made to each of the group assignments listed. Each column should add to 100 percent. For example, if there are five members in your group and all were present for Group Assignment 5-1, you would divide the 100 percent among the five members, including yourself. If you felt that all group members were prepared to discuss the assignment and contributed equally to the solution, you would give each person 20 percent. If only four members were present and you felt that one particular member contributed twice as much as the other three, you would give the heavy contributor 40 percent and the other three members 20 percent. The group member who was absent should be listed and given a zero percent.

	Group Assignment Number	
Group Members (List)	**5-1**	**5-5**
Myself		
Totals	**100**	**100**

Fill in this sheet after each group assignment is completed and turn in at the completion of Group Assignment 5-5.

MODULE 5 REVIEW

REVIEW QUESTIONS

After you have completed Module 5, you should be able to answer the following questions. If you are unable to answer these questions in a reasonable manner, you should go back and review the readings and/or go over the Module 5 cases and readings again.

1. Explain how exchange rates can fluctuate and have effects on financial statements.
2. How are financial statements of a subsidiary company consolidated with its parent financial statements?
3. How are financial statements denominated in foreign currency translated into the parent company's currency using appropriate exchange rates?
4. Explain how to analyze the stockholders' equity section of the balance sheet.
5. Describe how to compute and evaluate earnings per share.
6. How are financial statement ratios calculated? How are these ratios used to compare performance of companies within an industry group?
7. How are financial statement ratios used to estimate and evaluate the price of a company's stock?

REVIEW PROBLEM

The financial statements below are from two companies that started business on January 1, 2003. You are given a balance sheet, income statement, and statement of cash flows. Using these data, you may review the various ratios and material discussed in the Module 5 readings. Note that the depreciation for 2003 was 4 and 3 for the American Co. and the National Corp, respectively. No dividends were paid in 2003.

Requirements:

1. From a short-term liquidity perspective, which company has performed better? Use the appropriate ratios to explain your answer.
2. From a profitability perspective, which company has performed better? Use the appropriate ratios to explain your answer.
3. From a solvency perspective, which company has a better balance sheet? Use the appropriate ratios to explain your answer.
4. From a cash flow perspective, which company has a better CAR and FAR? (You will find the discussion of these ratios in Reading 1-2).
5. If each company paid a dividend of 3 to its shareholders, how would the financial statements change?

6. If the weighted average number of outstanding shares for American and National are 9 million and 6 million, respectively, what is the EPS for each company?

7. American Co. is a public company. Its stock is selling for $20 per share. National Corp. is privately held. Its owners want an estimate of the company's stock price. Based on EPS and BV, estimate National's stock price.

American Company and National Corporation
Income Statements For Year Ended 2003
(in millions of dollars)

	American Co.	National Corp.
Sales	$ 150	$ 110
Less:Cost of goods sold	100	35
Gross profit margin	$ 50	$ 75
Operating expenses:		
Fixed manufacturing expenses	10	35
Fixed selling and administrative expense	10	10
Income before tax	$ 30	$ 30
Income tax	12	12
Net income	$ 18	$ 18

American Company and National Corporation
December 31, 2003 Balance Sheets
(in millions of dollars)

	American Co.	National Corp.
Cash	$ 5	$ 6
Accounts receivable	15	8
Inventory	30	14
Fixed assets (net)	20	17
Total assets	$ 70	$ 45
Accounts payable	$ 5	$ 10
Accrued liabilities		12
Total current liabilities	$ 5	$ 22
Long-term debt	40	
Total liabilities	$ 45	$ 22
Stockholders' equity		
Common stock	7	5
Retained earnings	18	18
Total liabilities and stockholders' equity	$ 70	$ 45

8. Assume hypothetically that the fixed assets of American Company contain a $10 million investment in a European subsidiary that has no liabilities. The purchase of this subsidiary was made on January 1, 2003, when American was formed the subsidiary. How would the balance sheet of American change if the subsidiary posted neither an income nor a loss while the Euro exchange rate moved from $0.85 at the beginning of the year to $1.02 by the end of the year?

American Company and National Corporation
Income Statements For Year Ended 2003
(amounts are in millions)

	American Co.	National Corp.
Cash from operations		
Net income	$ 18	$ 18
Adjustments to obtain CFO:		
Depreciation	4	3
Change in accounts receivable	(15)	(8)
Change in inventory	(30)	(14)
Change in accounts payable	5	12
Change in accrued liabilities		10
Cash from operations (CFO)	$ (18)	$ 21
Cash from investing:		
Purchase of fixed assets	$ (24)	$ (20)
Cash from investing (CFI)	$ (24)	$ (20)
Cash from financing:		
Proceeds from long-term debt issue	$ 40	
Issuance of common stock	7	$ 4
Cash from financing: (CFI)	$ 47	$ 4
Change in cash	$ 5	$ 5
Beginning cash	0	0
Ending cash	$ 5	$ 5

Appendix

USING MICROSOFT EXCEL

INTRODUCTION

Microsoft Excel is a powerful spreadsheet software package with many complex capabilities. Excel is used extensively in business by all types of workers, including managers, salespersons, accountants, and small business owners. Spreadsheet usage is integrated throughout this book because techniques covered, such breakeven and budgeting, are typically implemented in practice by using spreadsheets. In addition, spreadsheets are a powerful learning tool because with them students can easily change assumptions and data to see the impact such changes. This type of "what if" analysis helps to assess risk inherent in decisions and to better understand interrelationships.

This appendix presents some Excel basics, while the web sites listed are more comprehensive. Although you may be familiar with spreadsheet software, the Excel instructions and web site tutorials assume no previous exposure to spreadsheets. These resources will not make you an expert in using Microsoft Excel, but will provide enough information so that you can complete the spreadsheet assignments in the course. To understand the instructions completely read the text and follow the directions while sitting at a computer. These instructions assume the use of at least Microsoft Excel version 8.

SUGESTED EXCEL TUTORIAL WEB SITES

The following sites offer excellent, free, hands-on Excel tutorials. If an address is no longer current, go the web site for this book (adams.swcollege.com) where the current link will be maintained.

1. www.fgcu.edu/support/office2000/excel
2. www.extension.iastate.edu/Pages/Excel

SELECTED MICROSOFT EXCEL TOPICS

Workbooks and Worksheets

When you open a new file within Excel, that file is called an *Excel workbook file*. The workbook itself has many different worksheets. Each worksheet in the workbook can be used and given an identifying name by the worksheet preparer. For example, Figure A1 shows the financial transactions for a company. The workbook file name is C3, as shown in the top left-hand corner of Figure A1. The worksheet that is currently displayed is named JWksht.

When a new workbook file is opened, all worksheets within the workbook have preassigned names such as Sheet1, Sheet2, Sheet3, and so on. To rename a particular worksheet, double click on the open worksheet tab at the bottom of the workbook. (The open worksheet tab is white whereas the other worksheet tabs are a darker color, usually gray.) A menu will pop up with a box called "Rename Sheet." Putting the mouse cursor within the box, delete the current sheet name, and type in the name you want to assign to the sheet. Then click "OK." If done correctly, your sheet should now have a new name. (Alternatively, you can get the same effect by selecting the Format menu, "Sheet," and then "Rename.")

Linking Worksheets

Having several different worksheets within the same workbook allows the spreadsheet preparer to easily link information from one spreadsheet to another. For example, when preparing the statement of cash flows in Case 1-2 or Case 4-2, you want to link the numbers from the balance sheet and the income statement to cells in the cash flow statement. To link worksheets, place the cursor on the cell that is the destination of the link and enter "=". Then go the cell in the worksheet where the link originates and hit enter. The contents of the origin cell will be linked to the destination cell when you return to the destination worksheet.

To illustrate, say you want to link cell C8 (the depreciation adjustment) in the cash flow statement on worksheet 3 with net income in cell D24 on the income statement in worksheet 1. Place the cursor on cell C8 and type in an equal sign. Then click on the worksheet 1 tab, put you cursor cell D24, and hit enter.

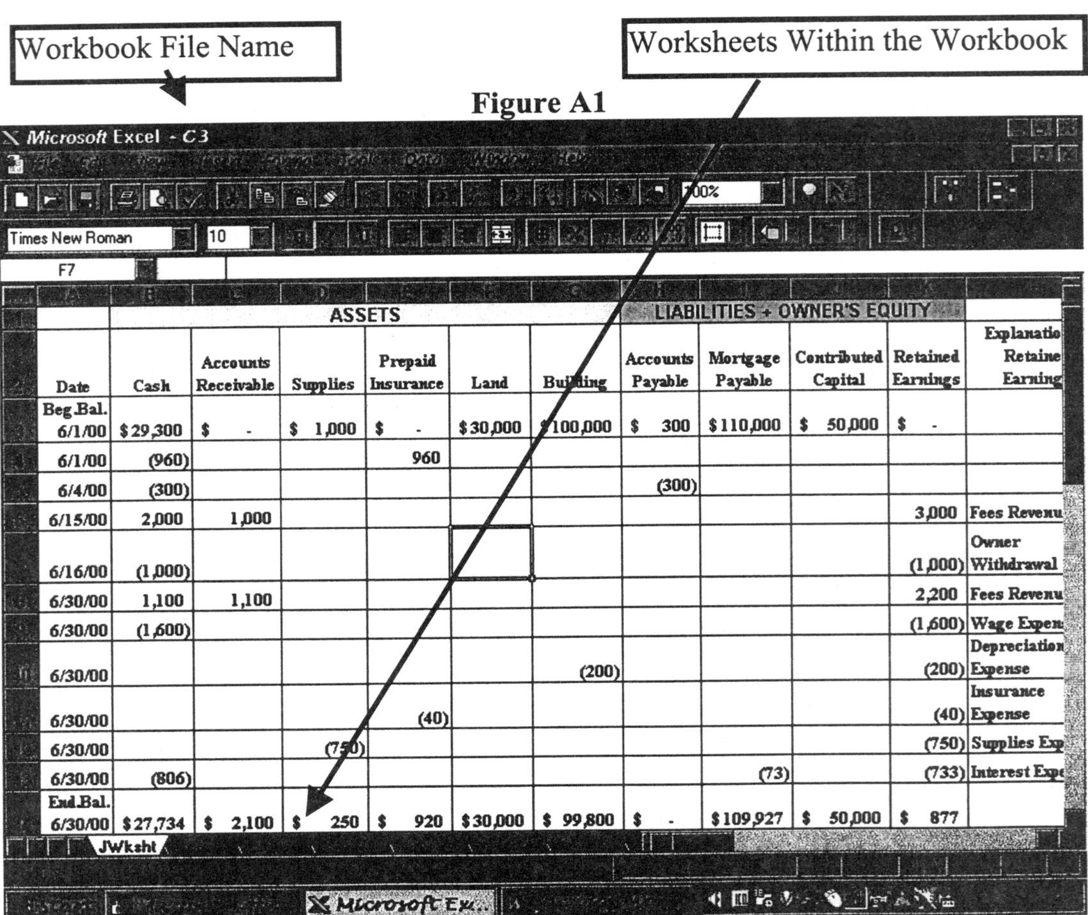

Figure A1

	ASSETS						LIABILITIES + OWNER'S EQUITY				
Date	Cash	Accounts Receivable	Supplies	Prepaid Insurance	Land	Building	Accounts Payable	Mortgage Payable	Contributed Capital	Retained Earnings	Explanatio Retaine Earning
Beg.Bal. 6/1/00	$29,300	$ -	$ 1,000	$ -	$30,000	$100,000	$ 300	$110,000	$ 50,000	$ -	
6/1/00	(960)			960							
6/4/00	(300)						(300)				
6/15/00	2,000	1,000								3,000	Fees Revenu
6/16/00	(1,000)									(1,000)	Owner Withdrawal
6/30/00	1,100	1,100								2,200	Fees Revenu
6/30/00	(1,600)									(1,600)	Wage Expen
6/30/00						(200)				(200)	Depreciation Expense
6/30/00				(40)						(40)	Insurance Expense
6/30/00			(750)							(750)	Supplies Exp
6/30/00	(806)							(73)		(733)	Interest Expe
End.Bal. 6/30/00	$27,734	$ 2,100	$ 250	$ 920	$30,000	$ 99,800	$ -	$109,927	$ 50,000	$ 877	

The main benefit of linking files together is that if you change the source file, any linked files will change automatically. For example, assume that the JWksht worksheet has been prepared as shown in Figure A1 above and that all the financial statements in this workbook have been properly linked to that worksheet. Row 7 of JWksht shows an owner withdrawal of $1,000. Suppose someone wants to see what effect a $1,200 withdrawal (instead of $1,000) would have had on her financial statements. If the amount of the withdrawal in row 7 is changed to $1,200, all the linked financial statements will change to reflect the revised amount.

Printing Spreadsheets

After completing your assignment, you will need to print the spreadsheet to turn in to your instructor. To print the spreadsheet once the file has been opened (see retrieving and saving files), follow these steps:

1. Click on "File."
2. Click on "Print Preview." This allows you to see what your spreadsheet will look like before printing it.
3. If your spreadsheet is more then one page, click on "Next" and "Previous" to see all of the pages.
4. Click on "Print" to print the document, or if you want to make any changes, click on "Close" to go back to your spreadsheet.

The amount that can be printed on one page depends on the capability of the printer and the size of the spreadsheet you wish to print. Following are some methods to change your page setup in order to get all or more of your spreadsheet on one page. Some of these methods will not be available to you, depending on your printer.

Printing Options. From the Print Preview window, you can do some or all of these options, depending on how much you need to get on a page:

1. Click on "Setup." In the Page Setup dialog box:
   a. On the Page tab under Orientation: click on "Landscape" (versus "Portrait"). This will allow more columns to be printed (but less rows.) Click on "OK" to see the changes in Print Preview.
   b. Also on the Page tab, under Scaling, you can click on "Fit to: 1 page wide by 1 tall." Click on "OK" to see the changes in Print Preview. Note: This method may reduce your spreadsheet to a type size too small to read.
   c. On the Margins tab, change the "Left:" and/or "Right:" to a smaller number. Click on "OK" to see the changes in Print Preview. Margin changes can also be made in the Print Preview window by clicking on "Margins."

Printing Gridlines. Printing gridlines can make it easier to see which information is in the same row or column. Under the "File," "Page Setup," "Sheet" tab, you have the option to print the spreadsheet with or without gridlines. The default is without. Click on the box next to the option to put an "x" in it, then press "OK."

Printing Row and Column Labels. Sometimes when printing a spreadsheet it is very helpful to have the spreadsheet printed with the row and column labels. This is especially helpful if you are also printing formulas because you can see the row and column designations that are mentioned in the formulas. Go to "File," then "Page Setup," then click on the "Sheet" tab. You have the option to print the spreadsheet with row and column labels or without them. The default is without. Click on the box next to the option to put an "x" in it, then press "OK." Your spreadsheet will now print with row and column labels. Figure A2 shows a partial spreadsheet with row and column labels.

Figure A2

	A	B	C	D	E
1	Date	Cash	Accounts receivable	Accounts Receivable	
2	1/1/00	1000	162		
3	1/1/00	500	300		
4	1/1/00	300	452		

Deleting Rows or Columns

Sometimes you may want to delete a row or a column. Perform the following:

1. Click on a cell(s) in the row(s) or column(s) you want to delete.
2. Now click on "Edit" (up in the Menu bar), then "Delete."
3. A dialog box will allow you to choose "Entire Row" or "Entire Column." Then click on "OK"
4. Row and column labels and formulas will adjust automatically.

Cut and Paste

If you want to move the contents of one cell to another cell, you can use the Cut and Paste commands. To cut and paste:

1. Click in the cell from which you want to cut the data.
2. Now click on "Edit" (up in the Menu bar), then "Cut." You will notice that the cell that you are cutting has been highlighted.
3. Move the mouse cursor to the cell in which you want to put the data.
4. Click on "Edit" (up in the Menu bar), then "Paste."

There is a quicker way to move the contents of one cell to another. First, highlight the cell you want to move. There will be a highlighted box around the cell. Next, touch the mouse to an edge of the cell so that you can now see an arrow. Press the mouse button, holding down without releasing, and drag the cell to its new desired location.

Changing the Column Width

For One Column

1. Make one of the cells in the column you want to enlarge the active cell.
2. Click on “Format.” Click on “Column.” Click on “Width.”
3. In the Column Width window the present column width will already be highlighted, so you just need to type in a new width (e.g., 12,) and click on “OK.” This column will now have the new width designated by you.

For More Than One Column

1. Put the mouse pointer in the first column, click and drag to highlight the desired columns.
2. Repeat steps 2 and 3 in the section for one column.

Or, if you do not wish to guess the appropriate column width, position the cursor on the right edge of the column header tab (A, B, C, etc.) of the column you wish to change. Your cursor should look like ✢. Drag the column edge until it is the desired width. (Double-clicking between two heading tabs will automatically adjust the column width of the left column to hold its cell contents.)

Spellcheck

Excel provides a spellcheck to check the spelling on the worksheet. To use the spellcheck, go to “Tools” and then to “Spelling.”

Showing and Printing Formulas

There are times when you want to show or print your formulas in their cells. In order to do this:

1. Click on “Tools.” Click on “Options.” On the “View” tab, under Window Options, click on the box to the left of “Formulas.” This will put an "x" in that box. Click on “OK.”
2. This will automatically widen the columns, and you will see all your functions and formulas rather than their numerical results.
3. If you need a printout showing the formulas, use the normal printing procedures (see below).
4. To put your spreadsheet back to its original state, repeat step 1. By clicking on the box next to “Formulas,” with the "x" in it, the "x" will be removed.

> There is a useful short cut to this command. Pressing Ctrl and ~ at the same time will allow you to see formulas without having to go through the menu process., If you press those two keys together again when you are viewing the formulas, the spreadsheet will return to normal. You can toggle the formulas on and off by pressing the two keys at the same time repeatedly. The ~ key is generally located on the top left portion of your keyboard.

=Sum Function

If you want to add data contained in 10 cells you can physically type all cell addresses. Suppose you want to add data contained in cells C1 through C10, then you could type:

=C1+C2+C3+C4+C5+C6+C7+C8+C9+C10

This is a very tedious and inefficient approach. Instead there is an easier approach. Type:

=Sum(C1:C10)

Suppose the cells to add were not in the same row or column. For example, say we wanted to add the numbers in cell A1, B2, C4, and D5. We can still use the sum function but it will look like this:

=Sum(A1,B2,C4,D5)

The terms A1, B2, C4 and D5 are called the function arguments.

Net Present Value (NPV) Function

During the second half of this course, you will learn present value and net present value (NPV) concepts. This section of the instructions does not explain these concepts but tells you how to compute them using Microsoft Excel once you understand present value and net present value.

The NPV function of Microsoft Excel computes the present value of a series of future cash flows, discounted at a specified interest rate. For example, assume it is now January 1, 2000, and a firm invests $3,000 to receive future cash flows of $800, $1,000, $1,400, $500, and $1,200 on December 31, 2000 through December 31, 2004, respectively. The appropriate interest (discount) rate is 10 percent. To compute the NPV of this investment in cell A1, do the following:

1. Enter the value -$3,000 in cell B1.
2. Enter the values $800, $1,000, $1,400, $500, and $1,200 in cells C1 through G1, respectively.
3. Move to cell A1 and type "=B1+NPV(.10,C1:G1)".
4. Press the Enter key.

The NPV of this stream of cash flows, discounted at 10 percent, will appear as $692.17 in cell A1. This indicates that the "true" interest rate, or the internal rate of return (see below), is higher than 10 percent.

In the function, "=B1+NPV(.10,C1:G1)," the investment is located in cell B1, the interest or discount rate is 10 percent, and the positive cash flows are located in cells C1 through G1. The interest rate may be entered as a percentage (10%) or a decimal (.1).

To compute a present value only (i.e., there is no original cash outflow in the present), simply enter a zero in the cell to which the initial investment part of the function refers. In the preceding example, if we wanted to find the present value of the five inflows with no initial investment in the present, a zero would have been entered in cell B1. The present value of $3,692.17 would appear in cell A1.

Internal Rate of Return (IRR) Function

In Module 4 you will learn the internal rate of return (IRR) concept. This section of the instructions does not explain this concept but tells you how to compute it using Microsoft Excel.

Briefly, the IRR is the interest or discount rate that equates the net present value to zero. Continuing the net present value example, we can compute what interest rate will give us a net present value of $0. Since the net present value at 10 percent was positive, we know that the internal rate of return is higher than 10 percent. To compute the internal rate of return, do the following:

1. Make sure you have the value of -3000 in B1.
2. Move to cell A2 and type "=IRR(B1:G1)."
3. Press the Enter key.

The IRR will appear as .1844 in cell A2. Your amount in cell A2 might differ depending on the number of decimal points you have specified in this spreadsheet session. For example, if only two decimal places are specified, you'll see .18, if three places, you'll see .184. The internal rate of return is 18.44 percent. This means that if the firm invests the $3,000 and receives the future cash inflows as specified, it will earn an 18.44 percent return on this investment.

GLOSSARY OF KEY TERMS

Accounting rate of return. The annual net income generated by the proposed project divided by the net investment in the project.

Accrual basis of accounting. Method of accounting in which revenues aren't recognized until earned and expenses are matched with revenues. An alternative is the cash basis of accounting where revenues are recognized only when cash is received, and expenses are shown only when cash is paid. Generally-accepted accounting statements found in business use the accrual basis of accounting.

Activity. A unit of work within a process. Preparing a customer invoice, repairing equipment, or preparing a midterm examination are examples of activities.

Activity-based budgeting. Budgeting costs by activity, with the intent to use the different activity costs to determine the cost of producing a product or providing a service. Thus, the focus of activity-based budgeting is on budgeting costs for activities, not by departments or other business segments.

Activity-based costing. The allocation of overhead costs directly to cost objects (products, customers, etc.) based on the cost drivers that cause costs to occur in overhead activities (maintenance, selling costs, etc.).

Activity-based management. The use of activity-based cost information to identify operational problems and to improve process effectiveness.

Activity improvement measures. Measures that provide guidance to employees on how to improve tasks or activities in a process. A statistical quality control chart is an example.

Additional paid-in capital. The difference between the par value of stock and the amount actually received by the firm when the stock is issued. Also referred to as contributed capital in excess of par.

Amortization. The process of matching the cost of using intangible assets with revenue. The same process as depreciation, except amortization applies to intangible assets while depreciation applies to tangible assets.

Applied overhead. The assigning of overhead costs to cost objects through the use of predetermined rates rather than allocating the actual overhead costs incurred. The two main reasons for applying overhead rather than assigning actual overhead costs are timeliness of information for making decisions and the preparation of monthly or quarterly financial statements. The process of applying overhead involves a two-step method of computing the predetermined overhead rate and multiplying that rate by the amount of cost driver causing the overhead cost.

Appraisal costs. Costs incurred to check that products, processes, and services are in conformance with specifications. These include all costs to inspect incoming parts and goods and services produced. Appraisal costs also include quality audit and testing costs.

Assets. Probable future economic benefits owned or controlled by the company that result from past transactions or events.

Attainable standards. Performance objectives that are challenging but achievable. Attainable standards are more motivating than impossible-to-achieve or easy-to-achieve standards.

Balanced scorecard. A performance report with measures, both financial and nonfinancial, that are linked to an organization's critical success factors.

Basic earnings per share. Presented below the income statement, this is the earnings per share number that most analysts focus on. It is computed by dividing net income less preferred stock dividends by the average number of common stock shares outstanding.

Benchmark standards. Standards that are set with the idea of moving a firm's performance toward matching the world's best organizations at performing that activity.

Benchmarking. Evaluating the effectiveness of a process by comparing that process to the best similar process in the world. For example, many firms benchmark their sales order processing against L.L. Bean's sales order process.

Bill of materials. A list of the parts used in the manufacture of a product or component. It normally includes the quantity of each type of part used.

Book value. For an entire firm, book value is the accounting value of the firm's assets less the value of its liabilities. In other words, it is equal to the amount of a company's shareholders' equity section of the balance sheet. For an asset, book value refers to the purchase price of the asset less accumulated depreciation recorded for the asset.

Breakeven point. The level of either unit sales or total dollar sales at which a firm or product earns exactly zero income. It is computed by dividing total fixed costs by either the unit contribution margin (for the unit breakeven point) or the contribution margin ratio (for the breakeven in total dollar sales). Breakeven point formulas are:

Breakeven point in unit sales: $\dfrac{\text{Total fixed costs}}{\text{Unit contribution margin}}$

Breakeven point in total dollar sales: $\dfrac{\text{Total fixed costs}}{\text{Contribution margin ratio}}$

Budgeted balance sheet. A component of the financial budget that shows what the balance sheet will look like if budget assumptions were to become reality.

Budgeted cash flow statement. A component of the financial budget that shows what the statement of cash flows will look like if budget assumptions were to become reality.

Budgeted income statement. A component of the financial budget that shows what the income statement will look like if budget assumptions were to become reality.

Budgeting. The formalized, detailed process of planning for the future. The budgeting process normally includes the preparation of operating, capital, and financial budgets.

Capital budget. List of spending on approved projects that benefit the firm for more than one year. Examples include expenditures for plant and equipment, new product development, new information systems, and other long-term investments.

Cash adequacy ratio. Cash flow from operations divided by current liabilities. It is a measure of the cash-generating muscle of the business compared to the short-term liabilities that must be paid within the coming year.

Cash flows. The amount of cash generated by a firm or an investment project. This is in contrast to accrual-based income for a firm, which is affected by noncash items such as depreciation and sales on account.

Committed costs. A special type of fixed cost that is locked in by past decisions and cannot easily be changed by future decisions. Depreciation on existing equipment is an example of a committed cost.

Comprehensive budget. A budget that includes both financial and nonfinancial measures. This is in contrast to a financial, budget that looks only at the financial dimension of planning and control.

Consolidated financial statements. The combination of the financial results of the parent company and its subsidiaries. These subsidiaries may be both foreign and domestic.

Consolidation. The process of creating one set of financial statements for a parent company and its subsidiaries.

Contingent liabilities. Potential liabilities which may result in future losses for a firm. Contingent liabilities which cannot be reasonably estimated at the current time are disclosed in the footnotes to the financial statements. An example is the possible loss from a major environmental lawsuit.

Continuous improvement. An organizational philosophy which holds that, for every process, procedures should be established to assist employees in managing and measuring ongoing improvement to their process.

Contributed capital. Portion of owners' equity contributed by owners.

Contribution income statement. An income statement constructed such that the major headings are: sales, variable expenses, contribution margin, fixed expenses, and net income.

Contribution margin. Unit contribution margin is unit sales revenue minus unit variable costs. Total contribution margin is total sales minus total variable costs. Total contribution margin is also equal to total fixed costs plus net income.

Contribution margin ratio. Contribution margin divided by sales. This is total contribution margin divided by total sales or unit contribution margin divided by unit selling price.

Control. The management function that seeks to ensure that the plans are being followed and appropriately modified as circumstances change.

Control chart. A plot of data measuring some aspect of a process with control limit lines drawn three standard deviations from the mean. Control charts are used to differentiate special cause events from common cause events and to help employees tell if they are improving the process.

Controllable (noncontrollable) cost. A cost which managers can cause to increase or decrease through their actions. Note that a cost that is noncontrollable to one manager may be controllable to a higher-level manager. A key concept of responsibility accounting is that managers should be evaluated only on costs over which they have control.

Core processes. Processes that are part of a firm's value chain. Examples include product development, order fulfillment, and customer service.

Corporate performance measures. Comprehensive measures of performance for an entire organization or large divisions of a firm. Examples include return on equity and market share. The object of the management control system is to link process output measures to corporate performance measures in a way that is meaningful to process managers and employees.

Cost base. The group of costs that a company selects to use as the basis of cost-plus pricing. An example of a cost base is variable manufacturing costs.

Cost driver. The primary factor causing the cost of an activity to increase or decrease. For example, total setup costs may be driven by the number of setups performed.

Cost management systems. Information systems used to support managers in their efforts to improve efficiency and to better meet the needs of the customer.

Cost object. Anything which requires a measurement of the cost of inputs into that item. Cost objects may include products, services, activities, departments, programs, and even customers. The choice of cost objects depends on the type of decision to be made.

Cost of capital. The rate of return required to attract investors to invest in a firm.

Cost of goods manufactured. The direct material, direct labor and manufacturing overhead costs of units completed during the period. In a job-order cost system, this is simply the summation of job cost sheets for all jobs completed during the period.

Cost of goods sold. The cost of all goods sold during the accounting period. It is computed by adjusting cost of goods manufactured for the change in finished goods inventory. Cost of goods sold is the first major expense item shown on the income statement. Sales less cost of goods sold equals gross margin.

Cost of goods sold budget. This schedule summarizes all of the planned factory cost information regarding the cost of planned units produced and sold.

Cost of quality. Term used to identify the total costs incurred by an organization to prevent poor quality plus costs incurred due to poor quality. Includes cost of inspection and lost customer goodwill due to poor quality products. Most firms discover that the cost of quality is about 25 percent of revenue and several times the level of income.

Cost-plus pricing. The use of cost information to set a selling price or set a target selling price. The selling price is usually computed by applying a standard markup to some cost base.

Cost pool. The aggregation of similar costs for the purpose of cost allocation. It is desirable that all costs in a cost pool have the same cost driver.

Critical (or key) success factors. The few key things an organization must do well to implement its strategy successfully. For example, quality is a critical success factor for CCC because its strategy is to pursue a high-quality segment of the LEV market.

Cross exchange rate. The exchange rate between two currencies that is developed based on each of these two currencies' exchange rates with a third currency. For example, in Reading 5-1 the exchange rate between the South African rand and the Japanese yen was computed by using the current exchange rate between each currency to the U.S. dollar.

Cumulative translation adjustment. Reported as a separate item in the stockholder's equity section of the balance sheet. Computed by summing:

value of assets at the reporting date
– value of liabilities at the reporting date
– historical translated value of stockholder's equity
= cumulative translation adjustment

Currency devaluation. An action by a country to reduce the value of its currency relative to other currencies. This is done by increasing the amount (exchange rate) of domestic currency required to purchase foreign currencies.

Current exchange rate. The exchange rate at the balance sheet date.

Current ratio. Total current assets divided by total current liabilities. This ratio is a measure of a company's ability to meet its short-term debt obligations.

Cycle (or throughput) time. The time it takes for one unit to progress from the start of production to either completion of production or sale.

Debt-to-equity ratio. Total liabilities divided by stockholders' equity. This ratio is a measure of the financial risk faced by a firm.

Decentralized organization. An approach to managing a large organization by dividing it into units and unit managers' responsibility for the performance of the units. Decentralized organizations require a sophisticated management control system.

Demand pull. A JIT production scheduling concept whereby products are not produced until there is customer demand for the product. Thus, demand "pulls" the production process.

Diluted earnings per share. A secondary measure of earnings per share. Diluted earnings per share is the net income divided by the number of common stock shares plus all potential new shares that could be issued to fulfill contractual arrangements such as the conversion of convertible preferred stock or stock options.

Direct labor. Manufacturing employees who are immediately involved in making a product. Assembly workers are an example. Direct labor occurs only in production departments.

Direct labor budget. A schedule that is part of the operating budget that details the direct labor hours and rate per hour for the budgeted units of production.

Direct labor efficiency variance. The difference between the actual direct labor hours worked and the hours that should have been worked to produce the actual output multiplied by the budgeted (or standard) direct labor pay rate.

Direct labor rate variance. The difference between the actual labor rate paid to employees and the budgeted (or standard) rate that was planned multiplied by the actual hours used.

Direct material. Materials or components that are part of the finished product.

Direct material price variance. The difference between the actual material cost per unit and the budget cost per unit, multiplied by the actual quantity of materials used.

Direct material usage variance. The difference between the quantity of materials used in production and the materials that should have been used to produce the actual output, multiplied by the budgeted material cost per unit.

Discretionary cost center. A department or other area that is not critical to the current operations of the organization. These cost centers perform functions that benefit the firm in the long term. Examples include research and development, advertising, maintenance, and employee development. Performance of discretionary cost centers is difficult to evaluate using financial data.

Earnings per share ratio. Computed by dividing net income less preferred stock dividends by the average number of common stock shares outstanding during the year.

Earnings/price ratio. Annual earnings per share divided by stock price. This ratio is the undiscounted rate of return a shareholder "earned" based on the market value of the stock. A shareholder's earnings, however, aren't realized until the firm distributes earnings in the form of cash. Analysts usually use the inverse of the earnings-price ratio, called the price-earnings (P/E) ratio. See price-earnings ratio for more detail.

Economic order quantity (EOQ). The optimum quantity of a part or material to purchase at one time. The EOQ minimizes the total order and carrying costs related to a purchased part or material.

Enterprise resource planning (ERP) software. Software that integrates accounting and other information from most functional areas of the firm. Modules include accounting, marketing, production, and human resources. Examples include SAP, Oracle, and Great Plains.

Entity concept. States that accounting information is accumulated and reported for a clearly defined economic entity regardless of its legal status. Accounting for the transactions of a sole proprietorship separately from the personal transactions of the owner of the business is one example of applying this concept.

Ethics. The moral principles that determine the “rightness” or “wrongness” of human behavior.

Exchange gain or loss. Also know as transaction gains or losses. The gain or loss that arises when the time at which a foreign currency transaction is recorded is different from the time cash payment is received or made. The gain or loss occurs because exchange rates change during the time a receivable or payable exists. For example, if you purchase goods from a foreign vendor on account and pay for them 60 days later, a gain or loss will occur to the extent that the dollar has changed value relative to the currency in which the invoice is denominated.

Exchange rate. The rate at which one currency can be converted into another currency.

External failure costs. Costs incurred due to the discovery of defects by customers. These include warranty, legal liability, and time involved in handling customer complaints. The largest external failure costs, the loss of existing and future customers due to loss of goodwill and reputation, are difficult to measure, and often are not formally reported.

Fair market value. This refers to the price an "arms-length" purchaser (that is someone not having a stake in the firm) would pay for an asset or the entire firm.

Financial budget. Creation of budgeted financial statements based on the operating and capital budget for the coming period. This budget allows managers to acquire the financial resources needed to implement the operating budget.

Financial performance measures. Process output performance measures based on information collected by a firm's financial and cost accounting systems. Examples include product and department cost information, sales revenue, net income, and return on investment. Most firms rely on these as their primary performance measures.

Financing assets ratio. Cash flow from operations (CFO) divided by the absolute value of cash flow from financing activities (CFI). A company with good operating cash flow is able to pay for most, if not all, purchases of new buildings and equipment with its internally generated cash, CFO.

Finished goods inventory. Units that are completed, but not yet sold. The cost of the units in the finished goods inventory is shown in the current assets section of the balance sheet.

Fixed costs. Costs or expenses which *in total* do not change in proportion to changes in the volume of production or sales. Fixed costs *per unit*, however, change as volume changes. Note that most fixed costs change from period to period; they just do not change in proportion to volume.

Forward exchange contract. An agreement to exchange one currency for another at a set rate at a specified date in the future. A forward exchange contract is a method of hedging.

Future value. The value at some future date of an amount invested or borrowed today, given a specified interest rate.

Future value factor. The value of $1 plus accumulated interest at some specified time in the future at a specified interest rate. The factor is multiplied by the total dollar amount invested to determine the total future value on an investment.

General and administrative expense budget. This schedule, part of the operating budget, contains all planned costs other than manufacturing, selling, and distribution costs.

Going concern concept. States that, for financial statement reporting purposes, it is assumed that the business will continue operating for the foreseeable future.

Goodwill. *Economic goodwill* is the value of a business in excess of the fair market value of its assets minus its liabilities. *Accounting goodwill*, which appears as an asset on the balance sheet, arises only when one firm purchases another firm for more than the fair value of its net assets.

Hedge. A financial transaction aimed to reduce risk. Many firms will engage in hedging to reduce the risk of losses due to changes in the valuation of currencies.
Historical cost concept. States that assets should be recorded in the accounting records and reported in the financial statements at their historical (original) cost.

Historical exchange rate. The exchange rate in effect when a transaction occurred. For example, if a building was purchased in 1975 by a foreign subsidiary of a U.S. firm, the historical exchange rate for that building is the 1975 rate.

Horizontal analysis. A comparison of changes in financial statements over time for the same company to assess its performance.

Incremental (out-of-pocket) cost (revenue). The amount a cost (or revenue) changes for a given decision. For example, total material cost will increase if a new order for 100 units is accepted. The amount of increase is the incremental material cost for the 100-unit order.

Indirect labor. All manufacturing employees who are not direct labor. Maintenance workers are an example.

Indirect material. Material used in the production process, but it does not become a part of the finished product. Grease used to lubricate production equipment is an example.

Inflation. A reduction in the amount of goods and services a unit of money will purchase. This is generally the result of governments expanding the money supply too fast.

Intercompany accounts receivable. The amount that a parent company owes a subsidiary for purchases of goods or services or visa versa. Since the transactions that give rise to these receivables are not with third parties, these receivables must be eliminated when a consolidated balance sheet is prepared.

Internal failure costs. Costs incurred to correct problems detected by inspection, testing, etc. These include the cost of rework, scrap, and downtime due to quality problems.

Internal rate of return. The interest rate that will cause the net present value of an investment to equal zero. It is used to compare the relative profitability of proposed capital projects.

Inventory turnover ratio. Cost of goods sold divided by average inventory. This ratio is a measure of how efficiently a firm uses its inventory. As discussed in Module 3, it also has become a critical measure of operating effectiveness for many firms.

Job. A unique, made-to-order product, or identifiable batch of different items being manufactured.

Job-order cost sheet. A document used to record direct material cost (posted from materials requisition forms), direct labor cost (posted from time tickets), and overhead costs for a job.

Job-order costing. The method of costing products that are produced in batches or are custom made. It is distinguished by the collection of manufacturing costs on job-order cost sheets. The alternative is process costing.

Joint venture. A partnership is a partnership of two or more entities that pool a part of their resources to pursue a new business opportunity.

Just-in-time (JIT) system. A process-oriented system that organizes work into cells and seeks to reduce cycle time and inventories through the use of demand pull, preventive maintenance, and continuous improvement.

Kaizen. The Japanese term for continuous process improvement.

Kanban system. The use of cards passed from operation to operation that signals an employee to begin production. Many firms use this system to implement demand pull.

Key success factors. Those few things that a firm must do well if its strategy is going to be successful. Examples include high quality, cost control, and new product development.

Lean production. A name commonly used to describe firms that have implemented JIT concepts throughout the value chain. Toyota is the original lean production firm.

Liabilities. Obligations to transfer cash, other assets, or services to other entities.

Liquidity. Refers to how quickly a company can convert its assets to cash and the length of time it takes for its liabilities to mature.

Make-or-buy. A decision in which management decides to make a component or an entire product itself or to purchase it from a supplier.

Management by exception. An approach whereby managers focus attention primarily on events that deviate from the plan. Large variances are important exceptions to review.

Management control system. Organizational structure that encourages individual parts of an organization to work toward common goals. The budgeting and performance evaluation subsystems normally form the heart of the management control system.

Managerial (or management) accounting. The collection, analysis and presentation of information to support managerial decision making.

Manufacturing overhead. Production costs other than direct labor and direct material.

Manufacturing overhead budget. This schedule contains all the planned costs in the factory area other than raw materials and direct labor.

Manufacturing process. A set of related activities that convert material and parts into finished products.

Market value. Amount of money an independent buyer is willing to pay for an asset or for an entire company. This amount is different than the accounting or book value of an asset or company which are based on historical cost.

Markup. The amount that a company adds on to its cost base to cover overhead and profit when computing a target selling price.

Markup percentage. Markup divided by cost base

Matching principle. Requires that all costs incurred in generating revenue be recognized in the same period as the related revenues.

Material requisition form. A document used to record the type and quantity of materials put into production and the job for which the materials are used.

Materials inventory. This inventory consists of parts and raw material waiting to be used in production departments.

Mixed cost. Cost item that is partially a fixed and partially a variable cost. An example is an electric utility bill, which is based on a flat monthly amount plus a rate per kilowatt hour used.

Monetary assets. Cash and other assets for which there is a contractual obligation with other parties to convert the assets to a specific amount of cash. Examples include accounts receivable and bonds issued by other entities held as investments.

Multinational corporation. A firm with subsidiaries located in more than one country. These firms tend to be more complex because of currency, legal, and cultural differences between countries.

Multiple performance measures. Used to better capture all dimensions of the activity being evaluated; helps reduce the behavioral problems created by measuring employee performance.

Net income. A firm's total sales revenue less its total expenses for the period (year, month, etc.). It is also referred to as net profit, profit, earnings or income.

Net present value. The difference between the present values of cash disbursements and cash receipts for a project.

Nonfinancial measures of performance. Process output performance measures based on information collected outside of traditional accounting systems. These measures are used extensively by firms employing TQM and JIT to provide appropriate incentives for employees. Examples include defect rates, cycle time, and training hours.

Nonmonetary assets. All assets except those defined as monetary. Examples include inventory, equipment and buildings.

Normal cost system. A product costing system in which a firm uses *actual* direct material and *actual* direct labor costs, but employs a *predetermined* overhead rate to cost products. CCC uses a normal cost system.

Operating budget. A detailed plan showing how many units of each product will be produced in which departments, how much material needs to be purchased, how much labor must be hired, etc.

Operations management. The study of how work is organized to meet the goals of an organization.

Ordinary annuity. A series of equal cash flows that are received or paid at the end of each time period in the series.

Overapplied (underapplied) overhead. When overhead applied to the jobs for the period is more (less) than actual overhead cost.

Overhead (or service) department. A manufacturing department that is not a production department. Overhead departments do not work directly on products. Maintenance is an example.

Paradigm. A personal perspective from which events are viewed. An example is a flat versus a global earth perspective.

Participative (budgeting). The involvement of those who will be held accountable for the budget in the development of their budget. It also requires agreement or "buy in" by those held accountable.

Par value of stock. An arbitrary valuation assigned to a share of stock, which becomes the valuation assigned the stock in the accounting records and on the balance sheet. The arbitrary valuation is done for legal reasons.

Payback period. The time (normally in years) it takes to get your investment back. If cash inflows are the same each year, the formula is initial investment ÷ annual cash inflows.

Performance (also control or flexible) budget. A planning or static budget that has been revised by using actual instead of planned volumes. It is used as the standard against which actual performance is compared.

Performance report. An accounting report showing the performance budget, actual results, and variances.

Period cost. A cost that accountants match to revenue on the income statement by time period. All selling and administrative costs are period costs. No manufacturing costs are period costs.

Planning. The management function of selecting goals, predicting results of specified plans, and deciding how to attain the selected goals.

Planning (static) budget. A budget that is prepared before the year (or other period) begins that is used for planning, motivational, coordinating, and communication purposes, but not for performance evaluation.

Plantwide overhead rate. Overhead allocation procedure whereby all manufacturing overhead costs are collected into one cost pool and allocated to products using one cost driver (usually direct labor hours).

Predetermined overhead rate. A rate computed before the year begins by dividing estimated annual overhead cost by the estimated volume of the cost driver used (direct labor hours in Module 2). This rate is used to apply overhead costs to jobs in work-in-process inventory.

Preferred stock. Stock that has first claim on dividends (dividends must be paid on preferred stock before common stock dividends are paid) and priority over common stock in the event of liquidation.

Present value. The value today of an amount to be received or paid at some future date, given a specified interest or discount rate.

Present value factor. The value today of $1 received at some specified time in the future discounted at a specified interest rate. The factor is multiplied by the total dollar amount received in the future to determine the total present value on an investment.

Present value of a lump sum. The value today of a one-time receipt or disbursement of cash at some point in the future discounted at some rate.

Present value of an annuity. The value today of a stream of equal cash receipts or disbursements spread over future periods discounted at some rate.

Prevention costs. Costs incurred to prevent defects. These include product design review, statistical process control, preventive maintenance, employee quality training, and vendor planning and production review costs.

Preventive maintenance. A JIT concept stipulating that factory operators be trained and held responsible for maintaining their equipment.

Price/earnings ratio. Stock price divided by annual earnings per share. The P/E ratio is a measure of a firm's stock price relative to its current income. It is used extensively by stock analysts as one measure of whether a stock is over-priced or under-priced. It is the inverse of the earnings/price ratio.

Process. A series of related activities or steps focused on achieving a specified output. Examples of processes at CCC are manufacturing, new product development, and billing and collection.

Process costing. Method of costing used when only one product or a family of similar products are produced on one set of equipment. It averages all costs across all units produced in the period.

Process output measures. Measures developed by accountants from key success factors. They are used to monitor how well each process contributes to a firm's success. These measures are part of the management control system.

Process quality improvement. A generic term used to describe any methodology used to improve process quality. Examples include total quality management and Six Sigma.

Product cost. A cost that accountants match to revenue on the income statement by products sold. These costs can be inventoried (work-in-process and finished goods). All manufacturing costs are product costs.

Production budget. A schedule that contains the projected units to be produced for the coming period. It uses information from the sales budget and takes into consideration beginning and ending finished goods inventories for the budget period.

Production department. A department that works directly on a product. The alternative is an overhead department.

Production process. The sequence of events involved in physically manufacturing products. The process involves all the manufacturing activities necessary to complete a product including the delivery of materials and the cutting, assembly, finishing, and inspection of units.

Purchases budget. A schedule that details the quantity of materials a firm must buy to meet its budget, considering the effects of both the planned beginning and ending material inventories.

Random fluctuations. Normal variations from the mean that occur in a process that is under statistical control. There are no explanations for these fluctuations other than that they are a natural result of the process.

Relevant cost. A cost that is incremental to a decision under study; that is, it will change if the alternative under review is implemented. Direct material cost in a special order decision is an example.

Relevant range. The range of operating activity (units produced) over which total fixed costs remain constant. This is usually the normal operating range of volume for a firm.

Responsibility accounting (reporting). A performance evaluation system, based on the budget, that holds responsibility center managers accountable for those areas over which they have control.

Responsibility center. A unit of an organization that holds its managers accountable for specific activities and outcomes that may included costs, revenues, or profits.

Retained earnings. Cumulative amount of past earnings (net income) retained in the business and not distributed to the owner or owners. Although this term is normally seen only in the balance sheet of corporations, the concept can apply just as readily to sole proprietorships or partnerships.

Return on equity ratio. Net income divided by average stockholders' equity. This ratio is a measure of how much the company is earning for stockholders relative to the amount of investment made by stockholders. The higher a firm's ROE, the better it is performing for stockholders.

Return on sales ratio. Net income divided by net sales (total sales less sales returns and allowances). This ratio, also known as the net profit margin, is an overall measure of a firm's relative profitability. For example, If firm A has a return on sales of .05 and Firm B in the same industry has an operating performance ratio of .10, it means Firm B earns twice the profit on each dollar of sales revenue as firm A. All other things being equal, Firm B will earn a higher return on equity.

Revenue recognition principle. A requirement that revenue be recorded when (1) the earnings process has been substantially completed and (2) an exchange has taken place. Revenue is *not* recognized when cash was collected or at any other time.

Sales budget. A schedule that contains planned unit sales and prices by product, by territory, and by other desired segments.

Sales revenue. The total amount a firm charges for goods and services sold during the period (month, year, etc.). Also referred to simply as sales or revenue.

Salvage (or residual) value. The amount received (or estimated to be received at a future date) when a long-lived asset is sold or scrapped.

Selling and distribution expense budget. A schedule that contains all the planned costs of marketing, selling, and distributing the product or service to customers.

Settlement date. The date at which a liability is paid.

Shareholders' (or stockholders') equity. Total assets minus total liabilities. It is composed of all the capital contributed by the stockholders plus earnings retained by the firm (not paid out in dividends) and any special accounting adjustments. Also referred to as owners' equity, shareholders' equity, and book value of the firm.

Six Sigma. A process management system with the objective to build quality into processes to the extent that each activity will have a defect rate of less than 3.4 defects per million.

Special cause events. An event that impacts the operation of an activity, but is external to the normal operation of that activity. An earthquake that causes large fluctuations in machine tolerance is an example.

Special order. The one-time sale of goods or services to a non-regular customer below the normal selling price.

Standard cost. Estimates made before the year begins of how much an item should cost.

Standards. Estimate made before the period begins on quantity, rate, or cost of an activity. If a standard is a cost, it is termed a *standard cost*. Other examples of standards include the number of pounds of material per unit of product and the expected defect rate.

Statistical quality control. The use of statistics, including control charts, to improve the quality of products or services.

Stock option. A contract that allows the purchase of stock at a preset price. For example, companies give managers options to purchase stock, often at a price higher than the current stock price. If the firm does well and the stock price increases, the managers can acquire the stock at a discount and then sell the shares at a profit if they wish.

Strategic planning. A description of how a firm plans to attain its goals. It includes the markets in which a firm will operate, the type of products or services it will sell, the pricing it will use, and the technologies it will employ.

Suboptimization. A systems concept stating that optimizing the individual parts of a system will not optimize the entire system. Traditional management control systems focus on the optimization of individual department performance, thereby causing suboptimization.

Sunk cost. A cost stemming from a past decision, which cannot be changed by decisions made today. A sunk cost is not relevant to decision about the future. An example is a past investment in a building.

Supply chain management. The integration of suppliers, producers and distributors of goods or services to minimize cost and optimize service. The essence of supply chain management is to have independent companies integrate their information systems to improve decision making.

Support process. A process that is not part of the value chain, but supports it. Examples include billing and collection, planning, and information systems processes.

Tampering. Attempts by management to improve a process by using common cause variations as a basis for action. Tampering only increases process variation.

Target cost. A pricing technique that begins by determining what customers will pay for a product and works back to an allowable cost for manufacturing the product. It is basically the reverse of cost-plus pricing.

Target price. The price at which a firm would like to sell its products or services so that all costs and an acceptable profit margin are covered. The firm may actually price the goods or services higher or lower based on market considerations.

Target rate of return. The rate of return a firm desires to obtain when investing in new projects.

Time ticket. A document used to record the number of hours a direct labor person worked on each job during a day.

Time value of money. The concept that money changes in value with time because it earns interest. For example, receiving money today is preferable to receiving the same amount of money at some later date because the money received today and invested will earn interest.

Total quality management. A management philosophy that focuses on the customer, processes, process variation, and measurement.

Trade balance of payments surplus (deficit). When the value of goods and services exported is greater (less) than the value of goods and services imported.

Traditional overhead allocation. Allocation of overhead based on one or more drivers that are highly correlated with production volume (for example, direct labor hours). Overhead allocation in Module 2 is an example of traditional, volume-based overhead allocation.

Transfer pricing. Determining the price charged for the purchase of goods or services by one business unit by another business unit within the same company. Transfer prices are an important issue for decentralized organizations.

Translation. The process of converting the financial statements of a foreign subsidiary into the currency used by the parent company.

Translation gains (losses). The increase (decrease) in the book value of a foreign subsidiary due to changes in exchange rates during the period.

Treasury stock. A firm's shares that it reacquires from shareholders. These shares are not counted as shares outstanding and do not receive dividends. The firm may reissue them at a future date.

Underapplied overhead. See overapplied overhead.

Under(over)-costed products. Assignment of less (more) overhead to a product than production of that product caused. Activity-Based costing reduces the under- and over-costing of products by more accurately assigning overhead to products.

Value-added activity. An activity that, from the customers' perspective, is worth more than the cost of that activity. Work-in-process inventory normally is a non-value-added activity because customers won't pay more for products just because a firm maintains high work-in-process inventories.

Value chain. Set of interdependent processes that add value, from the customer's perspective, to a product or service. In the value chain, the process normally includes research and development, product design, manufacturing, distribution and customer service.

Variable costs. Costs that change *in total* in proportion to changes in the volume of production or sales. Variable costs *per unit* remain constant as volume changes.

Variance. The difference between the performance (flexible) budget and actual results.

Variation. Differences in products or services that are produced in the same process. In the view of TQM advocates, the lower the variation, the higher the quality.

Vertical analysis. A restatement of one company's financial statements to a percentage of sales basis for the income statement and percentage of assets basis for the balance sheet in order to better assess performance.

Work cell. An area of a factory dedicated to producing one product or a family of similar products. It contains different types of equipment that perform different steps in the production process.

Work-in-process inventory. This inventory consists of all of a firm's partially completed units. The cost of these units is shown as a current asset on the balance sheet.

INDEX

A

Absorption income statement, 63
Account receivable, intercompany, 443
Accounting
- accrual basis of, 6
- corporate, 316–317
- environmental, 318
- financial and tax, 316
- forensic, 319
- governmental, 318
- just-in-time and, 282–288
- management, 85
- managerial, 316
- role of, in quality improvement, 255–259

Accounting-based performance measures, change in, for just-in-time systems, 287–288
Accounting careers, 313–319
Accounting employment outlook, 313–314
Accounting information systems, 315, 316
Accounting positions, types of, 314–319
Accounting rate of return, 382
Accrual basis of accounting, 6
Accumulated depreciation, 11
Activity, 223
Activity-based budgeting, 343
Activity-based costing, 223
- allocation of selling and administrative costs in, 225
- calculating costs per driver in, 226–230
- organizational fit of, 231–232
- overhead cost pools in, 228–229
- in practice, 231–234
- service application of, 232–233
- traditional versus, 223–226
- use of additional drivers in, 224–225
- using, to determine customer profitability, 225–226

Activity-based costing overhead allocation, traditional and, *illus.*, 231
Activity-based costs, computing, 226–231
Activity-based management, 234–235
Activity improvement measures, 257
Additional paid-in capital, 467
Amortization, 14
Annual report
- auditor's report, 464–465
- corporate, 463–466
- footnotes to financial statements, 465–466
- importance of financial information in, 466
- management discussion and analysis of operations, 464
- public relations section, 463
- ratio analysis, 467–473

Annuity
- ordinary, 373
- present value of, 373–374

Applied overhead, 133
Appraisal costs, 259
Assets, 9
- current, 11
- intangible, 14–16
- other, 12
- total, 13

Assurance services, 316
Attainable standards, 399
Auditing
- external, 315–316
- internal, 316
- quality, 319

Auditor's report, 464–465

B

Balance sheet, 9–14
- budgeted, 340–341
- comparative, 11–14; *illus.*, 12
- consolidation of parent and subsidiary, 447–448
- key concepts, 10
- links connecting income statement and, 17–18
- shareholders' equity section of, 467
- translation of, 446–447

Balanced scorecard, 391
- at California Car Company, 401

Balanced scorecard concepts, 399–400
Balanced scorecard performance report, 393–394
Basic earnings per share, 8, 470
Benchmark standard, 330
Benchmarking, 253
Bill of materials, 107
Book value, 13
Book value per share, 471
Breakeven analysis, 60–63
- impact of taxes on, 63
- including desired profit in, 62–63

Breakeven point, 60
Budget
- capital, 332
- comprehensive, 399
- control, 393
- cost of goods sold, 337
- direct labor, 336
- financial, 332
- flexible, 195
- general and administrative expense, 337–338
- manufacturing overhead, 336
- operating, 331
- performance, 195, 393
- planning, 131, 195
- production, 331
- purchases, 331
- reasons to, 329–331
- sales, 331
- selling and distribution expense, 337–338
- static, 131

Budget measures, three-step procedure for determining, 400
Budgeted balance sheet, 340–341
Budgeted cash receipts and disbursements schedule, 339–340
Budgeted income statement, 338–339
Budgeted statement of cash flows, 341–342
Budgeting, 329
- activity-based, 343
- comprehensive, 342

Business units, evaluating unit managers and, 396–397

C

California Car Company
- balanced scorecard at, 401
- comprehensive budget at, 402
- history and management structure of, 91–95
- organization chart, *illus.*, 92
- physical structure of, 95–96
- plant layout, 95–96; *illus.*, 97
- production process, 96
- strategy of, 91
- work cell performance evaluation at, 402

Capital
- additional paid-in, 467
- contributed, 9

Capital budget, 332
Capital budgeting techniques, 377–379
Capital investments, strategic nature of, 371–372
Cash adequacy ratio, 42
Cash flow, importance of, to financial statement users, 44
Cash flow from financing activities, 33–34
Cash flow from investing activities, 32–33
Cash flow from operations, 32
- illustration of, 38–39
- indirect method, 36–38

Cash flows, 31
- statement of. *See* Statement of cash flows

Cash receipts and disbursements schedule, budgeted, 339–340
Certified public accountants, 315
Chief financial officer, 316
Comparative balance sheet, 11–14, *illus.*, 12
Comparative income statement, 6–9; *illus.*, 7
Comprehensive budget, 399
- at California Car Company, 402

Comprehensive budgeting, 342, 399–403
Consolidated financial statements, 443
Consolidation, 443
- of parent and subsidiary balance sheets, 447–448

Continuous improvement, 250
- and process variation, 254

Contributed capital, 9
Contribution income statement, 63–64
- comparison of traditional and, *illus.*, 64

Contribution margin, 58
- variable costs and, 58–59

Contribution margin ratio, 58
Control, 391
Control budget, 393
Control charts, 257, 262–265
Core processes, 249
Corporate accounting, 316–317
Corporate annual report. *See* Annual report
Corporate performance measures, 256
Cost-based pricing formulas. *See* cost-plus pricing formulas
Cost center, discretionary, 330
Cost drivers, 133
- identifying in activity-based costing, 226–228
- use of additional, in activity-based costing, 224–225

Cost flows
- change in, in just-in-time systems, 282–284
- in job-order cost system, *illus.*, 283
- in just-in-time system, *illus.*, 284
- manufacturing, 175–179

Cost management systems, 221
Cost objects, 134
- applying overhead to, 136

Cost of goods manufactured and sold, 180–182
Cost of goods manufactured and sold schedule, *illus.*, 181
Cost of goods sold, 7
Cost of goods sold budget, 337
Cost of quality, 259–262
- example of, 261–262
- using information from, 260–261

Cost planning, 57–60
Cost-plus pricing, 151
Cost-plus pricing formulas
- determining cost base in, 153
- determining markup percentage, 154–155
- determining prices using, 152–155
- using, to make decisions, 152

Cost pools, 133, 228
Cost system
- normal, 176
- standard, 176

Costing
- activity-based, 223
- job-order, 175
- period, 183
- process, 175
- product, 183
- traditional versus activity-based, 223–226

Costs
- appraisal, 259
- computing activity-based, 226–231
- direct, 99
- estimating, for a department, 132
- estimating, for a job, 132
- estimating direct, 131–132
- estimating overhead, 133–137
- external failure, 259
- fixed, 59
- internal failure, 259
- manufacturing overhead, 100–101
- mixed, 60
- period, 101, 152
- prevention, 259
- product, 100, 152
- relevant, 65–66
- sunk, 65
- target, 151
- variable, 58

Critical success factors, 400
Cross exchange rate, 431
Cumulative translation adjustment, 443
Currency, gains and losses from sales and purchases of, 432–433
Currency devaluation, 423
Current assets, 11

Current liabilities, 13
Current ratio, 18, 468
Customer profitability, using activity-based costing to determine, 225–226

D

Debt-to-equity ratio, 19–20, 469
Demand pull, 280
Departments
    applying overhead to, 135–136
    estimating costs for, 132
    estimating overhead costs for, 136
    overhead, 132
    production, 99
    service, 132
Depreciation, accumulated, 11
Diluted earnings per share, 8–9, 470
Direct costs, 99
    estimating, 131–132
    for performance report, 197
Direct labor, 99
Direct labor budget, 336
Direct labor efficiency variance, 394
Direct labor rate variance, 394
Direct material, 99
Direct material price variance, 395
Direct material usage variance, 395
Direct method of statement of cash flows, 36
Discounted cash flow analysis, 378
Discretionary cost center, 330
Dividends, determining cash paid for, 41

E

Earnings per share
    basic, 8, 470
    diluted, 8–9, 470
Earnings per share ratio, 470
Earnings/price ratio, 470
Enterprise resource planning, 343
Enterprise resource planning software, 259
Entity concept, 10
Environmental accounting, 318
Ethical conduct, standards of, for management accounting and financial management, 363–365
Ethical decision making, 362, 365–367
    model of, 362–363
    steps in, 363
Ethics, 361
Excel, using Microsoft, 495–501
Exchange gain or loss, 433
Exchange rate, 427
    cross, 431
    historical, 443
    impact of changes in, 428–432
    profitability analysis and, 448–450
Expenses
    interest, 8
    operating, 8
External auditing, 315–316
External failure costs, 259

F

Financial accounting, 316
Financial budget, 332
    operating and, example, 333–342
Financial information, importance of, 466
Financial management, 316
    standards of ethical conduct for, 363–365
Financial statements
    consolidated, 443
    footnotes to, 465–466
    importance of cash flow to users of, 44
    ratio analysis of, 18–20
    translation of foreign, 443–450
Financing assets ratio, 43
Finished goods inventory, 96
Fixed costs, 59
Fixed manufacturing overhead, accounting treatment of, 183
Flexible budget, 195
Flexible manufacturing systems, 284
Forensic accounting, 319
Forward exchange contract, 426
Future value, 371
Future value factor, 372

G

General and administrative expense budget, 337–338
General Electric, quality program at, 254–255
Global Airlines, 258
Global business risks, 423–426
Going concern concept, 10
Goodwill, 14–16
Governmental accounting, 318
Gross margin on sales, 7

H

Hedge, 426
Historical cost concept, 10
Historical exchange rate, 443
Hybrid vehicle industry, 89–91
    current market situation, 90
    future demand, 90–91

I

Income, net, 8
Income statement, 5–9
    budgeted, 338–339
    comparative, 6–9; *illus.*, 7
    contribution, 63–64
    links connecting balance sheet and, 17–18
    translation of, 445
Income tax, 8
    impact of, on proposed investments, 378
Indirect labor, 133
Indirect material, 133
Indirect method of statement of cash flows, 36–38
    example of, 39–43
    popularity of, 43
Inflation, 427

Intangible assets, 14–16
Intercompany account receivable, 443
Interest expense, 8
Internal auditing, 316
Internal failure costs, 259
Internal rate of return, 375
Inventory
  finished goods, 96
  materials, 96
  work-in-process, 96
Inventory turnover ratio, 19, 469
Investments, choosing between alternate, 382–383

J

Job, 175
  applying overhead to, 135–136
  estimating costs for, 132
  estimating overhead costs for, 137
Job-order cost sheets, 176; *illus.*, 178
Job-order cost system, cost flows in, *illus.*, 283
Job-order costing, 175
  normal, 176–177
Joint venture, 423
Just-in-time
  accounting and, 282–288
  definition of, 278
  history of, 277
  impact of, 278
  principal elements of, 279–282
  relationship between process quality improvement and, 278–279
Just-in-time process output measures, 287–288
Just-in-time system, 277
  change in cost flows, 282–284
  cost flows in, *illus.*, 284
  overhead allocations in, 284–286

K

Kanban system, 280
Key success factors, 256

L

Labor, indirect, 133
Lean production, 277
Liabilities, 9
  current, 13
  long-term, 13
Liquidity, 42
Long-term liabilities, 13
Long-term pricing, 149–156
  factors in setting, 150–151
  traditional approach to, 151–152

M

Maintenance, preventive, 281
Make-or-buy, 159
Make-or-buy decisions, 159–160
Management
  activity-based, 234–235
  total quality, 250
Management accounting, 85
  standards of ethical conduct for, 363–365
Management control cycle, 392–399; *illus.*, 392
Management control system, 255
  behavioral aspects of, 397–399
  focus on processes, 257
  quality measures in, 255–257
Managerial accounting, 316
Manufacturing, accounting for, 99–101
Manufacturing cost flows, 175–179
Manufacturing overhead, 100
  accounting treatment of fixed, 183
  performance budgets for, 197–199
  reasons for applying, 133–134
Manufacturing overhead budget, 336
Manufacturing overhead costs, 100–101
Manufacturing performance report, 196–199
Manufacturing value chain, 96–99; *illus.*, 98
Market value, 13
Markup, 151
Markup percentage, determining, 154–155
Matching principle, 6
Material, indirect, 133
Material requisition forms, 176; *illus.*, 177
Materials inventory, 96
Measures of performance
  multiple, 399
  nonfinancial, 342
Microsoft Excel, using, 495–501
Mixed costs, 60
Multinational corporation, 444
Multiple measures of performance, 399

N

Net income, 8
  determinants of, 5
Net present value, 374
Net sales, 7
New manufacturing environment, 343
Nonfinancial measures of performance, 342
Nonvalue-added activities, 96
Normal cost system, 176

O

Operating budget, 331
  financial and, example, 333–342
Operating expenses, 8
Operations management, 277
Ordinary annuity, 373
Overapplied overhead, 182
  overhead performance variance versus underapplied or, 199
Overhead
  accounting treatment of fixed manufacturing, 183
  applied, 133
  overapplied, 182
  performance budgets for manufacturing, 197–199
  underapplied, 182
Overhead allocation
  in just-in-time systems, 284–286
  traditional and activity-based costing, *illus.*, 231

Overhead cost pools, creating in activity-based costing, 228–229
Overhead costs
 estimating, 133–137
 reasons for erratic, 134
Overhead departments, 131
Overhead rates, uses of predetermined, 182–184

P

Paid-in capital, additional, 467
Par value of stock, 467
Paradigm, 250
Participative budgeting, 399
Payback period, 381
Performance budget, 195, 199, 393
 applied and actual overhead compared to, 197–199
Performance budget report, using information from, 199–200
Performance measures, corporate, 256
Performance report, 393
 balanced scorecard, 393–394
 manufacturing, 196–199
Performance variance, 199
Period costing, 183
Period costs, 101, 152
Planning, 391
 cost, 57–60
 enterprise resource, 343
 revenue, 57
 strategic, 330
Planning budget, 131, 195
Plantwide overhead rates, 135
Predetermined overhead rates, 131
 computing, 135
 uses of, 182–184
Preferred stock, 467
Present value, 371
Present value concepts, using, 371–377
Present value factor, 372
Present value of an annuity, 373–374
Prevention costs, 259
Preventive maintenance, 281
Price/earnings ratio, 470
Prices, target, 151
Pricing
 cost-plus, 151
 long-term, 149–156
 special order, 156–160
 transfer, 156
Process, 249
Process costing, 175
Process output measures, 256
 just-in-time, 287–288
Process quality improvement, 249
 comparisons of traditional and, paradigms, 251
Product costing, 183
Product costs, 100, 152
Product mix analysis, 149
Production budget, 331
Production departments, 99
Production process, 96
Profit, including desired, in breakeven analysis, 62–63
Profitability analysis, exchange rates and, 448–450
Property and equipment, 11
Purchases budget, 331

Q

Quality
 cost of, 259–262
 principal elements of, 252–255
Quality auditing, 319
Quality control, statistical, 250
Quality improvement, role of accounting in, 255–259
Quality management, 250
 history of, 250–252

R

Ratios
 book value per share, 471
 cash adequacy, 42
 contribution margin, 58
 current, 18, 468
 debt-to-equity, 19–20, 469
 earnings per share, 470
 earnings/price, 470
 financing assets, 43
 inventory turnover, 19, 469
 price/earnings, 470
 return on equity, 18–19, 468
 return on sales, 19, 468–469
Relevant costs, 65–66
Relevant range, 59
Responsibility center, 96
Retained earnings, 9–10
Return on equity ratio, 18–19, 468
Return on sales ratio, 19, 468–469
Revenue planning, 57
Revenue recognition principle, 6

S

Sales budget, 331
Salvage value, 380–381
Selling and administrative costs, allocating under activity-based costing, 225
Selling and distribution expense budget, 337–338
Service departments, 131
Settlement date, 432
Shareholders' equity, 9
Shareholders' equity section of balance sheet, 467
Shares, assessing market price of, 472–473
Six Sigma, 250
Special cause event, 262
Special order, 156
 conditions for, 156–157
 example, 157–159
Special order pricing, 156–160
Standard cost system, 176
Standards, 392

Statement of cash flows
budgeted, 341–342
direct method, 36
example of, 39–44
indirect method, 36–38
popularity of indirect method, 43
structure of, 32–35
types of, 36–39
uses of, 31
Static budget, 131
Statistical quality control, 250
Stock
par value of, 467
preferred, 467
treasury, 467
Stock option, 470
Stockholders' equity
on balance sheet, 13–14
on income statement, 9
Strategic planning, 330
Suboptimization, 257
Sunk cost, 65
Supply chain management, 281
Support processes, 249

T

Tampering, 253
Target costs, 151
Target prices, 151
Tax accounting, 316, 318
Taxes
impact of, on breakeven analysis, 63
income, 8
Time tickets, 176; *illus.,* 177
Time value of money, 371
Total quality management, 250
Trade balance of payments surplus (deficit), 427
Traditional overhead allocation, 135
Transaction gain or loss, 433
Transfer pricing, 156
Translation, 443
of balance sheet, 446–447
of foreign financial statements, 443–450
of income statement, 445
Treasury stock, 467

U

Underapplied overhead, 182
overhead performance variance versus overapplied or, 199

V

Value-added activities, 96
Value chain, 96
manufacturing, 96–99; *illus.,* 98
Variable costs, 58
and contribution margin, 58–59
Variances, 195
direct labor efficiency, 394
direct labor rate, 394
direct material price, 395
direct material usage, 395
performance, 199
Volume-based overhead allocation, 135

W

Work cell, 279
allocating estimated shared overhead to, 285
estimating direct overhead to, 285
Work cell performance evaluation, at California Car Company, 402
Work-in-process inventory, 96